MW01484799

Pickled Herring and Pumpkin Pie:

A Nineteenth-Century Cookbook for German Immigrants to America

by Henriette Davidis

with an introduction by
Louis A. Pitschmann

Monographs of the Max Kade Institute

Max Kade Institute for German-American Studies
901 University Bay Drive
Madison, WI 53705

Copyright © 2003

The Board of Regents of the University of Wisconsin System
All rights reserved

Printed in the United States of America

ISBN 0-924119-06-3

Preface

It is a delight to present this reprint of Henriette Davidis' *Practical Cook Book*, a turn-of-the-century English translation of the most popular German cookbook of all time. Many people have helped bring this project to fruition, and for their excellent work I am very grateful. First off, I deeply appreciate the tireless efforts of my predecessor, former MKI director Joseph Salmons, for including this reprint into our growing mongraph series. Antje Petty, as part of her work as MKI assistant director and educational outreach specialist, has been actively involved in the reprint project from start to finish, including discussing the cookbook's historical significance at a number of public events. In this latter regard, Antje has worked closely with Ruth Olson, associate director of the Center for the Study of Upper Midwestern Cultures. Leng Lee was responsible for most of the scanning of the original, while Eric Platt prepared the final manuscript for publication. Nancy Zucker designed the dustjacket. Lillian A. Clark edited the introduction by Louis A. Pitschmann, to whom greatest thanks are due. This reprint was originally conceived by Lou, and he has assisted the MKI staff in numerous ways to ensure the success of the project.

Guten Appetit!

Mark L. Louden
Director, Max Kade Institute

Introduction: The History of Henriette Davidis' *Practical Cook Book* in America, 1879–1913

by Louis A. Pitschmann

More than fifty German-language cookbooks appeared in the United States between the middle of the nineteenth century and World War I. Of these, Henriette Davidis' *Practical Cook Book* [Praktisches Kochbuch] undoubtedly had the most lasting influence on German-American kitchens. Originally published in Germany in 1844, the first American edition appeared in Milwaukee in 1879, and by 1911 at least fifteen reprints, revised editions, and translations had been published. Several things account for its popularity during the years it remained in print and for its appeal to cookbook collectors and food historians today. Foremost among these is the author herself whose reputation as Germany's most highly regarded culinary authority went unchallenged during her lifetime and for nearly fifty years after her death. Today, Henriette Davidis' *Practical Cook Book* retains its significance not only because it represents an interesting chapter in the history of cookbook publishing in the United States but also because it sheds light on the food habits of one of America's largest immigrant groups. It remains an important source of authentic recipes that had their origins in Germany and that were the mainstay of many American kitchens until the mid-twentieth century when other ethnic cuisines began to exert greater influence on the American public.

Cookbook Publishing: The Historical Context

Recipes are among the oldest surviving written records in Western societies. Prior to the invention of printing, there existed from ancient times to the Renaissance a tradition of recording and compiling culinary recipes. Once the printing press was introduced, cookbooks were among the earliest examples of the printed word in many European countries, appearing as early as the 1470s. An undated Latin edition of Bartolomeo Platina's *De honesta voluptate et valetudine* [Of Honest Indulgence and Good Health], printed in Venice in 1474 or 1475, is considered by scholars to be the first cookbook produced using moveable type.[1] The first cookbook printed in a

---

[1] Katherine Golden Bitting, *Gastronomic Bibliography* (San Francisco: 1939) 373–374.

vernacular language, *Küchenmeisterei* [Kitchen Mastery], was published ten years later in Nuremberg, Germany, on November 10, 1485. This collection of German recipes enjoyed immense popularity, and no fewer than fourteen editions had appeared in six different cities by the year 1500.[2] A flood of cookbooks followed, and by the end of the eighteenth century literally thousands of cookbooks for both noble and more modest households had been published throughout Europe. In the nineteenth century another invention, the cooking stove, caused cookbook publishing to flourish in Europe and North America. In the United States some 800 cookery books were published between 1742 and 1860, and ladies' aid societies and other charitable groups published more than 2,100 cookbooks between 1865 and 1914 to raise funds for various causes. During the latter period, American commercial publishers released no fewer than 700,[3] while in Germany cookbooks appeared at a rate of approximately one every month during the fifty years preceding World War I. Great Britain, France, and other parts of Europe experienced similar phenomena.

Among the American cookbooks published prior to 1914 are nearly two hundred written in French, Swedish, Danish, Norwegian, Finnish, Czech, Polish, Yiddish, and German. The earliest known foreign-language books published in the United States to include cooking recipes were Heinrich Sage's *Die amerikanische Goldgrube* [The American Goldmine] (Lebanon, PA, 1810) and Johann Krauss's *Oeconomisches Haus- und Kunst-Buch* [Economical Household and Craft Book] (Allentown, PA, 1819). The first foreign-language book devoted solely to cookery did not appear until a generation later when George Girardey published his *Höchst nützliches Handbuch über Kochkunst* [Most Useful Handbook on Culinary Art] in Cincinnati in 1842. This was followed six years later by a pamphlet published for the Pennsylvania Dutch entitled *Die geschickte Hausfrau* [The Clever Housewife]. In 1856, the European-trained chef William Vollmer translated his *United States Cook Book* into German under the title *Vollständiges deutsches Vereinigte Staaten Kochbuch* [Complete German United States Cookbook]. Simultaneously, an anonymous American edition of a work originally published in Stuttgart, Germany, (Friederike Loeffler's *Oekonomisches Handbuch für Frauenzimmer* [Economical

---

[2] Hans U. Weiss, *Gastronomia: eine Bibliographie der deutschsprachigen Gastronomie, 1485–1914* (Zürich: Bibliotheca Gastronomica Buchantiquariat, 1996) 290.

[3] For the bibliography of American cookbooks see Eleanor Lowenstein, *Bibliography of American Cookery Books, 1742–1860* (Worcester, MA: American Antiquarian Society, 1972). Margaret Cook, *America's Charitable Cooks: A Bibliography of Fund-Raising Cook Books Published in the United States (1861–1915)* (Kent, OH: [The Author], 1971). Eleanor and Bob Brown, *Culinary Americana: Cookbooks Published in the Cities and Towns of the United States of America During the Years from 1860 through 1960* (New York: Roving Eye Press, 1961).

Handbook for Ladies]) appeared in Philadelphia under the title *Vollständiges Kochbuch für die deutsch-amerikanische Küche* [Complete Cookbook for the German-American Kitchen]. These works enjoyed various reprints and marked the beginning of German-language cookbook publishing in the United States that continued well into the twentieth century. As was the case with other foreign-language cookbooks published in the United States, a few of those printed in German were reprints of recipe collections previously published in Europe; others were American editions of European cookbooks, revised and adapted for the American kitchen. Still others were translations of American titles, and a number were original works. Most recipes included in these cookbooks reflected the traditional cuisines of the targeted ethnic groups. However, many included a large number of recipes for American dishes as well as some recipes for Old World dishes using American ingredients unknown, or at least not commonly known, in Europe at that time.

American authors, editors, and translators of German-language cookbooks were without exception European born, with the food habits of their homeland deeply ingrained in their memories and palates. They were also highly knowledgeable about American food, its character, and its preparation. The men were for the most part professionally trained chefs who had established their reputations in Europe before coming to America. William Vollmer, for example, worked in various major restaurants on the Continent prior to managing the dining room in Philadelphia's Union Club.[4] The women authors and editors, on the other hand, were either columnists for newspapers and magazines, teachers in cooking schools, or middle-class ladies recognized for their reputation as hostesses and managers of fine homes. In the case of American editions of Henriette Davidis' *Praktisches Kochbuch*, only persons equally well-qualified in German and American cookery were involved in preparing each edition. This deliberate striving for quality contributed greatly to the book's success in this country.

Henriette Davidis and Her *Praktisches Kochbuch*

Although Frau Davidis' *Praktisches Kochbuch* was in all probability the most widely used of the German-language cookbooks issued for the American market, the author never visited the United States and did not foresee an American edition when she died in 1876. Born on March 1, 1801, in Wengern in Germany's Ruhr

---

[4] William Vollmer, *Vereinigte Staaten Kochbuch. . . ; mit besonderer Berücksichtigung der klimatischen Verhältnisse & Produkte Amerika's* (Philadelphia: Schäfer u. Koradi, 1877). Below the author's name on both the title page and the cover appears "former head chef in various large hotels in Europe and restaurateur of the Union Club in Philadelphia."

Valley, Henriette Davidis was the tenth of thirteen children of a Dutch mother and German Lutheran minister father. She was home-schooled until she reached her fifteenth birthday, and following her confirmation in 1816, she attended a girls' school and later trained to become a teacher. Upon completion of her training, she worked for eight years as a governess, first in the home of an older sister and later for four years in the home of a wealthy family in Bremen. The ensuing years proved difficult. After the death of her father in 1828, she devoted the next ten years to her mother's care. During this time, she was twice engaged to marry only to see her fiancés die prematurely. Following her mother's death, she served as companion to a woman suffering from poor mental health. It was in this capacity that she resided in Switzerland for an extended period.

Henriette Davidis began to realize her full potential when in 1841 she assumed the leadership of a school specializing in household management. As headmistress, she conceived the idea of writing a series of practical guides to the domestic arts for the teenage girls under her supervision. The first of these took the form of a cookbook. Using recipes learned from her mother, her circle of friends, and her experiences while traveling, she began carefully testing and refining each recipe until it met with her approval. Writing with her students in mind, she recorded each recipe in a clear and concise style while providing sufficient detail to permit the reader to follow her instructions easily and successfully. Late in the fall of 1844, the publishing house Velhagen & Klasing issued her first collection of recipes under the title *Zuverlässige und selbstgeprüfte Recepte der gewöhnlichen und feineren Küche* [Reliable and Author-Tested Recipes for Everyday and Fine Cooking]. A second edition appeared in 1846, and in 1847 the third edition followed under the title by which the work would henceforth be known, *Praktisches Kochbuch für die gewöhnliche und feinere Küche* [Practical Cookbook for Everyday and Fine Cooking].

The sale of the third edition permitted Frau Davidis to relinquish her duties as headmistress and thereafter devote herself exclusively to writing. Among her published works were a cookbook for children, a book on kitchen gardening for housewives, a book on household management, a small collection of recipes for horse meat, and a collection of poetry. All but the latter two appeared in multiple editions over an extended period. Her career guide for young women, for example, continued to appear as late as fifty years after her death.[5]

Of all her writings it was the *Praktisches Kochbuch* that gained the widest popularity throughout German-speaking areas of Europe. Revised and augmented

[5] Willy Timm, "Henriette Davidis (1801–1876)," in *Westfälische Lebensbilder*, Im Auftrage der Historischen Kommission für Westfalen, hrsg. von Robert Stupperich, Band XII (Münster: Aschendorffsche Verlagsbuchhandlung, 1979) [88]–103.

editions followed in rapid succession as did translations into Dutch, French, English, and Danish. Sales of her cookbook not only contributed substantially to her publisher's profits, accounting for 17% to 20% of annual revenues between 1869 and 1876, but also helped to build Velhagen & Klasing's reputation as a publishing house.[6] At the time of her death on April 3, 1876, the twenty-first edition was already in print, and the sixth edition of the Dutch translation had appeared. Her cookbook had attained bestseller status, and her reputation as a cookbook author was similar to that of Fanny Farmer, Irma Rombauer, and Julia Child in this country. Her name became synonymous with reliable recipes for housewives and hostesses, and references to her and her cookbook occur repeatedly throughout German literature from the nineteenth to the late twentieth century as a literary allusion and as a source of indisputable culinary authority.[7]

The *Praktisches Kochbuch* in America:
Its Editors and Publishers and Their Contributions

The title page and foreword of the first American edition of 1879 do not attribute editorial responsibilities to any one person, but the role its publisher, George Brumder, played in introducing Frau Davidis' *Praktisches Kochbuch* to the American public was significant. As a bookshop owner in Milwaukee offering an array of books imported from Germany, he knew his customers' tastes. As an individual who possessed exceptional business acumen, he also knew a basic tenet of the book trade: publishing an edition of the Bible or a cookbook guaranteed almost certain profit. And, in 1877 while his bookshop was showing modest profits, Brumder had to face the fact that his investment in the Germania Publishing Company was not yielding the return his partners would have preferred.[8]

At the same time, another Midwestern publisher was experiencing considerable success as a cookbook publisher. Alfred Gould Wilcox, together with his wife, the

---

[6] Martin Tabaczek, "August Klasing (1809–1897)," in *Bielefelder Unternehmer des 18. bis 20. Jahrhunderts*, hrsg. von Jürgen Kocka und Reinhard Vogelsang, *Rheinisch-Westfälische Wirtschaftsbiographien*, Band 14 (Münster: Aschendorff, 1983) 118.

[7] Alois Wierlacher, *Vom Essen in der deutschen Literatur: Mahlzeiten in Erzähltexten von Goethe bis Grass* (Stuttgart: Kohlhammer, 1987) 78.

[8] Frederick J. Olson, "Foreword," in *A Bibliography and List of Library Holdings of Milwaukee Publisher George Brumder (1839–1910)*, compiled by Gerhardt Becker (Milwaukee: Golda Meir Library, University of Wisconsin–Milwaukee, 2000) 2.

former Estelle Woods, had acquired the copyright to the highly successful *Centennial Buckeye Cookbook*, which had been published in honor of the hundredth anniversary of American Independence to raise funds for the First Congregational Church in Marysville, Ohio. Mrs. Wilcox was a member of the church and served on the cookbook committee. A year after the book appeared, the Wilcoxes secured the publication rights from the church. Thus, beginning with the second edition in 1877, copyright was held by Mr. and Mrs. Wilcox's enterprise, the Buckeye Publishing Company. They modified the title to *Buckeye Cooking and Practical Housekeeping* and sold 27,000 copies in 1877 alone. In 1880 a German translation was published under the title *Buckeye Kochbuch und praktisches Haushalten*. By 1886 the English and German editions combined had sold more than 250,000 copies; by 1892, 750,000 had sold; and more than a million by 1900.[9]

The undeniable success the Wilcoxes experienced from the outset with *Buckeye Cooking and Practical Housekeeping* could not have escaped George Brumder's attention. Clearly, he saw an opportunity and seized it. As an importer of German books, he knew the German editions of the Davidis cookbook, and in all probability they were a regular part of his inventory. He also knew that the Centennial celebrations of 1876 had generated an extended wave of national pride which included identifying and recording examples of things uniquely "American." This documentation of what was considered uniquely American led in turn to the compilation of not one but two cookbooks honoring American cooking: *Centennial Cook Book and General Guide* by Ella Myers and *National Cookery Book* compiled by the Women's Centennial Committee. The goal of the Women's Committee was to gather and make more widely available recipes that were unique to the United States and that reflected the American identity.

Brumder built on these sentiments of national pride as he laid the groundwork for his American edition of Frau Davidis' cookbook, which he first published in 1879 under the title *Handbuch der Hausfrau* [The Housewife's Handbook].[10] In the same year, he republished the work with a new title page using a revised title, *Praktisches Kochbuch für die Deutschen in Amerika* [Practical Cookbook for the Germans in America]. Like Ella Myers and the members of the Women's Centennial Committee, he wanted to produce a cookbook that would appeal to the

[9] Andrew F. Smith, ed., *Centennial Buckeye Cook Book*, compiled by the Women of the First Congregational Church, Marysville, Ohio; with an introduction and appendixes by Andrew F. Smith (Columbus, OH: Ohio State University Press, 2000) xxxiv.

[10] Kevin Kurdylo, "Collection Feature: German-American Cookbooks," *Newsletter of the Friends of the Max Kade Institute* 10 (no. 4, Winter 2001–2002) 12.

sentiments of the 1876 centenary: pride in all things American. Rather than striving to preserve German cookery in America, he and his editors articulated a strong bicultural theme in their preface. Here they wrote that the German-American cookbook should retain the excellence, wholesomeness, and taste of German cuisine while simultaneously not neglecting the foods and products native to what they called "our American homeland."[11] This equal emphasis on German and American foods and methods of preparation was not intended to assure the survival of German culture in America, nor was it meant to encourage the Germans in this country to assimilate. Rather, Brumder used an important marketing strategy, namely, to take advantage of the strong sentiments of national pride sweeping the country.

Brumder's cookbook was the result of a close collaboration with his wife Henriette, an accomplished cook who learned much of what she knew about the culinary arts at an early age. She was only fourteen years old and fairly recently arrived in the United States from Germany when her foster mother announced that she was tired of the kitchen and thrust a cookbook—presumably an earlier edition of Frau Davidis' cookbook—into the girl's hands and informed her that henceforth she was responsible for the cooking. The teenager tackled the new assignment with vigor, and over the years "she tried out every recipe in the old German Davidis Kochbuch."[12] But Mrs. Brumder's role is not credited anywhere in the book. At best it is only alluded to through the repeated use of the German pronoun *wir* [we] in the two-page introduction.

In preparing their edition of 1879 for the American market, the Brumders labored to remain faithful to the twenty-second European edition of Frau Davidis' cookbook, but they did not publish a strict reprint. Instead, they modified the text to facilitate its usefulness in American kitchens by including North American ingredients unknown or uncommon in Europe as well as adding numerous recipes unknown to Frau Davidis. In their introduction the Brumders graciously acknowledged the various unnamed housewives and Mr. J. M. Riebs, chef at Milwaukee's Newhall House Hotel, for their generosity in providing the many American recipes they incorporated into the text. Like the housewives across America who had submitted their "American" recipes to the *National Cookery Book*, the Brumders' contributors provided a large number of recipes typically American and in many cases unknown outside the United States at that time. Thus, in the 1879 Milwaukee edition of *Praktisches*

---

[11] Henriette Davidis, *Praktisches Kochbuch für die Deutschen in Amerika* (Milwaukee: Georg Brumder, 1879) [iii].

[12] Herbert P. Brumder, *The Life Story of George and Henriette Brumder* (Milwaukee: Printed by the North American Press, 1960) 94.

Kochbuch one finds recipes for baking powder biscuits, buckwheat muffins, cookies, cornbread, cornmeal griddle cakes, catfish, Delicate Cake, Feather Cake, Gold Cake, Marble Cake, Pound Cake, Silver Cake, Spice Cake, Sponge Cake, pie crust, apple pie, cocoanut pie, lemon pie, squash (i.e., pumpkin) pie, sweet corn, catsup, and numerous other recipes calling for American ingredients not found in the German editions of Frau Davidis' cookbook.

The Brumders, however, did not limit their changes solely to inserting American recipes into Frau Davidis' cookbook. Relying on the highly respected German dietetic cookbook by Dr. Josef Wiel that had appeared in a special American edition a year earlier,[13] they inserted a sixteen-page chapter on special diets recommended for a variety of specific illnesses ranging from scarlet fever and gout to rickets. This supplementary chapter also included dietary guidelines for gaining and losing weight and reducing infant mortality. The Brumders also took the important step of converting Frau Davidis' original weights and measurements to their American equivalents. This daunting task required precision and testing lest slight discrepancies lead to cooking disasters. According to her grandson, Mrs. Brumder alone worked to refine the conversion of Frau Davidis' measures.[14] For example, one-eighth liter became one-eighth quart; 30 grams became one ounce; and 70 grams became one and a half tablespoons.

Brumder himself worked to assure that the edition would garner the increased revenues his business required by underscoring Frau Davidis' own emphasis on thrift and frugality in the kitchen. The years of prosperity that followed the Civil War through the end of Reconstruction had drawn to a close, and by the late 1870s many American homes knew firsthand the effects of a national recession. Brumder used this economic downturn to support the sale of the book. In the preface Brumder wrote, "The period of excess and waste has passed. . . . One should strive to learn frugality, and this cookbook is intended to teach frugality in the household. Especially in this country where not only the men but also the women to a certain extent are 'self made,' the will to save is not as lacking as the knowledge to do so." Further, he wrote that "our cookbook" would not fail to promote thriftiness by providing its readers with sound advice on how best to use leftovers and other small quantities of

---

[13] Josef Wiel, *Diätetisches Kochbuch mit besonderer Rücksicht auf den Tisch für Magenkranke*, nach der in Deutschland erschienenen 4. vermehrten und verbesserten Auflage, für Amerika bearbeitet von Karl Krohn (Milwaukee: Krohn, 1878).

[14] Brumder, 94.

ingredients. In the end, Brumder's edition of 1879 so successfully lent itself to the American kitchen and the economic realities of the day that only a year after its publication, the author of a Dano-Norwegian cookbook for Scandinavian immigrants in the United States cited the Milwaukee edition of the *Praktisches Kochbuch* as one of the *American* cookbooks that she had used as a source.[15]

Brumder's edition of Frau Davidis' *Praktisches Kochbuch* proved to be extremely popular and copies sold well. Following the first printing with its ornate peacock feather decoration on the edges of the text block, a less expensive printing appeared on lower quality paper without the peacock design but with solid red on all three edges. A variant and possibly third printing was issued on what appears to be even lower grade paper and without any coloring on the edges. Both these printings show a broken font in the numeral "2" used in numbering page 274. All these printings are bound in green cloth with blind stamping and gilt on the front and back covers and spine. Brumder issued yet another printing bearing the 1879 date. For this he used a medium quality paper with all edges colored bright red but a binding of brown pebbled cloth without blind stamping on the back cover. In all other respects (i.e., pagination and content), all printings with the 1879 date are identical.

These multiple printings suggest that a large number of copies sold. One might estimate this number by considering the sales of other German-language cookbooks published in the United States at approximately the same time. For example, *Die Hausfrau, Gattin, und Mutter* [The Homemaker, Wife, and Mother], published in Milwaukee and Detroit, appeared in four editions between 1879 and 1882 and sold 12,000 copies.[16] The reference to "achtzigstes Tausend" [eightieth thousand] on the title page of the German translation of *Buckeye Cooking and Practical Housekeeping*, however, is not indicative of the level of sales for other German-language cookbooks, as it refers to the *entire* number of copies printed of both the German and English-language editions of the work. The relatively wide availability of Brumder's edition today in antiquarian and used bookshops in this country, Great Britain, and Germany and in online auctions would suggest that sales of Brumder's edition exceeded the 12,000 copies of *Die Hausfrau, Gattin, und Mutter*, which today is quite scarce, appearing rarely on the used book market.

---

[15] [Anonymous] *Skandinavisk-amerikansk kogebog*, Af en husmoder (Chicago: Chr. Treiders Forlag, 1880) 2.

[16] Weiss, 212.

By 1889, Brumder had sold the copyright to his edition of *Praktisches Kochbuch* to Hoffmann Brothers, a competing publisher of German-language books and newspapers in Milwaukee. They issued an unrevised edition as a premium to subscribers of the Catholic newspaper *Columbia*. Their edition appeared without the lengthy subtitle Brumder had employed[17] and without Henriette Davidis' name on the title page although her name remained in the introduction and appeared prominently on the spine. Except for the slightly modified ornamentation on the spine, the decorative binding closely resembled that used by Brumder. The Hoffmanns, however, distinguished their edition by using black stamping on red cloth rather than gilt on the green or brown cloth used by Brumder. And they did not reset their edition, as evidenced by the same broken font used in numbering page 274 that is found in Brumder's later printings. The popularity of Frau Davidis' *Praktisches Kochbuch für die Deutschen in Amerika* also led the Philadelphia publishers Schäfer and Koradi to issue their own reprint of Brumder's 1879 Milwaukee edition for their Pennsylvania German market.[18]

During the twenty years following her death in 1876, Frau Davidis' reputation and the demand for her cookbook continued to grow. By 1896 her German publishers Velhagen & Klasing had issued fourteen new editions, making a total of thirty-six European editions in the fifty-two years since the first edition appeared in 1844. These posthumous editions were edited first by Luise Rosendorf and then beginning in 1892 by Luise Holle. Velhagen & Klasing's 1897 release of the thirty-sixth edition, combined with Frau Davidis' popularity in the United States, occasioned three Milwaukee publishers to issue two separate German-language editions as well as an English-language translation. C. N. Caspar adapted the thirty-fifth European edition, which had appeared in Germany only a year earlier, for his 1897 Milwaukee edition, but George Brumder, always the consummate businessman, acquired publication rights to the potentially more desirable, greatly revised and augmented thirty-sixth edition by Luise Holle that had just appeared in Germany. This business coup notwithstanding, Brumder's edition proved to be a far greater and indeed more lavish undertaking than Caspar's competing edition of that year. It was and remains aesthetically the more impressive because of its higher quality with respect to paper, illustrations, and recipe instructions. For example, Brumder's illustrations included twenty-nine numbered plates on coated paper as well as numerous line drawings.

---

[17] *Praktisches Kochbuch für die Deutschen in Amerika; zuverlässige und selbstgeprüfte Anweisungen zur Bereitung der verschiedenartigsten Speisen und Getränke, zum Backen, Einmachen u.s.w. eine Bearbeitung des anerkannt besten deutschen Kochbuches der Frau Henriette Davidis.*

[18] Weiss, 99.

Moreover, Brumder further distinguished what he called his second American edition by enlisting the aid of the Chicago hostess Hedwig Voß, who created a revised and considerably augmented cookbook that went far beyond the thirty-sixth German edition upon which it was based.

Frau Voß was a German immigrant and the widow of Arno Voß, who had left Germany in 1838 and eventually settled in Chicago in 1846 where he launched a highly successful career, being elected city attorney in 1853. During the Civil War, he organized the Twelfth Cavalry Regiment and served with the rank of colonel. Following the war he was elected to the Illinois State Legislature and received various political appointments thereafter.[19] Because of her husband's social position, Hedwig Voß was received in Chicago's finest homes and was an admired Chicago hostess. Her culinary skills were acknowledged when she was asked in 1891 to translate into German the highly successful *White House Cook Book* by Fanny Gillette and Hugo Zieman. Intimately familiar with German and American cuisines and cooking methods, she contributed far more than editorial revisions in preparing Brumder's 1897 edition. Her emendations and augmentations were extensive and exceeded revisions one would normally expect in a revised edition. Her resulting work exhibited several outstanding features. It introduced readers to literally hundreds of American recipes unknown to either Henriette Davidis or Luise Holle, including American-style pies, various cookies and layer cakes, and such items as Boston brown bread, Virginia brown bread, and five variations of cornbread. She vastly enlarged the sections on baking and preserving and inserted entirely new sections on bread baking, lunches, sandwiches, candy, and the use of leftovers. The rather minimal credit granted her on the title page of Brumder's edition greatly belies the extent of her contributions and the degree to which Brumder's second American edition deviated from the Davidis-Holle edition upon which it was based.

C. N. Caspar's Milwaukee edition of 1897 differed from Brumder's in several ways. Not only did Caspar use the thirty-fifth edition rather than the thirty-sixth, he also introduced several changes, of which three are of particular significance. To facilitate use of his edition, he compiled extensive German-English and English-German glossaries of culinary terms that remain of value today. He also deleted the last seven sections in the European edition devoted to the use of leftovers, time-saving tips, meats, advice for arranging large parties, the order of multi-course dinners, daily menus, and household management. In their place he substituted a 54-page chapter containing historically important American recipes, to which he gave the

---

[19] "Col. Arno Voss [Obituary]," *Chicago Tribune*, March 24, 1888.

title, "Die amerikanische Küche" [The American Kitchen]. Here one finds typically American recipes for soups, vegetables, meats, fish, shellfish, poultry, breads and related baked goods, cakes, pies and puddings, canning and preserving, and beverages.

Many of the American recipes that Caspar included are those recognized since George Washington's day as characteristically American. A number of them are also found in Amelia Simmons' *American Cookery* published in 1796,[20] which is generally acknowledged to be the first cookbook to include such distinctively American recipes as chowder (in the present edition see pp. 463, 464), biscuits (p. 488), Indian pudding (see boiled corn-meal pudding, p. 500), Johnny cake or hoe cake (p. 488), pumpkin pie (p. 499), soft gingerbread (p. 494), and cookies (pp. 494, 497). The undeniably American character of these and other recipes that Caspar added is underscored by a bill of fare written by the quintessential American, Mark Twain. In *A Tramp Abroad*, as Twain anticipated his return home, he composed a lengthy list of dishes that were considered typically American at the close of the nineteenth century.[21] Many of the items on his list can be found in Caspar's chapter "The American Kitchen": baked apples with cream (p. 501), fried oysters (pp. 480, 481), oyster soup (p. 461), American roast beef (p. 474), baked beans (p. 467), succotash (p. 468), stewed tomatoes (p. 468), catsup (p. 504), hominy (p. 488), hot biscuits (p. 488), hot buckwheat cakes (p. 486), American toast (p. 485), Johnny cake or hoe cake (p. 488), apple dumplings with cream (p. 501), apple fritters (p. 468), peach cobbler (p. 502), American mince pie (p. 499), and squash pie (p. 499). In addition to these, Caspar provided other recipes that were as American as those recorded by Amelia Simmons or cited by Mark Twain, *inter alia*, deviled crabs (p. 480), oyster fritters and clam fritters (p. 481), cornmeal puffs and corn dodgers (p. 487), Boston Brown Bread (p. 489), hickory-nut cake and other baked goods (pp. 490-498), lemon and cocoanut pies (pp. 500, 501), and maple cream (p. 515).

Caspar's and Brumder's competing editions of 1897 failed to satisfy the American appetite for new editions of the Davidis cookbook. Only two years later in 1899, demand permitted Brumder to issue a revised second edition, and a reprint of that edition followed in 1901. The market for American editions of the Davidis cookbook remained viable, and other Milwaukee publishers responded to the opportunity by publishing yet two more editions. Competitors in 1897, C. N. Caspar and H. H. Zahn combined forces in 1901 and jointly published a revised edition of their 1897 adaptation of the thirty-fifth European edition. They based this second

---

[20] Amelia Simmons, *American Cookery*. . . . Hartford: Printed by Hudson & Goodwin for the Author, 1796.

[21] Mark Twain, *A Tramp Abroad*, [1st ed.] (Hartford, CT: American Publishing Co., 1880) chapter 19.

edition on the thirty-sixth European edition used by Brumder and Hedwig Voß four years earlier. This they called the second revised American edition. On the title page they showed the publisher as "Verlag von C. N. Caspar, Co., Buchhandlung, H. H. Zahn Co. Buchdruckerei." In other words, they co-published the work by jointly sharing the cost of its production, marketing, and distribution, but each retained control over his respective area of expertise. Caspar the bookshop owner handled sales, and Zahn the printer was responsible for the production, typesetting, proofreading, and binding. As he had done previously, Caspar omitted end matter found in the thirty-sixth European edition and replaced it with the chapter devoted to American cooking, "Die amerikanische Küche."

Astonishingly, later that same year, 1901, the publishers of the German-language newspaper *Der Herold* reprinted the same edition using the Caspar and Zahn copyright statement on the verso of a significantly revised title page. The wording and layout, including the title, used by *Der Herold* show major differences from those used by Caspar and Zahn, while at the same time remaining so similar as if to intentionally confuse prospective buyers. The title page of *Der Herold*'s reprint states "Neueste Ausgabe" [Latest Edition] in a larger and bolder font than that used elsewhere on the entire page. Even the name Henriette Davidis did not merit as large or as bold a font, and only the title proper, *Praktisches Kochbuch*, was set in a somewhat larger but less bold typeface. That the edition statement is also centered on the page can only lead one to conclude that marketing was as important then as it is today. The other major difference between the two editions of 1901 is that the *Herold* printing attributes editorship to one Liese Haller. There may indeed have been a Milwaukee editor by that name, but it is also possible that a typesetting error occurred or a marketing strategy was intentionally employed, as the editor of all Velhagen & Klasing editions from 1892 to 1913 was not Liese Haller, but Luise Holle. Except for these points and Caspar and Zahn's half-page foreword, which is lacking in the *Herold* printing, the two Milwaukee editions of 1901 are identical. Even their bindings are virtually identical: the same decorative green cloth binding used by Velhagen & Klasing for their revised and enlarged German edition of 1891.

C. N. Caspar published a "third, corrected and illustrated" American edition in 1911. This, too, was based on the thirty-sixth edition that Luise Holle prepared for Velhagen & Klasing. Perhaps the greatest significance of this edition is that it was the thirteenth and last time an American publisher is known to have released a German-language edition of Henriette Davidis' *Praktisches Kochbuch*. In the spring of 1913, H. Carly in Hamburg published the only European edition of the *Praktisches Kochbuch* for the American market. This edition provided American weights and measurements for each recipe and included a German-English glossary. Carly's edition is of particular significance for it is the last of the German-language editions of the Davidis cookbook published exclusively for the American market.[22]

The American Translations

Because of the bestseller status achieved by the German-language editions of Frau Davidis' *Praktisches Kochbuch* in the United States, publishers attempted to increase their sales even further by marketing an English-language translation. Using the thirty-fifth European edition issued by Velhagen & Klasing in Bielefeld, C. N. Caspar and H. H. Zahn published the first American translation of Frau Davidis' cookbook in 1897 under the title *Henriette Davidis' Practical Cook Book, Containing an Appendix of Receipts for Dishes Prepared in Styles Peculiar to Cooking Done in This Country*. In March 1904, Caspar published the "second American augmented and illustrated edition" using a new title, *German National Cookery for American Kitchens: A Practical Book of the Art of Cooking as Performed in Germany*. Authorship of this edition is fully attributed to Henriette Davidis, but no reference is made to the translator or editor. Later, Caspar issued a third edition citing his Book Emporium as the publisher and using the 1904 copyright of the second edition but without any indication of the year in which it was issued. Even the date "March, 1904" that appeared in the second edition on page iv at the end of the "Publisher's Note" has been deleted although the "Publisher's Note" itself is otherwise unrevised. The reprint edition offered here is the third edition as published by "C. N. Caspar Co. Book Emporium, Milwaukee, Wis."

The second and third editions are the same in terms of content through page 530 with the exception that page iv in the third edition is unnumbered and the plates, which are not bound in their correct places in the second edition, appear with related recipes in the third edition. The most important difference between the two editions is the greatly expanded English-German and German-English glossaries that C. N. Caspar personally created for the third edition. These are extensive and serve as an excellent source of both German and English cooking terms. The only other differences between the second and third editions are their bindings and endpapers.

---

[22] Henriette Davidis, *Praktisches Kochbuch für die bürgerliche und feinere Küche: mit besonderer Berücksichtigung der Anfängerinnen und angehenden Hausfrauen*, neu durchgesehen und bearbeitet von Marie Wesenberg, Ausgabe für Amerika mit amerikanischen Maßen und Gewichten und deutsch-englischem Wörterverzeichnis (Hamburg: H. Carly Verlagsbuchhandlung, [1913]) 416 pp.

The second edition was bound in the identical decorative green cloth used for the 1901 Milwaukee edition that Caspar published in German, but "Practical Cook Book" is used in place of "Praktisches Kochbuch" on the front cover, and "Cook Book" replaced "Kochbuch" on the spine. The third edition differs only in the use of red rather than green cloth, and its endpapers are a dull undecorated turquoise, not the light green checkered pattern used for the second edition. It is interesting to note that the endpapers of the second English translation and *Der Herold*'s edition of 1901 are identical. Except for the fact that these are translations, the important aspects of the 1897 and 1901 German-language editions published by Caspar, Zahn, and *Der Herold* are retained: a faithful adaptation of Henriette Davidis' *Praktisches Kochbuch* and the uniquely American and historically significant recipes that appear in the separate chapter on "The American Kitchen." Interestingly, while the title pages of many of the thirteen German-language editions published in the United States between 1879 and 1911 clearly stated that the American editions were for "die Deutschen in Amerika," the translations merely stated "compiled and adapted for the United States." In so doing, the publishers revealed their desire to reach a broad market, one extending beyond the German-American community. They also revealed, although perhaps unknowingly, the degree to which many German Americans were losing or had already lost their knowledge of German, but not necessarily their love of German cooking, which, as editions of Irma Rombauer's *The Joy of Cooking* and other popular general cookbooks attest, continued to exert a major influence on American cooking long into the twentieth century.

Acknowledgments

I wish to thank Professor Joseph Salmons, former director of the Max Kade Institute for German-American Studies at the University of Wisconsin–Madison, for inviting this introductory essay. I also wish to acknowledge Antje Petty, assistant director of the Institute, for her interest in German-American cookbooks and her enthusiastic support in bringing about this reprint edition. I am especially indebted to Judith L. Tuohy, head of Interlibrary Services at the University of Wisconsin–Madison, and Angela J. Wright, head of Interlibrary Services at the University of Alabama, as well as Patricia Causey on Ms. Wright's staff for their persistence in locating and making available obscure publications needed while researching the history of foreign-language cookbooks published in this country.

GERMAN NATIONAL COOKERY

FOR

AMERICAN KITCHENS

A PRACTICAL BOOK OF THE ART OF COOKING AS
PERFORMED IN GERMANY

BY

HENRIETTE DAVIDIS

Compiled and adapted for the United States, according to the
Thirty-fifth German Original, with Weights and Measures
in American equivalents, and an Appendix of
Selected Recipes of Peculiar American
Dishes

Embracing also a Topically arranged List of over 550 Char-
acteristic German Dishes in German, with English translation, giving page where these Recipes can be found;
also a Vocabulary of Culinary Terms in both
languages, with full Table of Contents and
Indices

THIRD AMERICAN AUGMENTED AND ILLUSTRATED EDITION

PUBLISHED BY

C. N. CASPAR CO. BOOK EMPORIUM

MILWAUKEE, WIS.

Copyrighted 1904, by C. N. CASPAR COMPANY.

NOTE—Copies of our American edition in German of this Cook Book can also be
had from your dealer, or from the Publishers, C. N. Caspar Co., Milwaukee,
Wis. Price, in either language, $1.25, post-paid.

Publishers' Note.

"Henriette Davidis' Practical Cook Book" is recognized in Germany as being the standard authority in all matters pertaining to the culinary art. Its popularity and worth are evidenced by the fact that thirty-five editions have already been printed, and the demand for the book continues to be as great as at any time since its first appearance, because it is universally acknowledged as being the best and most practical of all cook books which have appeared in that country.

The original book of Mrs. Davidis has been constantly revised and kept up to date with each successive edition; in the preface to the German publication Mrs. Louise Holle, who, for a number of years past, has been in charge of this important work, says:

"The progress made in science and industrial methods during recent years has especially been the means of introducing manifold innovations in the culinary art, and I have endeavored to place all that has proved to be of real practical value in this direction at the disposal of the users of this Cook Book.

Furthermore, greater demands are to-day made upon the cook than formerly. Without any reference to luxury a greater variety of dishes is expected, owing to a general realization that this is conducive to a better nutrition of the body, and that such variety is often attainable with the simplest materials.—Food preparations for invalids have received proper attention, and the receipts in this book for dishes for the sick room will prove invaluable.

It may not be superfluous to say that none of the following receipts have been selected without a distinct knowledge of their value in each instance, many of them being of my own invention, and all having been tried in actual kitchen practice."

Appreciating the fact that we have in America many thousands of families comprising not only German-Americans, but among them many native Americans who are fond of cooking according to the German methods, the publishers determined to bring the Davidis Cook Book within the reach of those not familiar with the German language, and to this end we have made a careful compilation and translation of the thirty-fifth edition of the book, which we now take pleasure in placing upon the market. The German (metrical) weights and measures have been changed to conform to those in vogue and best understood in this country, and all designations of dishes and ingredients have been given in every-day English, avoiding the use of French appellations commonly found in other cook books. In an appendix are contained a number of receipts for the preparation of a variety of dishes specifically American in their character. Our edition has also been augmented by the addition of an English-German vocabulary of culinary terms. The typographical arrangement of this book conforms in its general character to the one published in Germany.

We trust that our American "Davidis Cook Book" will be found to meet every requirement anticipated in a practical, common sense handbook for the kitchen, and that it will prove to be as popular and gain as many friends as its European predecessor.

C. N. CASPAR COMPANY,

CONTENTS.

The American Kitchen.

Alphabetical Index.

Division A.—Miscellaneous Receipts.

ALPHABETICAL INDEX.

Division B.—Soups.

Alphabetical Index.

Division C.—Vegetables.

Division D.—Meats.

I. BEEF.

II. VEAL.

III.—IV. MUTTON. HARES.

Division E.—Meat and Game Pies, etc.

I. LARGE MEAT PIES.

II. SMALL MEAT PIES.

Division F.—Fish and Shell Fish.

I. FRESH WATER FISH.

II. SALT WATER FISH.

Division G.—Rare Dishes,

Division H.—Hot Puddings,

Division I.—Souffles, etc.

Division K.—Crullers, Omelettes and Pancakes.

Division L.—Dishes prepared with Milk, Rice, or Cornmeal.

Division M.—Jellies and Ices.

Division N.—Cold Sweet Dishes.

Division O.—Dumplings.

Division P.—Compots of Fresh and Dried Fruits.

Division Q.—Salads and Lettuces.

Division R.—Sauces.

Division S.—Pastry, Cakes, etc.

TARTS, COOKIES, Etc.

Division T.—Preserved and Dried Fruits and Vegetables.

Division U.—Dried and Pickled Vegetables.

Division V.—Beverages, Cordials, Etc.

The American Kitchen.

Soups.

Vegetables.

Meats.

Fish.

Shell Fish.

Poultry.

Bread, Fritters, Crullers, etc.

Cakes, Cookies, etc.

Pies and Puddings.

Preserves, Jellies and Pickles.

Beverages, Candies, etc.

Introductory Directions.

The proper preparation of our food should never be considered of secondary importance, even if regarded from a purely hygienic standpoint only. Every young girl, no matter what her station in life may be, should attain sufficient proficiency in this necessary accomplishment to enable her either to take charge of her kitchen herself, or, where this may not be imperative, to exercise that control over her subordinates which is always a part of the duties of a thorough housewife, and so necessary to keep expenses within bounds and to have the table well served.

The FIRST essential rule to be observed in order to achieve the best results in cooking, is scrupulous cleanliness. This consists in having the hands, the kitchen, all of the utensils and the table-ware perfectly clean, and also in being careful to rinse and freshen your vegetables thoroughly.

The SECOND rule is: Economy. An extravagant use of sugar, butter, and spices does not make your dishes any more palatable, but on the contrary, it detracts from their perfection, is unwholesome, and often spoils much that would otherwise be excellent food. Economy consists further in utilizing all odds and ends which can be used for our nutrition, and finally in a practical disposal of remnants of dishes which have once appeared on the table and oftentimes make a pleasing addition to our bill of fare, when skillfully prepared in another form.

The THIRD rule is: Care and deliberation. All cooking should be put on the stove at the proper moment—neither too early nor too late. The size of the kettles or other utensils should always be adapted to the quantity of whatever is to be cooked; this is particularly essential in cooking meats.—The fire must be carefully attended to, so that the cooking will proceed uniformly and the food neither be scorched nor served half-done.

The FOURTH rule is, to have all ingredients and materials necessary for the preparation of your dishes ready and handy before you commence cooking, so that nothing need be hurriedly done and you have abundant time to cook everything properly and can send it to the table nicely and orderly. Many excellent dishes are spoiled when improperly served. Plenty of hot water should always be ready while you are cooking in case any is needed for replenishing purposes; it is also better to warm platters, plates, etc., in hot water than to do this on the stove or in the oven, because they are not so liable to discolor or crackle.

*
*   *

In the following receipts the various quantities of each ingredient to be used have been given as accurately as possible, but the proportion of salt for each dish could not, in all cases, be definitely indicated; it would also be impossible to have scales and measures always at hand in order to minutely determine how much of this or the other article should be taken. Practice will soon enable the painstaking cook to judge correctly in regard to these particular matters of detail. Spices should, generally speaking, be used in accordance with the taste of those who are to partake of the dishes, but, on the whole, the directions given in the receipts should be adhered to. Pepper should always be added with caution, because its overabundant use is deleterious to health, especially for children. For the same reason, nutmegs and cloves should be used as sparingly as possible. Every dish should of course be properly spiced, but too much spicing must always be avoided.

Supplies for the kitchen should always be purchased at the most seasonable times, because then they can be obtained at the most advantageous prices. Always buy the best meats, poultry, vegetables, butter, flour, etc., because, while the best may cost a trifle more, yet it will be found in the end that, as in everything else, the best is here the cheapest also, and, beyond this, the most wholesome.

Flour must alway be stored in a dry, but airy place; when flour becomes damp, it should be turned and sifted frequently. Good wheat flour is almost pure white in color, with a very slight yellowish tinge; it possesses an agreeable sweetish taste, and when pressing it in the hand it balls very loosely. Poor flour is gray or reddish in hue and often darkly speckled, has a sour or musty odor, and when moistened feels clammy in the hand.— All kinds of starch flours, such as potato, wheat, and cornstarch flour, must be pure white in color and very smooth.—Carolina rice is the best; it must be clear white, hard, transparent, and the grains long, slender, and sharp-edged.

Pearl sago is superior to all others; inferior sago dissolves in cooking into a pasty mass.—Butter is most frequently used where fats are to be added to dishes; it possesses somewhat less nutritive qualities than other animal fats, but is more readily digested. Kidney suet (see A, 17,) is indispensable in cooking many fine dishes, because when used with meats which must remain in the oven a long time it does not brown so easily as butter; goose-grease and lard (see A, 16 and 18) are also of great value. Fats already used for roasts should not be preserved for any length of time, and in no case should they again be used for that purpose.—As a substitute for pure Olive oil, cotton-seed oil need not be despised—indeed the latter is more frequently sold as "Olive oil" than under its proper designation. Genuine Olive oil is quite expensive. All oils used in cooking must be odorless or but slightly aromatic when rubbed between the hands; a rancid condition of the oil is more readily discernible by that means than by the tongue.— It is almost superfluous to say that eggs should never be stale, but that the freshest obtainable must invariably be used.

* * *

Regarding the best cuts of meats and the proper handling thereof, explanations will be found in Division D, I, VI and VII, and Division F.—Concerning vegetables but little need be said, inasmuch as they can usually be obtained of good quality and in prime condition.

* * *

The quantity of meat, etc., necessary to prepare a meal will depend of course, upon the number of persons expected at the table.—For a large dinner party take ½ pound of beef for each person for a good soup or bouillon; veal ¾ pound. For a smaller dinner party take one-half more. Using but half of the quantity of meat and adding to each quart of soup ⅙ to ⅓ ounce of extract of beef and the same amount of salt, will make a plentifully strong bouillon at less expense.

One chicken will make enough soup for 4—5 persons.

Codfish—1½ pounds for 4—5 persons, if served with potatoes without any other meat-dish.

Rice boiled with milk, 3 ounces for each person.

Roasts, no matter whether beef, veal, mutton or lamb, should be reckoned at 1 pound (including the bones) for each person. As it would not look well to cut up the last shred, it will be impracticable to take less, even when there are a number of other dishes, unless the roast consists of a large cut without bone.

A good sized turkey, filled, will be sufficient for 10—12 persons, and when another roast is served with it, it will be enough for 18 persons.

Spring chickens, when quite small, one for each person; when of medium size four will be sufficient for 6 persons. If an additional roast is served, one-fourth less of the chickens will answer.

Pigeons—Six to eight for 4 persons; with a variety of dishes on the table a few less pigeons can be prepared.

One goose is enough for 8 to 10 persons, and one duck for 3 to 4 persons.

A shoulder of venison will be enough for 10 to 12 persons, and with an additional roast will suffice for 18 to 20 persons.

A leg of venison alone is enough for 8 to 10 persons, with another roast for 15 persons.

A.—Miscellaneous Receipts.

1. To clarify Sugar. Dip the sugar in cold water, put it in a medium sized kettle (preferably of brass or nickel), allowing it to dissolve over a slow fire, skimming off the broth until it is clear. In order to clarify it particularly quick and clear, add the beaten white of an egg, which will absorb the froth.

2. Frosting. To obtain very white frosting, which is essential for most puddings and cakes, the freshest whites of eggs are necessary. Beat in a large platter, in a cool place, until it is thick and stiff enough to turn, which will usually take from 5—10 minutes. A few drops of lemon juice added to the whites of the eggs will aid materially to stiffen the frosting. The frosting should be used immediately when done, otherwise it is apt to turn watery.

If the frosting is to be made into little balls for milk or beer soups, or is to be used for ices or cakes, a small quantity of pulverized sugar should be beaten with it.

3. Flour rubbed in Butter. Cook a piece of butter in an iron kettle, add a tablespoonful of flour and stir until it commences to curl and bubble. It must be well done, but only lightly yellow in color; if water, bouillon, or other liquid is stirred up with it, these should be cold, because then it will remain nice and smooth. If the floured butter is to be used in meat soups, stews, ragouts, etc., it can be added to the dish while cooking, after the latter has been skimmed, because it dissolves completely when cooked for any length of time.

4. Browned Flour. Stir a good sized piece of butter in a kettle until it commences to brown, add flour, stirring constantly until it is nicely browned, being careful not to scorch. Flour can be browned without butter, and preserved for future use. Put it into a small kettle and place over a slow fire, and stir constantly until lightly browned. A better process is to put the flour into a baking pan, and to brown in the oven.

5. Cleaning and scalding Rice. Rice should be carefully picked over, rubbed between the hands in water, and then put on the fire in cold water, and before it commences to boil pour it into a sieve. This process is particularly essential if the rice is to be used in the sickroom, or for milk-dishes, because the acids sometimes contained in the rice, causing the milk to curdle, are thereby removed.

6. To prepare Sago. Sago should also be carefully picked over, washed, placed on the fire in cold water, and after warming up, poured into a sieve. After repeating this once it is ready for use.

7. Browned Butter. Put the butter into an iron kettle on a slow fire and stir until brown; it dissolves at first, and then slowly commences to brown.

Whatever is intended to be browned, must be put into the butter after the latter is browned, otherwise the color will not be nice. Care must be taken, however, to prevent even the slightest scorching.

8. Clarified or Melted Butter, designed principally for Crullers, Doughnuts, Fritters, etc. Butter for this purpose must be clarified; if not, it will bubble and run over when the crullers, etc., are put into it. Put it into a medium sized iron kettle over a slow fire until it is light and clear, which will take about two hours. The froth not dipped from the top, partly settles at the bottom. As soon as the cooking sound is no longer heard, the butter is heated to the required degree; remove it from the fire, let it stand about ten minutes, take off the remaining froth and pour the clear butter into a perfectly clean stone jar, taking care to prevent any of the sediment being poured with it. After it is cool cover it with paper, put on this a layer of salt about one-half inch deep, and set it aside, uncovered, in a cool, airy place.

Butter clarified in the above manner is the very best for doughnuts and crullers, and for general cooking purposes it is unexcelled.

9. Crab Butter. Take about 20 crabs and stir them in clear water with a small whisk until they are perfectly clean, put on the fire and cook for 5 minutes. Pick the meat from the shells, put all the shells with about 6 tablespoonfuls of butter into a mortar and pound, but not too fine; put on the fire, stirring occasionally until the mass turns to a red color and commences to raise, then add one quart of water, boil and strain into a deep dish through a fine sieve; after cooling, the red butter is ready for use; the remaining liquor can be used for soups, particularly so if the crabs are boiled in beef broth, or extract of beef has been added to the water.

The tails of the crabs can be utilized in the soup or in a stew.

10. Anchovy Butter. Stir 1 pound of good butter to a froth, freshen 1 pound of anchovies (see No. 31), let them remain in fresh water 10—15 minutes to sweeten; chop them up fine, press the mass through a sieve, put into a small stone jar, cover, and keep in a cool place.

Anchovy Butter is spread on toasted wheat bread, and used in gravies, stews, etc. When put to the latter use it should be added just before serving, because it must not cook.

11. Parsley Butter. Bring a quantity of clarified butter to a boil, stir into it a good proportion of parsley and set aside for winter use.

12. Epicurean Butter. This is used to spread on toast. 4 boned anchovies, 4 small pickles, a trifle of chives and tarragon should be chopped very fine, pass the yolks of 3 hard-boiled eggs through a sieve, mix with 4 tablespoonfuls of butter, 1 teaspoonful of mustard, and then put the entire mass through a sieve.

13. Fairy Butter. An English receipt. The yolks of 3 hard-boiled eggs, 2 spoonfuls of sugar, 1 tablespoonful of orangeflower water and 4 tablespoonfuls of finest unsalted butter, well mixed and passed through a sieve. This butter is used to spread on cakes. Instead of the sugar and orangeflower water ¼ pound of crushed hazelnuts or grated almonds can be used, with the addition of a small quantity of lemon juice.

14. Fried Bread for Soups and Dumplings. (Croutons.) Put the butter on the fire, cut the bread into small pieces, or small figures if preferred, stir in the butter until it becomes yellow. Do not allow it to become hard.

15. Eggs in Soups, Gravies and Stews. Eggs are not added to dishes of this kind until they are cooked and taken from the fire. It is done in the following manner: The yolks, which must be fresh, are first stirred with a little cold water, then add some of the boiling soup or gravy, increasing gradually and continuing the stirring, then pour into the hot dish, constantly stirring, which will prevent the eggs from curdling. Whole eggs —the yolks and whites together—can be whipped up with a small quantity of water and some of the hot soup added, keeping up a continual stirring. A whole egg is equal to two yolks of eggs for the above purpose and more nutritious, but does not taste quite as well as the clear yolks of eggs, and should, therefore, not be used for fine dishes.

16. An excellent Goose Oil, which will remain sweet for a long time. The fat is first set aside for a day in a cool place in water and the latter changed three or four times. Then cut up the fat, add a small quantity of salt, put on the fire and slowly try it out, being careful to stir frequently. When the oil is quite clear and the remaining pieces of a light yellow color, the former is poured through a strainer into a stone jar and set aside for about a week. Then take the oil out of the jar, leaving the sediment and jelly. Put the oil on the fire again, adding a few sour apples pared and quartered, cook until the apples are soft and commence to roast, then again pour the oil through a fine strainer into the jar and the next day cover with paper perforated with a needle. If it is desired that the oil be of a firmer consistency, add a small quantity of tried leaf lard.

17. An excellent Way to prepare Kidney Suet. The firmer the suet, the better and richer it is. Cut it up into medium sized pieces, put it into fresh water, and let it stand until the next day, changing the water once during that time. Then chop the suet up fine, and take a small quantity of milk—about a small cupful to a pound of suet—cook it in an open kettle over a slow fire, straining frequently until the suet appears perfectly clear; it then does not need straining, but can at once be filled into a stone jar. The suet may also be cut into small cubes, then, after being tried out, it can be passed through a sieve; this method is preferable where the suet is to be used for fine dishes. If milk is added while trying the suet, it must *not* be stirred, and the kettle must not be placed directly on the fire. Should the suet be scorched it will be worthless, because it will thereby acquire a bitter taste. The cracklings, which at first should be loosened from the bottom of the kettle with an iron spoon, must not have a deeper color than light brown, and the clear suet, which has a sweet odor, like butter, is passed through a strainer. The cracklings when chopped with boiled beef, make excellent meat balls.

18. To Try Fat. Although it may seem that any directions how to try fat are unnecessary here, yet the fact is, it is too often very carelessly done.

The thick and firm pieces are the best for the purpose. Cut the fat into small cubes, as nearly alike in size as possible. Put them into an iron kettle or similar utensil, set over a medium fire, stir frequently until the pieces are yellow and crisp. This will prevent the fat from evaporating or receiving a scorchy taste, which is unavoidable if you have a very hot fire. Ham fat is well adapted for trying out in this manner, but the smoked outer crust must be carefully cut away.

19. Clear Broth for White Stew. To make a stew for 12 persons take 3 pounds of lean beef cut into small pieces, cover with water and put on the fire, skim carefully and add at once ½ of a celery root, 1 carrot, 1 parsley root, 2 onions, all cut into pieces, no salt, cover and cook for 2 hours. Pour through a sieve, set aside, and when it is to be used for the stew, take off the fat and pour carefully from the settlings.

20. Brown Broth for Brown Ragout. For 12 persons take ¼ pound of pork fat cut into slices, put it into an enameled kettle, add to this ¼ pound of raw ham (remnants of ham can also be used) and 2 pounds of beef, both cut into slices, also 2 onions, 2 bay leaves, 1 carrot, ½ of a celery root, 1 parsley root and whole spices. If you have any remnants of various kinds of raw meats they can be substituted for the beef. Put on a slow fire, cover and let it simmer for ½ hour. It will be of advantage if it turns brown without scorching. Then add a dash of boiling water and repeat this several times if the meat should adhere to the kettle. When brown enough, add sufficient boiling water to make the required amount of ragout. Salt is not used but is put into the finished ragout If the meats are well cooked after the elapse of 1 or 2 hours, the broth is passed through a sieve and the fat and settlings removed. Instead of the beef, 2 teaspoonfuls of extract of beef can be used.

21. To give Brown Soups, Ragouts and Sauces a good Color. Put 1 tablespoonful of sugar into a saucepan over the fire, and stir constantly until it has turned to a dark brown color. Immediately add 1 small cupful of water, take from the stove, stir, set it aside for coloring purposes in a closed glass receptacle. 1 teaspoonful is sufficient to give a large cupful of broth a nice yellow color.

An onion nicely browned in ashes, peeled, and then boiled with the soup after the latter has been skimmed, will give it a nice color.

22. Liver Force Meats. To ½ pound of tender veal, cut into cubes, add a few tablespoonfuls of finely chopped mushrooms, some parsley, half of a bay leaf, some salt, a little pepper and nutmeg, and 2 heaping tablespoonfuls of butter; let it cook slowly about 20 minutes. Take the livers of 10 or 12 fowls stiffened in beef broth or weak brine, put together in a mortar and pound until fine.

Instead of mushrooms, truffles rubbed in butter can be used; the liver of a goose or calf can be substituted for fowl liver, and finely chopped anchovies, to suit the taste, may be added. If goose liver is taken it can be used for making goose liver patties, or for goose dressing.

23. Beef Force Meat. ½ pound of lean beef and a little over 2 ounces of pork fat or kidney suet chopped fine, add salt, lemon peel, mace, a small piece of melted, yellow-browned butter, a trifle over 2 ounces of wheat bread soaked in cold water and then pressed, and 2 eggs, the white beaten to a broth. Stir well together, and it will make good force meat.

24. Veal Force Meat for Soup Dumplings. ½ pound of veal chopped with 1 ounce of marrow fat or kidney suet, 2 heaping tablespoonfuls of butter, salt, 2 ounces of wheat bread without any crust, which have been soaked in cold water and well pressed, and 2 eggs, the whites of which have been beaten. Stir well together.

25. Poultry Force Meat. After removing the skin from the breast of any kind of a fowl, it (the breast) should be pounded fine and passed through a sieve. Add 4 tablespoonfuls of unsalted butter to 1 pound of pounded meat and stir to a froth. Add the yolks of 4 eggs, nutmeg, a tablespoonful of chopped anchovies, 3 ounces of soaked wheat bread, which have been made into a paste on the fire, and salt; mix well together with the sifted meat. Instead of the creamery butter, crab butter (see No. 9), can be used, and the sifted meat need also be mixed only with the white of 1 egg and 1 large cupful of sweet cream, and all other ingredients be omitted. When prepared in this manner it makes good force meat for meat pies.

26. Fish Force Meat. Take 1 pound of fish (the best are pickerel or carp), cleaned and boned, ¼ pound of fresh pork fat, 2 stirred eggs, 1 small onion baked in butter, 1 anchovy, some finely chopped parsley, salt, ground white pepper and mace. After chopping this all up very finely, soak about 2 ounces of stale wheat bread in cold water, press it out well, stir into a dough on the fire with about 2 heaping teaspoonfuls of butter, then mix well with 1 or 2 raw eggs.

27. Force Meat Dressing for about 12 Pigeons or a Breast of Veal. Stir about 2 heaping tablespoonfuls of butter until soft, add the yolks of 3 eggs, some mace or lemon peel, salt, about 8 ounces of grated wheat bread, 1 large cupful of milk or cream, and the whites of the eggs beaten to a froth. One-third of this quantity mixed with some finely chopped parsley, is sufficient dressing for four pigeons. If desired, the finely chopped heart and liver of the pigeons may be added; in this case, however, more milk or cream will be needed.

28. Raisin Force Meat. Stir about 2 heaping table-spoonfuls of butter until soft and add the yolks of 3 eggs, some mace or grated lemon peel, about ½ pound of stale grated wheat bread, 3 tablespoonfuls of either sour or sweet cream, salt, ¼ pound of small raisins, about 2 teaspoonfuls of powdered sugar mixed with cinnamon. This is sufficient dressing for a turkey, 8 pigeons or 6 spring chickens.

29. Almond Force Meat. Take a coffeecupful of almonds and cover them with boiling water; as soon as the skins can be easily removed, take them out of the water, skin them, put in a mortar (a small quantity at a time), add a trifle of water and pound until very fine. Mix the pounded almonds with 3 tablespoonfuls of butter stirred until soft, the yolks of 3 eggs, mace and 2 coffeecupfuls of grated stale wheat bread. After stirring this all well together with a quantity of good cream, mix with the beaten whites of 2 eggs. This is sufficient dressing for a duck or 2 pigeons.

30. Cream of Anchovy for Meat Patties or Toast. Fresh butter and some flour lightly browned together, add sweet cream, finely chopped onions and lemon juice; cook thoroughly. Into this stir some finely chopped anchovies and the yolks of a few eggs, and then cook again.

31. How Anchovies should be prepared. Rinse the anchovies in water two or three times to clear them of salt, then let them stand in fresh water 10—15 minutes longer. Anchovies of an inferior quality must remain in the water a longer time, perhaps several hours. If good anchovies are laid in milk and the latter is frequently changed, they acquire a most delicious taste.

After the anchovies have been watered, pick off the fins from the back with the fingers, take them by the tail and pull them into halves, removing the spine and the rear fin. Then put the anchovies into a strainer and drain. They can be served with a dressing of olive oil and wine vinegar, or finely chopped onions, vinegar, olive oil and pepper. The best method of serving anchovies is to put them on a small platter in the form of a star, filling the spaces with capers, small onions, finely chopped herbs, and the grated yolks of eggs. The flesh of good anchovies is white and light; those of inferior quality are hard and dry and of a yellowish red color.

32. To prepare Celery and Parsnips for Soups, etc. Celery roots must be washed, peeled and cut into 4—8 pieces, the young unopened leaves need not be removed. Parsley roots must be washed, scraped and cut into pieces about 2 inches long, and split if very thick. Both are used for beef soups, the latter for chicken and veal soups only.

Parsley heads must be rinsed, the large heads cut away, take them in a bunch and cut them on a chopping board as finely as possible with a sharp knife. A little practice will enable one to cut parsley as fine in this way, as though it were chopped.

33. Truffles. Truffles must also be soaked from 1—1½ hours, they are then thoroughly cleaned, preferably with a brush, then cooked in a rich beef broth or claret; cut into pieces and serve in gravies.

34. Mushrooms. Remove the outer skin from the upper part of the stalk of the mushroom, cutting away the small leaves clustering under the head. Then wash in cold water, cut them up, put them in butter and on the fire, cook them rapidly in their own liquor and put them into the stew as they come from the kettle. They become hard if cooked too long.

Dried mushrooms must be soaked in water about 1 hour; should they happen to be of a brownish hue, previously boiling them will take out this color. Press them until dry, and add them to the stew or ragout when it is ready to serve.

35. To prepare Veal Sweetbreads for Stews and Gravies. Put the sweetbreads on the fire in cold water; as soon as hot pour off the water and renew, repeating several times until the sweetbreads are white. Then put them in cold water, take the skin from the longer pieces and cut off the fleshy parts from the others, cut the sweetbreads into cubes, and then cook in the stew for about 10 minutes.

36. Pistachios. Put them on the fire in cold water, let them come to a boil, hull them, lay them into cold water and leave until wanted for use. When used in stews they must cook not less than 30 minutes.

37. Crabs with Dressing. (Devilled Crabs.) Before cooking the crabs, stir them in clear water with a small whisk until they are perfectly clean. Put them into boiling water with vinegar and salt and cook until they are done. Break off the tails, pick out the shells, and then fill with force meats (see No. 23 or 27). The crab shells filled with dressing are then cooked or baked in the stew for about 15 minutes, and, with the tails, added to the stew when the latter is served.

38. To scald Onions. Peel the onions, then pour boiling water over them and after standing for about 8—10 minutes, dip in cold water and dry with a cloth. Scalded onions should always be used in cooking, because scalding them removes everything that is usually considered unpleasant in taste about this vegetable, and makes it very palatable.

39. Chestnuts prepared for various cooking purposes. If chestnuts are to be used in a stew or as a dressing for poultry, put the kernels into boiling water long enough to permit the removal of the hulls the same as with almonds, and then rinse them in cold water. Put them into an enameled kettle, with the addition of some water, butter and a small piece of sugar. Cover tightly and simmer slowly until done. In this way the chestnuts will be white, tender and not crumby.

Chestnuts as an addition to cabbage are prepared in the same manner. They can be either stirred into the cabbage before the latter is served, or be brought to the table in a separate dish.

Chestnuts for dessert or tea with bread and butter have their shells split and are either roasted in a coffee roaster or an iron kettle—adding a small handful of salt to a pound of chestnuts—and are roasted until soft and tender, which will take from ½—¾ of an hour; be careful to stir or shake them frequently.

Before serving the chestnuts rub them in a coarse cloth; they should be quite hot when put on the table.

40. Spice Extract for Stews. Cover the kernels of 60 sound walnuts with hot water for a few minutes, rub with a cloth to hull them, and when they are dry put them in layers into a stone jar with the following spices which have first been well ground together: ½ ounce of mace, some cloves (or, if preferred, garlic), ginger, 1 ounce of mustard seed, a pinch of whole white pepper, a piece of grated horse-radish, a handful of salt, 6 or 8 bay leaves, then add 1 quart of good wine vinegar well boiled. After the mixture has cooled, cover the jar, set it outside in the air, and after 2 or 3 weeks the extract can be filled into bottles which must be well corked.

The spices retain strength enough for another filling of boiled vinegar which has been cooled. 2 teaspoonfuls of this extract are sufficient for a stew for 6 persons.

41. Dill in Vinegar for pickling purposes. Dill is a favorite aromatic plant and is much used with pickles in vinegar. Dill is at its best immediately after the blossoming time, but very often when wanted for use, it is no longer green; for this reason it would be well to cut the dill when the heads are still fresh and green, and preserve them in a large glass jar covered with vinegar until they are wanted for use.

42. Pepper, Nutmeg, Cloves and Mace should be ground when needed and not before, because they otherwise lose a large percentage of their aromatic strength and flavor.

43. Mustard. As a usual thing, prepared mustards are of a very inferior quality, and it is advisable, therefore, to prepare them onesself. Take black and yellow mustard flour in equal parts, and to each ¼ pound add 1 heaping teaspoonful of white sugar, a pinch of ground cloves, ¼ teaspoonful of allspice, and enough white wine vinegar and white wine in equal parts to make a moderately stiff paste. When done fill into small wide-mouthed bottles, cork and let stand one week before using.

44. Almond Paste. Shell the nuts, pour boiling water over them and let them stand a few minutes. Then remove the skins, which will slip off easily, pound the almonds to the finest paste, moistening them occasionally with either water, the whites of eggs or arrac, as the receipt may require. Pounded dry makes the almonds oily. A stone or porcelain mortar is the best.

45. To wash Currants. After picking the currants over, put them into a sieve, place this in a deep pan containing lukewarm water, and rub hard between the hands. This loosens the small stems which will sink into the water; the latter must be renewed several times. Before putting them into cakes, currants and raisins must be dried.

46. To clean and stone Raisins. Remove the stems, pick them over carefully, rinse in lukewarm water, then dry and stone them. Large raisins may be cut into pieces before using.

47. Points about Lemons and how to keep them. There being so many lemons with a bitter taste put on the market, it is better to test them before use, which is particularly necessary when lemons are to be put into jellies, creams, blanc manges, or used for soups and beverages. Do not neglect to wash and dry the lemons before using them, and to remove the seeds and the white inner skin, which also imparts a bitter taste.

To keep lemons, they should be wrapped in tissue paper and laid in a cool place where there is a draft.

To keep lemon peel fresh, grate it on sugar, take off the yellow sugar very carefully, and preserve this lemon sugar in a widemouthed bottle well corked. As a substitute for the pure lemon juice, the extract of lemon can be used, which usually gives satisfaction.

48. The Use and Preservation of Orange Peel. Orange peel can in many cases be substituted for lemon peel; it gives a very nice flavor to most sauces. In order to keep well for a long time, peel the orange thinly with a sharp knife, chop the peel very fine, mix with 2 tablespoonfuls of pulverized sugar, keep in a well-corked bottle.

B.—Soups.

I. MEAT SOUPS.

1. General Directions for cooking Soup Stock. The kettle in which the soup is cooked should be used for this purpose exclusively and be kept perfectly clean. The best are made of heavy tin or enameled ware, and have a tightly fitting cover.

Dried peas, etc., can be softened by adding ½ to 1 teaspoonful of bicarbonate of soda (or saleratus) while they are cooking; it may be well to state, however, that this does not improve their flavor. The meat for soup stock must be fresh. The shinbone is generally used, but the joint and the neck or "sticking-piece," as the butchers call it, contains more of the substance that you wish to extract, and makes a stronger and more nutritious soup than any other part of the animal. However, nearly every kind of meat, such as mutton, veal, game or poultry, will make good soups of varying excellence.

For invalids who may partake of easily digestible food only, soups made from poultry or veal are the best. The meat from young animals will not make so strong a soup as that from older.

Where a strong soup is wanted without reference to the juiciness of the meat, as in case of a dinner party where the soup-meat is not brought to the table, take a piece of the joint without bone or fats, and although this may, apparently, after having been used for the soup, be of little account, yet when chopped up with fat boiled ham or nice pork fat, it will make very palatable meat balls. If the meat is to be served after the soup, however, or as a side-dish, it will be well to cut away all ragged pieces and then cut it up into smaller pieces, place it, covered with cold water, on the back of the stove for about 1 hour, bring to a boil and then add it to the soup when the latter begins to boil; whatever a soup made in this manner lacks in strength, may be supplied by the addition of some extract of beef.

Meats for soups should be washed very slightly and must not be laid in water, as this would tend to lessen their strength. Whenever possible, do not wash the meat at all, in any event it must not be kept in the water too long. When the meat is put on the fire, good judgment should be exercised as to the amount which will boil away and the quantity of water first put into the kettle gauged accordingly; adding water after the soup is done is very detrimental. Should it have boiled away too much, however, then a little *hot* water may be added. Soups cooked over a charcoal or peat fire are the best. Inasmuch as soups require long cooking and lose in quantity even in a tightly covered kettle, it is easy to oversalt, and this circumstance must be taken into consideration when the salt is first put in. It is always easy to add more salt if needed, but over-salting is an indication of either negligence or ignorance.

If a good, clear, palatable soup is wanted, a thorough skimming must not be neglected. At present many recommend that soup should not be skimmed, claiming that skimming weakens the soup. We cannot agree with this view, the albumen contained in the scum has but little nutritive value and a cloudy soup is not nearly so palatable (which should be the principal feature of a good soup) as one that is quite clear. But the skimming should not be done too soon—not before the meat has slowly simmered for at least ½ hour. Throw in a tablespoonful of cold water, which will bring the scum to the surface, when it should be immediately taken off.

Be careful in cooking the soup to keep the kettle closely covered, in order not to lose the flavor of the juices, and keep it simmering slowly, but without ceasing, until done, being careful to prevent boiling over. After cooking about 1 hour, take the precaution to pass the soup through a sieve, slightly rinse the meat to take off any scum which may adhere to it, and then place all back into the kettle (which has been cleaned in the meantime) and put on the fire again, having added the desired vegetables, etc.

Vegetables in Soups. A piece of celery root cooked in the soup gives it a pleasant flavor. If one wishes to add the celery plentifully, it is well to first cook it in water before adding it to the soup, so that the flavor of the celery will not be stronger than the flavor of the meat; for the same reason too large a quantity of vegetables, particularly celery tops, should never be put into the soup; in a weak beef broth, pea soup or potato soup vegetables, however, may be added to advantage. A red onion will give the soup a yellowish color, and is an agreeable seasoning.

Parsley and salsify should be added about an hour after the soup has cleared. Parsley, leek and asparagus will become tender in about ½ hour, celery root in a short hour. The preparation of soup vegetables is explained under No. 32, A.

To thicken Soups. If flour is to be used for thickening meat- or potato soup, it should be browned to a light yellow color with a piece of butter in a kettle or pan over a slow fire. Instead of this, however, flour may be kneaded with some fresh butter, make a small dumpling and put it into the soup at once after the latter has been passed through a sieve. The dumpling will dissolve completely and thicken the soup nicely. But the browned flour is preferable because it adds more strength to the soup.

When flour is used to thicken soups, it should never be put in raw, because this will impart an unpleasant flavor which will spoil even an ordinary potato soup.

Soups cooked for large dinner parties at which there are several courses, are usually served quite clear and without the addition of the usual soup vegetables. Small dumplings with a little fresh asparagus or cauliflower may be added. For the family table, soups can be thickened with slightly browned flour, as above, and the addition of rice, pearl barley, noodles, or sago will make them more nutritious. Sago, noodles or vermicelli are usually added to strong beef stock.

Quantities and Length of Time for cooking Pearl Barley, Rice, Sago and Fancy Noodles. 2 heaping table-spoonfuls of pearl barley or rice are sufficient in soup enough for 4 persons; 1 heaping tablespoonful of sago or fancy noodles in clear bouillon. Pearl barley and pure sago should be cooked in the soup 2½—3 hours, rice 1—1½ hours, potato sago (which can be distinguished by its small round grains) ¼—1 hour, fancy noodles and vermicelli, ½ hour.

When buying noodles be careful not to take those colored yellow and which ostensibly are made with eggs, for experience proves that the "saffron" used for coloring them is very harmful.

Dumplings. When dumplings are wanted in the broth or soup, take out the meat, lay it on a dish placed over boiling water, add 2—3 tablespoonfuls of soup fat and cover the dish at least until the soup is served. If the soup is to be entirely clear, it is better to cook the dumplings in slightly salted water to which a trifle of extract of beef has been added, and then take them out with a skimmer and put them into a tureen; the remaining broth, after having been put through a sieve, can be used for other soups or for cooking vegetables.

To make Soup stronger. A weak meat soup can be made stronger and more palatable by the addition of good extract of beef, of which small quantities are needed, perhaps as much at a time as can be taken on the point of a table knife; further on, directions will be given how good, strong soups can be made without any meat by simply using beef extracts.

All meat soups must be served as hot as possible.

2. Quick Beef Broth. Into a large cup put the yolk of a fresh egg, some salt, a very small quantity of mace or nutmeg, a piece of butter the size of half a hazelnut (the butter is not absolutely necessary) and ½ teaspoonful of extract of beef; stir well and gradually fill the cup with ½ pint of fresh boiling water. Instead of the butter a piece of beefmarrow the size of half a hazelnut is much better; chop fine, cook for about 10 minutes in the boiling water which is to be used for the broth, and then pass through a sieve onto the beef extract. In case the entire yolk of the egg is not wanted, half of it stirred up in a tablespoonful of cold water will keep until the next day if put in a cool place. Or the cup can be filled with boiling water to begin with and the salt and extract of beef stirred up with it.

3. **A palatable Soup for 8 Persons made of Beef Extract.** Figure on ½ pint of soup for every person; a small quantity of water should be added for the boiling. In all, therefore, 3 quarts of water must be brought to a boil; put in 1 pound of nicely washed beef without any bones, add a sufficiency of salt and skim carefully. Then add an onion cut up very fine, ¼ of a large celery root—if it is small take ½—and 4 tablespoonfuls of pearl barley, cover tightly and let the soup cook continually for 2½ hours over a moderate fire.

Just before serving put the yolk of an egg, nutmeg according to taste, and a scant teaspoonful of beef extract into the tureen, then pour in the soup gradually, stirring constantly to prevent the egg from curdling.

4. **Clear White Beef Soup.** For a large number of people take ½ pound of beef and for a smaller number take ¾ pound for each person, to make a good, strong soup. The broth will greatly gain in strength if a chicken is cooked with the beef. In this case less of the latter will be required. If the meat is not to be brought to the table, cut it up and put it on the fire in water, ½ pint for every ½ pound of meat; after the meat has simmered gently for about 30 minutes, skim carefully, immediately add a celery root peeled and cut into pieces, the white end of a leek or of an onion cut in pieces, a carrot cut in half and the necessary quantity of salt, and cook until the meat is done. Then pass the broth through a sieve, and after it has settled pour it into the soup kettle again, being careful to keep back all the settlings, and cook once more, adding little dumplings, asparagus tips or small cauliflowers. Crab tails can be put into the tureen if desired; these must not be cooked, because cooking makes them tough.

At the same time, rice, ½ tablespoonful to each person, may be scalded and cooked in clear broth; it should be of a thick consistency, but the grain should remain whole. The rice is served with grated parmesan cheese as a side dish with the soup; or the rice may be moulded in any pretty form, dusted with the grated cheese or dripped with crab butter. A modern side dish served with the soup consists of cooked tomatoes. The tomatoes are cut up, cooked in beef broth and passed through a sieve and served in sauce dishes.

Beef soup must be cooked from 2—3 hours, according to the age of the beef from which the meat is cut, sometimes even 4 hours, particularly the breast piece.

5. Hasty Beef Soup. For 6—8 persons, 2 pounds of meat are cut into small cubes or thin slices. Take a piece of butter the size of half an egg and in this lightly brown a few tablespoonfuls of flour, put in the meat, a finely chopped onion, a carrot, together with a small celery root which has been cut into 8 pieces, stir for a short time and add as much boiling salted water as is wanted to make the desired quantity of soup, cover tightly, cook 1 hour, and pass through a sieve. If rice is to be put into the soup it is cooked separately and added, with the celery, when the soup is served. Season with nutmeg according to taste.

6. Clear Brown Beef Soup. Directions for the preparation of a brown broth will be found under No. 20, A. For a party of 12 people, take from 5—6 pounds of beef, and about 1 to 1½ ounces of raw ham. Small dumplings can be cooked in this soup or brown sago if desired.

7. Tomato Soup. Lightly brown a good sized piece of butter with an onion, and in this stew 5—6 quartered tomatoes until soft, add 3 ounces of bits of toasted bread, a sufficiency of salt, and enough water to make 6 plates of soup. Before serving, the soup is strained, and strengthened with beef extract. It must cook 1½—2 hours and be well bound. If the bread is not liked in the soup take flour which has been lightly browned in butter instead.

Another way is to cook the tomatoes in meat broth until done, and pass through a sieve.

8. Beef Soup with Pearl Barley and Rice. Follow the directions given under No. 1, but pass the stock through a very fine sieve as soon as it has cooked ½ hour, then get a small piece of butter very hot in a small iron kettle and, for about 4 persons, stir with this about 1 heaping spoonful of flour until it is very lightly browned, and put the flour together with the broth (which must be poured from the settlings very carefully) and the meat on the fire again. If it is to be pearl barley soup the barley is to be added at once, also such soup vegetables as may be desired, but rice must be cooked only 1—½ hours, as observed in No. 1. An hour before serving a few button onions, asparagus tips or young kohlrabi can be cooked with the soup. Cauliflower makes a good addition to the soup, but must be cooked previously to putting it in, not so much, however, that it will fall to pieces; asparagus for this kind of a soup needs no previous cooking. Shortly before serving, drop a few fresh, finely chopped celery leaves or a trifle of finely ground mace into the tureen; dumplings can be added to the soup if desired.

REMARK.—Meat dumplings are preferable to all other kinds in weak soups, but the soup must not be made too thin, and it can easily be thickened by the addition of flour rubbed in butter, yet the latter should not be added sooner than 1 hour before serving. Those liking the flavor of celery can take 1 or 2 thick celery roots, clean them nicely, and cook them in the soup, then slice and serve with a dressing of olive oil, vinegar, pepper and salt as a salad.

9. French (Vegetable) Soup. Take vegetables of various kinds in their season; in the Summer peas, asparagus, kohlrabi, small carrots; in the Fall turnips, celery, savoy cabbage and kohlrabi. Cut up the vegetables and let them simmer in fresh butter, cover with a good strong meat broth, cook until the vegetables are well done, season the soup with mace and chopped parsley and serve with the addition of small egg dumplings or toasted bits of bread.

10. Ox=Tongue Soup. When the tongue is nicely prepared, an ox-tongue soup is not less palatable than any made from other kinds of meat. In the first place cut away the yellow spongy meat close to the bone, dip the tongue in hot water, rub thoroughly with salt, wash carefully and rinse until clean, then cover the tongue with plenty of water, add salt (not too much), put on the fire and cook slowly without interruption from 3—3½ hours. This broth can be used for potato soups according to Nos. 39 and 40. Any other soup can be made from a weak tongue broth by the addition of more or less beef extract, and will then be but little inferior to soups made from meats.

For a small table, dishes of various kinds can be made from tongue. Taken hot from the soup, it is palatable with cabbage or savoy. Parts of the tongue can be divided, sliced, and when fried with salt, egg, and cracker crumbs it makes a good side dish with Brussels sprouts, asparagus, spinach, cauliflower, or other vegetables; the remainder can be made into a stew, but in this case the necessary broth is taken from the tongue after it is cooked, and put into a cool place. It is best to make the stew the following day; do not forget to add a few slices of lemon.

The larger you can get the tongue, the more profitable it will be.

11. Ox=Tail Soup. Cut 2 ox-tails at the joints into pieces about 2 inches long, wash carefully, put on the fire in cold water, and leave until it begins to boil, then again rinse them in cold water. Clean the kettle carefully, and put in some onions, carrots cut into small pieces, parsley root, leeks and celery, to which may be added a bay leaf and 6—8 peppercorns. Let it simmer with a piece of butter and a little salt for about 10 minutes, then pour in 1½ quarts of meat broth and a pint of white wine. Then the ox-tail and a few slices of pork fat, and remnants of raw ham are cooked in this until nearly done. Take the meat out of the broth, strain the latter through a fine strainer, take off the superfluous fat, add one more glass of Madeira and enough meat broth to furnish the desired quantity of soup, say from 2½—3 quarts, and in this let the ox-tail cook until completely done.

Vegetables of various kinds, such as peas, asparagus or carrots which have been cooked in a separate vessel in some meat broth, are now put into the tureen and the soup, which has been seasoned with a trifle of cayenne, is poured in as hot as possible. Frequently the meat is cut from the bones and served in the soup.

According to the *English method*, the thick pieces are first fried with a few pieces of pork fat until they begin to color before putting them into the boiling broth, which has been made from the thinner pieces of the ox-tail, a piece of beef and a few pork kidneys.

No vegetables are put into this soup, but only 1 bay leaf, mace, and a piece of ginger for seasoning.

The soup is thickened with browned flour and butter, and receives an additional seasoning of Madeira and mushroom catsup.

12. Gravy Soup. Stew a thinly sliced onion with plenty of nice fresh butter, brown about 1—2 table-spoonfuls of flour in this and add enough boiling water to make the desired quantity of soup. After cooking rice and a sliced celery root in this until done add your gravy. Be careful in preparing soups from roast meat gravies that the latter have not become unpalatable or sour.

13. Veal Soup. Take the veal according to the number of persons as directed under No. 4; a somewhat larger quantity than there given is needed, however, because it does not yield so much broth as the beef. Wash, cook in water with a trifle of salt and skim carefully; after it has cooked for about 30 minutes pass through a strainer, rub some flour in butter, and onto this slowly pour the veal broth from the settlings, add a parsley root and, an hour before serving, some scalded rice. If in season, asparagus or cauliflower can be added; the latter should be previously cooked; 10 minutes before serving, meat balls or other kinds of dumplings may be cooked in the broth. Some people like a few purslane leaves or a little sorrel in veal soups. If you wish to substitute groats for the rice then leave out the flour, and put in a small piece of butter after the broth has been strained as directed under No. 8. When serving this soup, stir with it a little nutmeg or finely chopped parsley; the yolk of an egg is a palatable addition to veal soup, but in this case the latter must not be thickened too much. If the meat is to be brought to the table after the soup, the directions given under No. 4 should be heeded; serve with the meat prepared grated horse radish, or else turn it in a beaten egg with salt and pepper and fry in butter. The cooking will take from 1½—2 hours.

14. Calf's=Head Soup. Take the head of a well fattened calf, clean, cover with water and a little salt, boil until tender and pass the broth through a strainer. For 10 persons, 3 heaping tablespoonfuls of flour are lightly browned in butter, and then 5½ quarts of the broth are slowly poured over this; if the broth should have become reduced too much through the boiling, add some water. When the soup begins to cook, season with a pinch of saffron which has been previously dried and powdered, and add a dash of vinegar which has been made milder with a little sugar. A small cupful of vinegar of medium strength would be about the right proportion. Before serving stir the yolks of 5 eggs into the soup and also, according to taste, add about 6 ounces of bits of bread toasted in butter. In the meantime the calf's head should be split open; the brain taken out and put into the tureen, the meat taken from the bones and cut into pieces, fried in butter and served after the soup with boiled potatoes and pickles.

The boiled brain can also be cut into slices, sprinkled with salt and pepper, turned in eggs and bread crumbs and fried in butter to a light brown color.

15. Veal Sweetbread Soup. Prepare the sweetbreads according to A, 35, cut into small cubes and lightly brown in butter and flour. Cook for a short time in veal broth, salt slightly and stir with some finely chopped parsley or mace, and the yolks of eggs. This soup is also good for invalids, but then the seasoning must be omitted and the flour rubbed in a little butter but not browned, and ¼ of a teaspoonful of extract of beef added to a pint of the soup.

16. Princess Soup. Prepare 3 veal sweetbreads according to A, 35, and cook them for 15 minutes in a mild broth made from the extract of beef. Chop 2 of the sweetbreads very fine, simmer for a few minutes in melted butter and stir with the yolks of 5 hard boiled eggs to a uniform mass. Cook 3 ounces of lightly toasted bread in about 3 quarts of mild meat broth, then put in the sweetbread mass and cook the soup ½ hour longer. 3 hard boiled eggs and the other sweetbread are cut into cubes, placed in the tureen, and sprinkled with a small glassful of Madeira. Season the soup with cayenne pepper, strengthen with a teaspoon-ful of extract of beef if necessary, pour over the ingredients already in the tureen and serve.

17. Mutton Broth. After washing the meat put it on the fire in boiling water, add salt, but not too much, skim carefully, put in 1 small celery root, a small kohl-rabi, a finely sliced onion, flour browned according to No. 8, and some pearl barley or scalded rice, cover tightly and let it simmer slowly; clear off the fat as soon as it appears, for if it is cooked with the soup too long the latter will receive an unpleasant taste. If you desire to put groats into the soup, this should be done about 30 minutes before the soup is served, stirring thoroughly. Potato dumplings may be put into the soup or the yolk of an egg, mace or minced parsley stirred with it. The length of time for cooking this soup is about 3 hours.

18. Good Chicken Soup. For 5 persons take a large fat fowl which has been killed the day before and care-fully pick it clean and wash thoroughly in cold water. As fowls occasionally impart a strong flavor to soups, it is well to keep them in cold water for 15 minutes or so. The feet of the fowl can be utilized, if desired, by scalding them in boiling water, then take off the skin, chop off the points of the toes and put the latter in the soup with the heart and stomach of the fowl. The liver should be kept back until the last and cooked in the soup about 3 minutes before serving. All chicken or poultry soups gain strength if the breast piece is first cut out with the bone, the legs and wings are parted at the joints, and all other larger bones are cracked.

Put the fowl on the fire in 3 quarts of water and should it be an old one the water must be cold; add a little salt, skim and follow the directions given under No. 8 with reference to pouring off the broth and browning the flour; then add a piece of fresh butter the size of a large walnut and let the soup cook slowly but uninterruptedly for about 3 hours, keeping the kettle tightly covered all the time. Rice, pearl barley or fancy noodles can be cooked with the soup if wished, but of vegetables the only proper kinds are parsley roots, salsify or asparagus. Celery, leeks and onions are too strong for the delicate flavor of the chicken soup. Crab dumplings (see O, No. 2) or crab butter (see A, No. 9) are excellent in a good chicken soup, but bread-, groat- or egg dumplings are also good; a trifle of mace is an appropriate seasoning for chicken soup, or instead of this a little finely chopped parsley and the yolks of 1—2 eggs can be stirred into the soup.

Soup cooked according to the above directions, but without the addition of either noodles, rice, etc., leaving it entirely clear with all the fat taken off, and thickened simply with lightly browned flour, then adding 4 yolks of eggs whipped with 1 cupful of sweet cream or a glassful of Rhinewine and furthermore adding the roast meat of the chicken, which has been chopped very finely and passed through a strainer, makes what is known in Germany as "Queen's Soup".

Another German method is to omit the beaten yolks of eggs, and instead to mix the grated yolks of a few hard boiled eggs with the chopped meat of the chicken and then to heat them both in the soup. In some kitchens a glass of champagne is added before the soup is served.

The fowl may be served with the chicken gravy described under division R of this book, or if the roast meat has been used in the soup, the remainder can be used for chicken croquettes.

19. Windsor Soup. (A fine soup for a dinner party of 10 persons). Take 1 pound of chopped beef, ¾ pound of veal, about ¼ pound of raw ham and lightly brown this in 6 tablespoonfuls of butter together with 1 onion, 1 carrot and ½ celery root, cover the meat with 3—4 quarts of meat broth or broth made from the extract of beef, add a chicken from which the breast piece has been cut away and cook all together slowly for 3 hours. In the meantime take the meat from the breast of the chicken, chop very finely and then add 2 eggs, grated bread, salt, and a trifle of parsley, and make up into little dumplings which should be cooked in salt water just before serving. Macaroni broken into pieces are also cooked in salt water, soaked in an even tablespoonful of butter with 2 teaspoonfuls of sherry, and put in the soup which has been thickened with browned flour and butter and strained. The soup can be still further seasoned according to taste with a few glassfuls of sherry, or instead of the macaroni a baked rice pudding can be served as a side-dish.

20. Oyster Soup. For 12 persons make 6 quarts of good beef broth, taking for this purpose 6 pounds of beef with some soup herbs, skim off the fat, pour the broth from off the settlings, clean out the kettle and again cook the broth, then thicken with ¼ pound of fresh butter in which 4 tablespoonfuls of flour have been rubbed; in the meantime make 24 fish balls, open 48 oysters and take them out of the shells, cook the beards of the oysters in the liquor of the oysters, then pass through a sieve, add to the beef broth, and cook the dumplings in it for a few minutes, stir the yolks of 4 eggs with a little mace in a glassful of Rhinewine to which gradually add, stirring constantly, some of the boiling broth, and afterwards pour this into the soup, keeping up the stirring so that it will not curdle. After the soup commences to boil, take the kettle from the fire and then throw in the oysters, because cooking hardens them. Then immediately serve the soup together with buttered toast.

21. "Kaiser" Soup, Meat=Puree Soup of Wild Fowl and Rabbit or Hare. These soups are particularly nutritious for elderly persons or those in delicate health. Make a good brown meat broth and in this cook until done, 1 pheasant, 2 partridges, 1 snipe, 1 hare, take out the meat and let it partly cool. All of the meat is then taken from the bones, which are broken up, and cooked for another hour in the broth. The latter is then passed through a very fine strainer; the best parts of the meat, which must be free from skin and not stringy, are then pounded very fine in a stone mortar, pass through a strainer and mix with the broth, which, amounting to about 3 quarts or more, is salted according to taste, receives a piece of butter and should be frequently stirred with a wooden spoon, but heated only and not again boiled. To thicken the soup slightly soak about 2 heaping teaspoonfuls of bread crumbs with the meat broth and pound with the meat. This easily digestible soup contains all the strength of the game without any of the bones and sinews, combined with the best essence of the beef.

22. Crab Soup. Make a good beef broth according to No. 1 and for 12 persons take about 30—40 crabs, which have been cleaned and prepared according to directions already given, and cook them in boiling water for 15 minutes. Pick the meat out of the tails and claws, crush the shells in a mortar, but not too fine, and put them on the fire with ¼ pound of butter and stir until it begins to turn red and raise, then put in 4 tablespoonfuls of flour to thicken the soup. Pour over this 6 quarts of the beef broth, and then pass the whole through a sieve covered with cheese cloth. Shortly before serving add crab dumplings—(see O, No. 2) and sweetbreads (A, No. 35) into the soup which has been brought to a boil again. Asparagus tips and small cauliflowers are also favorite additions to crab soups. The tails of the crabs are put into the tureen, just before serving. When thickening be careful not to get it too thick, and, by the way, avoid this with all soups made for dinner parties.

23. Eel Soup (Bremen Style). For 3 quarts of soup boil 2 tablespoonfuls of fine pearl barley in a small quantity of water, then pour over this the necessary quantity of beef broth, and add shelled green peas, parsley or celery roots, cauliflowers, asparagus and a few small potatoes—the latter three ingredients should first be cooked — some chopped lettuce, celery, leek, parsley, purslane, salt and ground white pepper, taking proportionately smaller quantities of the stronger herbs, cook all together for 30 minutes and then put in nicely cleaned pieces of eel about 2 inches long, which have first been cooked in salted water, and cook until done.

Then make dumplings of fish force meat, cook them for a few minntes in the soup and stir this with the yolks of a few eggs, sweet cream, chopped thyme and a few drops of lemon juice; serve immediately.

24. Eel·Soup (Hamburg. Style). Two pounds or more of heavy eels are rubbed in salt—it is best to do this the day previous to cooking—then washed, cut into pieces of suitable size, the head and the point of the tail cut off, and cooked in white wine, a very little wine vinegar, salt, white and black peppercorns, and 1—2 bay leaves. Cook a number of pears the day before in white wine and cinnamon as for a sauce, but without sugar. The pears should be cooked whole so that they may receive the full flavor of the wine and vinegar. The eel and the pears should be set aside in a cool place.

When ready to cook, boil 2, 3 or 4 pounds of good beef in 1 pint of water to each pound of meat. Skim carefully and after cooking 1 hour throw in a soupplateful of carrots cut into little pieces, half as much parsley root also cut into small pieces, and 1 celery root, whole. At the same time take a handful of celery leaves, a handful of parsley, a few slips of sweet majoram, also a bit of thyme, burnet, houseleek, a few sorrel and sage leaves and some green leek, chop fine and put into the soup, and after it has cooked a few hours throw in a soupplateful of shelled green peas, a handful of purslane and of cauliflower. Shortly before serving rub a tablespoonful of flour in a good-sized piece of butter, and stir it into the soup with some pepper. When ready to serve pour as much of the soup as will be needed into the tureen and add as much of the eel and of the pears (which must first be warmed) as will be proportionately enough, bringing the remaining pieces of the eel and the rest of the pears to the table in separate dishes. Should it then happen that more soup is wanted than was prepared, the eel and pears can be passed around and the plates filled with what is remaining of the soup.

Dumplings made according to directions given under O, No. 2, are also put into the soup.

If the eel soup is wanted for the family table, prepare a simple strong meat broth and in this cook for an hour before serving a plateful of green peas, another plateful of quartered pears and celery roots until done. Then put in a few eels which have previously been skinned, cut into pieces and cooked in salt water until half done; put in such soup herbs as can be obtained, cook until done. Thicken the soup if necessary and put in sponge dumplings (see under O). Serve with sliced lemon.

25. Fish Soup. Pickerel, pike, carp or freshwater fish of every kind are cut into pieces, turned in flour and baked in butter together with some slices of bread until light brown, then pour in some meat broth which has been made with celery, parsley roots and onions, or else the strained broth of shelled green peas, let the soup cook a little longer, pass through a sieve, shortly before serving bring to a boil again and serve with finely chopped parsley. Buttered toast cut into small pieces is served in the soup.

If the broth has been prepared beforehand, this kind of soup can be gotten ready in 1 hour.

For an ordinary fish soup the water in which fresh-water fish have been cooked will answer. This soup is best thickened with dried peas, cooked and strained; strengthen with extract of beef.

26. Mock Turtle Soup. For 24—30 persons make a strong beef broth, taking 8—10 pounds of beef with the requisite soup herbs, onions, bay leaves, ground cloves and 2—3 whole cloves. Put on the fire a large well cleaned calf's head, a pig's jowl and ears, a nice beef bone and a smoked beef tongue; cook all together until done, but it must not be too tender. After the meats are cold, cut them up in small oblong pieces and also the tongue of the calf, which of course must be well cleaned, put all in the broth with the addition of small sausages, a pinch of cayenne pepper, several sweet-breads (see A, No. 35), and enough of the calf's head broth to make a sufficent quantity of soup, which should be thickened with browned flour and butter.

After everything has cooked for 15 minutes, cook a number of veal meat balls in some veal broth or salted water and add them to the soup, together with several hard boiled eggs cut into small pieces, and also the brain of the calf which must first be washed in water, scalded, the small veins taken out, then cooked in water with a little vinegar, afterwards cut it into slices, turn in egg and bread crumbs and bake in butter; further-more, put into the soup some catsup and, if they can be obtained, ½ bottle of Madeira and some oysters; the latter two, however, must not be cooked as long as the rest.

Then immediately serve the soup.

To make a very elegant mock-turtle soup small dumplings in imitation of turtle eggs must be added. Take the yolks of 3 hard boiled eggs, grate them finely

Vegetables — Gemüse.

1 French Bean—Veitsbohne; 2 Green Pea—Grüne Erbse; 3 String Bean—Welsche Bohne; 4 Kidney Bean—Schwertbohne; 5 Scarlet Bean—Scharlachfarb'ge Bohne; 6 Garlic—Knoblauch; 7 Sea Cabbage—Meerkohl; 8 Spinach—Spinat; 9 Endive—Endivie; 10 Sprouts—Sprossenkohl; 11 Mustard and Cress—Senf und Kresse; 12 Truffle—Trüffel; 13 Savoy Cabbage—Savoyerkohl; 14 Broccoli—Broccoli; 15 Horseradish—Meerrettig; 16 Radish—Radieschen; 17 Turnip—Weisze Rübe; 18 Beet—Rothe Rübe; 19 Radish—Rettig; 20 Asparagus—Schnittspargel; 21 Summer Cabbage—Schnittkohl; 22 Mushrooms—Pilze; 23 Onion—Zwiebel; 24 Carrots—Carotte; 25 Cabbage—Weiszkraut; 26 Cucumber—Gurke; 27 Artichoke—Artischoke; 28 Green Artichoke—Grüne Artichoke; 29 Red Cabbage—Rothkraut; 30 Tomato—Tomate; 31 Spanish Onion—Spanische Zwiebel; 32 Lettuce—Lattich; 33 Head Cabbage—Kohlkopf; 34 Parsnip—Pastinake; 35 Celery—Sellerie; 36 Potato—Kartoffel; 37 Lima Bean—Weisze Bohne; 38 Leeks—Porre; 39 Mark Pea—Markrbse; 40 Cauliflower—Blumenkohl; 41 Egg Plant—Eierpflanze.

and mix with a small teaspoonful of flour, the yolk of a fresh egg, 1½ tablespoonfuls of butter, salt and a trifle of nutmeg, make little balls the size of a marble, cook for a few minutes in boiling water.

The beef broth as well as the head of the calf can be cooked the day before without detriment to the soup.

A simple mock-turtle soup can be made by cooking the head of the calf together with the soup herbs, carrots and a beef jaw; thicken with browned flour and butter, strengthen with about ½ teaspoonful of extract of beef for each quart of broth and then add tarragon, the chopped meat of the calf's-head, 1 glassful of arrac and hard boiled eggs cut into cubes.

27. Hare Soup. When cleaning the hare, catch the blood; crack the bones and cut the meat, excepting the saddle, into pieces, cook together with several pounds of beef, some ham, spices and soup herbs slowly for 3 hours; in the meantime fry the saddle in butter, cut up into pieces and put into the tureen. Pass the soup through a strainer, thicken with browned flour and butter and then add the blood, being careful to stir vigorously, also 2 glassfuls of Portwine, some cayenne pepper and salt, cook thoroughly and serve.

According to the English method, only the hare is used and the time devoted to cooking does not exceed 2 hours. For this soup cut up the whole hare and after setting aside the best pieces of the saddle, fry the rest of the meat with carrots, sliced ham, soup herbs and seasoning in butter to a light brown; on this pour clear beef broth and cook as above. The saddle pieces are also fried, but they are then pounded very fine, mixed with some soaked bread or roll and ½ pint of Portwine and cooked with the soup.

Sometimes rice is cooked in the soup, but a rice pudding served with the soup is preferable.

A medium-sized hare will make enough soup for 6—7 persons.

28. Brown Soup made from the Bones of Hares, Game or Roasts. First remove all of the meat which may still adhere to the bones, chop very fine and stir with soaked and pressed bread, some fresh butter, several eggs, salt, pepper, nutmegs; this is to be made into small dumplings to be cooked in the soup later on. It is well to first test the dumplings to see whether they are too hard or too soft; in the first case put in another egg or some cream, in the latter some bread or cracker crumbs. The bones, in the meantime, are broken or cracked into small pieces and fried lightly in butter with sliced lean ham, onions, carrots and a parsley root, brown a few tablespoonfuls of flour and pour over all as much boiling water together with such lots of perfectly good gravy as you have left over. Cook the soup for 2 hours, pass through a very fine strainer in order to catch the chips of bones that may be in the soup, then pour the soup back into the kettle, being careful to keep back the settlings, cook the dumplings until done, strengthen the soup with extract of beef and season with Madeira, cayenne pepper and salt. Should there be no meat on the bones, thicken the soup with browned flour and butter, or else cook the dumplings or the hearts of cabbages in the soup. Ordinarily the frying of the bones can also be omitted and then they need simply receive a long and slow cooking in water with salt, spices and plenty of soup vegetables, but when thus made an addition of extract of beef is desirable.

29. Partridge Soup. Partridge soup is made like hare soup; instead of the dumplings, the meat from the breast can be sliced very fine and served in the soup.

30. Jacobine Soup. Put poached eggs, (see under L) into the tureen together with bits of toasted bread, cover with strong, hot beef broth and add chopped pieces of poultry roast.

31. Beef Tea. Take about 1 pound of lean beef free from sinews; it is necessary to have a vessel that can be hermetically sealed, and a large piece of absorbent or blotting paper. Cut the beef into small pieces, put into the vessel, close it and put into a kettle with boiling water and let it cook slowly 4 hours. Then pour through a very fine strainer into a warm cup, take off the fat with the blotting paper by absorption, season with salt and stir into it the yolk of an egg. The given quantity of meat will make a medium sized cupful of beef tea. The meat can be utilized for hash or for meat balls.

32. Pigeon Soup for Invalids. The broth is prepared as directed under No. 1, and scalded rice is added immediately after the broth is skimmed; a few fresh carrots or green peas, or ½ hour before serving some asparagus tips or a little cauliflower (the latter must first be cooked) may be added. The soup must cook not less than 2 hours, because only old pigeons are to be used; it should be well bound but not too thick, and if the invalid is entirely free from fever, the half of the yolk of a fresh egg may be stirred into it. Instead of rice, pearl barley is frequently put into soups of this kind; the barley must first be scalded, slightly browned in butter, cooked with a few spoonfuls of the broth and be allowed to draw on top of the stove until the pigeon soup has cooked for about an hour; then cook them in the soup until completely done, after which a few asparagus tips only are added.

33. Veal Soup for Invalids. Take a good chunky piece of veal, skim the broth through a strainer, put in a small piece of fresh butter and some scalded rice, and cook until done with asparagus and cauliflower which have first been separately cooked. The yolk of a fresh egg or a trifle of nutmeg or finely chopped parsley may be stirred in the soup if it is not contrary to the physician's directions.

34. Beef Broth Soup (Puree) for Invalids. Make a good clear beef broth according to No. 1; in 1 large cupful cook 2 heaping teaspoonfuls of grated wheatbread and after passing it through a sieve stir into it the breast of a chicken very finely chopped, which has first been thoroughly mixed with 2 tablespoonfuls of sweet cream. The soup must not be cooked again and the yolk of an egg can be stirred in if desired.

35. Game Soup with Tapioca. Take a partridge and make a clear broth free from fat, stir 2 even tablespoonfuls of tapioca with 4 tablespoonfuls of sherry, cook for 10 minutes in the broth, and finally add a few asparagus tips or small cauliflowers, which have previously been cooked in salted water until done. Any other kind of game can be used, but it must first be slightly roasted, covered with cracked veal bones, salt, soup vegetables and the necessary amount of water, and cook slowly for 3 hours before the broth is strained and other ingredients, as taste suggests, are added.

Besides the last five of these soups, Nos. 2, 16, 17 and 19 are well adapted for the sick room.

II. VEGETABLE AND HERB SOUPS.

36. Soup, Vegetables and Meat. This dish makes a palatable, nutritious and cheap dinner, and can be prepared either from fresh peas or such as have become slightly hard, (the latter must be strained after cooking) as well as from young kohlrabi, cauliflowers or even potatoes. Get a piece of butter or lard very hot, in this brown 2 heaping tablespoonfuls of fine flour, pour the necessary quantity of water over all, stirring it, and as soon as it commences to boil add the desired vegetables, either a heaping soupplateful of shelled green peas and soup vegetables cut into pieces, or 2 sliced kohlrabi, some salt, and cook until tender and the soup becomes rather thick. If the soup is to be made with potatoes follow the directions given under No. 38 for a potato soup, cook with either a piece of leek or a celery root, then with a tablespoon cut from the boiled meat 16 dumplings (see O, beef or veal dumplings) shaping them by turning them back and forth with the spoon; it is advisable, however, to try them to see that they are not too flabby or too hard; then cook the dumplings for about 5 minutes, that is to say, until done, after which the soup should not cook any longer, then stir a small head of finely chopped parsley into it. If no potatoes are cooked in the soup, serve them boiled as a separate dish.

37. Russian Cabbage Soup. (Borsch). (*Original receipt.*) Take about six pounds of beef for the stock. Clean 6 small red beets, cut into long thick slices, turn in flour, cover tightly and stew in butter for ½ hour. Besides this take a small head of cabbage, quarter it, cover with boiling water, put the lid on the kettle and set aside for ½ hour. After the broth has cooked for 1½ hours, put in the beets and then ½ hour later the cabbage; celery root, small carrots, and green leek must not be forgotten. After all is thoroughly well cooked add ½ pint of sour cream into which a heaping tablespoonful of flour has been stirred, and when the cooking is done, stir the yolk of an egg into the soup and serve with small sausages.

38. Potato Soup. Put the bones of fresh or roast meats on the fire, together with meat remnants of fresh meat, adding the proper amount of salt, skim, put in onions, leek and a celery root, and cook slowly for 1½ hours. In the meantime cook the potatoes in a separate kettle until they are almost soft, add them to the soup and after the cooking is well done, strain. Stir a finely chopped bunch of parsley or else grated nutmeg into the soup, then serve with bits of toasted bread.

Potato soup can also be made without meats, using water only, but in this case it must have plenty of vegetables, and also some flour browned in butter and a teaspoonful of extract of beef must be cooked with it.

39. A very fine Potato Soup. Fry 2 platefuls of sliced raw potatoes with a chopped onion in 2 even tablespoonfuls of butter to a light brown color until nearly done, throw them without the butter into 3 quarts of boiling water, in which some soup vegetables have been cooked for 15 minutes previously, add sufficient salt and cook the soup for ½ hour; then pass through a sieve, and in the fat which remains from frying the potatoes brown 1 tablespoonful of flour, add this to the soup, strengthen with a small teaspoonful of extract of beef and 2 tablespoonfuls of claret, let it come to a boil, and then serve with toasted bits of bread.

40. Oatmeal Soup with Potatoes. Soak the oatmeal in water, about 1 heaping teaspoonful for each person, and then cook in water with the addition of some good fat (broth from cooked smoked meats or ham mixed with water is excellently adapted for the purpose), kohlrabi, celery, parsley and green leek, or if these are not obtainable, take a few finely chopped onions, add nicely washed potatoes and the necessary salt; cook for about 2 hours until thoroughly done and of a medium thickness. A little extract of beef can be added to this soup advantageously.

Instead of oatmeal coarse pearl barley (groats) can be taken. Cook with pork fat until white and do not fill up with the broth or the water until the groats are entirely soft.

41. Early Vegetable Soup. Rub some flour in butter, add as much water as is wanted to make the desired quantity of soup, salt, and cook therein the following early vegetables until done: celery and parsley roots, lettuce, spinach, sorrel, purslane and peas. Stir some cream into the soup and add wheat bread toasted in butter. 1¼ hours are sufficient to cook this soup.

42. Green Pea Soup. Shell the peas, and, without washing them, let them simmer for a short time in a piece of melted butter and then, according to the quantity of soup desired, let 1—2 tablespoonfuls of flour draw in this, then pour on the requisite quantity of broth or boiling water and add a little extract of beef. When the peas are quite tender, put in salt and chopped parsley. Groat- or meat dumplings may be cooked in the soup and served with small pale sippets of bread fried in butter. Time of cooking, 1 hour.

43. Vegetable (Puree) Soups made from Extract of Beef. These easily digestible soups are made from carrots, beets or turnips. The kind of vegetable selected for the soup is nicely cleaned, cooked in water until tender, passed through a colander, stirred with some good beef broth and then cooked until quite thick with salt and bread crumbs, or, omitting the latter, stir constantly while cooking and then serve with a piece of butter and fried bits of bread placed in the tureen. In the spring of the year an asparagus puree soup made from chicken broth is very palatable. The asparagus, with the exception of the tips, is cooked in the broth until tender. The soup is passed through a strainer, thickened with browned flour and butter and then the tips of the asparagus are also cooked until tender. Stir into the soup a number of yolks of eggs whipped in sweet cream.

A soup can be made from the cauliflower, first cooking them until they are half done, then cook in butter until entirely done, pass through a strainer and make up with meat broth and stir an egg into it.

44. German Soup. (*Especially recommended for the months of August and September.*) Carrots cut into cubes, sliced string beans and kohlrabi are stewed in butter for ¼ hour; then cook in enough boiling salt-water to make the necessary quantity of soup; the vegetables should be tender but not overdone. Shortly before serving add a few well-cooked new potatoes, young cauliflower, hearts of cabbages and particularly the pulp of 6 large tomatoes and 1 teaspoonful of extract of beef; season with pepper and serve over small baked kidney slices.

45. "Schweriner" Soup. Take 1 sliced cucumber, the center leaves of several heads of lettuce, a few early eschalots and a plateful of shelled green peas, and simmer in hot butter until nearly done; as seasoning add parsley, chervil and burnet all finely chopped together with salt, pepper and a pinch of ginger; fill in the boiling broth and cook the soup for an hour, thicken with lightly browned flour and butter, stir into it the yolks of a few eggs and serve with small marrow bits.

46. Old Pea Soup.. Old peas can be utilized best in soups. Put them on the fire in boiling water with a piece of kidney suet, cook until tender and pass through a sieve; cook the broth once more, add salt, a piece of butter and lightly browned flour, and stir with chopped parsley and a little extract of beef. Meat balls make a very palatable addition to the soup. Time of cooking, 2 hours.

47. Split Pea Soup. Pick the peas over carefully, rub them between the hands in warm water and clean then nicely; put them on the fire in cold soft water and if the peas are very old, add a trifle of bicarbonate of soda (cooking soda, see No. 1) on the fire, and cook slowly for a short ½ hour, which will make them quite tender; after cooking put them on a colander, pour water over them and cook slowly in boiling water until

done, with the addition of some fat, a piece of beef or a
sausage, together with a celery root and green leek.

If it is desired to cook a smoked pork sausage or a
pickled pigshead in the soup (well liked by some), the
sausage must first be washed and cooked, in order to
take from it the smoky flavor which would injure the
soup. If the sausage has been kept for some time and is
consequently no longer juicy, it should be laid in warm
water for a day and night; salt pork should be first
cooked in water until done, and only as much of the
salty broth put into the pea soup as can be done without making the latter too salty. Peas, beans and similar vegetables do not require much salt.

After the peas have become quite tender take out
the meat and the celery root, put the latter into the
tureen, pass the peas through a strainer and cook them
with the meat until well done; if necessary, thin with a
little broth. If no onions were at first put into the
peas they can be added later on, first chopping them
up finely, then brown in butter and stir into the soup.
Bits of bread fried in butter may also be added if wished.

A mild flavor can be given to the pea soup by cooking 2 sliced carrots, 2 small bunches of fresh parsley
and a little sugar in it; this gives it the flavor almost
of a soup made of new peas.

The soup must not be thick but it should be nicely
bound. If its consistency is not just right, flour browned
in butter can be used; but this should only be done in
case the peas have either not been cooked long enough
or are too old, or if the soup has become too thin. The
pure flavor of the peas is impaired by the addition of
the flour. Ordinarily, a few small potatoes can be
cooked in the soup after the peas have been strained,
but they must not be overdone, and if the soup should
stiffen through cooking too long, it should be thinned
somewhat.

The time of cooking depends upon the quality of
the peas. If they are good they will be tender in about
2 hours, otherwise it will take from 3—4 hours.

48. White Bean Soup. The very small white beans
are the best because they taste nicer and need not be
strained. After washing the beans put them on the fire
in cold water—1 pound of beans for 6 persons—and let

them cook well for ½ hour; pour them on the colander and immediately put them back into the kettle, which has been cleaned in the meantime, with fat or butter and enough boiling water to cover; the beans are cooked until they are tender, being careful to frequently add a dash of boiling water; they must not be stirred very often so that they will remain whole and yet make a good thick soup; they are afterwards salted and reduced with boiling water to make the soup, and once more cooked after a small quantity of meat broth or extract of beef is added. A smoked pork sausage which has first been cooked, or a small piece of smoked ham, according to the opinion of some people, will improve the flavor of the soup, or 5 minutes before serving "Frankfurt" or "Wiener" sausages can be put into it and, if liked, a number of small potatoes which have first been separately cooked. In some German kitchens thyme or majoram are a favorite seasoning for bean soup.

A few tart apples cooked in the soup give it a very pleasant flavor, which can be still further improved by adding a teaspoonful of crab butter before serving.

49. Lentil Soup. Lentils should be cooked in an enameled vessel to prevent them from turning dark, and they will be much improved by pouring off some of the water and renewing it twice after cooking about 15 minutes at each time, and then let them cook slowly in not too much water but with plenty of fat. After this thin to the proper consistency with the broth of pickled meat and cook until done with small potatoes, some leek or sliced onions browned in butter. If this kind of soup is made with water and fat only, a large lump of pork forcemeat should be cooked with it until done. Serve with cooked prunes.

Lentil soup can also be cooked like a pea soup with "Frankfurt" or smoked pork sausages or a piece of pork, but the lentils should remain whole; flour should be browned with onions and some good fat, to thicken the soup if it should be too thin. Serve with vinegar.

Time of cooking, 2—4 hours.

50. Lentil Soup with Partridges. This is a meat puree soup and gains very much in nutritive qualities through the addition of the lentils. It is advantageous

to take an already roasted chicken, the bones of partridges or old partridges. The best meat is stripped
from the bones and the latter are then crushed in a
mortar and cooked 1—2 hours with soup herbs and an
onion, after which the soup is strained. In the meantime, cook ¼ pound of lentils with a piece of butter in
not too much water until thick, pass through a sieve
and stir with the partridge broth. If you have the
breast pieces of partridges, take out the sinews, clean
off the skin and all gristle, cut into fine slices and put
into the tureen at once, because cooking will harden
the meat. Should there be any meat left, pound it as
finely as possible, stir it into the soup, letting it cook
¼ hour longer, then pass through a strainer once more
and serve very hot, pouring it over the breasts of the
partridges and slices of wheat bread nicely fried in butter.

51. Sorrel Soup. Sorrel should be raised in every
garden. It is very wholesome and in the Spring it
makes a palatable and refreshing soup. Lightly brown
plenty of flour in good butter, rub nicely washed tender
leaves of the sorrel in this and cook in veal broth or
water, after supplying the necessary salt. Stir into the
soup nutmeg, thick cream and the yolks of a few eggs
and serve over fried wheat bread placed in the tureen.
Instead of the bread small egg dumplings can be cooked
in the soup. It should be nicely thickened, but must not
be too stiff. A little extract of beef will prove a desirable addition.

Time of cooking, ¼—½ hour.

52. Silesian Celery Soup. Clean 2 thick celery roots,
a piece of green leek and 1 parsley root, and boil tender
in 2 quarts of water, adding the necessary salt; then
brown 2 tablespoonfuls of flour in 1 tablespoonful of
good butter, stir the broth into this, add the herbs
(leaving out the celery) and serve as hot as possible. A
small addition of extract of beef improves the flavor of
the soup.

After the celery roots have been cooked until tender
they can be sliced and made into a salad with olive oil
and vinegar, and served as a side dish with the roast.

The French way of making this soup is much simpler; 4 celery roots are divided and cooked in water with

double the quantity of potatoes cut into pieces, salt, pass through a strainer, add a small piece of butter and little extract of beef and season with a small bunch of a chopped celery. Both kinds of soup are served with toasted bread.

Time of cooking, 1½ hours.

53. Hotch Potch or Scotch Soup. This very wholesome, nutritious and palatable soup is a favorite Scotch dish for the ordinary table. Although generally made from mutton and vegetables of all kinds, yet it is also very good when made with beef or veal, or fresh pickled pork.

In the Summer take for about 8 persons, 2 pounds of mutton from the shoulder, the neck or the ribs, 2 quarts of shelled green peas, not too young, 1 pint of large beans, 1—2 cauliflowerheads cut up fine, 1 quart of fresh kohlrabi cut into cubes, 1 quart of carrots also cut up, 1 head of cabbage, 1—2 heads of curled (savoy) cabbage cut into fine shreds, 1 dozen chopped white onions and a handful of purslane and celery leaves.

Cook the meat 2 hours in 2 quarts of water, then gradually add the above-named vegetables, putting in the cauliflower last; salt, and let the soup cook 2 hours longer until everything is nice and tender. The meat can be separated from the bones and served in the soup, or it may be brought to the table after the soup with the potatoes, butter and parsley or a gravy.

This soup can also be cooked as *Scotch* broth by making it thinner and chopping the vegetables as finely as possible and adding some salsify. If it is not to be the principal dish at dinner, cook the vegetable soup with a mild beef broth strengthened with a little extract of beef, and omit the meat. In the Fall and in the Winter enough of this soup can be cooked to last for several days.

In the Winter, take instead of the peas ½ pound of coarse groats, let them stand over night covered with water, and then cook with the meat and such vegetables as are obtainable.

54. Soup a l'aurore. Peel and scrape 3 carrots, 3 potatoes and 3 onions, cut into thin slices, add a few small celery leaves and cook together in 2 quarts of water until soft enough to pass through a sieve. After the latter is done, put the soup on the fire again with 1 heaping tablespoonful of butter, 1 even teaspoonful of extract of beef and the same quantity of salt, stir slowly until thoroughly cooked and serve with bits of toasted bread.

----

55. Herb Soups for Invalids. Take ½ pound of boneless beef and make 1 pint of clear broth with salt, but skim off all the fat, pass through a sieve and then cook in it for 10 minutes 1 ounce of bread- or cracker crumbs. Chop beforehand 1 ounce of sorrel and the same quantity of chervil, spinach and a piece of parsley root, simmer slowly in butter until tender and pass through a sieve, then mix with the yolks of 2 eggs and slowly pour the beef broth over this vegetable puree. The soup need not be cooked again—it is served immediately. When fats are forbidden the herbs are to be cooked in salt water until done.

Soups Nos. 41, 42, 43 and 51 are also adapted for the sickroom.

III. WINE AND BEER SOUPS.

56. White Wine Soup. 2 tablespoonfuls of fine flour and the yolks of 6 very fresh eggs are stirred with 1 bottle of white wine or cider, and 1 bottle of water sweetened with plenty of sugar. Put in a few lemon slices without the seeds, add a pinch of salt, and then cook over a hot fire in a clean kettle, stirring constantly with an egg beater, and pour into the tureen immediately, first putting in some mace. The whites of the eggs, beaten to a froth, can be made into little balls, put on the soup, sprinkled with sugar, and when the tureen is covered they will be done in a few minutes.

If the whole eggs are used instead of the yolks only and only ½ of the flour be taken, it makes a wine froth soup.

Serve with these soups small crackers or toast, which can also be dusted with sugar.

57. Another Wine Soup. Lightly brown 2 ounces of flour in 2 even tablespoonfuls of butter, stir this smooth with 1 bottle of white wine and 1 pint of water, add 3 heaping teaspoonfuls of sugar and a trifle of salt. This soup is seasoned variously with lemon or orange peel, peach or orangeflower water, or with fresh fruit, such as strawberries or raspberries, simply letting them boil up once in the soup. The yolks of a few eggs may be stirred in the soup if desired.

58. Sago Soup with Claret. Scald pure sago twice with water, then put on the stove with hot water, add a piece of cinnamon and cook until done, which will take from 2—2½ hours. Then add the same quantity of claret, sweeten the soup well with sugar, let it come to a boil, put in a few slices of lemon and serve with crackers or fresh toast.

59. Hasty Cracker Soup. Water, crackers, some butter, a few pieces of cinnamon, lemon peel and salt in proportions according to the quantity of soup desired are put on the fire and cooked until done; then pass through a sieve and stir into it the yolks of a few eggs, sweet cream, wine and sugar.

60. Pearl Barley and White Wine Soup. Put the barley on the fire with a little boiling water, a small piece of fresh butter, some cinnamon and lemon peel, and cook slowly in a scant broth (replenishing the hot water frequently) until done. After the soup has cooked for 2 hours, put in raisins that have first been washed, and let them cook until soft. When serving add wine, sugar and a trifle of salt, and stir into the soup the yolks of 1 or 2 eggs.

61. A nice Soup made from Coarse Barley Groats. Put 1 pound of groats on the fire in a little boiling water with a small piece of butter, a few pieces of cinnamon and a little salt, replenishing the boiling water from time to time and cook until quite soft. Then pass the whole through a sieve, during which operation some water should be poured over the barley in order to retain in the soup everything that will tend to thicken it. After about ¾ hour, cook about ½ pound of well-washed raisins in the soup until soft. The soup should be well bound but not thick. When ready to serve, stir the yolks of 2 fresh eggs together with ½ pint of white wine in the tureen and pour in the boiling soup gradually, stirring constantly, and sweeten with sugar. This will make enough soup for 8—10 persons Instead of the barley the soup can be made with very fine barley meal stirred in it, which is cooked about 10 minutes until done, first boiling the raisins in water with some butter.

This soup can also be made from grits (fine middlings); in this case first cook the raisins, stir the grits with sugar, salt and the proper quantity of water, add sufficient boiling water to make as much soup as is wanted, and after the grits are thoroughly cooked, stir the soup as above directed. In both soups cider or white currant wine can be used to excellent advantage.

Time of cooking, 3 hours.

62. Rice Soup with Raisins. Lightly brown a little butter in a spoonful of flour, take the necessary quantity of boiling water, scalded rice, cleaned and washed raisins and a small piece of cinnamon. Cook all until well done and stir the soup with salt, sugar, a litte wine, and the yolks of a few eggs.

63. Frothy Beer Soup. 1 quart of beer (which must not be bitter), 1 quart of water, 2 tablespoonfuls of fine wheat flour, 4 eggs, sugar, 2 slices of lemon and cinnamon according to taste are whipped with an egg beater over a hot fire until nearly cooked; pour into the tureen immediately. Serve with buttered toast or crackers.

A palatable addition to this kind of soup consists of a bread pudding made from pieces of rye bread mixed with fine sugar, ground cinnamon and scalded currants. Fry the bread in butter until of a light brown color, press tightly into a large funnel or similar mold and turn into the tureen.

64. Hasty Beer Soup. Take ½ pint of beer for each person and the same quantity of water, cook, and add the necessary quantity of sugar and a pinch of salt. Then stir the yolk of 1 egg and 1 heaping teaspoonful of flour together with some cold water and gradually pour the boiling beer over it, constantly stirring, and then put back into the kettle. The stirring should be kept up continually, even after the kettle has been taken from the fire, to prevent curdling.

If desired, the white of an egg can be beaten to a froth with some sugar, taken up with a spoon and put on the soup, or else the froth may be beaten through the soup.

65. Beer Soup with Raisins. Cook plenty of raisins with water and wheat bread until the raisins are quite soft, then add enough beer to give the soup good strength, sweeten with sugar and when it cooks put in according to the quantity of soup ½—1 tablespoonful of flour stirred in water, and then stir through the soup (which should not be too thin nor too stiff) the yolks of a few eggs and some cinnamon. When eggs are lacking the flour can be stirred up with good cream or milk.

66. Beer Soups with Milk. For 3—4 persons take 1 pint of milk with its cream, 1 pint of water, ½ pint of strong but not bitter beer, 2 ounces of currants, 1 table-spoonful of flour, 2 heaping teaspoonfuls of sugar, ½ teaspoonful of salt and the yolk of an egg. Put everything excepting the egg and the salt in a deep kettle on a hot fire and bring it to a boil, stirring constantly and briskly; take the kettle from the fire immediately, keep up the stirring for a few minutes longer, otherwise it will curdle easily, add some salt and then stir into it the yolk of the egg and some ground cinnamon. Serve with biscuits or toast.

If you have no time to devote to stirring the soup, and without which it will curdle, then the water, beer, currants and flour should be brought to a boil, cook the milk in a separate vessel, take both from the fire, pour together and stir the yolk of the egg into the soup.

67. Wine Soup for Invalids. Good claret, Portwine or sherry are absolutely essential for these soups, which, by the way, should never be served to invalids unless with the consent of the physician. Take pure sago or tapioca, pound the sago and soak in cold water for 3 hours. Then drain. and afterwards cook it with water and a small piece of candied ginger (the latter is omitted when claret is used) until transparent, add the wine, some lemon juice and sugar and serve with crackers. Tapioca is simply cooked in the water until done without any previous soaking. When claret is used, the addition of a few teaspoonfuls of pineapple, raspberry or strawberry jelly will greatly improve the flavor of the soup.

Nos. 57, 60 and 61 are also good soups for invalids.

IV. MILK SOUPS AND WATER SOUPS.

NOTE.—It is well to keep a particular kettle for cooking milk soups, because the milk scorches very easily and the flavor of food that has been previously cooked in the kettle is readily imparted to the milk. Scorching may be prevented by first greasing the bottom of the kettle with a piece of pork fat, or at least first rinsing the kettle with cold water.

68. Fine Milk Soups served either warm or cold. For 3 persons take 1 quart of fresh milk, 1 tablespoonful of cornstarch, the yolks of 2 eggs, sugar, lemon peel or a little vanilla, or a few pounded bitter almonds. Stir over a hot fire constantly until cooked and then pour into the tureen. Make a stiff froth of the whites of eggs, and form into little balls as directed under No. 56, or else the froth can be mixed with sugar and stirred into the soup until the latter is frothy through and through.

REMARK.—During the hot season, this soup, served cold, makes an excellent and convenient dish for the supper table and for this purpose it can be cooked in the forenoon.

69. A very nutritious Milk Soup. Bring 3 quarts of milk to a boil. Whip 1—2 eggs, stir up with fine flour and reduce the stiff dough with cold milk and pour into the boiling milk without stirring; pass a spoon over the bottom of the kettle several times to loosen the mass, and break it up into lumps, and then cook until these are done. Salt the soup moderately and pour into the tureen at once to prevent scorching.

70. Grits (Middlings) Soup with Milk. Put the grits into the boiling milk, constantly stirring, and cook with salt, sugar and some butter until nice and thick. It can consist of water to the amount of ⅓. For 1 person the right proportion would be ½ pint and 1 tablespoonful of grits according to quality.

71. Noodle Soup with Milk. This soup is cooked according to the directions given for the grits soup preceding.

72. Rice Soup with Milk. Wash the rice and put on the fire in cold water, and after the water has become quite hot, pour it off, because some varieties of rice are somewhat acidulous, causing the milk to curdle; after this cook the rice on a hot fire until done. If fresh milk is used for the soup, it can be reduced one-half with water, and ½ pint of milk with an even tablespoonful of rice will be the right proportion for each person.

Cook half of the milk with the water, put in a few pieces of cinnamon and the rice, and cook slowly until tender; then add the remainder of the milk and a little sugar and salt, and let the soup cook for a short time longer. If it is desired that the soup should be a little thicker, add at last some cornstarch stirred in water, but no flour because the latter spoils the flavor of the soup; the cornstarch should simply cook until done. As noted, flour impairs the flavor of the soup, but if it must be used then the soup should cook with the flour under constant stirring for 15 minutes.

73. Soup with Pearl Barley and Milk. Wash the barley, put on the fire with a small piece of butter and a little water and cook slowly with a scant broth until tender, replenishing the water as often as necessary, then add milk and a little salt, and cook the soup until thick; if not thick enough to suit, put in a little cornstarch which has first been stirred in water. It can be flavored with sugar and cinnamon or mace.

In the same manner good soups can be made from pure sago or from coarse barley which must be soaked the night before in water.

Time of cooking, 2 hours. The quantities and weights of ingredients are the same as given in the preceding receipts.

74. Pearl Sago Soup with Milk. Put the sago into the boiling milk which has been thinned somewhat with a little water, otherwise the sago will dissolve completely. After the elapse of ½—¾ hour the sago should be soft, then stir into it some cornstarch and salt, and add, according to taste, sugar and cinnamon; the yolk of an egg can also be stirred into the soup if wished.

Take a pint of milk and 1 ounce of sago for each person.

75. Oatmeal Soup with Milk. Drain the oatmeal several times and then cook in water until tender and of a medium thickness, stirring occasionally because it adheres to the kettle easily and scorches. After straining, put it on the stove again, add milk and some salt and let it cook 15 minutes more.

Take 1—1½ ounces of oatmeal and ½ pint of fresh or 1 pint of skimmed milk for each person; the first is preferable.

76. Cornmeal Soup. To cook this very nutritious and cheap soup, mix water and milk half and half and bring to a boil, stir in enough cornmeal until it has the proper consistency, and put in some salt.

77. Chocolate Soup. Put ¼ pound of chocolate on the fire in a cupful of water, and after it is soft stir until quite smooth, and then add 2 quarts of milk and sugar according to taste; as soon as it commences to cook, flavor the soup with vanilla or cinnamon and stir into it the yolks of 1—2 eggs. The whites of the eggs may be beaten to a froth and put on the soup in the form of little balls, sprinkled with sugar and cinnamon. This quantity of soup is calculated for 5 persons and is served over bits of bread toasted in butter placed in the tureen.

78. Buttermilk with Fine Pearl Barley, also good for Invalids. Put the barley on the fire in water and cook until tender; then add the buttermilk, into which some flour has been stirred, with salt, sugar and cinnamon according to taste.

79. Buttermilk with Prunes or Raisins. After carefully washing and rinsing them, cook until soft in water into which some anise seed can be put and, according to taste, grated rye bread. Grate some wheat bread and put it into the soup with the buttermilk into which some flour should be stirred to prevent curdling, and boil under constant stirring. When serving, stir in salt, sugar and some cinnamon.

80. Brown Flour Soup. Lightly brown the flour without any butter as directed under A, No. 3, boil the milk and stir into it enough of the browned flour and cold milk as is necessary to give the soup consistency, then stir through it sugar, cinnamon and the yolks of eggs, and serve over bits of bread toasted in butter which have been placed in the tureen.

81. White Flour Soup. Heat a piece of butter the size of half an egg, put in 3 tablespoonfuls of flour and stir until it commences to curl and bubble; then pour in the required quantity of boiling water, stirring carefully, so that the flour will remain smooth and not become lumpy. When done, stir the soup with salt, mace or lemon peel, a trifle of sugar and the yolk of an egg, or else serve without any spice or sugar, putting in salt, sour cream and finely chopped parsley.

82. Onion Soup (South Germany Style). For 4 persons, lightly brown 3 large onions, cut up into small cubes in 2½ tablespoonfuls of butter, in this also brown lightly 2 tablespoonfuls of flour, and then pour in enough meat broth to make the necessary quantity of soup, and cook thoroughly. Then pass through a sieve, cook once more, stir with 2 yolks of eggs, and serve over bits of bread toasted in butter, placed in the tureen.

83. Soup made with Pastry Dough. Break the dough into pieces and put it on the fire in cold water; after it has been cooked to a pulp put in a piece of butter or good fat and gradually pour on boiling water. Before serving, put in some finely chopped parsley, beat up the yolk of an egg in a tureen, with some sour cream, and then pour in the soup, being careful to stir constantly.

84. Barley Soup for Invalids. Fine pearl barley is cooked in a little boiling water with a small piece of fresh butter, frequently replenishing the water, until the barley is tender and of the proper consistency. It will improve the barley if it is to be used in the sick-room to first scald it several times. After it is cooked, season with salt, finely chopped parsley or nutmeg; the latter is preferable when there is stomach trouble.

Sweet Barley Broth is made by stirring into the broth through a fine sieve, the barley which has first been cooked until tender, add to the soup thus thickened salt and sugar, and stir into it the yolk of an egg. Barley broth made in this manner is excellent in cases of dysentery and diarrhœa.

85. Oatmeal Soup for Invalids. Fresh oatmeal is rinsed in hot and cold water alternately until the water remains clear, then cook the oatmeal 1 hour with a pinch of salt and 2 tablespoonfuls of fresh almonds, either pounded finely or grated, together with the necessary quantity of water, pass through a sieve and put in some sugar and toast.

86. Toast Soup for Invalids. Very finely pounded toast is cooked with water and the juice of 1 lemon, until it no longer sinks, add sugar and a trifle of salt, and if permitted by the physician, stir in the yolk of an egg.

87. Bread Soup for Invalids. Take rye bread and wheat bread half and half, and thoroughly cook in water, stir through a fine sieve and cook again with some salt, sugar, lemon juice and either currants or raisins until the latter are soft, and, if permitted by the physician, stir into it a little wine and the yolk of an egg.

88. Another Bread Soup for Invalids is made by taking rye bread only, grating it and then browning in a frying pan without any fat until dry, pour on enough water to make a thick pulp and let it stand for an hour on the back part of the stove, then stir the pulp with hot milk until it is smooth, add sugar and salt and the yolk of an egg. As a matter of precaution it will be well to stir this soup through a fine sieve before serving.

V. FRUIT SOUPS.

89. Strawberry Soup. Cook some finely pounded toast in water until thick, add wine, sugar and cinnamon, and in case the soup is not of the proper consistency put in some cornstarch smoothed in water. Then take from the fire and stir into the soup according to its quantity a number of saucerfuls of ripe strawberries which have been sugared 1 hour before. This soup is served with biscuits or toast.

90. Cherry Soup. Take sour cherries and cook them with some toast and lemon peel or 2—3 cloves and the required quantity of water, until the cherries are pulpy. Strain, put on the stove and bring to a boil again and serve after adding sugar, a little salt, cinnamon and claret, which must not cook. Sweet cakes can be put on the soup or it may be served with biscuits.

In the winter this soup can be made with dried cherries which are first cooked with some oatmeal and a few slices of lemon, before straining. Afterwards follow the above directions.

91. Apple Soup. Cook in water a soupplateful of sour apples (which have been cut into very small pieces), with a cupful of scalded rice until soft, pass through a sieve, add sugar, cinnamon, lemon peel and some salt, cook again and stir into it the yolk of an egg.

92. Apple Soup with Currants. Cook some wheat bread with the apples, and after passing through a sieve add some grated rye bread which has first been fried in butter, then put in the currants and a very few cloves and some salt, cook for a short time and stir into the soup cinnamon and a spoonful of thick cream.

93. Plum Soup. Stone a soupplateful of plums and cook in water with wheat bread until soft, pass through a sieve, then cook with the addition of some sugar and cinnamon, and serve with buttered toast placed in the tureen.

94. Plum Soup with Milk. This is a nice soup for the supper table and is made by taking a soupplateful of ripe plums, rub thoroughly to clean them, stir 2 heaping tablespoonfuls of flour in water until smooth, add 3 pints of milk and some salt, put on the fire with the plums and cook for a short time, stirring frequently until the flour is well cooked. The plums may burst but must not become pulpy. If they are entirely ripe no sugar need be added. The soup must be nicely bound, and is brought to the table when nearly cold.

95. Prune Soup for Invalids. Wash the prunes, cut them up, put them on the fire (with about half the quantity of oatmeal added) in an earthenware vessel in water, with sugar, cinnamon, lemon peel and a pinch of salt and cook slowly until all is soft. Strain, bring to a boil once more and stir up with the yolks of 2 eggs which have been whipped in 1 glassful of wine. A few of the prunes can be cooked separately and put into the soup at last.

96. Soup made from Dried Prunes. Wash the prunes nicely, rubbing them between the hands. Scald thoroughly, and then cook in water with lemon peel and a little wheat bread until soft, pass through a sieve stirring with sugar, cinnamon and, according to taste, a glassful of wine. Serve over toast placed in the tureen. For invalids omit the wine, spices and toast.

97. Mixed Fruit Soup for Invalids. Take huckleberries, strawberries, raspberries and stoned cherries in equal proportions. After picking them over and washing, mash them as finely as possible, pour on as much water as will make the required quantity of soup, boil slowly for ½ hour and strain; after bringing to a boil again, add sugar, extract of lemon, a pinch of salt and enough flour, which has been smoothed in cider, to bring the soup to the proper consistency. Stir through the soup the whites of 2 eggs beaten to a stiff froth.

COLD SOUPS.

98. Wine Cold Soup. 1 hour before serving put into the tureen macaroons or small sweet crackers (if large, break them into pieces) and add sliced lemon without the seeds, a few pieces of cinnamon, white wine and water half and half, sweetened with sugar.

99. Orange Cold Soup. Take various fruit syrups, wine and water half and half, a few pieces of cinnamon, and oranges which are first peeled, divided into 8 parts and turned in sugar. The sweet crackers put into this soup are first slightly soaked in wine but they must not become mushy; they are then covered with sugar, built up in little piles and passed as a side dish.

100. Apricot Cold Soup. Skin and stone the apricots and then cook them in water, being careful not to get them too soft, together with some of the apricot stones, cinnamon and plenty of sugar; put one-half of this into the tureen and pass the remainder with the broth through a fine sieve, and when cool add as much wine as water was used in the soup, sweeten with plenty of sugar and pour over the apricots. Crackers or toast are passed with the soup.

101. Cherry Cold Soup. Stone a soupplateful of sour cherries and cook them for 15 minutes in 1 quart of water together with 2—3 cloves and a few of the kernels of the cherry pits; then strain through a fine sieve and after it is cold put in 1 pint of claret, plenty of sugar and some cinnamon. Sweet crackers can either be broken into or passed with the soup. A cream froth (see directions under Division N) can be put into the soup.

102. Strawberry and Raspberry Cold Soup. The strawberries are first, if necessary, rinsed with water in a colander; this is not required with the raspberries. Put the berries into the tureen, add plenty of sugar, cover tightly and let it stand for 1 hour; then mix white wine and water half and half with sugar, the juice of a lemon and ground cinnamon; pour over the berries.

103. Sago or Rice Cold Soup. Scald ¼ of a pound of fine sago or rice, and then cook in water without stirring until soft and thick; the grains must remain whole; then pour into the tureen. Strew on it plenty of sugar, cinnamon and grated lemon peel and add nicely washed currants; scald these and pour in the liquor. When cold, add 1 bottle of claret and the same quantity of water sweetened with sugar.

104. Beer Cold Soup. Stale grated rye bread, plenty of rinsed and scalded currants without the liquor, cinnamon, a slice of lemon, beer (which must not be bitter) and sugar according to taste.

105. Westphalian Cold Soup. Take grated stale rye bread and whipped thick sour cream, and stir brown beer (which must not be bitter), sugar, cinnamon and the grated bread into the whipped cream.

106. Buttermilk Cold Soup. Grate rye bread and slightly brown it; for each 4 spoonfuls of bread add 2 spoonfuls of sugar, then again brown the whole lightly, stirring constantly. After this stir into the buttermilk some sweet cream or milk; shortly before serving crumble into it crackers or wheat bread and finally strew over it the bread after it has cooled. This cold soup is very palatable and refreshing.

107. Whipped Cream. Thick sweet cream is shaken to a froth in a shaker or whipped in any convenient vessel, but this should be done in the cellar or some other cool place. Then stir through it sugar and vanilla and serve with crackers and grated rye bread.

The vanilla can be put into the cream a few hours beforehand to draw, or else pound fine with sugar, thus requiring less vanilla.

108. Whipped Sour Cream. For this purpose the milk should be thick but its cream must be smooth. Whip as directed in the preceding receipt, and stir through it sugar and cinnamon.

C.—Potatoes and other Vegetables.

I. VEGETABLES.

1. Hints on cooking Vegetables. It is of such frequent occurrence that vegetables, which form so important and nutritious articles of food, are neglected in their preparation and cooking, that a few hints in this direction may be found useful and not out of place.

Cleanliness. Although before alluded to in the introduction to this book, the necessity of perfect cleanliness in respect to the utensils used for cooking and in cleaning the vegetables is again brought to your attention. But caution should be exercised not to leave them lying in water too long, because thereby the valuable salts they contain are extracted; particularly tuberous vegetables and celery roots, parsley, etc., should never be soaked in water.

How to economize in using Butter and how to rapidly cook Vegetables tender. To obtain a very palatable dish of vegetables and to have them done without cooking them too long a time, the following directions will be found serviceable. When the price of butter is unreasonably high, good kidney fat, prepared according to A, 17, will be found an excellent substitute for creamery butter when cooking most kinds of vegetables, without impairing their flavor. Put the fat in the water before putting in the vegetables, and when these are taken from the fire, merely drop a few pieces of butter over them, which will impart a nice butter flavor and the liquor will become much smoother. If fat from roasts is used, this can also be put into the boiling water and some butter mixed through it at the last. Lard, goose grease and mutton fat, which can also be profitably used as already explained in the first part of this book must, however, be put on the fire in cold water and be cooked thoroughly before the vegetables are put in the kettle.

In the meantime, the carefully cleaned and rinsed vegetables are put on a colander to drain; the entire quantity of vegetables should not be thrown into the kettle at one time, but, on the contrary, put them in gradually with the skimmer, but the water must be brought to a boil each time. In scalding vegetables this method should also be observed, because they will then become tender much sooner than if the cooking is delayed by putting in too large a quantity at a time. Salt should be added during the latter half of the time taken for cooking (except in the case of peas, beans, etc.); strew it over the vegetables uniformly and cover tightly and let the cooking go on uninterruptedly. Replenishing the water should be avoided as much as possible; careful attention will soon teach one the necessary quantity needed, but it is always better to take rather too little than too much. Always have enough boiling water handy for replenishing purposes.

Many vegetables must first be scalded on account of their strong flavor or perhaps their acrid taste; of course, some of their nutritive properties are thereby lost in the water. Scalding should, therefore, not be resorted to unnecessarily but be minimized as much as possible. When scalding vegetables, which require a rather long time in cooking before they are tender, for instance in the case of vegetables preserved for Winter use, water must be used rather plentifully and boiling water for replenishing purposes should also be provided for, because cold water is not adapted for it.

To preserve the fresh color of Vegetables. Spinach, green peas, sorrel, Brussels sprouts, etc., should always be boiled uncovered over a hot fire so that they will become tender rapidly and thus preserve their fresh green color.

To cook preserved Beans and Cabbages tender rapidly. Vegetables preserved for Winter use—beans and cabbage — should be cooked until quite tender and freshened in boiling soft water as long as is necessary. Vegetables in salt or brine become tender very rapidly after taking them out of the receptacle in which they are contained and cooked without being freshened in boiling water. Do not change the water until the vegetables are almost done.

When Vegetable Dishes should be thickened. Several kinds of vegetables should be thickened with flour or the yolks of eggs only when they are almost done.

Particular care should be taken to cook all vegetables until they are quite tender and juicy, but they should never be stirred enough to become pulpy and mushy. If fat and salt are added at the time directed, no stirring is necessary because they are absorbed equally well by the vegetables without stirring. How long a time is required for cooking each variety of vegetables cannot be designated with any degree of exactness, because this depends entirely upon their quantity and quality, and also upon the condition of the fire; nevertheless, the cooking time has been given as approximately correct as possible in each receipt. Vegetables grown in dry seasons require a longer time on the fire and this circumstance should, therefore, always be taken into account.

Warmed over Dishes. All varieties of cabbages and turnips are also good when warmed over, but it will improve them to first bring water or meat broth to a boil and then putting in the vegetables. Do not neglect to add some parsley, salt, sugar or butter according to the variety of the vegetables. If the better kinds of vegetables, such as green peas, beans, oyster plant, etc., are to be warmed over, follow the above directions, and then put them into a double kettle until they are thoroughly heated.

Serving. Only spinach and similar vegetables are smoothed with a knife when they are served. All other vegetables should be arranged neatly in the dish in which they come to the table, without pressing them; being careful to wipe off the edges, and have the dish warm.

2. Salsify or Oysterplant. Scrape thoroughly, stir a spoonful of flour or some sweet milk in water and lay the salsify in this, which will prevent it from turning black. Put on the fire in an enameled kettle with meat broth and butter and boil until tender, adding the necessary salt, but not too much. 15 minutes before serving add grated crackers or browned flour, and mace according to taste. Before bringing to the table meat dumplings are added to the dish, which is served either with boiled beef or without any side dish.

The salsify can also be boiled in salted water with a little vinegar until tender; serve with either a thick asparagus or Hollandaise sauce, or else make a sauce from browned flour and butter, meat broth, lemon juice, mace and parsley and stew the salsify in this.

In England the salsify is boiled until tender in salted water and then shaken on the fire with butter, grated parmesan cheese and ground pepper until the butter and cheese are melted; in South Germany it is usually cut into pieces, dipped in a batter and fried in hot lard.

3. Brussels Sprouts. The sprouts or buds are picked when fresh and closed, and the dried leaves and hard knots cut from the stalk, being careful not to break up the small buds; scald them in boiling water with salt, using as little water as possible, take them out with a skimmer and put them on a colander to drain, covering tightly so that they will remain hot. Before serving put them on a slow fire with a piece of butter, salt, nutmeg and a few bread crumbs, and as soon as hot turn them in the kettle several times.— Brussels sprouts may also be put into the dish, which should of course be warm; immediately after the water has been poured off, put pieces of butter between and over the sprouts.

Time for cooking is a short 15 minutes.

Smoked or roasted beef tongue, small sausages, cutlets, croquets, meat balls, or ham fritters can be served as side dishes.

4. Spinach. Spinach must be carefully picked over and rinsed 3 or 4 times in a deep vessel in plenty of cold water. In order to retain its rich green color, scald it for about 5 minutes in boiling water with some salt, leaving the kettle uncovered, then put it into cold water at once, pour it onto a colander, press well with a skimmer and chop until very fine. Then melt some kidney suet or butter, stir a little flour or some bread crumbs with it, put in the spinach, adding nutmeg and some butter, and cook with frequent stirring until done, putting in as much salt as may be found necessary, and, perhaps a small quantity of meat broth or water.

Some people consider the taste of spinach as being rather insipid; for such it should be seasoned by adding a trifle of chives, or onions fried in butter.

Spinach can be garnished in various ways; the simplest is to take bits of toasted bread and medium soft boiled eggs, quartered. A richer method is to first put on a border of baked crullers which have been formed in a thick mass, by means of melted butter and cheese; then inside of the border cover with plain fried eggs, each one surrounded by a ring of finely chopped cooked tongue. Serve small roasted potatoes as a side dish.

Omelets, croquets, fricandeaus, small sausages, roast or smoked beef tongue, kidney slices, crullers with a ham forcemeat or fried liver are all good side dishes with spinach.

5. Spinach, Saxony Style. Cook the spinach in salt water with an onion, chop it up with a boned anchovy very fine, brown some flour in melted butter, stir in as much meat broth as is necessary, then cook the spinach until well done and garnish with eggs.

6. Spinach, French Style. Cook the spinach as above directed and chop very fine. Stir some butter to a froth, add the finely grated yolks of hard boiled eggs, some nutmeg and salt, and stir all of this with the spinach on the fire, until it begins to boil.

Spinach prepared in this manner is greatly improved by the addition of a few spoonfuls of dark meat broth. Fried sliced sweetbreads are served as a side dish.

7. Spinach with Rice. Scald about ½ pound of rice in water several times, then boil it in milk or weak meat broth until soft and stir into it 3 whipped eggs and a few spoonfuls of sour cream. Four quarts of spinach are cooked in the meantime according to the directions previously given, chopped very fine and allowed to simmer in melted butter; then season with ground pepper and grated cheese and mix with it a few spoonfuls of grated wheat bread. The rice and spinach are separately pressed into a buttered mould, afterwards bake for 30 minutes, turn out of the cups, pour over it a dark meat broth and serve with roast spring chicken or veal cutlets.

8. Moulded Spinach. Spinach left over from the table is mixed with the yolks of 2 eggs, several spoonfuls of white gravy, grated wheat bread and a few finely chopped stewed mushrooms; mould the mass in small cups which have first been buttered, cook in a double kettle for ½ hour, turn out of the cups and serve with roast potatoes and baked ham.

9. Spinach Stalks cooked as a Vegetable. After the spinach has run to seed and is no longer good for cooking purposes, the stalks should be stripped, cut up, cook them until soft, soak, press tightly and simmer slowly the same as cauliflower (see No. 38).
Time of cooking, 1 hour.

10. Dandelions. In the Spring of the year the dandelion grows as a weed on many lawns and fields; when young and tender it makes a very palatable dish, if cooked in the same manner as directed for spinach.

11. Sorrel. Strip the large fresh leaves from the stems. Then rinse the leaves in plenty of water several times until perfectly free from sandy particles. Put on the stove in cold water and throw on a colander just before it begins to cook, otherwise it is apt to become too soft. After the acid has been absorbed by the cold water and the sorrel has been well drained and pressed out with the skimmer on the colander, lightly brown butter and some flour and add a few cupfuls of sweet cream or milk into which the yolks of 1—2 eggs have been stirred, also salt and nutmeg, and cook the sorrel in this thoroughly. The broth should be scant and of a nice consistency and not watery. Garnish with bits of toasted bread. Time of cooking, ½ hour.

Side-dishes: cutlets, tongue, smoked meats, boiled ham, liver, kidney slices, fish omelets, roast or stewed lamb.

12. Endives. Bleached endive leaves are among the nicest winter vegetables. Cut away the stalks and green leaves and boil the inner yellow leaves in salted water, cool in cold water, press them out and chop them fine. Then stew for ½ hour in a strong meat broth which has been thickened with lightly browned flour. Season with nutmeg, put in a little lemon juice and if desired, the yolks of a few eggs may be stirred into it.

The endives can be stewed in a cream sauce instead of the meat broth, or else after having been prepared according to either one of the described methods, pass through a sieve, stir with butter and serve as a puree. Serve with cutlets of all kinds, fried liver, meat balls, sweetbreads or spring chicken.

13. Greens from Stems and Stalks of Turnips and Beet Tops. Strip off the leaves (when quite young the stalks can be prepared unstripped) wash and cut the stems and cook in slightly salted water until tender. After draining cut the stalks very finely, brown some flour in butter very lightly, cook this either in milk or the broth of pickled meat, stew in it the greens until done and season with nutmeg. If the broth from pickled meat is used it should be first examined to see that it is not too salty.

Serve with cutlets, scallops, meat balls, boiled **or** raw ham and kidney slices.

14. Greens as above for the Family Table. First boil a piece of smoked bacon or fat pork for an hour, put some potatoes in the broth and then add the meat and the greens which have been cooked until tender and are well drained, salt and cook thoroughly until done. Then take out the meat and stir into the greens, according to quantity, 1 to 3 grated raw potatoes; this thickens the dish nicely and gives it a bright appearance, but it must not be cooked long enough to become dry.

Instead of cooking meat in the greens, sliced smoked bacon may be slightly fried on a slow fire, then take some of its fat and add to the greens, and serve the bacon separately. This is not only economical, but is preferred by a great many.

15. Asparagus. Scrape the coarse skin from each blade and cut from the bottom as much as is hard. A better way still is as follows: slit the outer skin from the bottom upwards and take it off at once; a little practice will enable one to do this rapidly. Then wash the asparagus, tie into bunches, making the tips even and cutting the lower ends all of one length. Cook with a little salt in not too much water, which should boil moderately, otherwise the tips will become too soft. The addition to the salt water of a pinch of sugar and a piece of butter the size of a hazelnut gives the asparagus a very delicious taste. As soon as the lower ends become tender (the usual time for tips is ¼ of an hour and for the whole blade ½ hour) put the bunches on a heated platter, cut the bands and serve.

Serve with either an asparagus sauce (see under R) or pass with it melted butter; frequently the grated yolks of hard boiled eggs accompany the butter.

In South Germany cream sauces are preferred; in England the asparagus is placed on large pieces of toast, and melted butter, into which the yolks of 3 eggs have been stirred, is poured over it; sometimes parmesan cheese is grated over it, and fried eggs laid on top. Appropriate side dishes are cutlets, roast poultry, meat balls, scrambled eggs, raw ham and smoked salmon.

It should be noted that asparagus must never be permitted to lay in water.

16. Stewed Asparagus. Scrape or peel the asparagus, cut into pieces, lay aside the tips and cook the rest until half done, because these pieces sometimes have a slightly bitter taste; then bring meat broth with a good sized piece of butter, a trifle of mace and some salt to a boil; put into this all of the asparagus pieces and let it simmer slowly until soft. Shortly before serving add some crushed toast and stir into the broth the yolks of a few eggs. Serve neatly, garnishing with bread dumplings and pour the thick broth over all.

Side dishes the same as above, with the exception of scrambled eggs.

The asparagus tips prepared alone make a very nice dish. Cook them until soft in a scant meat broth with the addition of salt and some butter. In the meantime prepare a cream sauce and have it ready so that the broth in which the tips are being cooked need only be brought to a boil, when the tips are placed on a warm platter and set over a vessel containing hot water. Then immediately pour over the sauce, garnish with medium soft boiled whole eggs, and serve with pickled tongue.

17. Asparagus with young Carrots. Take a quantity of young carrots, rub them in salt, wash and scrape them until clean and cut into 2 or 3 pieces; cook the carrots with the same quantity of asparagus according to the preceding receipt and serve in the same manner without the yolks of eggs.

18. Imperial (Kaiser) Asparagus. Cook the asparagus until tender as directed in No. 15, then whip in 1 pint of Rhinewine the yolks of 8 eggs, 3 tablespoonfuls of butter, a little salt and a pinch of sugar in a double kettle to a thick sauce, serve the asparagus on a hot platter with this sauce poured over it.

19. Asparagus in Rusks, (an elegant Entree). Peel the asparagus, take the tips only, cook in salted water until done. Make a thick sauce from veal broth thickened with lightly browned flour and butter, adding some finely chopped parsley; the tips are heated in this and then stir them with the yolks of a few eggs beaten up with cream. Soak small rusks after removing the crust, hollow them out and fill with the asparagus, tie the crusts over them as a cover and toast in butter until nicely browned. The ends of the asparagus together with the broth and some extract of beef will make an excellent soup.

20. Leipzig Hotch Potch. This dish is the most palatable during the asparagus season. Take the following early vegetables in equal quantities and cook each kind separately until done: asparagus in water with some salt, small carrots in beef broth, shelled green peas in water with a small piece of butter, kohl-rabi in water with a little salt, and cauliflower the same as kohlrabi. As soon as everything is thoroughly cooked, put it all into the dish carefully, placing the cauliflower on top, and mix through all the claws and tails of crabs. The shells of the crabs are filled with force meat made from the meat of the crabs and pie-crust dough. While preparations for serving are going on, place the vegetables over a steaming vessel, and then drench with a butter sauce made from cream and crab butter half and half, stirring into it the yolks of eggs. Garnish with the stuffed crab shells and little bread dumplings.

21. Early Carrots, Early carrots are scraped very lightly, and if quite young simply rub with a coarse towel; they are left whole and nicely rinsed but not laid into the water. Then cook them in boiling water with some sugar, butter and a very little salt (they can easily be oversalted) in a scant broth until done. Be-fore serving dredge over them ¼ teaspoonful of flour and put in some finely chopped parsley leaves.

The carrots can also first be stewed for about 10 minutes in butter, shaking them, then add some sugar, a small bunch of parsley, salt and a little lightly browned flour and butter, simmer slowly until tender, and serve after taking out the parsley. Sometimes an onion is also added, but this is objectionable to people with delicate palates.

Time of cooking, 1 hour. Serve with cutlets of var-ious kinds, baked meat balls, fried pork sausages, smoked and salted tongue.

22. Young Carrots and Peas. Put the carrots on the fire as above directed in boiling water with some butter. Then add the shelled peas, take half of each kind of vegetable and proceed as directed above. Shortly before serving a few bread dumplings may be added, but in this case more broth (which can be thick-ened with a little cornstarch) must be provided for.

23. Green Peas. Put plenty of butter in water and let it boil, throw in the shelled peas gradually, keeping the broth boiling. Peas must cook in plenty of broth rapidly; cooking them too slowly or for too long time, or letting them stand too long when done greatly impairs their flavor. Shortly before serving add some salt but not too much, because they are easily oversalted, and, if they are not sweet enough, put in a small lump of sugar. Stir into them finely chopped parsley, and cornstarch or flour smoothed in water (a quarter of a teaspoonful at a time). Or instead of this, knead flour and butter into a small dumpling and put this with the peas as soon as they begin to boil; it dissolves gradually, thickens the broth somewhat and imparts a pleasant flavor to the peas. If there is abundant broth, little sponge or bread dumplings can be cooked with it at the last. The preparation of dumplings is described under Division O.

Peas can also be cooked as directed in the second receipt for carrots, or, after boiling them in salt water, they may be stewed in a cream sauce or else drench in butter and scatter chopped parsley over them.—For a particularly fine dish the peas may be garnished with the tails of crabs or stuffed crab shells.

Peas are served with roast spring chicken, veal cutlets, croquettes, raw ham, hot or cold tongue, smoked salmon, fried eels and other crisply fried fish.

REMARK.—To retain the fine aromatic flavor of the peas they must be freshly picked, and in no case should they be shelled sooner than shortly before wanted for cooking.

24. Green Peas boiled with Spring Chicken and Crabs. Cook the chicken in salt water until all the scum has been taken off, then put in a piece of butter and cook slowly until tender. As soon as the broth is strong enough, put a large piece of butter into another kettle, put in the shelled peas, cover and let them simmer for a while, stirring them occasionally. Then fill up with part of the chicken broth, cook the peas until tender, stir through it some finely chopped parsley, and thicken the broth with a few egg yolks, whipped with a tablespoonful of water. Have ready some crabs with dressing and some crab butter, as directed under A, No. 37, and No. 9, also a lot of wheat bread dumplings. Carve the chicken nicely, place in the center of the dish, surrounded by the peas, then put in the dumplings and filled crabs, put in between them the claws and tails and pour over the whole the crab butter. Serve as an entree.

Time of cooking is the same as given for preceding vegetables.

25. Green Peas with Codfish (a favorite dish in Saxony). Cook the peas in a meat broth and butter until tender, then add some lightly browned flour and butter and sufficient salt; the codfish, together with some chopped parsley is then stirred through the broth, which must not be too plentiful, because the addition of the codfish in itself increases the quantity of broth. The codfish should be prepared in advance early enough as directed for cooking fish in another part of the book, take off the skin, bone and pick into small pieces, stir in plenty of melted butter, put on the stove, but do not allow it to stew or simmer, and then mix it through the peas.

26. Sweet Peas. The small variety is the best, those with long pods are not so nice. Sweet peas need not be shelled, simply string them carefully and wash thoroughly, cook in boiling water with butter and salt and finally stir through them some chopped parsley and some cornstarch smoothed in water. Time of cooking, from 1 to 1¼ hours.

Smoked meats, fried sausages, fried liver, baked fish, etc., are served with the peas.

27. Mixed Vegetables for a Dinner Party. Quarter pigeons or spring chickens, boil in salt water until free from scum, then add some butter, mace and some nicely browned flour and cook slowly. In the meantime carefully peel plenty of asparagus and cauliflower and cut into pieces; both are then cooked in salt water until half done. Pour the vegetables on a sieve to drain and then put in with the pigeons and cook until completely done. Be careful to keep the pieces whole. · After this cook a lot of crabs in boiling water for 15 minutes, pick the meat from the shells and prepare crab butter from the shells of the claws and the tails, according to A, No. 9. Lay the crab tails aside; the meat picked from the claws is chopped fine with butter, a small quantity of wheat bread crumbs, 4 tablespoonfuls of cream, 1 egg, some nutmeg and salt, and made into forcemeat; stuff a few of the crab shells with the forcemeat and cook them together with little meat or wheat bread dumplings in meat broth until done. Put the fowls with the vegetables into the dish. Stir the yolks of a few eggs into the sauce, add a little lemon juice, the tails of the crabs and some dumplings, garnish with the stuffed crab shells and put the crab butter over all.

This dish is excellent without the crabs, which, while adding to its elegance, cause some trouble in its preparation. It will take fully two hours to prepare this dish.

28. Early Turnips. It is best to cut the turnips into either large cubes or into narrow slices; they are occasionally bitter, and should therefore be scalded in boiling water; then put them on the fire in boiling meat broth or, with fat, in water, observing that this vegetable in itself contains a large percentage of water and consequently needs but a small addition of it, cook until tender, putting in the salt later on, then add ¼ to ½ teaspoonful of cornstarch smoothed in water or sprinkle some flour into the broth from the side and put a few pieces of butter on top; if meat broth is not used put in ¼ of a teaspoonful of extract of beef. After the turnips are served, grate nutmeg over them and serve boiled potatoes as a side dish.

The potatoes can also be cooked with the turnips and should be put into the kettle with the turnips when the latter are half done.

Pork or mutton chops and fried sausages are served with the turnips.

29. Early Turnips with Mutton. The mutton is either cut into cubes as for a stew, or else washed off whole and boiled in not too much salted water until the scum ceases to rise. After cooking for an hour pass the broth through a sieve, clean the kettle and bring the broth with the meat to a boil again. Then the meat can be either cooked in the broth until entirely done and the turnips also without being scalded if quite sweet, but if bitter, scald them and then cook until done with some of the mutton broth, putting in a few small potatoes at once if desired, or the turnips may be boiled together with the mutton.

Time of cooking the mutton is from 1½ to 2½ hours.

30. Mixed Vegetables with Mutton, English style.
Take a tender breast of mutton and cut it in cubes as
for a ragout, rinse thoroughly and boil, until scum no
longer appears, in sufficient salt water to cook the vegetables. In the meantime slice string beans into small
pieces, cut up savoy cabbage into pieces the size of half
an egg, and carrots into cubes after they have been well
washed and cleaned. After again carefully rinsing the
latter, they are put into the kettle with the mutton, the
first two kinds of vegetables, however, are previously
boiled for a short time and then also put in with the
mutton; add what salt may still be needed and some
pepper; cover the kettle and cook until all is tender,
nicely bound and juicy, but the vegetables must not be
cooked to a pulp.

31. Spanish mixed Vegetables or Hotch Potch. Very
palatable and nutritious. Cover a stewpan with slices
of fat pork, cut equal parts of lamb and beef into cubes,
kohlrabi into slices and separate the leaves of a savoy
cabbage. Fill the kettle with the meat and vegetables in
alternate layers, sprinkling salt and pepper on each
layer. Put in some butter and pour a cupful of meat
broth over all. Put on top a few small smoked sausages,
cover the stewpan as tightly as possible and then let it
cook slowly until done, which will take all of two hours.
Serve neatly, garnishing with peeled roast potatoes
placed around the edge of the dish and cutting the sausages into slices and laying them on top.

32. String Beans. Take beans that are tender but
not too young, and wash them nicely. Cook the beans
in plenty of boiling water, putting in the beans gradually as directed under No. 1 of this division, or else cook
them over a quick fire in an uncovered kettle until quite
tender in milk and water half and half, skimming carefully. Salt is added when the beans are about half
done but not before. After they are quite tender pour
them into an earthenware colander (tinware will give
the beans a bad color), pour boiling water over them
and cover quickly; they thereby retain their natural
color, but be careful that they remain nicely hot. Before serving stir lightly with plenty of butter and parsley, or else pour hot melted butter with parsley over the

dish when bringing it to the table. Time of cooking, 1 hour.

Serve with either boiled ham, spare ribs or bacon.

33. Another Method. Cut some bacon into cubes, fry slowly, and lightly brown some flour in it. Then stir with boiling water, a small piece of butter and salt; the beans which have first been boiled until tender and drained are then rapidly stewed until done, together with some chopped parsley or savory, care being taken that they do not become pulpy or stirred to pieces. Sliced pork can be lightly fried (see No. 14), stir the fat through the beans and lay the slices on the top.

Or, cook a piece of lean pork, take off the fat, heat it in another vessel until boiling hot, lightly brown a little flour in it, stir into it some of the pork broth, cook the beans in this as above directed and serve with the pork.

If the beans are old and have tough skins, they should first be cooked until half done, when they can be hulled; afterwards cook them as above directed.

34. Stewed Lettuce. Pick the heads over carefully and wash very thoroughly. Cook in plenty of boiling water, putting in a little cooking soda, pour on a colander then let it stand for about 1 hour in water to extract any bitterness there may be in the lettuce, press out and chop finely. Brown a little flour, grated toast or crackers in good fat, and add to this the lettuce, together with some boiling water, a small piece of butter, salt and nutmeg and then stew until done.

Another way is to take young lettuce and boil until tender, press it out, do not chop it but stew with milk and then proceed as directed in No. 14. Serve with veal meat balls, fried liver, cutlets, kidneys, baked fish, meat omelets, etc.

35. Vegetables with Barley Groats for the Family Table. Cut up several kohlrabi, together with parsley, celery and other roots, string beans and sliced onions, put on the fire with some water and soup fat, salt, season with spices and cook until half done. Then cook in this broth with the vegetables barley groats which have first been scalded and simmered until half done. When everything is thoroughly cooked stir through it fried pork cut into little cubes, and serve with poached eggs put on the dish, smoked bacon, spare ribs, beef roasted in a kettle.

36. Kohlrabi. After washing and peeling, cut them into fine slices or pieces, being careful to remove everything that is tough or hard, and then cook in boiling water until tender. Brown some flour in kidney fat or butter, add either fresh milk or meat broth according to taste, and also nutmeg and salt as desired, in which the kohlrabi is to be stewed. If the kohlrabi is quite young and tender, the small inner leaves are chopped quite fine, cooked in a separate vessel, butter and meat broth stirred through them and then used to garnish a dish of kohlrabi that has been stewed like cauliflowers. If the leaves are not tender enough for this purpose, then sliced sweetbreads or little pork sausages can be used to garnish, or else serve with cutlets, meat balls or steak.

Time of cooking, 1½ hours.

Remark.—The blue kohlrabi is preferable to the white because it is milder and does not become tough so easily as the other kind.

37. Filled Kohlrabi (*as an Entremet*). Peel the kohlrabi nice and round, and cook until partly done in weak salt water. Cut a slice from the end, hollow out the kohlrabi in cupform, fill with a good veal forcemeat, close by tieing on the slice that has been cut from the end, and then put them into a low kettle with the covered ends to the top, adding boiling meat broth, a good sized piece of butter and salt if necessary; then cook until done.

When serving put them on the dish with care, cutting the threads with which the covers were tied, stir some cornstarch into the broth and pour it over the kohlrabi. About 2 hours time will be necessary for the preparation of this dish.

38. Cauliflowers. Trim the stalk carefully, cut the smaller leaves away with a sharp-pointed knife, leaving the flowers whole, then lay into salt water which will expel any insects that may lurk in the vegetable. Cook slowly in not too much boiling water with salt, a piece of butter, and lemon juice until tender—but not soft—

and in order to prevent its not going to pieces lift it out with a clean napkin, put it carefully on a colander, drain well and cover immediately. Put it in a round dish with the flower to the top.

In Germany it is customary to pour over it a thick crab sauce, a cream- or a tart egg sauce; the English style is to simply pour over it melted butter and cover it with grated bread crumbs with a little grated nutmeg.

Serve with small sausages, beef tongue, raw ham, roast spring chicken, stuffed breast of veal, smoked salmon, forcemeat balls, meat fritters, kidney croquettes or pork sausages.

Time of cooking, 1¼ hours.

39. Cauliflowers with Parmesan Cheese. After cooking the cauliflowers set them into the proper dish, pour over them a thick cream sauce into which has been stirred a handful of Parmesan cheese, and afterwards cover it with grated Parmesan cheese. Pour over it melted butter and then bake in the same dish in a moderately hot oven until it receives a rich color.

In some kitchens broccoli, which is a species of cauliflower, is quite frequently cooked in its stead. The preparation of the flowers of this vegetable, which are separated into single pieces, is the same as with cauliflowers. The stalk of the broccoli can be peeled, cut into pieces, and cooked like asparagus, and it tastes quite similar to the latter.

40. Artichokes. Cut the stalks close, remove the hard leaves, and trim off the sharp points from the remaining leaves with a pair of scissors. After they have boiled for two or three hours in salted water, take out the fibres, cut off the bottom clear to the white of the artichoke and serve hot with Hollandaise sauce (Division R). In the winter artichokes filled with sweet peas (canned) are a favorite dish for genteel dinner parties.

Serve with the same dishes indicated for cauliflowers.

41. Egg Plant. Of this vegetable those shaped like a cucumber and of a violet color, and the white kinds are considered the best, but both varieties must be thoroughly ripe, otherwise they are quite apt to have a bitter taste.

To cook them first cut into halves the long way, make a few incisions into the pieces, turn them in bread crumbs, melted butter, pepper and salt, and then brown slightly in the frying pan. Or else cut into slices, season with salt and a little pepper, brown lightly with butter in a frying pan and serve with tomato sauce. If the egg plants are pickled for a few hours in vinegar, salt and water, they can be made into a very appetizing salad by the addition of either eggs, cresses, etc., with vinegar, olive oil, salt and pepper.

42. Butter Beans. String carefully, wash and put them into boiling water gradually. Put in the salt when the beans are more than half done, then cook until quite tender and put them on an earthenware colander to drain. Serve with an egg- or butter sauce (see Division R). Time of cooking, $1\frac{1}{4}$ to $1\frac{1}{2}$ hours.

Fresh herring, raw or boiled ham, pork chops, escallops, sausages, fried meat balls are usually served with this vegetable.

43. Another method of cooking Butter Beans. Clean and string the beans as usual, but instead of slicing them break into little pieces about 1 inch long. Then brown a little flour in hot kidney suet, stir with milk so that the beans can be cooked in it, add whatever salt is necessary and also some pepper. Cook the beans for a short time in this sauce and then take from the fire. Stir through the beans enough vinegar to give them a tart flavor, doing this carefully so that they will not mash, and serve with potatoes. Or when boiled the beans can be dressed simply with fresh butter and chopped parsley.

44. Sliced Beans. As sliced beans receive no preliminary scalding, they should be well washed after stringing; then cut them into thin long slices and cook in boiling water with a little butter, an onion, and a small piece of ham; afterwards take out the ham and onion, stir in some browned flour and add a teaspoonful of pulverized sugar, finely chopped parsley and, if necessary, some salt.

Time of cooking, about two hours. Serve with the same dishes indicated for butter beans.

45. Sliced Beans with Milk. Prepare the beans as already directed, scald in boiling water, drain, add milk, salt and butter, and cook until tender; before serving put in finely chopped parsley and peppergrass, also flour stirred in cream, 1 tablespoonful to a large cupful; stir through the beans and cook until done.

46. Savoy Cabbage. Remove the outer leaves, cut the head in two, take out the heart and the coarse ribs and cut the rest into small pieces, wash these nicely, cook in plenty of boiling water with not too much salt on a hot fire until done; put on a colander, drench with boiling water, press, and stew with meat broth, nutmeg and butter.

Time of cooking, 1 hour. Serve with roast duck, roast beef, cutlets, pork sausages, kettle roast of beef, or, for the family table, a nice piece of soup meat.

47. Duck in Savoy Cabbage. Cut the cabbage into 2 or 4 pieces, according to the size of the heads; remove the coarse ribs, taking care to leave the pieces whole; then wash and drain on a colander. In the meantime prepare a duck as directed under VII, Division D, salt slightly, roast it in butter to a light brown, lay a few slices of fat pork under it, and put 2 cupfuls of water and the cabbage to the duck, being careful that the cabbage pieces remain whole; put some salt between the layers, cover the kettle and let it simmer on a slow fire about 1½—2 hours.

In serving put the duck in the middle of the dish and place the cabbage around it. If it is not desired to cook the duck with the cabbage, the latter can be prepared with the gravy of the roast duck. which is served separately with it.

48. Red Cabbage (Kappes). Red summer cabbage is preferable to winter cabbage because the latter has a stronger flavor and takes twice as much time in cooking. First cut the head in two in the middle, remove the coarse outer leaves and thickest ribs, and then cut the cabbage into fine shreds which should be as long as possible. The cabbage will be better if it is first scalded; after draining, put in enough vinegar so that it will retain its natural bright color. Then bring water to a boil with either goose or duck fat or lard, or else with

butter and kidney suet half and half, and then add some
sweet grapes, 2 sour apples cut into pieces, a number of
small onions, a little sugar and salt, and in this cook
the cabbage until tender. Shortly before serving, dredge
a little flour over it, add a glassful of claret and according to taste, a few spoonfuls of currant juice, stew a few
quartered apples on top of the cabbage until soft, garnish with these and serve.

Cabbage prepared in this way does not need the
addition of any vinegar, it is tart enough without and
more wholesome than if it had received a stronger seasoning with vinegar. Small roast potatoes are served
with the cabbage, but boiled potatoes will also answer
if the time is short.

White cabbage can also be prepared in the same
manner, but instead of the claret take white wine and
leave out the apples; some prefer a rather tart flavor
to white cabbage which can be obtained by adding a
little vinegar and lemon juice. Serve with filet of beef,
roast beef, tongue, meat balls, fried sausages, roast
pork, hare, goose or duck, sour beef, roast or stuffed
spare ribs.

49. White Cabbage. After removing the outer green
leaves of the cabbage, cut it in two in the center. Take
out the core and the coarse ribs and then cut up into
large pieces; cook in plenty of boiling water on a hot
fire for 10, but not more than 15 minutes, leaving the
kettle uncovered, put on a colander to drain, bring
salted water to a boil, add some kidney fat or fat from
roast meats, put in the cabbage with a few pieces of
butter, cover tightly and let it simmer until very tender.
It does not need any stirring because the fat and salt
are absorbed equally well by the cabbage, and after it
is done it is taken out with the skimmer and placed in
the dish. Cabbage cooked in this manner is very palatable and looks nice. Potatoes can either be brought to
the table separately or else be cooked with the cabbage;
in the latter case put them on the cabbage after it has
cooked about 15 minutes, and put a little salt and a
few pieces of butter on the potatoes instead of the cabbage. The meat intended to go with cabbage—beef,
lamb or lean pork are the most appropriate—may be

boiled in water for about 1 hour beforehand, lay the cabbage on the meat and then cook as above directed.

Serve with stewed beef, soup meat, meat balls, spare ribs, fried sausages and the like.

50. Hunter's Cabbage (Jaeger=Kohl). Shred white cabbage the same as red cabbage and make a thick tart bacon sauce (see Division R), season with pepper, taking for the sauce about 1 ounce of fat pork and a heaping teaspoonful of fine flour for each person. Put nicely washed potatoes on the fire in a medium sized kettle with some salt; they should not be entirely covered with water. After the potatoes begin to cook, put in the cabbage evenly, a little higher around the edges, add whatever salt may still be necessary, pour the sauce over the cabbage, cover tightly and cook until the potatoes are thought to be entirely done. Lift the cover and, if, after the potatoes are done there is too much broth, then uncover the kettle and boil away the broth over a hot fire. Finally a good stirring must be given the cabbage which should be of a nice consistency, quite juicy and taste pleasantly tart.

Serve immediately with fried sausages.

51. White Cabbage with Mutton (Mecklenburg Style). Cut the mutton into small squares, wash nicely, salt and cook 1—1½ hours. In the meantime remove the outer leaves and the stalk of the cabbage, quarter, boil about 15 minutes and drain. Cover the bottom of the kettle with thin slices of fat pork, put on a layer of cabbage, then a few pieces of meat, sprinkle with salt and chopped onions, chervil, ground pepper and a few cloves, put on another layer of cabbage and meat and proceed in this manner, finishing with a layer of cabbage on top, pour in the mutton broth (which should be free from settlings) and cook for an hour to a rather thick consistency. When serving, turn out of the kettle and remove the slices of pork from the bottom before bringing to the table.

52. Stuffed Cabbage. Take plenty of large cabbage or savoy leaves, boil them for about 10 minutes, put a napkin into a colander and place in it the leaves (after removing the coarse ribs) evenly and thick all around. Spread over them forcemeat No. 23, A, put on another layer of leaves and proceed in this manner until a rather good sized head has been formed. Then gather the ends of the napkin, tie with a string and cook until done in meat stock or slightly salted water with which it should be barely covered, keeping the kettle tightly closed. When ready to serve, take the cabbage out of the napkin carefully and put it on a dish. Make a sauce of plenty of butter browned with flour stirred with some of the cabbage broth; season with extract of beef, mace and lemon peel and stir into it the yolks of a few eggs. Part of this sauce should be poured over the cabbage and the remainder passed at the table. This dish must cook fully 2 hours and is served with potatoes only, with no other side dish.

53. Filled Cabbage in another Style. Take a few white cabbages, cut away the outer leaves, remove the coarse ribs and also the heart or core. Wash the cabbages and cook in slightly salted boiling water until almost done. Drain, and after it is cool put it lengthwise into a pudding mould or perhaps into a narrow cooking vessel, in which case a cupful of beef broth should be poured over it, together with a pork forcemeat which is made as described further on, and then cook slowly. When put into the pudding mould in layers, the largest leaves should be placed on the bottom; spread on them the forcemeat about ¼ inch thick and continue in this manner until the desired quantity has been moulded. Finish with cabbage and a few pieces of butter on the top. Press down a little, cover tightly, put into boiling water and cook uninterruptedly for 2 hours.

The forcemeat is made for a large cabbage by taking about 1¼ pounds of finely chopped pork, about ¼ pound of grated wheat bread, 3 eggs, 2 tablespoonfuls of sour cream, some finely chopped onion, pepper, salt and nutmeg.

The sauce can be made in various ways. The simplest and most profitable is, to take gravy of roast beef or roast veal with some extract of beef, thicken with grated wheat bread and add to it previously stewed mushrooms. Or else lightly brown grated wheat bread in butter; again make a weak broth from cabbage leaves and remnants of meat, use this to thin some flour browned in butter and season according to taste with capers, chopped anchovy or mushrooms, and strengthen with a trifle of extract of beef.

54. Stewed Celery. After cleaning the roots, cut them into 4—8 pieces, boil until done, take them out and stew in a clear meat stock which gives the celery a good yellow color, together with butter, salt and nutmeg; finally thicken the broth with some cornstarch.

Time of cooking, 1½ hours. Serve with stuffed breast of veal, stewed ribs of veal, beef tenderloin, rolled steak, fried sweetbreads, forcemeat balls, roasted beef tongue, fried sausages, meat fritters and cutlets of all kinds.

55. Stuffed Celery is prepared in the same manner as directed for stuffed kohlrabi, omitting the crab butter.

56. Stewed Onions. Take onions of medium size and peel them. Cook until done in an earthenware vessel in meat broth, with butter, mace, salt and rolled crackers. Time of cooking, 1—1½ hours. Add some lemon juice according to taste.

Serve with escallops, cutlets, roast tongue, fried liver and fried sausages. This dish can be served with soup meat or used as a garnish for a string bean salad.

57. Stuffed Giant Onions. Spanish onions, which grow to the size of a saucer, are peeled, cut off one end to be used as a cover, hollow out, fill with good forcemeat, put on the cover and fasten with a little wooden peg or tie with a thread. Stew the onions for 5 minutes in melted butter, add beef broth, some salt, cloves, white pepper, 2—3 bay leaves, a little mace, some grated toast, and stew the onions covered tightly in this until they are done and the forcemeat is thoroughly cooked, which will take from ¾—1 hour. Remove the pegs or threads and serve the onions in their own sauce with lemon slices.

58. Stewed Cucumbers. Pare, take out the seeds, cut the cucumbers into pieces and cook in water and vinegar half and half, with salt. A simpler way is to lay them in a pickle of water, vinegar and salt for an hour.

Then stew them in a meat or beef extract broth with butter, nutmeg and rolled crackers. Three-fourths of an hour will be sufficent to prepare this dish. Serve with meat balls, cutlets, roast mutton, sausages and veal escallops.

59. Stuffed Cucumbers. Take large green cucumbers and pare them the evening before they are to be used, cut them in two lengthwise and lay them in vinegar after taking out the seeds. Towards the noon hour dry them and make a veal forcemeat, taking for this purpose a small piece of finely chopped veal, chopped mushrooms, a rusk which has been soaked in cold water and well pressed, a small piece of fresh butter, a whipped egg, nutmeg and salt. Mix well, stuff into the halved cucumbers, tie them together, put them on the fire in plenty of melted butter, brown them nicely all over and let them stew slowly until done. After the cucumbers have been taken from the fire, brown as much flour in the butter which remains in the vessel as is necessary to thicken the sauce; also put in the broth to make the sauce, or instead of this, water with the addition of beef extract. Furthermore, a lemon slice without the seeds, some mace, salt, a pinch of white pepper and capers. Stew the cucumbers in this for a short time and after removing the threads serve in the sauce stirred with the yolk of an egg.

60. Cooked Cucumbers. This makes a very easily digestible dish and while, perhaps, it may be considered as being a trifle insipid in taste, yet it is recommended because it can be prepared in 15 minutes. Pare the cucumbers, which should be of a good size, cut into long pieces the thickness of a finger, put into boiling salted water and cook for a few minutes; in the meantime brown a teaspoonful of flour in a small piece of butter, stir with it some fresh milk, season with nutmeg and after draining the cucumbers stew them until done, similar to cauliflowers.

After the cucumbers have come from the fire, a little vinegar can be added if desired. Serve with meat balls, roast spring chicken and all kinds of salted and smoked meats.

61. Fresh Mushrooms. The mushrooms should be closed as much as possible; cut away the sandy end of the stalk, wash them with great care, drain and put them on the fire in an earthenware vessel with some meat broth and butter; cover tightly and cook slowly for 15 minutes. Finally add a teaspoonful of cornstarch or some rolled crackers, a little lemon juice, pepper and salt and, according to taste, some chopped parsley, and cook until the broth has a nice consistency; stir the yolk of an egg through it.

If the mushrooms are old and large they must be peeled and cut into pieces. If they are to be served with the roast or as a stew, let them simmer slowly in butter and their own juice until tender.

Serve with smoked salmon, roast chicken, veal cutlets or veal stew.

62. Stuffed Mushrooms. Mushrooms to be stuffed must retain their stalks. After carefully peeling the mushrooms and the stalks, wash and let them dry, then make a good veal forcemeat as described for stuffed cucumbers, omitting the mushrooms; press some of the forcemeat on every stalk as far as the head so that it will adhere tightly. Then stew the mushrooms in plenty of melted butter until tender and serve with a sauce as described for stuffed cucumbers.

63. Fried Mushrooms. First cut off the sandy end of the stalk, break it from the head and peel; take off the mushrooms, rinse them in water and drain on a colander, cut them into thin slices and have some butter ready in a frying pan in which the mushrooms are fried over a hot fire until done.

They often yield considerable juice and must, therefore, be turned quite frequently, otherwise they will become tough. As soon as the slices begin to fry they should be salted plentifully; add some ground pepper and serve with bread or potatoes. They may be fried in fat without onions, and can also be cooked rapidly with butter and a little beef broth. When mushrooms are fried or cooked for too long a time they become tough.

64. Fresh Truffles. The truffles are not peeled but are cleaned with a brush in warm and then in cold water. Put them on the fire in 1 pint of Burgundy or other good red wine, all kinds of whole spices, a piece of fresh butter, salt, and a few slices of lemon and cook until they are tender. Serve on a folded napkin with fresh butter. Or they can be served in a dish with sauce poured over them.

65. Another method of cooking Truffles. Clean as directed just preceding. Put fat pork slices into a stewpan with a bay leaf, some thyme, salt and coarse ground pepper, lay the truffles on these and cover them with slices of fat pork; add 4 glassfuls of strong white wine and a piece of nice butter, cook for a good half hour and serve very hot on a napkin.

This makes one of the finest dishes that can be served and is brought to the table as an entre immediately after the soup, or else (garnished with escallops or veal croquettes) in a middle course.

66. Sweet Chestnuts. Shell and then blanch them. Put them in a stewpan, adding fresh butter, salt, some sugar and a strong beef broth, and simmer slowly until tender; the broth is nicely thickened with flour browned in butter. Serve very hot, garnishing with juicy cutlets, or else bring to the table with winter cabbage as a side dish.

67. Winter Carrots. After washing and scraping the carrots, wash them again and take the lower ends in order to get as much as possible a dish similar to early carrots; they should be cooked as directed for the latter, only sweetening with some sugar, and finally adding some chopped parsley.

Serve with the same meats, etc., as directed for early carrots.

REMARK.—Washing vegetables of every description before and after cleaning them, has a great influence in attaining good results in cooking, and this is particularly the case with all bulbs and roots, which should invariably be rubbed between the hands in water and then rinsed in fresh water several times, because the outer peel or skin usually imparts a strong flavor to the dish. Roots, however, should never be washed after they are cut, because some of their sweetness is thereby lost; carrots as well as turnips should be cooked as long as possible, for this increases their palatableness.

68. Another method of cooking Winter Carrots. Clean the carrots and cut them into very fine shreds, put them on the fire in not too much boiling water with a few finely chopped onions and some kidney suet; cook quickly until tender, adding the salt towards the last. Then melt a few pieces of butter on the carrots, thicken the broth with cornstarch or flour and stir with chopped parsley. Shortly before serving, pared sour apples cut into halves may be put on the carrots; let them simmer until cooked and lay the apples on top of the carrots when bringing them to the table.

Or else put a layer of potatoes of uniform size on the carrots ½ hour before the latter are quite done, add the necessary salt and when the potatoes are cooked put on them small pieces of butter, stir with some finely chopped parsley before serving, and, according to taste, add a little vinegar. Time of cooking, 1—1¼ hours.

Serve with smoked meats, fried sausages or head-cheese.

69. Stuffed Tomatoes. Take nice, ripe tomatoes, scoop them out carefully, pass the pulp through a sieve and make a dressing of either chopped mushrooms, grated stale wheat bread, creamed butter, salt and pepper, or else with finely chopped mutton, roast meat gravy, a few eggs, grated bread and fine herbs; fill the tomatoes with the mixture. Bake the tomatoes in butter for about 15 minutes, sprinkle with lemon juice and serve with toast as an entree or as a garnish for more important dishes in middle courses.

70. Spanish Tomatoes. Cut ripe tomatoes into slices, salt, cover and set aside for an hour. In the meantime boiled ham is finely chopped; butter a dripping pan, fill it with ham and tomatoes in alternate layers, cover the surface with pieces of butter and grated wheat bread; bake for 30 minutes. When done, turn out of the pan carefully, pour over it a brown sauce, garnish with small roasted potatoes and serve.

71. Parsnips. After washing the parsnips, scrape and then wash them again and cut them into short, thick pieces. Put butter into water, bring to a boil, put in the parsnips gradually, add salt and cook until tender, which will take about 1 hour. The broth should be plentiful and will be thick enough of itself without any addition; season with a little nutmeg. Parsnips can also be cooked in a meat broth with its own fat.

Serve with cutlets of all kinds and fried sausages.

72. Turnips. Wash them, pare and wash them again, cut into narrow slices and parboil if necessary; then cook until tender in not too much water with some good kidney suet and salt; put in a few pieces of butter and stir through the dish 1—2 tablespoonfuls of sweet cream and a little cornstarch. When serving, grate a little nutmeg over the turnips. Potatoes can be served with the turnips, either cooked or roasted, or else they may be cooked with them.

Serve with beef roasted like hare, warm or cold smoked meats, fried sausages and fried liver.

73. Winter Cabbage, Bremen Style. Green winter cabbage has not so strong a flavor as the brown variety and is therefore preferable to the latter. If the cabbage is frozen take the heart only and the leaves nearest the heart, together with the stalk as far as tender, washing carefully. It is best to prepare the cabbage the evening previous, letting it freeze again over night. Where the cabbage has a strong flavor it is well to first parboil it in plenty of water for about 10 minutes. Then put some boiling water with plenty of goose-grease or lard and butter on the fire, put in the cabbage in layers, with plenty of small onions, adding salt sparingly because cabbage is very easily oversalted, cover tightly and cook slowly. It must be thoroughly done but not soft and should not be stirred; ordinarily 2 hours will be sufficent time for cooking. If it should lack sweetness put in a piece of sugar early in the cooking. When ready to serve, the broth, which should be rather scant, can be bound with a little flour or cornstarch.

Garnish with stewed chestnuts (see A, 39,) which may, however, also be stirred through the cabbage or else be brought to the table in a separate dish. Serve as a side dish small potatoes, roasted raw to a nice brown color. Serve the cabbage with roast goose, stuffed spareribs, roast pork, roast beef, round of beef, fried pork sausages or pork chops.

In Bremen this cabbage is usually cooked with "Pinkel" sausages (made of beef kidney suet and oat-

meal); sometimes the cabbage is brought on the fire
after being put in the kettle with oatmeal layers between it alternately.

74. Shredded Cabbage, Westphalian Style. Take
the heart, together with all the green leaves of the cabbage, wash, cut into shreds on a chopping board, and
parboil for 10 minutes and then cook until tender in
not too much water with goose-grease or else butter
and lard half and half, adding a few small onions and
some salt. A little sugar and a trifle of cornstarch are
added towards the last. Serve with stewed chestnuts
and roast potatoes, but if a fat meat is served, roast
goose for instance, then boiled potatoes are preferable.
Time of cooking, about 2 hours.

75. Sourkrout. Take it carefully out of the keg or
other vessel in which it is contained, rejecting all that
may not be of the proper color. Press it vigorously
and if it should be too sour pour hot water over it, dry
quickly; it should not be rinsed. Kidney suet, butter
and lard in equal parts make an excellent fat for cooking sourkrout. Bring the fat to a boil in the necessary
amount of water, put in the sourkrout with a few pep.
percorns, cover tightly and cook with a quick fire, add.
ing some salt if necessary. If liked a little bunch of
juniper berries and carraway tied in a cloth can be
cooked with the krout. When ready to serve some cornstarch or flour, or still better grated potatoes, should
be stirred through the dish.
Serve with mashed potatoes or a puree of peas.
If the cabbage has been cut very fine and put up
without any salt, about ¾—1 hour is necessary for
cooking, otherwise it will take about 1½ hours, and if
made from winter cabbage it will take from 3—4 hours.
The following method is preferable for cooking sourkrout because it thereby retains its bright appearance:
Bring wine and water half and half to a boil, and then
put in the sourkrout with some salt and a few peppercorns and cook until tender. Shortly before serving
pour off all the broth and stir plenty of butter through
the sourkrout.
Sourkrout is usually served with partridges, pheasants, goose liver patties, liver dumplings, fried liver,

baked pike, headcheese, roast pig, roast pork, spare ribs, boiled ham, and particularly pickled pigs' feet. A puree of peas makes a very good side dish.

76.   Sourkrout for the Family Table.   Prepare in the first place as described just above.   Put water in sufficient quantity with lard on the fire, bring to a boil, put in the sourkrout and cook until done.   If one wishes to cook a piece of ham or bacon in the krout, it must not be too salty, and should be cooked until about half done before the krout is put into the kettle. Fat pork can also be used to advantage as described for the preparation of greens under No. 14 of this division; the melted fat can then be put to the sourkrout.   It is better to cook the potatoes alone because the acid of the sourkrout is apt to make them a trifle hard; stir them into the dish at last. 1—2 raw potatoes grated and stirred through the dish after it is thoroughly cooked gives it a nice consistency and a good color. Dried white beans cooked until quite tender together with their own broth can also be stirred through the krout, shortly before serving.

Time of cooking as above noted.

77.   Sourkrout with Pike.   Prepare the krout as directed in the last preceding receipt, clean the fish, cut off the head and put the liver into the mouth.   Put the fish on the fire in enough water to cover, together with some butter, peppercorns, bay leaves, cloves and salt; when the head is half done take it out and lay it aside, cooking the rest until done and then boning it. Put the sourkrout with the fish into the dish in layers, rounding it in the middle, pour over it a few spoonfuls of good cream and 1 to 2 whipped eggs, sprinkle over it rolled crackers, put the head of the fish with the liver on the rounding in the middle of the dish, and then bake in the oven for about 30 minutes.   To preserve the head cover it during the baking with a piece of buttered paper.

Crabs can also be cooked with this style of sourkrout.   Fill the shells with a crab forcemeat, cook in salt water or the fish broth and use them together with the crab tails to garnish the border of the dish.

78. Sourkrout with Stewed Oysters and Rhinewine.
Press the krout well and cook for 3 hours in boiling
water adding 1 pound of unsalted butter for every 3
pounds of krout; then put in 1 bottle of Rhinewine and
let it simmer slowly until little or no broth remains.
Serve the krout placed in the dish around the edges,
leaving the center open, which is filled with an oyster
stew. Bring to the table hot.

79. Sourkrout with Pheasants and Oysters. Prepare the pheasant as for a roast; then lightly press
about 2 pounds of sourkrout (if it should be too sour
freshen it), put it in a stewpan, pour over it white wine
and water half and half, enough to cover the krout, put
in a good-sized lump of lard and a chopped onion and
let it cook slowly for an hour. Then put in the pheasant and let it cook slowly for another hour and after it
is tender take it out and thicken the sourkrout slightly
with a sauce made of ½ tablespoonful of fine flour rubbed
in 1½ tablespoonfuls of fresh butter, together with 2
chopped onions, afterwards smoothed in a large cupful
of clear stock and cook for ½ hour; then stir through it
the same quantity of sweet cream, bring the sauce to a
boil, thicken with the yolks of 2 eggs and pass through
a fine sieve, season with salt and some lemon juice.

Remove the beards from 40—50 oysters, dry them
in a cloth, sprinkle each oyster with salt and pepper,
turn in flour and dip in egg and bread crumbs; have
hot lard or butter ready and fry the oysters to a nice
brown color shortly before they are to be served. Carve
the pheasant, garnishing first with the sourkrout and
with a border of the oysters. If one wishes to serve the
oysters in another style, remove the beards, put the
oysters on the stove and get them hot, but do not cook
them. Add the liquor of the oysters to the sourkrout,
thicken the latter with a sauce made as above directed,
adding a few drops of lemon juice. Serve with the oysters placed in the center of the dish encircled with the
sourkrout and the pheasant as a border.

80. To cook Beans salted for Winter use. Freshen
the beans early in the morning, cover them with water,
which should be renewed several times; then cook them
in an unglazed stone cooking vessel in the same manner

as fresh beans, but after they have cooked for a time put in plenty of boiling milk which preserves their natural color, being careful, however, to cook them rapidly and uninterruptedly until tender. After this proceed with their preparation the same as with fresh beans, and the difference between the two can be hardly noticed.

Time of cooking, and serve with the same dishes, as noted for fresh beans.

81. Pickled String Beans. Cook them until tender and then rinse them repeatedly to extract the salt and pour them on a colander; after this cook the beans in water with kidney suet and lard half and half with a scant broth, salting as much as is necessary. Afterwards put in the white beans which have been cooked until quite tender, together with their broth and stir well together, or else the string beans are put into the dish along the edges and the white beans filled into the center. Instead of the white beans, a number of small potatoes parboiled can be cooked with the beans until done, and a grated raw potato stirred through them as directed for sourkrout. Time of cooking, 1—2 hours, according to the quality.

Serve with smoked meat, boiled ham, fried sausages, pork chops, smoked tongue and freshened herring.

82. Pickled Salad Beans are parboiled, then freshened and stewed like fresh salad beans, or else the broth is poured off and a thick egg sauce is put over them.

Serve with meats as directed in the preceding receipt.

83. Dried Peas or Pea Puree. Prepare as directed for pea soup, and after pouring off the water cook them in a scant broth with the necessary fat until rather thick, add the salt, pass through a strainer, bring to a boil again, put into the dish, rounding them high in the center, smoothing the surface nicely, cover with onions browned in butter and put strips of toast around the edges.

Time of cooking, 2 hours. Serve with salt pork of every kind or nicely freshened herring.

84. White Beans. Cook them the same as peas until tender, but pour the water off twice and do not strain tnem. After bringing to a boil the second time stir in good fat and before serving stir salt and a little vinegar through the beans. The beans should not be too dry.

Or else cook the beans without either fat or vinegar, pour off the broth and serve with pork or onion sauce, or else with butter and vinegar.

White beans are excellent when stewed with crab sauce. Serve with boiled ham, roast beef or kettle roast, fried liver, fried sausages, calf's head jelly.

85. Lentils. Prepare as directed for peas, parboil, drain and serve with an onion sauce poured over them.

Or else, after parboiling, cook the lentils until tender with a small piece of pork and a few onions and then stir a little flour and vinegar into the broth, which should not be too scant.

Time of cooking, the same as for peas and beans.

86. Lentils in Mecklenburg Style. After the lentils have been well picked over and washed they are cooked until tender. Then pour off all of the water and put in a meat broth with chopped green leek and celery, cook for quite a while longer and thicken with flour rubbed in plenty of fat.

Or else, after cooking the lentils for an hour, pour off the water and then cook them in fresh water until quite tender. Then cut a piece of fat pork into slices and fry in butter with plenty of onions until it commences to froth, lightly brown in this according to quantity, 1, 2 or 3 spoonfuls of flour, stir with meat broth to make a thick sauce, add vinegar, salt and pepper, pour onto the lentils and cook them until done.

----

87. Artichokes for Invalids. Prepare the artichokes, cut them into pieces and cook in salted water until tender, pass through a sieve and mix with fresh butter, grated wheat bread and a few yolks of eggs whipped with sweet cream. A puree of cauliflowers can be made in the same manner for invalids.

88. Puree of white Beans for Convalescents. This should be served only when permitted by the physician.

Soak the beans over night, cook them in water until quite tender and then strain. In the meantime chop the meat of a few boiled crabs quite fine, mix with the puree of the beans, add some crab butter and 1 cupful of beef broth and cook all together. Stir into the puree the yolks of several eggs whipped in cream, and serve with tender cutlets or roast chicken.

Many of the vegetable dishes in this division are fit for invalids, among them Nos. 2, 4, 15, 16, 17, 21, 36, 38 and 60, but care should be taken to usually omit sharp spices or seasoning.

II. POTATOES.

1. How to cook Potatoes.   Far too little care is quite frequently exercised in cooking potatoes and yet when well cooked they make very palatable dishes, preferred by many to other perhaps more elegant articles of food. Without question, much depends upon careful paring, washing and cooking. Potatoes should be selected of medium and as nearly as possible of uniform size; before paring wash them and throw them into fresh water as soon as pared, rub them several times between the hands in the water, rinse and keep them covered in fresh water until wanted for use. Then drain them on a colander, pour clear water over them and put on the fire in a kettle which should not be too small and be used for this purpose only; have the water cover them and put in salt in the proportion of about ½ of a teaspoonful to a quart of water. It should be noted that new potatoes require more salt than old. Skimming should be carefully attended to and they should cook neither too rapidly nor too slowly until done. It is well to try them occasionally in order to determine whether they are done; if they can be easily pierced with a fork they may be considered done. They should not fall to pieces, neither must they be brought to the table half done. Pour the water off carefully—none must remain in the kettle—and put the kettle back on the fire for a few minutes longer, taking off the cover, shaking the potatoes so that all watery particles may evaporate, and then let them stand on the back of the stove. It is much better, however, to bring them to the table at once in a covered warm dish after they have been evaporated, because nothing loses in palatableness so much through standing as potatoes.

The longer or shorter duration of time for cooking potatoes depends upon the variety and, in a measure, upon the season; nice fresh potatoes need about 15 to 20 minutes. Potatoes grown in light sandy soil are the best.

2. Potatoes with various Kinds of Sauces. After cooking potatoes as directed above, cover them with a sauce made of either onions, fat and parsley, or else a slightly sour milk sauce, or a Bechamel, Maitre de Hotel or an anchovy sauce (see under R) and cover the dish tightly, or else the sauce may be served separately.

3. Potatoes with Herring. Cook the potatoes in their jackets with salt, then peel and slice, keeping them as hot as possible. In the meantime lightly brown a few onions in plenty of butter, add some flour, after this some water, salt, ground pepper, a little vinegar and, if handy, a few bay leaves; when this begins to cook put in the sliced potatoes and then the boned herrings cut into small pieces. After everything is thoroughly cooked and very hot, stir through it some cream. This dish should be very juicy and not stiff.

4. Potatoes with Parsley and Boiled Fish. Peel small potatoes, cook them in salted water on a quick fire until done, being careful that they remain whole. After pouring off the water carefully, shake the potatoes on top of the stove with plenty of fresh butter and finely chopped parsley. Serve at once.

5. Sour Potatoes with Bay Leaves. Slowly try out some pork fat or else get some other kind of good fat nicely hot, lightly brown in it finely chopped onions, stir with it water, salt and a little pepper, and boil the potatoes in it with some bay leaves until done. Before serving take out the bay leaves and add a dash of vinegar, and if they should not be of the proper consistency thicken with a little browned flour. Be careful to have the dish nice and juicy.

6. Breaded Potatoes. Take potatoes of a medium and uniform size and after washing, cook them in their jackets with some salt until done, but they must not be soft. Then peel them, cut into thick slices, dip into a whipped egg and turn in bread or cracker crumbs. Heat some good fat with plenty of good butter in a clean sauce pan, put in the sliced potatoes side by side and fry over a medium fire, lightly brown on both sides, keeping the pan uncovered; serve at once. This makes a nice side dish for spinach, Brussels sprouts, red cabbage and for various kinds of meats.

7. Roast Potatoes. Peel quite small potatoes of uniform size, wash and cook in salted water until half done and then drain until dry. Then heat some butter and good fat in one or two saucepans on a medium fire, put in the steaming potatoes side by side, cover the pan tightly and when the lower sides of the potatoes are brown turn them and cover again until they are done, after which they should be roasted in the uncovered pan until browned, being careful not to scorch them. In order to preserve their nice appearance and smoothness they should not be touched with a fork while cooking; the best way to turn them is to use a pancake turner. Dusting sugar over the potatoes when they are roasting makes them look glossy.

Should the potatoes accidentally have been cooked too long, be careful to put only those remaining whole and none of the broken ones into the pan. If potatoes cooked in their jackets are to be roasted, which, by the way, are not near as nice as the other kind, they are cooked until done in salted water, peeled while hot, roasted in an open pan, turning frequently.

Raw potatoes roasted are preferred by many to any other kind. Select small, round potatoes of a uniform size, wash them carefully and drain well, roast them in an open pan in hot butter until brown, sprinkle with fine salt, cover the pan or kettle and shake frequently until done. Serve immediately.

8. Potatoes with Buttermilk. Boil the potatoes until soft, add buttermilk and let them cook for a while longer with pieces of browned pork fat cut into cubes. When they do not fall to pieces, a little flour stirred with buttermilk may be added. Or else the potatoes are cooked in their jackets until soft and then cut into slices. Heat some fat, brown some flour in it, stir with buttermilk to a plentiful thick sauce, salt and then cook the potatoes until done.

9. Curried Potatoes. Curry powder is composed of various strong spices and can be obtained in most drug stores or first-class groceries.

Boil small potatoes and shake them several times with plenty of butter and 1 tablespoonful or more of curry powder, let the kettle stand for a short time on the top of the stove. Serve as soon as possible.

Curried potatoes are appropriate side dishes for all kinds of cabbages and roast meats.

10. Baked Potatoes with Sausages. Fry the sausages in butter with finely chopped onions, take them out of the pan, stir a spoonful of flour into the fat and afterwards some good meat broth, gravy fat from roast meats, salt and pepper.

Cook the potatoes in their jackets, slice them while still hot, put them into the pan with the sausages and simmer for a short time. Put a layer of these potatoes into a buttered dish dusted with bread or cracker crumbs, put on them the sausages cut into pieces 2 to 3 inches long, on these put another layer of potatoes, cover with bread or cracker crumbs, pour over it melted butter, then bake in an oven for about ¾ of an hour or until it is nicely crusted. Turn out of the pan and serve.

11. Potatoes, Spareribs and Sour Apples baked to= gether. Put the spareribs on a medium fire, half covered with salted water, in a rather shallow fryingpan, cover the pan tightly and let the meat cook moderately for 1—1¼ hours until of a light brown color. Then take them out of the pan and cover the latter with small, round potatoes, peeled, put on a little salt, lay the spareribs over them with the opening towards the top, and fill this with pared and quartered apples, add a cupful of water, cover and let the potatoes roast slowly until they are tender and brown, turning them once.

Serve the spareribs with the apples in a deep dish, using the potatoes as a garnish. This dish is best cooked in an oven.

12. Baked Potatoes with Cheese. Cut boiled potatoes into slices and put them in layers into a buttered
pan. Cover every layer with a sauce made of sour
cream, eggs and Parmesan cheese, continuing in this
manner until the pan is filled. For 4 persons take 1
pint of cream, 4 eggs and about 3 ounces of cheese.
Bake in an oven for about ½ hour and serve as a side
dish with ham, beefsteak and other meats of a similar
kind.

13.   Stuffed Potatoes (an original receipt). Peel
large potatoes, cut off a slice, scoop them out and fill
with a dressing made of roast meat remnants of any
kind, preferably pork; chop the meat very fine and mix
with a few eggs, chopped parsley, salt, pepper, nutmeg
and grated bread; put a tablespoonful into every potato and tie on with a thread the slice that has been
cut off. Bake slowly in plenty of fat until done; they
should be lightly brown in color. This makes an excellent side dish with greens and lettuce.

14.   Potatoes with Apples. This dish is prepared
best by cooking potatoes until done in salted water and
mashing them. Stir through them a piece of butter,
then mix with them an applesauce, which should be
rather thick but not too sweet, taking about ⅓ as many
apples as you have potatoes. In case the dish should
be too stiff, put in some boiling water and cook. When
done, put into an appropriate dish and cover with
browned bread crumbs, or else pass with it melted butter, sugar and browned cracker crumbs.

To save time the apples can be cut into pieces and
be put with the potatoes after the latter are fully half
done, pouring off part of the water. Cook until done,
stir butter through it and bring to the table as already
directed.

Serve with roast hare, sour beef, cutlets, fried liver,
sausage, ham and chopped meat balls.

15.   Potatoes and fresh Pears are best cooked with
a piece of lean pork which has already been boiled until
half done, otherwise with fat and butter; the pears must
be nearly done before the potatoes, which should first
be boiled until done, are put with them.

Before serving, stir through with some vinegar, but the potatoes must not become mashed. Instead of the vinegar a few sour apples may be added to the pears after putting in the potatoes. Like all other dishes made of potatoes this one should not be too stiff.

Instead of pears, plums can also be stirred through the potatoes after the latter have first been stirred through with butter, but in this case omit the pork and use any other kind of roast meat. Instead of the fresh fruit dried apples, pears or prunes can be taken, but they must then be stewed before putting them in with the potatoes, which should first be cooked until done and then mashed. Sometimes 2 eggs are whipped with 2 spoonfuls of milk and stirred through the dried fruit, and then fat pork, smoked sausage or ham is served with the dish.

16. Potato Balls (Rissoles). Cook the potatoes in salted water, drain entirely dry and mash. Mix them with a few eggs, a piece of butter, nutmeg according to taste, and a few spoonfuls of sour cream. Then roll into small balls, sprinkle them with rolled crackers and fry in butter. For the family table potatoes left over can be used, which are mashed, mixed with egg and fried as above.

These potato balls make a nice adjunct to greens or lettuce.

17. Potato Noodles. Take a deep plate full of peeled and grated potatoes cooked in their jackets the day previous in salted water, together with 4 eggs, 4 spoonfuls of cream or milk, the same quantity of melted butter and add whatever salt may be necessary. Put the potatoes on a bread board, make a hollow in the center into which put some flour and the eggs, cream, butter and salt, knead this to a dough, adding a little flour from time to time until the dough can be stretched and is compact and does not show any holes when cut. Roll the dough into oblong pieces about the size of a potato, cook for 8—10 minutes in boiling salted water, put them on a colander and after they are drained, fry them all around in butter until lightly brown.

18. Sliced Potatoes (German Style). Peel the potatoes, wash carefully and cut into very thin slices. Put plenty of lard and butter half and half into a pan or else brown some fat pork in it, put in the potatoes about an inch deep, sprinkle with salt, add a cupful of water and cover the pan tightly. After the potatoes have been browned over a medium fire until done, they may be sent to the table or else turned in the pan and browned on the other side.

Instead of raw potatoes, cold potatoes that have been left over may be cut into slices and fried in butter or other good fat. About ⅓ the quantity of sliced sour apples can be laid on the potatoes and, covered tightly, fried in butter to a nice brown; the potatoes can also be stirred with 2—3 eggs mixed with a little milk.

19. Roast Potatoes. Take good potatoes of a medium size, wash them very carefully, put them in an iron kettle, cover with water, cook until half done, pour off the water, sprinkle with some salt, cover tightly, put them on a medium fire or better still into a medium hot oven and roast until they are quite tender and nicely crusted. Serve with fresh butter.

Nos. 4, 16 and 17 are well adapted for invalids.

D.—Meats.

1. GENERAL DIRECTIONS.

Preparing the Meat. Meats should never be washed more than is absolutely necessary to clean them, and they should never lay in the water, because they thereby lose too much strength. Roast beef, beefsteaks and mutton roast are much improved by pounding, and this should be done immediately before cooking. Put the meat on the chopping board and pound on each side, whereby it more fully retains its juiciness, then rinse the meat, dry it with a towel and proceed with the cooking.

Veal and poultry are best scalded before roasting or stewing, pouring off the water immediately after. The meat is thereby improved in appearance and is more easily larded.

Larding. Larding makes roasts juicier and improves their appearance. Use salted water and smoked fat pork for larding, taking for this purpose a piece from the shoulder, cut obliquely into pieces 1½—2 inches wide, divide them into thin slices and from these cut the lardoons of the size required.

The meat which is to be larded should be laid on a meat board, put a lardoon into the larding needle, draw the pin and part of the fat, of which the two ends should be of equal length, through the meat. Proceed thus until the entire piece is covered with lardoons placed at regular intervals and in as straight a line as is possible. The grain of the meat should be taken into consideration when larding; it must run crosswise to the larding needle, then commence a new row.

In larding hares, put 2 rows of lardoons along each side of the back, making 4 rows in all; usually 2 are sufficient. Other kinds of game or poultry are larded in the same manner, but quite young and tender poultry, sweetbreads, etc., should be hardened before larding by pouring hot water over them.

Cooking Meat. All kinds of meat, including salted and smoked if it is freshened, should be put on the stove in boiling water, because it thus loses less of its juiciness and is done sooner. Regarding fresh meats for soups all necessary remarks have already been made in the chapter devoted to soups. The time necessary until the meat becomes tender, depends upon the age of the beef, and the size of the piece, but in general the following table can be depended upon: Fresh beef, up to 3 hours; smoked beef or a whole smoked ham, 3½—4 hours; pickled meats, 3—3½ hours; veal, 1½—2 hours; mutton, 2—2½ hours; poultry, 3 hours; spring chickens, ¾—1 hour; pigeons, ¾ hour at the furthest; a pig's or calf's head, 2—2½ hours; game, according to its kind, from 2—2½ hours.

If a soup is not to be made from the meat, allow it to simmer slowly because it thereby fully retains its juiciness. If cooked in vessels that can be tightly covered the meat can be put on the fire without any water, simply with fat or butter, otherwise put on the stove and not in the oven, and in this case with boiling water, which should be replenished as it evaporates. As soon as this broth begins to cook move the vessel to the back part of the stove where the meat will finish cooking slowly.

Roasting. Roasted meats are done quicker than when cooked in any other way. It is not advisable to roast meats on top of the stove; the meat is far better when roasted in the oven. Small cuts only, like chops, etc., should be fried or roasted in the frying pan, unless one prefers broiling.

In broiling, put the meat over glowing coals or on a hot fire-place; as soon as heated, butter and then put the meat on the broiler; turn when necessary. In turning, be careful not to pierce the meat with the fork, in fact this precaution is necessary with roasts of all kinds.

When roasting meat in the oven it should be properly heated before the meat is put in, because this tends to roast the meat uniformly all around and it loses little or none of its juiciness. Thereafter allow the heat in the oven to gradually diminish.

Baste the roast frequently with the added fat, or in case of a pork roast or roast goose, with their own fat. If the top heat is too great it is well to cover the roast with a piece of buttered paper; care should be taken to observe whether the heat radiating from the sides of the oven is of equal intensity or not, because it may be necessary to turn the roast *with* the pan—not *in* the pan.

For roasts that are to be well done an earthenware roasting pan is the best, and repeated basting with boiling water or meat broth is necessary. If, on the contrary, the roast is wanted rare the ordinary roasting pan can be used, the heat in the oven should be greater and the addition of water be avoided; plenty of fat should be put with the roast from the start. As the clear fat easily absorbs great heat, the roast receives a nice crust, retains its juice and is more quickly done, consequently the inner part of the roast does not receive heat enough to thoroughly cook it. If the fat should begin to brown the roast it can be taken out of the oven and set for awhile on the stove without detriment. If the roast is really scorched, however, which may happen to the best cook under an unfortunate conjunction of circumstances, it is still possible to save it by carefully cutting away the scorched parts and then cooking the remainder for several minutes in boiling water, which should be frequently renewed. The scorchy taste is thereby largely removed and the meat can then be roasted in fresh browned butter until done.

Roasts should never be left in the oven longer than necessary for them to become done; meats roasted for too long a time are dry and tasteless. It is advisable, however, to leave the roast in the pan and put it on the top of the stove for a short quarter of an hour before it is served; this prevents the juice from dripping away when carving. The gravy is made from the drippings in the pan.

Gravy. Plenty of good rich gravy is essential with a roast. Nothing is better than cream for roasts of all kinds, because it makes the meat milder and the gravy more palatable. But cream is not always easily obtained, and therefore the cook must provide for a substitute by setting aside some milk early enough. After the roast has been taken out of the pan stir some fine flour into the latter (for 6 persons a roast weighing 6—7 pounds will take about a small tablespoonful) and stir constantly until brown. Then stir in the requisite quantity of water, loosening everything adhering to the pan. If it should happen that the gravy is too salty or too dark in color, this can be remedied by pouring in some milk, which in itself is quite desirable when cream is lacking. Good gravy must not be too salty, but of a nice consistency and lightly brown in color; scorched or watery gravies spoil the best meat dishes. If not otherwise directed, all meat gravies should be strained.

Meat Remnants. As soon as meats are brought from the table, they should be taken out of the gravy or juice and immediately placed into a refrigerator or into the cellar.

I. BEEF.

2. Roast Beef. The best cut of beef for roasting is the sirloin or English cut; that most commonly used is the rib roast; the former has the tenderloin under the rib-bone. After removing the greater part of the fat, wash, dry it with a towel and pound as directed in No. 1. For a large roast put a pound of thick, solid kidney suet into water over night, cut it into small cubes (kidney suet and fat pork, half and half, can also be used); put it on the fire in a perfectly clean dripping pan and try it out slowly, then sprinkle the beef with fine salt and put it in the pan with the tenderloin to the top, drip half of the fat over it and then place it uncovered into a hot oven in order that it may roast rapidly, basting very frequently because both are necessary to prevent the juices from running out of the meat; afterwards have a more moderate fire and finish roasting without turning the meat or piercing it with a fork.

The fat should remain clear and is poured out of the pan before making the gravy, which is prepared as already described. Mushrooms are much liked in roast beef gravies and are either stewed in butter previously to putting them into the gravy, or else let them simmer in meat broth until tender, using the broth instead of water to finish the gravy.

3. Kettle Roast of Beef. For kettle roasts, the meat need not necessarily be taken from young beef, but it should be well pounded. Put a pound of kidney suet into water over night, cut it into small pieces (instead of the suet half as much pork fat can be used), put into a kettle and try it out, then put in the meat and roast it until it is nicely browned all around; move it from side to side frequently, being careful not to pierce it with the fork. Then cover it with a part of the pieces of fat, pour in from the side 1—2 cupfuls of boiling water, cover the kettle tightly, put it on the stove where it will roast uninterruptedly but not too vigorously. Roast in this manner for 2—2½ hours according to the size of the piece; after roasting for about 1 hour turn the meat once with a skimmer and sprinkle with a little salt, always being careful not to pierce the meat. Make the gravy as previously directed; a cupful of sour cream is a favorite addition to gravy of this kind of roast.

4. Rolled Roast. Take a rib roast and have the ribs cut out, pound well and rub with salt, pepper and ground cloves, roll it tightly and tie it with a cord. Then roast for 3½ hours as directed in No. 3, basting often; make a sauce as described in No. 1.

Serve with compots, salads or with brown winter cabbage. The broth will make a good mushroom- or truffle sauce, in which the roast can be served with macaroni or roast potatoes in a middle course.

5. Fillet of Beef. After larding, put it in the oven in an earthenware roasting pan with plenty of hot butter and roast rather gently for about ½ hour, basting frequently and covering with thick cream. When serving, stir a little water through the gravy; the cream usually makes it thick enough.

A Bearnese sauce (see division R) is excellent with every kind of fillet of beef roast, which should be covered with the sauce immediately before serving. These roasts may be varied by means of numerous different kinds of gravies, such as truffle-, mushroom-, Madeira- and Burgundy sauces, etc. A further variation is attainable by serving the fillet roast with all kinds of vegetables (filet a la jardinere). The vegetables are taken according to season: in the Spring, peas, carrots, kohlrabi, asparagus and the hearts of lettuce; in the Summer, string beans, cauliflowers, mushrooms and small potatoes; in the Fall, small heads of savoy cabbage, artichokes, cauliflowers, tomatoes and stewed onions; in the Winter, salsify, savoy cabbage, sweet turnips and endives. All of the vegetables must be gotten ready neatly, removing stalks and cores where necessary.

6.   Fillet of Beef with Madeira Sauce. Brown some flour in butter, with it stir dark soup stock or other good meat broth, add a bay leaf, pepper, salt, some cayenne pepper and 2 glassfuls of Madeira, stir well together and put into this sauce pieces of veal sweetbreads, little dumplings, mushrooms and a few sliced truffles. The meat is first roasted until half done, then put into the sauce, roast it slowly for another half hour and serve with all of the additions with which it has been cooked. Frequently macaroni are cooked in salted water until half done and then finished in meat broth with Madeira; they are then placed around the roast in the form of a wreath. Before serving with the roast shake the macaroni with butter and grated cheese.

7.   Rossini Fillet. Cut the meat into slices, salt and turn in egg and bread or cracker crumbs, and roast in melted butter until juicy and well done. At the same time slice a nice goose liver (in the Summer take the half of of a calf's liver) and also dip in bread and roast it. Serve the slices in layers arranged in the form of a pyramid, and pour the gravy over them; make the gravy from the drippings of the meat, some sour cream, meat broth, a glassful of Madeira, thickening with a little rice flour.

8.   Beef a la mode. Take about 8—10 pounds of the round, pound it, rub with salt, pepper, and ground cloves; it can also be larded if wished. Put about 2½ ounces of kidney suet, prepared as directed in A, **17**, into a kettle, heat it, put in the meat, dredge a table-spoonful of flour over it, and roast until brown all over, turning from time to time. Then pour in from the side enough boiling water or better still half claret and half water to partly cover it, then put on the lid tightly and cook slowly, turning it after the elapse of 1½ hours, adding a cupful of pickles cut into cubes, together with 1 spoonful of vinegar, 4 bay leaves or a few lemon slices, cover again and cook slowly until tender, which will usually take from 2—2½ hours. Then put the meat into the dish in which it is to be served, skimming most of the fat from the gravy; if the latter should be too thick add water to it, and if too thin thicken with a little corn-starch, put some of this gravy over the meat and bring the remainder to the table in a gravy boat. If the meat is to be served as an entremet, truffles, mushrooms or chestnuts may be served with it. It is usually served with vegetables of various kinds but macaroni are par-ticularly recommended. Very often the meat receives no preliminary roasting, but is immediately put into the kettle, which is lined with sliced fat pork, carrots, etc.; cover with white wine and meat broth and season with spices of various kinds, according to taste. In France this kind of a roast is served with a tomato sauce; in Bavaria, with a mushroom sauce, using for this purpose the broth from the roast.

9. Sour Beef (Sauerbraten) No. 1. For a sour roast take a good, fat piece from the round. In the Summer let it lay in vinegar 3—4 days and in the Winter 8—10 days. Then add bay leaves, cloves, allspice and perhaps a few juniper berries to the vinegar; put it on the stove and bring to a boil; the meat should first be freshened, then pour over it the boiling vinegar, which prevents the juices from being lost from the meat. If the vinegar is very sharp mix with a little water. As onions harden in vinegar they should not be added until ready to cook. In the Summer the meat should be kept uncovered in a refrigerator or other cool place, turning it frequently, being careful not to do this with the hands. Before cooking, lard the roast as follows, there-by making it juicier: Cut fat pork into strips the length of a finger, turn them in a mixture of salt, pepper and ground cloves, puncture the meat all over with a sharp knife and put in the lardoons; sprinkle some more salt over the meat, but not too much—oversalting makes the meat tough. Get plenty of good fat quite hot in an iron kettle, put in the meat and allow the broth which gathers to steam away rapidly, lightly browning the meat all around, being careful to often turn it in the fat. Then put a heaping tablespoonful of flour into the fat, also browning it, and immediately pour in from the side enough boiling water to cover the meat, covering the kettle at once so that none of the flavor may be lost. After a few minutes add for a piece of meat weighing from 5 to 6 pounds, 2 small carrots, 3 to 4 large onions and a piece of rye bread crust, and if necessary some of the spiced vinegar in which the meat has laid; then cover the kettle tightly and cook slowly but uninterruptedly for about 2—2½ hours, turning the meat during this time and occasionally lifting it with a fork without piercing; add a little boiling water if necessary. A cupful of sweet cream put in during the last half hour of cooking greatly improves the gravy. When ready to serve put the meat on a warm dish and set it in the oven while the gravy is being prepared. If the latter should have become too thick during the cooking it can be thinned with water; if not thick enough, put in a little flour; if it should be too sour and the color brown enough, put in a cupful of milk, then pass it through a sieve and cook rapidly; part of the gravy is poured over the roast and the remainder served in a gravy boat.

Instead of the carrots, onions and breadcrust, a piece of honeycake is frequently taken to thicken the gravy, and where possible use a thin meat broth instead of the water. If one wishes to impart a gamey flavor to a sour roast, roast it in pork fat with a few juniper berries with a medium fire until half done, add plenty of chopped onions and a pint of thick sour cream and then roast until done, basting often. Skim the fat off the gravy, stir into the latter a cupful of milk and bring to the table in a gravy boat.

10. Milan Roast. Lay a piece of beef weighing about 6—7 pounds in wine and vinegar half and half for 2 days; this liquor is afterwards poured boiling hot over the roast; lard and salt the meat, line the roasting pan with slices of fat pork, ham, onions, turnips and veal; lay the meat on these, pour over it 2½ tablespoon-fuls of melted butter and roast for 1 hour in the oven. Then gradually add 1 glassful of Portwine, ½ glassful of the pickle and a large cupful of boiling meat broth; leave the roast in the oven until tender, which will take 1½ hours longer. A full half hour before serving cook about 10 tablespoonfuls of rice quite tender, but keep the grains whole, stir through it the whipped yolks of 2 eggs and about 1 dozen finely chopped steamed mush-rooms, and put where it will keep hot. When the roast is done cut it into slices, lay them in the form of a wreath in the dish on a layer of rice, put a border of rice around the meat and drip a little of the gravy on it. The gravy is made from the drippings of the roast, which are passed through a sieve, thickened with a little rice flour and seasoned with extract of beef and ½ tea-spoonful of mushroom extract.

11. Beef prepared like a Hare Roast. The tender-loin is the best for the purpose, but a piece of the round weighing about 4—5 pounds, the same as is taken for steaks, can also be used. In the Summer let it lay from 2 to 3 days, according to the temperature, in the Winter from 5 to 6 days; wash and pound, as directed in No. 1, until quite tender, press it back to its original form and lard it (3 rows) like a hare. Then sprinkle with fine salt, let it brown all around in plenty of butter, add a cupful of fresh milk and repeat this as often as the gravy, which should be of a light brown color, thickens too much. Cover the meat tightly and let it roast slowly but unin-terruptedly, basting often, until tender, which will take about 2 hours. About 1 quart of milk will be necessary; stir 1 teaspoonful of flour with the first cupful of milk to prevent curdling.

12. To warm left=over Roast Beef. In order that a warmed-over roast should taste as good as when fresh the warming must be properly done. Heating the roast over an open fire or on the hot stove is decidedly objectionable; a warmed roast must never cook, be-cause that makes it tough; always warm it in a double boiler. Put the meat into the inset whole or cut into slices, cover it with the gravy, which can be easily in-creased if too scant by the addition of some cornstarch

and dissolved extract of beef with a piece of butter, and
then let it remain on the stove for ½—1 hour according
to the quantity of meat, keeping the kettle well covered.

13. Round of Beef. For a rib roast weighing about
24 to 28 pounds from which the ribs have been removed,
take 1 pound of coarse salt, ¼ pound of brown sugar, ½
ounce of cloves, 1 ounce of ground cloves, 1 cupful of
brown syrup and 1 tablespoonful of pulverized saltpetre, mix well together and rub the beef with it all
over, then roll it very compactly, tieing it closely with a
cord. Let it lay for 4 weeks in a large vessel, which
should be preferably of wood, turn it daily, and pour
over it the liquor which runs from it. When ready to
cook put it on the fire, cover with boiling water and
some of its own liquor, cover tightly and cook slowly
and uninterruptedly for 4 hours, afterwards leaving it
in the broth for ½ hour longer. In Bremen it is served
with sourkrout, puree of peas covered with fried onions
or brown cabbage and fried potatoes.

REMARK.—This kind of roast can be kept for a long time and is very nice
when eaten cold and even the remnants can be made over into palatable dishes,
such as round of beef omelets, round of beef puffs with potatoes, etc.

14. Beef stewed in Beer. Take a piece of beef weighing about 8 pounds and from 2 days to a week old,
according to the season, pound it thoroughly and sprinkle with salt. Line the kettle with a few slices of fat pork,
2 onions, 1 carrot, bay leaves and whole spices, put on
this the meat and pour in enough water and beer (which
should not be bitter) half and half to cover it, add a
cupful of vinegar, 1 spoonful of pear sauce or syrup,
cover tightly and let it cook slowly for 3 hours. When
ready to serve take off the fat, brown some flour in
butter and add it to the gravy, strain and serve with
the roast.

15. Roast Beef with Dressing. Take the kernel of
a beef joint and stew it until done, but not too tender,
in meat broth and white wine half and half, adding
some spices, a bay leaf and various soup herbs, let it
cool and cut a slice from the top. Then carefully hollow
it out, leaving the walls of the meat about ¼ of an inch
thick. Heat it in the broth, chop the meat taken out
of the hollow together with mushrooms very fine, mix

with a batter of 6 eggs, finely chopped herbs and 2 spoonfuls of broth, and fill this dressing into the beef. Cook the broth of the meat until thick, finishing it with flour browned in butter and strengthen it, if necessary, with extract of beef and Madeira; pour a part of this gravy over the meat (which has been covered with the slice first cut from it) garnishing it with small boiled onions; serve the rest of the gravy separately with macaroni.

16. Beefsteaks. The best steaks are prepared from a beef tenderloin which has been exposed to the air for a few days. Next to this in quality is the sirloin taken from a young animal; be particular not to have the slices too thin, they should be at least ¾ to 1 inch thick. Pound the meat slightly with a beefsteak pounder, trim nicely and dip in clear melted butter. When ready to cook, brown some butter in a pan, put in the meat and set it on a rather strong fire, leaving the pan uncovered; sprinkle with salt and pepper and fry on both sides from 1 to 2 minutes, according to the thickness of the slices. Pour melted butter over them and serve.

Another and entirely different method of preparing beefsteak is as follows: The slices should be fully ¾ of an inch thick; they are pounded and brushed with water in which onions have been soaked for 1 hour, sprinkle with pepper and salt, lay the slices tightly one on the other and set aside for 2 hours in a cool place; get a frying-pan hot, put in the steaks side by side without any fat, and fry for 4 minutes, turning them constantly. After this put in the butter and during the time it is browning each steak is covered with a plain fried egg and afterwards garnished with mushrooms stewed in butter. Serve with the browned butter in a gravy boat. This makes exceedingly tender and juicy steaks.

In England the steaks are taken with as much fat as possible, dipped into melted butter and broiled 10 minutes before serving, they are then set over a glowing coal fire, sprinkled with salt and pepper and broiled for a few minutes longer. They should be rare. Put on the platter with a pat of nice fresh butter on each slice, and pour a little of the juice over them.

Beefsteak can be served in various ways—either

covered with plain fried eggs, sliced onions fried in butter or garnished with sliced pickles, fried potatoes, etc.
It is very nice when covered with fried oysters. In England beefsteak is served without gravy but with mustard or mushroom catsup. In France beefsteaks are
garnished with olives or served with an olive gravy.

17. Beefsteak chopped. If it is impossible to obtain
good steak proceed as follows: Take a pound of clear
lean beef and about 2½ ounces of solid kidney suet which
is cut into cubes, removing the skin and sinews, chop
both together very fine, make up into 4—5 pats about
½ inch thick and sprinkle on both sides with pepper and
salt. Brown a piece of butter, or butter and fat half
and half, in a fryingpan, put in the patties, brown them
nicely, moving them about with a fork frequently without piercing them, turn them over and fry to a nice
brown. They should fry for a few minutes only and be
slightly rare. Serve at once, pouring a little water into
the pan and stirring the gravy until it has thickened
somewhat and then put it into a gravy boat.

18. Raw Beefsteak. Chop good tender beefsteak
very fine, mix with plenty of salt, finely chopped onions,
pepper and the yolks of raw eggs, or else chop with salt
and onions and mix with coarse ground pepper. Or
else mix 1 pound of finely chopped meat with 3 beaten
eggs, some vinegar, olive oil, pepper and salt, form into
little patties, cover them with chopped onions and serve
with mustard. Some prefer chopped beefsteak with but
little pepper and salt, nicely rounded, creased with a
knife and with depressions in the center; into this
depression carefully put the yolk of a raw egg and garnish the patties with dots of chopped onions, capers,
sliced pickles and rolled anchovies, serving with vinegar,
oil and mustard.

19. Stewed Beef. Take a piece, weighing from 2
pounds upwards, of not too fresh beef from the round.
Pound it as directed in No. 1 until it is tender. Sprinkle
with pepper and not too much salt, turn it in flour and
let it simmer with plenty of hot butter or fresh hot kidney suet for ¾ of an hour in a small iron kettle, keeping
the kettle covered tightly.

Then add enough boiling water to not quite half cover the meat, immediately put on the cover again and then simmer for ¾—1 hour longer. Serve the meat in its own gravy with boiled potatoes. If the gravy should be too scant add a little water, and it can also be thickened with cornstarch if necessary.

20. Escallops with Mustard Sauce. Make the escallops the same as beefsteaks made from chopped meat. When they are served make a sauce of 1 spoonful of mustard, 1 spoonful of sour cream and a little cold water, and pour it over the escallops. Instead of the water it is better to take meat remnants and make a meat broth and use it in preparing the sauce.

21. Brown Ragout of small Beef Dumplings. Make dumplings as directed under O, No. 5. At the same time get a piece of butter very hot, stew in the butter a number of chopped onions, lightly brown a proportionate quantity of flour in it and stir with bouillon or water to a thick gravy and strengthen this with roast meat or other left-over dark gravy. Season with pepper and dill according to taste. The dumplings should be nicely moulded with a tablespoon and cooked for 5 minutes in meat broth or salted water (which can also be used for the gravy), until they are done; put them into the ragout and serve with boiled potatoes.

22. Goulash (an Hungarian Dish). Cut a tenderloin of beef into slices and divide these into smaller pieces. For each 2 pounds of beef take ½ pound of fat pork and a few small onions, cutting both into cubes, and lightly brown them. Put the meat on a quick fire, together with the browned fat and onions, and stew until the juice has nearly all been cooked away, then add salt, coarse ground pepper and a little finely ground cayenne pepper; stir well together and serve very hot.

Another way of preparing goulash is to take a piece of rib roast, carefully remove all sinews and cut the meat into cubes. Melt 2½ ounces of beef marrow for every 2 pounds of meat and get it hot. Put in the meat and the necessary salt, cover tightly and simmer for 20 minutes. Then add not quite a pint of boiling bouillon and stew until quite tender, cut 2 ounces of fat pork and 2 large onions into small cubes, try out the fat and stir with 3 spoonfuls of cold bouillon and some cracker crumbs and strain. As soon as the meat is done add the pork fat and onions, flavor with capsicum and serve very hot with salted potatoes.

For that matter, goulash can be made from various kinds of meat and is then equally as palatable as when made from beef.

23. Spanish Fricco. Take a tenderloin or other juicy piece of beef, pound it slowly until tender, cut it into cubes weighing about ½ ounce each and mix through them fine salt and cayenne pepper. In the meantime cook potatoes with salt until done, cut them into slices of medium thickness, keeping them hot. For each pound of meat take two pounds of potatoes. Line the bottom of a kettle having a tight cover with plenty of butter, then put in a layer of potatoes, some more butter, a layer of meat and a layer of finely chopped onions which have first been stewed—not roasted or fried—in butter; continue in this manner and then cover the kettle tightly and put it on a slow fire at first. As soon as the contents begin to roast stir very carefully and then have a stronger fire. In the meantime stir a spoonful of cornstarch with 1 large cupful of thick sour cream and a small cupful of claret and set aside; after stirring the meat carefully several times and it has turned to a grayish color, the sauce is poured over it. After the sauce has been well cooked with the rest, the fricco is brought to the table in a well warmed dish without any extras.

This dish is generally preferred highly seasoned, but this of course should be regulated according to the taste of your guests.

24. Breakfast Stew ("Pickelsteiner Fleisch"). Take a large parsley root, a carrot of the same size, a celery root, a large green leek and 4 medium sized potatoes, wash them very carefully, scrape or peel them, rinse in cold water and cut into fine slices. Cut 1 pound of beef tenderloin into very thin slices and mix everything well together, adding salt and ground pepper. Heat in an open pan ¼ pound of fresh beef marrow or butter, put in the meat and vegetables and fry until of an amber color, turning often, cover the pan and let it simmer on top of the stove for 15—30 minutes or until done. Serve with wheat bread.

25. Breakfast Stew, No. 2. Take beef tenderloin and chop it very fine or cut into cubes. In the meantime fry sliced onions in butter lightly, put in the meat with pepper and salt, stir it for a few minutes on the fire and serve. For each pound of tenderloin take 4 large onions.

26. Ox Tongue Brown Ragout. As tongues easily become tainted they must be used when quite fresh. Cut away the bone and the yellow spongy meat, rub the tongue with salt and a little water, then wash until the water remains clear; cook until tender in a small kettle with not too much water and a little salt, skimming carefully; this will take from 2—3½ hours. The tongue is thoroughly done as soon as it can easily be pierced with a fork. After the tongue is cooked, take off the skin, cut it into slices about an inch wide, dividing the larger pieces in two again. For the rest proceed as directed under D, 183, or stew the tongue with a thick raisin sauce; it can also be prepared with plenty of onions, like "Hasenpfeffer" (ragout of hare). For 12 persons 1 large ox tongue will suffice.

27. White Fricassee of Tongue. After the tongue is cooked as directed above and cut into slices, melt plenty of butter, brown in it 1 large finely chopped onion and 2 tablespoonfuls of flour, add to it some of the tongue broth and, according to taste, some mace; also fine ground pepper and if judged best ½ glassful of white wine; put in the tongue when the broth begins to boil. After it has cooked slowly for ¼ of an hour (it should not become too soft) serve with small round meat dumplings which have been cooked in water or some of the tongue broth. Strain the gravy, which should not be too thick, stir the yolk of an egg through it over the tongue, and garnish with lemon slices.

The fricassee can be given a flavor of anchovy or capers, or mushrooms can be cooked in it; the latter should then be prepared as directed in A, No. 34.

REMARK.—If one wishes to prepare this dish for a large dinner party, it may be done the day previous, without hesitation. It is then necessary to put it in the oven for 1½ hours in an old tureen with a cover. Or else heat it with boiling water in a double kettle; it need not then be stirred, neither is the yolk of the egg added until the dish is sent to the table.

28.   Fried Tongue as a side dish.   After the tongue
has been cooked until tender and peeled as described
under No. 26, it should be split in two.   Then sprinkle
with fine salt, and a very little fine ground cloves. Or else
rub it with a mixture of chopped eschalots, tarragon,
sage, salt, nutmeg and cloves, turn it in egg and cracker
crumbs, and then fry it in butter to a light brown, being
careful that it retains its full juiciness.   Fried tongue
can also be served with an anchovy-, caper-, Madeira-
or tomato sauce.

29.   Sliced Tongue (a nice side dish).   The tongue
should be cooked until very tender, peeled, cut into
slices ½ inch thick, cutting the largest pieces in two once
more.   Then whip an egg with 2—3 tablespoonfuls of
water to which a little lemon juice may be added with
advantage, put in some nutmeg, fine salt if necessary,
dip the tongue slices into this, turn them in stale bread
crumbs and fry in melted butter in an open pan over a
quick fire until light brown and crisp.

30.   Salted Tongue for Sandwiches or as a side dish.
Clean a heavy beef tongue as directed under No. 26, and
rub it with 4 ounces of salt after it has been rubbed all
over with a little saltpetre.   Sprinkle a little of the salt
into a stone jar, put in the tongue, sprinkle the rest of
the salt over it and let it stand in this pickle in a cool
place for 6 to 8 days in the Summer, or a fortnight in
the Winter, turning it daily.   Before serving the tongue
it should be cooked in boiling water a few days previously; cook uninterruptedly until it is so tender that
it can easily be pierced with a fork, which will take about
3½ hours. Then take off the skin and put the tongue into
the cold broth, into which it should be returned every time
after it is cut, thus retaining its juiciness to the last slice.
If the tongue is to be kept during the Winter for any
length of time, the broth should be heated again after
the elapse of about 1 week.

31.   Fried chopped Beef.   To every 4 pounds of clear
beef take 1 pound of kidney suet, add some salt, and
chop together very fine, mould into round flat cakes,
turn them in an egg mixed with cloves, ground black
pepper or grated nutmeg, dredge with grated crackers
and fry in melted butter similar to beefsteak.

32. "Charles X." Pound a piece of lean but juicy beef, take off the skin, lard it, then put it into the oven with water and vinegar half and half, plenty of seasoning (particularly onions) and a little garlic, some butter and leave it in the oven partly roasting and partly cooking until it is done, basting often and being careful not to pierce it. Let the meat stand over night, chop plenty of eschalots very fine, mix them with pepper, salt and grated wheat bread; cut the meat into slices, brush an egg over them, turn in the mixture and then fry in a pan like cutlets.

33. Fried Meat Loaf made from fresh Meat. No. 1. This is very nice and palatable when made with beef, veal and medium fat pork in equal parts finely chopped together, and then taking 3 tablespoonfuls of butter to each 1½ pounds of chopped meat. When these meats are not to be obtained take 1½ pounds of beef from the joint and ¼ pound of kidney suet or fresh pork fat and chop them together very fine, add 4 whole eggs, salt according to taste, nutmeg, 2 ounces of grated wheat-bread or cracker crumbs, and 1 cupful of cold water. Mix well together, mould with the hands into a smooth round or oblong loaf, dredge with rolled crackers and crease with a knife. Have some hot butter ready, put in the loaf and bake in the oven until light brown, basting often; when possible pour over it from time to time a few spoonfuls of thick cream and then bake for ¾—1 hour to a light brown color. If the oven should not be hot enough, the meat can first be fried on top of the stove for ½ hour, keeping the pan covered and then put it in the oven; the meat should not be turned. Before serving, a few pulverized juniper berries can be sprinkled over the meat.

34. Meat Loaf, No. 2. To 1½ pounds of chopped lean beef free from skin or sinews add ¼ pound of chopped kidney suet, about 6 ounces of stale wheat bread without the crust, which has been soaked in cold water and pressed dry in a napkin, 3 eggs (slightly frothing the whites) about ½ ounce of salt and ¼ of a nutmeg. Mix well together, mould nicely round and smooth and turn in the toasted and grated crust of the bread. Then put a good-sized piece of butter into an earthenware vessel and melt it, adding about 12 to

15 chopped fresh juniper berries, put in the meat, cover tightly and after a little while put the vessel on the stove with a very slow fire; turn and lift the meat frequently to prevent it from scorching. As soon as browned on the under side turn once, roasting in all about 1 hour.

35. Hasty Meat Balls. From the quantity of meat directed in the preceding receipt, make 9 small balls; bread them, put into hot butter and fry on the stove all around for a few minutes, so that they do not become dry. Juniper berries can also be put into the butter if desired.

36. Stewed Meat Loaf. Prepare as directed in both preceding receipts. After browning in plenty of butter, pour in enough boiling water to barely half cover the meat, add a few lemon slices, a parsley root, and 2 slips of mace to the gravy and then cook, tightly covered, for ½ hour. Then add a little browned flour to the gravy, cook thoroughly and stir the yolk of an egg through it.

Instead of making 1 large loaf the meat can be rolled into balls the size of a hen's egg, and then proceed as above, which will make a very nice fricassee. The balls, however, must be on the fire no longer than about 10 minutes; take them off as soon as they are no longer rare in the center.

Serve with potatoes.

37. Meat Balls made from roast or boiled Meat Remnants. Chop the meat remnants with an onion or parsley very finely, stir with it a few eggs, salt, a trifle of cloves or nutmeg, grated bread browned in butter and such meat broth or gravy that happens to be left over, or instead of this sour cream and a little grated lemon peel. Mould into balls the size of an egg, turn them in the toasted and grated crusts of the bread, and then fry in the butter. If you have any boiled ham handy, chop some of it with the meat and then take less butter. In place of the wheat bread cold boiled potatoes can be used, first grating them.

38. Small Forcemeat Balls. After chopping meat remnants of all kinds together with some ham very fine, mix with chopped onions stewed in butter, a few eggs,

salt, pepper, nutmeg and some grated bread. In the
meantime make a few thin omelets, spread one side with
the forcemeat, roll them up, cut them into oblique slices
and fry in plenty of butter after spreading an egg over
them and sprinkling with bread or cracker crumbs. If
your meat should be scant mix what you have with the
omelet batter and make up into balls.

39. Beef au Gratin. A deep pan is buttered and
lined with a mixture of grated bread, chopped mushrooms, a few eschalots, parsley and spices. Dip sliced
beef remnants into melted butter or pork fat and put
them into the pan. Sprinkle the remainder of the seasoning on top, put on pats of butter and pour over all
½ cupful of salted beef extract bouillon into which 4 eggs
have been beaten. Sprinkle according to taste with
grated cheese and then bake for 30 minutes. Serve with
potatoes.

40. Beef Roll. Pound a piece of beef taken from
the upper round, which should not be too fresh. Cut it
into oblong slices which should again be pounded with
a meat pounder (not with a knife), sprinkle sparingly
with a mixture of fine salt, cloves and pepper, or else
with a few ground juniper berries. Put on some thin
pork slices and roll into small tight rolls tied with a
thread. The rolls are much improved when spread with
the following mixture: Pass a number of yolks of hard
boiled eggs through a sieve, stir with the yolk of a raw
egg, 2 spoonfuls of tomato pulp (or sour cream), a little
chopped parsley and a grated eschalot with pepper and
salt, and spread this on the rolls before putting on the
pork slices. Melt plenty of butter in a medium sized
saucepan, turn the rolls in flour, put them into the pan
closely side by side, cover tightly and let them fry
slowly in their own juice as long as possible. After the
elapse of 5 minutes turn them. Then pour in from the
side enough boiling water to fully half cover the rolls.
and let them simmer slowly on top of the stove with a
low fire for not longer than ¾ of an hour at the most,
because frying the rolls for too long a time with too hot
a fire makes them dry. Then cut the threads and remove them and serve the rolls with a good thick brown
gravy.

41. A crusted piece of boiled Soup Meat. Take a good piece of beef and make a soup; after the meat is done put it into a saucepan, add a few spoonfuls of soup fat, 2 onions and 3 bay leaves, sprinkle the meat with salt, nutmeg and grated crackers and bake in a hot oven until of a golden brown. Or if any of the soup stock is left the meat can be covered with a few eggs and rice, seasoned with grated cheese and then proceed as above directed. Serve with an anchovy-, caper-, or mushroom sauce.

42. Stewed Soup Meat served with Potatoes after the Soup. Put the soup meat on the fire a little earlier than usual and after it is tender cut it into small pieces, melt some butter and lightly brown this also, stirring constantly, and take some of the soup stock and make plenty of rich thick gravy, which is to be seasoned with a few cloves, some bay leaves and pepper; add the necessary salt and 1 to 2 tablespoonfuls of thick sour or sweet cream. Let the meat simmer in the sauce for ½ hour over a slow fire and when serving put in a few drops of lemon juice.

43. Soup Meat Cutlets. Cut the meat remnants into slices, lay them into vinegar over night, turn in egg, salt and nutmeg, dredge with rolled crackers and fry lightly in butter.

44. Irish Stew made of Roast Meat Remnants. A rare piece is the best for this purpose and the sinews should be carefully removed from it; cut into small cubes and for each plateful of meat take 2 platefuls of sliced raw potatoes, ½ plateful of onions, pepper, salt, a little ground cloves, mix well together and cook in soup stock, shaking frequently until done. The kettle should be buttered and then make the broth from the bones of the roast with water and whatever gravy is left; cover the kettle tightly.

45. Irish Stew No. 2. Turn the meat slices in soup fat mixed with a little stock and then turn them in a mixture of grated bread, finely chopped onions, parsley, pepper and salt. Then heat some good fat in a saucepan, put in the slices with a dot of butter on each and bake in the oven to a light brown. In the meantime make a mustard sauce as directed in Division R. When serving and not before, put the sauce into the dish with the baked slices of meat and then serve after the soup.

46. Soup Meat Salad. See Division Q.

47. Hash. Cook a fat piece of beef until tender in salted water, skim well, take out all the bones and chop. At the same time boil for 1½ pounds of meat ¼ of a pound of rice and then cook it with the meat broth until thick and tender, lightly brown some butter and stir the meat, rice, ground cloves, nutmeg and the necessary salt with it. Let it simmer until done and serve hot. Instead of the rice, good fresh oatmeal soaked in water can be cooked in meat broth until thick. Stale grated wheat bread cooked in the broth is also good and especially recommended if the broth is to be used for a soup. This kind of hash tastes very good with apple sauce.

48. Hash made from Soup Meat or Remnants of Roast. Chop the meat very fine and cook some rice, barley or oatmeal in water with a small piece of butter or good fat and salt until tender and thick ; then brown plenty of butter and kidney suet half and half, turn the meat in this or else in some left-over roast meat gravy and afterwards let it simmer until done in the rice with seasoning as above.

49. Left=over Soup Meat with Onions. Cut the meat into thick slices with the fat, put the salt into the water, pour it over the meat and turn so that it will absorb the water. Heat some butter or fat in a saucepan, add plenty of chopped onions and brown them lightly, put in the meat, cover and cook, turning it once. Put it into the dish, brown some flour in a pan, stir some water or meat broth to a scant, thick gravy and pour this over the meat.

50. Left=over Soup Meat stewed with Apples. Cut the meat into thin slices, put the fat pieces in the bottom of a small kettle and the rest on top of them, sprinkle with salt and a few cloves, cover and simmer. Peel some sour apples, take out the cores, slice, cover the meat with them, pour a few tablespoonfuls of water in from the side, cook the apples until done and serve without stirring.

51. The same with a Raisin Sauce. Make a raisin sauce as described under Division R, cut the meat into small pieces and cook slowly in this sauce for ¼ hour. The meat can also be prepared with caper-, mushroom-, anchovy-, pickle-, mustard- or onion sauce, which are all described in Division R.

52. Soup Meat Ragout. Cut the meat into small pieces, melt roast meat fat or butter, lightly brown in it 1—2 chopped onions, and, according to the quantity, 1—2 tablespoonfuls of flour, add bouillon or water with roast meat gravy, some pepper and cloves or else ground cloves, 2—4 bay leaves and some sliced pickles. Cook the latter until tender and let the meat simmer for a short time in the gravy, which should be of a good consistency. If liked better sweet, add a teaspoonful of syrup or pear sauce.

53. Meat Fritters ("Dominikaner-Schnitte"). Besides the soup meat remnants a lighter-colored meat, as pork or veal, is necessary. Both kinds are cut into large slices of a uniform size; on each slice of beef spread some forcemeat made of 3 ounces of grated wheat bread, 1½ ounces of Parmesan cheese, 2 tablespoonfuls of chopped herbs, the same quantity of anchovy butter, 3 eggs, lemon peel, salt and pepper, and lay the lighter colored meat on this. Put butter into a saucepan and lay in the fritters with alternately a light and a dark slice to the top, sprinkle over them hot melted butter and ½ glassful of Madeira, cover tightly and heat through and through. Serve neatly, garnishing the border of the dish with lemon slices and parsley, pour the sauce over the meat and bring to the table with potato salad or lettuce; if with the latter, small potato dumplings should also be served.

54. Meat Cream. Chop soup meat with a freshened herring (a few anchovies are better) and onions and some parsley. Let the meat simmer for a few minutes in melted fat, then stir with it a few spoonfuls of capers, 2 eggs, 2 spoonfuls of sour cream, 1 spoonful of claret, salt, pepper and grated wheat bread to a jellylike consistency, stew in unsalted butter for 15 minutes and serve with mashed potatoes or boiled rice.

55. Meat Pudding a la Zurich. (A good Dish made from Remnants for the Supper Table.) Mix with 1 pound of chopped meat 3 ounces of chopped pork fat, 1 tablespoonful of fine herbs, 2 spoonfuls of capers, a chopped pickle, salt, pepper and four eggs, mould in a round pan or other vessel and cook for ½ hour in a double kettle. Leave it over night and the next day turn it out of the mould and serve with a brown or Remoulade sauce. It can also be covered with meat jelly and is then served with olive oil, vinegar and mustard.

56. Fried Sour Roll (see Division W). Cut the roll into slices ½ inch thick, and if they are wanted particularly nice, turn them in egg and cracker crumbs, then fry them in hot butter or hot kidney suet together with a few apple slices to a light brown color.

Or else each slice can be covered with a spoonful of griddlecake batter, and then fry the apple slices alone.

The roll is very good when the slices are stewed for about 10 minutes in a claret sauce.

57. Fried Minced Collops (German "Panhas"). This is a very economical and palatable dish for the family table, and can be prepared at any time (see Division W) taking beef as well as pork; soup meat or tough roast will answer, but then plenty of fat pork should be chopped with it. When cooked long enough panhas can be kept in the Summer for a week when put in a cool place, and in the Winter for 2 weeks, and will then be very often found to come in handy when a dish is lacking for the table. After it is cooked it is fried as follows: Heat some butter or good fat in a frying pan, cut the loaf into slices about ¼ inch thick, put them into the frying pan close together and let them fry uncovered on both sides until crisp; they should not become dry. Serve with potato dishes of various kinds, especially with potatoes and apples.

58. How to cook Pickled Beef. If the meat has simply been pickled with salt freshen it over night or for a few hours, according to its saltiness; then put it on the stove covered with cold water, and cook slowly for 3 hours. If water is added while it is cooking it must be hot. Meat which has been pickled in brine with spices and herbs is put on the fire in boiling water with the addition of a little salt, and then be careful that the cooking is not interrupted nor continued too long, otherwise the meat will receive an insipid taste.

REMARK.—The broth will make a nice barley soup with potatoes or a bean or pea soup and all Fall and Winter vegetables can be cooked with it nicely.

59. How to cook Smoked Beef. It should be well washed the evening before cooking; this is done best with a clean whiskbroom and a handful of wheat bran; then soak over night in water, rinse it again the following day, put it on the fire covered with boiling water and cook slowly for 2—4 hours. After it is done it can remain in its own broth for ½ hour longer, keeping the kettle covered; this makes the meat more tender and juicier.

REMARK.—This broth can also be used for the same purposes as in the preceding receipt. But to have the remainder of the meat retain its juiciness put it in an open tureen with the broth and set it into a cool place; it may be necessary to heat the broth again after a few days.

60. Smoked Tongue. Soak the tongue for 24 hours, cook it the same as smoked beef, then put it under a little slab or something similar with a weight on it; after it has cooled take off the skin and keep it until wanted in the broth in which it was cooked. Pressing the tongue gives it a better form. Serve in slices and garnish with parsley. It is very nice when served with fresh peas, kohlrabi, spinach, or for sandwiches.

---

61. Ribs of Beef for Invalids. Take out the bones and remove the fat and sinews, pound the meat and then fry it in butter for 10 minutes, turning frequently and sprinkle with salt and pepper; make a sauce, taking for this purpose the bones and sinews for a broth and mix through it flour lightly browned in butter and a glassful of Madeira.

Nos. 2, 3, 5, 7, 11, 16, 17, 27, 28 and 29 may also be served to invalids.

II. VEAL.

NOTE.—A good roast can only be expected if the meat is continually basted; adding water or meat broth must be absolutely avoided, neither must the meat be pounded—veal is too tender for pounding and it only makes it stringy. A perfect roast should be finished with sweet or sour cream, but this must be added not sooner than ½ hour before serving.

62. Roast Leg or Loin of Veal. After preparing the veal for the stove, heat plenty of butter in the pan and if you have any nice fat pork handy, put in a few slices and on these the veal with the round part to the top. Put it into a hot oven and roast it for 1½ hours with a strong fire at first, which should gradually decrease; baste often but do not turn the roast. A small roast should not be kept in the oven longer than 1¼ hours, otherwise it will become soft and dry; to prevent the gravy from becoming dark or scorching, put in a piece of butter occasionally.

The gravy will receive a nice amber color and be improved in taste by the addition of 1—2 cupfuls of cream. After the roast has been taken out of the pan pour in the cream, let it turn to a rich yellow color, stir up everything remaining in the pan with boiling water and let it cook for a few minutes longer to a rather thin gravy; the cream will give it the proper consistency. Should you have no cream a half tablespoonful of flour may be browned with the roast and add some weak broth or water to make the gravy, which should always be strained before it is served.

If the gravy is to be seasoned with mushrooms, they should be stewed in butter quickly and then added to the gravy.

63. Roast Neck of Veal. Take the best end of the neck of a calf, cut off the ribs on both sides to half their length and take out the kidneys, peel off the skin and lard the meat like a hare; roast in the oven with a medium fire, with plenty of fat pork and butter, from 1—1½ hours until done. Salt is not sprinkled over the meat until it has been in the oven for ¾ of an hour. When nearly done cover the roast with thick sour cream.

The gravy is made as directed in the preceding receipt. Serve the meat either with a salad or a compot, or else macaroni mixed with butter and Parmesan cheese are served with the meat.

64. Veal Kettle Roast. Wash and dry the roast. Melt butter and fat in the kettle and add a few slices of fat pork if desired. Then put in the meat, and roast uncovered until partly done, moving it about in the kettle, being careful not to pierce it. Gradually pour in a few half cupfuls of cream, cover the kettle tightly and proceed as directed for veal roasted in the oven, basting frequently. The round side should lie to the top.

65. Minced Kidneys with Roast Veal. Chop the roasted kidneys with their fat very fine, lightly brown a chopped onion in butter and cook the kidneys with salt, nutmeg, a tablespoonful of sour cream and ½ tablespoonful of mustard until done   serve to the roast with toast.

66. Stuffed Breast of Veal. Take out the breast bone (it is best to let the butcher do this), wash and dry the meat, with a knife enlarge all round the opening left through the removal of the bone, being careful not to puncture the outer skin, and fill with the dressing A, No. 27, or a dressing made of wheat bread; take a needle and thread and close the opening, rub the meat with a little salt, put it on a strong fire with plenty of butter, which can be mixed with good fat. Roast for 1½—3 hours, according to the size of the piece, basting frequently and gradually adding some strong bouillon. Do not neglect removing the threads when serving. Stir some cold water into the gravy and cook it until of the proper consistency. Breast of veal prepared in this manner is very nice when served cold for the supper table.

After removing the threads brush the meat with the gravy which will, when cool, make a brown jelly. The cold roast should be brought to the table with a Ravigote Sauce (see Division R).

67. Stewed Breast of Veal. For a middle course, stewed instead of stuffed breast of veal is often preferred. After it has been stiffened in hot water it should be larded, slightly roasted in butter, then pour in some meat broth and add mushrooms and parsley root. Thicken the gravy with grated bread, flavor with lemon juice and pour it over the meat before serving. In first-class kitchens this breast of veal is surrounded with truffles and small baked chicken croquettes, finishing with a border of mashed potatoes. For the family table any suitable large piece from the breast can be stewed without the mushrooms.

68. Fricandeau of Veal. Raise the flesh of the finer part of the loin clear from the bones, pound and lard it as for a hare. Sprinkle with lemon juice, dredge with flour, melt plenty of butter in a pan, put in the meat with the larded side to the top, together with an onion and parsley root. The oven must be hot enough to soon lightly color the lardoons. After this sprinkle with fine salt and then roast the fricandeau, basting often, for ½—¾ of an hour until done. If the fricandeaus are intended for a dinner party, bring them to the table with a Madeira-, truffle- or herb sauce, surround them with a border of boiled rice, or serve with roasted potatoes. Fricandeaus sliced make an excellent garnish for a dish of fine vegetables.

If the fricandeau is to be stewed, cook a brown broth from the rest of the meat together with soup herbs, and spices, pepper, ground cloves, onions and a bay leaf and strain. As soon as the fricandeaus are nearly done, pour in a large cupful of the broth, close the oven and afterwards baste them once; serve with the gravy which has been bound with a little flour browned in the pan with the broth. After straining the gravy, a few lemon slices may be added to it. Truffles cooked with this dish improve it very much.

Time of cooking, 1¼—1½ hours.

69. Hunter's Fricandeau of Veal. Take a piece from the loin, pound it well until it has the appearance of a beefsteak about 2 inches thick. Then make a batter of 6—8 eggs whipped with 8 spoonfuls of sweet cream, salt and a little nutmeg, mix with 3 ounces of chopped ham and a few finely chopped mushrooms, spread this mixture over the meat, then roll it and tie pieces of fat pork around it. Bake the fricandeau in melted butter in the oven for about ½ hour until done; make a sauce taking some meat broth, lemon juice, cornstarch and a spoonful of Portwine, and pour it over the meat, which is served with small round roasted potatoes.

70.   Veal Kidney Fritters. Chop a veal kidney with 1 to 2 roasted sweetbreads or a small piece of veal very fine, adding grated lemon peel and nutmeg. Melt a piece of butter, add a little chopped onion and afterwards a trifle of rolled cracker, and when this has been well browned, with constant stirring, put in the roast veal jelly and also the juice of a lemon, and cook it to make a thick ragout gravy. When cool, mix into the gravy a few eggs, the chopped meat and the necessary salt; mould into small oblong fritters, turn in egg and cracker crumbs and fry in butter to a light brown color. The fritters can be garnished with minced parsley fried in butter, and served with various kinds of vegetables, such as carrots, peas, cauliflowers, asparagus or artichokes.

71.   Sweetbread Fritters (Entree). Scald veal sweetbreads and slice them thin; chop eschalots and anchovies very fine and stew the onions in butter. Then cook the sweetbread, anchovies, wine, salt and either mace or nutmeg, some grated wheat bread and, according to the amount of the dish, 2—4 eggs and a few tablespoonfuls of roast beef gravy, meat jelly or milk, until of a fine consistency, stirring constantly. Instead of the anchovies and eschalots, crab butter or crab tails can be used. Let the mass stand over night and mould it into oblong rolls the next morning. Turn these twice in a beaten egg, sprinkle with cracker crumbs and fry over a quick fire in enough butter or fat to swim the fritters. Garnish the dish with fried or fresh minced parsley.

72.   Stewed Ribs of Veal. Take a very good piece of meat, trim out the ribs smoothly, pound thoroughly without separating them, so that they will be about ½ inch thick, and then cut them down to about half their length. Line a pan thickly with butter, put in the ribs, sprinkle with salt and nutmeg and add butter, lemon slices, cracker crumbs, and to 3 pounds of meat

about 1 large cupful of wine and water half and half.
Cover tightly, lay a damp cloth over the lid and stew
for 15 minutes.

73. Vienna Veal Steak ("Wiener=Schnitzel"). Cut
pieces the size of a small beefsteak from the center of a
loin of veal, pound slightly, rub with fine salt and
pepper, turn them first in egg and flour, then in rolled
crackers and fry in plenty of butter until tender. When
serving, sprinkle the steaks with lemon juice, garnish
with lemon slices and a few capers and serve with a
lattice of anchovy slices and a plain fried egg.

74. Veal Cutlets. Loosen the meat at the bone
and then pound it slowly until tender, chop off the bone
to half its length and cut the meat round and smooth
to the thickness of a finger; sprinkle with salt and
pepper. Dip the cutlets in egg, turn them in bread or
cracker crumbs (in South Germany the crumbs are
mixed with grated Parmesan cheese), and then lay them
in the pan in melted butter. Fry for about 6 minutes
in the open pan, turning them once, frequently basting
them with the butter. Fry until of a golden brown and
tender. Serve with fresh vegetables, such as peas, asparagus and cauliflowers. In the Winter they are very
nice when served with macaroni mixed with a few tablespoonfuls of tomato sauce.

Cutlets can also be served as a middle course, but
then they should be larded with pork lardoons, or else
with lardoons of tongue, anchovy, truffles, or pickles;
they can be pickled for a few hours in white wine spiced
with fine herbs. They are then brought to the table
with a fine sauce, for which the marinade is partly
used.

Veal cutlets can also be broiled like mutton chops.
The scraps from the cutlets can be used for the sauce of
an ordinary ragout or for headcheese.

75. Veal Stew or Fricassee. A breast of veal should
be well pounded and cut into small squares, and in
order that the meat may look very white it should be
blanched by laying the pieces into nearly boiling water,
then bring to a boil once, afterwards putting them in
the cold water and drying them. Then heat some
butter in a kettle, put in the meat and let it simmer

slowly for 15 minutes, turning once, keeping the kettle covered but being careful that the meat does not brown. Pour in enough boiling water to make the requisite quantity of sauce, add salt, parsley root and some salsify, cut into 2-inch lengths and add mushrooms if desired; cover tightly and cook slowly until tender but not too soft; this will take about 1½ hours. 15 minutes before serving, the following can be added: Sweetbreads, parboiled asparagus tips, small sausages, a few lemon slices, mace, and to bind the sauce, rolled crackers. When serving stir the yolk of an egg through the sauce; a glassful of white wine can also be cooked in it to advantage. Bring to the table with crab-, meat- or bread dumplings which have been cooked in salted water, and pour the sauce over them. This kind of veal stew can be varied in many ways; the sauce can be seasoned with anchovy butter, the sweetbreads may be omitted and instead of them, sweetbread dumplings (see Division O) can be substituted, or else it may be brought to the table with a border of boiled rice or puff paste. For the family table all the fancy ingredients may be omitted and only bread dumplings and cauliflower buds, in the Spring bits of asparagus, in the Winter salsify or chervil roots, and when all these are lacking, quartered celery roots may simply be put with it.

76. Paprican (an Hungarian Dish) can be prepared from veal, as well as from pigeons or Spring chickens. Divide the meat into small pieces, if veal, about the size of a small walnut, Spring chickens into 10 parts, and pigeons into 4 parts. Heat plenty of fat with a finely chopped onion, put in the meat, sprinkle some salt over it and cover the kettle tightly. After the meat has browned on a slow fire, which should be the case after it has cooked an hour, stir through it, without turning the meat, a heaping tablespoonful of flour and add beef extract bouillon and some sour cream. When cooked the sauce must be of a good consistency. Serve in a hot dish with boiled or crusted potatoes.

77. Stuffed Veal Roll. Cut from the loin about 4 pounds of meat and divide it into medium-sized slices. Stew the scraps of the meat in butter chopped finely with lemon peel, season with ¼ pound of anchovy and make up into a forcemeat by adding 3—4 eggs, some wheat bread and a little cream or milk. Spread the forcemeat over the meat slices, roll them up, tie with a thread and fry slowly. For the gravy take the broth from the roast, about 1 ounce of mushrooms, a little cornstarch or rice flour and simmer the meat in this for a short time longer. These rolls can be pickled in vinegar and spices for a time, they are then slightly fried in fat and afterwards stewed slowly until done. Cut them in two lengthwise and either surround a fine ragout—as for instance one made from veal sweetbreads and mushrooms—with them, or use as a border for a dish of fine vegetables.

78. Calf's-Brain Ragout. Wash the brain, bring it to a boil in water with a few onions, cloves, pepper, vinegar and salt, then take off the fine skin and also remove the veins. Then brown a tablespoonful of flour in butter, stir in some broth and put in the brain, (which has been cut into pieces) together with a few lemon slices and some wine. Cook for a little while and stir into the sauce the yolks of 1 or 2 eggs.

79. English Calfs-Head or Mock Turtle Ragout, (enough for 20 Persons). Take a fresh calf's head, wash, singe and cook it, together with 2 beef palates, in salted water long enough to clear it from scum, and then cook with onions or eschalots, cloves, peppercorns, and a few bay leaves for 2—2½ hours until done. The beef palates should be cooked for at least 2 hours beforehand, so that they will be done simultaneously with the calf's head. Cut the meat into small pieces, add ½ pound of veal sweetbreads, (A, No. 35) meat dumplings, ½ pound of small sausages, which should be previously fried; if possible also add ½ of a roasted hare. Then brown flour in butter, stir with it a good beef bouillon cooked with a few vegetables and eschalots and put in the meat, together with mushrooms, capers, lemon slices, ground pepper, whole and ground cloves, a pinch of cayenne pepper and ¼ bottle of Madeira, cooking until the sauce is of the proper consistency.

When served with puff paste sippets this ragout is an excellent substitute for a meat pie; in fact, if filled into a pie crust it will make a good meat pie.

80. Veal Sweetbreads. Prepare them as directed in A, 35, divide into two pieces, lard and season with salt and nutmeg, then fry in hot butter to an amber color and serve with fine vegetables. Or else parboil the sweetbreads, slice them, turn in egg, nutmeg, a little salt and cracker crumbs, bake in butter and after sprinkling them with lemon juice, use as a garnish for fine vegetables. Or boil in broth for 15 minutes, cut them up and serve in gravies or stews. Sweetbreads must always be thoroughly cooked or fried.

81. Boiled Calf's=Head with Gravy. Clean a fresh large calf's head very carefully, cut off the upper lip, ears, and take out the eyes, break off the lower jaw, take out the tongue, because it will become tender sooner, then wash out the head, split it and tie it together again. Cover with water, add salt, skin, and cook with whole spices, fresh herbs, onions and bay leaves until tender, which will take about 2 hours. Leave in the broth until ready to serve, then put into the dish and cover the brain with bread crumbs browned in butter, split the tongue and lay it on both sides of the brain, make a Hollandaise sauce (see Divison R), put some of it over the meat and bring the rest to the table in a gravy boat.

It is much nicer to cook this meat in white wine and thin meat broth half and half instead of water; instead of serving the entire head the meat can be sliced and brought to the table with some fine broth or Hollandaise sauce, laying around it the tongue slices and bits of the brain scooped with a teaspoon. The gravy is served separately.

For the supper table this dish is served with a French sauce of mustard, olive oil, vinegar and savory herbs.

82. Baked Calf's=Head. After cooking a fresh calf's-head as described in the preceding receipt, the meat is cut into fine slices and put into a buttered pan; then sprinkle with salt and pour over it a mixture of 1 large cupful of sour cream, the yolks of 4 eggs, nutmeg, salt and grated Parmesan cheese. Bake in the oven.

83. Calf's=Head Brawn. The head, heart and foot of a well-fattened, freshly killed calf are washed clean,

Beef—Ochſen= und Rindfleiſch.

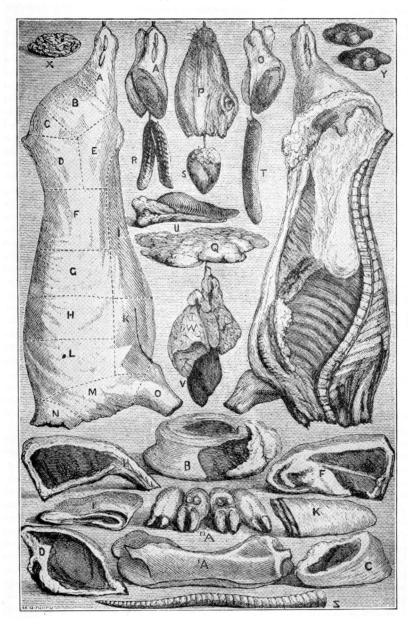

A Hind shank—Keule; B Round—Rundstück; C Rump—Schwanzstück; D Sir-loin—Lende; E Flank—Untere Flanke; F Porterhouse—Mittelstück; G Ribroast—Vorderrippe; H Chuckroast—Mittelrippe; I Nablepiece—Dünne Flanke; K Breast—Bruststück; L Chuck—Rippenstück; M Shoulder—Kamm; N Neck—Oberer Kamm; O Front shank—Schienbein; P Check—Backen; Q Kidney suet—Nieren-fett; R Sweetbreads—Saum; S Heart—Herz; T Milt—Milz; U Tongue—Zunge; V Liver—Leber; W Lungs—Lunge; X Brain—Gehirn; Y Kidney—Niere; Z Tail—Schwanz; 'A Paunch—Kaldaunen; "A Feet—Füsze.

lay in fresh water for 1—2 hours to draw out all of the blood, put them into an enameled kettle and cover fully one-half with water and vinegar, add salt and skim carefully. For the rest proceed as directed for pork brawn in Division W.

84. Brown Calf's=Head Ragout for the Family Table. Cook a calf's head, the heart and if liked the lungs until quite tender, and then cut up into small pieces. Brown 2 chopped onions in butter, add 2 tablespoonfuls of flour and stir until it is also brown, put in some of the broth in which the head was cooked, add raisins or dried currants, pepper, cloves and salt, 1—2 tablespoonfuls of pear sauce or syrup and some vinegar, and cook until the meat is thoroughly well done. The gravy must be smooth and have a tart, spicy flavor.

85. Escallops for 6 persons. Take a pound of veal and if this is not obtainable, beef may be substituted, chop as finely as possible with ¼ pound of pork fat or freshened kidney suet, then mix thoroughly with ¼ pound of wheat bread (without the crust) soaked in cold water and pressed, the yolks of 2 eggs and a little salt and pepper, and then mould into flat escallops the size of a silver dollar; fry in plenty of fat with a quick fire, taking them out as soon as they have turned yellow. Then brown a spoonful of flour in the fat, add chives, parsley, etc., about a handful in all, also bouillon and a little sour cream to make a rather thick sauce, which is poured boiling hot over the escallops.

Escallops can also be made from rib roast, chopping the meat very finely and moulding the escallops without any other addition, add the necessary salt, then turn the escallops in an egg and grated cracker crumbs and bake. The sauce is cooked with sour cream only and the escallops served with fine vegetables.

86. Veal Rolls. Chop 1 pound of veal very fine with 3—4 ounces of beef marrow, mix with salt, pepper, nutmeg and a few eggs, rolling the mass between thin slices of fat pork, tieing them with a thread; put the rolls into a medium-sized vessel, pour meat broth over them, stew until done and before serving cover with a caper sauce.

87. Veal Forcemeat Sausage. (A *Swiss* Dish.) 4 parts of clear veal without sinews or veins are finely chopped with 1 part of pork fat or kidney suet; for each 2 pounds of this meat take 4 whole eggs, 4 table-spoonfuls of bread or cracker crumbs, 4 tablespoonfuls thick cream or wine, salt and nutmeg, mix well together and fill into a sausage stuffer or else roll into small sausages with the hand, afterwards turning them in cracker crumbs. Melt some butter in a flat pan, put in the mass in the form of a tightly rolled-up sausage, moisten with melted butter, sprinkle a little fine bread crumbs over it and bake in a hot oven.

88. Stewed Liver. The liver must be very fresh, because even if only one day old during the hot season, it may become tainted and unwholesome; wash the liver, which is best done by putting it into cold water for 1 hour and changing the water frequently. Take off the skin, and lard as follows: A large number of short slips of fat pork are turned in a mixture of salt, pepper and ground cloves, then take a sharp knife and gash the liver and insert the lardoons. Afterwards melt a good-sized piece of butter and let the liver simmer in it for 15 minutes, keeping it covered tightly; then half cover it with boiling water, add ½ plateful of finely chopped onions, 2 bay leaves, a little more salt, ground cloves, and a piece of butter, and when the liver is almost tender put in bread crumbs, either a large spoonful of pear sauce, syrup or a piece of sugar, some vinegar and according to taste a glassful of claret. There must be plenty of sauce of a nice consistency.

Time of cooking, 15 minutes. Serve with boiled potatoes.

REMARK.—Liver is easily over-salted, which should be borne in mind when preparing the above dish and the succeeding ones.

89. Fried Liver. Take a fresh liver, wash it, if possible let it lay for a few hours or half a day in sweet milk, remove the outer skin and all sinews, cut into slices about ½ inch thick, sprinkle with pepper according to taste, turn in flour and fry in an uncovered pan in heated butter and fat pork for 10 minutes until crisp, turning once. If the liver is fried too long it will become dry.

When blood no longer appears if the liver is pierced with a fork, it is done and must be taken from the fire. Immediately pour a cupful of water into the pan, stir until it is properly thick and pour it over the liver.

A few fresh pounded juniper berries can be added to the hot butter according to taste; they impart a nice flavor to the liver.

90. Liver Dumplings. Directions for making liver dumplings will be found under Division O.

91. Cold Veal Slices fried. Cut ½ inch thick slices from a cold veal roast, dip them in an egg with nutmeg, turn in grated crackers mixed with a little salt and then fry in plenty of hot butter over a quick fire on both sides to a light brown and serve at once.

92. Sausages or small Meatballs made from Cold Veal Roast. Take cold roast veal, remove all sinews and chop the meat very fine. Heat a good-sized piece of butter, brown some cracker crumbs in it and mix with the meat a few eggs of which the whites have been slightly frothed, together with some nutmeg and salt. Then roll into the form of sausages, brush with egg, turn in cracker crumbs and fry in butter to a light brown. This makes a nice side dish for all kinds of fresh vegetables, particularly spinach.

93. Meat Balls made from Boiled Veal and fried in Lard. Cut boiled veal into small cubes, brown flour in butter, add some bouillon and water, but not too much, because the sauce should be thick, together with salt and lemon peel, stir the yolk of an egg through it, then cook the meat in it thoroughly and put it into a dish to cool. Beat an egg with some salt and turn in it the meat balls which have been formed from the cold mass, then turn them in cracker crumbs and fry in hot lard to a light brown and send to the table. Garnish with slips of celery which have been fried in the hot lard.

94. Warmed-over Roast Veal. Slice the roast, put it into a deep porcelaine dish, pour over it the gravy from the roast together with some fat and add some salt if necessary. Then cover tightly and put the dish into

a hot oven or over boiling water. It will take an hour
or longer to finish, according to the heat of the stove.
The meat should be basted frequently with the sauce,
but it should not cook.

95. Warmed-over Roast Veal a la Gourmand. Cut
the roast into slices, put them into a buttered pan,
sprinkle with capers, chopped anchovy, chopped parsley
and some lemon juice and dot with butter. Put the
dish into a double kettle, cover and put live embers on
the lid. After heating the roast thoroughly for ½ hour
it should be garnished with a border of sc mbled eggs
and small roast potatoes.

96. Roast Veal Ragout. A good-sized piece of butter
or roast meat fat is browned with a few chopped onions,
add a large spoonful of flour and stir until brown; also
add some bouillon made from the cracked bone of the
roast with a little water, white vinegar, a few bay leaves,
ground cloves, sliced pickles, sugar and salt, and finally
the roast veal slices.
Time of cooking, ½—¾ hours.

97. Veal Roast for Invalids. For this purpose take
the broad thin upper part of the loin, pound it, take off
the skin, lay it out flat and roast it with a very slow
fire for not longer than 20 minutes, turning frequently.
When serving, sprinkle with fine salt, cook some cream
and brown gravy in the pan to a thick consistency, and
serve with mashed potatoes and cauliflower puree.

98. Veal Steak for Invalids. Take a piece from the
loin the same as directed in the preceding receipt, cut
it into slices of medium thickness, remove all of the skin,
pound a little and lard nicely. Use the scraps together
with some pieces of beef to make a meat broth, melt
butter and fry the steaks carefully; pour off the butter
and then cover the steaks with bouillon which has been
thickened with cornstarch and seasoned with lemon juice
and Madeira.
Serve with mashed potatoes.

99. Veal Sweetbreads for Invalids. Prepare the sweetbreads according to A, 35; all scraps are lightly fried with a slice of lean ham in butter, covered with a large cupful of water and thoroughly cooked. Cut the sweetbreads into slices and lard if wished, fry in butter, pour over it the broth and stew slowly until done. Remove the fat from the sauce, thicken it with corn-starch and strengthen with extract of beef.

100. Veal Sweetbread Pudding for Invalids. Prepare 2 veal sweetbreads according to A, 35, stew in butter until tender and cut into cubes. Soak some wheat bread in milk, press it well and stir it into some frothed butter. add the yolks of 3 eggs, chopped parsley, pepper, salt and the sweetbread cubes, whip the whites of the eggs to a froth and stir through the mass. Cook the pudding in a small buttered mould for a good ½ hour, turn it out and add a brown sauce.

101. Veal Tongue for Invalids. Boil a nice veal tongue in salted water until tender, let it lay for a moment in cold water and then take off the skin. The tongue broth is then strengthened with extract of beef and seasoned with lemon juice; stew the tongue in a little of this broth, replenishing from time to time; after ½ hour the tongue should be perfectly tender, then thicken the broth with a little cornstarch smoothed in Madeira, and sauce the tongue with it.

Other veal dishes suitable for the sick-room are Nos. 62, 63, 64, 68, 71, 72, 73, 74, 76, 78 and 79.

III. MUTTON.

NOTE.—Inasmuch as mutton fat cools very rapidly, all dishes in which mutton is to be served, and also the plates on the table, must be warmed.

102. Saddle or Leg of Mutton prepared like Game. For a dinner party the saddle is usually taken; if the leg is chosen it is chopped off smoothly to about ½ its length and not cut in two at the point like a leg of veal.

Wash the saddle and pound it thoroughly, put it into an appropriate vessel together with plenty of onions and eschalots, bay leaves, cloves and peppercorns, garden-rue, majoram, tarragon, 1 quart of vinegar, and, if you have any heavy claret, a bottleful, this giving the meat the brown color.

Pour this liquor boiling hot over the meat and let it remain in it for 8 days, turning it daily. Instead of preparing the mutton as above it can be laid in sour milk only, or else a day before using and after it is skinned rub it with the following essence, which will impart an excellent gamey flavor to the meat: Put 2 grated onions, purslane, chives, chopped thyme, ground spices and pounded juniper berries into 2 glassfuls of claret and let it draw for a few days, strain through a sieve and brush the roast all over with it from time to time, until it is all used up. Then lard the roast like a hare, sprinkle with fine salt and put it into a pan in which plenty of fat pork and butter has previously been heated, and roast until light brown. Afterwards gradually pour either some of the vinegar in which the meat has lain, together with the herbs, over the roast, or else gradually some sour cream, and then roast until tender, basting often and keeping it covered, at least during the earlier part of the time it is in the oven; according to the size of the roast and whether it is to be rare or well done, this will take from 1½ to 2 hours. During the last hour gradually stir 2 cupfuls of thick cream into the gravy and let the roast finish, uncovered, to a golden brown, basting often. When serving rub ½ tablespoonful of flour in a pan for a few minutes until brown, add enough water to make the gravy and then strain it, The roast may be garnished with either small potato dumplings or with a border of stewed onions; mushrooms are also very nice for this purpose.

For a middle course at a dinner party the piece from the saddle over the tenderloin is often taken only; lard, stew in the oven with meat broth, parsley root, etc., or with claret, until tender, and when done drip off until dry and glaze with the broth which has been made in the oven. Then slice the meat and serve it as a garnish for a fine veal sweetbread ragout, or mushroom ragout, or even to good bouillon rice, which has been well shaken with Parmesan cheese and butter, formed into a high cake and brushed with tomato sauce.

103. Roast Leg of Mutton. The meat should not be taken for use before the time noted and then pound it, without removing the fat, according to No. 1, wash and dry with a cloth, and put it into boiling fat (butter and pork fat) roast until of a light brown and add boiling water—if the meat is to have a slightly sour flavor, take 1 part of vinegar to 3 parts of water; season with eschalots or onions, some bay leaves, cloves and pepper and sprinkle with fine salt. If fresh cucumbers are to be had cut ½ plateful into cubes and put them into the pan at once, which will greatly improve the flavor and appearance of the gravy. Roast for 3 hours, basting often; it is best to cover tightly. An hour before serving gradually add 2 cupfuls of either cream or milk to the gravy. If no vinegar has been used, a spoonful of mustard can be stirred into it at last. To prepare the sauce proceed generally as directed under No. 1.

104. Stewed Leg of Mutton. The meat, which should not be too fresh, is well pounded and put on the fire with water and white ("Weiss") beer, which must not be bitter; skim and add cloves, peppercorns, 3 bay leaves, a few whole onions, and a bunch of green herbs, such as garden-rue, majoram, and sweet basil, let it cook slowly for 2 hours, keeping it covered tightly. Then pour off the broth, sprinkle the meat with fine salt, dredge a spoonful of flour over it, put in some butter and brown the meat on both sides, moving it back and forth to prevent scorching. Take the fat from the broth, strain the latter and put it into the kettle, add lemon slices without the seeds, pickles sliced lengthwise, or fresh cucumbers, a cupful of vinegar, a handful of button onions and a glassful of claret. Stew until done, which will take about 2½ hours, serve with some of the gravy and bring the remainder with the onions and pickles to the table in a gravy boat.

105. Roast Lamb. Take a leg of lamb, wash, dry it with a towel, rub well with ground cloves, put it into a pan containing hot butter, afterwards sprinkle fine salt over it, and roast like a loin of veal, not too tender; a short hour will be sufficient.

Instead of the ground cloves a few juniper berries may be put into the butter.

Take the fat off the gravy and bind the latter with cornstarch, adding either ½ cupful of sour cream or ½ glassful of Madeira. If the lamb is a very small one, both legs can remain together; bend them inwards after they are larded, tying them with a cord.

106. Saddle of Lamb roasted like Venison. Take the saddle of a Spring lamb, remove the skin, and rub thoroughly all over with the following mixture: eschalots, majoram, rosemary, and 2 to 3 bay leaves, all chopped very fine, pepper, cloves, and 4 to 5 fresh pounded juniper berries. Then add vinegar and claret half and half and let the meat lay in this for 3—4 days, turning it in the pickle frequently. It is then larded if wished and roasted in an earthenware or enamelled pan for 1 to 1¼ hours, sprinkling fine salt over it and basting often.

107. Mutton and Lamb Chops are prepared like veal cutlets, taking off all of the fat. When serving, a bit of anchovy or vegetable butter can be put on each chop. Lamb chops can also be served with tomato sauce and mixed with pickles. When served cold they should be covered like stuffed breast of veal, with a thick brown gravy.

108. Broiled Mutton Chops. Trim the chops nicely, remove the fat, dip in melted butter, sprinkle with salt and pepper and with cracker crumbs, which are often mixed with Parmesan cheese. Broil them 5—8 minutes according as they should be rare or well done, 4 minutes on each side. Serve hot. To broil them successfully have a glowing coal fire, but no blaze.

109. Stewed Mutton with Claret. Cut pieces ½ inch thick from the loin, pound and sprinkle with salt and pepper, put them into a kettle with melted butter, roast very slightly and pour in enough hot claret to half cover the meat. Season with 1 bay leaf, 2 sliced onions, 6 cloves and allspice, stew slowly until tender, thicken the gravy with browned flour, pour it over the meat and serve with mashed potatoes.

110. Mutton Fricassee. Cut a breast of mutton into medium-sized pieces, put on the fire with water and salt, an hour afterwards add 2 or 3 onions, with a clove in each, to be removed before serving; if carraway is liked a little may be added. The flavor can also be improved by the addition of some mushrooms. Boil the fricassee slowly for two hours, but do not get it too soft, skim off the fat, lightly brown a spoonful of flour and stir it through the fricassee, cook slowly for 10 minutes longer and serve.

111. Fricassee of Lamb with Capers and Anchovy. Cut the meat into small squares, wash, and lay it in boiling butter together with a few cloves, mace, sweet basil and whole onions. Let it simmer in this for a while, then add a little boiling water, salt, cover and cook slowly. When nearly done, which will be after about 1 hour, add flour smoothed (not browned) in butter, lemon slices without the seeds, capers and some wine, stir finely chopped anchovy through the fricassee just before serving, because cooking impairs their flavor. The fricassee can also be prepared without the capers and anchovy, in fact this is preferred by many.

112. Mutton Ragout. Wash the meat, cut it into small squares, put it on the fire in boiling water with salt and season with bay leaves, peppercorns, cloves, onions, and if agreeable, a little dill; for a large quantity a small bunch of the latter is sufficient. Cook the meat with this until quite half done, take off the fat from the broth, strain the latter and bring it to a boil with flour rubbed in butter, and then put in the meat with a few lemon slices without the seeds, button onions, pickles or fresh cucumbers (if the latter, add a little vinegar), and cook until done. The meat must be easily pierced with a fork, but it should not fall to pieces, and the sauce be neither too thin nor too thick.

The ragout may also be prepared wholly like brown ragout of hare ("Hasenpfeffer").

It can also be improved by the addition of mushrooms, stewed onions, veal sweetbreads, kidneys or fowl livers; the gravy can be spiced with claret and the ragout brought to the table in a puff paste or surrounded with bits of toast. A border of boiled rice is also suitable.

113. Ragout of Roast or Boiled Mutton. Stew sliced onions until tender in butter or good fat (not mutton fat), stir the flour in this until brown and gradually add a little boiling water, constantly stirring, season with sweet basil, pepper, cloves, 1 to 2 bay leaves, salt and a little vinegar; if convenient put in ½ or an entire spoonful of thick sour cream, and pickles peeled and sliced. Cook the sauce slowly for a while, keeping it covered, stewing the boiled meat in it thoroughly; the roast meat should become hot only.

114. Fried sliced Mutton. Cut boiled mutton into slices, turn in egg, salt and ground cloves, dredge with flour and fry in butter or fat.

115. Remnants of Mutton with Pickles. Cut the meat into oblong slices and 3 to 4 sweet-sour pickles into cubes, and mix well together. Then rub an ounce of flour in 1 heaping tablespoonful of butter, together with several sliced onions, add the left-over gravy, a trifle of extract of beef, a little ginger, cloves, pepper and salt, flavor the gravy with a little vinegar, a pinch of sugar, heat the meat and the pickles in this, and serve with boiled potatoes.

116. Mutton Curry. Cut the meat into cubes and heat it with small pieces of onions, salt, pepper and a little curry powder, add a large cupful of boiling meat broth, and let it simmer for ¼ hour. In the meantime put about 6 ounces of rice into plenty of salted boiling water, boil rapidly until done, drench with cold water so that the kernels will be firm and loose, and then surround with it the curry, which has been put into a deep dish.

117. Lamb Chops for Invalids. Take fresh lamb chops, remove all fat and trim them nicely, pound lightly, lard neatly, dredge with flour and sprinkle with a little salt. Fry the chops to a light brown in melted butter, gradually add a small cupful of good boiling meat broth, and simmer until done, keeping them covered; put them on a warm dish, thicken the gravy with a spoonful of cornstarch smoothed in Madeira, strain, and if permitted mix with it a few spoonfuls of tomato pulp.

Nos. 100, 103, and 109, without the capers, are also suitable dishes for invalids.

IV. TAME HARES OR RABBITS.

118. NOTE.—Although the value of tame hares or rabbits as articles of food has long been recognized, it is only of late years that particular attention has been paid to raising them. They are now so frequently to be found in most kitchens, however, that a separate chapter of this book may be profitably devoted to a description of the various modes of preparing them for the table.

Killing the hare is accomplished in the easiest manner as follows: Insert a sharp knife into the neck, between the forelegs, this will pierce the heart and kill the animal without any struggle. In order to have the flesh retain a light color, which is desirable in the preparation of so-called white dishes, and also in order that it may keep longer, let all blood drip away. Catch the blood in a dish containing a little vinegar and set it aside in a cool place; it is used for brown hare ragout ("Kaninchenpfeffer"). After being killed the skin of the hare should be immediately taken off and it must also be emptied. Tame hares are skinned in the same manner as wild ones (see No. 156) and they are also cut up the same as these.

119. English Hare Soup. Cut the meat into very small pieces, melt some butter and brown the meat in this lightly together with 6 onions with a clove in each, stirring carefully; then add a heaping tablespoonful of flour and shortly afterwards meat broth or water, a small parsley root cut into pieces, 2 bay leaves, 1 tablespoonful of black peppercorns, and salt. The onions and spices are taken out before serving. After the meat is tender the broth is strained, brought on the fire again and then cook enough sago in it to bind the soup.

A piece of finely chopped raw meat together with some wheat bread soaked in cold water, butter, egg and mace, prepared like beef dumplings, can also be cooked in the soup for a few minutes. The liver of the hare is frequently cooked in the soup; after it is done it is chopped fine, passed through a strainer and mixed with a small glassful of Portwine, salt and pepper and made up into little dumplings for the soup. Most other soup dumplings are also suitable for hare soup.

120. Fresh Roasted Hare. For the various kinds of hare roasts the large kinds are the most suitable: the hare should be full grown but quite young; when a little older they are better adapted for brown ragout of hare, and when old they should be used for soups.

Cut off the head, neck, breast and forelegs, remove the skin, wash the saddle and lard, or else lay a few slices of fat pork on it. Sprinkle with fine salt, put the roast into a hot pan containing plenty of melted butter and a few slices of fresh bacon and add a tablespoonful of mustard. Baste frequently and as soon as the meat begins to turn yellow it is best to add sour cream and continue the roasting with a slow fire, basting often. As soon as the roast can be readily pierced with a fork, and has a dark yellow color, which will be after half an hour or so, according to the age of the hare, it should be put on a hot dish, stir what is left in the pan with ½ tablespoonful of flour and cook with salt and water to a well bound gravy, pour part of this over the roast and bring the remainder to the table in a gravy dish.

Apple sauce is the most suitable accompaniment.

121. Roasted Tame Hare like Wild Hare. Lay the saddle of a large hare into an earthenware vessel for 3 days in a pickle made as follows: 1 large cupful of vinegar, 1 large cupful of claret, 4 medium-sized chopped onions, 1 heaping teaspoonful of fresh coarsely pounded juniper berries, 1 teaspoonful of pounded peppercorns, 3 bay leaves and a little bunch of thyme. Drench the meat three times daily with this liquor and also turn it once a day. Lard the meat, salt, and roast with the addition of sour cream.

This mode of preparing a hare can be well recommended, and it may be observed that every dish of hare will gain in flavor, if first pickled for a few hours.

Pear sauce, compot of apples and cranberries are suitable accompaniments.

122. Brown Ragout of Hare ("Kaninchenpfeffer").
When killing the hare catch the blood in a dish containing some vinegar, as already noted, and set it aside. Cut the meat into pieces and put with it the heart, lungs and liver, put it into a rather narrow vessel and cover it fully one-half with vinegar which has been boiled with a few bay leaves, plenty of peppercorns and cloves. In order that the meat may be thoroughly penetrated by this liquor, it should lay in it for 3 days at least and be turned once a day. Then melt a piece of butter (for the sake of economy pork fat cut into cubes can be taken) brown it in a handful of finely chopped onions, stirring constantly, then also stir through it a heaping tablespoonful of flour to a light brown, and add the liquor in which the meat was pickled, together with salt and enough water to make the necessary amount of gravy; should through this the gravy be too sour, however, do not put in all of the vinegar. Cook until the meat can be readily pierced with a fork, but not too tender, then stir in the blood of the hare without any further cooking; add a piece of sugar to give the gravy a sweet-sour taste. The gravy must have a nice consistency. Serve with hot boiled potatoes.

123. Fricassee of Hare (White Ragout). Cut the hare into good-sized pieces, laying aside the head, neck lungs and liver. Wash the meat, lightly brown a heaping spoonful of flour with a piece of butter, put in the meat together with salt and 2 finely chopped onions, and simmer on both sides for a while. Then add as much boiling water as is wanted to make the gravy, put in some mushrooms if possible, and cook until tender. If the gravy should not be thick enough, this can be remedied by putting in a very finely rolled cracker; a little finely grated nutmeg will improve the flavor of the gravy.

If dumplings are wanted in the fricassee, make them of the meat of the hare or from beef, or else from beef marrow, and in serving the fricassee mix them between and around it.

V. PORK.

NOTE.—Pork does not need to hang for any length of time to become tender, nor need it be pounded. The slightest taint renders it unfit for use.

124. To bake a whole Ham. After cutting away the bone and point from the ham of a young pig, rub with salt, put it into a small crock and pour over it hot vinegar in which have been boiled a handful of chopped eschalots or onions, a little tarragon, a spoonful of peppercorns, a teaspoonful of cloves and 3 bay leaves, let it lay in this for a week; if it is only one-half covered it should be drenched and turned daily. If a small piece only is to be baked, the spices should be taken in proportion. If the ham is to be boiled, put it on the fire with half of the liquor and about 1 or 2 quarts of water, with the skin to the top, cover tightly and boil until almost tender. Then pour off all of the broth and strain it; put a piece of butter into the pan and either take a sharp knife and criss-cross the skin of the ham and insert a clove in the corner of each little square, or else take off the skin and thickly dredge the ham with finely rolled crackers mixed with nutmeg, bake uncovered in a hot oven until quite tender and brown, gradually add the liquor, ½ cupful at a time. Baste the sides of the ham frequently but with care, so that the upper crust will become crisp. When serving, take part of the fat from the gravy, put into it a heaping spoonful of flour, stir for a few minutes, make up as much gravy as is wanted and put in a few lemon slices.

The ham can be garnished as follows: Boil several celery roots in salted water until half done, slice lengthwise and cook them not too tender in the ham broth before the latter is poured off. Set aside until ready to serve, and when the gravy is done, simmer the celery in this for a few moments, and use to garnish the dish.

To cook a whole ham will take about 3 hours.

125. Fresh Loin of Pork with a Crust (Mecklenburg Style). Take off the skin and rinse the meat with cold water, point with cloves at intervals of 3 inches, sprinkle with salt and put into the oven in a pan containing water; the oven should not be too hot at first, otherwise the meat will be roasted on the outside while the inner part remains rare. Baste frequently and add boiling water as often as is necessary. When done, which can be ascertained by piercing the side of the meat with a fork, skim off the fat from the broth and then dredge the skinned side with a mixture of grated bread crust, sugar and some finely ground cloves; put the meat back into the oven and leave it there without basting until the crust is crisp.

Time of roasting, at least 3 hours.

126. To prepare a Ham like Wild Boar. Take from a young pig a ham weighing about 8 to 10 pounds, remove the skin and rub the meat well with the following mixture: 1 pint of claret, 1 large cupful of vinegar, some sugar, 2 large grated onions, 6 bay leaves, ground pepper, whole and ground cloves, a teaspoonful of each, 30 fresh juniper berries, the chopped peel of half a lemon and a little ginger. Then put the ham into this liquor and leave it in the same for a few days, drenching it daily Sprinkle with salt, put it into a pan with butter and let it brown lightly, add a few cupfuls of boiling water and some of the liquor. Then roast until tender for 2—2½ hours, basting frequently; an earthenware or enameled pan is the best. 1 hour before serving put 2 cupfuls of cream into the gravy, which is thickened with a little flour before serving, after taking off part of the fat as directed in No. 124.

127. Roast Pork. A cut from the neck has the mildest meat and is the most profitable on account of the small bones it contains. It is the best when taken from a young pig and cut towards the middle in such a manner that it is covered with a thin layer of fat.

The roasting can be done in a kettle as well as in the oven. The fat on the meat is usually sufficient to finish the roast, or some of it may be cut away if found necessary. Put some water into the pan, sprinkle salt over the roast, and leave it in the oven covered tightly until done, turning it once. The oven should have a medium heat only; according to the size of the piece— say from 3 to 5 pounds,—it will take from 2 to 2½ hours to finish the roast. Baste frequently with the sauce, which has been spiced with pepper and juniper berries, occasionally adding a little boiling water. When the roast is served skim off the superfluous fat from the gravy and cook the latter with the addition of a teaspoonful of flour and a little water and salt, if necessary stirring with it all that remains in the pan.

128. Roast Pork, No. 2. After rubbing the meat the evening previously with salt, pepper and mace, put the kettle on the fire with water and enough vinegar to impart to it a decided sour taste; there should be enough of this liquor to cover the meat about one-third; add plenty of finely sliced onions, peppercorns, a few cloves and bay leaves, bring the broth to a boil and put in the meat, cover tightly and let it cook slowly until it is quite half done, turning it once. If the broth should then not be wholly cooked away it will make no difference—it can be poured into a separate vessel; put the fat back with the roast, together with a little kidney suet if necessary, and then keep the roast on the fire until it is done and of a medium brown color, adding from time to time a little of the broth or instead of this a few tablespoonfuls of boiling water.

The gravy, which has been thickened as directed in the previous receipts, should be strained before it is served. Add 1 or 2 tablespoonfuls of milk to the gravy if it should be too sour, provided it is brown enough.

According to the French method, a neck of pork, after being salted is put in the pan with some quartered apples, plenty of small onions and small potatoes, drench the meat with melted butter, roast for 15 minutes and then pour in a large cupful of seething hot water with which it simmers until done. When serving put the roast into the center of the dish, and place a wreath of apples, onions and potatoes around it.

129. Boiled Smoked Ham. Put the ham into water over night and the next morning wash it thoroughly with hot water and a handful of wheat bran. Rinse it well and put it on the fire with the skin to the top, covered with water or else in a steamer. The ham must be brought to a boil rapidly, afterwards, however, it should cook slowly but uninterruptedly for 3½ hours, and then let it lay in the broth for ½ hour longer. A whole ham will be particularly excellent if it is put on a hot stove without cooking it the day before it is to be used, and then finishing the cooking the day after in the same broth. This makes the meat extremely tender yet it does not drop to pieces in the least on the outside. If it is to be brought to the table whole put it into a dish, trim all around very nicely, make a straight cut through the skin about 2 inches from the end, and in such a manner that it will adhere to the inner side and form a border all around; roll up the skin from the point and fasten it, (the thin piece of bone can be taken from the leg), roll the end of the leg into a frill of paper, fastening it, put a wreath of parsley around the edge of the dish and garnish the top of the ham with chopped parsley.

130. Ham with Madeira Sauce. Boil a smoked ham until tender as directed in the foregoing receipt, take off the skin, remove all fat excepting a single narrow strip, then cut the ham into thin slices and put them into a deep dish side by side, so that the fat edges lie to the top, and pour over them a hot sauce made as follows: Take a meat broth made according to A, No. 20, brown 1 to 2 tablespoonfuls of flour in butter, stir some of the broth into it, season with salt, and cook with ½ bottle of Madeira until clear. Then add truffles or mushrooms, which have been prepared according to A, 33 and 34. After the ham has been served in this sauce surround it with a rice border made as follows: Scald 1 pound of rice and then cook it in water until tender and thick with a piece of butter and a little salt; the kernels, however must remain firm. Then mix with the meat broth 1 cupful of Madeira, 1 cupful of cream, the yolks of 2 eggs, and ¼ pound of grated Parmesan cheese and stir this through the rice carefully.

Serve as hot as possible.

131. Ham with Burgundy Sauce. Wash a well smoked ham and lay it into water over night, wipe it off carefully, put it on the fire in cold water and bring to a boil, after which it should simmer for 2 to 3 hours, rather than boil, but it should not be soft. Then take it out of the broth, remove the skin with part of the fat, bring about 1½ to 1¾ quarts of strong beef broth together with a bottle of Burgundy and 1 tablespoonful of sugar to a boil, pour this over the ham and cook until nicely brown and tender, basting often. Before serving take the fat from the gravy and strain. If you have no broth use extract of beef.

132. Stuffed Spare Ribs. Take the spare ribs connected in one piece, rub well with salt, cut off the small bloody end, crack the ribs in the middle without injuring the meat and then fill with quartered apples or stewed prunes, or both mixed, bend the edges together and sew them. Put the meat into boiling butter, brown both sides, pour in some boiling water and roast for at least 2½ hours, keeping it covered tightly and adding a little boiling water from time to time; spare ribs are best roasted in the oven. The meat should at first be only half covered with water in the pan, and roasted from 1 to 3 hours according to the age of the pig from which it is taken; turn once only. At the end of the time mentioned the water must be cooked away and then baste the meat quite often with the fat in the pan, sprinkle with a little salt and roast for ½ hour longer until nicely brown. Thicken the gravy with a little browned flour and some of the liquor of the stewed prunes. The superfluous fat is best skimmed off after taking out the roast, and then prepare the gravy.

Spare ribs are frequently filled with sourkrout, which has first been stewed for ¾ of an hour in butter with a little sugar and a glassful of white wine, after which boiled chestnuts or small stewed mushrooms are stirred through it. The roast is otherwise prepared as above directed, but a little wine added to the water is an improvement. Do not neglect to remove the threads before serving.

133. Pork Headcheese. See directions in Division W.

134. Roast Pig. The pig should be well cleaned, skinned and washed; cut off the feet and take out the eyes, rub inside with salt, dry the outside and pierce it lengthwise with a wooden skewer; then put it into a pan containing a little water and brush thoroughly with olive oil or a piece of fat pork. Puncture with a larding needle to prevent blistering. Roast pig is not basted like other roasts and salt is not sprinkled over it until it is crusted to a light brown. It is then brushed again with pork fat and after roasting for 1 hour, served hot without any gravy, putting a lemon between its jaws. As a side dish serve the following: First boil the lungs and then chop them finely together with the liver and the heart and simmer in butter until it is done. Stew some eschalots in butter in which a spoonful of flour has been lightly browned, stir with some meat broth to a thin pulp, add salt, nutmeg, ground cloves, lemon juice and some chopped lemon peel and cook all of this until done.

135. How to cook a smoked Pig's Head. Cover it over night with water, wash it off the next morning with warm water and then cook slowly in boiling water for 3 hours with the meaty side to the bottom. Is most appropriate with sourkrout and salted beans.

136. Pickled Pork is cooked in the same manner as directed for pickled beef (D, No. 58).

137. Pork Sausages. Take some nice streaky pork and chop it very fine, add salt, nutmeg and lemon peel or chopped eschalots, a few eggs, some grated wheat bread and a little cream. Mix well together and then roll between the hands into little sausages or balls, dredge with cracker crumbs and fry in butter. Serve with spinach and most varieties of cabbage.

138. Pork Chops should be cut from a young pig. Prepare like veal cutlets, but they should fry slower and 2 minutes longer. They are an agreeable accompaniment to all kinds of cabbages.

139. Chopped Pork Cutlets. To make 4 cutlets take 1 pound from the neck of a young pig, chop it fine together with some salt and pepper, divide into 4 parts, mould into the form of cutlets and cross-hatch the surface somewhat, by means of which they can be easily breaded. Then beat up 1 egg with a tablespoonful of water which will be sufficient for 6 cutlets, have ready plenty of grated bread crust or stale grated wheat bread, heat butter or kidney suet as directed in A, 17, dip the cutlets in egg so that they will be covered all over, turn them in bread crumbs and fry quickly in an open pan on both sides for a few minutes until of a light brown color, moving them about in the pan frequently so that the fat will not scorch. When done through and through take them from the fire at once so that they will retain their full juiciness. These cutlets are appropriate with the finest kinds of vegetables or potato dishes. A gravy made of extract of beef with capers, anchovy, etc., can be made for the cutlets, sprinkling a few drops of lemon juice over them, or else they may be garnished with large apple slices stewed in butter.

140. Smoked Raw Ham Steaks. Cut the slices about ½ inch thick and lay them in milk over night, which is particularly essential when the ham is very salty or dry; pound the slices on both sides with the edge of a dull knife, dip into a beaten egg with a little pepper, turn in bread or cracker crumbs and fry in hot butter in an open pan on a very moderate fire—a hot fire will harden the meat; turn them quite often until they are of a golden brown color.

141. Chopped Pork Steaks are prepared like chopped beef steaks, (see No. 17). Fry them with browned onions or in melted butter.

142. Pork Tenderloin. Pound the meat slightly, sprinkle with a little salt, put it into the pan with melted butter, fry until slightly browned and then keep them tightly covered on a slow fire for 15 minutes longer, turning once. Then add some cream and fry 15 minutes longer, basting frequently, until they are tender enough to be easily pierced with a fork. Before serving add a little flour as usual, and a few minutes after enough bouillon or water to make the gravy, which is flavored with a few lemon slices.

143. Sweet-sour Ragout of Pork. A piece from the neck or any cut from the breast can be taken. Divide the meat into pieces of appropriate size and proceed precisely as directed for ragout of hare ("Hasenpfeffer").

144. Pork Croquettes in South Germany Style. (Sueddeutsche Schnitzchen.) These can be made from any kind of meat besides pork. Chop 1 pound of tender fat pork very finely together with a small onion or an eschalot steamed in butter. Then stir with 12 freshened, boned and chopped anchovies, 1 tablespoonful of coarsely chopped capers, some ground pepper and nutmeg, 2 ounces of wheat bread grated without the crust, 3 eggs and 3 tablespoonfuls of thick sour cream to a smooth forcemeat, make it up into cakes of a medium thickness about the size of a silver dollar, put into each a slip of parsley root to serve as a bone and fry them over a quick fire on both sides until brown.

Served with the butter in which they are fried they are nice with fine vegetables, without the butter and the parsley root they are good with bread and butter and tea.

145. Fried Sausages and Apples. Cut 6 pared apples each into 8 pieces, sprinkle with sugar and a little cinnamon and let them stand for a few hours. At the same time put some cleaned dried currants into lukewarm water and let them soak on top of the stove. Melt a good-sized piece of butter in the pan, put in ½ pound of sausages, lay the apples around and the currants and a little lemon peel over them, cover and fry slowly. As soon as the apples are soft underneath turn them, and take out those that are done to prevent them from dropping to pieces. As soon as the sausages are fried add a glassful of Rhinewine to the gravy and serve them garnished with the apples.

146. To fry fresh Sausages (so=called "Mettwurst"). If the sausage meat has been cut into cubes put it on the fire in a pan containing some water, cover and cook for ¾—1 hour, then take off the cover so that any remaining water will steam away, put in a piece of butter and fry the sausages on both sides to a light yellow so that they will remain quite tender. Fresh sausages made from *finely chopped* meat are put into melted butter at once; fry for 15—20 minutes. After the sausage has been fried on both sides in the melted butter to a light brown, beer (which should not be bitter) can be added, in which the sausage is stewed until done.

147. To cook smoked Pork Sausage. Smoked sausage is cooked principally in browned cabbage or in pea-, bean-, lentil- and potato soups. As long as it is juicy,

wash it in warm water and put it on the fire in cold
water and cook until done. If it is dry this procedure
will not be sufficient to make it tender; it must then be
washed 2 days before cooking, covered with water and
set aside in a cool place.

148. "Frankfurt" Sausages. These and "Wiener"
sausages are covered with boiling water and then set
on top of the hot stove for 10 minutes. Serve with
grated horse-radish. They are an appropriate accompaniment to all cabbage dishes and to potato or bean
salad.

149. Ham Croquettes. Take ham remnants and
chop them very finely with some fat, and for a soupplateful add 3 eggs, 2 ounces of grated wheat bread,
3 tablespoonfuls of cream and some pepper; mix thoroughly. Soak slices of wheat bread in milk and egg,
cover smoothly with the meat, turn in bread and cracker
crumbs and fry in butter to a light brown. This is a
very palatable dish after the soup and is also nice when
served in a middle course, or with salads, greens or
beans.

150. Fried Slices of pickled Pork. Cut boiled pickled
pork into slices, turn in egg and ground cloves, then in
flour and fry in butter until of a light brown and crisp.
Excellent with various kinds of coarser vegetables.

151. Warmed=over Pork Remnants. Cut the remnants into slices. Slightly brown 2 handfuls of small
onions in butter, also some flour, and cook with a
glassful of claret, 1 cupful of meat broth, salt, pepper,
bay leaves and a little thyme to make a rather thick
sauce, in which the meat slices are thoroughly heated:
serve with mashed potatoes.

152. Roast Pork in Packages. Cut the meat into
slices, lay them together two-by-two, spread top and
bottom with butter, turn in bread crumbs and chopped
herbs and then wrap them in strong white paper thickly
covered with butter. Put these "packages" on the shelf
in a hot oven for 10 minutes and then bring them to
the table at once. Serve with potato salad and pickles
in a separate dish.

153. Remnants of Ham with Asparagus. Entree. If the remnants should happen to be very dry, lay them in milk for a few hours, then cut them into cubes and mix with the same quantity of asparagus pieces, which have been cooked in salted water; make a thick sauce, taking 3 eggs, 2 teaspoonfuls of flour, 1 large cupful of the asparagus broth, a little lemon juice, a trifle of extract of beef, salt and nutmeg, mix the meat and asparagus through the sauce, fill into little buttered cups, cover the tops with bread crumbs and bake in the oven to a golden brown.

No. 138 is the only pork dish suitable for invalids.

VI. GAME.

154. General Rules for the Disposition and Prepar= ation of Game. When purchasing game be careful to observe that the flesh has not been injured or torn through the killing. It should, furthermore, not be too old, that is to say, it should not have laid too long because the slightest "houtgout" will seriously impair the meat.

Game must never be freshened in water; the following method, in vogue in France, has proven to be the most practical for cleaning game. Remove all bloody parts, dip a cloth in lukewarm water and rub the meat with it all over, repeat the process with cold water and then lard or otherwise prepare the meat as desired.

The meat must be well cooked in order to bring out perfectly its fine flavor. A roast must be well larded (see D, II) and the oven should not be overheated. Game is roasted in plenty of butter with fat pork and sour cream and frequent basting; no water should be added.

The head is the least valuable part of all varieties of game, excepting the wild boar, and can only be used in an ordinary ragout, like a pork ragout, and in this case the neck can also be used; the tongue, on the contrary, is very good. The breast, particularly if it has become bloody in consequence of the shooting, is not an especially choice part and it is also then best for a ragout. Then follow the sides and joints, which, when from an older animal, are best stewed, and from younger ones are best for roasting, and finally the buttock piece, which is best of all for roasts.

155. To keep Game. A cleaned hare with its fur on will keep in cold weather for a week longer, but if necessary it can be put into vinegar for a few days more, yet this does not tend to improve it. Venison will keep well as follows: Divide the meat into roasts, sprinkle moderately with salt, then roast very slightly all around in a pan. When the meat is quite cold pack it into a keg or a stone jar with a few onions, peppercorns, fresh juniper berries, a sliced lemon and some salt and pour enough fresh lard over the meat to entirely surround it. It will keep in good condition for a week, and can be either stewed or roasted and is then handled like fresh meat.

156. To skin Hares. When purchasing the hare, be careful to observe that the saddle is not injured, otherwise it will be dry and of a poor quality. The forelegs of a young hare are easily broken and their ears can be readily torn, and up to their second year they have a light spot on the forehead. For that matter, old hares are also good when properly cooked. The meat of an old hare is more tender if it is first laid in buttermilk for a few days. The skinning and preparing of a hare for a roast is somewhat troublesome and is done as follows:

Usually the hare has been cleaned before it is sent to market, and only the liver, heart and lungs come with it. Lay it on a chopping board or hang it up by the hind legs, first on one leg and then on the other; the back or saddle is on the board or against the wall. Then with a sharp pointed knife cut the skin from the paws to the point where it has been opened for cleaning, and pull it over the stubby tail and both joints, assisting at the latter places with the knife so that none of the meat adheres to the skin, which can now be easily drawn forward as far as the forelegs; the aid of the knife will again be necessary when the body is reached, where the fat is found. Cut the paws from the forelegs, after which they can be easily drawn out of the skin, which is then pulled over the head, at the same time cutting off the ears. Then take the knife and remove the skin from around the eyes and the front part of the head. The bones of both hind legs are cut off at the point where the opening was made for cleaning the hare, then slit the body as far as the breast, take out the liver, lungs and heart and catch the blood which has gathered in the cavity of the chest, in a dish containing a little vinegar. Cut the breast bone in two and divide the skin of the neck up to the head, pull out the wind-pipe and put the hare on the meat board to cut it up, separating the head from the body at the point where it is joined to the saddle. Finally shorten the ribs on both sides of the hare enough to leave them about 1½ inches long to protect the tender meat of the saddle when it is being roasted. After the hare has been washed in cold water several times, the inner skin should be removed and larding next in order.

Every bit of the rest of the meat together with the lungs and the heart must be washed very carefully, picking out any shot that may happen to remain in the flesh, but need not have the inner skin removed like the piece intended for the roast. If the ragout cannot be gotten ready at once, cover the meat with vinegar so that it will keep for a while longer. The gall bag, which adheres to the liver and is scarcely to be distin-guished from it, must be removed very carefully; fry the liver as fresh as possible (or after it has lain in sweet milk for a few hours) in browned butter, a little flour, bread crumbs and a few crushed juniper berries. It should not be fried for too long a time, otherwise it will lose its juiciness.

157. Roast Hare. Take the entire saddle and the two hind legs, the remainder is used for brown ragout. Wash carefully, remove the inner skin from the saddle, and lard. Sprinkle the hare with salt and put it with its back to the top into an enameled pan with plenty of butter, cover the feet with paper and have a hot oven; the heat from below should not be too intense, because otherwise the gravy will be apt to scorch. As soon as the roast is turned lightly brown, pour over it 1—2 cup-fuls of thick sour or sweet cream. Plenty of butter and cream and frequent basting will make the roast juicy, so that the meat of the legs will be nearly as tender as that of the saddle. A young hare should not roast longer than ½ hour and older ones 1—1¼ hours, and as soon as the meat can be easily pierced with a fork take it out of the oven even if you are not quite ready to serve, because leaving it in the oven will make the meat dry. When the table is ready put the pan back into the oven again for about 10 minutes, bearing in mind to baste and not neglecting to remove the paper when serving the hare. Prepare the gravy according to No. 1.

Instead of using cream, an old hare may be prepared with good buttermilk; after the meat has become lightly brown, gradually add a pint of buttermilk, and in this case the heat from below should be stronger so that the gravy will be brown.

If it is desired that the roast hare should have a slightly sour taste, let it lay in vinegar for 12 hours previously to cooking.

REMARK.—The preparation of a palatable soup from the remnants of a roast hare or its bones is described under B, No. 28.

158. Stewed or Steamed Hare. This is the best method of cooking an old hare; it should first be larded, divided into pieces and very slightly roasted in browned butter, then pour the butter into a stone jar, put in the fat pork slices and spices, on these the meat, sprinkle with salt and pour over the whole a small cupful of sour cream, into which a teaspoonful of flour has been stirred. Then seal the cover of the jar with a strip of paper thinly covered with flour smoothed in water, and simmer in the oven for 2 hours with a slow fire; the meat will become quite tender and juicy and should be served in a hot dish. What remains in the jar should be strained, thinned with meat broth and poured over the meat, which should be brought to the table with boiled potatoes. If the cover of the jar is perfectly tight, it need not be sealed as above directed.

159. Ragout of Hare ("Hasenpfeffer"). Divide the forelegs and the lower part of the body into pieces, wash thoroughly, being careful to rinse off any hair that may adhere to the meat; split the head and wash it together with the heart, liver and lungs. If the meat is to be preserved for a few days prior to cooking, cover with vinegar and turn it daily. It should not be kept so long, however, that it will have an unpleasant odor. When cooking, heat some pork fat in order to economize with your butter, brown some finely chopped onions in it, stirring frequently, and afterwards a heaping tablespoonful of flour, then stir in enough boiling water to make plenty of gravy, taking into consideration that some of it will evaporate, add salt, a few pounded cloves, a good-sized pinch of pepper, a few bay leaves, a large piece of butter and a sufficient quantity of the vinegar in which the meat was pickled. Cover tightly and cook until done, but the meat must not fall to pieces. Then stir in the gravy a piece of sugar, or, according to taste, a glassful of claret. The gravy should have a spicy, sweet-sour taste and be well bound but not too thick. Boiled potatoes are the most appropriate accompaniment.

A nicer method is to first scald the meat and to divide it into pieces of proper size after removing the bones, and then after heating the fat, very slightly roast the pieces together with chopped onions. Instead of the water use boiling meat broth and add claret to the gravy.

160. Roast Haunch of Venison. Pound the meat slightly, remove the skin and lard lengthwise in rows in such a manner that the larding needle is inserted between the lardoons of each preceding row. In this manner the larding will be richer and add greatly to the juiciness of the venison, which is naturally lean and tender. Line the bottom of a pan with fat pork slices which are first roasted. Then put in the meat and roast until the lardoons are yellow, basting frequently with the pork fat; after this cover the roast with pieces of butter or sour cream, salt and roast until done according to taste, a few finely pounded juniper berries can at last be sprinkled over the roast.

Time, from 1—1½—2 hours.

161. Roast Loin of Venison. The loin is very seldomly roasted in one whole piece; fricandeaus can be cut from it and larded and roasted like No. 160—or veal fricandeaus No. 68, not longer than 1 hour. If the roast should be a large one, take either the front or back part of the loin without any bones, pound it slightly, remove the skin, lard, and roast for 1½—2 hours according to the size of the piece and the age of the animal. The rest of the loin will make excellent steaks, or can be utilized for meat balls, etc., while the bones, after being split, will make a palatable brown bouillon. The meat taken from an animal chased to death is absolutely useless and unwholesome.

Venison from older animals, especially pieces from the forejoints, can be pickled for a longer or shorter time in vinegar with onions and spices, after which it is larded; then stew and roast in an oven with a little water, or cook until almost tender and then roast in the oven with butter or fat for ½ hour longer. The addition of sour cream always makes it more tender and more palatable.

162. Ragout of Venison. The best for this purpose are the upper parts of the forejoints, the breast, neck and ribs. These pieces must be carefully examined and washed, especially if they are very bloody and badly torn through shooting. Cut the meat into pieces of proper size, turn them in flour, brown all round in pork fat and butter, pour in some salted boiling water, cover the kettle immediately and a few minutes later, after skimming, add a little lemon peel, some pepper, cloves, a few bay leaves, a few finely sliced onions, a few pickles sliced lengthwise and some vinegar. A glassful of claret is added later on and also a lump of partly browned sugar, but only enough to take off some of the acidity of the vinegar. The gravy must be abundant and of a nice consistency. Serve with roasted or boiled potatoes.

163. Venison Chops ("Mailænder Rehrippchen"). Cut the chops from the saddle and prepare them like veal cutlets; lard on one side and salt. Slice some ripe tomatoes and boil to a thick pulp together with some chopped raw ham, finely chopped onions, salt, pepper and a piece of butter; strain. It must be thick enough so that it can be served in pats; cracker crumbs can be used to make it firmer if necessary. In the meantime boil some macaroni in salted water and mix on the fire with butter and Parmesan cheese; keep in a hot place until the cutlets are done. The cutlets are fried in butter until brown, turn and put them on a hot dish, cook the gravy with flour browned in butter and some Madeira until it binds. The tomato pulp is put into the center of the dish, the macaroni around it in a wreath and on this the cutlets side by side. Serve the gravy in a boat.

164. Stewed Shoulder of Venison. Cut off the shoulder at the second joint of the leg, remove the skin carefully, lard and put the meat into a kettle which has been lined with fat pork slices. Pour claret and meat broth over the venison and add some sweet herbs, a piece of ginger, some toasted bread crust, a bay leaf, and stew in the oven until tender. Then lay it on a hot dish and glaze by holding over it a ladle heated in the fire; surround it with a border of small potato balls and serve. The gravy should be strained and served in a boat.

165. Game Hash. Chop very finely remnants of roast game; grate a few onions, steam them in browned butter, add some flour, 1 spoonful of chopped parsley and whatever gravy is left over, taking off the fat, and cook this to a nice gravy. The chopped meat is thoroughly heated but not cooked in this gravy, then add some lemon juice according to taste, some pepper and salt if necessary. Serve the hash with a border of small potato dumplings and cover it with button onions and egg slices.

166. Game Headcheese. Take the juicy remnants of roast game and chop them finely, and for each 2¼ pounds of meat take 3 ounces of wheat bread soaked and pressed, 2 ounces of boned and chopped anchovy, a little over 2 ounces of grated eschalots browned in butter, a batter of 5 eggs, about 5 ounces of pork fat, 4 ounces of grated Parmesan cheese, salt, pepper and 4 spoonfuls of roast meat gravy. Mix this very carefully and then stir the whites of 3 eggs beaten to a froth through the mass, which is cooked for an hour in a buttered mould. When cold tip out of the mould and serve with a Remoulade sauce.

All game dishes, with the exception of Nos. 158, 159, 162, 165 and 166 are suitable for invalids.

VII. TAME AND WILD FOWL.

167. Points of Difference between Old and Young Fowl and the best Season for purchasing. It is quite essential that every housekeeper be informed as to the points of difference between fowl that are good and those that are not. Of course the greatest safeguard against obtaining unwholesome poultry is to buy it when alive. Poultry in good health has clear shiny eyes, smooth plumage, lively movements and bright red combs. When purchasing killed poultry, first examine the place or wound where they were killed, which should open outwards; the skin should be white, the flesh firm and the bill retain its natural color. If the skin has a bluish tinge or is slimy, and if the bill has changed color, the meat is unwholesome.

The distinguishing points of young fowls are: A white, tender skin, an easily indented breast-bone, a light-colored bill and skin of the legs, and a slender body. With the exception of the turkey, which has a dark skin on the legs when young, all old poultry has a dark, hard, horny skin on the legs. The windpipe of young turkeys and geese can be easily compressed and with geese an infallible indication that they are young consists in the fact that the head of a pin can be inserted into the skin of the breast, which cannot be done with an old goose. Young wild fowls have soft bills with a yellow ring and light colored feet (partridges have yellow feet); the ends of the quills of the plumage of any young fowl are quite soft and filled with blood.

Besides the age and wholesomeness of poultry, the time of the year has some influence regarding its adaptability for cooking. Young—so-called "Spring" chickens—are best from May to November, capons in the Winter months and turkeys from September to March, although the latter are the nicest in September, December and January. Young pigeons are the plumpest in June and July. Fat geese can be obtained from October to January and ducks are in season at the beginning of November. The game laws of the various States of course govern the time when game can be obtained in the market.

168. Preparation of Poultry. According to its kind, poultry should be killed one or more days before it is to be cooked, spring chickens and pigeons the previous evening, old chickens, capons, ducks and turkeys 2 days and geese 3—4 days beforehand. If it should be necessary, however, to cook the smaller varieties of poultry at once, they must be put on the fire immediately after being killed. Poultry intended for roast or brown ragout should be plucked immediately after killing and while the flesh is still warm, but it must be done carefully so as not to injure the skin. After geese and ducks have been drawn and singed, they should be rubbed with warm bran water, or flour and water; to singe the finer varieties of poultry use a spirit lamp; this does not discolor the skin, neither does it impart a smoky taste. If geese are to be kept for a long time they should not be washed after being drawn, at any rate they must be carefully wiped inside and out with a clean cloth until dry.

Fowl for soups or stews should be put into cold water for ¼ hour immediately after killing and they will fully retain their natural white color. Then take by the legs, let the water drip off and hold in seething hot water for a few minutes; if the feathers do not come out easily, repeat, but for young fowls the water must not be too hot, otherwise the entire skin will come off.

Before turkeys or capons are drawn, crush the breast bone by laying the fowl on its back on a cloth, fold a cloth over its breast to prevent the skin from being injured and then carefully crush the breast with a meat pounder; it is better, however, to do this only when the breast bone projects so prominently as to spoil the appearance of the roast, because crushing somewhat lacerates the meat. The breast bone of a tender Spring chicken can be quite easily pressed down with the thumb; it can then be easily taken out, which greatly improves the appearance of the roast.

Then cut off the head and feet, clean inside and out, carefully dry it and wrap in a cloth; it should be laid in a dish until wanted, otherwise the action of the air will injure the whiteness of the skin. When ready to cook wash slightly once more and truss according to its kind. The liver and stomach of small fowls are roasted in the body if they are not intended to be used in the dressing; the filling should be attended to before the fowl is trussed.

a. Turkeys are prepared as follows for a roast: Bend the wings toward the head so that the tips will lay flat on the back, then turn the turkey on its back, draw the head under the left wing so that it will lie beside the breast, and fasten it with a thin wooden skewer, being careful not to injure the meat. Then press the legs upwards towards the head, thus pushing forward the breast, run a wooden skewer through the drumsticks to hold them up closely. Fat pork slices are tied over the breast of the turkey before it is put into the oven.

b. Chickens, capons, Spring chickens and pigeons are prepared in the same way; chickens and pigeons are not larded, capons and Spring chickens are stuffed and larded according to taste. After stuffing, the legs are crossed and passed through the laps of the skin under the breast.

c. The greatest caution is necessary in drawing *geese*, so that the valuable grease is not spoiled by coming in contact with the entrails; after making a large opening under the breast extending to the tail, loosen the skin from the leafy fat. Take this fat with the right hand and loosen it from under the breast bone, to which it adheres, loosen it to the right and left from the ribs and stomach and pull it out in one whole piece, putting it into a covered dish containing cold water. Then carefully take out the liver and separate the gall bag from it; the latter is enclosed in a very thin skin which must not be ruptured. Then take out the stomach, together with the entrails and the crop, which has been loosened from the neck. The entrails must be separated from the fat with great caution, as they break open very easily and are almost always filled, and the fat surrounding them is necessary for the roasting; this, like the leaf fat, should be laid into cold water also, but use a separate dish; the water for both should be renewed daily until the fat is to be used. Cut open the stomach, clean it very carefully and with a sharp knife remove the thick inside skin. Cut off the head and neck of the goose and its feet and wings about

2 inches from the body, using this together with the heart and stomach for giblet soup. Wash the goose thoroughly, dry it inside and out with a clean cloth and hang it into the larder for a few days. The stuffing can be done when ready to roast (or the day previously if preferred) according to the directions already given. The liver is roasted separately.

Geese should be killed and prepared in very cold weather at least 2 days previous to cooking; they can hang in the air for 2—3 weeks, but they are the nicest when cooked a few days after they are killed. The blood, which is indispensable for black giblet dishes, will keep in cold weather for several days when mixed with plenty of vinegar and set uncovered in a cool place.

d. *Ducks* are treated like geese; the skin of the neck is drawn backwards, then the neck is cut off and the skin is forced in the opening; they are sometimes stuffed according to previous directions.

e. *Pheasants, partridges and grouse.* The feet are not cut off as in the case with other kinds of fowl, but they are held for a time in boiling water, after which the skin is taken off and the spurs removed. The tips of the wings are cut away, the liver and stomach are not used; the wings are bent towards the head the same as with other poultry and the legs are turned from the second joint from below in such a manner that the feet point towards the head. Then pass a thin, small, wooden skewer through the drumsticks.

f. *Snipe* are prepared in the same manner with the exception that they are not drawn; the bill is bent over and turned in the breast.

169. To bone Poultry. After the fowl has been plucked, drawn, washed and singed, cut through the skin, down the center of the back and raise the flesh carefully on either side with the point of a sharp knife until the sockets of the wings and the thighs are reached, being careful not to damage the skin. Occasionally the wings and legs are also boned. As a rule boned poultry is filled with forcemeat and this should be done with some care, so as to preserve as much as possible the original form of the bird. When securely trussed and sewed the bird may be either boiled or stewed with a rich gravy, serving it hot with mushrooms, capers, truffles or oysters; or it may be roasted after being boned and forced.

170. Roast Turkey. If the turkey has been killed for a few days or a week before cooking and after it has been prepared as directed in No. 169, bend the joints upwards before cooking, lard if desired wherever there are no fatty portions, or else omit the larding and fill with a forcemeat, (see A, Nos. 27, 28 or 29). Sprinkle with fine salt, line the pan, which should be very clean, with thin fat pork slices and some of the same should be laid on the breast; put in plenty of butter and boiling water and then put the turkey on the fire, cover tightly, and let it cook in a scant broth for 1½ hours, or long enough until the meat is almost tender; the cooking should proceed slowly but uninterruptedly, but the heat must not be too great. Pour the broth into a separate vessel, lay a large piece of butter on the breast of the turkey and bring it into a hot oven, roast until quite tender and of a yellow (not brown) color; frequent basting is very essential and should be carefully attended to. The broth is added gradually; the addition of cream will make the gravy much thicker. When ready to serve stir 2 tablespoonfuls of flour in the pan for a few minutes, adding enough cold water to bind the gravy, stirring in everything that remains in the pan or adheres to it. Add whatever salt is necessary. Serve the turkey on a hot platter, garnishing with a border of thin lemon slices.

A young turkey will require about 1½ hours until it is tender; old birds from 3 hours and upwards.

REMARK.—The heart, stomach, wings, etc., of a turkey, together with some veal, may be cooked to make a good fricassee, to which dumplings, mushrooms, etc., can be added, or else, with a little veal, they make a clear soup.

171. Turkey with Forcemeat. Make a forcemeat of ¾ pound of chopped veal, ¾ pound of streaky pork, also finely chopped, ½ cupful of melted butter, 3 eggs, the whites of 2 eggs beaten to a froth and stirred in at last. Furthermore, 4 ounces of stale wheat bread soaked in cold water and pressed, ½ ounce of sliced mushrooms or, better still, truffles, the turkey liver finely chopped, 4 veal sweetbreads cooked until half done and with the skin removed, salt, nutmeg, capers and finely chopped parsley. This forcemeat is filled into the craw and body of the turkey, after which it is roasted.

A turkey can also be filled with a dressing made of wheat bread, to which dried currants can be added according to taste.

A very fine flavor or aroma can be imparted to the turkey by means of truffles. Get a freshly killed turkey ready for roasting and in the meantime steam about 1¼ pounds of truffles with some sweet herbs, salt, ⅛ pound of very thinly sliced pork fat, and ½ glassful of claret for about 20 minutes. Let the truffles cool, fill the turkey and sew; dress it, cover with fat pork slices (tied over the body) and let it hang for 6 days in a cool place. The turkey is then roasted as usual, but instead of putting cream into the gravy it is flavored with Madeira. Turkey roasted in this manner is the nicest, but it is also very expensive.

When filled in the above manner the turkey will suffice for quite a large party, and can be brought to the table either hot or cold.

172. Turkey in Vienna Style. After the turkey has been prepared for roasting, fill it with the following dressing: Shell and blanch 1⅛ pounds of chestnuts, simmer in meat broth until soft, let them dry and pound finely in a mortar together with some salt, pepper and nutmeg. Stir ¼ pound of butter to a froth, mix with the yolks of 4 eggs, the chestnuts, 3 ounces of cracker crumbs, and also mix a few dozen chestnuts with the forcemeat, which is then filled into the craw and body of the turkey, whereupon the latter is larded and roasted.

The gravy is prepared according to No. 170, but a glassful of Madeira is added at last.

173. Hen-Turkey in a Fricassee Sauce. A hen-turkey is prepared as for a roast; the legs can be inserted as directed in 168, b., then put it on the fire with ¼ pound of fresh butter and a few eschalots, cover tightly and cook slowly until yellow. Add some boiling meat broth or water together with the yellow part only of a lemon peel, nutmeg, and half an hour later plenty of mushrooms, cover tightly and stew in scant broth until done. Have ready some strong meat broth and half an hour before serving put in some flour browned in butter and, according to taste, some sweetbreads (see A, 35), asparagus or cauliflower, cook until tender, but it should not in the least be broken up. Take the fat from the turkey gravy and add to it the cooked gravy, which, like every other fricassee gravy, should be well bound, together with a few lemon slices without the seeds; stir through it the yolks of 2 eggs and then serve the turkey in its own gravy with bread-, sponge- or veal dumplings, which have been brought to a boil in salted water. Send to the table with croutons which are served instead of pastry. If the hen-turkey was not a young one it should be parboiled at least 1 to 3 hours before cooking it entirely done in the fricassee gravy as above described.

174. Roast Capon. The capon is gotten ready like the turkey, well larded and covered with fat pork slices and slowly roasted in butter about 1½ hours, according to age.

175. Stewed Capons with various kinds of Sauces. After the capon is ready for cooking line the bottom of a clean kettle with fat pork slices and put in celery slices, carrots, parsley root, parsnips, eschalots, lean raw ham, coarse spices and salt, then the capon; cover it with fat pork slices, add bouillon and stew slowly until done, but not too soft. Serve with either oyster-, mushroom- or crab sauce. For a small capon take from 1—2 cupfuls of bouillon.

Instead of serving the capon with a sauce, it may be brought to the table in a fine ragout if preferable; or else it may be cut up. Pour over it a truffle sauce and put a border of boiled rice around the edge of the dish.

176. Baked Puffs of Capon Remnants. Entree. Remove skin and sinews from all the remnants and chop the latter very finely. Crack all the bones and boil them thoroughly, cooking with the broth flour lightly browned in butter, add a cupful of thick sweet cream and a trifle of extract of beef, salt and pepper, and cook the whole to a thick, smooth sauce. Mix the chopped meat with the sauce, add the yolks of 4 eggs, 2 heaping tablespoonfuls of fresh butter, stir the frothed whites of the eggs through the mass, fill it into a mould and bake for 30 minutes. Send to the table without any sauce.

177. Roast Spring Chicken. The best method of roasting young spring chickens is to lard them thickly the same as a hare, as is customary in Bremen and Hamburg; it makes them juicier and gives them a fine appearance on the table. They should be roasted in a kettle with a tight cover, and the kettle should be of fitting dimensions—not too large. If the cover is so arranged that embers can be placed upon it, so much the better, if not, the kettle must be put into a hot oven after the chickens have become tender so that they will rapidly become lightly brown on top.

After the chickens have been prepared according to the directions in No. 168, *b.*, sprinkle moderately with fine salt because some salt is contained in the butter, put a piece of butter together with the liver into the body of each chicken and then put them into the kettle closely side by side with a piece of butter; roast with the kettle uncovered at first on a slow fire until lightly brown, then put on the cover and roast until tender, which will take about 1½ hours. According to the requirements of a fine table, poultry must never be roasted too strongly but should have a beautiful golden brown color, and to attain this end it must at first be covered with fat pork slices.

Spring chickens will retain their juiciness if covered on the back and sides with fat pork slices, and are then wrapped in grape leaves which have first been carefullly washed and dried.

A good ¼ hour after they are done, dredge with finely rolled cracker crumbs (especially if the chickens have not been larded) which enhances their appearance and improves the quality of the gravy; in this case, however, the latter should be served without anything else being added. Instead of the cracker crumbs, some thick sweet cream can be added gradually during the last half hour of cooking. The fire should then be stronger and basting more frequent. Care should be exercised that the gravy does not become too brown.

178. Baked Spring Chicken in Gravy. After the chickens have been prepared for cooking they are divided lengthwise and then roasted until tender and juicy as directed in the preceding receipt. Take them out of the pan, brown some flour in the butter remaining in the pan, stir with it some strong beef broth, chopped mushrooms, a little mace, some lemon slices and, perhaps, a glassful of white wine; cook everything together to a thick gravy. After stirring through it the yolks of a few eggs, fill each half of the chicken with the mass, heaping it somewhat in the center, sprinkle with grated Parmesan cheese, put into a pan side by side and bake in the oven for 15 minutes, after which serve without any additions.

179. Baked Spring Chicken in South Germany Style, ("**Backhænel**"). The chickens should be about 6 or 8 weeks old; after plucking and washing, hold them in hot water for a minute, then in cold water, and with a sharp knife divide them lengthwise into two pieces, take out the backbone and cut each half in two sideways, thus dividing the chicken into quarters. Sprinkle with fine salt and turn in flour, dip in eggs beaten with water, then turn in bread crumbs which can be used, if preferred, with Parmesan cheese, and immediately bake in plenty of lard which must not be too hot, to a light brown. 8 pieces can be put into the hot lard at a time, moving the pan gently to prevent scorching. Only about 4 minutes are necessary to bake the chickens nicely and give them a good color.

Drain off the fat by laying the pieces on bread slices until all are done, and lightly brown a handful of fresh parsley, which has been washed and dried in a cloth, in some lard, but to prevent overheating the pan should first be taken from the fire. Then serve the chicken on a warmed platter and garnish with the parsley, which has been sprinkled with a little salt; lay a little bunch of fresh parsley on the meat.

180. A dainty Fricassee of Capons, young Spring Chickens or Pigeons with Crabs. Divide the chicken into quarters and the pigeons lengthwise in two, so that the one kind can be readily distinguished from the other, but this may be done according to preference; capons are not cut up. Put on a medium fire with some salt and plenty of butter, cover tightly and after a time turn them; in ½ hour add some boiling bouillon, a few lemon slices without any seeds, some mace and finely rolled cracker crumbs; cover and cook slowly until tender but the meat should not drop to pieces. During the last 15 minutes of cooking add to the stew the following ingredients, prepared as described under A, 35 to 37: Veal sweetbreads, crabs with dressing, mushrooms, asparagus tips, small sausages and when serving add wheat bread dumplings which have first been cooked in salted water or bouillon, oysters, crab tails and crab butter, stir the yolks of 1 or 2 eggs through the gravy. Send to the table with croutons, which will take the place of pastry.

REMARK.—A plain fricassee is cooked similarly, excepting that the finer ingredients are omitted and boiling water is taken instead of bouillon.

181. Chicken Fricassee in Rice with Crabs. Cook 30—40 crabs, pick the meat out of the tails and claws and pound the shells (not too fine) in a mortar, and stir them on a medium fire until the butter begins to raise and turn red. Pour in some meat broth, boil for ¼ hour and strain through a fine sieve covered with a clean cloth. Boil from ¾—1 pound of scalded rice in bouillon until quite thick, adding some salt. In the meantime cook a chicken fricassee, using for this purpose the crab bouillon made as directed, putting in sweetbreads, small sausages, crab tails and crab dumplings (see under Division O). Put the rice into a deep dish; have a hollow in the center large enough to contain the fricassee without any gravy. Then close the opening with the rice and smooth the surface nicely, pour over it melted butter and brown in the oven to an amber color, basting it occasionally with some of the sauce. The rest of the sauce should be cooked in the meantime, stirring through it either lemon juice or wine and the yolks of eggs or crab butter. When on the table an opening is made in the top of the rice, put in a few spoonfuls of the sauce and pass the rest of the latter in a boat.

182. A fine Ragout of young Spring Chickens and Pigeons. For 12 persons take 4 spring chickens or 8 pigeons. Get them ready as directed in No. 180 and stew them in butter until done. Brown a piece of butter the size of a hen's egg, throw in some flour and also brown it, being careful not to scorch. The browned flour is stirred with the broth in which the birds have been cooked, afterwards adding a brown meat broth (which can be made of extract of beef) together with a sliced lemon, some ground cloves, pepper and salt; as soon as this commences to boil add according to pleasure any of the following: A small handful of either fresh or canned mushrooms cut into small pieces, or 6—8 sliced truffles, ½ pound of veal sweetbreads, ½ pound of large sweet chestnuts, ½ cupful of capers and 1 teaspoonful of pistachios and besides these, dumplings made from ½ pound of finely chopped meat. The preparation of the above ingredients and the length of time they should cook in the ragout is described in Division A; the dumplings are boiled in meat broth or salted water, and put into the ragout at last when it is sent to the table. The gravy should be rather thick and just slightly sour.

183. Spring Chicken in Sauce. Put on the fire in a little boiling water with salt, a good-sized piece of butter and some parsley root, skim thoroughly and cook until not quite tender. Then use the chicken broth to make a caper-, mushroom-, anchovy- or crab sauce, which is put over the chickens when they are served.

184. Fricassee or Ragout with a Rice Border. Put ½ pound of rice on the fire in cold water; as soon as it begins to boil pour off the water, renew with cold water and bring to a boil again. After the last water has been poured off, drench the rice with cold water and cook with 1 pint of meat broth, 1½ tablespoonfuls of fresh butter, salt, a few sliced onions and 12 white peppercorns and cook until tender and thick. Then butter a round mould, press the rice into it, put it into a hot oven for 10 minutes, and then turn it out on a hot dish; however, the rice can be turned out of the mould without first being put into the oven. A dainty ragout, fricassee or chicken hash is then filled into the rice ring; send to the table hot.

185. Chicken Souffle. Cut the chicken very fine and mix it with several spoonfuls of white sauce (see receipt), a piece of butter stirred to a froth, salt, several spoonfuls of grated Parmesan cheese, and the yolks of 2 or 3 eggs, frothing the whites and stirring through the mass. Butter several small souffle cases and fill with the mass, put on a tin and bake them in a medium oven to a light brown. This dish must be eaten immediately. The souffle can be made from chicken remnants if desired.

186. Chicken with Macaroni or Rice. Cook 5 ounces of macaroni in salted water and cool in cold water, butter a smooth pudding mould, in the center of it arrange a star of mushrooms, winding the macaroni around and about the star, brush with the yolks of eggs, cover thickly with forcemeat A, No. 24, and put diced remnants of chickens, veal sweetbreads, ox tongue, truffles, mushrooms, crab tails and small dumplings into the mould in layers; fill around the edge of the mould thickly with the macaroni, also brushed with egg, and then pour a very thick crab- or Bechamel sauce over the contents of the dish, put on another layer of the forcemeat, and finally cover the surface closely with the macaroni. Cook in a double kettle for an hour, turning out of the mould and serve with the remainder of the crab- or Bechamel sauce. Rice may be substituted for the macaroni, and various kinds of the finer varieties of vegetables can be used instead of the sweetbreads, etc.

187. Chicken with Pearl Barley. Put a nicely prepared chicken on the fire in some salted water as for a soup, using less water, however, (see chicken soup, B, No. 18,) skim well, add a piece of butter and a little mace and cook slowly under a tight cover; often chickens are fat enough so that the butter is unnecessary. In the meantime cook 3 ounces of pearl barley with chicken broth until quite tender—it should at last be quite thin enough to be eaten with a spoon instead of a fork; the chicken broth is not put in at once, but is added gradually. The chicken is then placed whole, or, if preferred, divided into pieces, into the bottom of a round dish with the pearl barley surrounding the meat. Browned butter may be put over this dish, but it is not absolutely necessary.

188. Chickens in Rice. Boil the chickens in salted water, skim and cook with a large piece of butter until done. Scald the rice, add the chicken broth gradually and cook slowly until the rice is quite tender but not pulpy; ½ hour before it is tender add, according to taste, some nicely washed raisins to the rice and gradually fill in the remaining broth to prevent the rice from becoming too thick. Cut up the chickens, keep them hot and put them into the middle of the dish, surround with the rice and garnish with small dumplings according to taste.

189. Chickens with Tomatoes. Cut up two spring chickens before they are cooked, bone them and after smashing the bones fry them with the wings and drumsticks in 4 spoonfuls of the best olive oil. Then add 3 chopped onions, a bunch of parsley and salt, pepper and the breast pieces, furthermore 10 sliced tomatoes and 1 small cupful of strong bouillon, and stew all together until tender. Arrange the meat with a rice border, strain the gravy, thicken if necessary and pour it over the meat.

190. Roasted young Pigeons should be killed a day or two before cooking, plucked and drawn, but must not be exposed to the air after being plucked. Fill with forcemeat A, No. 26, if desired, put on a medium fire in a vessel having a tight fitting cover, with plenty of good butter and a few grains of salt (they are easily oversalted); roast slowly but continuously until they are quite tender. Pigeons should roast to a yellow color only and the gravy must not in the least be too dark.

Great care in preparing pigeons is particularly necessary when they are intended for the sickroom. When ready to serve, a few fresh chopped juniper berries (not ground or pounded) may be put into the butter and a small spoonful of sweet cream be added during the roasting; however, both are matters of taste, the main point is that the color be light and the meat tender, especially if for invalids.

191. Young Pigeons with Asparagus Tips. After preparing the pigeons scald them for a minute in seething hot water, cool in fresh water and salt them. Then fry in butter until yellow all over, add 1 onion, 1 carrot, parsley, and after dredging some flour over the pigeons, a cupful of meat broth; then stew the pigeons until tender. Put them where they will remain hot, strain the gravy and thicken it, if necessary, with some bread crumbs, and stir the yolks of 4 eggs through it, add lemon juice, a little pepper and fine sugar; have ready asparagus tips cooked in salted water, mix them through the gravy, put into the center of a deep dish and arrange over it the pigeons divided into halves.

192. Roast Duck. Ducks can be roasted with or without filling. They are filled with currants and quartered apples, or else with the following dressing which is preferable: Chop the heart, lungs, liver and stomach (which must have the skin removed) very finely, add a piece of butter the size of half an egg, 2 eggs, about 5 ounces of wheat bread soaked in cold water and then well pressed, nutmeg and salt.

In England a filling is made consisting of a mixture of onions stewed in butter, bread crumbs, sage and a little salt. The forcemeats used for filling turkeys are also well adapted for ducks.

In Saxony a sprig of mugwort is simply placed in the duck; in Bavaria a filling consisting of potatoes and pork sausages is considered good. It is made of peeled and diced boiled potatoes and the sausages are fried and sliced; the diced potatoes are stewed until done with sliced onions, parsley, pepper and nutmeg, shaking frequently, then mixed with the sausage slices and filled into the duck.

Rub the duck with some salt, put it on the fire with plenty of butter and a little water, cover tightly and roast slowly for 2—2½ hours according to the age of the duck, if necessary occasionally adding a dash of boiling water along the side of the vessel. Basting must not be neglected. As soon as the duck is tender prepare the sauce as directed for turkey.

193. Ducks stewed with Onions. Boil the duck in salted water and skim; add ½ soupplateful of sliced onions, some wheat bread and cloves, cook all together until tender. Strain the gravy, cook it with lemon slices and spread it over the duck.

194. Ducks with Claret. The duck should be lightly roasted in butter with a few sliced onions, being careful not to get it too brown, otherwise the butter will be apt to lose its flavor. Then add boiling water, some lemon peel, cloves, cardamon seeds and salt, afterwards some flour lightly rubbed in butter, dark meat broth, and when ready to serve, a large glassful of claret and a few lemon slices. The gravy must have a brownish color and be of a good consistency. Truffles cooked in the gravy improve the dish.

195. Ducks a la Française. Chop the liver with some pork fat and eschalots, and make up into a force-meat with some wheat bread soaked in water and pressed, 2 eggs, nutmeg and salt, fill into the duck and sew. Line the bottom of the kettle with butter or fresh bacon and roast the duck in it to a yellow color. Add a handful of parsley, 3 or 4 whole onions and when the broth is all cooked away, some carrots. Pour in 1 pint of water or weak bouillon, and cook the duck in this until light brown in color and well done. Stir through the gravy a little browned flour, boiling water, a trifle of vinegar and, according to taste, a piece of sugar, and stew the duck in this for a few minutes longer.

196. Ducks with Dumplings. Line a kettle with a number of pork fat slices, put in the duck, and add peppercorns, cloves, 2—3 bay leaves and a few onions. Cover the kettle tightly and stew the duck on a medium fire, turning it once. After half an hour, add some lemon peel in small pieces and enough meat broth so that the duck can cook in it until tender. Have ready ⅓ of the quantity of forcemeat A, No. 26, add to it some ground cloves and the finely chopped liver, heart and stomach of the duck; roll up into little dumplings. Then thicken the gravy with flour lightly browned in butter, add a few lemon slices and some wine, and stew the duck in this for a little while longer. During this time boil the dumplings in bouillon or salted water, garnish the duck with them when served, strain the gravy through a fine sieve, adding to it the mushrooms cooked until white; the gravy is poured over the duck.

197. Stewed Duck in a Brown Gravy. For a full grown young duck take 1 pint of water, a piece of butter the size of an egg, 6 eschalots, the necessary salt, cover tightly and stew slowly until tender so that the gravy will not be too scant. When the duck is done, stir with it a spoonful of flour browned in butter, ½—1 glassful of wine, 4—6 ground cloves, a little sugar, and stir the duck in this for a little while longer.

198. Ducks with New Turnips. Prepare the ducks as directed in No. 196. Peel small new turnips, cut them into pieces of uniform size, boil in hot water, and after cooling them in fresh water, steam them with butter, a little meat broth, salt and some sugar until tender, but they should not become too soft. Keep the ducks in a hot place, take the fat from the gravy, thicken the latter with flour browned in butter, mix with a cupful of thick, sweet cream and then put part of the gravy with the turnips. Cut up the ducks, heat them in the gravy and serve them with the turnips arranged around the meat as a garnish. Bring to the table with roasted potatoes.

199. Jellied Ducks. (See directions in Division M.)

200. Wild Ducks are prepared for cooking the same as tame ducks, wrapped in slices of pork fat and roasted without filling in a pan with butter and pork fat slices until juicy and tender; thick cream may be added if desired.

201. Wild Ducks. The best methods of cooking according to the age, etc., of the duck are the same as directed for a wild goose under No. 209. If intended for a roast, rub it with fine salt and pepper, wrap in fat pork slices and roast with butter for 1 hour in the oven, basting frequently; or else put on the fire with plenty of butter and nice kidney suet, 2 bay leaves, 2 lemon slices and 8 juniper berries; cover tightly. As soon as the duck is yellow on both sides pour over it a very little boiling water and then roast slowly until tender and of a light brown color. The addition of thick cream will be found an improvement. Stir up the gravy with some cold water and cook it with a little extract of beef and a glassful of claret and serve. An old wild duck should be cooked like brown ragout of hare ("Hasenpfeffer"), using plenty of onions, but no sugar.

202. Roast Goose. After the goose has been gotten ready as directed under D, VII, No. 168, *c.*, fill the body with quartered apples, which can be mixed with raisins or dried currants, or else with diced toasted bread; sometimes the filling consists of boiled chestnuts or small potatoes and salt, after sewing the opening put the goose into the pan with salt, pour in a pint of water, cover tightly and then roast until tender; as soon as this point has been reached, take off the cover and proceed with the roasting and baste, adding boiling water from time to time. To make the crust nicely crisp quickly pour a few spoonfuls of cold water over the skin about half an hour before the roast is done. The goose as well as the gravy must have a light brown color. When serving, be sure to remove the thread and finish the gravy as directed for roast turkey. Very young geese are roasted without water but with plenty of butter because usually they have very little fat. Small-sized geese, if young, require about 1 hour for roasting, large-sized ones from 2—2½ hours.

For a very fine roast the following filling is considered very superior. Chop the liver of the goose together with 9 ounces each of calf's liver, veal and pork very fine, strain, add about 12 ounces of shredded pork fat, a little thyme, salt, pepper, the yolks of 2 eggs and some soaked and pressed wheat bread, stirring all of this to a smooth dressing.

203. Goose in Jelly. See Division M.

204. Fried Goose Liver. Lay the liver into water and milk for a few hours; dry it and cut into slices, or, if very small, leave it whole, salt, turn in egg and bread crumbs, and then fry in butter—if sliced fry for 2 minutes, and if whole for 10 minutes. Serve with a border of steamed apple slices, or cover it with a truffle or Madeira sauce; in the latter case it need not be turned in the egg and bread crumbs.

205. Goose Giblets in Westphalian Style. For this dish take everything that is not wanted for the roast: neck, wings, liver, heart, stomach and, perhaps, the legs; the latter are laid in hot water and skinned. The neck as well as the rest is divided into several pieces. If the meat is not to be used at once, set it aside in some vinegar. When ready to cook put it on the fire with not too much salted water, adding a few onions, 4 bay leaves, pepper and cloves and, according to taste, 2 handfuls of scalded prunes; cook until done. Brown flour in butter, being careful not to scorch, stir it through some of the broth and add to the giblets, together with some vinegar and a piece of sugar to impart a sweet-sour taste to the gravy. In some parts of Germany it is customary to use grated honey cake instead of the browned flour, to bind the gravy. If any of the blood of the goose has been caught this is cooked with the giblets, greatly improving the color and flavor of the dish, but in such case very little flour must be used because the gravy is sufficiently thickened by the blood. The gravy should be plentiful, nicely thick and have a spicy and tart flavor. Potatoes are a proper accompaniment.

If the giblets should be insufficient in quantity, add a small piece of diced pork fat; peeled and sliced pears can be cooked with them and if there should not be enough blood to properly thicken the gravy, use some flour rubbed in butter. In Mecklenburg bread dumplings previously cooked in salted water are added to the dish.

REMARK.— When killing the goose the blood may be caught and stirred with vinegar, and it will keep in the Winter from three days to a week if the weather is cold enough and it is set aside in a cool place; without the vinegar, however, it would spoil very soon.

206. Goose Giblets are cooked in a variety of ways in different parts of Europe. According to the Stettin receipt, the meat is put on the fire in salted water as directed in No. 205 and cooked in a rather scant broth until done. After this some butter is browned, a few finely chopped onions and also some flour are lightly browned in it, the whole stirred with some broth and added to the giblets, sharply seasoned with pepper and thyme and cooked for a few minutes longer in the gravy.

In North Germany apples and dried currants are preferred cooked with the giblets, omitting the blood; in Brandenburg finely sliced new turnips and potatoes are added; in Pommerania, kohlrabi, celery root, carrots and parsley roots are cooked with the broth of the giblets, which are also seasoned with parsley; and in Russia a mixture of the giblets with steamed dried fruit of various kinds, such as pears, apples, plums and cherries is considered a delicacy. No blood is used in cooking giblets according to any of these modes.

207. Stuffed Goose Neck. This makes an excellent dish for the supper table and is prepared as follows: Take the thick outer skin of the neck, rub it inside and out until very clean and fill it two-thirds full with the forcemeat A, No. 24, or else with a dressing made of the finely chopped liver, stomach and heart of the goose, mushrooms, fresh bacon, pork, a little majoram, eggs and bread crumbs. Sew the neck at both ends, fry in goose oil until done, press it between two flat weights and send to the table in slices. Instead of frying the neck it can also be cooked in meat broth mixed with some white wine.

208. Brown and White Ragout of Goose. The whole goose is cut into pieces and cooked until tender in salted water with the heart, stomach, liver, a few onions, 3 bay leaves, ½ of a sliced lemon—removing the seeds and white inner skin—and a pinch of fine pepper. If it is to be a brown ragout, add some ground cloves, flour browned in butter, vinegar, a small piece of sugar and at last the blood of the goose. If the ragout is to be white, omit the vinegar, blood and sugar, and instead of these add lightly browned flour, a few lemon slices and ground nutmeg, and the yolk of an egg is stirred through the gravy.

209. Wild Goose. An old wild goose is decidedly tougher than an old tame one, consequently young wild geese only are fit for roasting. Otherwise cut into small pieces as directed in D, VII, No. 168, c., and let it stand for a week in a pickle of boiled vinegar, bay leaves and cloves, turning it daily. Proceed as with ragout of hare ("Hasenpfeffer"), omitting the sugar.

For roasting, the goose is rubbed inside and out with salt, pepper and mace and roasted like a tame goose—without stuffing, however—in butter and kidney suet, until yellow and tender. ½ cupful of cream added during the last half hour of cooking improves the gravy.

210. Roast Pheasant. The pheasant should be hung in its plumage for 2 or 3 days before cooking. After the pheasant is plucked, singe over burning spirits and

Mutton — 𝕳𝖆𝖒𝖒𝖊𝖑.

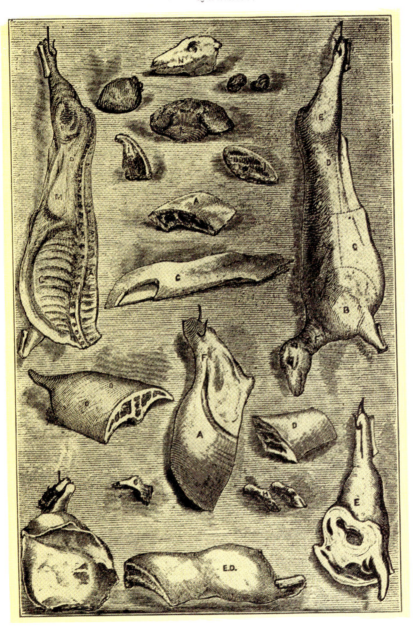

A Chops—Hals; B Shoulder—Schulter; C Breast—Brust; D Loin—Lende; DD Saddle—Rücken; E Leg—Keule; F Neck—Das Dünne Stück am Ende des Halses; G Tongue—Zunge; H Feet—Füsze; I Chop—Lendenrippchen; J Shoulder Chops—Rundes Rippenstück; K Liver—Leber; L Heart—Herz; M Kidney—**Niere**; **N** Head—Kopf; ED Hindquarter—Schenkel.

Pork — Schwein.

A Hind loin—Hintere Lende; B Foreloin—Vordere Lende; C Shoulder Butt—
Rippenstück; D Shoulder—Blatt; E Ham—Schinken; F Bacon—Bauchstück; G
Feet—Füsze; H Heart—Herz; J Lung—Lunge; K Liver—Leber; L Kidney—
Niere; M Head—Kopf; N Tongue—Zunge.

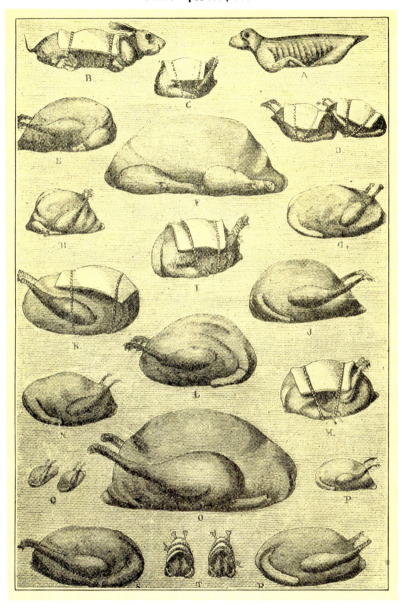

A Rabbit—Kaninchen; B Hare—Hase; C Grouse—Haselhuhn; D Quail—Wach-
tel; E White grouse—Schneehuhn; F Goose—Gans; G Teal—Kriechente; H
Woodcock—Waldschnepfe; I Partridge—Rebhuhn; J Grouse—Birkhuhn; K Pheas-
ant—Fasan; L Mountain cock—Auerhahn; M White grouse—Schneehuhn; N
Widgeon—Pfeifente; O Turkey—Truthahn; P Snipe—Becassine; Q Lark—Lerche;
R Duck—Ente; S Wild duck—Wilde Ente; T Pigeon—Taube.

Poultry — Geflügel.

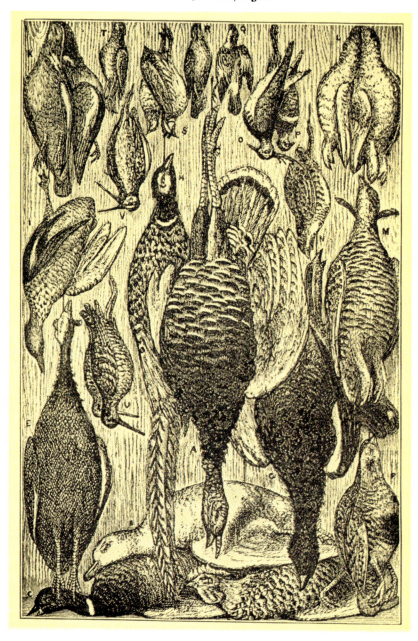

A Turkey—Truthahn; B Goose—Gans; C Duck—Ente; D Hen—Huhn; E Guinea-hen—Perlhuhn; F Partridge—Rebhuhn; G Mountain cock—Auerhahn; H Pheasant—Fasan; I Teal—Kreichente; K Wild Pigeon—Wild Taube; L White grouse—Schneehuhn; M Prairie Chicken—Prairiehuhn; N Land-rail—Wachtelkönig; O Green Plover—Grüner Brachvogel; P Gold Plover—Goldbrachvogel; Q Wheat Bird—Weizenvogel; R Ortolan—Ortolan; S Quail—Wachtel; T Lark—Lerche; U Snipe—Landschnepfe; V Snipe—Becassine.

prepare otherwise as usual with fowls, draw, and dry inside carefully with a cloth, sprinkle with fine salt and tie a slice of pork fat over the breast. Roast the pheasant in plenty of butter for 1—1½ hours until juicy, tender and of a golden brown color.

Partially take up all of the fat that remains in the pan, then stir into the latter browned flour and cold bouillon, cook to a nice gravy which is served in a boat. The most fitting compot to serve with the pheasant is one of peaches or apricots; a celery salad or water cresses are also appropriate accompaniments.

211. Pheasants with Sourkrout. Take for this dish older birds which are not so well adapted for roasting, prepare them as for a roast, wrap in pork slices and then roast in butter until about half done. In the meantime cook about as much sourkrout as is necessary (about a quart for 2 pheasants) in an enameled stew pan, together with a cupful of onions lightly browned in butter, 2 cupfuls of strong meat broth and ½ bottle of white wine; put in both of the pheasants and let all stew together slowly until done; cut up the pheasants, cook a few spoonfuls of dark meat broth through the sourkrout; serve.

212. Pheasants with Macaroni. This is an excellent dish for which the remnants of pheasants can be utilized. All of the skin is removed from the meat and the latter cut into little pieces, crush the bones and boil them slowly for an hour with a pint of water; strain the broth and thicken it with flour browned in butter, season with ¼ teaspoonful of extract of beef, ½ teaspoonful of mushroom catsup, a glassful of sherry, pepper and salt. Heat, but do not cook, the meat in this thick gravy. In the meantime cook about 6 ounces of broken macaroni in salted water, mix butter, a little bouillon and grated Parmesan cheese through the macaroni. Serve immediately, filling the meat with the gravy into the center of the dish, placing the macaroni around it in a border.

213. Partridges, Grouse or Prairie Chickens are prepared for roasting like other fowl and sprinkled with fine salt. Tie a thin slice of pork fat over the breast of the bird and roast it either on the spit or else in the

oven with plenty of butter and a little water. Cover
tightly and roast for ½—1 hour with great care, basting
frequently and towards the last occasionally adding a
spoonful of sweet or sour cream. When ready to serve,
all that remains in the pan is loosened and stirred up
with some cold water, a teaspoonful of rice flour and a
little extract of beef, so as to bind the gravy somewhat,
which is then finished with perhaps the addition of a
little salt.

A very dainty accompaniment to a roast of this
kind is made as follows: Mince the heart and liver of
the bird very fine, mix with them a few crushed juniper
berries and stew for a few minutes in butter shortly
before the meat is done. Toast a number of neatly
trimmed slices of bread, spread with the paste prepared
as above directed and surround the roasted birds with
them. These patties must be ready at the same moment the meat is to be sent to the table.

214. Partridges in Saxony Style. After preparing
the partridges as directed in the preceding receipt, lard
the breast, sprinkle with salt, lay a piece of pork fat
over it and wrap two clean grape leaves around each
bird; put the partridges into hot butter, cover and
roast slowly, occasionally adding a little water. After
about ½ hour put sour cream (a spoonful at a time)
over them and also bread or cracker crumbs and at the
very last some melted butter. The grape leaves and
pork fat, which will drop off during the roasting, are
served separately.

215. Cold Prairie Chickens with Gravy. Quarter
the chickens, arrange them neatly in a dish and cover
with the following sauce: 3—4 tablespoonfuls of good
olive oil, 2—3 tablespoonfuls of white calf's foot jelly,
2 tablespoonfuls of best vinegar, very finely minced
eschalots, a trifle of estragon, pepper and salt, stir
together until bound to a thick sauce.

216. Roast Snipe. After the snipe is prepared for
roasting as directed in 168, f., cover the breast with
thin slices of pork fat and turn the head so that the bill
will point upwards. Put on the fire in cold butter,
cover and let them roast slowly for 1—1½ hours. Put
a number of thin slices of toasted wheat bread under

the snipe to catch everything dropping from the inside. This toast ("Schnepfenbrot") is served in a hot dish, laying the birds on it. The snipe can also be drawn before roasting; remove the stomach and then chop the trail very finely with some pork fat, an eschalot, a trifle of lemon peel, some wheat bread soaked in cold water and pressed, salt and pepper. Mix with beaten egg and spread on the toast, which is then fried in lard until crisp and juicy. Send the snipe to the table surrounded with the toast, cover with the gravy and lay a number of lemon pieces onto the dish.

217. Salmi of Snipe, Grouse and Wild Duck. Line the bottom of a kettle with a few slices of raw ham, put the birds on them, add a little salt, a few carrots, a few sliced eschalots or onions, and butter; cover tightly and roast until yellow, pour in some meat broth and keep on the stove until quite tender. Then with a sharp knife divide the birds into small neat pieces; all that cannot be cut up is ground in a mortar, together with the livers and the ham. Boil in the broth in which the birds have been cooked, put on a strainer and pour over it a little of the meat broth, but do not stir, in order to prevent any bone splinters from passing through the sieve. Add some chopped eschalots and a pinch of pepper and bring to a boil once with the meat. The gravy for a salmi should really receive its consistency from the strained meat only, but when necessary, browned flour or bouillon jelly can be added, or instead of both of these toast a piece of wheat bread, roll finely and add to the gravy. If the salmi is to be particularly dainty mix a little Madeira or claret through the gravy, adding truffles and mushrooms at the last.

218. Curried Meats. In the East Indies, curries are usually made of fowl or fish, but they are also very good when made from any other kind of meat. Roasted and boiled meats are quite well adapted for curries, indeed many prefer a curry made from a roast, or boiled meat remnants, instead of having them warmed over or made into meat balls.

It is undeniable that spices are under certain conditions beneficial, improve the appetite and aid digestion. They should never be used to excess, however, and the consent of the physician should first be obtained before spicing the food of sick or debilitated persons. In making curries fresh milk is used as a substitute for cocoanut milk. The meat for the curry, whether raw or already cooked, should always simmer very slowly so that it will become very tender. A curry must never be cooked on a quick fire and is always eaten with boiled rice, which renders the sharpness of the spicing more agreeable to the palate.

For a curry of fowls, divide Spring chickens or pigeons into small pieces as for fricassee and turn them slightly in flour. Brown a piece of butter in a kettle, put in the meat and roast rapidly until light brown, frequently shaking the kettle; take out the meat with a skimmer and brown a few sliced onions in the butter until done, stirring them frequently. Then put the meat back into the kettle with the onions, move the kettle from over the fire and add enough sweet milk or a good bouillon made of extract of beef to cover the meat; cover the kettle tightly and simmer very slowly for at least 1 hour, but during this time stirring should be frequently attended to. After the elapse of half an hour smooth 2 teaspoonfuls of curry powder with sweet milk. Mix it through the meat, salt and simmer for 15 minutes longer. At the last, boil for 1 or 2 chickens about ¼ pound of rice in weakly salted boiling water, and put it on the colander to drain. The rice should not be lumpy and the grains should remain whole. Put the rice around the sides of a warmed dish and fill the curry into the opening in the center. Serve.

A little flavoring of lemon juice can be added according to taste. The gravy for the curry should not be thin.

219. Partridge Cutlets for Invalids. Take from the partridge all of the meat that is free from sinews, pound it finely and mix with it salt and a spoonful of sweet cream. Crush the bones and fry them slightly in butter, excepting the wings and drumsticks which are used for the cutlets, and cook them with celery or parsley root and salt. Mould the minced meat into the form of cutlets and put a bone into each one; each partridge will make 4 cutlets, which are turned in egg and bread crumbs and fried in butter until done. Stir what remains in the pan with flour browned in butter, some of the bone broth, Madeira and sweet herbs to a gravy for the cutlets.

220. Minced Remnants of Poultry for Invalids. Take the best meat from the remnants of any kind of fowl or poultry, mince very fine, stew in butter for a few moments with a little flour, a trifle of extract of beef and 3 spoonfuls of thick sweet cream until it is thoroughly hot; serve immediately.

Besides the above, nearly all dishes of fowl or poultry are nutritious and well adapted for invalids, with the exception of fat ducks or geese; Nos. 172, 173, 175, 176, 179, 183, 184, 187, 189 and 209 are especially recommended for the sick room.

E.—Meat and Game Pies, etc.

I. LARGE MEAT PIES.

1. General Directions. The dough must be adapted to the kind of pie that is to be made. Chicken-, pigeon-, lamb- or veal pies, for which the meat has been fricasseed, are made with a fine puff paste or a good butter crust; the latter should be used if the meat is to be cooked until done in the pie. The butter crust is used for hare or venison pies; a water crust, which, of course, is not to be eaten, can also be made.

Meat pies that are not intended to be served at once after they are ready, must not be seasoned with lemon juice or vinegar, and majoram must be put into fine dishes with great caution, if at all.

Always serve a good jelly with cold meat pies of every description, excepting with goose liver patties.

2. Goose Liver Patties ("Strassburger Gænseleber-Pastete") No. 1. Divide 6 large goose livers into halves, cutting them in two where they are joined. Remove the yellow spot where the gall bag was attached and wash the livers with sweet milk; *water must not touch them.* Peel some truffles, cut them into pieces about the length of the little finger and lard eight of the pieces of liver with them. Slice the remaining livers and pound very finely, season with a tablespoonful of finely sliced eschalots stewed in butter, double this quantity of finely sliced truffles, fine salt, a little fine white pepper, nutmeg, and pound all this very fine. During the pounding, however, gradually add 2 pounds of fresh bacon which has previously been boiled for an hour and sliced and pounded after cooling; then pass the whole through a sieve. Line a goose liver tureen with thin pork fat slices, put in a layer of the forcemeat, then some of the whole pieces of liver sprinkled with salt and white pepper, another layer of forcemeat, some more of the liver and so on until the tureen is filled; a layer of the forcemeat must be on top. Cover the top with pork fat slices and put the lid on the tureen; if it does not close tightly seal it with strips of paper, using as a paste a little flour and water, put into the oven and bake slowly for about 2 hours. For a smaller pie 1½ hours will perhaps be sufficient. As it sometimes happens that fat will drip from the tureen, it should at first be set on an old plate and afterwards on a low tripod.

Goose liver patties can be made as large or as small as desired; a nice one can be made from 2 or 3 livers, which are then divided into smaller pieces.

The two following receipts are also according to the Strassburg formula and many prefer them to the preceding one, because the patties are not so rich and consequently more wholesome.

3. Goose Liver Patties, No. 2. Remove every bit of skin from 3 pounds of veal and then chop the latter very finely with a handful of eschalots, the thin peel of a lemon (yellow part only), 10—12 freshened anchovies and a handful of chopped capers; add thereto a handful of whole capers, a handful of grated wheat bread, pounded spices the same as in the preceding receipt and enough white wine to make a smooth dough. Take ¾ of a pound of butter, 4 eggs, salt, water, and enough flour to make a stiff dough, knead it thoroughly: butter an appropriate mould, sprinkle with grated bread, roll the dough, line the mould with it so that it will extend somewhat over the edges.

Sprinkle the dough with grated wheat bread, put in a layer of forcemeat, then a layer of the truffles cooked with spices in wine, a layer of sliced goose livers, another layer of forcemeat, truffles, goose livers, and so on until the mould is filled, the last layer must consist of forcemeat. The contents are then entirely covered with pork fat slices and over these place strips of dough to bind the whole together; then make a cover of dough with a knob in the center; the dough extending over the mould is turned inwards onto the cover and the edges then pressed together. Bake in the oven until light brown, which will take about 2 hours. When cold, turn out of the mould. Take 2 goose livers for this patty.

4. Goose Liver Patties, No. 3. The whiter and fatter the liver the better will be the patty. For a patty of medium size take 2 large goose livers that have lain in sweet milk for half a day, 1 pound of lean pork, 1 pound of leaf lard and 1 pound of truffles. Cut the livers into pieces, clean the truffles as already directed, sprinkle them with salt and white pepper and insert the truffles into the liver. Make a forcemeat of the pork, leaf lard, fragments of the liver all minced very finely and seasoned with pepper and salt, pass through a sieve, salt the livers and then pack them into a pastry mould in layers, alternately with truffles and the forcemeat. Bake for 2—2½ hours in a medium hot oven; if one wishes to keep the patty for any length of time pour over it melted clear lard.

Turned Meat Pies (Timbale). NOTE.—Timbales are a variety of hot meat pies now very frequently prepared. They are cooked in a cylindrical double bottom mould made of tin; after the pie is done it is turned out of the mould and takes its name (timbale—drum) from its shape; serve as a hot entree before the roast.

Small timbales are made in the same manner in little tin forms, but are then served after the soup (see No. 39). The filling for timbales is made in a variety of ways, but a good, firm chicken-, veal- or wild fowl forcemeat is always necessary, as well as a very fine ragout of veal sweetbreads, fowls, goose livers or fish with mushrooms, truffles or small dumplings; the ragout should be made with a strong, well cooked and thick brown or white gravy. The timbales will drop to pieces immediately if the forcemeat is too thin or if the ragout gravy is not well bound.

Sometimes the outer wall or ring of a timbale consists of boiled rice, macaroni or a fine crust; it is occasionally sent to the table sweetened.

5. Timbale of Grouse. Pluck 3 grouse, singe over burning spirits, draw, and clean inside and out with flour and water. Cut off the drumsticks, fry the breasts very juicy in butter, allow them to cool and then cover with buttered paper.

Butter the timbale mould very carefully, and line the sides and bottom with the breasts of the grouse, sliced cold, with truffles between. The slices will adhere to the buttered mould if pressed against it slightly. Spread over this lining (covering the bottom first and then the sides), three quarters of the forcemeat about ½ inch thick, taking care to fill all intervening spaces, and then put in the ragout, cover to the thickness of ¾—1 inch with the rest of the forcemeat, with a sheet of buttered paper on top. An hour before serving the timbale is put into the oven in boiling water, and shortly before sending it to the table turn it out onto a round dish. The mould is not taken off at once, but should remain about 1 minute longer after which it is cautiously lifted out; pour some of the gravy over the timbale, and serve the remainder in a boat. Frequently the forcemeat contains all of the meat of the birds and the mould is lined with sliced truffles only, then with the forcemeat, with the ragout in the center of the dish. Or the roasted breasts of the grouse are slightly warmed and laid on the timbale after the latter is ready to send to the table.

The forcemeat is made of two parts of meat, consisting of the flesh from the chicken's drumsticks, carefully skinned, with the sinews taken out and mixed with veal, one part of fat and one part of crust. The fat used for a fine forcemeat is taken from a fat calf, and is that part from which the udder finally develops; when not obtainable, substitute for it veal kidney suet or good pork fat.

To make the crust take 1 pint of water and 1 teaspoonful of butter. As soon as this begins to boil, dredge in enough flour, constantly stirring, to make a thick dough, which is then taken out of the kettle. Partially dry it on a slow fire, put it on a plate, cover with buttered paper and let it cool. The meat and fat for the forcemeat is chopped very finely, each separately, then pound together in a mortar, gradually stir into it the crust together with 2 whole eggs and the yolks of 2 eggs, season with salt and nutmeg and pass through a sieve. This forcemeat is very nice and will keep for a long time.

The ragout is made of well prepared sweetbreads which have been cooked in bouillon. Brown 2 table-spoonfuls of flour in butter, make a sauce of water, extract of beef and 1 large glassful of Madeira and cook in it the sweetbreads cut into slices, sliced truffles and mushrooms, salt, and stir through it the yolks of 2 eggs. Pound and crush the remnants and bones of the birds and cook with the scrapings of the roast in the pan, some water and extract of beef, take off the fat and then cook with Madeira and flour browned in butter to a thickish gravy; then salt and strain. When the timbale is on the dish pour over it a little of the sauce, and serve the remainder in a boat. Or else the timbale is sent to the table without any gravy and the extract from the bones used for the ragout sauce.

6. Timbale of Macaroni and Loin of Venison. Take ½ pound of macaroni and break them up into small pieces of uniform size. Cook for ½ hour in salted water, drain, mix with 2 tablespoonfuls of melted butter and 4 tablespoonfuls of grated Parmesan cheese, butter the timbale mould carefully and line it all over thickly with the macaroni. Make a veal forcemeat, taking about ½ pound of clear veal without any sinews, 3 ounces of fresh bacon, 5 eggs, salt, pepper, grated nutmeg and chopped herbs, using the crust described in the preceding receipt. Blanch a few veal sweetbreads, cut them up and fry slightly in butter, slice ½ of a pickled tongue, stew some mushrooms and neatly lard a tenderloin of beef; the latter is then cut into slices ½ inch thick, and spread over them a mixture of about 3 heaping table-spoonfuls of butter stirred with a pinch of salt and cayenne pepper, 2 teaspoonfuls of chopped parsley and the juice of a lemon, all passed through a sieve together; fry the meat on both sides in butter. Then cover the macaroni in the mould with the forcemeat, put in all of the other ingredients that have been prepared, cover with a layer of the forcemeat and finally put on a thick layer of the macaroni and then bake the timbale in the oven for 1½ hours. Turn the timbale out of the mould, pour over it a thick Madeira sauce (see Division R) and serve the other gravy in a boat.

7. Timbale with Ragout. Butter a round timbale mould, dust it with finely grated wheat bread, beat 4 eggs in lukewarm butter with salt and grated Parmesan cheese to a thickish but liquid mass, pour into the mould to cover all around and then sprinkle again with grated bread. Have ready a pound of rice that has been washed, scalded and then cooked in bouillon with a piece of butter, salt and some mace until tender and firm, and afterwards mixed with 2 tablespoonfuls of meat gravy and 6 spoonfuls of grated Parmesan cheese. A ragout consisting of mushrooms, fowl livers, veal sweetbreads and slightly roasted pigeon breasts and a thick, strong Madeira sauce should also have been prepared in the meantime. Line the mould uniformly with the rice, fill in the ragout and cover it very evenly with rice. Bake the pie for 1 hour, turn it out of of the mould, cover with Madeira sauce and serve the remainder of the sauce in a boat.

8. Game Pie. In Water Crust. To make the crust for a medium-sized game pie, boil ¼ pound of butter and ¼ pound of kidney suet in ½ pint of water; put 3 pounds of flour on the moulding board, make a depression in the center and gradually stir the boiling water into the flour; this will make a strong dough which must be well kneaded and be very firm. The meat, whether hare or venison, should be previously washed and the skin and all sinews removed, cut into pieces of appropriate size and mixed with good-sized pieces of pork fat. Then take eschalots or onions, sweet basil, majoram, cloves, pepper and ground cloves all chopped finely, and rub the meat with this seasoning. Line the bottom of a kettle with slices of pork fat, put in the meat with a few bay leaves and a small piece of butter, cover tightly and cook until half done. The meat can also be pickled the day before in the following manner: Stir the herbs and spices named in wine or vinegar, turn the meat in this liquor and put it into a flat dish, pour the liquor over it and cover. The next day it should also be cooked with pork fat until half done. Make a forcemeat consisting of either 4 parts of meat from game, free from skin or sinews, or else 6 parts of lean pork to 1 part of fresh pork fat chopped very finely, to which add lemon peel, eschalots stewed in butter, a trifle of capers, all chopped very finely, some wheat bread soaked in cold water and then pressed, salt, the yolks of a few eggs, with the whites beaten to a froth, everything mixed well together. Then roll a piece of the dough for the under crust about the thickness of a finger, put it into the buttered pan, roll a piece of the dough between the hands for the rim and flatten it with the rolling pin to the width of about 2 inches, cutting off both ends smoothly. The rim must be higher than the meat in the pan to leave room for the gravy, which is added later on. Now brush the lower crust with eggs, set around its edge the long strip of dough to make the side wall, put a few thin slices of pork fat on the lower crust and along the sides, spread the forcemeat over it and then put in the meat a trifle higher in the middle and not too tightly packed, so that the pie will receive a good form. If there is plenty of forcemeat roll some of it into small dumplings and scatter them through the meat. After the contents of the pie have been covered with pork fat slices, brush its edge with the yolk of an egg, roll some of the dough for a cover, put it over the pie and press the edges together gently; trim the edges, indent them and ornament the top of the pie with little globes made of pie crust, or leaves or other ornaments made from the same material. An opening about the size of a penny should be left in the center, with a little tube made of the pie crust to serve as a vent, otherwise the pie will burst. When sent to the table a round slice is cut out of the top, the pork slices removed and either the dark meat gravy or a truffle sauce filled in. The rest of the gravy is served in a boat.

9. Venison Pie, No. 2. Take a haunch of venison, pound it well, wash, remove the skin, cut into slices and lard. Pickle for 24 hours as in the preceding receipt; the forcemeat, however, is additionally·seasoned with anchovies and the loosely filled in contents of the pie covered with a few spoonfuls of herb broth.

10. A Hare or Wild Fowl Pie with Butter Crust. Clean the hare and after washing remove all sinews and skin; cut the meat from the backbone, divide into pieces of fitting size and then lard it. The wild fowl are also cut into pieces. Both kinds of meat are pickled as directed in No. 8 and afterwards cooked slowly until nearly done. Line a pan thickly with butter, dust with cracker or bread crumbs and put in the meat, alternating with little dumplings made of the forcemeat described in No. 8, above, or No. 22, A, so that it will be heaping in the middle. Take some of the butter out of the pan, stir all adhering to the latter thoroughly with water and claret, add some of the herb broth and pour through a sieve over the meat. For a medium large meat pie take for the crust ½ pound of flour (see English pie crust, Division S), roll until it is about ⅛ inch thick, dust with a little flour and lap crosswise, because it then can be laid onto the pie easier; brush the edge of the pan with egg, put the crust cover on the meat, open it out flat and trim around the edge. From the remainder of the dough make a rim, brush the pie with egg, put on the rim and brush this also, but not entirely all over, otherwise the crust will not rise. Then make 2 small incisions in the middle of the pie to serve as vents, and bake in the oven with 1 degree of heat (see Division S, No. 1) from 1¼—1¾ hours, according to the tenderness of the meat in the pie. Before sending to the table cut a round piece out of the top crust and pour a brown meat gravy into the pie, replace the piece of crust, cover the edge of the dish with a napkin or frill of paper and serve.

11. Mixed Meat Pies. For these pies take any kind of tame or wild fowl, or hare or tenderloin roast, making the dough of 1½ pounds of flour (English pie crust, Division S). Butter a deep pie mould and lay in it crosswise two pieces of muslin buttered on both sides, which will assist in taking the pie out of the mould more conveniently. Roll half of the dough moderately thick and line the mould with it as directed in No. 2, or else roll into a large flap, line the mould with it and trim along the edge. The wild fowl must be previously rubbed with a mixture of chopped onions, salt, cloves, pepper, sweet basil and wine, put it on thin pork fat slices, cover tightly and let it simmer until almost done. With tame fowl omit the coarse spices and use nutmeg. Hares with the backbone removed and tenderloin (the latter pounded) are also divided into pieces, larded,

pickled over night according to No. 8 and then simmered until nearly done. At the same time take 1½
pounds of veal and pork, half and half, and make a
forcemeat as directed in No. 8 of this Division. The
livers and hearts of tame fowl are chopped and added
to the forcemeat. Then with a knife make an opening
clear through to the bottom; roll a cover for the meat
from some of the remaining dough, trim this cover
smoothly all around, brush with egg, lay a border on it
and also brush it, ornament the top of the pie with
figures made from scraps of dough and then cut an
opening in the center about the size of a penny. According to the contents of the pie it must bake from 2½—3
hours. If it should begin to color too soon, cover it
with a piece of buttered paper. If the contents of the
pie consist of wild fowl, add to it a brown meat gravy
or truffle sauce poured into it from the opening in the
top. After the pork fat slices have been removed as
much as possible, the opening must again be closed.
For tame fowl take an oyster-, anchovy-, caper- or
mushroom sauce, in which the broth of the stewed meat
can be utilized. This pie can also be served cold; in
this case pour 1—2 cupfuls of strong bouillon into the
opening through a funnel as soon as the pie is taken
out of the oven; when the pie is cold close the opening
with a little wad of paper.

12. Mock Turtle Pie. Take 2 pounds of flour for a
puff paste as described in Division S, cut it into 2 parts
of unequal size, for the bottom roll the smallest piece
about ¹⁄₁₆ of an inch thick, lay the dish in which the
pie is to be baked on the dough and cut the latter
to the size of the dish; this flap is then placed into the
dish, which must first be buttered. Form a few sheets
of paper into the shape of a ball and cover it smoothly
with a few damp napkins and put the ball so formed on
the bottom of the middle of the dish so that the inner
space of the pie can be raised as desired, or else the
space can also be filled with dried peas. The remainder
of the dough is then also rolled to the thickness of the
under crust, and large enough so that a rim about
2 inches wide can be cut from around the edge of the
pie. The upper crust is put onto the dish over the
ball in the center; brush with egg and then put on the

rim which is also brushed on top but not on the sides.
Bake for ½ hour, then cut out the cover nice and round,
remove the contents carefully so that the crust will not
be injured, fill in a ragout and cover with the top crust.
The finished pie is then immediately filled with the mock
turtle ragout, D. No. 79, which should be rather thick.
To simplify matters a puff paste cover need only be
prepared, which is then used to cover a ragout filled
into a deep dish.

13. Forcemeat Pie. For this pie take 1½ pounds of
flour for a puff paste and make a forcemeat as follows:
1 pound of beef, 1 pound of veal, 1 pound of pork and
1 pound of bacon are finely chopped together with the
requisite amount of salt, and then mix with it 8 eggs
beaten to a froth, nutmeg, white pepper, a chopped
onion stewed in butter, finely chopped sweet herbs,
about ¼—⅓ pound of cracker crumbs and a few cupfuls
of wine or bouillon. Then line a meat pie mould to the
top with crust and fill in the forcemeat, put on the rim
and upper crust, finish it with an ornament and brush
with an egg. Cut an opening in the top for a vent and
serve with a caper-, oyster-, mushroom-, anchovy- or
brown meat sauce.

**14. Hot Meat Pie of Spring Chickens, Pigeons or
Veal.** First make a hollow pie crust as described in
No. 12, and a fine fricassee of chicken, doves or veal as
described in D, No. 75, and fill it into the crust with
some of the gravy, serving the remainder in a boat.
Veal fricassee can be improved by the addition of sweetbread dumplings (Division O).

15. English Meat Pie. For a pie sufficient for 8
persons take ½ pound of flour, 3 heaping tablespoonfuls
of butter, 1 egg and ½ cupful of cold water, make up
into a well kneaded dough and then divide it into two
unequal parts, roll the smallest piece and cut it into
strips about 1½ inches wide with which line a buttered
pan. Then take cold roast meat, poultry or meat remnants of various kinds, cut up into small pieces, put a
few slices of pork fat into the bottom of the pan and
the meat on these, adding salt, ground cloves and meat
dumplings according to taste. Pour 1—2 cupfuls of
strong bouillon over the meat, roll the other piece of

dough to a round flap a little larger than the dish, and cover the meat with it; turn the projecting edge of the flap inwards and press it against the edge with both fingers to form a rim. Brush the whole with egg, make two incisions into the top and then bake the pie for 1—1¼ hours. Send to the table in the dish in which it was baked.

16. Fine Meat Pie. Not only mutton, but also beef tenderloin or the best cuts of any kind of meat can be used for this pie. Ordinarily it is baked in the oven in a buttered porcelain dish and lined with puff paste.

For a mutton pie use the chops near the neck. Cut away the fat and remove the skin, take out the bones, pound the meat until tender, sprinkle with salt and pepper and add a few finely chopped onions.

Veal is treated in the same manner, omitting the onions, but some chopped bacon and about 1 cupful to 1 pint of meat broth are added.

For a pigeon pie the pigeon should be cut up and boned, seasoned with salt, finely chopped onions and slices of lean ham; fill the mould with sour cream instead of water.

For all of the above pies make a puff paste, taking ¾ pound of flour according to the preceding directions, rolling part of it for a cover. Then butter the bottom of a mould, line it with a crust, fill to the top with the meat, alternately sprinkling in a layer of fine bread crumbs and salt. Then pour in enough water with dissolved extract of beef to nearly cover the meat, turn back the projecting edges of the crust and put on the top crust, which should be large enough to closely cover the pie and then bake in the oven from 1—1¼ hours.

17. Macaroni Pie with Ham and Cheese. See Division I.

18. Crab Pie or Fricassee with Pie. See D, No. 181.

19. Fresh Fish Pie. Clean and bone the fish, wash and cut into pieces. Remove the gall bag from the livers, set the fish aside in salt for a few hours and put them into a pickle as described in No. 8, until the next day, after which they are dried with a cloth, put into a frying pan with a large piece of butter, leaving them long enough to stiffen; they must not be soft. Have ready a puff or butter paste, taking 1½—2 pounds of flour and the following forcemeat: 3 pounds of fish cleaned and boned, salt, chop finely and then heat thoroughly with the butter some chopped onions or eschalots. Add ¾ pounds of wheat bread soaked in water and pressed, together with eggs and stir the mass over the fire until it no longer adheres to the kettle, after which let it cool. Then mix with it ¼ pound of butter stirred to a cream, 3 more eggs, nutmeg and finely chopped parsley. If this forcemeat should be too solid, which can easily be tested by rolling a little of it into a ball and boiling it in hot water, add a little cream or cold water. Then roll the bottom crust as directed in No. 10, spread some of the forcemeat on it, cover this with pieces of the fish, put on another layer of forcemeat and so on alternately. Towards the center the contents, like those of all other pies, must be raised somewhat, the last layer of forcemeat be covered with pork fat slices, and a round opening left in the middle of the contents of the pie. For the rest the pie is moulded and baked like No. 11. Send to the table with a crab-, oyster- or anchovy sauce or else with a sauce made as follows and of which, as usual, a few cupfuls are put into the pie: Lightly brown some flour in butter and stir with it bouillon, salt, mace, lemon peel, or instead of the latter some of the pickle; when crab tails or pickerel livers are handy, chop and add them to the gravy; they should not be cooked but stirred in at last. Some of the forcemeat can be reserved and colored red with the crab butter or else it may be colored green by the addition of spinach, which has been cooked and rubbed through a sieve. Then roll the forcemeat into little balls the size of marbles, but cook in meat broth or salted water and put them into the gravy; into the latter stir some finely chopped parsley and the yolks of a few eggs.

20. Pie of Whole Fishes. After cleaning the fish, bone them as follows: Slit them down the back with a sharp knife, clean out the inside and wash carefully, remove all bones, cut off the head, taking care not to injure the skin under the body, then pickle according to No. 19, fill with the same forcemeat and arrange them on a bottom crust covered with pork fat slices. For the rest proceed according to No. 11.

21. Eel Pie is made according to the receipt No. 19, the spine, however, is not taken out of the eel and a few minced sage leaves are added to the forcemeat. If you have no fish to make the forcemeat with, bread crumbs with pieces of butter under and over the eel may be substituted. The crust for this pie must not be too rich; "Good crust for pie and pastry", Division S, is suitable.

22. Salmon Pie. Clean the fish, cut it into slices, pickle for a few hours according to No. 19 and get it hot in the broth. Prepare a forcemeat according to No. 19 and take ½ pound of flour for a puff paste and roll it. Butter the mould, put in half of the forcemeat, spreading it evenly to the thickness of ¼ inch, put on the salmon slices and cover them with the rest of the forcemeat, then cover with the puff paste, finish it with an edge and other ornaments and make several incisions in the top. Bake the pie for 1½—2 hours.

Send to the table with the same sauces described in No. 19; a good crab sauce, however, will probably be the nicest.

23. Russian Salmon Pie. Take 2¼ pounds of salmon and remove the skin, bone and cut into thin slices. Sprinkle the latter with salt, pepper and nutmeg and let them simmer in butter with sweet herbs until about half done. A large goose liver first laid in milk is cut into slices and stewed in butter; boil a dozen eggs hard, and cook ½ pound of rice in good bouillon with butter and salt until tender. When this is ready butter the mould, line it with a butter paste, spread the bottom and the sides with rice and then put in half of the salmon. Sprinkle over them the eggs grated, next put in some of the goose liver slices also sprinkled with egg and continue in this manner until everything is used. Then brush the butter in which the fish and goose liver was stewed over the top layer, cover with rice, then cover the top with slices of pork fat and bake in the oven to a golden brown.

Send to the table with a crab sauce.

24. Cold Veal Pie. Take a piece of veal weighing about 2—3 pounds, cut it into cubes and cook it with wine and salt until half done. Then add a few bay leaves, cloves, pepper, mushrooms, a celery root and an onion, cover and cook slowly for an hour. Get ready a pig's liver, first soaking it in hot water and then chop it very fine, strain in order to remove all skin and then mix with 1 pound of chopped pork, salt, pepper, nutmeg, mace, pounded thyme, majoram, capers, and 2 whole eggs, and add the mushrooms which have been cooked with the veal and then finely chopped to this forcemeat, which must be well mixed. Then take the veal from the stove, put it on a sieve, put the broth back on the fire, cover and cook thoroughly. The pie mould is lined with pork, then put in a layer of forcemeat, then some of the veal and continue in this way with a layer of the forcemeat on top. Pour some of the veal sauce between each layer and then bake with a good fire for 3 hours. After taking the pie out of the mould the pork slices are cut away all around; then with a sharp knife divide the pie into neat slices and serve with bread and butter.

25. Picnic Pie. Prepare a hollow crust as described in No. 12 and in the meantime fry 12 small tenderloin beef steaks nicely brown in butter; boil 10 eggs until hard and cut them into dices with about 6 ounces of boiled ham and stew 20 small mushrooms in bouillon until tender. Take off the top crust and then fill in with beefsteaks, ham, eggs, and mushrooms in layers, cover each layer with button onions and capers and drip over it a few spoonfuls of meat jelly. The jelly is made by cooking the meat bouillon and mushroom broth with 1 pint of water, ½ glassful of Portwine, 1 spoonful of estragon vinegar (the latter can be omitted if a sour flavor is deemed undesirable), and ½ teaspoonful of extract of beef. Stir ½ teaspoonful of dissolved white gelatine through this mixture and use the jelly when half cool. Let the pie stand in a cool place for a day after putting on the cover before serving it. A Remoulade sauce can be added according to taste.

II. SMALL MEAT PIES OR PATTIES.

26. Baking small Meat Pies. A puff paste is the best, but a butter crust may also be taken. Roll it out thin, and with a tumbler cut as many tops and bottoms as there are to be patties; put half of these flaps into a baking pan lined with paper and then with a smaller glass cut out the centers, thus forming the rims. Before these are placed on the patties the edges of the lower crust should be brushed with cold water to make them adhere better.

The patties are filled according to directions either before or after baking.

Have a medium fire and after the elapse of about 10 minutes break the upper crust of one of the patties to ascertain whether they are done or not. The force-meat should be thick but not stiff and be filled into the patties while hot; when the latter are made with puff paste they must previously be indented somewhat in the center. Send to the table hot.

27. Puff Paste Ornaments (Fleurons) are used to decorate a dish of ragout or are served separately with the latter. Roll puff paste to the thickness of about $1/16$ of an inch, stamp out with a wineglass or other utensil, brush the pieces with diluted egg, turn them over in the shape of a half moon, brush the upper side of these also and bake to a light brown.

28. Chicken Patties. Take ½ pound of roast chicken (weighed after being boned), 2 tablespoonfuls of capers, 6 freshened and finely chopped anchovies, ¼ pound of butter, the yolks of 4 eggs, ¼ pound of wheat bread soaked in bouillon and pressed, a few spoonfuls of strong roast meat gravy, a little salt and the whites of 2 eggs beaten to a froth.

Chop this to a smooth forcemeat and fill into patty moulds lined with butter paste; bake with a good fire for 15 minutes until done.

29. Nice Chicken or Veal Patties with Cheese. Cook a strong, nicely prepared ragout in a scant broth and stir it up with the yolks of several eggs. Roll butter crust very thin and line with it the patty moulds; fill the mould one-half with the meat cut into small pieces, adding some of the sauce and bake with a medium fire for fully ¼ hour; during this time stir a piece of melted butter about the size of a walnut, 2 whole eggs, some thick sour cream and grated Holland cheese to a thick sauce, fill 2 teaspoonfuls into each patty and bake for ¼ hour longer.

30. Sweetbread Patties. 1 veal sweetbread is sufficient for 4—5 persons. Set on the fire in cold water and as soon as it begins to boil take it out and put it into cold water again, remove the skin, fry in butter with a few eschalots, chop finely and then mix together with wheatbread soaked in cold water and then pressed, 3 eggs, of which half of the whites are beaten to a froth, lemons, a large piece of butter stirred to a cream, and, according to taste, a few freshened and chopped anchovies; a number of oysters with their liquor can also be added. Fill the patties before they are baked, which is done as directed in the first patty receipt.

31. Veal Patties. Mince a piece of cold veal very finely, season with nutmeg and salt, put it on the fire and stir up with a good-sized piece of crab butter, or instead of this with fresh butter and some good meat gravy, bouillon or sour cream to a rather thick forcemeat, and after taking from the fire, stir through it the yolk of an egg. If you have no crab butter stir through the forcemeat at last some chopped parsley, but omit the parsley if crab butter is used. A teaspoonful is filled as soon as possible into each patty.

32. Anchovy Patties. Cut roast veal into small dice or chop it very fine, chopped eschalots are lightly browned in butter with a little flour, season the meat with salt, nutmeg and lemon juice, then add to the eschalots together with some good roast meat gravy or strong bouillon to make a smooth forcemeat; after the latter has been stirred over the fire until thick, add the anchovy finely chopped with some fresh butter—they should not cook but only become thoroughly hot—and stir with the yolks of a few eggs and some white wine. Fill this forcemeat into the patties while very hot and send them hot to the table.

33. Oyster Patties. Stir a large piece of crab butter or when this is lacking, a piece of fresh butter to a cream, add in proportion the yolks of 2—3 eggs, lemon juice, mace and salt, the liquor of the oysters (3—4 oysters for each person), furthermore chopped mushrooms, capers, rolled crackers and finely chopped roast veal with good roast veal gravy. Half of the whites of the eggs are beaten to a froth and stirred through at last. If the forcemeat should be too stiff, add a little sour cream or strong bouillon or white wine. Fill the patties before baking, and after they have been in the oven, which should be moderately hot, for 10 minutes, lay 3—4 oysters on top of each patty after brushing the latter with egg yolk and lemon juice and sprinkling with very finely rolled cracker crumbs; then bake for 5 minutes longer.

34. Crab Patties. Stew a few eschalots in butter and brown in it a tablespoonful of flour, add some strong boiling bouillon and cook for a short time with the addition of 5—6 carefully washed and finely chopped truffles or mushrooms. Cook ½ pound of veal sweetbreads in bouillon until done, remove the skin and fleshy parts, cut the sweetbreads into small cubes and add to the bouillon. Cook all of this together until smooth, add 30 crab tails chopped into little cubes, stir with the yolks of 2 eggs and fill into the baked patties.

35. Brown Gravy Patties. Put a piece of butter into the kettle and add 1 pound of lean beef, 1 pound of veal and 1 pound of lean ham all cut into pieces, stew in the butter until light brown and then add the onions, 2 carrots, part of a celery root, (all sliced), together with some mace and 4 cloves, pour in some extract of beef broth, cover tightly and let it cook slowly until the meat is tender and the gravy amounts to only about 1 pint. Press the meat in a clean cloth until dry and let the gravy stand until clear, after which pour it off carefully from the settlings. Then beat up 12 fresh eggs, gradually stir in the above mentioned quantity of gravy and pass through a sieve. This gravy is filled into half the depth of small buttered tin moulds or cups as cylindrical and high in shape as possible, stand into boiling water reaching to half their height and cook

until the contents are firm. Turn the patties onto an
appropriate platter and sprinkle them with lean ham
and parsley chopped together very finely.

These patties can be made from remnants of meat of
most any kind, and the admixture of the meat of game,
for instance of wild hare, will be found an improvement.

36. Rice Patties. Thoroughly scalded rice is cooked
with milk and salt until tender and firm; in the meantime mix some finely chopped boiled ham with sour
cream, butter and dredge small moulds with cracker
crumbs, fill them with the ham, rice and Parmesan
cheese in alternate layers and bake.

37. Hasty Patties made from Meat Remnants. Chop
some remnants of veal roast or any other kind very
finely together with some fat meat, such as ham, add
nutmeg, salt, a piece of butter, a few eggs, parsley or
some minced eschalots or onions and stir all on the fire
to a smooth forcemeat. Cut the upper crust from rolls
or rusks, take out the center, fill in the forcemeat, cover
with the top crust and bake.

38. Mushroom Patties. Grate off the brown outer
crust from small rolls, cut them into halves, take out the
center, soak them in milk in which an egg has been
beaten and then turn in the crumbs. For each roll take
1—2 large mushrooms; clean the latter very carefully
and cut the heads into pieces about ¾ inch in size.
Mince the other parts of the mushrooms with parsley,
burnet and tarragon, rub a finely chopped eschalot in
butter and then add the mince together with the salt,
pepper, a little grated lemon peel, a little over ½ ounce
of very finely chopped fresh bacon, several whole eggs,
a few spoonfuls of roast meat gravy and 1 tablespoonful
of Portwine, and mix all of this with the pieces of mushrooms. Fill some of the forcemeat into the rolls, dredge
the surface with bread crumbs, put a piece of crab butter on each half roll, sprinkle with a few drops of lemon
juice and then bake the patties in the oven with a very
moderate fire.

39. Patties in Moulds. Butter a lot of small tin
moulds and fill them to three-fourths of their depth with
the forcemeat described for the ragout pie under No. 7;

press the forcemeat towards the sides and bottom of the mould to form a hollow, into which fill a tablespoonful of the ragout prepared as directed in the receipt mentioned (No. 7). Then spread enough of the forcemeat over the top to completely cover the ragout, cover each patty with a piece of buttered paper and stand them in hot water, which should not come higher than half the depth of the mould, for ½ hour before serving. To cook the patties until they are done the water should not be more than boiling hot, and the vessel in which they stand must be covered. After turning them out of the moulds, put a round slice of truffles or beef tongue on each patty. Serve after the soup with or without a sauce.

40. Baked Chicken Patties. Take the tenderest parts of 2 baked Spring chickens, chop finely and mix with 4 tablespoonfuls of thick Bechamel sauce and the yolks of 6 eggs; if the mass should be too thick add a little cream, and if too thin, bread crumbs; fill into small buttered cups. Stand in a double kettle, leaving them there until done and firm, which will take about 20 minutes, then turn them out, cover with a crab sauce and serve.

41. Talleyrand Patties. Butter a lot of small patty moulds and line with truffles cut in the shape of noodles, and beef tongue slices. Mince remnants of baked chickens together with a few stewed mushrooms, some bacon and a little boiled ham, mix this with a few eggs, salt, pepper, nutmeg, bread crumbs and spread the interior of the moulds thickly with this forcemeat. Fill the center with a thick mushroom ragout which is prepared by stewing small mushrooms in butter and meat broth until done, cutting veal sweetbreads into cubes and heating both in brown meat gravy. Spread a layer of forcemeat over the ragout, then cook the patties in a double boiler for ½ hour, turn them out of the moulds, cover with Madeira sauce and serve.

Meat pies and patties are not adapted for the sickroom, because they are too rich and not easily digestible.

F.—Fish and Shell Fish.

---

1. General Directions for Preparing and Cooking Fish, together with a Table showing when they are in Season. All fresh water and unsalted fish should be prepared while quite fresh; they become tainted very rapidly and are then absolutely unpalatable and unwholesome. A fish is best when placed on the market immediately after being caught and cleaned. Fish injured in catching are sometimes allowed to remain in water to keep them alive; this is not only cruel, but when it dies slowly, it is detrimental to the quality of the fish. Fresh fish have the following characteristics: The eyes and scales must be clear, bright and shining, the gills of a lively red color and the body must be firm. If the gills have a bleached appearance the fish is unfit for use. Fish that have been transported long distances and received even a slightly unpleasant odor must be carefully washed at once; it is best to use for this purpose water containing chloride of soda.

A good turbot is thick, and full fleshed, and the under side is of a pale cream color or yellowish white; when this is of a bluish tint, and the flesh is thin and soft, it should be rejected. The same observations apply equally to soles.

The best salmon and codfish are known by their small head, very thick shoulders, and small tail; the scales of the former should be bright and its flesh of a fine red color; to be eaten in perfection it should be dressed as soon as caught, before the curd (or white substance which lies between the flakes of flesh) has melted and rendered it oily. In this state it is really *crimp*, but continues so only for a few hours; and it bears therefore a much higher price in the market then, than when mellowed by having been kept a day or two.

The flesh of the codfish should be white and clear before it is boiled, whiter still after it is boiled, and firm though tender, sweet and mild in flavor, and separated easily in flakes. Many persons consider it rather improved than otherwise by having a little salt rubbed along the inside of the backbone and letting it lie from twenty-four to twenty-eight hours before it is dressed. It is sometimes served crimp like salmon, and must then be sliced as soon as dead, or within the shortest time possible afterwards.

Herrings, mackerel and whitings lose their freshness so rapidly that unless newly caught they are quite uneatable. The herring may, it is said, be deprived of the strong smell which it emits when broiled or fried, by stripping off the skin, under which lies the oil that causes the disagreeable odor. The whiting is a peculiarly pure flavored and delicate fish, and acceptable generally to invalids from being very light of digestion.

Eels should be alive and brisk in movement when they are purchased; they are easily killed by piercing the spinal marrow close to the back part of the skull with a sharp pointed knife, or skewer. If this be done in the right place all motion will instantly cease. Boiling water will also immediately cause vitality to cease, and is perhaps the most humane and ready method of destroying the fish.

Lobsters, prawns, and shrimps are very stiff when freshly boiled, and the tails turn strongly inwards; when these relax, and the fish are soft and watery, they are stale; and the smell will detect their being so instantly even if no other symptoms of it be remarked. If bought alive, lobsters should be chosen by their weight and "liveliness". The hen lobster is preferred for sauce and soups, on account of the coral; but the flesh of the male is generally considered of finer flavor for eating. The vivacity of their leaps will show when prawns and shrimps are fresh from the sea.

Oysters should close forcibly on the knife when they are opened; if the shells are apart ever so little they are losing their condition and when they remain far open the oyster is dead, and only fit to be thrown away. Small plump varieties are always preferable to the larger and coarser kinds.

To clean Fish. Let this be done always with the most scrupulous nicety, for nothing can more effectually destroy the appetite than fish sent to the table imperfectly cleaned. Handle it lightly, and never throw it roughly about, so as to bruise it; wash it well, but do not leave it longer in the water than is necessary, for fish, like meat, loses it flavor from being soaked. When scales are to be removed, lay the fish flat upon its side, and hold it firmly with the left hand, while they are scraped off with the right; turn it, and when both sides are done, pour or pump sufficient water over it to float off all the loose scales; then proceed to open and empty it. Be sure that not the slightest particle of offensive matter be left in the inside, wash out the blood entirely, and scrape or brush it away, if needful from the backbone. This may be easily accomplished without opening the fish so much as to render it unsightly when it is sent to the table. The red mullet is dressed without being emptied, and smelts are drawn at the gills. When the scales are left on, the outside of the fish should be well washed and wiped with a coarse towel, drawn gently from the head to the tail. Eels, to be wholesome, should be skinned, but they are sometimes dressed without; boiling water should then be poured upon them, and they should be left in it for five or ten minutes, before they are cut up. The dark skin of the sole must be stripped off when it is fried, but it must be left on, like that of the turbot, when the fish is boiled, and it should be dished with the white side upwards. Whitings are skinned, and dipped usually into egg and bread crumbs when they are to be fried; but for boiling or broiling, the skin must be left on.

To keep Fish. All the smaller kinds of fish keep best if emptied and cleaned as soon as they are brought in, then wiped gently as dry as they can be and hung separately by the head on the hooks in the ceiling of a cool larder, or in the open air when the weather will allow. When there is danger of their being attacked by flies, a wire safe placed in a strong draught of air, is better adapted to the purpose. Soles in winter will remain good a couple of days when thus prepared; and even whitings and mackerel may be kept so without losing any of their excellence. Salt may be rubbed slightly over codfish, and well along the backbone, but it injures the flavor of salmon, the inside of which may be rubbed with vinegar, and peppered instead. When excessive sultriness renders all of these modes unavailing, the fish must at once be partially cooked to preserve it, but this should be avoided if possible, as it is very rarely sc good when this method is resorted to.

To sweeten tainted Fish. The application of pyroligneous acid will effect this when the taint is but slight. A wineglassful, mixed with two of water, may be poured over the fish, and rubbed upon the parts more particularly requiring it; it must then be left for some minutes untouched, and afterwards washed in several waters, and soaked until the smell of the acid is no longer perceptible. The chloride of soda, from its powerful antiputrescent properties, will have more effect when the fish is in a worse state. It should be applied in the same manner, and will not at all injure the flavor of the fish, which is not fit food when it cannot be perfectly purified by either of these means. The chloride may be diluted more or less, as occasion may require.

Salting and cooking Fish. Careful use of Bay Leaves. The proper application of salt—neither too much nor too little—and the art of cooking fish until done without permitting them to become too soft, is a test cf a good cook. Fish put on the fire in boiling water must have plenty of salt, because they remain in contact with the brine but a short time. They are done as soon as the fins can be easily pulled out and the meat loosened from the bones, which is readily discernible when the fish is cut into pieces. Be careful to send the fish, with the potatoes and sauces, to the table as hot as possible.

Bay leaves should be added to fish as well as meat dishes of every kind very sparingly, because their flavor is quite strong. Fish served with olive oil and vinegar must not cool in the broth in which they are cooked; they should be taken out, slightly pickled in good olive oil, vinegar, pepper and salt and then set aside in a cool place.

To bake or fry Fish Fish should always be baked in an open pan with plenty of butter; the fire should not be too strong, so that they will bake through and through, and not scorch on the outside while the inside remains raw. Serve on a warm, uncovered dish.

For fish in jelly, see Division M.

Fish are in season as follows: Salmon from May to August; can be obtained earlier but are scarce.

Eels are in season all the year, but not in prime condition in April and May.

Pike and perch are in the best condition from September to January.

Carp are best from October to the end of March.

Shad, April, May and early part of June.

Trout, May to August.

Red mullet through the Summer, but may be had all the year.

Crab and lobster, April to October.

Haddock — best season, October, November and December, but in the market to the end of April.

Turbot in season all the year.

Soles are the best from the end of April to September.

It would be impracticable to give rules for cooking every kind of fish; they are too numerous. Suffice is to say that the directions for cooking one will apply to any other of the same size.

I. FRESH WATER FISH.

2. Boiled Salmon. Scale, empty and wash the fish with great care. Cut into slices about 1½—2 inches thick, put on the fire in boiling water with salt, peppercorns, whole and ground cloves, a few bay leaves and lemon peel; cook for a few minutes, skimming thoroughly. Let it stand on the back of the stove until the fins pull out easily, which will indicate that the fish is done. Send to the table with potatoes, melted butter, which should not bubble but simply be hot, minced parsley and the grated yolks of hard boiled eggs.

Boiled salmon may also be served with a Bearnese-, yellow caper-, oyster- or Hollandaise sauce; a few drops of lemon juice should be added to the melted butter.

If the salmon is to be served cold with oil and vinegar, take the pieces out of the kettle, let them cool and immediately put them into a pickle of some of the cold fish broth, olive oil, vinegar, pepper and salt. Less salt is required for cooking salmon than for any other fish.

3.   Salmon with Savory Herbs. Clean the fish thoroughly and cut it into pieces, sprinkle with salt and let it stand for 1 hour. Then mix the following herbs: Parsley, eschalots and capers, together with freshened and boned anchovy and ground pepper and put them into fresh melted butter with enough lemon juice to slightly acidulate it, put it on the fire and when warm add the fish and leave it for 2 hours, turning quite often; the butter should be melted but must not scorch. Heat some butter in another pan and fry the salmon in it for 10 minutes, brushing the minced herbs over both sides of the fish frequently.

The sauce is made by boiling the rest of the marinade with 2 glassfuls of white wine with a few spoonfuls of good meat broth, and if it should not be tart enough add a few drops of lemon juice and stir through it the yolks of a few eggs.

4.   Pickled Salmon. Take 2 pounds of salmon and without washing or skinning it cut it into slices about 1 inch thick, put into salt for about 1 hour, dry with a cloth, brush with the best olive oil and then fry them on a quick fire until done and of a light brown color; the slices are then placed into an earthenware jar. Boil 1 pint of mild vinegar and 1 pint of white wine, ½ ounce of salt, 2 lemon slices, 2 bay leaves, tarragon, a pinch of white pepper and when this liquor is cool pour it over the fish; cover the jar by tying a cloth over it and let it stand until wanted.

5.   Boiled Eels. After the eel has been killed it is not taken out of the skin, but the latter is rubbed down with salt; the eel is then emptied, cut into pieces and hot vinegar poured over it; afterwards put it on the fire with a dash of vinegar, salt, a bay leaf, lemon slices, eschalots, peppercorns, cloves, a small piece of butter, some sage, thyme and tarragon; cook slowly for 10 or 15 minutes. Send to the table hot with potatoes, butter and mustard; garnish with lemon slices and parsley leaves, and serve with it vinegar and olive oil or else a horse radish-, caper- or lemon sauce.

It is advisable to save the eel broth, because whatever is left over of the eel can be set aside in it. Less salt is required for cooking eels than for other fish.

If the eel is to be kept for any length of time and to be served with a Remoulade or other similar sauce, it should be cooked in the same manner, only taking vinegar and water half and half. After the eel is cooked take it out of the broth until it has cooled completely, then put it back again, cover and set aside until wanted. Garnish the dish in which the eel is served with meat jelly, sliced eggs, beets, capers, pickled walnuts, etc.

6. Fricassee of Eel, Bremen style. Clean the eel as directed above, cut into pieces, cover with salt for an hour, washing it before cooking. Bring to a boil in a slightly salted strong bouillon of which there should be enough to nearly cover the eel, add a few mushroom slices, cook until the eel is done, take out of the broth and set it on the back of the stove. Roll fish forcemeat into oblong dumplings, cooking them in the ragout for not to exceed 5 minutes. Should there be say 2 pounds of the eel, rub some flour and butter, cook in the eel broth to a thick sauce, stir through it the yolks of 2 fresh eggs, season with lemon juice, a little mace and white pepper, stir until it begins to boil, put the eel with the dumplings into a warm dish in which they are mixed with the gravy. To improve this dish cook a glassful of Madeira with the sauce and in addition to the fish dumplings, get ready chicken force meat dumplings. Stew mushrooms and veal sweetbreads in bouillon until tender, mixing all of these ingredients together with crab tails into the fricassee. This fricassee can be served in a rice crust, garnishing the top with puff paste slices (see under "Meat Pies", Division E.)

7. Stewed Eel. Cook 2 calf's feet until the meat drops from the bones, strain the broth and immediately pour it back into the cleaned kettle, put in the washed pieces of eel—they should not be entirely covered with the broth—add 2 tablespoonfuls of vinegar in which a trifle of extract of beef has been dissolved, together with a slip of mace, 2—3 small sliced onions, pepper, salt and a few lemon slices without seeds, cover tightly and stew slowly until done. Try the broth to determine whether it needs more vinegar or salt, then arrange the eel in a dish and pour over it the broth, which should be slightly cool.

8. Fried Eel. Salt the pieces, turn in bread and egg crumbs and fry in an open pan in melted butter with fresh sage leaves until done—golden brown and crisp.

Or the eel may be covered with salt for a few hours, cover and set it aside, dry it with a cloth, wrap it into sage leaves, and then fry it in butter, pork fat or olive oil.

Eel is most delicious, however, when baked in the oven; it is then rolled into a coil fastened with thin wooden skewers. Put it into a buttered pan and cover with sliced onions, pour over it a marinade consisting of vinegar, white wine and savory herbs, enough to half cover the eel, and then bake in the oven. As soon as done lay the eel on a clean cloth which will draw out the fat, glaze it with meat jelly and serve with a tomato sauce. Eel prepared in this manner is the most wholesome, because the greater part of the fat is drawn from it. Serve with sliced lemons and mustard or lettuce; a Remoulade sauce is also a fitting accompaniment. Eel is also nice when served with early green peas.

If the eel is a large one the spine can be taken out immediately while it is being prepared, and the pieces can then be filled with a fish or veal forcemeat, afterwards tying them so that the forcemeat will not fall out; then bake as directed above.

9. Rolled Eel. After the eel has been cleaned, cut off the fins, slit along the back instead of underneath, empty, wash nicely and take out the entire spine. Then put the eel on a chopping board, with the inner side turned out, flatten it, sprinkle with minced yolks of hard boiled eggs, onions and parsley, pepper and salt, or instead of the latter cover with anchovy slices. Cut the head and tail from the eel and then roll it up, beginning at the head, and wrap this roll into a piece of clean muslin, which should be closed at both ends. Put water and vinegar, half and half, into a small kettle, and cook the roll with onion slices, spices, 2 bay leaves and salt for ½ hour until done; the liquor should barely cover the roll. Afterwards take the roll out of the kettle, and draw the muslin, which loosens during the cooking, tight again. When cool press the roll slightly and unwrap the muslin; the roll should be sliced and neatly arranged on the dish, garnish with lemon slices and send to the table with meat jelly or a Remoulade sauce.

10. Eel Stew, English Style. Clean the eel, cut off the head and tail and the remainder into medium sized pieces, which are turned in flour, pepper and salt. Bake in butter to a light brown. After the eel is cold cook the head and tail with some good bouillon, several chopped anchovies, a few mushrooms, 1 glassful of wine vinegar, 1 glassful of sherry to a strong broth; strain and thicken with flour rubbed in butter. Stew the baked eel in this sauce for 15 minutes, send to the table in the sauce.

11. Eel in Cases. Clean a large eel, salt, cut it into pieces and stew until tender in bouillon containing a little white wine, mixed spices and savory herbs. In the meantime boil about 6 ounces of rice in bouillon until tender, finely chop 1 dozen mushrooms, 3 eschalots and some parsley, mix and stew for a few minutes in butter; brush the inside of a large paper case with olive oil, put a layer of rice on the bottom, then a layer of the eel sprinkled with the minced ingredients and continue in this manner until the case is filled. The last layer should be of rice, dot it with crab butter, cover with bread crumbs, and bake with a slow fire for ½ hour. Serve immediately on a folded napkin.

12. Pickled Eel. Skin the eel, wash, salt for 1 hour, cut into pieces, dry it with a cloth, fry in a clean pan with olive oil, and lay on absorbent or blotting paper to cool. Then cook for ¼ of an hour with eschalots, peppercorns, mace, a few bay leaves, lemon slices (without the seeds) and enough vinegar to cover the eel, together with water and salt. When the liquor is cold pour it over the eel; set aside in a cool place until wanted. Another method is to put the eel in salt for a few hours; then cook it for about 15 minutes until done in an enameled kettle in which water and vinegar, half and half, and the above mentioned spices have first been brought to a boil; arrange the eel in layers in a stone jar, remove the fat from the liquor, acidulate it with lemon juice, pour it into the jar and set it aside.

The fish can be served without any further preparation, or else the pieces can be mixed with medium hard boiled eggs quartered, small pickles, pickled button onions and beets; sprinkle with capers.

13. To boil Brook Trout with a blue Color. Like all other kinds of fish that are to have a blue color after cooking, trout should not be scraped, simply empty them and this is done best by laying them on a wet chopping board and handling them as little as possible so that the glutenous substance enveloping the fish, and which produces the blue color, will not be rubbed off. Afterwards rinse and lay them on a flat dish, pour boiling vinegar over them, and let them stand for half an hour in a cool draft. Bring water to a boil with plenty of salt, put in the fish with the vinegar, cover the kettle and let it stand on top of the stove for 6—12 minutes, but the fish must not cook. Serve hot with fresh butter, or with melted butter as preferred. They can also be sent to the table with minced parsley or a Hollandaise sauce, or they may be served cold with olive oil, vinegar and pepper. Butter used with fish must never become hot enough to cook, because it thereby loses greatly in quality.

Brook trout require more salt than most other kinds of fish.

REMARK.—Where brook trout are not to be cooked with a blue color they are simply boiled in water according to directions. Brook trout will keep for a few hours only after being caught, and should therefore be cooked when quite fresh.

14. Trout Steaks with various kinds of Sauces and Vegetables. Take trout of medium size, empty, skin and bone them and divide into quarters. Put the steaks into a buttered pan, sprinkle with salt and minced savory herbs, and fry on both sides for 2 minutes. Then pour off the butter, add to the fish some of the sauce with which they are to be served, let it come to a boil once, arrange the fish in a deep dish and send to the table with either a crab-, caper-, tomato-, Bearnaise- or rich brown sauce. Instead of serving with a gravy separately, the fish, fried in butter without the addition of any herbs, can be served with peas, asparagus or other fresh vegetables.

15. Baked Trout. Select trout of the smallest size, scrape off the scales nicely, empty, and wash. Cut a slit about $\frac{1}{16}$ inch deep along each side, salt for $\frac{1}{2}$ hour before baking. Then dry them with a cloth and turn them first in flour and then in egg and cracker crumbs, fry, serve on a napkin placed over a fish plate. Lettuce is a fitting accompaniment.

16. Carp cooked blue. Empty the fish as directed in No. 1, wash, divide lengthwise into halves and cut each part into 2—3 pieces. Carp can be cooked blue the same as trout, and as it is a very fat fish, it should be boiled for a few minutes and served quite hot. Send to the table with hot melted butter and minced parsley, or with a plain horse radish sauce. The milt of carp is considered a delicacy. Carp require a great deal of salt.

17. Carp with a Claret Sauce. When killing the carp catch its blood in a small cup half full of vinegar, scrape off the scales and proceed as directed in the preceding receipt. After washing the pieces put them into a saucepan with salt, sliced onions, coarse ground pepper and cloves, sliced lemons and bay leaves, add water and enough claret to just cover the fish. Take off the scum as carefully as possible, add a large piece of butter and finely rolled crackers and then cook slowly. Shortly before serving stir in the blood and a piece of sugar, put the fish into a dish and strain over it the sauce, which should be well bound.

18. Carp with a Polish Sauce. Kill the carp and catch the blood in vinegar, scrape, divide in half and cut each part into pieces. For 3 pounds of fish take 3 carrots, 1 parsnip, 2 parsley roots, 3 onions and $\frac{1}{4}$ celery root; cut everything into slices and put it into a saucepan with some ginger, a few cloves, peppercorns and about 2 bay leaves, add beer and water half and half and boil for ¼ hour. Then put in the fish, add the necessary salt and 2—3 tablespoonfuls of butter, ½ of a lemon without the seeds, a wineglassful of vinegar (including that mixed with the blood) cover tightly and cook for 15 minutes longer. As soon as the fish is tender take it out of the broth and set it on the back of the stove, add ginger bread ("Pfefferkuchen") or grated wheat bread and 1 glassful of claret to the sauce, strain the latter and put part of it on the fish and the remainder into a sauce boat. Serve with potatoes. The beer should not be bitter and the sauce quite thick.

19. Stuffed Carp. Scrape the scales from the fish, empty it and carefully loosen the meat on one side between the head and tail, so that both parts remain attached to the skin and be careful not to injure the latter. After boning the meat that has been cut out, chop the latter very finely, stir a piece of butter to a cream, add 2 eggs, some wheat bread soaked in water and then pressed, 1—2 eschalots, lemon peel, salt, mace and finally the chopped meat of the fish. If this force-meat should be too soft add some grated bread and if too firm put in some water. Fill this forcemeat into the body of the fish so that it will regain its original shape, sprinkle with cracker crumbs, put it into the pan with pork fat slices and some butter with the filled side to the top and bake in the oven, basting often, until brown and done. After the fish has been carefully laid on a fish plate cook the gravy in the pan with ½ tablespoonful of flour rubbed in butter, bouillon and salt. Season according to taste with chopped anchovy, strain and add capers or lemon peel. If it is possible to put a cover containing live embers over the pan, the fish will be greatly improved.

20. Carp and Eel mixed. Take the same quantity of both fish (about 2¼ pounds of each), scrape and skin the fish, cut them into pieces about 2 inches long, salt lightly and set aside for an hour. During this time cook some pickled pork until half done, cut it into pieces the same size as those of the fish and put it all into a vessel, mixed with small onions and mushrooms and with about 6 heaping teaspoonfuls of butter added. Season with 1 bay leaf, peppercorns and a few cloves, add 1 pint of bouillon and the same quantity of claret, and stew the whole slowly until done. Set the various ingredients on top of the stove to keep them hot, strain the broth, thicken with flour browned in butter and pour it over the mixture. Garnish the edge of the dish with egg dumplings and slips of toast and send to the table with boiled potatoes.

21. To bake a whole Carp. Scrape the fish, slit down the back but not under the body, empty, salt and after an hour dry it with a cloth, sew the back, turn in egg and bread crumbs and then fry in a flat pan with hot butter or lard until of a golden brown color. Remove the thread and serve. The pan must not be covered when frying the fish, otherwise they will become soft and this will also be the case if they are not sent to the table at once; to draw out the fat, however, they should be laid on absorbent or blotting paper for a moment. Left-over carp or other fried fish can be utilized in fish soup (B, No. 25) or with sour cabbage and fish.

22. Hungarian Carp. Prepare the carp and cut it into pieces, salt and set aside for 15 minutes, then cook them in boiling salted water containing a dash of vinegar, as directed in No. 16, until done. Serve on a hot dish and pour over it the following sauce. Brown 2 chopped onions and ½ ounce of flour in 2 tablespoonfuls of butter, and cook this with a large cupful of sweet cream, a small cupful of fish broth and 1 tablespoonful of bouillon to a well bound sauce. Season with cayenne pepper, being very careful not to take too much. After straining the sauce stir through it the yolks of 2 eggs and then a piece of fresh butter.

23. Fillet of Carp. Raise the flesh from the bones of a medium-sized fish and chop it finely, mix with some shredded bacon, anchovy butter, 2 or 3 eggs, 2 to 3 spoonfuls of sour cream, salt, pepper and enough grated bread to make a smooth but not crumby forcemeat, which is shaped into the form of a loaf. Lard along the top closely with small pork fat lardoons, sprinkle the surface with bread crumbs and bake in the oven in butter with frequent basting until done. ¼ of an hour before serving add a cupful of sour cream. Thicken the sauce with cornstarch and send the fish to the table with boiled potatoes and lettuce.

24. Cold Carp with a Sauce. After the fish has been cleaned and emptied, nicely rinsed and salted for an hour, put it into a frying pan with a large cupful of wine, spices, tarragon, parsley and 1½ tablespoonfuls of butter, baste and cook slowly until done. After it is cool put a Remoulade sauce or sauce a la Diable, (Division K), into the dish with the fish and garnish around the sides with eggs and parsley.

25. Carp in Mayonnaise Sauce. Take a fish weighing 4 to 4½ pounds, rub it with salt and stew it slowly until done with a large cupful of wine, salt, pepper, spices, onion, a small bunch of parsley and 1½ tablespoonfuls of butter. Leave in the broth until cold, and make a good thick Mayonnaise sauce as directed under Division O; after the fish is taken out of the broth and dried, cover it evenly with the sauce. Garnish the dish with sliced eggs, capers, button onions, gherkins and parsley, and surround with a border of meat jelly. Serve for supper.

26. Pickled Carp. Clean and empty the fish and cut the gall bag from the liver. Wash, rub on the in- and outside with salt and let it lay for a while. Put the roes back into the fish and dry it. It can also be divided in two and cut into pieces. Then brush with olive oil. broil slowly until done and of a golden brown color; if you have no broiler a sauce- or frying pan will answer the purpose, but in this case it must be shaken frequently, so that the fish will not adhere to the pan. Let it cool, boil vinegar with lemon peel, eschalots or onions, whole spices, mace, some salt and a bay leaf, and after the liquor is cold pour it over the fish. After a few days, the carp can be sent to the table; it will keep for several weeks if the liquor is boiled once more in the meantime.

27. Perch Hollandaise. The fish is scraped under the body only and emptied, leaving the milt and liver in the fish, rinse carefully and boil for 5 minutes in a little salted water, in which a piece of butter, peppercorns, and plenty of small parsley roots with a few sprigs of parsley have been previously cooked until done. When serving the fish the parsley roots should be interspersed between them; send to the table hot in the broth in which they were cooked. If sent to the table without the broth, then serve with melted butter and chopped parsley, grated yolks of eggs, and mustard, or with a Hollandaise sauce, using some of the strained fish broth in making the sauce.

28. Another method of boiling Perch. The perch are scraped all over; empty and put them on the fire in boiling salted water with onions, peppercorns and bay leaves and cook until done. Then mince 2 hard boiled eggs with parsley, stir in some nutmeg and rolled crackers, put the fish into a dish, dredge with the above mixture and send them to the table with hot melted butter with either a caper-, Maitre de Hotel- or a brown herb sauce.

29. Perch in a French Sauce. Take perch weighing about ½ pound apiece, scrape, empty and wash nicely, salt and put them into a saucepan with plenty of butter. As soon as they are heated on both sides dredge some flour over them, turn the fish in the flour and add enough white wine to cover. At the same time add finely ground cloves, minced parsley and eschalots, cover tightly and let the fish cook slowly until done, but they must not fall to pieces.

30. Blue Pike with Butter and Horse Radish. Select fish of a small size, empty and bend them with their tails in their mouths. They should not be handled much, however, because otherwise the blue color cannot be given them. They are then cooked blue as directed in No. 13, but should remain on the fire longer than trout. Send to the table garnished with sprigs of parsley and a few apples; in addition to melted butter serve grated horse radish prepared with vinegar, sugar and hard boiled eggs. The liver of the pike, which is considered a great delicacy, must not be forgotten, being careful, of course, to first remove the gall bag. Salt the same as perch.

In England the fish is cut into pieces and is then cooked in boiling salted water with vinegar, butter and spices until tender, sprinkled with grated horse radish and covered with plenty of browned butter.

Instead of being served with butter, pike may be sent to the table with a caper-, Hollandaise-, or sour egg sauce.

31. Stewed Pike. With a sharp knife shave the scales close to the skin to leave the latter white, divide the fish in two and cut up each half to the size desired, wash nicely and cook in salted water for 5 minutes and put into another kettle. In the meantime boil some capers in white wine with some fish broth, lemon juice and lemon peel, a good-sized piece of butter and some grated wheat bread, pour over the fish and let it stew in this gently for 15 minutes. The sauce can be slightly seasoned with anchovy if wished. Then stir with it the yolk of an egg and send to the table as hot as possible.

32. Larded Pike. Take a fish of medium size, clean and skin it, lard on both sides closely with fine lardoons and sprinkle with fine salt. The fish is then baked as follows, either in its natural form or with the tail inserted in its mouth: Melt plenty of butter in a frying pan, put in the fish, baste it thoroughly and bake until done and nicely brown; have a slow fire, but the cover of the pan should be so arranged as to hold live embers. The fish can, however, be as nicely baked in the oven in the open pan; it is then frequently dredged with grated wheat bread and basted with several spoonfuls of sour cream. In this case the juices in the pan are made into a gravy with the addition of some extract of beef, a little Portwine, lemon juice and thickened with flour rubbed in butter and used instead of the browned caper sauce.

Larded pike baked according to the directions first given should be served with a brown caper sauce made with some anchovy and plenty of lemon juice; pour some of it into a hot dish and put in the fish. The rest of the gravy together with the browned gravy in the pan is sent to the table with it.

33. Chopped Baked Pike. The spine is taken out of the fish in such a manner that the head and tail remain attached to the body. Put the spine into an earthenware dish and lay the meat into boiling water for a few minutes, after which all the other bones can be easily removed. Then chop the meat very finely and make into a forcemeat with the addition of a large piece of butter, 2 eggs, grated wheat bread, mace and salt. Press this forcemeat onto the spine so that it will e moulded into the original form of the fish, sprinkle with cracker crumbs and bake in the oven. Baste frequently with butter, being careful not to wash away the cracker crumbs and season with lemon juice. If the fish comes to the table on a hot platter, serve it with a caper- or anchovy sauce. Other varieties of fish can be chopped and served in the same way.

34. Baked Pike. After cleaning the fish nicely, split the larger ones, cut them into pieces, and leave the smaller ones whole, removing the heads and tails. Slit them closely, but only through the upper skin, and salt. After the elapse of ½ hour dry them with a cloth, turn in egg and bread crumbs and then fry crisply to a golden brown in an open pan in which plenty of butter or lard has been heated.

To prevent the fish from becoming soft again, it should not be fried until just before it goes to the table. It can be served with sourkrout or lettuce.

35. Pike with Parmesan Cheese and Onions. A large fish is best adapted for this purpose. Scrape off the scales, remove the spine, cut into pieces about 2 inches in size and sprinkle with salt. For about 5 pounds of fish melt 2—3 tablespoonfuls of butter in a saucepan, add a handful of finely chopped onions and in this stew the fish until done and take them out of the kettle, then rub a tablespoonful of flour in butter, add 1½ pints of thick sour cream, constantly stirring; pour the sauce into a deep dish. Remove the bones out of the pieces of fish as carefully as possible, turn the latter in grated Parmesan cheese, put them in layers into the dish containing the sauce, and sprinkle with a handful of the cheese. The stewed pieces of fish, after having been turned in the cheese, can be covered with a sauce made of a cupful of sour cream, a cupful of meat broth and ½ teaspoonful of mushroom catsup, then sprinkle with capers and proceed as above directed.

36. Pike with Egg Sauce. Put the tail of the fish into its mouth and set it on the fire with vinegar and water half and half in a medium-sized saucepan; there should not be too much broth, add some onions, 2 bay leaves, a few peppercorns, the half or the whole of a parsley root and the necessary salt. As soon as the fish is done place it carefully on a warm dish, and cover after pouring over it the following sauce: Rub 1 spoonful of flour in some hot butter, in the meantime stirring the yolks of 10 eggs in about 1 quart of bouillon (which can be made of extract of beef), add to the flour and bring to a boil under constant stirring; then add previously prepared mushrooms, crab tails, crab butter and lemon juice and serve the fish with the sauce over it.

37. Baked Pike with Sour Cream. Cut the fish into pieces of proper size and put them into an earthenware baking pan. To 3 pounds of fish add 2 bay leaves, a few onion slices, salt, 2 tablespoonfuls of butter, 1 cupful of sour cream and then bake in a hot oven for about 20 minutes, basting the fish several times with this sauce and sprinkling it with grated crackers or Parmesan cheese. When serving stir through the sauce some bouillon, season with vinegar or lemon juice and pour it on the fish. Remove the bay leaves and onion slices before sending to the table.

38. Baked Pike. After nicely cleaning the fish lard it on both sides, salt and bake it in butter, add finely sliced onions and when these are thoroughly heated pour in some water. After cooking for about 10 minutes add a freshened thinly sliced herring, pounded crackers, some vinegar, ground pepper and nutmeg, and, if necessary, some more salt. The sauce must be well bound.

39. Fricassee of Pike. Put a good-sized piece of butter into an earthenware dish with the fish nicely cleaned and cut into pieces; add white wine, a few lemon slices without the seeds, finely chopped anchovy and salt, dredge with finely grated crackers or grated wheat bread, and cover. After stewing the fish for about 15 minutes until done, stir a few tablespoonfuls of thick sour cream through the sauce, pour it over the fish and serve. Put a border of ragout rice (see Division L) around the fricassee.

40. Pike Steaks with Savory Herbs. Divide a medium-sized, cleaned and emptied pike in two lengthwise, remove the bones and skin from each part, cut into pieces about 2 inches in size, salt, sprinkle with pepper and stew in plenty of melted butter with several spoonfuls of minced savory herbs for about 20 minutes in a medium hot oven until done. Send the steaks to the table arranged neatly around the sides of a dish of green peas, or a brown sweetbread ragout, using the juices in the pan for a Bechamel- or Madeira sauce, taking the first when the dish is served with green peas or the latter when served with the ragout. For the family table the steaks may be arranged in a spiral form, then pour over them the greater part of the butter in which they were fried, put a border of mashed potatoes around the dish and serve with lettuce or a vegetable salad.

41. Pike Salad. (See Division Q.)

42. Eel Pout or Burbot. Empty the fish, leaving the liver but removing the gall bag, rinse thoroughly and then boil them for 15 minutes in water, salt and vinegar, let them lay in this broth for a little while and send to the table hot with a sour egg sauce or a tomato-, crab-, or fresh herb sauce (see Division K), together with boiled potatoes. Serve cold with vinegar, olive oil and pepper. The liver of the burbot is considered a delicacy; it is boiled with the fish a few minutes before the latter is served. But little salt is required, the same as with eels.

43. Fried Burbot. Burbot and other fresh water fish should be fried generally in the same manner as carp or pike; it will be well, however, to pickle them an hour beforehand in olive oil and lemon juice with parsley and sliced onions. A fitting accompaniment to sourkrout and salads.

II. SALT WATER FISH.

44. Boiled Sturgeon. After the fish is emptied wrap it into a cloth and let it lay on a stone slab in the cellar for 1—2 days, because its meat is tough when cooked fresh. Before boiling, rub it thoroughly with salt and water to remove all slime, then cut it into 5—10 pieces according to its size. Put it on the fire in cold water containing a handful of nettles, which assist in making the fish tender and in extracting the oil; let it draw slowly for ½ hour and take off the scum carefully. Then put the fish into fresh boiling water, add 6—10 onions, a few bay leaves, some cloves, peppercorns, a bunch of thyme, sage and majoram, and cook very slowly for another hour, taking off all of the fat with great care. Salt must not be added until the fish is quite tender, and then leave it in the broth a little while longer so that the salt may be absorbed. Take the fish out of the broth, remove all projecting gristle, cut into smaller pieces and send to the table with butter and a good mustard- or a parsley sauce (see Division R).

The left-over pieces can be preserved for several days in the fish broth after adding a little vinegar; serve with olive oil, vinegar, pepper, finely chopped onions and mustard.

45. Sturgeon Steaks. Take the left-over pieces out of the broth, cut them into slices about the thickness of a finger, dip them into eggs, pepper and minced eschalots, turn in cracker crumbs and fry on both sides in hot butter over a quick fire to a light brown. Send to the table with young carrots or with onions browned in butter.

46. Sturgeon a la Epicure. Cut a piece of sturgeon weighing about 4½ pounds into slices and lard them. Line the bottom of a large saucepan with fresh bacon, ham, onions, carrots and parsley roots, all sliced; on these lay the fish slices, sprinkle with salt, pour over them a veal bouillon and then add 1½ tablespoonfuls of butter, 1 bay leaf and a few peppercorns, cover the saucepan with a lid holding live embers, and let the fish simmer on a slow fire for a good half hour. When done strain the broth, thicken with flour rubbed in butter, add 1 glassful of white wine, and then pour the sauce so made over the fish slices which have been neatly arranged in the dish.

47. Boiled Cod Fish. If the fish is to be cooked on a Friday it should be put into water for freshening not later than the Tuesday forenoon preceding. Before putting it into the vessel for freshening, cover the fish for half an hour with water and then pound it with a wooden mallet, gently at first and with gradually increasing force and long enough until the meat has lost its firmness; it should not, however, be pounded into shreds; then divide it into pieces of uniform size. To soften the meat use either potash or soda; the latter is preferable because it is not so liable to leave an unpleasant taste. About 1 ounce of pulverized soda to each pound of fish is the proper proportion. Put the fish into a stone jar in layers sprinkled with the soda, cover with plenty of water and let it stand in a very cool place until the following Thursday morning, that is to say, for two days and two nights; then press the fish until dry, scrape off the scales and otherwise clean very nicely, cut off the fins, rinse and lay into fresh water. The water should be changed at least three times and the pieces pressed dry each time.

When preparing the fish lay the pieces on top of each other on a cloth; three hours before they are to be used put them on the fire in a kettle with cold water with a plate in the bottom of the kettle. Wrapping the pieces in the cloth keeps them in better shape. Heat the cod fish slowly and then let it draw, but it should never boil even in the slightest degree. When serving put the drained fish on a hot platter, sprinkle with fine salt, cover and send to the table with potatoes. About $\frac{1}{3}$—$\frac{1}{2}$ ounce of salt is the right proportion for dried cod fish. If the fish is to be salted in the water add the required quantity of salt about 15 minutes before serving, after taking out part of the fish broth. Most people prefer as a sauce simply plenty of good butter and mustard. Another sauce is made by boiling water, milk and fish broth, bind with cornstarch and then stir through it butter and mustard; do not cook the latter.

REMARK.—If more cod fish has been prepared than is consumed during the meal, what is left over can be warmed with butter over boiling water, or a pie can be made from it as directed in E, 21.

48. Fresh Cod Fish. Scrape and empty the fish, cut off the fins, remove the head and tail and divide the body into pieces 1—2 inches in width. The head, which many consider a delicacy, is divided in two if not too large, and scalded in sharply salted water for about 5 minutes beforehand, afterwards add the remaining pieces and boil for 10—15 minutes longer, carefully taking off all the scum. As soon as the fish is done put it on a warm dish, garnish with parsley and add butter, mustard and boiled potatoes; other kinds of sauces are appropriate, for instance parsley-, sorrel-, or an oyster sauce. For large parties the fish is served with another sauce besides melted butter. If it is to be sent to the table whole, whereby it remains much juicier, cook it on a quick fire in salted water. The liver cannot be used on account of its pungent flavor. Cod fish and all other salt fish are the nicest when boiled in milk and water half and half; they thereby receive a milder flavor and the meat becomes flakey.

In England cod fish is most generally served with the following sauce. Grate 8 hard-boiled eggs, mix with it 1 tablespoonful of chopped parsley, a teaspoonful of mustard, a little mace, salt and lemon juice, add a few spoonfuls of fish broth and ½ pound of fresh butter and stir the sauce on the stove until boiling hot.

A Hollandaise-, oyster- and Bechamel- or crab sauce can also be served with the cod fish.

49. Stewed Fresh Cod Fish. Cut off the head and tail, wash, salt and lay them into an earthenware vessel, add plenty of butter. rolled crackers, nutmeg or mace, a sliced lemon without the seeds, a large cupful of wine, cover and stew on a slow fire until tender. The body of the fish is cooked in the same way.

50. Fresh Cod Fish Roulades. Take a number of small fresh cod fish after they are cleaned and emptied, divide in two lengthwise, remove the skin and take out the bones, and then cut each half into 2 or 3 pieces, according to the size of the fish. Make a forcemeat of the scraps of the fish with the addition of savory herbs, sour cream, eggs, salt, pepper and grated bread, spread the forcemeat on the pieces of fish, roll them up and wrap in buttered paper, put them into a buttered pan with white wine, bouillon, savory herbs and bake slowly for ¾ hour. Then take off the paper, spread the rolls with a thick Remoulade sauce, sprinkle with grated bread, dot with crab butter and bake for a little while. Slice the rolls and serve with salsify.

51. Boiled Haddock. Scale, empty and wash the haddock and divide according to size into 3—4 pieces and after rinsing these once again, put them into boiling, rather strongly salted water, and take off the scum. After the fish has boiled for a few minutes leave it in the broth for a while longer to absorb some of the salt and send to the table hot.

Before transporting haddock they are frequently emptied and salted. In this case put them on the fire in cold water and exercise careful judgment in the application of salt. Serve with hot boiled potatoes, melted butter and mustard, or else with a mustard sauce.

52. Haddock with Savory Herbs. After cleaning the fish divide it into pieces and remove skin and bones carefully. Pickle these pieces for an hour in a glassful of white wine, the juice of a lemon, salt, pepper and minced herbs, then stew a dozen chopped mushrooms in butter with a handful of minced herbs and a few sliced eschalots. Simmer the fish in this for 10 minutes, add to it ½ of the marinade with a little more white wine, and stew the fish for 5 minutes longer. Strain the fish broth and stir through it flour rubbed in butter and extract of beef bouillon to a rather thick sauce, which is served with the fish.

53. Stuffed Haddock. Take 2 fish of medium size and after they are cleaned wash them, dry and fill with veal forcemeat A, No. 24, sew them, sprinkle with salt and brush all over with anchovy butter. Then lay them in a well buttered pan, bake in the oven for ½ hour to a light brown color, and in the meantime prepare the sauce as follows: Finely chop a few gherkins, eschalots and capers and rub with a tablespoonful of flour in brown butter and then boil with 2 cupfuls of hot bouillon. Strain the sauce and season, if necessary, with a little lemon juice and with pepper, salt and a spoonful of chopped parsley. Put the fish on a hot platter, garnish with sprigs of parsley and serve with the sauce.

54. Haddock in Hamburg Style. Take off the head and cut into slices about ¾ of an inch thick, salt and set aside for an hour, butter a pan and put in the pieces of the fish together with sliced raw potatoes alternately, sprinkle each layer with chopped onions heated in butter and with some pepper, and pour over all a large cupful of sour cream whipped with 3 eggs. Bake in the oven for a good half hour and send to the table with lettuce or a bean salad.

55. Boiled Turbot. In Germany turbot are considered the finest of all fishes and many esteem the head and tail as being particular delicacies. After rubbing the fish with salt and emptying, being careful to remove the gall bag from the liver, wash the fish with salted water, trim the fins, cut off the tail fully a hand's length and also the head with at least ½ inch of the flesh with it. Then divide the middle piece smoothly in two lengthwise, and cut the two halves into pieces of proper size. Cook in strongly salted water for about 10 minutes, skimming carefully; the fish is done when the fins can be easily pulled out. If the fish is to be boiled whole put it into a fish kettle, or when this is lacking wrap it in a napkin and put it on the fire in salted water with a plate in the bottom of the kettle. As soon as done drain and put the fish with the white side to the top on a warm dish and garnish with parsley. When sorrel is in season and quite young make a good sorrel sauce, at any other time a crab-, shrimp- or butter sauce, and particularly a Bearnese sauce, (see Division R). Nice boiled potatoes with melted butter, lemon juice and mustard are also very good.

56. Baked Turbot. The turbot is prepared the same as in the above receipt, divided into pieces, salted and baked the same as codfish. The same sauces are used as given for cooked turbot.

57. Crusted Turbot. Use for this purpose remnants of the fish. Remove all skin and bones and cut the meat into small pieces; stew them for a few moments with butter and chopped eschalots, mushrooms and parsley, add salt and pepper and put into a baking pan with the pieces heaping towards the middle, pour over it a few tablespoonfuls of white sauce, sprinkle the sur-

Fish — 𝔉𝔦𝔰𝔠𝔥𝔢.

1 Grayling—Aesche; 2 Lobster—Hummer; 3 Sea-mullet—Meeräsche; 4 Tench—Schleie; 5 Haberdine—Klippfisch; 6 Perch—Barsch; 7 Smelt—Stint; 8 Shiner—Weiszling; 9 Plaice—Scholle; 10 Groundling—Gründling; 11 Sardine—Sardine; 12 Flounder—Flunder; 13 Herring—Häring; 14 Trout—Forelle; 15 Mackerel—Makrele; 16 Roach—Roche; 17 Lamprey—Lamprete; 18 Crab—Krabbe; 19 Codfish—Stockfisch; 20 Haddock—Schellfisch; 21 Carp—Karpfen; 22 Crawfish—Krebs; 23 Barbel—Rothbart; 24 Long-nose Skate—Glattroche; 25 Sprat—Sprote; 26 Pickerel—Hecht; 27 Halibut—Hellbutte; 28 Pearl—Brill; 29 Eel—Aal; 30 White Shrimp—Seeheuschrecke; 31 Whitefish—Weiszfisch; 32 Peter's fish—Goldfisch, Petersfisch; 33 Turbot—Steinbutte; 34 Shrimp—Taschenkrebs, Garnele; 35 Barbel—Barbe; 36 Shad—Alse; 37 Sturgeon—Stör; 38 **Grunter—Knurrhase**; 39 Salmon—Salm; 40 Sole—Seezunge; 41 Minnow—Elritze.

face with bread crumbs and dot with butter. When this gratin is of a nice brown color send to the table at once with a dish of creamy mashed potatoes into which the yolks of a few eggs have been stirred.

58. Boiled Soles. Soles have a white and a gray side, the first is scraped and skinned from the tail upwards. Cut off the head, the point of the tail and the fins, empty the fish, wash several times with cold water and let it lay for an hour in salted water. Then cook in boiling salted water with onions and coarse spices for a few minutes until done. Garnish the dish with sprigs of parsley, sliced lemons and serve with boiled potatoes and a crab- or butter sauce (see Division R), with mustard according to taste.

59. Fried Soles. After the fish is cleaned, sprinkle with salt, let it stand for an hour or two, dry with a cloth, cut slits into the skin over the entire fish, brush with a beaten egg mixed with a little water, dredge with rolled crackers and fry on both sides in hot butter or lard in an open pan on a quick fire, to a crisp and light brown color.

60. Fried Soles, Bremen Style. After the fish have been cleaned they should be cut into several pieces if they are large, otherwise leave them whole, salt and let them stand for an hour. Then dry them, turn in melted butter first and then in egg and bread crumbs and fry. In the meantime stir 6 tablespoonfuls of creamed butter with 2 tablespoonfuls of anchovy butter, the juice of 2 lemons, salt, nutmeg, 1 tablespoonful of mustard and 1 tablespoonful of minced parsley to a cream. Put the fish into the pan in layers, and the cream between them, and serve with boiled potatoes and a dish of potato salad.

61. Fillets of Soles. The fillets are cut the same as pike, salted and laid in lemon juice for 1 hour. Make a forcemeat of remnants of poultry, crab butter, eggs, salt, pepper and grated wheat bread and spread over the fillets. Melt some fresh butter, lay the fillets in this with sliced truffles and over these some pork fat and then a buttered paper, and bake in the oven for 15 minutes. In the meantime stew young mushrooms in butter, bouillon and lemon juice until done, fill into the middle of the dish and surround them with the fillets which have been taken out of the paper and pork fat.

62. Baked Fillets of Soles with Sauce. When baking or making a fricassee of the soles it is better to skin the fish on both sides. This is easily done by loosening the skin at the end of the tail and rapidly pulling it off. Cut the sole into 4 pieces, take the flesh from the bones, pickle these 4 fillets in lemon juice, salt and parsley leaves. Shortly before serving take them out of the pickle, dip in egg and nutmeg, sprinkle with cracker crumbs and fry in browned butter, basting often, until crisp and of a dark yellow color. Garnish the same as given for boiled soles and serve with a- Remoulade-, anchovy-, caper- or crab sauce, (see Division R), or serve as is usually done in Holland, with good fresh lettuce. Potato salad is often served with it in Bremen.

63. Baked Soles with Lemon Juice. The soles are prepared as directed in the above receipt and laid for 1—2 hours in lemon juice, salt, chopped eschalots and spices. Before baking dry the fillet, turn in flour and then in egg and bread crumbs and bake in plenty of lard to a light brown color. The soles are sent to the table hot on a napkin and garnished with a bunch of parsley. Serve with a highly spiced sauce, or as a side dish with young peas, asparagus, etc.

The fish can also be fried in butter and served with a fine ragout of oysters, crabs, and the like.

64. Boiled Mackerel. The mackerel is a nice, fat fish. Cut off the head and lay it in strongly salted water with a little vinegar for an hour, in one large or a number of smaller pieces. If it is boiled whole, lay it on a plate and pour hot vinegar over it. In the meantime, cook some onions, tarragon, thyme, sweet basil, pepper and cloves in salted water, put the mackerel into a fish kettle and cook for a few minutes, skim, add some vinegar and serve with a Travemunder sauce, (see Division R).

The mackerel is also fried and left in a pickle of lemon juice and salt for a little while like other fish.

65. Boiled Smelts. Wash and clean the fish thoroughly and boil in salted water for a few minutes, skimming carefully. Then pour into it a little cold water; serve the fish with hot potatoes, butter and mustard and a sour egg sauce, (see Division R).

66. Baked Smelts are prepared the same as boiled smelts, nicely washed, put on a colander and sprinkled with fine salt, turned in flour and fried crisp in plenty of hot fat to a light yellow color. Potato salad is served with it.

REMARK.—The smelt is a dry fish, and plenty of fat must be used in frying.

67. Fish Rice. ¼ pound of rice is cooked in salted water with a little butter or in bouillon until thick and done, boil 3—4 eggs until hard, cut the whites into small pieces and grate the yolks. In the meantime bone about ¾ pound of fish, taking out all the skin, and break the meat into pieces. Then mix the rice with the fish and the whites of the eggs, stir over the fire until hot with 2 spoonfuls of melted butter, a little salt, cayenne pepper and nutmeg, put the fish rice on a hot dish and sprinkle over it the grated yolks of the eggs. Using half cream and half crab butter mixed with stewed mushrooms and the whole stirred with a few whipped eggs, will make the dish much nicer.

68. Caviar Sandwiches. Butter wheat bread toast, spread thickly with caviar and serve with lemon slices and finely chopped onions.

69. Anchovy Sandwiches. Either toast wheat bread slices or brown them in butter, or else soak the bread in milk and egg and rapidly brown it in melted butter. Then spread the bread with a sauce as described further on and cover with anchovies prepared as directed under A, No. 31. Line the inside of a dish with these bread slices in such a manner that they overlap shingle-fashion. Put hard boiled eggs divided into halves into the middle of the dish with the square edges to the top and pour over them the following herb sauce: Grate the yolks of 4 hard boiled eggs and gradually stir with them minced herbs such as estragon, parsley and burnet, also a small cupful of bouillon, 2 tablespoonfuls of olive oil, 1—2 tablespoonfuls of wine vinegar, capers, mustard and some pepper.

70. Fried Fresh Herring. After the fish are cleaned and emptied, wash, salt and dry them. Then pickle for an hour in lemon juice, a little salt and pepper, turn in egg and then in cracker crumbs and mace. Fry in hot butter. Herring can be filled and fried and are then very delicious. Melt 3 heaping tablespoonfuls of butter, stir in as much rye bread as will absorb the butter, add 2 eggs, 2 chopped eschalots, salt and pepper and fill into the fish.

71. Boiled Fresh Herring. After the fish have been cleaned and washed, sprinkle with salt, dip into vinegar, turn the tail of the fish into its mouth and then cook in boiling salted water for about 10 minutes. Garnish the dish with sprigs of parsley or grated horseradish and serve with a parsley or butter sauce.

72. Fried Salt Herring in Mecklenburg Style. Remove fins, bones, roes or milt, and put the herring into milk to freshen. Then dry them, turn in a sauce made of wine, the yolks of a few eggs and flour and fry in hot butter. Serve with sourkrout.

73. Pickled Herring. After cleaning the herring take out the milt without opening the body. Wash carefully and lay them preferably into milk, or else into water, for two days to freshen them. Then for 12 herrings take 1 nutmeg, 1 ounce of white mustard seeds, 8 eschalots, and 12 white peppercorns, pound finely and put part of the mixture into each herring. Put the fish into a jar in layers with small onions, peppergrass, tarragon, thyme, bay leaves; stir up the milt with vinegar and pour into the jar.

Herring can be pickled in a simpler way by omitting filling them with the above mixture, or else the vinegar may be stirred to a thick sauce with the strained milt; the sauce is then poured over the fish. Before pickling, herring are frequently cut into thin slices.

74. Broiled Herring. After the fish has been freshened and dried, trim the head a little smaller on both sides, take out the eyes, and brown on a broiler, then lay them into a dish with lemon slices, bay leaves, coarse ground pepper and cloves and pour over them some beer, vinegar and salad oil.

They are served for breakfast, also with pea soup.

75. **Herring for Tea.** About 1½ cupfuls of sour cream are well beaten, add 3 teaspoonfuls of mustard, 2 tablespoonfuls of olive oil, the same quantity of vinegar, ½ of a grated onion and a little pepper, and stir well together. To the above quantity take 6 freshened boned herrings, cut into long pieces and mix with the sauce. Serve with bread and butter for tea.

76. **Herring with Remoulade Sauce.** After the herring have been freshened and skinned tear into halves down the middle, bone, cut into pieces and pour over them a good Remoulade sauce. Serve for breakfast or supper.

77. **Herring Cream.** Freshen 6 herring for 24 hours and then cut them into pieces. Lay the pieces into a dish, take 1 cupful of not too strong vinegar, and beat into this the yolks of 6 eggs, ½ pound of butter, 2 large grated onions, 1 heaping teaspoonful of mustard and 1 tablespoonful of sugar, stir on the fire to a cream, let it cool and pour over the herring pieces. Garnish with hard boiled eggs, mushrooms, gherkins or button onions.

78. **Herring Rolls.** The herring are freshened, split down the back and divided into two pieces. After they are carefully boned, spread the inner side with mustard and grated onions, then with capers, roll tight, tie with a white thread (which is taken off when the fish is sent to the table), and serve with a sauce as directed for pickled herring. A very nice and quickly made dish to serve with cold meat.

79. **Broiled Bloaters.** If they are to be cooked on a broiler, split them down the back, empty, but leave in the milt, put a piece of butter on the fish, clap them together, wrap into buttered paper and cook until done. If you have no broiler, open the body of the bloaters instead of the back and after they have been emptied fry them nicely in butter.

80. **Boiled Lobster.** The lobster is killed by putting it head first into seething hot water with plenty of salt. Carraway seed is often put into the water, also a bunch of parsley. The water must be kept boiling during the entire time the lobster is cooking. The lobster should

boil according to size from 10—15 minutes, if very large 15—20 minutes; leave it in the water 15 minutes longer to cool, and after taking it out brush with a piece of pork fat or good olive oil, which will give it a bright appearance. Before serving, split it lengthwise into two pieces and cut it crosswise into smaller pieces, break the claws so that the meat can be easily taken out, put the pieces together so that it will have its original form, and garnish with parsley leaves.

Serve the lobster warm with butter, chopped parsley and a lemon cut into 8 pieces. When the lobster is brought to the table cold, serve it with olive oil, wine vinegar and parsley.

81. American Lobster. After the lobster is cooked as given under No. 80, take off the meat, cut the meat from the tail into slices and the meat from the claws into small pieces, and stew both for $\frac{1}{4}$ hour in a sauce made as follows: Stew a few eschalots in butter, add 1 cupful of white wine, take 6 tomatoes, stew and then pass them through a sieve and then stir through it 1 cupful of brown sauce. Season the sauce with cayenne pepper, stew the meat and fill the dish in such a manner that the larger pieces of the lobster form a border around the smaller pieces heaped in the center. A border of rice around the whole is very delicious.

82. Lobster Fricassee with Fish Balls and Asparagus. Take fat young spring chickens, clean and boil them in not too much salted water with a piece of butter and mace, skimming carefully. About $\frac{1}{4}$ hour before they are done add some cleaned and parboiled asparagus. When the chickens are done, cut all the meat into cubes, pour the broth with a little fat over this, put in the asparagus, cover, and set aside in a warm place. In the remaining broth cook some fish dumplings (see Division O) which are put with the asparagus. Then stir as much flour and butter as is needed to a fricassee sauce, let it cook, and pour the chicken broth to it; cook for $\frac{1}{2}$ hour and strain through a fine sieve. This sauce is put into a rinsed dish with the meat of the chicken, asparagus and dumplings and cooked for a few minutes, add the lobster pieces, which must not boil again, take the dish from the stove, stir the sauce with

1—2 yolks of eggs, put the fricassee into a hot dish and serve with croutons.

83. Lobster Salad with Caviar Sandwiches. This receipt will be found under Salads, (see Division Q).

84. Crabs. The crabs are put into cold water and cleaned with a whisk broom. In the meantime heat a piece of butter in a kettle, pour in a little vinegar, add a bunch of parsley, pepper and salt, and when the water boils put in the crabs and stir them a few times. After about 10—15 minutes they will receive a red color, take from the fire, put them on a napkin, pile in pyramid form and garnish with parsley.

85. Fried Oysters. Sprinkle a few drops of lemon juice on the oysters, add a very little mace, turn in egg and mace, then in grated crackers and fry in a pan in hot butter; frying the oysters too long makes them hard. They can also be baked in butter for a few moments.

Another way is to dry the oysters with a cloth and sprinkle with wheat flour. Then fry 2 small onions in butter until light brown, fry the oysters in this for a few seconds, sprinkle with salt and pepper and drop over them a few drops of lemon juice.

86. Oyster Stew. Open a few dozen oysters, cut off the beards, sprinkle with lemon juice, put the beards of the oysters together with the liquor and pepper, mace and lemon peel into a stew pan, let it boil for half an hour, thicken the broth with flour lightly browned, add 1 cupful of thick sweet cream and stir the broth until thick. Heat the oysters in this and serve immediately.

87. Fish Pudding. See Puddings, No. 41.

Boiled trout, pike-perch, pike and oysters are the only kinds of fish that should be served to invalids. With these fish serve only a butter sauce, which is stirred with a few yolks of eggs and seasoned with a little lemon juice, or fresh butter stirred to a cream; a Bechamel- or Hollandaise sauce can also be served.

G.—Rare Dishes of Various Kinds.

---

1. Turtle Soup. Medium-sized turtles are better than the very large ones, because the meat of the latter is usually tough. The day before the turtle is cooked, hang it up by the hind legs and as soon as it puts out its head, cut it off; then let it bleed for about 4 hours, lay on a meat board, cut the under side all around from the shell and empty carefully, cut away the gall bag which is attached to the liver. The liver and heart, also the eggs if there are any, are laid in fresh water. After the turtle is emptied cut the forefeet with quite a piece of the flesh from each side, and smaller pieces from the hind feet. The fins are cut off and the feet and the under side scalded in boiling water, so that the skin can be taken off. It is not advisable to cook the turtle whole, as it is very slimy and has quite a strong flavor.

Wash the meat carefully, lay for a few hours in cold water, changing the water frequently, and then hang up the meat over night to let it air. The next day put the heart and meat with some thin beef bouillon on the stove to cook, (the bouillon can be made the day before), with the necessary salt, skim carefully and put into the broth a bunch of tarragon and thyme, finely chopped onions and a bottle of white wine, and let the meat cook in this until done. Then take the meat out of the broth, and after it is cold cut it into long, neat pieces. The liver is not cooked with it, but is stewed in butter until tender, then cut into pieces and laid into the tureen.

The turtle soup is served clear, also thickened; the latter kind is preferred. When it is to be thickened, brown some flour in butter, stir with it some of the broth and put into the soup. The turtle meat is cooked in the soup for ¼ hour and seasoned with powdered ginger, cayenne pepper, cloves and mace; dumplings may also be added and are made of some of the raw turtle meat as follows: Chop the turtle meat with some beef marrow, pound it in a mortar, and then mix with some bread, eggs, salt, mace, grated lemon peel and white pepper and make small dumplings. Instead of these, veal dumplings can also be used. As dumplings when cooked in a thickened soup make the latter too thick, it is well to cook the dumplings in the soup before the browned flour is put in, and when the dumplings are done put them into a tureen with some of the bouillon while thickening the soup.

If it is desired to put turtle sausages into the soup, take the same forcemeat described as above for the dumplings. Mix with it a small glassful of brandy, some finely chopped eschalots rubbed in plenty of beef marrow, a little white pepper and some minced liver and fill this into very small sausage casings, boil the sausages until done, cut them into oblique pieces and put them into the tureen when the soup is served. Should there be any eggs in the turtle put them into the soup together with a bottle of Madeira. Serve the soup very hot over the liver and dumplings.

A medium-sized turtle will take about 1½—2 hours in cooking, and an old one from 3—3½ hours.

2. Soup made of Canned Turtle. In cooking the soup the green fat, which has an oily flavor, should be removed as much as possible by means of hot water. Then cut the meat into small cubes, bring to a boil once in a strong Espagnole sauce with Madeira, and serve.

The Espagnole sauce is made as follows: Line the bottom of a deep saucepan with fresh butter about ¼ of an inch thick, put in a pound of sliced, lean, raw ham, then 3—4 large sliced Spanish onions, 1 pound of lean veal, 2 old partridges or 2 old pigeons, an old chicken and the remnants of uncooked or roasted poultry, pour in 2 bastingspoonfuls of bouillon and put the pan on a slow fire, allowing the whole to simmer slowly and to draw until it is of a light brown, being very careful not to scorch. Then fill up with the bouillon, bring to a boil, skim off the fat very thoroughly, put in some carrots, green leek, parsnips and cook slowly. In the meantime lightly brown some flour in ½ pound of fresh butter for 1 hour over a slow fire, stir with bouillon until thin and smooth and cook for 2 hours slowly and uninterruptedly, taking off all the fat and scum frequently and carefully; then pass the broth through a fine sieve, add ½ bottle of Madeira and then cook until rather thick, constantly stirring, adding at the last the juice of a lemon.

3. Snail Soup. The vineyard and the spiral species are the only kinds that can be used for this soup, and then only when they are closed. Boil for an hour in boiling salted water, pull them out of their shells with a fork, take off the little patch of skin from the top, cut away the ring which encircles the snail and remove the front point. Sprinkle with a handful of salt which will loosen the slime, wash them 3 or 4 times in warmed water and press them dry. Boil about 50 snails in bouillon, take them out of the kettle, chop 2—3 of them very finely, stew in butter for a short time, add as much bouillon as is required to make the soup, put in a little mace and boil for a few minutes, stir in the yolks of a few eggs and serve the soup with wheat bread toast and the rest of the snails in the tureen.

If the soup is cooked during Lent, boil all of the snails in water until tender, chop all of them finely with 4 hard boiled eggs, 2 onions, minced parsley and a few rolls soaked in milk, stew this in butter for 15 minutes. Then pour in part of the snail broth, ½ bottle of light wine and a pint of pea broth, season with salt and pepper and stir through the soup the yolks of a few eggs.

4. Snails in Sauce. Take a few washed and boned anchovies, and chop fine with a little parsley. Then knead a tablespoonful of stale grated wheat bread, a little flour and 2 heaping tablespoonfuls of butter, mix the chopped anchovy and parsley with this, stir with good bouillon, lay the snails into this with a little mace and pepper and cook for ¼ hour. A very nice dish is made by serving the snails in their shells, which should be nicely cleaned and dried. Then take anchovies, parsley, the spices already mentioned, butter, wheat bread, flour, knead all together, fill some of it into a shell, lay a snail on this and cover with some of the mixture. After the shells have all been filled in this manner, put them into a saucepan with the openings to the top, add a bastingspoonful of bouillon and serve after cooking for ¼ hour.

5. Snail Salad. The snails are cleaned as directed in No. 4 and cut lengthwise into pieces, or else leave them whole and mix with salt, pepper, finely chopped onions and two parts of olive oil to one part of vinegar

6. Ragout of Frog Legs. Put the frog legs into a deep dish with water, vinegar and salt and wash thoroughly with a whisk. Then melt some butter, lay the frog legs with a few eschalots and a little salt into this, cover and simmer until nearly done. Then sprinkle over it some flour, add some strong bouillon, made of extract of beef, mace and a few lemon slices, cook the frog legs until done and stir the sauce with a few yolks of eggs. Wheat bread or meat dumplings cooked in either salted water or bouillon can also be laid around the ragout.

7. Frog Leg Pie. Make a ragout as directed in No. 6, with good meat dumplings and fill into the pie.

8. Ptarmigan or White Grouse is cooked the same as prairie chicken, but the entire skin must be pulled off with the feathers.

9. Coot. The skin of the coot has an oily taste and must be taken off; then tie pork fat slices around the bird and roast it like wild duck.

10. Guinea Fowl are only fit for use when quite young; roast like prairie chicken.

11. Roast Peacock. A Suabian Receipt. The half-grown peacock is the best for a roast. It is killed about three days before wanted for use, plucked up to half of the neck, the head taken off, emptied and washed clean. Rub inside and out with salt and pepper, fill into it a bay leaf, some parsley and some sweet basil, lay some pork fat on the breast, or lard the breast and legs with fine pork fat lardoons and roast slowly. If it is to be roasted on a spit, tie over the breast some buttered paper. When serving, lay the head with the peacock, garnish the dish with water cresses and serve with an oyster- or brown sauce; season with lemon slices.

If liked a well-seasoned veal forcemeat may be filled into the peacock.

13. Suabian Peacock Pie. Kill a young half-grown peacock a few days before it is to be used; cut off the head, pluck, empty, wash very thoroughly, rub inside and out with spices and salt. Put a piece of butter into a saucepan, let the meat simmer in this for a little while, mince the liver with a small piece of pork fat and an onion, brown a handful of bread crumbs in butter, simmer the mince in this, pour the butter out of the pan and substitute for it the minced liver, etc., together with ¼ bottle of wine; boil an ounce of truffles in wine and put them in with the wine, a large spoonful of bouillon, a few lemon slices, a little sweet basil and a few bay leaves, cover the pan tightly and when the peacock has been cooked slowly until nearly done, let it cool in this sauce. Make a good butter crust, put in the bird with a piece of pork fat on its breast, close and brush the crust as usual and bake in an oven for ¾ of an hour to a light brown. The remaining sauce is thinned with bouillon and a little lemon juice and kept hot. When the pie is taken out of the oven remove the upper crust and pour in the sauce, then put the head of the peacock on the cover, close the pie and send it to the table hot.

Old birds can be used for small pies only, for instance, pies of various kinds of meat (see E, No. 11); it may be well to lay the meat into a seasoned broth some time beforehand.

14. Mountain Cock or Grouse. For roasting, young birds only should be taken as the older ones are almost invariably tough and fit for ragouts or fricassees only. Fill with the following forcemeat: Chop a piece of good veal with some raw ham and its fat very finely, then add a few yolks of eggs with a couple of ground cloves, some thick sweet cream, grated wheat bread, salt and the frothed whites of the eggs, mix well, fill into the bird and roast like turkey.

15. Mountain Cock Pies. Cut the bird into small pieces, take out all of the bones, slightly roast the meat in butter and let it lay in wine vinegar with pepper, nutmeg and button onions for a few hours. In the meantime finely chop equal parts of veal, beef and fresh pork, add the yolk of an egg and the chopped yolks of several hard boiled eggs, some wheat bread and nutmeg. Line the bottom of the pie mould with pork fat and butter, put on a layer of the meat, then a layer of the chopped meat and so on until the mould is filled. Put a few lemon slices on top, sprinkle with salt and pour in ½ bottle of wine. Cover the mould tightly and cook on a slow fire for 4—5 hours. If the pie should become too dry, add a little more wine. After the pie is done, remove the lemon slices, bind the gravy with egg yolks and send the dish to the table cold.

16. Roast Badger. A young badger is quite palatable and tender, similar to pork tenderloin. Let it lay in vinegar for 2—3 days, with onions, carrots, sage and all kinds of kitchen herbs, bay leaves, pepper, cloves and salt; lard and roast it like young hare, but for a shorter length of time.

17. Ragout of Badger. All of the meat which is not used for the roast is cut into pieces and prepared like ragout of hare ("Hasenpfeffer"). If there should not be enough of the meat some pork may be added.

18. Bear's Paws. Bear's paws are by many considered to be a great delicacy, in fact the best part of the bear. Clean the forepaws very nicely, boil in salted water until tender, dip them in melted butter, egg, and then in bread crumbs, broil with frequent basting until lightly brown. Garnish with lemon slices and capers and send to the table with any kind of a spicy gravy. Sometimes the paws are pickled in vinegar and savory herbs for a day beforehand; then boil in bouillon and part of the marinade instead of water before broiling them.

19. Roast Bear. The hindquarters and the saddle of a young bear are the best for roasting. Meat from an old bear should be pickled in vinegar for a few days and then laid in milk for another day before roasting. Put the roast into the oven with a little water, add salt, baste freqently and roast for 3—4 hours. Take the fat from the gravy, stir into it a little sour cream, and serve with the roast.

20. Roast Beaver Tails. The flesh of the beaver is usually braised, but the tail, which is considered a delicacy, is roasted after it has lain in a marinade for a day. Scrape it carefully, boil in vinegar, water and some salt until tender and then turn it in whipped egg yolks and rolled crackers. Pour melted butter over it, roast on a broiler and serve with sliced lemons.

H.—Hot Puddings.

1. **How Puddings are cooked.** The pudding mould should never be used until it has been tested by pouring water into it to see if it is perfectly tight. The slightest leak in the mould will inevitably spoil the pudding.

Before using the mould rub it thoroughly on the inside with a dry cloth and carefully and plentifully butter it, and afterwards dredge with rolled cracker or finely grated wheat bread. If the mould has not been carefully buttered the pudding will adhere to it and tear or crumble in taking out. When through using, it is important to at once clean the mould and keep it in a dry place.

A trifle of salt should be put into all puddings, puffs and other sweet dishes, otherwise they will be apt to have an insipid taste.

The pudding dough must be vigorously stirred and the whites of the eggs used should be beaten until stiff, if possible by an assistant, so that it will not be necessary to interrupt stirring the pudding. As soon as the froth has been slightly stirred through the pudding, it should be put into the mould immediately, setting it into boiling water, except in case of yeast puddings.

When making yeast puddings the mould should be filled only about one-half and put on the fire in lukewarm water, at other times it is usual to fill the mould about three-fourths. Then cover tightly and close the edge with a thick paste of flour and water; put the mould into boiling water, but not too deep, in order that the water in boiling may not penetrate through the edge of the cover and thus spoil the pudding. To prevent the mould from lifting in the kettle, which sometimes occurs, secure it by putting some weights on it or tying it to the cover with a string. A false bottom in the kettle, either a piece of slate, an old plate, etc., will be advantageous and if through neglect the water should boil away, the pudding will not then scorch. Puddings should cook continuously and uniformly, replenishing the boiling water whenever necessary, and also being cautious not to jar the mould, which is apt to make the pudding fall.

When cooking puddings in a cloth the latter should be rinsed in hot water, then wring dry, brush with butter and dredge with flour as far as the pudding will cover the cloth. As soon as the pudding is filled into the cloth tie it tightly with a string, leaving enough loose cloth for expansion; the water should boil vigorously and uninterruptedly, otherwise the pudding will become heavy and spoil. A mould is always preferable.

Puddings should always be served in a hot dish during the cold season, or if the kitchen happens to be at some distance from the dining room, take the pudding out of the mould just before it is set on the table.

All puddings will be best when cooked in a double kettle.

2. English Plum Pudding, No. 1. For 12—14 persons use 4 eggs, (the whites beaten to a froth), about 1 pint of sweet cream, ½ pound of fine flour, ½ pound of kidney suet, ½ pound of nicely washed currants, ¾ pound of stoned and finely chopped raisins, 2½ tablespoonfuls of sugar, 1 ounce of citron, 1 ounce of orange peel, ½ grated nutmeg, ½ wineglassful of rum and a little salt.

If not liked, the orange peel and citron may be omitted. Stir all well together, put into a mould and cook for 4 hours. When serving pour arrac or rum over the pudding, light and bring to the table flaming. A white cream sauce (see Division R), is very appropriate.

For the family table make a plain sauce of butter rubbed with flour, add boiling water with sugar, cinnamon and a little salt, 1 glassful of wine and a dash of rum.

REMARK.—This pudding can be made the day previously, as warming over in the mould will not hurt it any.

3. English Plum Pudding, No. 2. For 12—14 persons take ½ pound of raisins, ½ pound of currants,

½ pound of kidney suet, ½ pound of cracker crumbs, ½ pound of sugar, ¼ pound of citron, 2 ounces of sweet pounded almonds, 2 ounces of orange peel, ½ grated nutmeg, 1 wineglassful of rum, a little salt and 4 whole eggs, of which the whites should not be frothed.

A pudding which is to be cooked in a pudding cloth must be quite thick and the bread or cracker crumbs must be moistened with a little milk, so that it will stir nicely in the pudding.

The dough is thoroughly stirred and then cooked in a pudding cloth for 6 hours.

4. Plum Pudding with Wheat Bread. For 24 persons beat 6 whole and the yolks of 6 eggs, and stir to them alternately, so that the flour will not become lumpy, ½ pound of flour, 3 cupfuls of milk, 1 pound of stale wheat bread crumbs, ¾ pound of finely chopped kidney suet, ½ pound of stoned raisins, ½ pound of currants and a little salt.

Stir all well together, put it into a large mould or into a pudding cloth, first rubbing a little flour over the latter to prevent the pudding from adhering to it, and tie it, leaving room for the pudding to raise. Put the pudding into the kettle and cook for 3—4 hours.

5. Rolled English Pudding. For 16 persons take 1 pound of flour, ½ pound of kidney suet, 1 egg, 1 small cupful of cold water and 1 spoonful of sugar. Stir well together and then roll the dough into an oblong sheet, lay on this stoned cherries or plums and sprinkle well with sugar. Or take preserves of any kind, or a compot, roll, lay in a napkin, close at both ends and cook in boiling water fully 2 hours.

This pudding is eaten with powdered sugar. It can be served cold as a cake but in this case butter instead of kidney suet is used.

6. English Apple Pudding. 1 pound of flour, ½ pound of kidney suet, which has lain in water over night and then chopped fine, 1 teaspoonful of ginger and 1 teaspoonful of salt. Rub all well together and take water enough to make a dough, which is then kneaded like bread until it will not stick to the hands. Then roll out the dough, lay a napkin into a deep dish, dust a little flour over it, lay the dough over this, fill with quartered pared apples, a few whole cloves, cover the dough over this, tie the napkin over the pan and cook in slightly salted water for 2 hours. Serve with sugar without a sauce.

This pudding can also be made by covering the apples with pieces of butter, 3 ounces of currants, 3 ounces of raisins, 1½ ounces of orange peel, some sugar and a little rum before it is filled into the dough.

7. English Chestnut Pudding. Take 1 pound of chestnuts, slit the shell and roast until the kernel is easily freed from the shell and brown inner skin. Take half of the chestnuts, pound them with 3 ounces of butter, mix with 6 ounces of finely chopped kidney suet, 4 tablespoonfuls of sugar, a little over ¼ pound of raisins, 4 whole eggs and the yolks of 3 eggs, 1 cupful of cream, a little nutmeg, 3 ounces of rolled macaroons, the remainder of the chestnuts and 2 ounces of flour. Put into a pudding mould or a buttered napkin, steam the pudding for 2½ hours and serve with a rum sauce.

8. Suet Pudding. 1 pound of flour, ½ pound of minced veal suet, 1 pint of milk, 3 eggs, 3—5 tablespoonfuls of sugar, a little salt, (if liked, a few finely pounded almonds and a little lemon peel), stirred well together, and put into a pudding mould which has been lined with fine bread crumbs; cook for 2 hours. The pudding is eaten with a compot made of fresh cherries, pears or plums, also dried plums and apple sauce.

9. Rice Pudding with Macaroons. For 12—14 persons take ½ pound of rice, 1 quart of milk, a little cinnamon, some salt and lemon peel, ¼ pound of butter, ¼ pound of sugar, 10 eggs and ¼ pound of bitter macaroons. If wished, instead of the macaroons ¼ pound of washed and dried raisins can be used and spiced with a few pounded bitter almonds. If the raisins are omitted add 6 ounces of pounded sweet and a few bitter almonds.

Scald the rice and cook it in the milk, adding the cinnamon and lemon peel and cook until done; the rice must be thick. After the rice has cooled stir the butter to a cream, add the sugar, lemon peel and yolks of eggs to the rice, and after mixing, lightly stir the beaten whites of the eggs through the pudding. Put the pudding into a buttered mould with the macaroons and steam for 2½ hours. A cream sauce is served with this pudding.

10. Grits Pudding. For 12—14 persons take ¾ pound of grits, nearly 1 quart of milk, ¼ pound of butter, ¼ pound of sugar, 12 eggs, the grated rind of a lemon, a little salt or 6 finely pounded bitter almonds. Boil half of the milk and stir the grits with the rest and half of the butter until all is thick. Then stir the rest of the butter to a cream and add, continually stirring, the yolks of eggs, almonds, sugar, the grits after they have cooled somewhat, and gently stir through this the beaten whites of the eggs. Instead of using grits, rice flour can be substituted, although the rice flour must be dissolved with cold milk. A good way is to fill the form three-fourths full and then take macaroons that have been soaked in wine and put them over the top.

Let the pudding steam for 2½—3 hours and serve with cream, rum or claret sauce.

11. Cabinet Pudding, No. 1. For 12—14 persons take ¼ pound of flour, ¼ pound of sugar, 1 large cupful of milk, ¼ pound of butter, 10 fresh eggs, 1 ounce of lemon and 1 ounce of orange peel cut into small pieces, 3 ounces of currants, 3 ounces of stoned raisins and 2 heaping spoonfuls of pounded bitter almonds. The flour is stirred in one-half of the boiling milk, to which is added one-half of the butter and cooked until it leaves the sides of the kettle. Then stir the rest of the butter to a cream, stir the other ingredients together, add to the pudding and then stir in the beaten whites of the eggs. The pudding is cooked for 2½ hours and is served with a cream sauce.

12. Cabinet Pudding, No. 2. Butter a pudding mould and line it with a buttered paper. Take 6 ounces of stoned raisins, 3 ounces of currants, a little sugar and a glassful of Marascino liquor, and cook until soft; put 6 ounces of canned cherries on a colander to drain. Make a dough of 6 ounces of sugar, 12 eggs, 6 ounces of flour and a little lemon peel, then bake four layers a little smaller than the bottom of the pudding mould. Stir 2 whole eggs and the yolks of 6 eggs with 6 ounces of sugar, 1 pint of thick cream and 1 glassful of Marascino and pass this through a sieve. When this is done put a layer of raisins in the bottom of the mould, a layer of the baked biscuits over this, then a few table-spoonfuls of the cream, one-fourth of the cherries and raisins and so on alternately, finishing with a biscuit layer on the top. Put over this a buttered paper, steam the pudding 1½ hours and after taking out of the mould serve with a Marascino sauce.

13. Figaro Pudding. For 15—18 persons take ⅔ pound of grits or rice flour, nearly 1 quart of milk and a little over ¼ pound of butter, 14 eggs and 6 ounces of sugar. Cook the rice with the milk and one-half of the butter until done and thick, stir the remaining butter to a cream, add the yolks of eggs and some sugar to the boiled rice and divide this into four equal parts. To one part add chocolate (see Division S—"To color Frosting") and a little vanilla. The second part is colored with a little spinach juice and seasoned with orange peel. The third part is colored with a trifle of cochineal and to this part add a little grated lemon peel or cinnamon. The last part remains white and is seasoned with 1 ounce of finely pounded almonds mixed with a few bitter ones. Then beat the whites of 12 eggs to a stiff froth, divide this froth into four parts and stir lightly through the four different parts of the pudding mass which are put alternately into the pudding mould. The pudding is steamed for 2½ hours; serve with a cream sauce.

14. Currant Pudding. For 14—16 persons take ¼ pound of butter, ½ pound of flour, a little over a pint of milk, 8 large eggs, 3 heaping tablespoonfuls of sugar, the grated rind of a lemon or one-half of a nutmeg, ½ pound of washed currants, 6 ounces of grated wheat bread and a wineglassful of arrac or rum.

A new way to make the dough for this pudding is to let the milk come to a boil and while this is being done take the flour and butter, knead it into little balls and then drop these balls one by one into the boiling milk, stirring constantly until they dissolve, and cook until the mass is thick and no longer adheres to the sides of the kettle. When this has cooled add the yolks of eggs, sugar, seasoning, currants and wheat bread, then lightly stir through this the beaten whites of the eggs mixed with the rum; fill into the buttered pudding mould, cover and steam for 2½—3 hours. Serve with a cream or fruit sauce.

15. White Sago Pudding. 6 ounces of sago cooked in milk until done and thick, 10 eggs, ¼ pound of sugar, ¼ pound of butter, the rind of a lemon grated on the sugar, 2 tablespoonfuls of grated wheat bread, 1 cupful of good, sweet cream. This pudding is cooked the same as rice pudding and served with the same sauces. Enough for 14 persons.

16. Brown Sago Pudding. Wash ¼ pound of sago in cold water, then in warmed water and cook with claret and water half and half until done; stir 3 heaping tablespoonfuls of butter to a cream, to this add the yolks of 6 eggs, 2 ounces of grated bread, ½ cupful of sweet cream, ¼ pound of sugar, a little cinnamon, lemon peel and the beaten whites of the eggs. Cook this pudding for 2 hours and serve with a cream sauce. For 12 persons.

17. Portuguese Pudding. For 16—18 persons take 1½ pounds of wheat bread, 2 ounces of butter, 2 ounces of beef marrow or instead of this ¼ pound of butter, 10 eggs, 3 ounces of sugar, 3 ounces of stoned raisins, 3 ounces of cleaned currants, the grated rind and juice of 1 lemon, a little salt and a wineglassful of rum. Cut off the crust of the wheat bread and soak it in milk and press, stir on the stove with the butter or beef marrow until it no longer adheres to the kettle. After it has cooled, gradually stir in the yolks of eggs, sugar, the juice and grated rind of a lemon, raisins and currants; then lightly stir in the beaten whites of eggs with the rum, and fill into the buttered mould.

This pudding must cook for 2 hours and is served with a cream sauce.

18. Cream Pudding with Macaroons. For 12 persons take 5 ounces of butter, 5 ounces of flour, 10 eggs, a little over ¼ pound of sugar, the grated rind of a lemon, 1 pint of milk, a little salt and 10—12 bitter macaroons.

Bring the milk and butter to a boil, gradually add the flour, constantly stirring, and cook until it no longer adheres to the sides of the kettle. After it has cooled, slowly stir in the yolks of eggs, sugar and lemon peel, beat and then lightly stir in the beaten whites of the eggs. Fill half of the pudding into the buttered mould, cover with grated crackers, lay on this the macaroons and then the rest of the dough. Cook for 2 hours and serve with a cream sauce.

19. Suabian Pudding. 4 tablespoonfuls of flour, 4 tablespoonfuls of finely pounded almonds, 4 tablespoonfuls of butter, 4 tablespoonfuls of sugar, 9 eggs, 1 large cupful of milk, a little salt and the grated rind of a lemon. The pudding is gotten ready as directed in the following receipt. Cook for 2 hours and serve with any kind of sauce.

20. Vermicelli Pudding. For 15—18 persons take ½ pint of milk, 3½ heaping tablespoonfuls of butter, 3 heaping tablespoonfuls of sugar, ½ pound of vermicelli, the grated rind of half of a lemon, 2 heaping tablespoonfuls of pounded almonds mixed with a few bitter ones, a pinch of ground mace, a little salt and 12 eggs.

Bring the milk, sugar and half of the butter to a boil, crush the vermicelli and add to the milk, constantly stirring until it no longer adheres to the sides of the kettle. Then stir the remaining butter to a cream and add it to the pudding, together with the almonds, spices and yolks of eggs, and lightly stir through this the beaten whites of the eggs.

Cook the pudding for 2½ hours and serve with a warm sauce of sour cherry or currant juice or serve with a wine sauce.

To give this pudding a pretty appearance, take some of the vermicelli out of the kettle before they are thoroughly cooked, drain and bake to a light brown. Then put the yellow and brown vermicelli into the mould and mix scalded and stoned raisins between each layer.

21. Biscuit Pudding served either Warm or Cold. For 12—14 persons take ¾ pound of biscuit (see "Biscuits" in Division S), cut into slices, also 10 eggs, 1 pint of milk or sweet cream, a little salt, sugar and vanilla.

Lay the biscuits in the buttered mould, beat the eggs and add to these the vanilla and cream or milk and sugar and pour over the biscuits. This pudding is cooked for 2 hours, taken out of the mould and served with a cream sauce. If it is not to be eaten warm, leave in the mould until nearly cold.

22. Uncle Tom's Pudding. (Cheap and good.) Stir together ½ pound of flour and ½ pound of syrup, and into this ½ pound of minced kidney suet mixed with a little flour, ⅛ pound of sugar and 1 teaspoonful of ginger, 1 teaspoonful of cinnamon, cloves and mace, 1 teaspoonful of soda and a little salt. Then take 1 cupful of buttermilk and beat in 2 eggs, stir through the dough and fill into the buttered pudding mould and steam for 2 hours. A white cream sauce is served with it.

23. Chocolate Pudding. For 12—15 persons take ¼ pound of butter, ½ pound of sugar, 12 eggs, ½ pound of crushed almonds, 6 ounces of grated chocolate, a little vanilla or cinnamon and some salt.

Stir the butter to a cream, then slowly add sugar, yolks of eggs, almonds, chocolate and vanilla, beat for ¼ hour, then lightly stir through it the beaten whites of eggs and bake the pudding for 1 hour in a moderate oven. If the pudding is to be served cold, steam it for 2 hours and serve with a vanilla sauce.

24. Berlin Pudding. Bake 5 thin layers of a good cake dough. Then take 6 ounces of flour, 1 large cupful of cream, vanilla, salt and 3 ounces of butter and mix to a dough, boil and stir until it no longer adheres to the pan, then add slowly 4 whole and the yolks of 4 eggs, and lightly stir through this the beaten whites of 4 eggs. Then butter a pudding mould, lay in the bottom a piece of buttered paper, put some fruit juice on this, then a quarter of the cream, a layer of the cake, and so on, having for the top a layer of the cake. This pudding is steamed for 1½ hours, then take it out of the mould and serve with an apricot sauce.

25. Warm Vanilla Pudding. For 12—15 persons take 1¼ pounds of stale wheat bread, cutting off the crust, about 1 quart of fresh cream or milk, ¼ pound of butter, 5 spoonfuls of pounded almonds, 5 spoonfuls of sugar, some salt, 10 eggs and a little vanilla.

The wheat bread is soaked in the milk and the butter stirred to a cream, then gradually add the yolks of eggs, almonds, sugar and vanilla, stir for ¼ hour and then lightly stir through it the beaten whites of the eggs. Steam for 2—2½ hours and serve with a cream sauce.

26. Bread ("Zwieback") Pudding. For 12—16 persons. Take ⅔ pound of bread spread with butter, 1 quart of milk, 9—10 eggs, ¼ pound of currants, ¼ pound of stoned raisins, both washed and dried, ¼ pound of crushed almonds, 2 heaping tablespoonfuls of sugar, and the thinly peeled and finely chopped rind of a lemon. Line a pudding mould with slices of the buttered bread. Then stir eggs, milk and sugar together, pour a little of this sauce over the bread, add some more bread and sauce and finish with bread. Then pour over this sauce a cupful at a time, so that it will be evenly distributed over the pudding. Let the pudding bake for 2—2½ hours and serve with a good cream-, claret-, or fruit sauce. The sauce of the latter should be thickened a little and there must be plenty of it.

27. Bread Pudding with Currants or Cherries. The pudding is prepared the same as in the preceding receipt, taking 8 eggs; instead of raisins take ½ pound of currants and ⅔ pound of sugar and prepare the same as given in the above receipt.

The pudding is served without a sauce and is of a fine flavor. This pudding is for 10—12 persons.

28. Potato Pudding. For 15—18 persons. Take 4 ounces of butter, 6 ounces of sugar, 1 ounce of sweet almonds mixed with a few bitter ones and pounded, lemon peel, cinnamon, a little salt, the yolks of 12 eggs, 1½ pounds of grated potatoes and ¼ pound of grated wheat bread.

The potatoes, which should be mealy, are cooked the day before in their jackets until they are almost done, then peeled and weighed. Stir the butter to a cream, then add, one by one, the yolks of eggs, almonds, lemon peel, cinnamon, also the potatoes. Stir for a few minutes, then add the wheat bread and at last the beaten whites of the eggs.

Let the pudding bake for 1¼ hours, or steam for 2 hours and serve with a cream-, rum- or fruit sauce.

The butter may be omitted, as the pudding is very good without it.

29. A fine Pudding with Yeast. For 8—9 persons take 1½ pounds of flour, 6 ounces of currants, 6 ounces of stoned raisins, 6 ounces of butter, yeast, 6—10 eggs, 1 pint of lukewarm milk, ¼ pound of sugar, the rind of a lemon and one-half of a nutmeg. After the butter is stirred until soft add, one by one, the whole eggs, flour and milk and the other ingredients, adding at last the yeast soaked in a little milk, then beat all together with a flat wooden spoon until it bubbles, put into the buttered mould, set into lukewarm water and steam for 2½ hours. If the whites of the eggs are beaten to a froth, the pudding will be much nicer.

Serve with a rum sauce; it can also be served without a sauce and eaten with roast meats or boiled fruits.

30. A common Pudding with Yeast. For 12—15 persons. Take 1¾ pounds of flour, some yeast, ¼ pound of melted butter, 4 tablespoonfuls of sugar, ½ pound of raisins and currants if liked, a little more than 1 pint of lukewarm milk, some salt and 2 eggs.

Stir all well together, let it raise in the form before steaming or set the pudding into lukewarm water and slowly bring to a boil.

Serve with fruit sauce or melted butter or cooked fruits with a good quantity of sauce.

31. Flour and Bread Pudding with Fruit, particularly Pears or Fresh Plums. A scant pint of milk, 3 ounces of butter, not quite ½ pound of flour, 8 eggs, ½ teaspoonful of mace, 6 ounces of grated wheat bread, 2 tablespoonfuls of sugar and ½ glassful of rum.

Melt half of the butter, add the milk and flour to this and stir until it no longer adheres to the sides of the kettle. After it has cooled add the yolks of eggs, mace and sugar and beat, then add sugar, wheat bread, the beaten whites of the eggs and at last the rum. Steam for 2½ hours and serve with cooked fruit.

32. Prince Regent Pudding. For 15—18 persons take ¼ pound of stoned raisins, ¼ pound of currants, ¼ pound of finely cut almonds, 14 eggs, 1 pint of milk, a little over 1 pound of stale wheat bread weighed without the crust, and ⅛ pound of sugar.

Cut the bread into slices, fry in butter to a light yellow, and then break into small pieces.

Beat together the eggs, sugar and milk with the lemon peel. Pour over the bread and proceed the same as in Bread Pudding, No. 26.

Let the pudding steam for 2 or 2½ hours and serve with raspberry or currant sauce.

33. Roll Pudding. One-half pound of butter stirred to a cream, the yolks of 12 eggs, ¼ pound of sugar, ½ pound of stoned raisins, ¼ pound of currants, ¼ pound of pounded almonds, ¼ pound of citron, half as much candied orange peel, 1 pound of finely grated wheat bread without the crust, 1 large cupful of milk or sweet cream, and 1 wineglassful of rum.

After the butter, yolks of eggs and sugar have been well stirred together, stir in the wheat bread which has been soaked in milk, add the orange and citron, stir through this the beaten whites of the eggs and at the last a glassful of rum, and let the pudding steam in the buttered mould for 2 hours. After taking it out of the mould pour over it some rum and light it, serving with the following sauce: 4 whole eggs, 2 teaspoonfuls of flour, lemon peel and whole cinnamon, 2 large glassfuls of wine, 6 ounces of sugar, beat well on the stove until thick and done.

34. Fruit Pudding. For 12—15 persons: A little over 2 pounds of stale wheat bread, nearly 1 quart of milk, ¼ pound of butter, 10 eggs and according to the sweetness of the fruit 6 ounces to ½ pound of sugar, lemon peel and cinnamon, and, if wished, ¼ pound of currants. The wheat bread is cut into thin slices, then broken into small pieces and put on the stove with the milk and butter and cooked until it leaves the side of the kettle, then take from the fire and let it cool. Stir the other ingredients into this, adding the beaten whites of the eggs at last, then put into the form alternately with the dough, add sliced sour apples or cherries and cook for 2 hours. This pudding can be served without a sauce.

35. Grape Pudding. Take ¼ pound of butter, 8 eggs, ¼ pound of finely pounded almonds, ½ pound of sugar, cinnamon, and if liked, a little lemon peel, ¾ pound of bread and a soupplateful of grapes.

Stir the butter to a cream, add yolks of eggs, sugar, seasoning with bread and beat, then lightly stir through this the beaten whites of the eggs with the grapes.

36. Neckar Pudding. For 12 persons take 1 celery root, 6 large carrots, 6 ounces of butter, the same amount of sugar, 12 eggs, ½ pound of currants, ⅔ pound of wheat bread, 1 tablespoonful of pounded almonds, juice of a whole and rind of ½ of a lemon and a little salt.

Clean and peel the celery and carrots and cook until nearly done and then grate them. Then stir the butter to a cream, add yolks of eggs, sugar, almonds, currants, grated and soaked wheat bread, seasoning and salt, stir all together, then add the beaten whites of the eggs. Put the pudding into the form and cook for 1½ hours in a double boiler and serve with it rum or wine sauce.

37. Indian Pudding. For 10 persons take a large cocoanut and grate the meat, cook in 1 large cupful of milk and then let it cool.

In the meantime stir 4 tablespoonfuls of butter to a cream, add ¼ pound of sugar, the yolks of 6 eggs, the meat of the cocoanut and 3 ounces of grated rolls, with a little ginger and salt. Fill into a pudding mould and if wanted extra nice line the mould with a puff or butter paste; cook for 1½ hours or bake in the oven for not quite 1 hour. Take the pudding out of the pan and serve with a strong claret sauce.

38. English Warm Meat Pudding. Take 2 pounds of beef, free from sinews, and chop with 1 onion until very fine. Then stir ¼ pound of butter to a cream, add, one by one, 8 whole eggs, a few spoonfuls of cream, lemon peel, a little pepper and cloves and one fresh, cleaned and finely chopped herring, 3 ounces of stale wheat bread with the crust removed, and soaked in cold water and pressed, finely chopped mushrooms and a little salt. Stir well together and fill into a well-buttered mould and cook for 2 hours. It is served with a crab- or a mushroom sauce.

39. Pudding made of Cold Veal Roast. For 12—14 persons take 1¾ pounds of cold roast veal, freed from sinews and chopped very finely, 8 eggs, 5 tablespoonfuls of butter, 2 heaping tablespoonfuls of stale, grated wheat bread, ½ cupful of sweet cream, 6 finely chopped eschalots, salt and a little nutmeg. Rub the eschalots with 1 ounce of the butter, then beat with 2 eggs and 2 tablespoonfuls of water and mix thoroughly. Stir the remaining butter to a cream and add, one by one, the yolks of 6 eggs, and beat for a few minutes, then add the minced eschalots, bread, cream, mace, veal, salt, and stir well together, adding at last the beaten whites of the eggs. The pudding is steamed in a well-buttered mould for 1½ hours and is served with a mushroom-, crab-, or a good brown gravy. If served cold, a gravy made of the yolks of a few hard-boiled eggs, grated, mixed with olive oil, vinegar, sugar, capers, mustard and pepper, stirred well together.

40. Crab Pudding. For 14—16 persons. 1⅓ pounds of stale grated wheat bread, 1 pint of fresh milk, 3 ounces of crab butter, 10 eggs, ¼ pound of sugar, ½ ounce of bitter macaroons or the rind of a lemon, a little salt, 7 ounces of finely chopped kidney suet and 10 crabtails cut into pieces.

Remove the crusts of the wheat bread, soak it in milk, press it and then stir with it the crab butter. Add one by one the yolks of eggs, sugar and macaroons, kidney suet and crab tails, and at last stir in the whites of the eggs, and steam for 2½ hours. A sauce is made of cream or milk to which add some crab butter and stir through it the yolks of a few eggs.

41. Fish Pudding. To 1 pound of fish take a little over 3 ounces of grated rolls or wheat bread, ¼ pound of butter, 4 eggs, 1 cupful of sour cream, a little nutmeg, mace, chopped parsley and salt to taste. The fish is cooked and finely chopped.

Stir the butter to a cream, add yolks of eggs, the chopped fish, grated bread and the other ingredients, mix well together, and then add the beaten whites of the eggs. If it should be too thick add a little sweet milk.

This pudding is cooked for 2 hours. It is served with an oyster- or anchovy sauce. In case you have neither, use butter, because this kind of pudding is somewhat dry.

42. Liver Pudding. For 10—12 persons, take a nice calf's liver, 4 tablespoonfuls of pork fat, 2 grated onions, 2 heaping tablespoonfuls of soaked wheat bread, 6 egg, 3 ounces of Parmesan cheese, salt and 4 chopped truffles. The calf's liver is skinned, chopped fine with the pork fat and then passed through a sieve. The grated onions and soaked wheat bread are mixed with the butter and then added to the liver, then mix with the yolks of eggs, cheese, salt and seasoning and mix well together. Then stir in the beaten whites of the eggs, and cook the pudding for 1½ hours and serve immediately with caper-, truffle- or anchovy sauce.

43. Pudding made of Remnants of boiled Cod Fish. For 12—15 persons take ½ pound of butter stirred to a cream, 10 eggs, a few finely chopped eschalots, nutmeg, salt, ½ pound of grated wheat bread, 2½ pounds of finely chopped codfish, stir well together and fill into a well-buttered mould and cook for 1½ hours. With this pudding the following sauce is served: A few finely chopped eschalots are stewed with some butter and thickened with a little flour, add some boiling bouillon, quickly gotten ready by using extract of beef, stir together, add nutmeg, lemon juice and salt, stirred with the yolks of 2 eggs which have been mixed with a little sweet cream.

Hot puddings should never be taken into the sick room, as they are not easily digested.

I.—Souffles

And Various Dishes Made of Macaroni and Noodles.

I. SOUFFLES.

1. Form of the Mould, etc. The mould for souffles should be treated the same as the pudding form, buttered and sprinkled with grated bread. It may either be of stoneware or porcelain. If you have no souffle mould, any kind of a china dish that will stand heating will answer.

In baking, the heat should never be too low nor too intense, and if possible do not get the heat as strong from below as from above.

A lid that will hold live embers is admirably adapted to increase the requisite heat from the top. The mould is best placed on a small griddle which will permit its turning without shaking the souffle. If the latter should brown on top too soon it may be protected by covering it with paper, but the first sheet should be buttered to prevent its adhering to the souffle.

Souffles are not turned out of the mould, but are served in the dish in which they are baked, putting them on a plate and enveloped in a napkin.

2. Souffle of Bitter Macaroons. For 8 persons take 1 pint of milk, ¼ pound of bitter macaroons, ¼ pound of grated rolls, 8 eggs, 3—4 ounces of sugar and fresh or canned fruit according to taste. Cook the milk, grated wheat bread and macaroons until thick. When this has cooled somewhat, stir in the yolks of the eggs and sugar and at last the beaten whites of the eggs. Then add fruit seasoned with sugar and cinnamon, fill into the buttered mould and bake for 1 hour.

This souffle can also be made by taking instead of the milk half cream and half good rum or brandy, and 1 ounce of butter stirred to a cream. The first may then be omitted.

3. Sago Souffle. For 10 persons take ½ pound of sago, milk, 6 eggs, 3 ounces of butter, 3 ounces of sugar, lemon peel according to taste, 2 heaping tablespoonfuls of finely pounded almonds, mixed with 6 bitter ones.

The sago is scalded, cooked in 1 quart of milk until done and thick. Stir the butter to a cream, and then one by one add the yolks of eggs, sugar, lemon peel, almonds and stir into the partially cooled sago and at last the beaten whites of the eggs.

The lemon and almonds can be omitted and the souffle is then seasoned with vanilla. Let it bake for 1 hour.

4. Rice Souffle. For 10—12 persons take ½ pound of rice, ¼ pound of butter, 8 eggs, ¼ pound of sugar, lemon peel and cinnamon, a few sweet crackers, ¼ pound of washed and stoned raisins and 1 quart of milk.

Scald the rice and then stir the boiling milk with it, put it on the fire and cook until done and thick, but it must not be stirred, then cream the butter, stir into it the yolks of eggs, sugar, seasoning, and to the cooled rice add the rolled crackers and raisins, lightly mix through it the beaten whites of the eggs and bake the souffle for 1 hour.

Rice souffles can be made in different ways. Instead of the lemon take pounded almonds or vanilla, or orangeflower water, also fresh or canned fruits can be filled into the mould and then baked.

5. Brussels Rice Souffle with Frosting. Scald 2 ounces of rice, boil it in 1 quart of milk, add sugar and lemon peel and cook until done and thick. Then stir through it the yolks of 4 eggs and the beaten whites of the eggs and fill into the mould with the frosting. The frosting is made in the following manner: Beat the whites of 5 eggs to a stiff froth, stir through it ½ pound of powdered sugar and spread a buttered mould with this frosting. Bake in a hot oven until of a light brown. Then fill in the rice, put the remaining frosting over the top and bake in a moderately hot oven until done.

As soon as the souffle is done serve with jelly.

6. Rice Souffle with Pineapple. Cook some rice as directed in the above receipt, stir into it sliced pineapple stewed in a sugar syrup until soft, or take canned pineapple. Then fill the rice into a buttered souffle mould which is lined with pounded bitter macaroons, and bake for about 1 hour. Turn the souffle out of the mould and pour over it the following sauce, which gives this souffle a very nice flavor: Cook 3 cooking apples of the best variety with 1 pint of sugar syrup and white wine (6 ounces of sugar, ½ glassful of water, 2 glassfuls of white wine) until done. Strain, mix with the juice of the pineapple, cook until like jelly and pour over the rice.

7. Chocolate Souffle. For 8—10 persons take 2 tablespoonfuls of butter and stir until soft, add 5—6 yolks of eggs, 3 ounces of sugar, 2 ounces of grated chocolate, a little vanilla, 6 ounces of bread soaked in milk and pressed, stirred together and then mix with it the beaten whites of the eggs and bake the souffle for ¾ of an hour.

8. Grits or Rice Flour Souffle. For 10—12 persons take ½ pound of rice flour, a little over a pint of milk, ¼ pound of butter, 2 heaping tablespoonfuls of lard or 6 ounces of butter, 7 eggs, 3 ounces of sugar, 6—8 pounded bitter almonds and a little salt.

Let the rice flour, milk and some of the butter boil until done and very thick, then stir the remaining butter to a cream, add the yolks of eggs, sugar, almonds, salt, the cooled rice flour, and, when this is all stirred together, add the beaten whites of the eggs. If the souffle is to be particularly nice, mix fruit jelly or marmalade through it when filling into the mould. The souffle is baked for 1 hour; serve in the mould and sprinkle over it sugar and cinnamon.

9. Flour Souffle. For 12—14 persons take the same ingredients as given in H, No. 18, for cream pudding and bake 1 hour. Put ¼ pound of bitter macaroons in layers into the form or before adding the whites of the eggs, stir through it 3 ounces of grated stale wheat bread.

10. Convent Souffle. For 6—7 persons, take 6 ounces of flour, ¼ pound of sugar, ¼ pound of butter, 2 ounces of finely pounded almonds, 4 eggs, nearly 1 pint of milk seasoned with vanilla or lemon peel, put all on the fire and stir until it is a thick cream. Then rub 1 ounce of butter until soft, add the yolks of 5 eggs and mix all thoroughly and then lightly stir through this the beaten whites of the eggs, and bake in a mould for 1 hour in a moderately hot oven. Serve with preserves or compots.

11. Dauphin Souffle. For 12 persons stir 6 ounces of butter, the yolks of 12 eggs, ½ pound of sugar over a moderate hot fire until it is a thick cream, which is seasoned with lemon peel and then stir through it the beaten whites of 8 eggs. Put this into a buttered souffle mould and bake for 1 hour, take it out of the mould and let it cool. Then cut the cake into thick slices and spread with a fruit marmalade and then put the cake together again. Pour over it a frosting made of the whites of the remaining 4 eggs, sugar, a dash of fine liquor and a little lemon juice. Bake the souffle in the oven until the frosting is of a golden brown color, and serve with a wine cream sauce.

12. Bread and Walnut Souffle. For 8—10 persons take 30 fresh walnuts; if you cannot get them fresh, take half almonds and half walnuts, 6 ounces of wheat bread free from crust, ¼ pound of butter, ¼ pound of sugar, 6 eggs, and ½ cupful of sweet cream. After the nuts have been finely pounded or grated, soak the bread in a little milk and press it, stir the butter to a cream, add the yolks of eggs one by one, also the sugar, wheat bread, cream and nuts, and then lightly stir through it the beaten whites of the eggs and stir thoroughly. The souffle is baked in a buttered mould for 1 hour and served hot with either a wine- or cream sauce.

13. Potato Souffle. For 10 persons, take ¼ pound of butter stirred to a cream, the yolks of 8 eggs, ¾ pound of sugar, ½ ounce of pounded almonds mixed with 6 bitter ones, and if liked, lemon peel or cinnamon; all is stirred well together for a few minutes. Then take nearly 1 pound of potatoes boiled in their jackets the day before, peel and grate them and mix with 3 ounces of wheat bread and then the beaten whites of the eggs. Bake for 1 hour.

14. Egg (Omelette) Souffle. No. 1. For 4 persons take 4 tablespoonfuls of sugar, salt, 4 eggs and a little grated lemon peel.

Stir the sugar briskly with the yolks of the eggs and lemon peel for 10 minutes, then lightly stir through it the froth of the eggs and cook the whole in a buttered omelette pan over a moderate fire for not more than ¼ hour. Serve immediately.

15. Omelette Souffle. No. 2. For 6 persons take 6 eggs, 4 tablespoonfuls of fine sugar, 1 tablespoonful of flour and 2 teaspoonfuls of butter.

The yolks of the eggs are stirred with the sugar for ¼ hour, and the flour and beaten whites of the eggs are not added until just before baking. Then melt unsalted butter in a pan over a slow fire, and pour the batter into the pan, evenly distribute it, often piercing with a sharp knife so that the batter will not brown too quickly on the bottom and leave the top uncooked. As soon as the omelette is browned nicely and the top is set, put it on a plate, fold and sprinkle over it sugar and vanilla. Sugar and the juice of a lemon may be sprinkled over the omelette, and rum can be poured over it and then lighted.

16. Omelette, "plain". For 4 persons. A heaping tablespoonful of flour, a very small cupful of warm milk and 2 tablespoonfuls of water are stirred together. Then beat 4 fresh eggs and stir all together. Put plenty of fresh butter into a pan, or take butter and fat half and half, put the batter into this and, turning the pan frequently, bake it to a light brown color until it is set. The omelette is turned and baked to a light brown on the other side also, folded and put on a hot plate and sprinkled with sugar, or before folding spread over it some apple or cranberry sauce.

17. Sponge Souffle. For 4—5 persons take 1 tablespoonful of thick sour cream, 6 eggs, sugar and vanilla

Stir the cream, yolks of eggs, sugar and vanilla for some time, then mix with the beaten whites of the eggs and bake in a quick oven.

18. Sour Cream Souffle. For 6—8 persons take 1 quart of thick sour cream, 8 eggs, 4 tablespoonfuls of flour, or 1 tablespoonful of cornstarch or 4 tablespoonfuls of grated bread, sugar, cinnamon, vanilla or instead of this grated lemon peel and a little salt. The cream is whipped and to this are added the yolks of eggs with the other ingredients, and then the beaten whites of the eggs; bake for ¾ of an hour. The batter can also be poured over cooked or fresh fruits and in this way a good cream souffle of fruit is made.

19. Souffle with Sour Cherries. For 9—10 persons take ⅔ pound of stale wheat bread without the crust and soak it in milk and scald it. Then stir with the bread a piece of butter the size of an egg, add the yolks of 9 eggs, some pounded almonds, a little lemon peel, 2—3 spoonfuls of sugar, the beaten whites of the eggs, 1 pound of stoned cherries stirred with a little sugar and bake for 1 hour.

20. Marmalade Souffle. For 8—10 persons, take ½ pound of peach or apricot marmalade or else apple sauce, stir the juice of a lemon through it together with the beaten whites of 12 eggs. Then fill into a buttered porcelain mould, have the top of the souffle smooth, sprinkle with finely chopped almonds mixed with sugar or coarsely pounded macaroons, take a knife and pierce through the souffle to the bottom several times and bake in a hot oven. This souffle is baked for 10—15 minutes only and must be eaten immediately, otherwise it will fall.

21. Vienna ("Wiener") Apple Souffle. Take 30 good cooking apples, ½ pound of sugar, 6 ounces of apricot marmalade, ¼ pound of fresh butter, and wheat bread. To the apples may be added 4 to 6 ounces of nice raisins, in which case 2 ounces less of sugar are required.

Pare the apples, quarter them, take out the core and then cut them each into 6 pieces. These apple slices are put on a slow fire with the sugar, marmalade and butter until they are heated through, then let them

cool. In the meantime butter a round mould, cut oblong slices from a loaf of not too stale bread, dip in
melted butter and line the mould with these, placing
the bread, one slice on the other, around the sides. When
the mould is lined, fill with the apples, cover with some
more bread slices, sprinkle the top with butter and bake
in the oven for ½ hour, in which time the bread will be
of a golden brown and crisp, and the inside of the
souffle heated through. This souffle is turned out of
the mould and served hot.

22. Apple Souffle. No. 2. For 8—10 persons take
good cooking apples, some marmalade, ¼ pound of butter, ¼ pound of flour, ¼ pound of sugar, 6 eggs, 1 large
cupful of milk and ½ of a lemon peel.

Pare the apples and core them, leaving the apples
whole, fill with some of the marmalade and put them
side by side into a buttered mould in which they can be
baked. Then melt half of the butter in a pan, add the
flour—which was stirred with the milk—to the butter
and then put on the stove until it no longer adheres to
the sides of the kettle. In the meantime stir the butter
until soft, add the yolks of the eggs, sugar, lemon peel
and the partly cooled batter, stir all well together and
lastly add the beaten whites of the eggs, and then put
all over the apples. The souffle is baked in a moderately
hot oven for 1 hour.

The apples can be quartered and instead of the
marmalade take 2 ounces of washed and dried currants,
mix with the apples and then cover this with the batter.

**23. Plain Souffle of Apples, but can be made of any
kind of Fruit.** For 10—12 persons. Take ½ pound of
flour, 2 heaping tablespoonfuls of butter, nearly 1 pint
of milk, 2 tablespoonfuls of sugar, 6 eggs, lemon peel or
8 bitter almonds and 1½ teaspoonfuls of salt.

After these ingredients have been well stirred together as directed in the above receipt, put one-quarter
of it into a buttered mould, put 2 heaping soupplatefuls
of quartered apples over this, sprinkle with sugar and
cinnamon, proceed in this manner and bake the souffle
for 1¼ hours.

The same can be made with most any kind of fruit
as well as stoned dried fruits, but before being stoned,

cook until done. When taking juicy fruits, such as sour cherries, huckleberries, currants, etc., grated wheat bread is mixed with the fruit, and according to their acidity add the required amount of sugar.

24. Apple Souffle. Another style. Take 2 soup-platefuls of apple marmalade, ¼ pound of butter, the yolks of 8 eggs, 1½ pounds of grated wheat bread, sugar and cinnamon, stir the beaten whites of the eggs through the batter and bake in a buttered mould for 1¼ hours. For 10 persons.

25. Chestnut Souffle. Remove the shell from about 2¼ pounds of chestnuts, put them into boiling water until they can be freed from their outer skin, cook in 1 quart of milk until soft and then press them through a sieve. Stir 4 tablespoonfuls of butter to a cream, add the yolks of 10 eggs, the strained chestnuts, 5 ounces of sugar, 6 tablespoonfuls of Marascino, Curaçao or other fine liquor, and then lightly stir through it the beaten whites of the eggs. Bake the souffle for ¾ hour in the oven and serve immediately.

26. Leipzig Punch Souffle. For 8 persons take 12 eggs, 5 ounces of sugar, 1 lemon, a glassful of rum, stir the eggs and sugar to a cream, add the lemon juice, and if liked the grated rind of a lemon, rum, and then the froth of the eggs beaten lightly through it; bake the souffle in a hot oven for 10 minutes and serve. The souffle must be of a yellow color on all sides, the inside soft like cream. Omitting the rum and taking the lemon peel and juice only, makes a very nice lemon souffle.

27. Rice and Apple Souffle. For 18—20 persons take ½—¾ pound of rice, milk, 4—6 ounces of sugar, 3—5 ounces of butter, 4—6 eggs, 12—14 good cooking apples, wine, lemon and an orange.

Boil the scalded rice in milk with a piece of butter until tender. Then cook the pared apples—cut into halves—in water, wine, sugar, lemon juice and peel of the lemon, until done, but they must remain whole, take them out of the juice, add to the juice enough sugar so that it will cook to a jelly, and then add the juice of an orange to this. Stir the remaining butter with the yolks of eggs, sugar, and add to the rice, and then lightly stir through it the beaten whites of the eggs. Put a layer of rice and a layer of apples into a well buttered mould and cover again with the rice; the apples must not touch the sides of the mould, neither must they come through the rice on the top. Then cover the rice, sprinkle some bread crumbs and a few small pieces of butter on the top, let the souffle bake for about 1 hour, or until it receives a nice yellow color; turn out of the mould and serve with the jellied juice of the apples.

A simpler way is to fill the souffle mould with rice and apple marmalade and strew over this grated bread and sugar and bake for about 1 hour.

28. Herring Souffle. For 10 persons. This is made the same as potato souffle (see No. 13), omitting the almonds, sugar and the spices, and adding plenty of nutmeg and the meat of 2—3 well freshened and boned herrings, with a saucerful of onions fried in butter and a little pepper and cloves.

29. Cheese Souffle, to be served after the Soup. For 6 persons take 5 tablespoonfuls of grated cheese (a good way to utilize dry cheese), mix with 1 large cupful of milk, the yolks of 5 eggs, salt, pepper and nearly ½ ounce of cornstarch, stir through it the beaten whites of the eggs and bake the souffle for 20 minutes.

30. Meat Souffle is made like cold roast veal pudding (see H, No. 39).

31. Souffle of Rice, Sweetbreads and Crab Butter. (Served after the soup with a ragout of fish). For 12—15 persons take ½ pound of rice, bouillon, mace, crab butter, 1 glassful of Madeira, and ½ pound of veal sweetbreads. The rice is scalded and cooked with bouillon, some mace, the necessary salt and crab butter until done and thick, and at last stir through it 1 glassful of Madeira.

In the meantime cook veal sweetbreads in bouillon until done, chop fine, and then fill into a buttered mould some rice and then the sweetbreads and so on, and bake for 1 hour.

32. Italian Rice Souffle for Poultry and Fish Ragout. For 15—18 persons take ¾ pound of rice, bouillon, butter, ½ pound of boiled and finely chopped ham and ¼ pound of Parmesan cheese. Scald the rice and then cook with it good bouillon, salt and butter until done and thick, but the rice kernels must remain whole. Then put the rice into the souffle mould, then the ham and Parmesan cheese, and so on and bake for 1¼ hours.

33. Noodle Souffle. For 4—6 persons. Make a noodle dough as described in No. 24, Division L, using 2 eggs. Then cook the noodles in salted water, take them out and put them into cold water, stir for a minute and then take them out of the cold water and put on a sieve to drain. After this is done take the yolks of 6 eggs, 5 ounces of pounded sugar and ¼ pound of clarified butter, stir for a few minutes, then add the noodles, ¼ pound of washed and dried currants, 2½ teaspoonfuls of pounded sweet almonds, the grated rind of half a lemon, a little grated bread and some cinnamon; when this has all been well stirred together, lightly stir the beaten whites of the eggs through it and then bake in a mould for 1¼ hours.

34. Pineapple Souffle for Invalids. The dough is prepared like the receipt given for Leipzig Punch Souffle, but omit the rum and instead of this mix a cupful of finely sliced pineapple through the dough, line the bottom of the mould with buttered paper and cover this with pineapple slices. This souffle is made in different ways; instead of the lemon juice take a few spoonfuls of apricot- or other fruit marmalade; other finely sliced preserved fruits can also be mixed through the dough.

35. Strawberry Souffle. Take ½ pound of fresh strawberries and put them through a colander, mix with ¼ pound of sugar, a little lemon juice and the beaten whites of 3 eggs, fill this into a mould and bake for 10—15 minutes in a moderate oven. Instead of the strawberries, cooked apples can be used and any kind of fruit marmalade or about 5 tablespoonfuls of chocolate or cocoa. This souffle must be served immediately when taken out of the oven.

There are but few souffles that are fit for the sickroom; Nos. 7, 14, 15 and 18 can be given to invalids.

II. VARIOUS RECEIPTS FOR MACARONI AND NOODLES.

NOTE.—Rice noodles and rice macaroni are of great value in the kitchen, and the "star" and "thread" noodles (vermicelli) are excellent in soups and puddings.

36. Macaroni, Ham and Parmesan Cheese in equal parts. Cut ½ pound of macaroni into pieces 1 inch long, cook in salted water until done, put on a colander and then pour boiling water over them. After cooling, stew some finely chopped eschalots in butter, add ½ pound of ham, then the macaroni, ½ pound of cheese and at last a small cupful of sour cream and bake in a buttered mould for 3—4 hours.

37. Souffle of Macaroni, Ham and Parmesan Cheese. ½ pound of macaroni, 1 pound of boiled and finely chopped ham, 2 ounces of grated Parmesan cheese, 4 eggs, nutmeg, 2 ounces of butter and 1 pint of milk.

The macaroni is cooked in salted water, but not to pieces, pour off the water and then fill into the mould with ham, cheese and nutmeg and pour over it milk with melted butter and eggs. The souffle is baked in a hot oven for 1 hour.

38. Macaroni Pie with Ham and Cheese. Make a puff paste of 1½—2 pounds of flour and ¾ pound of macaroni cooked in bouillon or boiling salted water, pour into a colander and drain; then add a heaping soupplateful of boiled ham mixed with a little of the fat, ¼ pound of butter, 2½ heaping tablespoonfuls of Parmesan cheese and 6 eggs.

The butter is stirred until soft, mixed with the cheese and the yolks of eggs and then added to the macaroni and mixed with the beaten whites of the eggs. Roll out the paste, on this a layer of ham, then the macaroni batter, then ham and so on until all is used, after which cover with the puff paste.

This pie can also be made without the crust and baked in a form and instead of Parmesan cheese white Swiss cheese can be used. Vermicelli or vegetable noodles can also be substituted for the macaroni.

39. Macaroni with Parmesan Cheese. Take ½ pound of macaroni, 2 ounces of butter, 2 ounces of grated cheese, cook the macaroni in boiling water until done, pour on a colander, put the macaroni, butter and cheese into a mould in alternate layers, and bake in a hot oven to a golden brown color. Then turn onto a plate and serve with roasts, spare ribs, forcemeat balls, etc. Also served with sourkrout.

40. Macaroni with Sauce, (Hamburg Style). Boil ½ pound of macaroni in salted water until done and then make the following sauce: Take nearly 1 quart of milk with 2 ounces of flour and 1 heaping tablespoonful of butter, put it on the stove and stir until it is thick, stir with it the yolks of 4 eggs, salt, pepper and 1 ounce of grated Parmesan cheese and mix the macaroni well together with the sauce. Fill into a pan and bake for ½ hour.

41. Macaroni, Potatoes and Roast. Take a fillet of beef for this dish. It can be roasted in different ways—either like a rabbit, or according to the English method, frying about 8 minutes with plenty of strong, rich gravy. In the meantime boil macaroni in salted water, drain on a colander, pour boiling water over them and cook with some browned butter. Then fry some medium-sized potatoes until done and of a dark yellow color. Slice the meat, put it into the pan in its original shape with the macaroni around the meat, pour the sauce boiling hot over all and then put the potatoes around the dish in the form of a wreath. Serve hot.

Instead of taking potatoes, fried eggs mixed with minced ham may be used as a garnish.

42. Macaroni with Kettle Roast. The macaroni are boiled in salted water and mixed with 2 ounces of grated cheese, 4 tablespoonfuls of strong bouillon, 4 tablespoonfuls of tomatoes, 2 truffles cut into small strips, 2 ounces of butter, salt and pepper. Heat the macaroni in this and serve.

43. Ham Noodles. If you have no rice noodles, make a stiff dough of 2 whole and the yolks of 2 eggs, as directed in Divison L, No. 24, and roll very thin. As soon as each piece is dry, cut into strips the width of a finger, cook in boiling salted water, put into a colander and pour boiling water over them. Then chop an onion with parsley and stew in butter, cut 1 pound of lean boiled ham into very small pieces, add 6 whole eggs and the yolks of 6 eggs with 1 pint of thick sour cream, ½ teaspoonful of mace and to this the stewed onion and parsley, and stir all together with the noodles. Then butter a mould, fill with the mixed noodles, sprinkle with grated bread and bake for ½ hour in a hot oven.

Serve with veal roast, kettle roast, or with all kinds of cutlets and pork sausages. Rice macaroni prepared in the same way are very palatable; break them into pieces 1½ inches long and cook in salted water.

44. Remnants of Ham baked with Noodle Dough. A very nice dish served with sourkrout and spinach. Use 1 egg in making the noodle dough as directed in Division L, No. 24, cut into pieces about the size of a visiting card, cook in boiling water until done, and put into cold water and then on a colander to cool. In the meantime take the remnants of boiled ham, chop as finely as possible and mix with nutmeg, pepper and grated Swiss cheese. Butter the mould, line the bottom and sides with the noodles so that there is no space between them. Over this put a layer of ham, then noodles, and so on for two or three layers, having noodles on top. Then beat up 4 eggs, add some milk and a little salt in case the ham is not very salty, pour the milk and eggs over the dish and bake in a hot oven for 1 hour, turn out of the pan and serve.

45. Rice Noodles. Rice noodles are cooked in salted water for ½ hour, put on a colander and pour boiling water over them, which must not be forgotten. Then bring to a boil with some milk, butter and nutmeg and serve covered with grated cheese.

Another way is to mix scalded noodles with melted butter and a broth prepared of extract of beef; if liked, stir through it finely chopped ham. Then serve, covering with some of the noodles browned in butter.

The noodles can be prepared with bacon cut into cubes and fried to a light brown color.

Excepting the rice noodles, none are fit for invalids.

K.—Crullers, Omelettes and Pancakes.

1. General Directions. The pan should preferably be of steel, those of enameled ware are not so good; they should be used for pancakes and the like exclusively, and beefsteaks, onions, etc., should never be fried in them, as is so frequently done. The pan should be well wiped with soft paper after each time it is used, so that when again wanted it will only be necessary to simply rub it dry with a clean piece of absorbent paper. If this is not done the pan should first be put on the fire and cleaned with some salt. If the pan is washed the cakes will adhere to the bottom. Stir the batter with warm instead of cold milk and beat it briskly before adding all the milk; this method will improve the cakes very much. Whether it is best to froth the whites of the eggs depends on the taste. If this is done the cakes will be nicely puffy and light, and it will take 1 egg less. Using the unbeaten eggs will permit of baking the cakes nicely crisp externally.

A medium fire is always best for baking pancakes; a glowing coal fire will give the most satisfactory results.

The best fat to be used consists of butter and sweet lard, half and half, or else slowly tried out pork fat; see A, No. 18. In order to bake the pancakes nice and crisp put plenty of fat into the pan and let it melt, being careful to prevent its getting brown or even too hot, put in the dough uniformly thick over the bottom of the pan, pierce it with a knife occasionally, especially along the edges of the pan, until no more of the liquid dough will appear on the top. Turn the pan cautiously so that the cake will bake nicely brown all over. If it should adhere anywhere put a little butter under it. Finally turn with a pancake turner and bake on the other side in the same way. In a few receipts cornstarch is put down instead of flour; be careful to test this before using as it is apt to be sour.

2. German Wafers, ("Plinsen"). No. 1. (To be served alone or as a side dish with spinach.) 4 heaping tablespoonfuls of flour, 4 large or 5 small eggs, 1 large cupful of milk mixed with cream or milk and water, 2 tablespoonfuls of melted butter, 2 ounces of washed and dried currants, grated lemon peel or mace and a little salt. When adding the eggs whip the dough as directed under No. 1, and bake four thin cakes. Then divide each cake in two, sprinkle with sugar and cinnamon and roll them out.

These cakes are served for supper with tea and bread and butter. When served as a side dish send to the table with a white wine sauce or fruit jelly. If served with spinach leave out the sugar, lemon peel and currants, and stir through it some finely cut chives.

3. Sour Cream Wafers. No. 2. 2 ounces of cornstarch, 4 eggs, 1 large cupful of thick sour cream, mace, cinnamon and a little salt. Smooth the cornstarch in 2 tablespoonfuls of cold water, stir with it the yolks of eggs, cream and spices, beat briskly and then lightly mix through it the beaten whites of the eggs, bake four large wafers and roll each one, sprinkle with sugar and cinnamon and bring to the table hot. When served with preserves they are very nice.

4. Wafers filled with various Remnants such as Cooked Fruit or Veal. No. 3. Bake the wafers as directed in No. 1, spread with cooked apples, cherries, plum marmalade or cranberries. Boil rice until thick, mix with sugar, cinnamon, and mace, spread over the wafer, roll it, and sprinkle with sugar. When using veal roast, chop it very fine, brown a large piece of butter, stir a little grated wheat bread and the meat in this, add sour cream or bouillon, wine, mace or nutmeg and a little salt, and cook for a few minutes. Spread the wafer with this forcemeat, which is then baked, rolled and served on a hot dish.

When using remnants of ham, which are then served with spinach, soak the ham in milk over night, then chop it very fine and mix with thick sour cream. Spread this on wafers that have been baked, split them, turn in egg and grated bread and fry in lard to a golden brown.

5. Cracknels. 4 fresh eggs, 1 heaping tablespoonful of cornstarch, 1 small cupful of lukewarm milk mixed with a little water, a pinch of mace or grated lemon peel, salt and some preserves.

The whites of the eggs are separated from the yolks and whipped to a stiff froth, which is mixed with the dough just before baking. The heat must be moderate and the pan very smooth. Melt a little butter in the pan, put the frothed dough into this, a hot tin cover over it and bake the cracknels on one side, turn the pan without shaking it, and let it stand until the dough is set and browned on the under side. Then spread this with preserves, either apple or currant compot, marmalade or jelly, fold, put on a dish and sprinkle with sugar and cinnamon.

The cracknels can be spread on top with sugar and cinnamon and served with a wine-, fruit- or rum sauce. A nice way is to serve a compot of currants, which can also be spread over it; the sauce is then omitted.

A little baking powder mixed with the egg batter will help it to raise. For a simple dish make two tarts instead of one. Sprinkle one with lemon juice, put the other on top of this, and on this put a little fruit of any kind, or sugar.

6. Omelette, No. 1. 8 fresh eggs, 1 heaping tablespoonful of fine flour or cornstarch, 1 large cupful of warm milk mixed with a little water, some mace and salt; all of this is mixed well together as directed under No. 1. Put butter into the pan and the batter into this and with a spoon lift it up so as to let the batter run evenly under the omelette. As soon as the omelette is set and no longer adheres to the pan—it must remain soft and is not turned—sprinkle with sugar and cinnamon, put on a plate and fold.

They are very nice when served with cranberries, also with Summer sausage, smoked meat and smoked tongue. The batter must then be stirred with finely chopped chives; the sugar and cinnamon are omitted.

7. Cream Omelette. No. 2. 6 eggs, 1 ounce of corn-starch, 1 large cupful of two-thirds milk and one-third boiling water, and, if liked, mace and a little salt.

The eggs are beaten to a stiff froth, the other ingredients well mixed together and baked as in the preceding receipt. As soon as the omelette begins to set, pour over it the beaten whites of the eggs, cover with a hot lid until it is no longer soft, sprinkle with sugar and cinnamon and, if wished, fold it.

8. Omelette with Remnants of Meat. Remnants of beef, smoked meat, cooked ham or soup meat are chopped fine. Stir up a good omelette- or pancake batter and stir the meat with it, season with nutmeg or finely chopped chives. The whole eggs can be put in at once or else beat the whites to a froth and stir lightly through the batter. The batter can be dropped into the pan a spoonful at a time and baked in little cakes.

9. Bouillon Omelette. Make a batter of 8 eggs, 3 tablespoonfuls of flour, 9 tablespoonfuls of good bouillon with chopped parsley and chives, salt and pepper and bake as directed in No. 8; spread over these some capers and fold. In the meantime make a thick, strong sauce of flour browned in butter, bouillon and a glassful of Madeira, pour over the omelette and serve.

10. Omelette of Wheat Bread. Make an omelette batter, soak wheat bread slices in cold milk, turn in the batter, bake on both sides, lay pieces of butter between them and put the omelette over them. By piercing with a sharp knife the batter will go to the bottom of the pan, bake on both sides and put the omelette on a plate as soon as it no longer adheres to the pan; sprinkle with sugar and cinnamon. Canned cranberries are very good with these omelettes.

11. Pork Omelettes. For every egg use 1 tablespoonful of milk, a little salt and beat thoroughly. Then cut some lean pork into slices, fry on both sides to a light yellow color and pour the milk and eggs over them. After the omelette is set put it on a plate so that the eggs will remain soft. If liked, finely chopped chives may be mixed with the egg batter.

12. Plain Omelettes. For 3 omelettes take 6 fresh eggs, 6 small tablespoonfuls of flour, 1 large cupful of milk, 1 pint of sour cream and a little salt. Flour, cream, the yolks of the eggs and salt are stirred well together, then add the milk and shortly before baking the beaten whites of the eggs.

If the cakes are to be baked in butter, which is best for cakes made with cream, use less salt and proceed as directed under No. 1.

13. Common Omelettes. Take the yolks of 5 eggs, 1 heaping tablespoonful of flour, 1 cupful of fresh milk, salt and the beaten whites of the eggs and follow directions in the preceding receipt.

14. Four=colored Omelettes. (Served instead of a souffle). Make a good omelette batter as given under No. 12, but use one-third more. Divide this batter into four parts. The first part is colored red with cochineal, the second green with spinach juice, the third brown with grated chocolate, while the fourth is not colored. Before baking make a thick vanilla cream filling for the red omelette (2 yolks of eggs, 1 cupful of milk, 2 spoonfuls of sugar, 1 spoonful of cornstarch, vanilla, salt); for the green omelette a chocolate cream (1 heaping tablespoonful of chocolate, 1 cupful of milk, ½ spoonful of cornstarch, a little sugar, salt and the whites of the eggs used in the vanilla cream). Cover the brown omelette with light colored apple jelly, and the yellow omelette with red currant prserves. Roll the omelettes after being spread with the different sauces, cut through the middle, sprinkle with sugar and drop over them some canned cherries before sending to the table.

15. Cornstarch Omelette. 4 fresh eggs, 2 ounces of cornstarch, 1 large cupful of warmed milk, using one-third water and a little salt. The yolks of the eggs, cornstarch smoothed in milk, and salt are well beaten together and mixed with the beaten whites of the eggs and baked in clarified butter as directed under No. 1.

16. Plain Pancake. 3 ounces of flour, 3 eggs, 1 pint of milk and a little salt. If only 2 eggs are used, take less milk.

17. Currant Cake. For this use a good omelette batter, taking a little sugar and salt, 1 small soupplateful of ripe currants, ¼ pound of sugar and ¼ pound of grated wheat bread. Heat the butter in the pan until quite hot, put in the batter, lay the currants on this, and before turning sprinkle over it a little finely grated bread. After the omelette is baked on both sides, put on a plate and strew a little sugar over it.

18. Apple Pancake. No. 1. Take 2 soupplatefuls of finely sliced apples, cook them until done with sugar, lemon peel and enough wine until there is no more juice.

Then beat the yolks of 6 eggs with a cupful of thick, sour cream, 2 tablespoonfuls of cornstarch, a little salt and cinnamon, mix the beaten whites through this and bake two cakes on one side to a light brown. After the second is baked, spread with apples, put the cakes one on the other and put them into the oven for a few minutes, sprinkle with sugar and serve.

19. Apple Pancake. No. 2. Take 12 sour apples, ¼ pound of butter, 12 crackers soaked in milk, 6 eggs, ¼ pound of currants, 2 tablespoonfuls of sugar, lemon peel and cinnamon. Pare the apples, slice and cook with butter over a slow fire until done. Then pour over the crackers enough milk to soak them, beat 4 eggs to a froth, stir the ingredients with the crackers, adding at last the apples and the whites of the eggs; 2 tablespoonfuls of rum may also be stirred with the apples. Bake the omelette on a slow fire.

20. Small Apple Cakes. Pare large cooking apples, cut into slices the thickness of a finger and take out the core. Then let them heat through with a little arrac and sugar. Take 1 small cupful of milk, ¼ pound of flour, the yolks of 4 eggs, a little salt and stir through the dough a little mace or cinnamon. Beat well together and just before baking add the whites of the eggs. Mix the apples through the dough and bake with butter on a hot pan on both sides until done and of a golden brown color.

21. Prune Omelette. Make a batter as directed in No. 16. Heat a pan with plenty of butter and put in about one-third of the batter after the omelette has set, lay in the prunes side by side with the opening to the bottom and bake on both sides until done and of a golden brown color. Sprinkle with sugar and cinnamon and serve hot.

22. Huckleberry Omelettes. Are made the same as prune omelettes, or, after turning them, put a thick layer of huckleberries on the baked side, sprinkle with grated crackers, cover until the under side is baked and by that time the berries will be baked through. The omelette is put on a plate and sprinkled with sugar.

23. Cherry Omelettes. Are made the same as prune omelettes, taking stoned cherries.

24. Macaroon Omelettes. Take ¼ pound of macaroons and mix with a few bitter ones, 2 tablespoonfuls of flour, 1 pint of water mixed with milk, 4 eggs, lemon peel and a little salt. Stir the flour and milk together, add the yolks of the eggs and lemon peel and beat thoroughly, and then add the macaroons and whites of the eggs. Heat a pan with some butter, pour into it the batter and bake on both sides, sprinkle with sugar or else bake on one side only, lay on it some jelly or preserves, fold and sprinkle well with sugar.

25. Roll or Bread Omelette. Take 1¾ pound of stale wheat bread, 1 pint of milk to soak the bread, ¼ pound of butter, ¼ pound of sugar, ¼ pound of currants, ¼ pound of crushed almonds, 6 eggs, 1 teaspoonful of cinnamon or a little lemon peel. Cut the crust off the bread, toast and finely pound it, break the bread into pieces and soak in the milk. Stir the butter to a cream, add the yolks of the eggs one by one, the soaked bread, the washed currants, almonds and spices, and after stirring all together add the beaten whites of the eggs. Then butter a pan, sprinkle with one-half of the finely pounded crust of the bread, on this put the batter, cover and bake to a golden brown, but it must not be moved. Strew over it the remaining bread, turn and bake this side to a light brown and sprinkle with sugar.

26. Anise and Carraway Omelette. 2 ounces of grated bread, 2 ounces of rolled crackers, 1 heaping tablespoonful of flour, 3 eggs, 1 pint of milk, 1 tablespoonful of anise seed and a little salt.

Beat the whites of the eggs to a froth, stir the batter together and mix with the froth, heat some butter with a little lard in a pan, bake to a golden brown color and sprinkle with sugar. Instead of anise, carraway can be used and bake with fresh bacon.

27. Omelette with Rice. ½ pound of rice boiled in milk with butter, a few pieces of cinnamon or a little salt, ¼ pound of raisins; also 4 eggs, 2—3 tablespoonfuls of sugar, a little grated wheat bread or crackers. The eggs, sugar and crackers are stirred with the rice and then mixed with the whites of the eggs. Heat some butter in a pan on a brisk fire and bake one large or several smaller cakes. Pounded crusts of bread sprinkled into the pan before putting in the batter, and over the batter before turning, give the omelette a better appearance and improve the taste.

Sprinkle with sugar and serve.

28. Noodle Omelettes. For 2 omelettes take a soupplateful of noodles, 1 tablespoonful of flour, the yolks of 3 eggs, 1 cupful of milk, a little mace or nutmeg and salt, stir well together and add the beaten whites of the eggs.

29. Baked Noodles. Heat some butter in a pan, spread the noodles on this and bake to a golden brown on both sides.

It is a very nice side dish with spinach and other greens, and is also good with cooked fruits.

30. Potato Omelettes. Heat some butter or lard in a pan until very hot, grate enough cold potatoes into the pan to cover it, and sprinkle with a little salt. In about 10 minutes make a common batter, beat the whites of the eggs to a froth, stir into the batter, cover the omelette and bake to a dark brown and until crisp. Serve immediately. An omelette of this kind is very nice with any kind of salad, or with a compot.

31. Small Wheat Cakes. One quart of warm milk, 2 ounces of melted butter, 3—4 eggs, 1 tablespoonful of sugar, yeast, 1 pound of warmed flour, 4—6 ounces of currants, cinnamon or mace and a little salt.

Stir the milk with the flour, add the other ingredients, whip the batter well, mix with it the currants (warmed) and put in a warm place to raise. If after about 1½—2 hours the dough is risen bake in an open pan in butter, or butter and lard mixed, in little cakes the size of a saucer, which are turned once, and then only when the dough is set.

32. Common Wheat Cakes. No. 1. 1⅓ pounds of flour, 1 quart of lukewarm milk, ¼ cupful of melted butter or lard, 3 eggs, yeast and a little salt are made into a dough as in the above receipt and are then baked in butter, making 2 large cakes.

33. Common Wheat Cakes. No. 2. Take 2 pounds of flour, yeast, 1 cupful of melted butter, ¼ pound of currants, 3—5 eggs, if wished some lemon peel, about 1 pint of milk and bake in an oblong pan. Serve warm or cold with butter.

34. Buckwheat Cakes. No. 1. To every cupful of flour take a cupful of hot water, a large tablespoonful of thick sour cream, or if you have no cream, take melted butter or lard, yeast and a little salt. Currants can also be added. After all is stirred together take a spoon and beat the dough well, set it aside to raise and make into small or large cakes like the above.

35. Buckwheat Cakes. No. 2. Two cupfuls of buckwheat flour, 3 cupfuls of hot water, 1 cupful of thick sour cream and salt are stirred well together and baked immediately in hot butter to a golden brown color.
The cream can be omitted and instead use 1 cupful of cold grated potatoes. Buttermilk can be substituted for the water if desired.

36. French Toast. ("Arme Ritter".) Take rolls, large ones are preferable, split them and for 6 rolls weighing 1⅙ pounds add not quite 1 quart of milk and 6 eggs. Season the milk with a little salt, lemon juice or cinnamon (boiled milk is not so good, as it makes the toast sticky), and divide with a spoon and lay the rolls on a dish. Then beat the eggs, lay the rolls in this so that they will soak up the egg; bake in butter to a light brown color. Sprinkle with sugar and serve with a compot.

37. Spanish Bread Pudding. Take 6 stale rolls, grate off the crust, cut the rolls into slices, lay them into a deep pan and cover with a thick wine sauce made of 1 pint of claret, ¼ pound of sugar, the yolks of 6 eggs, salt, lemon peel and 1 ounce of cornstarch; let them lay in this for ¼ hour, sprinkle through them the grated crust and bake in the oven as directed in the above receipt. Then let them cool, spread over them some good apple or other fruit marmalade, arrange in the form of a mound and pour over this the beaten whites of 6 eggs, sweetened to taste. Put into the oven for a few minutes until the frosting is of a nice yellow color and serve for dessert instead of a souffle.

38. Karthusian Dumplings. Grate off the crust from milk rolls and then cut them in two. For 3 rolls take 3 cupfuls of milk, 2 eggs, 1 tablespoonful of sugar, a little lemon peel, mace or cinnamon, beat well together, pour over the rolls and let them soak for 2—3 hours. After they are well soaked, sprinkle over them the grated crust and bake in plenty of butter to a dark brown color. Serve with any kind of fruit preserves, or with a wine or fruit sauce.

39. Rice Dumplings. Boil ½ pound of scalded rice in milk until thick, stir through it butter the size of an egg, sugar and grated lemon peel if liked. After the rice has cooled form into dumplings the size of a pear, roll in egg and cracker crumbs and bake in butter to a light brown. Serve with a vanilla-, wine- or fruit sauce.

Very few of the cakes, etc., described in this division, can be served to invalids as they are not easily digested on account of the butter used in preparing them; No. 6 and 9 can occasionally be sent to the sickroom.

L.–Dishes prepared with Eggs, Milk, Rice or Cornmeal.

1. Boiling Eggs. To boil eggs so that they will be just right, they should not be put into the water until it boils. Soft boiled eggs require about 3 minutes, and medium hard boiled eggs 4 minutes. Eggs for decorations, where the whites must be firm and the yolks somewhat softer, require 5 minutes. When a number of eggs are to be boiled at a time they are best put into a wire basket, by which means they can be easily taken out of the water.

When eggs are to be used for decorating vegetable dishes, put them into cold water, and as soon as cold take them out of the shell and warm them in salted water.

2. Scrambled Eggs. Take 1 tablespoonful of milk, a little salt and a piece of butter the size of half a walnut for each egg. Beat the eggs, milk and salt together, melt the butter (a small earthenware vessel is the best for this purpose), pour in the eggs, and stir over a very slow fire until thick. Stir only until thick and done, then serve. Using water and bacon instead of the milk and butter, will make the eggs more spicy and is preferred by many.

Scrambled eggs are served with asparagus, lettuce, smoked herring, Summer sausage, cold tongue and smoked meats. With the last three, some finely chopped chives should be mixed with the beaten eggs.

Scrambled egg dishes can be varied in many ways by the admixture of stewed and sliced mushrooms, small boiled asparagus tips, a few pieces of boned anchovy, minced salmon and a few spoonfuls of grated cheese of any kind.

If this dish is to be served as an entree after the soup, it should first be filled into warmed sauce dishes, mix with it sliced truffles and diced sweet breads boiled in bouillon, and afterwards cover with strips of salmon. For the family table mix cheese with the eggs before they are beaten and after the cups are filled brush with puree of tomatoes or else cover with bits of bologna (cervelat) sausage and put a border of slips of toasted wheat bread on each cup.

In the Spring a nice dish of scrambled eggs can be prepared for the supper table as follows: Clean some young red and white radishes, leave a blade of green on the top, slit the peel towards the top with a sharp knife and loosen without removing them from the radish, then lay them into cold water for a few hours, which will cause the skin to curl nicely, after which let them drain. Cut some round slices of wheat bread, hollow them out in the center, toast slightly and fill with a small bunch of cresses dressed with olive oil and a trifle of salt. Boil 3 truffles until tender and slice them. 10 eggs are then scrambled, lay them into the center of a hot dish, cover with the toast and surround with the sliced truffles and the radishes as a border.

4. Poached Eggs. Bring some water to a boil with a little salt and vinegar. Break into it some fresh eggs rapidly, but they must be dropped in side by side. As soon as the whites are set (they must not become hard) take them out of the water, if desired they can be sprinkled with a little vinegar, trim the edges smoothly all around, sprinkle with fine salt and serve either on a dish of spinach or with the latter as a side dish.

As an entree after the soup, poached eggs can be served for the family table with an anchovy-, herring-, sorrel- or Remoulade sauce over the eggs, ornamenting the dish with slips of toast. For a dinner party line a dish rather thickly with the following well bound sauce: Lightly brown a few onions and slices of ham in butter, rub in this 2 spoonfuls of flour and add bouillon and cream half and half to make a well-bound sauce, which is then strained; then put in about 2 ounces of grated

Parmesan cheese, stir through it the whites of 2 eggs beaten to a froth and line the dish with half of this sauce. Arrange the poached eggs in the dish, pour over them the remainder of the sauce, sprinkle with bread crumbs and cheese and then bake to a light brown.

5. Fried Eggs. Heat some butter in a very clean pan and break the eggs into it very carefully, keeping each egg whole; sprinkle over them a little fine salt, and when the whites are set put them on a dish without turning them, trim the edges and serve with spinach or other similar vegetables.

Fried eggs can be served with the following sauce and they then make an agreeable dish for the supper table: For 4 persons take about 2 eggs, 1 heaping teaspoonful of flour or cornstarch, 1 large cupful of water, vinegar according to taste and enough sugar to make the vinegar mild. Stir all of this until it commences to boil, and stir through it a piece of butter the size of half an egg. Pour the sauce over the eggs while they are still hot, cover and set aside for a few minutes on top of the stove. If fried eggs are to be served as an entree after the soup, prepare them as follows: Cut a long loaf of wheat bread into slices, remove the center without breaking the crust and fry these rings in lard to a golden brown. Lay the rings on a flat dish lined with anchovy butter, brush them with thick sour cream, break an egg into each, salt, dot with some sour cream, cover with buttered paper and bake until the whites are set. A border of whole filled tomatoes is very pretty.

6. Eggs with Mustard Sauce. Shell medium soft boiled eggs, divide them in two lengthwise, put them into a dish with the yolks to the top, sprinkle lightly with salt and pour over them a mustard sauce (see Division R), or else melted butter stirred with mustard.

7. Filled Eggs. Take hard boiled eggs and cut them in two, remove the yolks, mince and mix one-half of them with chopped anchovies, mushrooms, small pieces of tongue or ham and the yolk of one raw egg. Stir the remainder of the yolks to a thick sauce with mustard, olive oil, tarragon vinegar, salt and pepper, mix a part of this with the mince to make a smooth forcemeat, fill it into the hollowed whites of the eggs, and pour over them the remainder of the sauce. Hot filled eggs make a nice entree after the soup. The filling can be prepared in various ways, taking either a fish forcemeat or else a finely minced veal sweetbread- or chicken ragout. A simpler method is to grate the yolks of the eggs and mix them to a forcemeat with savory herbs, grated bread, grated cheese and some bouillon. Part of the filling should always be used to line the bottom of the flat dish; arrange the filled eggs on this, dot with butter, sprinkle with bread crumbs and bake to a golden brown.

8. Egg Mound. Cut the whites of 6 hard boiled eggs into fine strips, stew them in a Bechamel sauce, (see Division R), and put them on a small hot dish in the shape of a mound. Rub the yolks with a piece of fresh butter and some salt and press through a sieve over the whites. Cover with bits of toast, and then get it nicely hot in the oven.

9. Eggs in Marinade. Shell 18 hard boiled eggs and put them into a stone jar. Boil 1 quart of vinegar, ½ ounce of pepper, ½ ounce of Jamaica pepper and ½ ounce of ginger for about 10 minutes; pour through a sieve over the eggs. After the vinegar is cold, tightly cover the jar by tieing over it a piece of paper. After 3—4 weeks serve the eggs with bread and butter.

10. Raw Whites of Eggs for Invalids. Beat the whites to a stiff froth, slowly add 1 tablespoonful of thick sweet cream, 1 spoonful of brandy, 1 teaspoonful of fine sugar. Administer to the patient at once, a spoonful at a time.

11. Egg Cheese. 9—10 eggs are well beaten and then stirred over a slow fire with 1 quart of milk and a little salt until it curdles; it should not become too hot. Pour it into a mould rapidly so that the eggs may remain soft. A few currants previously scalded in boiling water can be scattered through the mass. If not wanted for immediate use the cheese will be milder if the milk mixed with the eggs is first poured into a stone jar and this put into a kettle containing boiling water, and then continuously boiling the milk until it curdles. Drop pieces of almonds over the cheese and serve with a sauce made of sour cream beaten to a froth with sugar and cinnamon and mixed with arrac. A cold wine- or fruit sauce is also appropriate.

12. Egg Jelly. 1 quart of milk, 4 beaten eggs and the yolks of 5 eggs, 1 grated lemon, sugar and cinnamon are put into a deep vessel, cover and set over boiling water until thick. As soon as cold sprinkle with sugar and serve with a cranberry sauce or some other well flavored compot.

13. Beaten Milk. Beat thick milk and its cream with a beater briskly for 15 minutes. Stir through it sugar and cinnamon and serve with toast. A glassful of claret can also be beaten with it.

14. Sour Milk Cheese. Set a pan of thick milk without the cream near the stove so that it will gradually separate from the watery parts. Pour into a muslin bag and afterwards press through a sieve. Mix with it fresh cream or milk and sugar and vanilla according to taste. Another method is to fill the cold sour milk into the bag and let it hang during the night to permit the watery parts to drip away. This makes the cheese smoother and mellower than if the milk is warmed, but it is mixed with sugar and cream or fresh milk in the same manner. After putting it into the dish and smoothing the top, sprinkle with sugar and a little ginger, or else pour over it some sour cream beaten to a froth with sugar and cinnamon. If no cream is mixed with the cheese it must not be made too thick, and it should be taken into consideration that this cheese thickens naturally when done, similar to boiled rice. Many like sour milk cheese with cranberries, grapes or cherry compot.

15. Rice Pudding. Take about ½ pound of rice and 2 quarts of milk. Scald the rice as directed in A, No. 5, melt a piece of butter in the milk which will thereby be prevented from scorching, and bring it to a boil. Put in the rice together with a few pieces of cinnamon— those not liking the flavor of cinnamon may prefer vanilla—afterwards add a little sugar and a trifle of salt, put the rice into a dish and sprinkle with sugar; it is often dressed with melted butter. If the rice is to be served cold, remember that it thickens materially when cooling. Before serving stir through it the yolks of a few eggs together with a dash of rum or cordial, otherwise the pudding will be apt to have an insipid taste.

Remnants of rice pudding can be used for rice omelette, (K, No. 27), or to fill wafers (K, No. 4), or it may be made into small dumplings which are baked in melted butter and turned in grated chocolate while still hot.

16.   Rice with Claret for Invalids.   Let 3 ounces of rice come to a boil in cold water, pour in 1 pint of claret, 2 teaspoonfuls of lemon sugar and a little cinnamon; boil until done. Serve hot with sweetened cream stirred with the yolk of an egg.

17.   Rice with Apples.   Scald the rice, which should be of the very best quality; then melt a piece of butter in a pan, put in the rice with boiling water, a piece of cinnamon and a little salt, and boil slowly. When the rice is almost tender put in the apples with a large piece of sugar, cook until done, but it must not be too thick; stir carefully so that the kernels will remain whole. A glassful of white wine can also be stirred through the rice. Sprinkle the top with sugar and serve.

For ¼ pound of rice take 6 medium-sized apples, pare and cut into eight parts. This will be sufficient for 3 persons.

18.   Rice with Raisins.   (A nice dish for convalescents.)   After the rice is scalded, boil for ¼ hour as directed in the above receipt, then add raisins and cook until both are tender, but they must not become mushy.

19.   Rice for Ragout.   For 2 dishes take 1 pound of rice, scald and cook in bouillon until tender, stir through it a glassful of Madeira, 1 cupful of cream, the yolks of 2 eggs and ¼ pound of Parmesan cheese, and surround with it a ragout of poultry or veal.

20.   Arabian Rice.   Boil some scalded rice in salted water for 20 minutes, pour off the water and set it in a warm oven for 10 minutes, stirring often, before bringing to the table. Serve this rice with roasted or boiled meats.

21. Turin Rice. ½ pound of rice is washed in cold water, dried with a cloth and fried in a pan with grated onion and 3 ounces of butter to a light brown color. Then mix 1 glassful of white wine with a little lemon juice and 1 small cupful of strong bouillon and boil the rice until tender; before sending to the table stir in salt and pepper. Serve with stewed meat. Substituting Madeira for the white wine, and the addition of sliced and stewed truffles will add greatly to the excellence of this rice preparation.

22. Rice in a Bag. 1½ pounds of rice, or ¾ pound of rice and ¾ pound of barley, or ⅔ pound of prunes and ¼ pound of raisins. Rice, raisins and prunes are washed, scalding the latter. Then take a very clean cloth, dip into boiling water, wring it dry, put the ingredients into the cloth in layers with a little salt, tie, leaving room for the rice to expand, put this into a pan of boiling water, first putting a saucer into the bottom to keep the cloth from scorching, and boil for 2 hours. Serve with browned butter and sugar, or with roast meat and gravy or raw ham. The following is a nice sauce, and smoked meats are a fitting accompaniment: For the above quantity take 1 tablespoonful of flour, milk, the yolk of an egg, a piece of butter, sugar and a little salt, put on the stove until it commences to boil. The sauce must not be too thick. To have this dish just right be careful not to leave too much room for the rice, as then it will become too thin, neither must the bag be drawn up too tightly, for then the rice will become too thick; it is advisable to examine the bag during the cooking to ascertain whether it is too tight or not.

23. Sago Compot. Cook ¼ pound of pearl sago in 1 cupful of water, 1 cupful of wine, 2 spoonfuls of raspberry juice, 2 ounces of sugar and a little pineapple extract. Then mix with the sago some preserved pears and cherries, put the compot into a pan, pour over it an icing made of 1 ounce of pounded almonds, 1 ounce of sugar, the yolks of 3 eggs, bake the compot for ¼ hour in a moderate oven and serve while still hot. For a plain dish take sugar, water, lemon peel and juice and at last a few spoonfuls of raisins or currants, or some quartered apples stewed in wine and sugar.

24. Noodles. For 8—10 persons. 4 whole eggs, 4 tablespoonfuls of milk and as much flour as the eggs and milk will take. Put the flour into a dish, make a depression in the center, put in eggs and milk, stir with a knife to a light dough and then mix with the hands until it is smooth. The longer the dough is kneaded the better the noodles will be. Then cut into four parts, roll each part as thin as paper and set aside to dry. When the fourth piece is rolled, take the first, dust with flour, cut in two, roll each piece, cut it into narrow strips, and then let it dry; they can also be used immediately. Cook the noodles in plenty of boiling salted water for about ½ hour, drain on a colander and then pour boiling water through them.

Serve with browned butter. Or boil milk with a large piece of butter and a little salt, let the noodles boil in this, then serve, covering the noodles with rolled cracker browned in butter. Then, too, the noodles can be covered with crisp noodles, by frying some uncooked noodles until crisp in butter; or the noodles can be covered with grated brown bread. Roast veal or dried prunes are a nice dish with noodles; apple marmalade is also a fitting accompaniment.

25. Rice with Tomatoes. After frying some scalded rice for ¼ hour in butter, cook it in bouillon until tender and thick, then stir in some finely cut onions stewed in butter, salt and pepper, some pieces of ham and some ripe stewed tomatoes. Serve the rice with beefsteaks and lamb chops. Use what rice remains for tomato soup.

26. Barley with Sour Cream. Scald the barley and fry it in butter for 10—15 minutes and then cook in milk until done. Add the necessary salt, stir through it some sour cream whipped with a few eggs, put the barley into a mould and bake for half an hour to a light brown color. Serve with sweet cream for supper.

27. Boiled Flour Groats. Make a dough the same as noodle dough, roll very thin, divide into small pieces and cut them as fine as groats with a chopping knife. If the dough is very stiff it can be grated. This is very nice when used in milk soups.

For Invalids Nos. 1, 2, 4, 8, 10, 12, 15, 17, 20, 23 and 26 are adapted.

M.—Jellies and Ices.

1. **The various Stocks for Jellies** are prepared from isinglass, calves' and pigs' feet, and gelatine. Isinglass makes the finest, clearest and handsomest jellies. The leaf like variety, which when held to the light has a bluish tint, is the best. Break the isinglass into small pieces, put it into a very clean stone jar, cover with water, let it stand over night and the next morning boil it for a quarter of an hour on a slow fire or, better still, on top of the stove, which should not be too hot, until dissolved. If the quality is good it will dissolve almost completely and have the appearance of clear water. Strain through muslin and use according to directions. For 2 quarts of jelly take 1 tablespoonful of isinglass.

Calves' feet jelly is more troublesome to make than when using isinglass, but it is much cheaper and at the same time very palatable. The stock can be prepared in the following manner: The calves' feet for jelly of every kind should be singed so that the skin will be perfectly clean, then wash them thoroughly and let them lay in lukewarm water for a few hours to draw and bleach. Cut them into small pieces and put them on the fire in an enameled kettle containing cold water; as soon as the water has boiled and the scum has been carefully taken off, pour off the water, fill up again with fresh water and put onto the stove again with a quick fire. Then boil the calves' feet uninterruptedly for 3, 4 or 5 hours with frequent stirring until they drop to pieces, take them out of the kettle, pour some water over them, and this water should then be added to the other broth, which must be well boiled down, and after taking off the fat pass through a fine sieve into a porcelain or earthenware jar and set aside until the following day. Before using the jelly the fatty outer skin and the settlings at the bottom should be removed.

To prepare 2 quarts of jelly use 6 calves' feet in the Winter and 8 in the Summer, and the broth of these should be boiled down to about a pint. This kind of stock can be used for wine-, meat- or fish jellies. In making stock of pork rind or pigs' feet, be careful to have everything perfectly clean, cut into very small pieces and boil the same as calves' feet. Take 1 pound of rind for each quart of jelly, which is also very good.

Gelatine is used very much the same as isinglass and although not quite so good as the latter, it is much cheaper and for this reason extensively used. It is obtainable in small cakes of a yellowish white, clear or even of a pretty red tint. The best gelatine comes in thin cakes and is very clear.

Gelatine is used not only in the preparation of blanc-mangers, meat- or fish jellies, but also for clear sweet jellies. It is dissolved in the following manner: Cut it into small pieces with the scissors, for each ounce of gelatine put a cupful of cold water into a small vessel and set it on top of a hot stove; it will be fully dissolved after ½ or 1 hour, and then take off the scum with great care. In case the gelatine is wanted for immediate use, put it on a medium fire with a little more water; keep it on the fire until it is dissolved and stir frequently so that it will not adhere to the sides of the vessel. For clear jellies the gelatine should be strained or otherwise clarified, but this is not necessary with the best kinds. For a quart of liquid jelly take a tablespoonful of gelatine in the Winter, and 1¼ tablespoonfuls in the Summer, but the quantity depends altogether on the kinds of dishes for which it is to be used. ¾ of a spoonful of gelatine is sufficient to transform a quart of milk into a jelly firm enough to turn onto a dish. Water, wine, bouillon, etc., require about 1¼ tablespoonfuls to a quart. If cold meats are to be sliced and jellied, the jelly should be firmer and for every quart of fluid jelly take a good ounce of gelatine. It is advisable to make a test of the stock before preparing the jelly in order to ascertain beyond any doubt whether it possesses the required consistency; at all events it is necessary to prepare the jelly the day before it is to be used, especially in the Summer.

2. Jelly in Moulds, etc. Porcelain and enameled moulds are the best and easiest to keep clean. In order that jellies may drop out of the mould readily, the latter should be thinly brushed with almond or olive oil. Then put in a layer of sour jelly broth about ¼ inch thick for fish or meat. As soon as firm ornament it with a star or border, using for this purpose parsley, lemon, beets, hard boiled eggs, pickles or capers; cover the ornamentation with jelly broth and as soon as it is firm, nicely arrange the meat or fish on it and pour over the whole the remaining broth and let it stand until entirely firm; if the mould can be placed on ice it will be done so much the quicker. To turn the jelly out of the mould put the dish in which it is to be served accurately onto the mould, then grasping them both tightly turn quickly, trim the edge neatly and garnish with parsley if it is a sour jelly, and with flower buds if it is a sweet one.

If, after the jelly is cool and firm, it will not drop out of the mould easily after all, soak a towel in hot water, wring it dry and wind it around the mould for a few moments, or else hold the mould over boiling water for a short time; the jelly will then drop out.

3. Coloring Jellies. Jellies may be colored in various tints if they are to be used in layers, or a clear jelly can be ornamented with some colored jelly. For red jelly dissolve some red gelatine, but boil it thoroughly, which will improve the taste.

To obtain a yellow tint put a small quantity of saffron into water to draw and use enough of the yellow liquid to give the jelly the desired color. Saffron should be used with caution as it is poisonous in undue quantities; for that matter, a trifle of bouillon color will produce an equally nice yellow tinge.

Sweet jellies can be colored brown with dissolved chocolate; spiced jellies are colored to a dark yellow with Madeira, and brown with extract of beef.

Spinach juice is used for green jellies, and a few drops of cochineal with some lemon juice produces a beautiful yellow color. After the jelly broth has been colored put a thin layer of it into a prepared porcelain dish and let it stand until cool.

If a number of jelly dishes are to be served at a large dinner party, prepare one of them in red and the others in light colors, and then ornament them with contrasting colors; for instance make some triangular ornaments of red jelly and arrange them around the edge of a light jelly. Then cut a rose or other flower of red jelly and put it into the center of the dish. Red jellies can be very prettily decorated with white or yellow ornaments.

I. SOUR JELLIES.

4. Sour Jellies of Calves' Feet for Fish and Meat. Jellies can be quickly and easily prepared by using extract of beef and gelatine, which will make a strong and clear thick jelly. When cooking the jelly an enameled kettle is the best. Iron is not well adapted for cooking jellies, as the acid in the jelly acts upon the iron and gives the jellies an unpleasant flavor.

For a sour jelly 4—5 blanched calves' feet, as given under No. 1, and 2—4 pounds of beef, washed, a piece of veal, remnants of any kind of fresh meat or poultry can be used (but nothing from the head, through which the jelly will become dark), and some raw ham cut into small pieces. Cover with boiling water, add some salt, cook rapidly, skimming carefully, and add 2 teaspoonfuls of white peppercorns, half as many cloves, 10 eschalots or 4 large onions, 2 fresh bay leaves, 1 carrot, parsley root, half of a celery root, the juice and the thinly peeled rind of 1 lemon, and enough vinegar to give the broth a pleasant flavor. Let the vegetables cook for an hour, boil the meat in this until tender and let the feet cook until the bones can be taken out. Then pour the broth (which will amount to about 2 quarts) through a sieve into a porcelain kettle; the next day take off the fat and settlings and mix ½ bottle of wine with the jelly and the juice of a lemon and set on the stove; taste it to see if it is sour and salty enough. Then clear the jelly in the following manner: Beat up the whites of a few eggs with a little water, stir into the warm broth and set on the hot stove until the broth is quite clear, then strain through a flannel bag; if not perfectly clear it can be strained again, though once will usually suffice.

5. Sour Jelly for Fish and Meat. Take a nice lean piece of beef, say about 2½—3 pounds, put it into an enameled kettle and pour over it enough cold water with salt to make a strong bouillon, bring quickly to a boil, skimming carefully. After it has cooked for half an hour take out the meat, rinse off any scum that may adhere to it and set the broth aside to settle. After it has settled, pour off the top into a clean dish, add half of a celery root, a piece of parsley root, 4 white onions, the peel of a lemon with the juice, 2 fresh bay leaves, 2 teaspoonfuls of white peppercorns, ½ teaspoonful of cloves and enough wine vinegar to give the jelly a sour taste; add a little salt if necessary. Cover the kettle and let the bouillon cook until the meat is tender. Then pour the broth, of which there should be about 1½ quarts, through a muslin cloth, set aside in a warm place so that it will not cool too rapidly, and when it is cold take off the settlings. In the meantime dissolve 1½ ounces of gelatine in 1 pint of water, strain through muslin, bring to a boil with the bouillon and pour over the fish or poultry.

6. Jelly of Beef or Poultry, etc. The meat should be nicely washed and freed from fat. Poultry, excepting geese, can be larded, turning the lardoons in salt and cutting the ends smooth; take the bones out of the turkey and the goose as given under D, No. 169. Put the meat into an enameled kettle in water and enough white wine vinegar to give it a sour taste, put in the necessary salt, skim carefully, add the spices as given in the above receipt, cover, let it cook slowly and then take it out of the broth and set aside to cool. Put into one large or several small dishes; the small dishes are preferable. Pour through a sieve and the following day take off fat and settlings and for each quart of broth take 1 pint of stock made of 4 calves' feet, or for the same quantity take 1 ounce of dissolved gelatine.

7. Salmon in Jelly. Boil some water and white pepper, lemon slices without seeds, onions, mace, a little salt, 2—3 bay leaves and the necessary vinegar (it is better to use fruit wine, lemon juice and vinegar half and half) in an enameled kettle for a while, pour through a sieve, then add to this the salmon, first cut into pieces and salted for an hour. Boil until tender, then take out the salmon and set aside to cool. For each 2 pounds of salmon there should be 1 quart of jelly; make the latter by using a strong, clear, white beef, veal or poultry bouillon. Cook this with 1 pint of white wine and 1 ounce of gelatine, salt and spice and season with a little lemon juice and pour this lukewarm over the salmon pieces. Decorate the edge with pickled crabtails.

8. Eel in Jelly. This makes a very pretty dish if the right mould is used. The eel is not skinned but is divided into pieces, first rubbing it with salt to take off any slime, empty, take off the fins, pour warm vinegar over it and let it come to a boil in unsalted water. Then lay the pieces into a stew pan with bay leaves, lemon slices, eschalots, salt, peppercorns, sage leaves and parsley, with enough water and vinegar, half and half, to cover the eel. After it has boiled for ¼ hour, take out the eel, skim off the fat and pour through a sieve; dissolve 1 ounce of gelatine for each quart and add to the broth, bring to a boil again, salt, pour into a mould putting in the pieces of eel and sliced lemon. Then let the jelly cool and turn into a dish. Serve with a Remoulade- or a good Mayonnaise sauce.

9. Jelly of Sardines or Caviar. Make a clear meat jelly as given under No. 4 or 5, let it cool until lukewarm, and pour into a round form to the thickness of about ½ inch. Bury in ice until frozen, then dry the sardines between blotting paper, and arrange them in the mould in the form of a rosette, cover these also with the jelly and when this layer is frozen fill the empty space in the middle with caviar; close the mould with aspic and bury in ice until wanted. After the mould has been turned on a round dish cover it for a moment with a cloth dipped in hot water and wrung dry; by this means the mould can be emptied more readily.

10. Jelly with Rabbit. The hind legs and the back of a rabbit are washed, skinned, washed again but not laid in the water, and boiled in an earthenware or enameled (not iron) kettle in water with enough vinegar to give it a sour taste; skim carefully. Then add a sliced lemon, 8 eschalots or 4 onions, 2 teaspoonfuls of peppercorns and 2 teaspoonfuls of cloves, let the meat cook slowly until tender, take it out and after the broth is strained set it in a cool place. In the meantime make a strong bouillon and a jelly of 3—4 calves' feet as given in No. 1. After it is cold take off fat and settlings, and bring to a boil with the bouillon and the rabbit broth, freed from settlings. The jelly broth must have a strong sour taste. There should be about 1½ quarts; should there be more than this quantity color it as given under No. 3, and use for decorating. Gelatine and extract of beef can be used instead of the calves' feet, saving time and trouble in preparing.

Then make a liver forcemeat as follows: Wash a calves' liver, skin, wash, pound finely and press through a sieve. Cut ¼ pound of bacon into small pieces, chop with ½ pound of pork and mix with a cupful of crackers or grated wheat bread, the yolks of 2 hard boiled eggs, 1 cupful of butter melted and cleared from settlings, salt and pepper. The forcemeat is put into a buttered souffle mould and baked in the oven until done. When cold cut into slices; the rabbit is also sliced. Then rub the jelly mould with oil, fill the bottom with jelly broth, and when cold lay the meat and forcemeat on this in layers, and over each layer put some jelly broth, let it cool and proceed in this manner until all the broth is used.

This jelly will keep in the Winter for 10 to 14 days if the jelly is made quite thick, and set aside uncovered in an airy place. When serving, turn out of the pan, decorate prettily with a wreath of small parsley leaves and red beets cut into long slices. Serve with an a la Diable sauce (No. 55, R,) or a sauce for jellies.

11. Jelly of Salted Tongue with Extract of Beef. After the tongue is salted and cooked until tender as given under Division D, No. 30, boil ½ pound of beef according to No. 5 of this Division with the ingredients there given together with 1¼ quarts of bouillon, pour off the settlings, dissolve 1 ounce of gelatine and bring to a boil with the broth which must not be more than 1½ quarts, try the sauce to see if salty and sour enough, take from the fire and proceed as directed under No. 2. In the meantime cut the tongue into slices of even size and cut off the rind. If the broth when cold is sufficiently thick, stir through it enough hot extract of beef to give it a pleasant flavor. Then let a layer of the jelly cool in the mould, lay the tongue slices on this, and around the dish some button onions boiled until tender in water with plenty of wine vinegar and a little salt, over this put the remaining broth and proceed as given under No. 2.

12. Beef Royal. A piece of nice beef, weighing from 8—10 pounds is laid into vinegar for a week. Lard, cook slowly with 8 calves' feet, bay leaves, eschalots, a sliced lemon, white pepper, salt and 1½—2 bottles of claret for 3 hours, covered tightly. Then take out the meat, add some browned sugar, and pour the broth over the meat through a sieve.

13. Veal in Jelly. No. 1. Cut a piece of veal into small square pieces, wash in hot water and bring to a boil with 4 scalded calves' feet, and salt. After skimming add plenty of vinegar, peppercorns, onions, whole and ground cloves, a few bay leaves, lemon peel and a few blades of mace, cook the meat slowly; then take out the meat and if there is still too much broth, boil it down with the calves' feet until it will form jelly when cold; then take out the calves' feet, stir through it the beaten whites of a few eggs, and let the broth stand on the back of the stove for an hour, it must not boil, then pour through a jelly bag. Take the meat from the bones, remove all unnecessary fat, put into a buttered pan and pour the jelly broth over it. Instead of calves' feet gelatine can be used.

Serve with an a la Diable sauce, (R, No. 55). To keep the jelly for any length of time it should be placed uncovered in a cool place.

14. Veal in Jelly. No. 2. (Very nice in the Summer). Cut pieces of veal as for a fricassee, lay into a deep earthenware jar with sliced lemon and cloves between the slices, and when the jar is filled sprinkle with the necessary salt; then pour over them a mixture of ⅔ vinegar and ⅓ water, cover the jar by tieing over it a piece of parchment or something similar. Then put it into an iron kettle filled with water and boil for 3 hours.

A few bones are necessary to fill into the jar with the meat so as not to have the meat packed too tightly together, in order that the jelly will form. Serve an a la Diable sauce (R, No. 55), or mustard and sugar with the meat.

15. Calves' Head Jelly will be found under veal, (D, No. 83).

16. Pork Ribs in Jelly. This will be found in Division W.

17. Filled Capon in Jelly, with Sauce. Bone a capon and fill with the following forcemeat (which is enough for 2 capons): Grate ⅛ pound of bread and stir on the fire with ¼ pound of butter, then take from the stove, add to it the finely chopped livers of both capons, 2—3 yolks of eggs, 1 pound of minced veal, ¼ pound of minced pork fat, some thick cream, salt, mace, a little chopped lemon peel and juice with the beaten whites of the eggs.

Stir well together and fill the capon with it, and tie around the capon some large thin pork fat slices, put it into some good bouillon, cover tightly and boil for 2—2½ hours. Then take out of the broth, lay on a flat dish, let it cool for 1 hour, take off the slices of fat and put a weight on the capon to press it a little. The broth in which the capon was cooked is stirred with gelatine (about 1 ounce to a quart), add the necessary salt, and as much lemon juice as will give the broth a nice sour taste, bring to a boil again and then strain through a jelly bag. If it is clear, straining once will answer. Then pour enough of the broth into the form to make a layer, let it cool, lay the capon into the pan with the breast to the bottom (it can also be cut into slices), pour over it the remaining broth, the next day turn out on the dish on which it is to be served, and pour around it the following sauce; One large spoonful of thick cream, or the yolks of 4 hard boiled eggs are stirred with 2 teaspoonfuls of mustard and the same quantity of sugar; then gradually stir with it 4 tablespoonfuls of vinegar, 4 tablespoonfuls of salad oil, some finely chopped tarragon, a little pepper and salt, and

some of the remaining jelly broth. Stir all of this well
together, pour around the capon and decorate with
capers.

18. Spring Chicken in Jelly. When the chickens are
prepared as directed for roasting, press in the breast
bone and then take it out. Then rub with salt, and
stew with butter and water—covering the pan tightly—
until tender, take out of the dish and let it cool. In the
meantime put a layer of jelly broth into the dish and let
this cool also. The form must not be larger than the
dish on which the jelly is to be served. Then lay the
cold meat on the cooled jelly, and cover this with the
somewhat cooled jelly broth. The next day turn onto
the dish and decorate as given under No. 2, or with
chopped sour jelly.

19. Chicken Mayonnaise with Jelly. After the chickens are cleaned, stew them in butter, bouillon and lemon
juice until tender, set aside to cool, take out the bones
and cut into pieces, lay into a porcelain dish, sprinkle
with salt and pepper, pour over it tarragon vinegar and
salad oil, and leave in this marinade for a few hours.

In the meantime brush a pan with olive oil, fill with
sour jelly, and after it is cool, turn onto a flat dish.
Then put the pieces of chicken into the center of the dish
in the shape of a mound; decorate with crabtails and
hearts of lettuce after dipping them into the sauce.

20. Turkey in Jelly. The turkey should be young
and should be killed 2—3 days before using. It is filled
with a dressing as directed for capon in jelly, No. 17, or
in the above receipt. Prepare as above.

21. Ducks in Jelly. The duck must be young and
prepared the same as for capon in jelly, cut it into
slices, lay around a long dish, put the jelly on this and
serve with a Remoulade sauce (Division R, No. 56).

22. Filled Goose in Jelly. Take a young but not
too fat goose, which must be killed 2—3 days before
using. After perfectly cleaning it cut off the legs, wings,
head and neck, which are taken for giblets together with
the heart and stomach (see D, Nos. 205—206). Bone
the goose and fill it the same as capon in jelly, using the
liver, or as given for roasted turkey. Calves' feet stock,

or else gelatine, 1 ounce for each quart, can be taken to make the jelly. When using calves' feet put them on the fire with the goose barely covered with water, with not too much salt, skim carefully, add the spices as given in No. 1, also some vinegar, take off all of the fat, cover tightly, and cook slowly until tender, which will take 2½—3 hours. Then take out of the broth, which should be boiled down to about 2½—3 quarts, clear the broth and proceed as directed for capon in jelly.

The goose can also be prepared without filling, the same as a capon; lay the pieces into the form and pour the jelly over it.

23. Veal in Jelly. Cut 2 pounds of veal into thin slices, spread with a nice forcemeat seasoned with chopped truffles or mushrooms stewed in butter, roll, tie with a strong thread and cook in a rich bouillon with 1 glassful of wine, a little salt, pepper and onions until tender, then take out of the broth. Take the fat off the broth, dissolve about ⅔ ounce of gelatine in water and ⅔ ounce of extract of beef for each 1 quart of broth, add the necessary salt, and bring to a boil with some lemon juice. Clear with the beaten whites of 2—3 eggs, as given under No. 4, and pour through a sieve. After removing the thread from the roulades, lay them into a deep dish, pour the lukewarm jelly over them and when serving, turn them onto an appropriate dish. A large roll can be made of a boned calves' breast spread with forcemeat. It is improved by the addition of truffles, eggs, tongue, cucumbers and pork fat slices, also anchovies, pistachios, capers, etc., before rolling; then stew until tender. Press between two slabs over night, cut into slices, arrange in a mould in the form of a wreath, cover with jelly and when cold turn out of the mould. Put endives or lettuce dressed with a mayonnaise sauce into the center of the jelly border and serve the mayonnaise separately.

Nos. 10, 13, 17, 18, 20 and 23 can be used for making sour jellies for invalids, but they should not be served with rich sauces.

II. SWEET CLEAR JELLIES.

NOTE.—It may be well to repeat here that when jellies cannot be placed upon ice in the Summer, they should be prepared the day before. Directions for coloring and ornamenting jellies are given under No. 3 of this Division.

24. Wine Jellies made with Calves' Feet. For 4 quarts of stock take 12 large calves' feet and cook as directed in No. 1. Then put on the stove with 1½ pounds of sugar, ½ ounce of stick cinnamon (if cinnamon is not liked it can be omitted), the juice of 12 and the peel of 3 lemons, add the whites of 6—8 eggs beaten on the stove until watery, and proceed as given under No. 1. Serve the jellies in glasses or in moulds, or turn them out of the mould, which has first been spread with almond oil. For 30—36 persons.

REMARK.—For 1 bottle of wine take 4 calves' feet; for invalids use only 2, because the jelly must be milder. All sweet jellies must not be made too thick, the lighter the better; but they should be thick enough so that they will not break when turned out of the mould.

25.   Wine Jelly made with Gelatine. Take 1 quart of white wine, ½ pound of sugar, the juice of 2 lemons and the yellow rind of half a lemon, put into wine for a while to draw, and about an ounce of white or red gelatine.

Soak the gelatine in 1 small cupful of water or wine, dissolve the sugar in the wine and put the juice of the lemons and the sugar into an enameled vessel with the dissolved gelatine, cover and let it come to a boil. Then strain it through muslin, put into a dish, and set aside in a cool place. This jelly can be turned out of the dish if wished.

26. Wine Jelly of Gelatine in Jelly Dishes. Take 1 quart of white wine, ⅔ pound of sugar and the peeled rind of a lemon, which should be left in the wine for a while. In the Summer take about 1 ounce of gelatine, in the Winter a little less. The gelatine is dissolved in a cupful of water and strained through muslin into a jelly dish.

Sometimes the wine jelly will not be quite clear and transparent, particularly if the gelatine was not quite perfect. In this case it will be best to only put about an inch deep of the jelly into the jelly dish, put the rest of the jelly into a large vessel, surround it with ice and beat until it is thick and bright. This frosting is then put onto the jelly and set aside in the chest until wanted.

27. Wine Jelly. Cook a white wine jelly as directed in the above receipt and set aside to cool. Then boil 5 ounces of washed rice in water until tender, add 1 small cupful of white wine, 2½ ounces of sugar, a little salt, lemon peel and juice, also 2 cakes of dissolved gelatine, let the rice boil until the water has all boiled away, and then spread on a flat dish to cool. After the wine jelly and rice have cooled, put a layer of the jelly into the mould, then with a spoon make dumplings of the rice and put these on the jelly side by side. Fill these into the dish in layers, having the last layer of wine jelly. Turn out of the mould and dot with candied orange peel.

28. Fruit Jelly with Cherry=, Raspberry= or Currant Syrup and Gelatine. Dissolve some gelatine in not quite 1 pint of water, strain through muslin and add enough white wine so that with the fruit syrup you will have nearly 1 quart. The color must be a pretty red. 2 heaping teaspoonfuls of sugar will be found to be about right, but the sugar should be added according to the acidity of the juice; sometimes the sugar can be omitted. Heat the juice, then pour through muslin into a dry mould (see No. 2), and before serving turn out of the mould.

29. Wine Jelly with Eggs, or "Eggs in the Nest". ¾ quart of milk, ½ ounce of gelatine (white), 2 ounces of grated sweet almonds, a few bitter ones, vanilla and sugar according to taste.

The gelatine is dissolved in 1 small cupful of water, and cooked until clear, then strained through muslin and set in a warm place. When this is done, boil ¾ of a quart of milk (cream is better) with the almonds, sugar, vanilla and pour into a large mould to cool. Then stir the eggs in the warm gelatine and pour into the egg shells. For this purpose the eggs must be opened at the large end, but the opening should be only large enough to permit emptying the shell without breaking it; put the pointed end of the egg into salt. The boiled blanc-manger, which can be divided into three parts and colored red with cochineal, brown with chocolate and green with spinach juice, is poured into the egg shells through a funnel and set aside to cool.

In the meantime make a jelly of 1 bottle of wine (¾ quart) with 1 ounce of gelatine dissolved in 1 small cupful of water, 6 ounces of sugar and the juice of 2 lemons with the grated peel, pour into a jelly ring and let it cool. When it is to be served turn the jelly into a round dish, peel the eggs and put them into the center of the ring.

A prettier way is to make a nest of sugared strings. Boil 1 pound of sugar with 1 cupful of water until the sugar when dropped into cold water will form into little balls. Then put the sugar syrup into a dish of hot water to keep it warm, brush a round mould with almond oil and fill the syrup into the form with a fork, spinning it out in threads to cover the bottom and sides of the mould. When the sugar is cold it can be taken out of the form in the shape of a nest.

Another way is to make a nest of chestnuts for the eggs. Boil 1 pound of scalded and peeled chestnuts until tender, with the addition of 1 cupful of cream and a little vanilla, and strain. Mix the almonds with a thick sugar syrup, butter a smooth mould, line it with fine paper and press in the chestnut mass evenly about ½ inch thick. After it is cold turn out of the mould, take off the paper, let the nest cool and pour over all a chocolate icing.

30. Ribbon Jelly. Prepare a blanc-manger as in the above receipt, also a fruit jelly as in No. 28. Fill into a form in layers, letting each layer cool before the other is put on. The best way is to put the mould on chopped ice and keep the jelly warm on the hearth.

31. Lemon Jelly. This is made of 1 pint of calves' feet stock as given under No. 1, 1 quart of white wine, 10 ounces of sugar, a little cinnamon, a few cloves, the juice of 4 and the peel of 2 lemons, a little saffron about the size of a pea, and the whites of 4 eggs prepared as directed under No. 25. The jelly is decorated with candied lemon slices.

Instead of calves' feet stock, 1 ounce of gelatine can be used to prepare this the same as wine jelly.

32. Punch Jelly. 1 ounce of gelatine is dissolved in 1 cupful of water (see No. 1), 1 pound of sugar is brought to a boil with the grated rind of a lemon, ¾ quart of wine, the juice of 6 lemons and the beaten white of an egg, then take the dish from the stove, set where it is warm and as soon as it is clear pour through flannel or muslin. Then stir through it 1 pint of rum and pour the jelly into a glass dish and set aside to cool, or put into any form desired if wanted to turn out of the dish.

33. French Liquor Jelly. 1 ounce of gelatine, ⅞ quart of water, ½ pound of sugar, 1 lemon, 2—3 small glassfuls of arrac.

Dissolve the gelatine as described under No. 1, mix with the water, beat the whites of 2 eggs with the crushed shells, pour in the cooled gelatine and beat. Then add the sugar and put the mass on the fire. When it begins to boil add the juice of a lemon, let it boil for a few moments, strain through muslin, then add the arrac, rum, or any desired liquor, fill into sauce dishes or glasses and set in a cold place.

34. Jelly of all Kinds of Fruit. Make a wine or lemon jelly sweeter than usual, pour into a glass dish, and to this add fruit of various kinds: strawberries, currants, cherries, raspberries, etc., arrange neatly without the juice and let the jelly cool. Or sweeten the jelly as usual and sugar the fruit for a while before using.

35. Apple Jelly. 1½ pounds of sour apples are cooked until tender in 1 pint of water, stirred through a sieve, and while still warm mix through the pulp 1 cupful of white wine in which 1¼ ounces of gelatine have been dissolved. Then put in the peel of half a lemon, the juice of 2 lemons, 1 pound of sifted sugar and a little arrac. Let the mass, of which there will be about 2 quarts, come to a boil, stir constantly and put into a form which has been spread with olive oil. The jelly is stirred often before it is put into the form, and before cold turn out of the form, and serve, if liked, with a vanilla sauce.

36. Orange Baskets filled with Jelly. Cut an orange in two smoothly in the center with a sharp knife, take out the pulp to the skin with a silver spoon. Then cut a strip along both sides of the hollow peel of the orange, leaving the strips fast at the ends, bend these strips upwards to make a handle like on a basket, and catch them in the middle with a dainty piece of ribbon tied in a bow.

In the meantime make a wine jelly with the juice of the oranges, fill into the baskets and set aside in a cool place on a dish. As these baskets hold but little jelly, an extra dish of jelly should be handy so that if any of the guests wish for more their baskets can be refilled.

All plain wine wine or fruit jellies are excellent for invalids; Nos. 29, 32 and 33 are particularly nice.

III. ICES.

37. General Directions. The preparation of ices is not so difficult an affair as it was a number of years ago. A freezer of good construction and easy manipulation is now within the reach of all at a reasonable price. The ice should be broken into small pieces, using plenty of salt, packing the ice and salt firmly around the freezer. Rock salt is the best for the purpose, but if it is not obtainable common salt will do.

38. Vanilla Ice. The yolks of 16 fresh eggs, 2¼ quarts of fresh cream, ¾ pound of sugar and vanilla, and keep on the stove, constantly stirring, until just before it commences to boil. Then pour into a deep dish, and stir until no longer warm, so that no crust will form. After it is cold put into the freezer and finish.

It is best to bring the cream to a boil in a double boiler so as not to scorch it.

39. Quince Ice. The quinces are peeled and cooked in water with a few pieces of cinnamon until tender, then pressed through a sieve, mix with sugar and then put into a freezer. To every pound of strained quinces take ½ pound of sugar.

40. Orange Ice. Dissolve ½ pound of sugar with 1 cupful of water, the rind of an orange grated on some sugar, the juice of 8 oranges and 2 lemons, ½ bottle of Malaga, ½ ounce of gelatine and 1 cupful of wine.

41. Punch Ice. 1 quart of water, 1 quart of wine, 1 pound of sugar, vanilla, cinnamon, the peel of a lemon grated on sugar, the juice of 4 lemons, and the yolks of 12 eggs. Stir this constantly until it commences to boil, then pour quickly into a deep dish. When it is freezing pour in gradually 4 cupfuls of arrac.

42. Raspberry Ice. The juice of 2 pounds of raspberries, ¾ pound of sugar dissolved in 1 pint of white wine, and a few pieces of cinnamon. Mix well together and let it freeze.

43. Frozen Westphalian Pudding. Boil 1 pint of milk together with 6 ounces of sugar, flavor with vanilla, and stir into it 3 whole or the yolks of 6 eggs with some cold milk and mix through the milk on the stove until thick. Let it cool, pour through a sieve and freeze. Then gradually stir in ¾ quart of whipped cream, sugar according to taste and 1 ounce of brown bread ("pumpernickel"), 2—2½ ounces of pounded macaroons with a few bitter ones, a little Marascino and stir until quite thick, fill into a pudding mould which can be covered tightly and bury in cracked ice with plenty of salt, and set aside in the cellar for 2—3 hours. When serving dip the mould into hot water, turn the pudding on a dish and surround with any kind of small cakes.

44. Baked Ice. Whip the whites of 6 eggs to a stiff froth, mix with it 6 ounces of sugar, and spread half of this into a deep porcelain dish. Bake in a warm oven to a nice yellow color, and let it cool. Then make a vanilla ice as directed in one of the preceding receipts, fill into the mould and pour the remaining frosting on top of this, sprinkle thickly with powdered sugar, hold a hot shovel over the sugar so as to form a crust. Decorate the edge of the pudding with preserved fruits and serve.

45. Fruit Ice Pudding. Make a vanilla ice as directed in No. 38, put into a round mould, when cool put in some fruit—without the juice—cherries, apricots, strawberries, etc., put the fruit inside of the pudding so that when it is turned out of the mould it cannot be seen, cover the mould tightly and set in ice. Whipped cream with sugar and vanilla is also set in a cool place. When it is to be served dip the mould into hot water, turn out of the mould and pour the cream over it.

46. Nesselrod Ice Pudding. Carefully peel 1 pound of chestnuts, cook in 1 pint of milk until tender, mash them, mix with ½ pound of sugar, a little vanilla, the yolks of 3 eggs, and 1½ quarts of cream. Stir on a slow fire until thick, then strain through a hair sieve, whip until cold and fill into a freezer. Let the cream freeze and then mix in 1 glassful of Marascino, ¼ pound of scalded raisins, ¼ pound of currants, 2 ounces of finely cut citron, fill into a mould and bury in ice for 2 hours. When ready to serve turn out of the mould, and serve this pudding with whipped cream as directed for fruit pudding.

Ices should not be served to invalids unless with the physician's consent.

N.–Various Cold Sweet Dishes,

SUCH AS

Puddings, Blanc=manges, Whipped Cream, Fruit Sauces, and Wine=, Milk= and Fruit Ices.

---

1. General Directions. Clean utensils are absolutely essential; the best kinds are deep enameled or tin kettles.

When finely grated almonds are required they should be prepared on an almond grater or pounded in a mortar.

As creams are apt to curdle very easily the following hints should be regarded: They should be whipped at the start but as soon as they become warm the beating should become more rapid and continue without interruption until just before they commence to boil, but they should not boil unless plenty of flour has been mixed with the eggs. Then put them into a tureen or deep porcelain dish and whip for a little while longer until cool.

Before jellies, puddings, etc., are held in hot water to loosen them from the mould, press the fingers around the edges, by which means you can easily determine whether it is necessary to warm the mould.

The jellies should never be dissolved in milk, but always in water or wine, much less can they be boiled in milk without curdling. In order to prevent curdling the jellies should be added to the cooled mass, either beating or stirring them, the milk should not be boiled with wine, the latter may be added cold at last and if the mass is not quite cool stir or beat it. If this precaution is not heeded the creams, etc., will be sure to curdle.

For dishes where the egg yolks are added at last, these should be stirred with a little cold water—a tablespoonful to each egg yolk—take the kettle from the fire, stir some of the boiling liquid to the egg yolks, gradually adding more, pour this to the cooked mass, stirring briskly and proceed as directed.

To prevent a skin from forming over the cream, stir them occasionally until they are cool. Let them stand 1—2 hours before using, then stir them once more and fill them into glasses or cream dishes as the case may be.

Before turning creams, etc., out of the moulds, it is particularly necessary to let them cool. The mould should either be lined with almond oil, or else, when directed, rinse in cold water or leave them dry.

As noted for the preparation of puddings or souffles, a pinch of salt should be taken when making creams.

2. Ornamentation of Creams. Creams can be ornamented with candied fruits cut into very thin slices, red or white "kisses", or with dots of cranberry- or black currant jelly, or with appropriate flower leaves. Thick sweet cream beaten to a stiff froth and mixed with the addition of sugar and a dash of arrac, then scooped with a teaspoon, makes a very pretty ornament for creams. Raspberry-, gooseberry- and other fruit jellies can also be used, stirring each heaping tablespoonful of the same with 2 tablespoonfuls of pulverized sugar and the white of 1 egg until it forms a stiff mass, which is then used to ornament the cream.

3. Victoria Pudding. Into a very clean iron kettle put 2 tablespoonfuls of sugar, put it on the fire, constantly stirring so that it will not scorch. Then stir 1 pint of sweet milk with the yolks of 6 eggs, a little salt and ¾ pound of sugar into the kettle and just before boiling take from the stove without stopping the twirling, gradually pour into it 1 quart of sweet cream and at last 1 tablespoonful of red gelatine boiled in 1 cupful of water until clear. If it begins to thicken pour into it

1 glassful of Marascino, quickly pour some of it into a dry mould, cover with some small crackers or macaroons, pour over these some more of the batter and so on, until all is used. ¼ pound of macaroons and half as many crackers are sufficient. This pudding must be made quickly or else it will be too stiff. The mould may be put into boiling water if necessary, before turning out the pudding.

4. Wine or Lemon Pudding. 1 tablespoonful of gelatine is dissolved as described in Division M, No. 1. Then take the yolks of 12 eggs with 3 glassfuls of white wine and 5 tablespoonfuls of sugar, a little salt, put on the stove over a slow fire and whip until it is smooth (it must not boil), then take it from the fire, constantly whipping it. After it has cooled, stir into it with a spoon the juice of 2 lemons and a little grated lemon peel, the dissolved gelatine and then slowly add the beaten whites of 12 eggs. The pudding can be put into a glass pudding dish to cool.

5. Lemon Pudding. Boil ½ pound of sugar with 1 quart of water, leaving 1 cupful of the water to dissolve 3 ounces of rice flour. After the flour has been smoothed in the water beat into it the yolks of 6 eggs, the grated peel of half a lemon, a little salt and the juice of 2 lemons, pour into the boiling water, let the batter boil until the flour is done, and at last beat in the whites of 6 eggs. After the pudding is brought to a boil again, put it into a porcelain mould to cool, and serve the pudding cold with raspberry juice or tutti-frutti made from preserved fruits.

6. Rum Pudding. Stir the yolks of 5 eggs to a thick froth with ½ pound of sugar, season with grated lemon peel, salt, and the juice of a lemon. Then stir ½ ounce of dissolved and boiled gelatine in a small cupful of water to the batter, with a small glassful of rum and 1 pint of white wine, and at the last the beaten whites of five eggs. The batter will then begin to be smooth and is then poured into the mould to set. It is served without a sauce.

7. Sago Pudding. For 10 persons take 5 tablespoonfuls of sago, 6 large eggs, 3 ounces of sugar, a little salt, not quite ½ ounce of gelatine dissolved as directed in Division M, No. 1, lemon peel and cinnamon. The sago is scalded and then cooked slowly with 1 quart of milk, lemon peel and pieces of cinnamon until done and thick. Add the yolks of the eggs and a little milk, constantly stirring into the sago, let it come to a boil, take from the fire, beat the gelatine into the sago then beat into it the beaten whites of the eggs and fill into a mould.

After the pudding has cooled turn out of the mould and serve with a fruit- or claret sauce.

8. Chocolate Pudding without Eggs. Boil 1 quart of water with a little vanilla, a little salt and 6 ounces of sugar with 3 ounces of rice flour dissolved in a little water, and 2 ounces of grated chocolate, then put into a dry mould to cool. After it has cooled it can be turned out of the mould, and decorated with thick beaten cream and small red "kisses" alternately and with a ball of whipped cream in the center.

9. Red Rice Flour Pudding. 1 pint of currant or raspberry juice, 1 pint of claret, ¼ pound of rice flour or grits and sugar according to taste; wine, juice and sugar are boiled, stir into it the rice flour, boil until done, but it must not be either too thick nor too thin, fill into a mould that has been rinsed with cold water and when cooled turn onto a dish.

A very palatable sauce to this as well as the following pudding is made of whipped cream with vanilla and sugar, or use a cold vanilla sauce, or thick cream with claret, sugar and a little rum whipped with it.

Instead of currant or raspberry juices, fresh fruits can be used; also fresh blackberries. Leave the berries on a dish so as to extract the juices. Then take the juice of 1 quart of berries, 1 pint of claret, 8—9 ounces of sugar, 4 tablespoonfuls of potato or rice flour or potato sago, and mix with 1 cupful of fresh berries that have been sugared for a few hours. Proceed as above and serve with the same sauce.

10. Red Cream Pudding. For 10—14 persons take 1 quart of claret, or currant or cherry juices, mixed with water, sugar, 3 ounces of cornstarch, the whites of 6—9 eggs and if liked a small piece of cinnamon. After

the juices are brought to a boil, the dissolved cornstarch is stirred with it and boiled. Then take the dish
from the fire, stir through it the beaten whites of the
eggs, let it come to a boil and pour into a mould;
sprinkle with sugar. Turn the pudding out of the
mould and serve with a vanilla sauce made of the yolks
of the eggs.

11. Rice Pudding. For 14 persons take ¾ of a
pound of rice, ¾ of a pound of sugar, a little salt, 1 pint
of wine and 4 lemons.

The rice is scalded and boiled in water until done
and thick but not stiff, the kernels must not be mushy.
In the meantime grate the rind of a lemon on some
sugar, peel the rind of 2 lemons very thinly so that you
have only the thin yellow outer skin, boil the peel in
water until soft and cut into thin strips.

Then boil some sugar and water until clear, put
the lemon peel slices into the syrup, stir often until they
are candied, then take them out and dry them.

The lemon juice is boiled with the wine and sugar
and then stirred through the rice, then carefully stir into it the candied peel, and fill into a dry mould. After
it is cool turn onto a dish and decorate with preserved
fruits.

Serve with a cream or claret sauce, or with strawberry juices.

12. Rice Pudding with Fruit. For 12 persons take
½ pound of rice, milk, salt, sugar, pieces of cinnamon,
almonds, wine, lemon, currants and sliced apples.

Boil the scalded rice in milk, sugar and a few pieces
of cinnamon until done but not thick. Then cook some
almonds, cut lengthwise, in a little water until half
done, add 2 cupfuls of wine, sugar, lemon peel and juice,
currants and the apple slices, and cook until done,
thickening the sauce with a little cornstarch. Fill into
a mould a layer of rice, then the apples and so on, finishing with the rice on the top.

After the pudding has cooled put it on a dish and
serve with a wine- or vanilla sauce.

13. Baden=Baden Pudding. For 10 persons take ¼
pound of rice, ¼ pound of sugar, 1 quart of milk, vanilla,

½ ounce of gelatine and 1 large cupful of cream whipped to a froth.

The rice is scalded and then boiled in milk, vanilla and sugar until thick; add the dissolved gelatine and after the rice has cooled add the whipped cream and if liked a glassful of Marascino, and fill into a mould which has first been rinsed in cold water; then put the pudding on ice.

14. Cold Rice Pudding. For 24 persons. Take 1 pound of rice, 1 pound of sugar, 6 lemons, 2 table-spoonfuls of rum or fruit jelly.

Grate the rind of 2 lemons on the sugar and set aside. In the meantime scald 1 pound of rice, cover, and then boil it slowly for 1 hour with 3½ quarts of water and the sugar. Then stir into it the grated rind and juice of 6 lemons and the rum, put the partly cooled mass into a mould rinsed with water, in layers, alternating with a teaspoonful of the fruit jelly, and after it has cooled turn onto a dish. For a sauce take cream, whip it in a cool place and just before serving stir through the cream some vanilla.

15. Spanish Rice. 1 bottle of white wine, ½ pound of best rice, ⅔ pound of sugar with the grated rind of a lemon, juice of 2 lemons and 1 large cupful of arrac.

The rice is washed and scalded, boiled with water until done and thick; the kernels must remain whole. When this is done, heat the wine, sugar and lemon juice, stir this through the rice, add the arrac and then let the rice cool. The rice will thicken while cooling, but it must not be stiff. Before serving stir it with a salad fork, fill into sauce dishes and garnish with jelly. Serve with a boiled cold claret sauce or fruit juice.

16. Rice Jelly. For 14—16 persons take 1 pound of rice, 1 pound of powdered sugar on which has been grated the rind of 1 lemon, the juice of 2 lemons and 1 wineglassful of arrac. Scald the rice and boil it in 4½ quarts of water, cover and cook for 1½ hours uninterruptedly but slowly without stirring.

In the meantime put the sugar into water, boil until clear, pour the rice water into this through a sieve and bring to a boil again with the juice of a lemon; then take from the fire and mix through the arrac. As this takes some time to cool, it should be prepared the day previously. A good fruit- or claret sauce is served with it. A nice way is to serve a sauce of fresh raspberries or currant juices (as described in Division R, Nos. 85—86). Preserved fruit juices are also good. If the rice jelly is wanted with a nice red color mix with it some red fruit juice.

17. Beer Pudding. 1 pint of beer (which must not be bitter), the same quantity of water, 1 small cupful of white wine, ½ pound of sugar and a little lemon extract are brought to a boil with not quite 1 ounce of dissolved gelatine, and filled into moulds to cool. Serve with whipped sweet cream seasoned with vanilla.

18. Common Sour Milk Pudding. 1 pint of thick, sour milk is stirred with 6 ounces of sugar, the juice of ½ and the rind of ¼ lemon, ½ glassful of rum and about ⅓ ounce of dissolved gelatine, fill into a mould rinsed with water, and just before turning out the pudding hold the mould in a pan of hot water so that the pudding will come out easily. Serve with whipped cream or vanilla sauce; some prefer fruit juices.

19. Pudding with Whipped Cream and Macaroons. 1 pint of milk, ¼ pound of sugar, 6 yolks of eggs, ¼ pound of sweet macaroons, 2 ounces of bitter macaroons, ⅓ ounce of gelatine, ½ pint of whipped sweet cream and a little vanilla.

The milk, sugar and vanilla are brought to a boil, then the yolks of the eggs are added, and boil again until the eggs are done. As soon as it is smooth turn into another dish and stir until nearly cool. In the meantime dissolve and boil the gelatine until clear and stir into the batter until cold. Then stir through it the pieces of macaroons. At the last the cream is stirred through it. Then put it into a mould to set, after which it can easily be turned out. The pudding can be served with a tutti-frutti sauce or it can be sent to the table without a sauce.

20. Marbled Blanc=mange. Make a nice blanc-mange with cream. Then in an iron kettle heat some sugar until brown, not black, cook with it 3 tablespoonfuls of sweet cream, stir with it ¼ pound of chocolate and ¼ of the blanc-mange. First put into the mould some of the white mass, then divide over it some of the brown, then some of the white and so on, until all is used. This must be done while the blanc-mange is still hot. Let the blanc-mange cool in the mould and then turn out onto a dish.

21. Cup Blanc=mange. For 12 persons take 1¼ quart of milk, 2½ ounces of grated almonds, 2½ ounces of cornstarch, 3 ounces of sugar, the whites of 10 eggs, and the grated rind of a lemon. Boil the same as blanc-mange. Fill into 12 sauce dishes and serve with fruit juice.

22. Whipped Cream. Take good, sweet cream, which, in the Summer, must not be more than 24 hours old, whip it without sugar and put on the ice. If the cream is wanted sweet add a little powdered sugar just before using.

23. Charlotte Russe. For 8—10 persons. Take 1 large cupful of sweet cream, ½ pound of sugar, the yolks of 10 eggs, some vanilla, a little salt, ½ ounce of gelatine and nearly 1 quart of thick sweet cream, which is whipped as directed in the above receipt.

The vanilla is put into the cream and sugar and brought to a boil. Let it cool, stir the yolks of the eggs into it and then whip it on the stove until it is thick— it must not boil—take from the fire and pour into a mould. Then the gelatine is stirred into it and whipped again, and after it has cooled mix the whipped cream through it. Butter a mould, line it with "lady fingers", fill with the cream and then put on the ice. When cold turn out of the mould, which is best done the day following.

Instead of lining the mould with cake before putting in the cream, it may be done just before serving. If liked, the cake may be spread with apricot marmalade and then filled into the mould.

24. Orange Sauce. For 6 persons take 3 oranges, 1 lemon, ¼ pound of sugar, a little salt, ½ ounce of gelatine and about 1 pint of thick whipped cream, as directed in No. 23.

Grate the rind of an orange on the sugar, mix the juice of the 3 oranges, the lemon juice and the gelatine as directed in Division M, No. 1, and bring to a boil in a small enameled kettle, take it from the fire and stir until nearly cold. Then mix through it the cream, fill into a buttered mould and set aside.

25. Sultan Cream. 1 pint of milk, 6 ounces of sugar, 8 eggs, the rind of 1½ lemons grated on sugar, and a little stick cinnamon. Half of the sugar is put into a copper stewpan on a moderate fire, constantly stirring until of a chestnut brown, then add cinnamon and sugar, let it boil for a few minutes very slowly, pour through a sieve and let it cool. In the meantime grate the rind of a lemon on some sugar, add the yolks of the eggs, also the milk, pour through a sieve again, put into a kettle of boiling water or a double kettle, and cover with a lid holding some live embers. As soon as the custard is set let it cool, beat the whites of the eggs to a stiff froth, add to it the sugar with the grated lemon, make a ring of the cream around the custard and a ball of it in the center, put into the oven a moment to color the cream, or hold over it a hot shovel.

The cream can be eaten warm or cold; if cold omit the frosting and bake into "kisses".

26. Holland Cream. 1 pint of white wine (or cider), 3 ounces of sugar, the yolks of 8 eggs, a little salt and the juice of a lemon with the grated rind are cooked over a moderate fire until it is a thick cream, and mixed with ½ ounce of white and red gelatine, half and half, and then let them cool. When it begins to set stir through it the froth of 5 eggs and 1 pint of whipped cream and fill into a glass dish.

27. Pineapple Cream. Dissolve in 1 small cupful of pineapple juice and 1 small cupful of white wine about ½ ounce of half red and half white gelatine, mix this with 10 tablespoonfuls of finely cut pineapple slices and some vanilla, and put this on the ice until it commences to set. Then stir through it 1 pint of whipped cream and the beaten whites of 2 eggs and fill the cream into a buttered mould or a glass dish. Instead of pineapple you can take half strawberries and half apricots.

28. Swiss Cream. A scant pint of milk, the yolks of 8 eggs, ¼ pound of sugar, bitter macaroons and

1 pint of thick whipped cream, vanilla, sugar and 3 tablespoonfuls of rum are whipped as directed in No. 22 of this division   The yolks of the eggs are mixed into the milk with a teaspoonful of cornstarch or flour and sugar, put on the fire and stirred to a custard as directed in No. 1, poured quickly into a dish and stirred until nearly cold. Then line a dish with bitter macaroons, which must not become soft, fill the custard into this and pour over it the whipped cream.

One-quarter of the cream may be mixed through the custard when it is being prepared, and instead of taking vanilla, 5 ounces of apricot marmalade may be substituted.

29. Coffee Cream. Whip nearly 1 quart of cream, add ¼ pound of sifted sugar and 1 cupful of coffee extract made of 2 ounces of coffee. This is stirred together just before wanted for use.

30. Sour Cherries with Whipped Cream. (A Swiss dish.) Sour cherries are stoned and laid into a deep dish, cover them with the necessary sugar and put on this some whipped cream as directed under No. 22.

31. Wine Cream. 1 bottle of white wine, the rind of 1 lemon grated on ½ pound of sugar, 10 fresh eggs, the juice of 2 lemons, a heaping tablespoonful of cornstarch smoothed in cold water.

Whip all together in a dish as directed under No. 1 until just before it boils, then pour into a dish, whip for a few minutes longer, fill the cream into small glass dishes and serve the same day that it is made. Serve with macaroons or other small cakes.

32. Lemon Cream with Strawberries or Raspberries. Make a cream as directed under No. 31, but use only 1 lemon and fill into a glass dish in layers with strawberries or raspberries, which have first been sugared. The top layer must be of cream. Decorate with large ripe strawberries and serve with biscuits.

33. Orange Cream. 1 large cupful of white wine, 2 oranges, 1 lemon, ¼ pound of sugar, 6—8 eggs, a little salt. The rind of the oranges and lemon are grated on sugar, but do not use too much of the orange peel; press out the juices, and then beat all on the fire until it comes to a boil. Pour the cream into a dish, beat for a little while longer and then pour into a dish in which it is to be served.

34. Russian Cream. Make a wine cream as directed under No. 31, taking 2 heaping tablespoonfuls more of sugar, 1 egg and 1 teaspoonful of cornstarch. As soon as taken from the stove pour into it 1 large cupful of arrac, constantly stirring. Then whip every once in a while until it is cold.

35. Vanilla Cream. 1 quart of cream or sweet milk, a piece of butter, the yolks of 11 eggs, 1 tablespoonful of cornstarch, 3 ounces of sugar, a little vanilla and a little salt.

After the cream and sugar have been heated, stir the yolks of the eggs, the vanilla and the dissolved cornstarch with the milk and whip until just before it boils; pour into a dish, whip for a few minutes longer so that there will be no crust on top.

36. Tutti=Frutti. Into a deep dish lay some preserved cherries, currants, small pieces of pumpkin, apricots, etc., strew over it some finely cut citron, lay over it some sweet biscuits and macaroons soaked with the juices of the fruit or some wine. Then boil 1 pint of milk with 2 ounces of sugar, a pinch of salt, a little vanilla, smooth ⅔ ounce of cornstarch in a little milk, add to the cornstarch the yolks of 4 eggs, and pour this into the boiling milk, constantly stirring. Then beat in the whites of 4 eggs. The boiling custard is poured over the fruit, smooth the top and pour over it the froth of the eggs, smooth the top also, sprinkle over it a little sugar, then hold over it a hot shovel, to make a thin crust, but not so that it will turn yellow. A better way is to set the dish into a hot oven for a few minutes so that the froth will become done.

37. Almond Cream. 1½ quarts of fresh milk, ¼ pound of grated almonds, 3 ounces of sugar, the yolks of 8—10 fresh eggs, vanilla or lemon peel, a little salt and 2 tablespoonfuls of cornstarch smoothed in milk.

Let it come to a boil, stirring constantly, pour the cream into a mould, stir until it is almost cold and then serve.

38. Chocolate Cream. ¼ pound of chocolate, 1 quart of milk, sugar to taste, the yolks of 10 eggs, vanilla and 1 tablespoonful of cornstarch, also a little salt.

Let the chocolate melt on the fire in a little water and boil slowly with the milk and sugar for 5 minutes. Then stir the yolks of eggs and cornstarch with some of the milk, add this to the chocolate milk, constantly stirring, pour it into the boiling milk, take the pan from the fire, keeping up the stirring, and serve the cream when cold.

39. Chocolate Cream without Eggs. 1 quart of milk, 3 ounces of bitter chocolate and 6 ounces of sugar, or 4 ounces of sweet chocolate and about 5 ounces of sugar, vanilla to taste and 1 tablespoonful of cornstarch. Let the chocolate dissolve on the stove in a little water and boil it with milk, sugar and vanilla. In the meantime dissolve the cornstarch in a little water, and before adding it to the boiling chocolate milk stir until it comes to a boil, and serve after the cream is cold. This is a very nice cream when eggs are scarce.

40. Macaroon Cream with Almonds. About 1 quart of milk, the yolks of 8 eggs, 8 grated macaroons, 3 ounces of sugar, a little salt and 2 ounces of shelled and finely chopped almonds.

The milk is slowly brought to a boil with 1 ounce of sugar, lemon peel and a piece of cinnamon, then take out the spices, stir in the grated macaroons and boil for a few minutes. Add the yolks of the eggs after they have been stirred with a little milk, let the cream come to a boil once more, constantly stirring, because if ·not stirred it will remain thin, and then take from the fire. After it has cooled, mix the almonds with the sugar, strew them on the top, and brown the top by holding over it a red-hot shovel.

41. Rice Flour Pudding. 1 quart of milk, ¼ pound of ground rice, 2 ounces of sugar, 4 eggs, a little salt, about 1 ounce of grated almonds, a little piece of cinnamon and lemon peel, or a few drops of orangeflower water.

Milk, almonds, sugar and spices are put on the fire, and then stir the rice flour with some of the milk and a little salt, pour into the boiling milk, constantly stirring, and boil slowly for 10 minutes; it must not be too soft. Then stir the yolks of the eggs with a little milk and add to the cooked rice. Let it boil until the eggs are done, stir through it the beaten whites of the eggs and pour this into a dish.

A sauce can be served with it as with a blanc-mange. Another way is to put some milk and 2 ounces of currants on the stove, omitting the almonds, and instead of the above mentioned spices boil a little cinnamon in the milk. If you wish to make this in a hurry, beat the whole eggs with 1 tablespoonful of water, and after taking the kettle from the fire stir this into it.

42. Snowball with Vanilla Sauce. No. 1. 1 quart of milk, 8—10 eggs, 3 ounces of sugar, 1 cupful of almonds, a little vanilla, a few pieces of cinnamon and a pinch of salt.

The almonds are pounded or grated finely and brought slowly to a boil with milk, sugar and spices. Beat the whites of the eggs to a froth and mix with the sugar. Put on a flat dish and shape it into a mound, slide it onto the boiling milk and cover until the froth is done, which will take but a few minutes. Carefully take out with a large flat spoon, put into a deep dish, stir the yolks of the eggs with cold milk which must be stirred for a few minutes before it is filled around the snowball, being careful that the snowball remains white.

43. Snowball. No. 2. After beating the whites to a stiff froth, take a spoon and make small balls, lay into the boiled milk as directed in the above receipt, let it come to a boil, keeping the kettle covered, then lay them into a dish and cook the remaining froth in the same manner until all are done. Make a sauce as directed in the above receipt, put a layer of the balls into a dish, pour some of the sauce over this, then put in some more balls, and so on until all are used and the balls have formed a moundlike pile, pouring the sauce over all. Sprinkle with pounded macaroons or sugar and cinnamon.

44. German Blanc=mange. Boil 1½ pints of milk with ½ pound of sugar, a little vanilla or lemon peel and a pinch of salt; stir with it 3 ounces of cornstarch dis-

solved in milk until it bubbles. Stir the beaten whites
of 10 eggs through it, fill the pudding into a mould
which has been rinsed with a little milk, and let it cool.
After the pudding has been turned out of the mould,
pour over it a sauce made of the yolks of 10 eggs, 10
tablespoonfuls of white wine and 10 tablespoonfuls of
sugar syrup and a little salt, bring to a boil, stir for a
few minutes and put where it will cool.

45. Orange Marmalade. After the oranges are
peeled, cut them into small pieces and lay them lengthwise into a deep dish. Sprinkle with plenty of sugar,
pour French white wine over them and serve instead of
a cream.

Ripe strawberries laid around the edge make the
dish look very pretty.

46. Strawberries and Oranges as Dessert. Very
ripe strawberries are laid into a deep dish and sprinkled
with sugar, small pieces of oranges are put over this
and the edge decorated with orange slices.

47. Cold Apple Cream. 10 large baked apples, ½
pound of sugar, the whites of 3 fresh eggs, juice and
rind of a lemon, or vanilla, and if liked 2 tablespoonfuls
of arrac.

The apples are pared and the core taken out, put
through a sieve, and whip for ¼ of an hour with the
beaten whites of the eggs, sugar, vanilla and lemon. All
ingredients are put with this and whipped for ½ hour
longer and then served.

48. Fine Apple Pudding. Pare and thinly slice 20
apples, slice ¼ pound of citron into small pieces and
cook with ¾ pound of sugar and 1 bottle of white wine
until done, then stir a good ½ ounce of dissolved gelatine through it and fill into a glass dish and let it cool.
It is served without a sauce, but whipped cream
seasoned with vanilla and sugar is passed with it.

49. Cherry Cream. Take 3 pounds of nice ripe
cherries, ½—¾ pound of sugar, 6 eggs, lemon peel, cinnamon and 4 cloves.

The cherries are stoned, and ⅓ of the stones are
pounded, and boiled for ¼—½ hour with a little water,
cloves and a few pieces of cinnamon, and then poured

through a sieve. The strained juice is cooked with a glassful of white wine and the sugar on which the lemon rind was grated. Add the cherries to this, cook until done, put through a sieve and then bring the marmalade to a boil, being careful to stir. Then rub a tablespoonful of dissolved cornstarch into this, let it cook, take from the fire, stir through it the yolks of the eggs as directed under 1, also the beaten whites of the eggs.

The cream is filled into a glass dish, sprinkle over the top some pounded bitter macaroons.

50. Gooseberry Cream. 2 pounds of ripe gooseberries, 1 pound of sugar, 6 eggs, 1 glassful of wine and a little cinnamon. The gooseberries are cleaned, and cooked in water until done and then stir them through a sieve. Then cook some sugar and wine, add to it the marmalade and a little cinnamon and proceed as given in the above receipt.

51. Gooseberry Sauce. 1 quart of green gooseberries are cleaned and cooked in 1 quart of water, then pour off the water, pass the berries through a sieve and sweeten to taste. Then put the marmalade on the fire and add to it ½ pound of rice flour stirred with the juice of the gooseberries, boil for a few minutes, constantly stirring, and then pour the sauce into a mould which has first been rinsed with water. Serve cream with it.

52. Strawberry Cream. 2 pounds of ripe strawberries, ½—⅔ pound of sugar, the whites of 6 eggs and 1 glassful of claret.

The strawberries are put into a sieve, pour water over them, drain and press them through the sieve. Then cook the wine with the sugar, add to this the strawberries, bring to a boil, take them from the fire and add the beaten whites of the eggs.

After the cream is finished and just before serving, decorate the cream with nice ripe strawberries.

A prettier way is to add ⅓ ounce of red gelatine to the strawberries, add the sugar and stir all together until it commences to get thick. Then stir through it 1 large cupful of thick whipped cream, fill the cream into a mould and decorate as directed in the forepart of this receipt.

53. Sago and Currant Cream. Take ¾ pound of currants freed from the stem, 2—3 pounds of sugar, 2 ounces of sago, the whites of 6 eggs, and a few pieces of cinnamon. The currants are sprinkled with the sugar, cinnamon and sago in layers, cover and cook slowly for ¼ hour, shaking the kettle once in a while. Then carefully mix through it the cream so as not to crush the berries, and serve the cream.

54. Raspberry and Currant Cream served in small Dishes. 1 pint of raspberry- and currant juice, half and half, 10 eggs. Sweeten the juice according to its acidity; to fresh juices add ½—⅔ pound, to cooked juices add whatever sugar is necessary. Juice, sugar and yolks of eggs are beaten together on the stove until it comes to a boil, take the kettle from the stove, whip for a little while longer and then mix through it the beaten whites of the eggs.

If this pudding is to be filled into small glasses, put each glass on a small plate and serve with a few bitter macaroons or small biscuits.

55. Raspberry Cream filled into Glasses. The whites of 5 eggs are whipped to a stiff froth, mix with 3 table-spoonfuls of raspberry jelly and 3 tablespoonfuls of sugar. Instead of the raspberries, 5 tablespoonfuls of preserved cranberries, which have first been stirred through a sieve can be taken; when this is used the cream has a tart flavor. Make a thick vanilla sauce of the yolks of the eggs and put a tablespoonful in each glass.

56. Strawberry Cream in Glasses. 1 quart of ripe, wild strawberries, not quite 1 pint of thick sweet cream, ½ pound of sugar, a trifle of grated lemon peel or cinnamon. The berries are stirred with the cream, then passed through a sieve, seasoned with sugar and the spices, whipped and filled into the glasses.

57. Arrac Cream. 1 quart of thick sour cream, ½ to a cupful of arrac or Madeira, sweeten to taste. Whip and fill into glasses.

58. Cream of Roses. Take ½ ounce of red gelatine and dissolve it in a cupful of white wine, and mix with it 1 cupful of cherry juice, the rind of ½ and the juice of

2 lemons, about 2 ounces of sugar and stir until it commences to thicken, then mix with it the beaten whites of 5 eggs and fill into glasses.

59. Whipped Cream filled into Glasses. Take the whites of fresh eggs and whip with sugar to a stiff froth; for each white take 1 tablespoonful of thick sweet cream beaten with sugar and vanilla or grated lemon peel. Whip each of these separately and then mix together.

60. Whipped Cream (Sillabub) filled into Glasses. 1 quart of thick sweet cream, ½ pound of sugar upon which is grated the rind of 1 lemon, add the juice of 2 lemons and 3 glassfuls of French white wine. All is mixed together and whipped in a cool place. As soon as it turns to a cream on the surface, fill into glasses and continue the whipping until all is creamed. All the ingredients can be mixed together and put on the ice some hours before whipping.

61. Strawberries with Whipped Cream. Take nice ripe berries; those that are dirty are put into a colander and fresh water is poured over them, clean them carefully, lay them on a glass dish, sprinkle with powdered sugar and put over this some sweet whipped cream. In the summer this is a very refreshing dish.

62. Ambrosia. Peel a small pineapple, cut it into slices, divide 3—4 oranges into pieces, sugar well and set the dish in a cool place. Then grate a large cocoanut, put the fruit into a glass dish in layers, sprinkle each piece with cocoanut and pour over all a glassful of Madeira.

Sweet puddings should be served to invalids with caution, and then the simplest kinds only; when permitted Nos. 9, 16, 22, 26, 27, 31, 32, 46, 47, 52, 53, 54, 55, 56, 59, 60 and 61 can be recommended.

O.—Dumplings.

I. DUMPLINGS FOR SOUPS AND FRICASSEES.

1. Directions for preparing Dumplings. The bread for dumplings must not be fresh nor soaked in warm water, because, in both cases, the bread will become sticky. Lay the bread into cold water for a few moments, put it into a cloth, gently press out the water and then rub it. Stale grated wheat bread and rolled crackers are also used in dumplings.

For the finest kinds of dumplings, and also for fish dumplings, only the white part of the bread is used, the crust being cut off.

Although in every receipt the quantity is given it is always best to try a small dumpling to see if they are right. If needed, a little bread, butter, egg or water can be added.

Meat dumplings to be served with fricassee and soup are either rolled with the hands, the hands being kept moist by dipping them into cold water; or, better still, they are moulded with a tea- or tablespoon, which is dipped into the boiling water after each dumpling is formed, put them into the boiling soup and cook for 10—15 minutes. If many dumplings are to be cooked it will be found better to mould and lay them on a dish so as to put them all into the soup at once, otherwise those put in first will cook for too long a time. If the dumplings are made of flour, potatoes or bread and they are dry on the inside after cooking, they are done. Meat dumplings are ready when the meat is done. Dumplings for fricassees are not cooked in a thick gravy because this makes them solid, but instead cook them in bouillon or salted water. All dumplings must be served immediately.

2. Dumplings for Crab= or Eel Soup. Stir 2—3 tablespoonfuls of crabbutter until soft, add the yolks of 2 eggs, 1 saucerful of finely chopped fish, or crabmeat taken out of the shell, the same quantity of soaked and pressed bread, mace, salt and the beaten whites of the eggs, stir all well together, form into small round dumplings, and boil in the soup for 5 minutes. When serving, the crab tails are laid into the tureen, as they must not cook.

3. Fish Dumplings. Take 3 ounces of butter and simmer with 1 finely chopped eschalot, then add to it while on the stove 3 ounces of grated bread, 2 table-spoonfuls of cream, the yolks of 3 and 1 whole egg, stir well together and then pour into another pan to cool. In the meantime take ½ pound of raw fish, cleaned and boned and freed from skin, and 2 heaping tablespoon-fuls of marrow or fresh bacon with salt, chopped fine and rubbed in a mortar. Mace, white pepper and finely chopped parsley are then stirred with the mass and put into a flat pan. The dumplings are formed with a tea-spoon, put into the bouillon and cooked for 5 minutes.

4. Dumplings for Brown Soups. ½ pound of lean pork and ¼ pound of veal without sinews are chopped finely together; stir 2 ounces of butter to a cream, add the yolks of 2 eggs, 2 ounces of soaked wheat bread, salt, lemon peel and mace, then the chopped meat and at last the whites of the eggs. Make into small dump-lings and cook in the broth until done. They can also be rolled in cracker crumbs and lightly browned in butter.

5. Beef Dumplings. Take ½ pound of beefsteak chopped finely, removing all the sinews, add 2 ounces of butter stirred to a cream, the yolks of 2 eggs, 2 ounces of wheat bread, nutmeg, salt and at last the beaten whites of the eggs. The batter should be soft but must be well bound. Form with a spoon and cook in the soup for 5 minutes. Instead of the beef, veal may be used; in this case add a little parsley.

6.   Sweetbread Dumplings for Veal Fricassee or Veal Pie. ½ pound of fresh firm kidney suet, and ⅔ pound of sweetbreads.   Take out the skinny parts, slice and then pound together until they cannot be distinguished. Then add salt, a little pepper and 1 egg and pound again, then another egg.   Then add, pounding constantly, as much water as half of an egg shell will hold, and as the mass absorbs the water repeat several times. Form the dumplings into balls the size of a walnut, cook in the broth and put them into the fricassee.

7.   Soup Dumplings of left=over roast or boiled Meat. Proceed with these dumplings the same as directed under No. 4, take out all of the sinews, chop as finely as possible, stir the soaked bread on the fire until it is lightly colored, put into a dish, add the ingredients mentioned, using some mace or nutmeg or finely chopped parsley, roll into small dumplings and cook in the soup for a few minutes.

8.   Sponge Dumplings. Take the whites of 3 eggs and beat to a froth, stir the yolks lightly through it with a spoon, add 3 teaspoonfuls of flour and a little salt.   The batter is put into the boiling soup, cooked for a few minutes, turned with a skimmer, then put into a tureen; divide into small pieces with a knife.

9.   Brain Dumplings. Take 2 calves' brains and boil in salted water for a few moments, cool in cold water, take off skin and veins, and chop fine.   Then mix with a finely chopped eschalot, 1 spoonful of chopped parsley, some soaked and pressed wheat bread, 3 eggs, salt and mace to a firm batter, make small dumplings and cook in salted water and serve with any kind of soup.

10.   Green Dumplings (a Suabian Receipt). A handful of parsley, the same quantity of spinach, half as much chervil and chives, chop all together and stew in butter for a few moments.   Then mix with 2 grated rolls, 2 eggs, salt and pepper, form into little balls and let them come just to a boil in the finished soup, or they will fall to pieces.   These dumplings are very nice in the Spring.

11. Cracker Dumplings. Take butter the size of half of an egg and stir to a cream, add 2 whole eggs and nutmeg, then add, constantly stirring, 4 heaping tablespoonfuls of finely grated crackers. The dumplings are cooked in boiling bouillon; let it come to a boil, take from the fire, put on the back of the stove for 5 minutes, keeping the kettle tightly covered. Cooking the dumplings too long makes them heavy.

12. Groat Dumplings. For 8 persons take 2 heaping tablespoonfuls of groats and 1 small cupful of water and milk half and half, and butter the size of a walnut; stir on the fire until it no longer adheres to the kettle. Then rub a piece of butter the size of a walnut until soft, add nutmeg, salt, the yolks of 3 eggs, the cooled groats and at last the whites of 2 eggs. Make into small dumplings with a teaspoon and cook in the boiling soup.

13. Egg Dumplings. 1 large cupful of meat broth or milk is beaten with 4 eggs, adding parsley, nutmeg and salt and put into a buttered pan. Put it into boiling water until thick, but not hard, mould into dumplings and put them into the boiling soup. This can be prepared some time before wanted for the soup.

14. Bread Dumplings. 2 heaping tablespoonfuls of butter are creamed, then add the yolks of 2 eggs, nutmeg, if wished some finely chopped parsley, ½ pound of soaked bread and the beaten whites of 2 eggs. Form into small dumplings with a spoon and cook slowly in the soup for 5 minutes.

15. Marrow Dumplings. For 4—5 persons take marrow the size of ½ of an egg, slowly melt and stir it. After it has cooled add 5 ounces of grated bread, 1 large egg, nutmeg, a little salt, stir together until well mixed, add enough cold water to make the dumplings smooth and light but not enough so that they will fall to pieces in cooking. When first making these dumplings it is well to try one and if too firm add a little cold water, or if not firm enough a little of the bread. Form into small dumplings with a teaspoon, put into the boiling soup, cook until they are done and then take from the fire.

16. Another Marrow Dumpling. ¼ pound or less of fresh marrow is cut into small pieces, stir grated wheat bread with 3 tablespoonfuls of sour cream and 3 whole eggs, add to the marrow with salt, pepper and nutmeg, make into a thick batter that can be formed into dumplings with the hands and cook in boiling bouillon.

17. Ounce Dumplings. 1 ounce of water, 1 ounce of flour, 1 ounce of butter are stirred together on the stove, cooled, then add the yolks of 2 eggs, the whites of 1 egg, some mace, form into balls with a teaspoon and cook for 10 minutes.

18. Almond Dumplings. 2 tablespoonfuls of butter are stirred to a cream, add 2 whole eggs, 2 ounces of finely grated sweet almonds, some sugar, and as much bread or cracker crumbs as will make a dough thick enough to form dumplings. Sour cream can also be added.

19. Common Soup Dumplings made of Flour. Take a piece of butter the size of an egg, stir it to a cream, add 1 whole and the yolk of an egg, nutmeg, chopped parsley, salt and 2 heaping tablespoonfuls of flour. Stir for 5 minutes, form into small dumplings with a teaspoon and cook in the soup for 10 minutes.

20. Potato Dumplings. A piece of butter the size of an egg is stirred to a cream, then stir in the yolks of 2 eggs, 1 saucerful of grated bread, the same quantity of cooked and grated potatoes, which must not be watery, lemon peel, nutmeg and salt and at last the beaten whites of the eggs. Of this make small balls and cook in the soup for 10 minutes. A piece of butter the size of an egg, 1 egg, some nutmeg, salt and 1 teaspoonful of sugar and grated potatoes stirred together also make nice dumplings in large quantities.

21. Egg Froth Dumplings for Wine=, Beer= and Milk Soups. Beat the whites of the eggs with sugar to a stiff froth, mould into dumplings with a spoon, lay them on the boiling hot soup, sprinkle with sugar and cinnamon, cover tightly and they will be done rapidly.

II. DUMPLINGS TO BE EATEN WITH SAUCE OR FRUITS.

22. Karthusian Dumplings. The receipt for this dumpling is given in K, No. 38, as a dumpling to be eaten with a fruit compot.

23. Egyptian Dumpling. 9½ ounces of butter rolls, ¼ pound of butter, 8 eggs, 2 ounces of finely cut almonds, 1 lemon, milk and 1 pound of prunes.

Grate the crust of the rolls and soak the crumbs in milk. In the meantime rub butter to a cream, add, one by one, the eggs, then the almonds, lemon peel, the soaked crumbs and the grated crusts. After the elapse of ¼ hour form into a dumpling and lay it on the prunes, which should be cooked ½ hour before. Let this boil for 1 hour in an open kettle and turn after cooking about ½ hour. The dumpling is served with the prunes.

24. Fine Wheat Bread Dumplings. No. 1. Melt a piece of butter the size of an egg and stir with it the yolks of 4 eggs, salt, nutmeg, 2 small spoonfuls of flour, ¾ pound of wheat bread without the crust, soaked in water and pressed, and at last mix through it the beaten whites of the eggs. Put this mass, a spoonful at a time, on fruit which has been cooked with plenty of sauce until nearly done, cover the dumplings and let them cook for ½ hour or cook them in salted boiling water for ¼ hour.

25. Wheat Bread Dumplings. No. 2. Cut the crust from ¾ pound of wheat bread into small pieces, or fry in butter or fat until yellow, pour enough milk on the bread so that it will become soft, stir, add 4 spoonfuls of flour, 4 eggs, salt, nutmeg, 1 spoonful of melted butter and the fried crust, stir all together and cook the dumplings as directed in the above receipt.

26. Nice Potato Dumplings. 2 soupplatefuls of grated potatoes boiled the day before in their jackets, 4 bastingspoonfuls of flour, nutmeg, salt, 1 cupful of melted butter or lard, 6 eggs, the whites beaten to a froth. Stir all well together and mould into dumplings with a spoon, cook in boiling salted water for ¼ hour. Serve with browned butter or currant juice.

27. Potato Dumplings. No. 2. 1 pound of grated potatoes, 1 pound of wheat bread, grated, ¼ pound of melted butter, 5 whole eggs, a little salt and nutmeg. Mix well together and form into dumplings, which are cooked in boiling salted water for ¼ hour. Serve with browned butter or cooked fruit.

28. Large Potato Dumplings. Peel potatoes which have been cooked in salted water until nearly done, and after they are cold, grate them. Then to 3 parts of potatoes take 1 part of grated wheat bread and fry, with the crust cut into small cubes, in butter or fat until brown. To each soupplateful of the mixture take 2 eggs, the whites beaten to a froth, 1 ounce of melted butter or good lard, nutmeg if liked, and mix well together. Make dumplings the size of the closed hand, dust with flour and cook in boiling water until they are dry on the inside. Serve with browned butter and cooked fruit.

29. Henneberg Dumplings. Peel and grate nicely washed potatoes and pour lukewarm water over them until the starch is all removed. Then press, pour over it enough boiling milk with a little salt to make a soft dough, to which add the starch that was in the potatoes when the water was poured over them. Then grate cold boiled potatoes and add some fried bread cut into cubes, make into large balls and cook in boiling water for ½ hour. Serve with fat roasts, such as goose or pork, with plenty of gravy.

30. Baked Dumplings with Fruit. 2 pounds of flour, 1 pint of lukewarm milk, 3 eggs, 1 cupful of melted butter, 1 ounce of yeast and 2 tablespoonfuls of sugar. Stir half of the flour with the milk, salt, eggs and yeast and let it raise; then stir the remaining flour, butter and sugar to this, make into a dough, beat, and let it raise once again. Then form into small balls which is most easily done in the following manner: Roll the dough, and with a very small glass make dumplings, which are again raised and then fried in melted butter for about 10 minutes.

31. Puff Noodles. ("**Dampfnudeln**".) The dough is made as directed in the above receipt. After they have raised for the third time, put them into a deep pan with plenty of butter, pour over them 1 cupful of milk, lightly cover and lay a damp cloth over them. After about 10 minutes and when the under side is brown, turn and take off the cover and brown the other side. They can also be cooked in salted water for ½ hour. Serve with browned butter and fruit.

32. Yeast Dumplings. Take 1 pound of flour, 3 ounces of butter (kidney suet can also be used when prepared as directed in A, No. 17), ¼ pound of raisins or currants, 1 cupful of lukewarm milk, 2—3 eggs, ½ ounce of yeast, and salt. Make into a dough which is beaten with a spoon, set it to raise in a warm place, form into dumplings with a spoon, and cook in boiling salted water. Cover the dumplings and cook for ¼ hour and serve with browned butter and fruit.

33. Baked Middlings Dumplings. 1 pint of milk, ½ pound of middlings, salt and a piece of butter the size of an egg are stirred on the stove until the mass no longer adheres to the dish. After it has cooled, add 5—6 eggs, lemon peel or mace, make into dumplings the size of an egg, sprinkle with bread crumbs, fry in butter or kidney suet and serve with sugar and cinnamon. Can also be served alone with a wine- or fruit sauce, or serve with cooked fruits with or without a roast.

34. Apple Dumplings. Take 1 soupplateful of finely sliced cooking apples, 2 cupfuls of milk, sugar, lemon peel and enough wheat bread to make a nice dough (about ¾ pound) adding 5—6 eggs, the whites beaten to a froth, and a piece of butter the size of an egg. Mix all together, make into little dumplings and cook in salted water until done. Sprinkle with sugar and serve with a wine sauce.

35. Cherry Dumplings. 1 pound of stoned juicy cherries are cooked slowly without water, but with sugar, lemon peel and 3—4 cloves. After it has cooled, stir into it a small piece of butter, 4 eggs and add as much grated wheat bread as will keep the dumplings compact when cooking. Cook for 5—10 minutes and serve with a cream sauce.

36. Poppy Seed Dumplings. (A Silesian receipt.)
For 8 persons ½ pound of poppy seed is scalded and
stirred; the inferior seeds which rise to the surface must
be carefully taken off, then pour off the water and dry
the seeds by spreading them on paper or a napkin.
Then pound very fine with ¼ pound of sugar, put into
1 quart of boiling milk, add 3 ounces of nicely washed
currants, the grated rind of ½ lemon, 3 ounces of sweet
almonds mixed with a few bitter ones, a little cinnamon
or vanilla and boil, constantly stirring, for 5 minutes.
Then put a layer of sliced stale wheat bread (boiled
noodles can also be used) into a dish, pour the warm
poppy seed milk over it, a few spoonfuls at a time, then
bread and poppy seed milk and so on until all is used.
Serve cold as a dessert.

37. English Dumplings. Cut ½ pound of kidney suet
into very small pieces, mix with ⅓ pound of flour, ½
pound of currants, 1 teaspoonful of salt, a little ginger,
3 eggs, a cupful of milk, beat all to a light dough and
form into flat dumplings. Cook for ¾ of an hour in hot
water, sprinkle with sugar and serve with a rum sauce.

38. Hamburg Dumplings. Stir 3 ounces of butter to
a cream, add 1 whole egg, also the yolks of 3 eggs, 4
tablespoonfuls of flour, a little more than 1 ounce of
finely cut and fried bread, 2 soaked and pressed rolls,
mix together with salt, nutmeg and chopped parsley,
and stir through it 3 ounces of chopped smoked pork
fillet. Make into large dumplings and cook for 10
minutes, sprinkle with grated wheat bread and pour
browned butter over them.

39. Wheat Bread Dumplings. Take 1½ pounds of
flour, 1¾ pounds of wheat bread, 3 whole eggs, ¼ pound
of melted butter and 1½ pints of milk mixed with a little
water. The crust of the bread is cut into small pieces
and fried in butter or kidney suet; soak the bread in
the milk and stir with the eggs, butter and salt, then
add the flour and at last the fried pieces of bread.
Form into small dumplings with a spoon, cook in
salted boiling water for ¼ hour and serve with browned
butter and fruit.

40. Bread Dumplings with Fruit. The dough is
made as in the above receipt, adding a little yeast. Let

it raise for 1 hour, then pour over the fruit and let it cook for 1 hour longer.

41. "Pint" Dumplings. Take 1 pint of flour, 1 pint of grated wheat bread, 1 pint of whipped eggs, 1 pint of milk. Cut the crust of the bread into small pieces and fry in butter, stir the remaining ingredients together, put into a kettle with 3—4 ounces of butter and cook until it no longer adheres to the sides of the kettle. When it has cooled make into dumplings with the hands, dust with flour and cook for 10 minutes, covering the kettle. Serve with browned butter and fruit.

42. Giant Dumpling. For 4 persons take 1 pound of flour, 2—4 eggs, 1 cupful of warmed milk, ½ ounce of yeast, a good sized piece of butter or lard, 1 heaping tablespoonful of sugar and a little salt.

Make a depression in the center of the flour, first put in the milk and then the other ingredients, knead well together with the hands and put in a warm place to raise. After the dough is well risen, knead again, put it into a cloth which was first buttered and then sprinkled with flour, tie (leaving room for the dumpling to raise), put into a dish, let it raise for a while and then cook in salted boiling water for 2 hours. Serve with brown butter and fruit or with a milk sauce.

43. Browned Dumplings with baked Fruit. To be served after a strong soup. For 3—4 persons. About 1 pint of milk, a piece of butter the size of a walnut, ¼ pound of flour, ¼ pound of stale bread, 2 ounces of clear pork fat, 4 eggs and a little salt.

The flour, milk and butter are stirred together, put on the fire and stir until the flour is done, and it no longer adheres to the sides of the kettle. Take from the fire, pour into a mould and let it cool. Then cut the crust of the bread into small pieces, grate the bread, cut the pork fat into small cubes, fry, take out the cracklings, and fry the bread crusts in the fat until hard and dark brown, stirring a few times. Stir the yolks of the eggs through the browned flour, then the remaining ingredients and at last the beaten whites of the eggs. Make small dumplings, cook 5 minutes in salted water, serve in a hot dish with any kind of fruit, and plenty of sauce. The dumplings, slightly thickened, do not become heavy so easily as those made with raw flour.

44. Cornmeal Dumplings. Boil some cornmeal as for cornmeal soup only making it thicker, let it cool, stir with it a few eggs and some flour, make into dumplings and bake in butter or good lard. Serve for tea.

45. Liver Dumplings. To a calves' liver of moderate size, which is skinned, pounded and passed through a sieve, add a finely chopped piece of pork fat the size of an egg, 4 eggs whipped in ½ cupful of cold water, salt, nutmeg and a little pepper, 3 ounces of finely cut bread fried in butter and kidney suet, and if liked a finely chopped onion and as much flour as is needed to keep the dumplings together. Form into dumplings with a spoon and cook in boiling salted water, wetting the spoon in the water, so that the dumplings will not stick to it. Boil for about 10 minutes, and serve on a hot dish with grated bread fried in either butter or kidney suet. For a sauce cook butter, salt and water, and thicken with a teaspoonful of cornstarch.

The dumplings are served alone or with sourkrout.

46. South Germany Liver Dumplings. Take 1 pound of calves' liver and prepare as in the above receipt. together with about 6 ounces of wheat bread, 1 handful of flour, 6 eggs, 2 onions fried in butter, parsley, majoram, nutmeg, pepper and salt. The finely cut bread is put into 1 pint of boiling milk, then the eggs are stirred through it with the seasoning, the pounded liver and then the flour is mixed through it thoroughly, after which proceed as above directed.

47. Ham Dumplings with Sourkrout. Take the remnants of a ham and boil them after they have lain in milk for a day. On the following day, for 6 ounces of ham, soak 8 rolls, cut into pieces in some bouillon (made of extract of beef), cut the ham into very small pieces with half as much pork fat, fry the fat until brown with a few sliced onions, mix fat, onions and ham with the pressed wheat bread, some eggs, salt, chopped parsley and 4—5 spoonfuls of flour, and let the dough stand for a few hours before making into large dumplings, which are turned in flour and boiled in salted water until nearly done.

Dumplings cannot be served to invalids.

P.—Compots of Fresh and Dried Fruits.

---

1. General Directions. All kinds of fruits, fresh as well as dried, must be cooked in enameled ware, for when they are cooked in iron they receive an unpleasant taste.

Dried fruits must be nicely washed. When washing prunes, take warm water, change it a number of times, rub well between the hands and then rinse in cold water. Fresh plums are rubbed in a towel before cooking, apples and pears are peeled and then washed and rinsed.

Another way is to wash dried fruit once, then leave it in water over night and the next day put on the stove in water and cook. The compot is much nicer when cooked in this way and can be prepared in half of the time.

Fresh juicy fruit, such as raspberries, currants, huckleberries or fresh stoned plums, need only a little water, just enough to wet the bottom of the kettle; they are cooked in their own juices until done; for dried fruits plenty of water must be added, cover, put on the stove and cook slowly until done.

The sauce must be neither too thick nor too thin, With dried fruits a little cornstarch can be stirred through, them but it must not be any thicker than in preserved fruits.

After cooking the fruit it should be placed on a flat dish, pour the juice into the boiling liquor, when serving form into a mound shape, leaving the edge of the dish untouched, put the best appearing fruit on top, being careful never to pierce with a fork. The upper layer of fruit should be covered with some of the sauce, and add the remaining sauce when the dish is sent to the table.

In cold seasons never send the fruit to the table icy cold, but if it has been cooked the day before, always slightly warm it.

Compots intended for the family table can receive an addition of 1—2 tablespoonfuls of common sago, added when the compot is put on the fire. Pearl soup noodles can also be added.

When compots need a flavoring, lemon- or orange peel may be used; prepare the latter as directed in A, No. 48.

I. FRESH FRUIT.

2. Rhubarb Compot. No. 1. Take off the skin, cut into small pieces, wash, put on the stove in cold water containing a pinch of bi-carbonate of soda to lessen the acidity of the plant, and let it come to a boil; put on a sieve and then into the sugar, which can be seasoned with white wine and vanilla or with a little lemon peel, and cook quickly until done. Thicken the compot with a little finely grated bread or else after taking out the rhubarb cook the sauce with a little sugar, and then pour it over the rhubarb on which bread toasted in butter can be placed.

3. Rhubarb Compot. No. 2. Put the prepared rhubarb on the fire with water and the necessary sugar, let it cook until done, and if necessary thicken the sauce with some dissolved cornstarch or finely grated bread; serve cold.

4. Green Gooseberry Compot. Take gooseberries when about half grown, pick and wash clean. Then bring some water to a boil with sugar and a few pieces of cinnamon or vanilla, put some of the berries into this and as soon as done take them out of the syrup with a skimmer, doing this carefully as they are easily mashed. Put in some more berries and continue until all have been cooked. Then boil the syrup as much as is needed and pour over the compot. Another way is to put the berries on the fire in cold water, and when nearly boiling pour off the water and proceed as above; in this way a great deal of the acid is taken out of the berries.

The gooseberries can also be used in sweet dishes by taking the juice and whipping it to a cream on the fire with 1 glassful of white wine and the yolks of 4 eggs, mixing through it the beaten whites of the eggs. Then carefully stir the berries into the cream, garnish the dish with preserved fruits and serve, if wished with cream seasoned with vanilla.

5. Compot of ripe Gooseberries. After the gooseberries have been cleaned, put them into boiling water, and after a few minutes when they are done put them on a colander. Then stir them through the colander and put on the fire with sugar and cinnamon or vanilla, stirring frequently, bring to a boil, and thicken as wished with either grated bread or cornstarch, and when cold cover with whipped cream before serving.

6. Compot of Strawberries and Apples. If good apples can be obtained during the strawberry season, prepare them as usual, divide into 8 pieces and wash. In the meantime bring the water to a boil with sugar and wine or lemon juice, add the apples and cook until done. Then put in plenty of strawberries with a little more sugar, cook for a short time longer and after it has been stirred carefully, send the compot to the table.

7. Wild Strawberries for Dessert. Rinse the berries in water 1 hour before wanted, sprinkle plentifully with powdered sugar, pour a little water over them, cover and set aside.

8. Cherry Compot. Sour as well as sweet cherries may be used. Take off the stems, and stone them. Then pound 4—6 cherry pits, cook them for ¼—½ hour in a little water, or water and wine, whole cinnamon and a few cloves, pour on a sieve, put the strained juice on the fire with the sugar (5 ounces to sour cherries and 2½ ounces to sweet cherries), and when it boils throw in the fruit. If the cherries are sweet cook slowly for ¼ hour, if they are sour let them simmer a few minutes longer, stirring occasionally. After they are done take them out of the juice with a skimmer, let the juice cook to a syrup and serve with the cherries.

9. Currant Compot. Take from the stems but do not wash them, sprinkle with sugar, in layers, and do not cook longer than until the berries are done, pouring the juice over the berries, then take them out with the skimmer. Cook the syrup for a little while and serve cold with the compot.

10. Raspberry Compot. Pick over the berries and slowly and carefully cook them the same as currants, as they must be served neatly.

11. Huckleberry Compot. The berries are cleaned and washed and put on a colander, and after they are drained, cook with sugar and cinnamon until done, as they lose too much juice when cooked longer. Then either lay a roll into the bottom of the dish and pour the juice over this, or take the berries out of the dish, let the juice cook a little while longer and when serving stir through it a spoonful of thick cream or a little dissolved cornstarch.

12. English Huckleberry Compot. After the berries are washed let them drain on a sieve, put into a stone jar, sprinkle in layers with plenty of sugar and cinnamon, cover with a china plate and put the jar into boiling water and cook uninterruptedly until the berries are done. Send to the table without any further addition.

13. Mulberry Compot. Take wine, sugar and a little grated lemon peel, put it on the stove, throw in the cleaned mulberries and proceed as in cooking currants.

14. Peach and Apricot Compot. The fruit is peeled, stoned, halved and cooked for 5—10 minutes with sugar, a little white wine and a few of the stones, but not too soft. Then lay them into a glass dish, the round side to the top, cook the juice for a few minutes and proceed as given under No. 1.

15. Half-Frozen Peaches. Peel very ripe peaches, cut them into halves, sprinkle well with sugar and put into a freezer. Keep the freezer in ice until the peaches are half frozen, then place them on a glass dish in the form of a wreath, sprinkle again with sugar and fill some whipped cream, seasoned either with vanilla or Marascino, into the middle of the dish.

16. Melon Compot. If the melon is hard and you do not wish to serve it in its natural state, a good compot can be made of it. Peel, cut into long pieces, and cook in water, wine, sugar and plenty of lemon slices until done, and serve with the sauce, which must be well boiled down.

17. Pear Compot. Peel the pears, cut off the blossom end and half of the stem, wash, cook in plenty of water, a glassful of claret, sugar, cinnamon and a few cloves, or else make a sauce of preserved plums or currant juice. Put into an enameled pan, cover and leave them until of a nice red color and done. Cook the juice for a while and pour over the pears, first straining it.

18. Pears cooked Brown. Peel some good pears, cut them in halves, take out the core and lay the pears into water. Put a piece of fresh butter into a stewpan with some sugar and the pears with only the water that remains on the pears. Let them stew slowly. When they commence to brown sprinkle a little more sugar over them, stew a little while longer until they are done; they are nice served with any kind of roast game.

19. Pears with Cranberries. See preserved fruits, Division T.

20. Pears with Plums. Peel the pears, quarter, take out the core, wash and cook in an enameled kettle with not too much water until they can easily be pierced with a fork. Then take the same quantity of plums, clean and stone them, lay them on the pears, let them cook until done, mix with the pears (being careful not to break the fruit), and serve the compot cold. There should not be too much sauce. The plums will give the sauce the proper thickness and will replace both sugar and seasoning. This compot is nice with dumplings or pancakes. Quartered apples can also be put onto the pears before the plums.

21. Common Pear Stew is made the same as apple sauce; a few sour apples can also be cooked with the pears until done. Serve with pancakes.

22. Plum Compot. Put the plums into a sieve and hold them in boiling water for a few moments, then take off the skin. After removing the stones put the plums on the fire with sugar and cinnamon, cook slowly for a little while, but not too soft and serve with the juice. The juice can also be mixed with 1—2 teaspoonfuls of rum.

23. Compot of Plums, Pears and Apricots. Take ripe plums, pears and apricots, skin and leave them 1 hour in sugar before serving. This makes an excellent compot.

24. Plum Marmalade. The plums are skinned and stoned. Add a few tablespoonfuls of water to them, cook, pass through a sieve, add grated bread roasted in butter, sugar, cinnamon, lemon or orange peel, bring to a boil again and serve.

25. Blackberry Compot. Pick out all of the large berries, press the smaller ones and cook the large berries in the juice for a few minutes, after adding sugar, a few cloves, cinnamon and lemon slices; then take them out and after the juice has cooked for some time longer pour it over the fruit.

26. Compot of whole Apples. Pare medium-sized apples, take out the core with an apple corer, slit lengthwise and rinse. Then put wine sweetened with sugar into an enameled dish, together with a few pieces of cinnamon and lemon peel and let it boil. A little strawberry juice makes the compot nicer. Lay in side by side as many apples as the dish will hold, and let them boil, turn with a spoon and cover, frequently pouring over them some of the juice; when the apples are done take them out, lay them on a flat dish and cook the remaining apples until all are done. Then pour the juice which drips off the apples back into the dish and boil for some time. In the meantime arrange the fruit as directed under No. 1, press half of the juice onto the fruit through a sieve and put on each apple a little apricot marmalade, apple- or currant jelly. Before serving the compot, pour over it the remaining cold juice of the apples.

The apples can also be filled after they are cold with a mixture of stoned raisins, currants and finely sliced citron, and are cooked with sugar and white wine until done. A layer of whipped cream mixed with apple marmalade can also be put into the dish, and a layer of the fruit over this, decorating with different colored fruit jellies. The juice of the apples is used in making fruit soup or sauce.

27. Apple Marmalade. Cook 15 nice apples as for a sauce, spice with a glassful of cherry cordial and a little vanilla, then mix through the hot sauce 4 preserved pears, 4 preserved apricots, 5 ounces of finely sliced candied fruits and 3 ounces of fresh grapes. Get a milk bread, hollow it and fill with the sauce. Pour over the bread a chocolate icing, leave it in the oven for a few moments, put on the top a spoonful of peach juice and serve.

Instead of the bread bake a rice cake as directed in S, No. 64, cut off the top and hollow out the cake and fill as above directed. This cake is not covered with an icing, but is dotted with the fruit juices, sprinkled with sugar and set in the oven for 5 minutes.

28. Halved Apples covered with Fruit Jelly. Peel the apples, cut them into halves, take out the core, wash and cook as directed in No. 26, putting the round side into the wine. Then let the apple jelly become fluid, cool it on a wet plate and just before serving pour the jelly over the apples, which have been put into a glass dish, and arrange some preserved fruit around the edge of the dish.

Instead of cooking the apples in wine, they can be cooked in water with lemon juice and sugar, or in wine and fruit juices half and half (strawberry-, cherry- or raspberry juices) until done.

29. Baked Compot of Apples. The apples are pared, cored and cooked in wine and sugar until done. Strain through a sieve, mix with apricot marmalade and put into a dish. Then beat the whites of 2 eggs, mix with 2 tablespoonfuls of sugar and some grated lemon peel, brush smoothly over the compot, which is sprinkled with sugar and baked to a light yellow color. Serve cold with a roast.

This compot can also be iced with an almond icing before baking, by taking a handful of almonds, grate and then mix them with sugar, vanilla, lemon juice and 2—3 eggs and spread over the compot. After it has cooled decorate it with different colored fruit jelly.

30. Sliced Apple Compot. To a medium-sized panful of apples take ½ bottle of white wine, 4—5 tablespoonfuls of sugar, some lemon peel and cinnamon and cook the apples slowly in this in a covered dish until done. If wished preserved quince or strawberry juice may be added to the sauce.

31. Apple Sauce. The nicer the apples the better the sauce will be. Pare and quarter the apples, take out the core, wash and cook until done in a little wine, or wine, water, sugar, cinnamon (vanilla can be used instead of cinnamon) and lemon peel. Then take out the spices and stir the apple sauce; the best way is to pass the sauce through a sieve. Smooth the sauce nicely on top before serving and after it has cooled drop a little fruit jelly or grated chocolate over it.

32. Apple Salad. (A nice compot of raw apples and oranges.) Take good apples, pare and core them, cut sweet oranges into thin slices, take out the seeds and lay the fruit into a dish alternately with sugar and wine. There should not be any sauce; the last layer must be of oranges and sugar. The compot is made some hours before wanted for use and is served with a roast.

33. Apples with Anise Seed. Take small apples, cut out the blossom, slit the peel from the blossom to the end 3—4 times, wash and put them into a jar, with 1 cupful of water or wine and a piece of butter, a little anise seed, cinnamon and lemon peel, cover and let them stew, shake a few times and at last put in some sugar.

34. Cooked Sweet Apples. After the apples are peeled, quartered and cored, put them on the fire with water, anise seed, a little butter and ½—1 cupful of vinegar (plenty of lemon juice is better) and cook until tender. The vinegar will cause the apples to become tender sooner.

35. Apples with Rice. Take apples of medium size, pare and core them and put them into water which has been seasoned with a little lemon juice. Then boil the apples in 1 quart of water with 1 pound of sugar and the rind of a lemon; when done take out of the juice with a large spoon. Scald 1 pound of rice and boil it in water with 1 pint of white wine, lemon juice and lemon peel until thick and tender, but the kernels must remain whole; mix the broth of the apples with a small glassful of arrac and the necessary sugar, and put into a dish. After the rice has cooled, put it into an appropriate dish, heap the apples in the center, fill some preserved fruits into the core, and pour over all the remaining juice of the apples. If you have no rice mould, form the rice wreath around the dish with a tablespoon.

36. Carrot Compot with a Roast. Peel the cleaned carrots with a small knife, so that they will curl (the hard core is removed), cook with the peel of 1 lemon until done, and pour on a sieve. Then for 1¼ pounds of carrots cook ½ pound of sugar, the juice of 2 lemons and a little vinegar, let the carrots boil for a few moments and then take them out, cook the sauce for a little while and pour it over them.

37. Compot of Quinces. Peel the fruit, halve, take out the core and cook the fruit in water with sugar and whole cinnamon until done. Then pour in 1 glassful of wine, put the quinces into a dish, let the sauce cook for some time and pour it over the quinces through a strainer.

The core will make the sauce thicker and the seeds will produce a nice red color.

38. Mixed Compot. 10—12 apples are pared, halved and stewed until tender as directed in No. 28. Peel 3 oranges, slice them, take out the seeds, and sugar for a few hours. Some time before this stew about 2 ounces of plums and let them cool. Arrange the cooked fruits neatly in a dish, mixing together orange slices, preserved cherries, apricots and sweet-sour beans, and pour over the compot the apple juice which has been boiled down with a few spoonfuls of preserved fruit until thick.

39. Currants and other Fruits as Dessert. Select nice grapes, currants, strawberries, cherries, dip each berry into whipped whites of eggs and then in powdered sugar and lay on a sieve to dry. When the fruit is dry it will have a frosted appearance, and look very pretty when mixed with fresh unsugared fruit.

40. Peaches for Dessert. Peel ripe peaches and for 15 peaches cook ⅔ pound of sugar and a little water to a thick sugar syrup and lay each peach into this syrup for 2 minutes. After all the fruit is sugared, which must be done with a very moderate fire, put it into a glass dish, mix the syrup with 3 tablespoonfuls of Marascino and pour it over the fruit. Put the fruit on the ice for 4 hours before serving and it will be found very delicious.

41. Pineapple Compot for the Sick. Take a pineapple, cut it into slices of uniform size, and boil the juice of the fruit with sugar and lemon peel until thick. Stew the pieces of pineapple in this for some minutes, lay into a dish, pour the syrup of the fruit over this and decorate with strawberries.

All compots may be given to the sick excepting Nos. 18, 21, 33, 34, 36, 38.

II. DRIED FRUITS.

42. Compot of Prunes. No. 1. Take good prunes, wash in hot water, rub between the hands and then put on the stove in cold water to boil; the water is subsequently poured off, after this is done put the prunes into a porcelain dish 2—3 days before wanted for use, covered with white wine and the necessary sugar, a piece of cinnamon and lemon peel; cover tightly, bring slowly to a boil, then set aside until wanted; they must be stirred often before using.

43. Compot of Prunes. No. 2. Prepare the prunes as directed in the above receipt, the evening before put them into a jar with plenty of water, cover and set them into the oven while it is still warm so that they will swell and become tender. The next day take them out of the broth, lay them into a dish, boil white wine, sugar, lemon peel and a few pieces of cinnamon with the prune juice, add a little currant juice and pour the hot juice over the prunes.

44. Prune Marmalade. After the prunes are scalded, they are put into a porcelain dish and cooked with wine and water, half and half, until done. Then pass them through a sieve, cook again with grated bread roasted in butter, sugar, finely cut lemon peel and cinnamon and put into a dish.

45. Dried Cherries. These are washed in hot water and then put on the fire with water, sugar and whole cinnamon; boil down to a nice thick sauce.

46. Dried Sour Apples. Wash them thoroughly in cold water, rubbing them between the hands, then put them into a porcelain dish, boil slowly with water, sugar, cinnamon and some preserved orange peel (see A, No. 48). When this is done take them out of the juice and if it is thin, boil until thick enough, or add a little dissolved cornstarch and strain the juice over the fruit.

47. Dried Pears are cooked the same as dried sour apples, but require a longer time.

48. Fig Compot for Invalids. Cut ¼ pound of dried figs into pieces and lay in water over night. Then cook them the following day in the same water until tender, pass through a sieve and cook like a jelly with lemon sugar and a glassful of Malaga. Serve either warm or cold.

All compots of dried fruits are given to invalids; some are very nourishing, as for instance the compot of dried prunes.

Q.—Salads and Lettuces.

1. In General. Lettuces of every description must be carefully examined before preparing, for slugs and insects are quite apt to be concealed in the leaves, and all of the latter that are withered or otherwise unfit for use can, at the same time, be removed, but it is a mistake to take away the ribs from closed bunches of lettuce, because they are deemed the best part thereof. After removing the outer leaves divide the remainder of the bunch into about three parts and cut the closed inside part into small pieces. When the lettuce is not of good quality, however, the stems or ribs must also be removed, because they are tough. In the opinion of many cooks, lettuce is improved by keeping it in the cellar for about 2 hours after taking it out of the garden.

Lettuce should not lay in water unless it has become withered. Rinse in a deep pan in plenty of cold water before preparing; this will cause all sandy particles to drop to the bottom of the pan; hold the bunches in the hand loosely and raise and lower them in the pan of water until clean. Then twirl in a sieve until all of the water has been removed. To press the lettuce with the hands is apt to crush and bruise it, thereby impairing its fresh appearance.

The addition to lettuce of certain herbs, such as tarragon, onion tops, peppergrass or cresses, burnet, etc., imparts to it an agreeable flavor. When onion tops are not in season, finely sliced onions are indispensable with some varieties of lettuce; inasmuch, however, as the flavor of onions is disliked by some, they may be cut into fine slices and served separately in vinegar.

Salt should be added to lettuce with great caution, because it is easily oversalted. Good olive oil should always be used. Hints on keeping salad oils in good condition will be found under General Directions in the forepart of this book. For a salad sauce in which the yolks of hard boiled eggs are used, the yolks should first be rubbed as finely as possible, then stir in some vinegar and finally add the oil gradually; the sauce when prepared in this manner will bind more readily; then mix it under constant stirring to the other ingredients. Good vinegar is essential for the preparation of a good salad, and care should always be observed not to obtain an adulterated article.

An excellent substitute for the yolks of eggs for sauces for lettuce, endives, etc., consists of 2 boiled potatoes, rubbed while still warm until very smooth. Then stir to a well bound sauce with vinegar, milk, olive oil, salt and such lettuce herbs as desired.

Many cooks add sugar to lettuce; as directions for the addition of sugar may be omitted in some of the following receipts, it may be well to say here that it can readily be added; instead of using the cream directed to be added to many of the salads, a rather plentiful addition of olive oil is then in order.

The sauces should be added to lettuce shortly before serving, because the latter, when in the sauce for too long a time, becomes tough and loses its fresh appearance. To make the lettuce milder, first mix the oil through it gently, and then the sauce. Horn or wooden salad spoons or forks are the best for this purpose, and the mixing should be done rapidly and carefully, so as not to mash or bruise the lettuce. Meat-, fish- and herring salads gain in palatableness when mixed a few hours, if possible a whole day, before serving. Meat salads absorb a large quantity of juices, and neither vinegar nor water should be added to them plentifully; the latter should be mixed with extract of beef, which will improve the flavor of the salad.

2. Chicken Salad. For 24—30 persons. Boil 6 young chickens with plenty of butter and salt until done but not too tender. Cut up when cold; the bones are taken out of the breast and legs, and the meat used for the salad. The back, wings and neck are cooked with a small piece of veal, add a little browned flour and, after cooking for ½ hour, strain the broth. Mix the yolks of 4 eggs with some nutmeg, ½ glassful of white wine, salt and a little white pepper and stir in the boiling broth which is then poured over the meat. Take nice crisp lettuce and cut it into 4 pieces, or else take tender endives, and mix with the following sauce: The yolks of 6 hard boiled and 2 raw eggs are rubbed together, add a little vinegar, a few spoonfuls of salad oil, stir well together, also finely chopped tarragon or tarragon vinegar, or better still some extract, 2 teaspoonfuls of sugar, 1 teaspoonful of mustard and the broth which was left from the chicken. This salad is put into the dish with the meat in the form of a star.

If remnants of poultry are used, cut them into cubes, mix with finely cut hard boiled eggs, boiled white beans and small onions, mix with a mayonnaise sauce and garnish with the hearts of lettuce.

3. Turkey Salad. If the whole turkey is to be used, follow the directions given in No. 2, and garnish with crabtails. In making a salad of remnants of turkey, cut the meat into little pieces. In the meantime boil a few celery roots until done, halve and then cut them into 3—4 pieces. Cut good Summer sausage into pieces, make a sauce as in the above receipt and into it carefully mix the meat, celery, sausage and sliced pickles; serve neatly. Slice some red beets and lay them around the salad in the shape of a wreath, cut some hard boiled eggs lengthwise into 8 pieces and lay them in with the beet slices with the rounded side to the top.

4. Fish Salad. For a dinner with several courses the following salad is very nice. For 20 persons take 1 pound of eel, 1 pound of pike, ½ pound of trout, ½ pound of turbot, ½ pound of soles, ¾ pound of salmon and 5 lampreys. Boil the fish in salted water the day previous with peppercorns and the juice and rind of a lemon. The eel is cooked first because it requires less salt, then it is taken out of the broth and the pike is cooked, which will need a little more salt, then the trout, soles, turbot one after the other, with the necessary salt. The salmon is cooked in separate water with salt. After the broth in which the other fish were cooked has become cold, keep the fish in it until the next day. Fish must not remain in the broth while it is cooling, as it gives them an unpleasant flavor.

When making the salad, after boning the fish, cut it into small pieces, cut the lamprey crosswise into pieces about 1 inch in length, serve with ½ cupful of capers to which may be added 30—40 oysters and 20 crabtails, either whole or cut into pieces.

The following sauce is poured over the fish: 3 hard boiled eggs and 1 raw egg are rubbed together with 1 cupful of strong meat bouillon, about 4 tablespoonfuls of salad oil, 2 teaspoonfuls of mustard, 1 teaspoonful of sugar, a little white pepper, 1 tablespoonful of thick cream, vinegar and a little salt, all stirred together.

5. Pike Salad. Medium-sized pike are emptied, washed, cleaned and cooked in salted water with plenty of onions until done. Take from the stove and leave them in the water for 10 minutes as the fish will be salted better in this way. Then put the pike on a dish to cool, take out the bones, skin and divide into pieces. In the meantime cook large crabs in salted water with a little vinegar. The vinegar will give the crabs a prettier red color. Then take the meat out of the crabs. In the meantime boil a few eggs until hard, rub the yolks and stir with vinegar, (the yolks will not bind as well in oil), mix with finely chopped eschalots and chopped anchovies, briskly stirring in vinegar, olive oil and a little pike broth, pass the sauce through a sieve and stir in a little mustard and chopped parsley. After the anchovies have been prepared as for bread and butter, cut some lemons into thin slices, lay the pike into a deep dish, mix with the meat of the crabs, pour over it the sauce, put over this the capers and garnish the dish as follows: Around the edge put the crabtails with the points turned to the outside of the dish, put the anchovies over the fish crosswise or in the form of a star, between these the lemon slices, put a quartered lemon around the edge and at last the cut crab claws between the tails.

6. Lobster Salad with Caviar. The lobster is boiled as directed in Division F, the meat taken out of the shells, cut into long pieces and laid into a salad bowl. Pour over it a sauce made of the yolks of hard boiled eggs, pepper, salt, olive oil, vinegar, white wine, finely chopped tarragon, parsley and a few eschalots. The salad is garnished with anchovies, capers, hard boiled eggs, each egg cut into 8 pieces and the edge of the dish surrounded with bits of bread spread with caviar. Some prefer the lobster without the bread; others like it simply with pepper, oil and vinegar. Salt is usually not necessary.

7. Anchovy Salad. The anchovies are freshened and torn through the middle, so that the bones may easily be taken out. Put them into a salad bowl with capers, small pickles, preserved sour plums, Summer sausage cut into slices, and pickled eel which is divided lengthwise and cut into pieces the thickness of a finger. The dish may be garnished with lemon slices; pour over it a sauce as directed in the above receipt or else vinegar, oil, pepper, salt and the grated yolks of a few hard boiled eggs. Some prefer the salad with olives, roast veal, button onions, mustard, pickles and a few apples, all cut into small pieces, and put into a marinade of bouillon, sugar, vinegar, onions, pepper and salt for a few hours before mixing with the salad.

8. Shrimp Salad. As soon as caught shrimps are boiled and shipped. They are taken out of their skins and eaten with bread and butter, or else served as a salad, putting the shrimps into the center of the dish, surrounded with the whites of hard boiled eggs, capers, on this the grated yolks of eggs, then surrounded again with hearts of lettuce or water cresses dipped in a mayonnaise dressing and then with boiled beets, sliced and put into hot vinegar. An a la Diable or mayonnaise sauce is served with the salad. A simpler way is to serve it with vinegar, oil, pepper, grated onions and hard boiled eggs; vinegar must not be poured over the shrimps, as it will tend to harden them.

Shrimps are also used to garnish fish dishes and for lunches.

9. Fish and Vegetable Salad. All kinds of vegetables in their season, such as asparagus, cauliflowers, cut into small pieces, small salad beans, savoy cabbage cut into pieces, young carrots, celery and parsley roots, etc., are boiled in salted water, and after they are cool put them into a dish with the fish, such as pike, eel, also crabtails, garnish with pickled beets cut lengthwise, and pour over them a sauce made as directed under No. 4.

10. Herring Salad. A dozen herring will make enough salad for 24 persons. The herring are emptied, washed and freshened in milk over night, and if very salty for a longer time. Then take off the skin, bone them and cut into small pieces. Take potatoes boiled in their jackets, peel and cool them together with plenty of veal roast, pickles, beets, some sour apples, 8—12 hard boiled eggs, leaving 4 to garnish the dish, a celery root cooked until tender, ½ pound of boiled ham and a few onions, all cut into very small pieces. Then mix this with a well-stirred, plentiful sauce made of olive oil, wine vinegar, claret, dissolved extract of beef, pepper and a trifle of mustard. The milts of 3—4 herrings can be used by mixing them with vinegar and passing them through a sieve. In case the salad is prepared the day before wanted for use, which will make it better, leave it over night in a porcelain dish, stir it before using and then garnish the dish in the following manner: Take pickles or parsley, beets, the yolks of 4 hard boiled eggs, and also the whites, each chopped separately. Smooth the top of the salad, make a figure with the back of a knife—a star for instance—and in the points put a teaspoonful of the minced ingredients, a different color in each point, hold the knife in the left hand and place it over the line so as not to have the figure uneven. Around this make a wreath of any color; if white or yellow is chosen, leaves of curly parsley are very pretty; freshened, divided and rolled anchovies and capers can also be used for ornamenting the salad. As a great deal of time is taken in cutting the ingredients of the salad separately they may be chopped, but each must be chopped separately, and not too fine or the salad will become pulpy.

11. Herring Salad with Bread and Butter. All the ingredients as given in the above receipt, excepting the potatoes and beets, are chopped fine and mixed with oil, vinegar, pepper, and, if necessary, a little salt; serve neatly, garnishing with capers.

12. Meat Salad. For 12 persons. 5—6 lampreys, ½ pound of anchovies, 3—4 freshened herring, celery, beets, mustard pickles, potatoes and veal roast, taking of each ⅓ soupplateful, and of the veal roast 1 soupplateful, 8—10 preserved sour plums, all cut into long pieces and put into the dish in layers. For the sauce take 8 hard boiled eggs, pass them through a sieve, also 1 small cupful of oil, then 4 teaspoonfuls of mustard, 2—3 teaspoonfuls of sugar, 2—3 grated onions and a little salt. Pour into this enough vinegar, or if wished, a little claret or bouillon, to make a thick sauce and spread it over the salad.

13. Soup Meat Salad. About 1 hour before wanted cut the meat into pieces and mix with a good horseradish sauce (see Division R). Take the nicest pieces of the meat, dip into the sauce and put them on top of the salad. Cucumbers cut into slices are very nice with soup meat salad, also the finely cut whites of the eggs used for the sauce. This salad is served with lettuce or with potato dishes of all kinds, and is also nice for supper.

14. Polish Salad. Cold roast of any kind can be used. Cut the meat into small pieces, adding some lettuce or endives, and mix with it salad oil, vinegar, mustard, pepper, salt, finely cut onions and soft boiled eggs.

REMARK.—All lovers of salads will find this one to be very nice and refreshing.

15. Truffle Salad. The fresh truffles are not peeled, but washed with a brush first in warm, then in cold water, then slice like cucumbers and instead of vinegar use lemon juice, oil, pepper, salt and mustard.

Sometimes the truffles are mixed with potatoes. When using potatoes stew the truffles in bouillon and oil until tender, take them out of the broth and heat some boiled peeled potatoes in this broth, mix with salt and pepper and cover them. Then peel the truffles, cut them into slices and mix with the potatoes; pour over them some vinegar, lemon juice, white wine, a little dissolved extract of beef and let the salad stand for about 3 hours before serving. A dozen pickled oysters may also be added to this dish.

16. Tomato Salad. Put 6—8 tomatoes where they will become cold so that they will harden and can more readily be cut into slices. Just before serving slice them, taking out as many of the seeds as possible. Then make a dressing of 4 spoonfuls of salad oil, salt, pepper, a little sugar, if liked a few teaspoonfuls of chopped onions, add 1 tablespoonful of vinegar, pour over the salad and serve.

17. Mixed Salad. Take beets, pickles, celery roots cooked until tender, and potatoes boiled in their jackets, in equal parts; slice and pour over them the following sauce: Hard boiled eggs stirred with vinegar, salt, mustard, a little sugar, oil, and thick sour cream, taking for each egg 1 tablespoonful of cream. As the beets and pickles are sour, be careful not to put in too much vinegar.

18. Mushroom and Potato Salad (Flanders Salad). Nice potatoes are boiled in their jackets, peeled, cut into slices, sprinkled with salt and pepper, and a few spoonfuls of oil and bouillon poured over them. Slice medium soft boiled eggs and some mushrooms stewed in butter and bouillon, and mix with the potatoes. The whites of 2 eggs, an eschalot and a sour apple are chopped fine and the yolks of 2 hard boiled eggs put through a sieve; mix all with 4 tablespoonfuls of salad oil, 1 teaspoonful of mustard, a little sugar and 4 spoonfuls of vinegar, stir to a thick sauce, and mix through the sliced potatoes and mushrooms. Set the salad aside for a few hours, and then send to the table garnished with endives, dressed with oil, vinegar, salt and a little sugar.

19. Potato Salad. Boil potatoes of uniform size in their jackets in salted water until tender, peel, cut into slices and pour 1 cupful of boiling water over them, cover and set aside until the dressing is made. Slice a tender boiled celery root. For a dressing for 6 persons take 6 tablespoonfuls of salad oil, the same amount of claret or a bouillon made of extract of beef, 4—6 spoonfuls of vinegar (if very strong dilute it), plenty of pepper and salt and if liked a little mustard and finely chopped onions. By putting into a dish a layer of potatoes then a spoonful of dressing, then potatoes and so on, the potato slices will remain whole. Dip potato slices of equal size into the dressing and put them over the top of the salad.

Another way is to peel the potatoes, slice and pour over them the dressing of oil, salt, pepper, grated onion and a little sugar. Then mix some good vinegar with a few spoonfuls of boiling bouillon or hot claret, white wine or else only seething hot water, whichever is preferred, and with this carefully stir the sliced potatoes. If liked a little tarragon or finely chopped chives can be added; set the salad aside for a while before bringing it to the table.

Excepting lettuce, any kind of greens can be served with potato salad. When mixed with the salad the lettuce wilts too easily. Serve with veal or pork brawn, or veal in jelly and with warm and cold roast.

20. Potato Salad. No. 2. Cut boiled potatoes into slices, keep them warm and mix through them the following dressing: Stir together oil, vinegar, milk, pepper, salt and finely cut onions. Put the sliced potatoes into a dish, pour over them half of the sauce, put a dish on this and shake the salad; then pour over it the remaining sauce and shake again so that the potatoes will be juicy. Goose oil can also be used instead of the salad oil.

21. Potato Salad with Bacon. Fry a saucerful of bacon cut into small pieces; after it has fried take out the pieces and fry in the fat some finely cut onions together with the necessary vinegar, salt and a little pepper, stir through it a few spoonfuls of sour cream or water, cut the potatoes into the warm broth, turn them in this and serve the salad.

22. Water Cresses. Water cresses make a very healthful salad, and are used as long as their leaves are tender. Cut off the stems, wash thoroughly without crushing and rinse them on a colander. Then mix with olive oil, vinegar and salt, and send to the table immediately before they wilt. Serve with or without potato salad with roast meats, especially with roast pheasant.

23. Salad of Garden Cresses. These cresses can be had all the year. Cut off all of the leaves that are tender, wash thoroughly and serve with oil, vinegar and a little salt

A dressing of oil, vinegar, finely grated yolks of eggs, mustard and sugar is also well liked.

24. Asparagus Salad. The asparagus is cleaned as directed under Vegetables (C, No. 16); tie into bunches and cook in boiling salted water until tender and then put it on a colander to drain. After it is cool cut the threads, lay the asparagus neatly into a salad dish and pour over it oil and vinegar in equal parts mixed with salt and pepper. The asparagus can also be cut into pieces and cooked in salted water until tender.

25. Lettuce. Directions for cleaning, washing, rinsing and mixing lettuce are given under No. 1. For a dressing according to the French method, for 6 persons take the yolks of 2—3 hard boiled eggs, 2 tablespoonfuls of salad oil, a little salt and vinegar and, if liked, a little mustard and pepper, also some finely chopped tarragon, a few young onions, etc.; to this can be added 2 spoonfuls of thick sour cream, taking the yolk of an egg and 1 tablespoonful of salad oil less.

In North Germany they take sour cream and sugar and mix them with the salad, or a little vinegar is mixed with the cream. The sauce can also be made in the following manner: 1 cupful of thick sour cream is stirred with 2 spoonfuls of vinegar, salt, sugar, chopped tarragon and the yolks of 3 raw eggs, pour this dressing over the lettuce just before serving, first moistening it with salad oil.

A mixed salad of lettuce and sliced beans cooked until tender is also nice; ½ hour before serving, mix through it a dressing made according to one of the foregoing receipts. Finely sliced cucumbers can also be used, in which case take only oil, sugar, vinegar and salt. When served with ham for the supper table mix with sliced, hard boiled eggs.

26. Cauliflower Salad. The cauliflowers are prepared the same as usual, and then cooked in salted water until tender. Drain on a colander and arrange in the dish so as to have the heads to the top, pour over them a dressing made of a few hard boiled eggs, vinegar, oil, pepper and salt.

27. Cucumber Salad. When peeling cucumbers be careful to cut off all of the bitter end. Often they are bitter all the way through and then must not be used. Slice, pour a little salad oil over them and just

before serving pour over the salad a dressing made as
follows: Hard boiled eggs or thick sour cream are
stirred together with vinegar, pepper, salt, chopped
parsley and tarragon. Onions may also be added or
can be served separately with vinegar. Some people
prefer to wilt the cucumbers by first sprinkling salt over
them and setting them aside for a short time and then
pressing. This does not only take away their nice taste,
but makes them tough and harder to digest. The
salad can also be mixed with sliced potatoes with a
dressing of oil, vinegar, sour cream, salt, pepper, tarragon and sliced onions. For persons with impaired
digestion who cannot eat fresh cucumbers, peel the
cucumbers, boil them for a few minutes in salted water
and then prepare the same as fresh cucumbers.

28. Bean Salad. After the beans have been cleaned,
cook in boiling salted water until tender, then mix with
onions, oil, vinegar, pepper and salt. Bean salad can
also be mixed with sliced cucumbers; when doing this it
is well to first cook the cucumbers for a few moments.
Lettuce can also be mixed with bean salad.

29. Red Mixed Salad. Take potatoes boiled in their
jackets, and to 1 part of potatoes take 1 part of sliced
beets and a little more of finely sliced red cabbage than
of beets. Carefully mix through it some oil, vinegar,
the broth of the beets, pepper and salt, and serve with
warm roast.

30. Red Salad. Red early cabbage is finely shredded, pour over it plenty of oil, then mix with vinegar,
salt and pepper. Serve with meat and hot potatoes.

31. White Cabbage. Shred the cabbage very fine,
scald and press it, mix with it oil, vinegar, salt, pepper,
or a good cooked sour cream sauce, or else with a warm
bacon sauce with pepper and salt and serve with warm
potates.

REMARK.—This cabbage is good for salads only in the Fall, for later it
becomes tough. Salad made of white and red cabbage put into the dish in layers
is very attractive and nice.

32. Mixed Winter Salad. 3 parts of potatoes boiled
in their jackets, 1 part of sour apples, 1 part of red
beets, 1 part of pickles, all sliced; mix carefully with

a sauce made of plenty of oil and some sour cream, or a sauce of milk, vinegar, pepper and salt so that the slices will remain whole. Put around it a border of lettuce mixed with oil, vinegar and salt and garnished with eggs that are not boiled too hard, each egg cut into 8 pieces. Serve with warm roast or cold meat and herring.

33. Endive Salad. When using the curled endives take only the yellow leaves and cut off the stems; the smooth endives are cut with the stem. The endives are washed shortly before making the salad, and mixed with oil, vinegar and salt, or, as directed in No. 1, with mashed potatoes, oil, vinegar, salt and pepper, or else serve it with a warm sour cream sauce and potatoes.

34. Celery Salad. The celery roots are washed and cooked in salted water until tender; peel, take out the hard parts and cut into slices and pour over them oil, vinegar, pepper and salt; the dish is garnished with celery leaves. Celery salad will keep for several days.

35. Swiss Salad. 1 part of beets, 1 part of celery roots cooked in salted water until tender (both cut into slices), 1—2 parts of endives or garden cresses are mixed with a dressing of oil, vinegar, pepper and salt.

36. Salad of Pickled Cucumbers. Salt or large vinegar pickles are finely sliced; put over them plenty of oil and if the pickles are not very sour add a little vinegar. This salad is very nice with soup meat or roast and also with potato salad.

37. Salad of Salted Salad Beans. Pour boiling water over the beans, leave the beans in this for a little while and then pour over them a dressing of salad oil, pepper and salt. A bacon or warm cream sauce can also be served with it.

38. Russian Salad with Beef. Good sourkrout made of Summer cabbage—krout made of Winter cabbage is too tough—is taken out of the cask, put into a cloth, pressed and cut; then pour over it oil and pepper.

Salads of all kinds must never be served to invalids.

R.—Sauces.

1. Hot and Cold Sauces for Fish, Meat, Vegetables and Pickles.

A. HOT SAUCES.

1. General Directions. Sauces should not be considered as of secondary importance, on the contrary they should always receive particular attention.

It is impossible to give exact directions regarding the right proportion or quantities of sauce to be prepared for the several dishes; good judgment must be your guide in this particular, but a few hints will be found useful.

For the lighter colored strong sauces or gravies the flour should be rubbed in hot butter until it curls, rises and turns yellow; for brown sauces it is stirred in the butter until it is of a good brown color (see Division A, No. 4); bouillon or water must be hot when added and then let the flour cook as long as possible to make the gravy clear and remove the flour taste entirely. Jelly-like bouillon is well adapted for preparing sauces of all kinds. Gravies must always be smooth, never lumpy, and by no means resemble a porridge, and be seasoned exactly right, that is, neither too much nor too little salt and vinegar must be used.

All gravies should possess an agreeable flavor of salt, spices or herbs, but none of these should be too prominent. For this reason English (Worcestershire) sauce, which is used to give sauces and ragouts a spicy flavor, should be added, a teaspoonful at a time only;

using too much will spoil the gravy, while when added in proper quantity it greatly improves it. When nutmeg or cloves are used in light sauces be careful to remove the heads, which will discolor the sauce. Cloves should be added very sparingly anyway.

Strength is the great desideratum in gravies, and when it is lacking or when a strong gravy must be made in haste, extract of beef is of inestimable value. It obviates the costly and time-consuming preparation of coulis, and the addition of ¼ or ½ teaspoonful of the extract to a finished gravy is all that is necessary to give it plenty of strength.

Sauces made with butter will be smoother and milder if cold butter is stirred through the finished gravy. If the yolks of eggs are to be stirred into the gravy, then this should be done just before serving, otherwise, if done on the fire, they will curdle. To prevent curdling altogether stir a pinch of flour with a tablespoonful of water to each egg yolk, gradually add under constant stirring some of the gravy, and then pour this into the boiling sauce, stirring it thoroughly.

Inasmuch as anchovies are frequently used in cooking, and a single stale anchovy will spoil the best dishes or gravies, it should be observed that anchovies of a yellow hue that have become dry and always have a rancid taste, must be rejected. They must furthermore be freshened until the water remains clear. After boning, again rinsing and chopping them, they must be cooked in the sauce for the shortest possible time to prove of value as a seasoning only.

2. Clear Meat Broth (Coulis). This broth is used for a good brown gravy. Take about ¼ pound of raw veal, a small piece of raw ham, a few eschalots, or 1 onion, 1 celery root, 1 parsley root, 1 carrot, 1 bay leaf, cloves and peppercorns. The meat and ham are cut into small pieces, coarsely pound the spices and all of this is put on the fire with ¼ pound of butter, stirring occasionally; it will be white for a time and then turn brown. When making a white broth put in some flour when the broth has turned yellow, let it turn yellow, then at once pour in some boiling bouillon.

When making a brown coulis brown the above ingredients, then put in the flour, stirring constantly until all has browned, add bouillon and brown broth or mushrooms, soup herbs, such as tarragon, sweet basil, etc., let it cook for at least 1 hour and then strain it. The broth must be very thick because it must be thinned when using. It will keep in the Winter for 2—3 weeks when left uncovered in a cool place and cooked once again in the meantime.

3. Brown Sauce. Brown a finely chopped onion in some butter with flour, browning the butter before putting in the flour and onion, add 1 carrot, ½ of a parsley root, tarragon, peppercorns and 1 bay leaf; after it has stewed for a short time add some boiling water and cook for 1 hour, strain, bring to a boil again, add as much extract of beef and a little salt as will make a strong sauce, and season with a little lemon juice. Capers, finely chopped anchovies or mushrooms can also be added. The last named must be very tender.

4. White Sauce is made as directed in the above receipt, using white instead of browned flour.

5. Truffle Sauce. Make a sauce as directed in receipt No. 4, adding nicely cleaned and cooked truffles cut into slices. A mushroom sauce can also be prepared according to receipt No. 3 or 4.

6. Robert Sauce. Fry 2 finely chopped onions in butter until brown, cook with white broth No. 2 or brown sauce No. 3, and make the necessary quantity of sauce, taking 1 pint of white wine, and just before serving add 2 tablespoonfuls of mustard. If the sauce is to be served with fish, mix with it at last a piece of butter.

7. Bearnease Sauce. Cook 1 tablespoonful of finely chopped eschalots or onions with 4 tablespoonfuls of vinegar, a few peppercorns, ½ bay leaf and a little estragon. When the vinegar is about half boiled away, pour it through a sieve, then stir the yolks of 4 eggs with 1 small cupful of strong bouillon made of extract of beef, put this into a pan containing boiling water (or into a double kettle), add ⅛ pound of butter in small pieces, stirring constantly until the sauce is thick, and at last the vinegar and, if liked, some finely chopped tarragon. All rich sauces, where plenty of butter and eggs are used, are apt to curdle when the sauce is stirred too long or when allowed to stand for even a moment. If this happens it can be remedied by twirling through the sauce a small piece of ice or a few drops of cold water.

8. Oyster Sauce. Take the beards from the oysters and cook the former in strong beef bouillon with a little pepper and a bay leaf. Then rub some butter and flour (see A, No. 3), stir this with the bouillon, nutmeg, 1 glassful of wine, the juice of a lemon, and just before serving add the oysters with their liquor as they will become hard if cooked, also the necessary salt and then stir through the sauce the yolks of a few eggs. 30 oysters are enough for 6—8 persons.

9. Bechamel Sauce. Take 8—10 onions and some lean ham, cut into small pieces and stew over a medium fire until tender; add a spoonful of flour rubbed in butter and 1 quart of milk (it is better to use half cream and half bouillon), let it boil thoroughly, stir through a colander, add to it a little white pepper and salt and heat the broth. Instead of using so many onions take half the quantity of sliced carrots or kohlrabi. The addition of a few finely chopped mushrooms and using cream instead of milk will greatly improve the sauce.

10. Diplomat's Sauce. Add to a Bechamel sauce 2 spoonfuls of crab butter and 1 spoonful of anchovy butter. This will make a very nice sauce for poultry, stewed sweetbreads and fish.

11. Yellow Caper Sauce for Pike and Salmon. Stir ½ spoonful of flour with a little water and add to this about 1½ pints of bouillon, 3 lemon slices without the seeds, a little finely pounded mace, bring to a boil, stirring constantly, and stir the yolks of 3 eggs through it. Then add ½ cupful of capers, but do not cook the sauce again, and ¼ pound of fresh butter, stirring in a little at a time. Serve hot over and with the fish.

12. Pike Sauce with Sour Cream. Take a good-sized piece of butter, rub it in flour, add to this the yolks of 4 eggs, 3 tablespoonfuls of sour cream and as much bouillon with a little pike broth to make the sauce of the proper consistency; then season with a little lemon juice or, if liked, a little nutmeg. Bring this sauce to a boil, stirring constantly.

13. Sauce with Boiled Fish, Salmon, etc. On a slow fire stew in 2 ounces of butter 1 large onion, 6 mushrooms, 1 carrot—all cut fine; add to this a little parsley and thyme, 3 cloves, 1 bay leaf and 1 blade of mace. When the onion is tender pour in ¾ quart of bouillon, let it cook for 1 hour, pour the broth through a sieve and then cook until well bound and clear with a little browned flour, using 1 tablespoonful of butter, the same quantity of flour, 1 glassful of wine, a little pepper and salt and the juice of a lemon.

Shortly before serving add to the sauce 8—10 finely chopped and cleaned anchovies and bring it to a boil once more.

14. Recamier Sauce for Fish, particularly Turbot. Bring 1 large cupful of bouillon, the same quantity of white wine and 1 glassful of champagne almost to a boil, stir the yolks of 8 eggs into the broth so that it will be well bound and bright, and then mix through it 3 ounces of the finest creamery butter. Season the sauce with lemon juice and serve immediately, as it loses its nice flavor if it stands for any length of time.

15. White Anchovy Sauce. Cook the bones of the anchovies and add to them a little coarsely pounded pepper and ground cloves, 1—2 bay leaves, a little lemon peel and some strong bouillon which can be made of remnants of meat. Then rub a few finely chopped onions or eschalots in butter, lightly brown 1—2 spoonfuls of flour in it, pour into this the boiling bouillon and then strain. Bring the well bound sauce to a boil, season with anchovy butter or a few anchovies chopped fine with butter (see Division A, No. 10), a little lemon juice, ½—1 glassful of white wine, a little finely pounded mace and stir into this sauce the yolks of 1—2 fresh eggs and a piece of fresh butter.

16. Herring Sauce. Freshen a herring in milk and chop it finely. Then rub a few finely chopped onions or eschalots in butter, lightly brown 1—2 spoonfuls of flour in this and stir as much water into it as will make a well bound sauce. The sauce is cooked with the herring, a little pepper, 1 bay leaf, 2—3 lemon slices or a little vinegar; stir into it a little meat extract, the yolks of 1—2 eggs and a piece of butter. Serve with fish or meat.

17. Spanish Sauce ("Espagnole"). Make a sauce as directed in No. 3 and cook with it 1 glassful of Madeira, skim and take off the fat and then add a little extract of beef.

18. Olive Sauce. Peel the olives from the stones with a small sharp knife in such a manner that they will roll together again. Then take some flour browned in butter, meat gravy or extract of beef bouillon, lemon peel and juice, mace, pickles peeled and finely cut, some peppercorns and a few eschalots. When this has cooked for a while pass it through a sieve, put in the olives and capers and cook for a few minutes longer.

19. Cucumber Sauce. Peel some cucumbers and divide them in two, take out the seeds and cut them into small pieces. They are cooked until tender in bouillon with vinegar, eschalots, some flour browned in butter, salt and a bay leaf.

Serve with veal and mutton. If you have onions pickled in dill and tarragon, add some of them with their vinegar and let the sauce cook until half done; the eschalots and vinegar are then omitted. The eschalots give the sauce an excellent flavor.

20. Hollandaise Sauce with Wine. Stir the yolks of 3 eggs and 1 teaspoonful of flour with white wine and water half and half until smooth, add some mace, stir until it comes to a boil, take from the fire and mix with the sauce ¼ pound of butter and a few drops of lemon juice. Serve with artichokes, mushrooms, fish and also with tongue.

21. Hollandaise Sauce. Stir the yolks of 3 eggs and 1 teaspoonful of flour in 1 pint of water and salt, mace or nutmeg, bring to a boil, stirring constantly, then quickly take from the fire. Then stir ¼ pound of butter and a little vinegar through the sauce. To this sauce can be added oysters, chopped anchovies, capers and mustard.

**22. Shrimp Sauce for different kinds of Fish, par=
ticularly Soles and Turbot.** Rub ½ tablespoonful of flour
in some fresh butter, stir to it 1 cupful of bouillon,
lemon juice and a blade of mace, and when it boils add
¼ pound of butter and plenty of scalded shrimps, then
take the sauce from the fire and stir into it the yolks of
2 eggs and a little salt.

23. Crab Sauce. Make a sauce as directed in the
above receipt, using crab butter. Instead of shrimps use
crab tails. Both are cut into small pieces and must not
cook in the sauce.

24. Holstein Sauce for Salt Water Fish. For each
person take 1 ounce of butter and a trifle of flour. Let
the flour get hot in the butter, stir into it ⅔ parts of
fish water and ⅓ part of white wine, or enough boiling
bouillon to make a well bound sauce, add some nutmeg
and fine white pepper and if necessary a trifle of salt,
stir the sauce until it commences to boil, take it from
the fire, stir through it a piece of butter and some
lemon juice. If wished the yolks of a few eggs may be
stirred through the sauce.

25. Saxon Fish Sauce. Rub some flour and butter
in a pan, add to this some finely chopped eschalots,
fish broth—but not enough to make the sauce salty—
a little white wine, lemon slices, plenty of mustard,
vinegar, and if wished a little sugar. Cook the sauce
slowly for a few minutes and before serving stir through
it a good-sized piece of butter.

26. Butter Sauce for boiled Salt Water Fish, as Soles
or Turbot. Put some unsalted butter into a double
kettle to melt, stir until it commences to bubble, then
put in slowly, constantly stirring, some fish water, also
a little finely chopped parsley, stir the sauce some five
minutes longer, but do not let it boil.

27. Butter for Fish and Potatoes. Take half of the
butter which is to be used and rub it in some flour. If
the butter is but slightly salty put in some fish water,
if quite salty use clear water and bring to a boil. The
remaining butter is added to the sauce when it is taken
from the fire and the yolk of an egg stirred through it.

28. Mustard Sauce for Fish. Take a good-sized piece of butter, several tablespoonfuls of mustard, fish broth and water, half and half, cook with 1—2 teaspoonfuls of dissolved cornstarch and then stir the yolk of an egg and a piece of butter through it.

29. Fish Sauce. 5 onions cut into small pieces and 1 spoonful of flour are rubbed in some butter and cooked with the fish water; afterwards stir in a small piece of sugar and a little vinegar and nutmeg.

30. Mustard Sauce for Fish and Potatoes. (Also served with eggs.) Melt some kidney suet the size of an egg and prepared as directed under A, No. 17, and stir into it an even tablespoonful of flour and a little salt, and then pour in enough boiling water to make a well bound sauce. Let it cook for a few minutes, take from the fire and stir through it a piece of butter the size of an egg and a few tablespoonfuls of mustard.

31. A Mustard Sauce for Soup Meat, etc. Cream ¼ pound of butter, stir into it the yolks of 6 eggs, a small cupful of mustard, a little flour, the juice of half a lemon, sugar according to taste, 2 cupfuls of claret and enough bouillon (about 1 cupful) so that the sauce will be well bound. Put the sauce on the fire just before serving, and stir constantly until it comes to a boil. This quantity of sauce is sufficient for 10 persons.

32. Sorrel Sauce for Fish and Soup Meat. Take a handful of sorrel leaves, wash and cut them finely. Then brown 1 heaping tablespoonful of flour, a piece of butter the size of an egg, add the sorrel, stir for a few minutes until tender and pour in as much bouillon as is necessary to bind the sauce, stirring constantly; add some nutmeg and salt and when it boils stir with it some butter and the yolks of 1—2 eggs, or instead of the eggs 1—2 spoonfuls of thick sour cream.

33. Boiled Horse Radish Sauce for Soup Meat. The horse radish is grated and kept covered so that it will not lose its strength. In the meantime cook bouillon with plenty of fat, currants, a little vinegar and a piece of sugar, salt, butter and rolled crackers, and stir through the horse radish. The sauce must be quite thick Serve with beef, veal or smoked meats.

34. Parsley Sauce for Soup Meat; also served with Potatoes. Rub kidney suet in flour, add salt and water and after it has boiled stir through it a piece of butter, finely chopped parsley and extract of beef.

35. Chestnut Sauce for Smoked Meats. Put the chestnuts on the fire in boiling water, cook until tender and then peel. Put them into a dish in which a half or a whole spoonful of sugar was lightly browned, and pour over them sauce No. 3, but without capers, anchovies and mushrooms.

This sauce is served with smoked meats and brown or winter cabbage.

36. Claret Sauce with Raisins, for stewing Beef Tongue, Sour Rolls and Beef. 2 tablespoonfuls of flour are browned in butter and stirred with tongue broth and water; to this add 2 ounces of raisins cooked in water until tender, 1 cupful of claret, lemon juice or some vinegar, lemon peel, mace, a few pounded cloves, a little sugar and salt. The tongue, either whole or cut into slices, is put into this sauce until it comes to a boil; then add a little extract of beef, which gives the sauce a better taste and a nicer color.

37. Raisin Sauce. No. 2. Heat a piece of kidney suet the size of a walnut, brown in this a finely sliced onion and 1—2 spoonfuls of flour, stir with boiling water to a well bound sauce, add some ground and whole cloves, salt, plenty of raisins, and pickles cut into small slices, let the raisins cook until tender and stir together with a trifle of sugar or syrup with ¼ of a teaspoonful of extract of beef. Cut the meat into slices and stew slowly in the sauce for 10—15 minutes.

38. White Sauce for stewing Tongue or Boiled Beef. Brown onions cut into small pieces in butter and flour, pour into this some of the broth in which the tongue was cooked, add 2—3 bay leaves, a little white pepper, nutmeg and a glassful of white wine or some pickles peeled and cut into slices. Stew the tongue slices in this for ¼ hour and when serving strain the sauce and stir through it the yolk of an egg.

39. Sauce for Head of Veal. Brown a few eschalots or 2 onions in butter, stir in 2 tablespoonfuls of flour, some veal broth and boiling water to make a well bound sauce and let this boil for ½ hour with 2 carrots, parsley roots, 1 bay leaf, a little cayenne pepper and lemon peel. Then pass the sauce through a sieve, put in a few lemon slices, a little sugar and salt, let it cook and then stir in a small teaspoonful of extract of beef, a little butter and a glassful of Madeira or white wine.

40. Sauce for Veal, Lamb or Chicken. For 6 persons take 2 teaspoonfuls of flour and rub it with a piece of butter, pour into this 1 cupful of strong chicken broth, nutmeg, lemon juice and salt, cook the sauce and stir with it the yolks of 3 eggs, and a piece of fresh butter. A little chopped parsley can be stirred with the yolks of the eggs, or else 1—1½ tablespoonfuls of capers can be added. The sauce must be well bound.

41. English Crab Sauce for Cauliflower. The yolks of 4 eggs, 1 tablespoonful of flour, nutmeg, salt, 1 cupful of crab butter. Add to this 1 pint of bouillon, constantly stirring, until just before it commences to boil, then take from the fire and stir for a short time longer. The sauce must be well bound. This sauce served with cauliflower makes a nice dish.

42. English Butter Sauce for Vegetables. Rub ½ pound of butter with 2 tablespoonfuls of flour, add salt, pepper, some nutmeg and the necessary bouillon to make a well bound sauce; a double kettle is necessary for its preparation. This sauce is served with vegetables cooked in salted water only.

43. Sauce for Cauliflower. Rub ½ tablespoonful of flour in some fresh butter, pour in some fresh milk or bouillon, or what is better half bouillon and half cauliflower water, nutmeg, salt, and stir until the sauce is quite thick; stir through it at the last the yolks of 1—2 eggs and a piece of fresh butter.

44. Asparagus Sauce. No. 1. For 4 persons take the yolks of 2 eggs and a heaping tablespoonful of flour, stir into this 2 tablespoonfuls of sweet or sour cream and 1 cupful of asparagus broth or water, add nutmeg and a little lemon juice or vinegar, and a piece of sugar the size of a hazelnut, beat the sauce over a quick fire with a beater just before it boils, take from the fire, stir into it a piece of butter the size of an egg and pour into the sauce boat. If the sauce is not salty enough add a trifle. The sauce must be well bound.

45. Asparagus Sauce. No. 2. For 4 persons take a large piece of butter, 3—4 tablespoonfuls of asparagus broth, or water, a little salt, and 1 spoonful of rolled crackers. Give the sauce a seasoning of lemon juice or vinegar and bring to a boil, constantly stirring.

46. Sauce for Asparagus, Cauliflower, etc. 1 pint of Rhinewine is stirred with the yolks of 8 eggs, 3 ounces of butter, 1 cupful of the vegetable broth, 1 cupful of bouillon, a little salt, pepper, a trifle of sugar and about 1 teaspoonful of cornmeal in a double kettle, and cooked until thick. Pour over the vegetables and serve.

47. Sour Egg Sauce for Salad Beans, also for Pota=toes. Take 1 cupful of cold water and mix with it enough vinegar to give the sauce the required acidity. Stir into this the yolks of 3 eggs and 1 teaspoonful of flour, a piece of butter, some nutmeg and if the butter is but slightly salty, add a very little salt. Beat the sauce constantly with a beater until just before it boils, take from the fire and stir for a few minutes so that it will not curdle, then stir into it another piece of butter.

48. Sour Milk Sauce for Bean Salads, Hot Potatoes and Endives. Take a piece of kidney suet, try it out as directed under A, No. 17, heat and stir into it ½—1 tablespoonful of flour, pour into it enough milk to make a well bound sauce, season with pepper and salt, or if liked a little nutmeg, and bring to a boil quickly. Then take the sauce from the fire, stir into it a large piece of butter and a little vinegar, stir through the beans, put them on the stove until heated through, take from the fire, and serve them in the sauce with the potatoes.

49. Sauce made of Onions pickled in Tarragon and Dill, for stewing Soup Meat or to pour over Potatoes. Take a piece of butter or kidney suet, heat it and brown in it 1 tablespoonful of flour, stir into it some good broth or some water with some dissolved extract of beef, salt, pepper, 1—2 bay leaves, some pickled onions and as much of the onion vinegar as is necessary to pleasantly acidulate the sauce, and then cook. Stew the meat in this for about 10 minutes, or pour the sauce over the potatoes.

50. Brown Onion Sauce with Bacon for Potatoes. Cut some bacon into little pieces, fry slowly until brown, turning the pieces; then take plenty of onions, also cut into small pieces, add to the bacon, brown them, then add 1—2 tablespoonfuls of flour, and stir this all together. Add vinegar, water and salt to taste and let the sauce cook.

51. Light Onion Sauce with Bacon for Potatoes. Cut some bacon into small pieces and try slowly, lightly brown some flour in this and pour in some boiling water. Then put in plenty of onions cut into small pieces, cook until tender, and add a little salt, pepper and a little vinegar.

52. Poor Man's Sauce. In 2 ounces of butter brown a tablespoonful of flour, add to this a tablespoonful of grated brown bread and a tablespoonful of grated roll, cook this for ¼ of an hour with 2 cupfuls of water, a little extract of beef and a glassful of wine. Season the sauce with pepper and lemon peel and serve with boiled veal or lamb.

53. Bacon Sauce for Salad. Cut the bacon into small pieces and fry to a light yellow color, stir with the yolks of 2 eggs, 1 spoonful of flour, 4—5 spoonfuls of vinegar, a little water and salt, and bring the sauce to a boil, constantly stirring until it is well bound. It must be cold before serving with the salad.

54. Syrup Sauce for Salad or Meat. For this sauce take butter, fried out bacon or other good fat, lightly brown in this 2 tablespoonfuls of flour, and if liked 1—2 finely sliced onions, stir with boiling water to a smooth sauce and add as much vinegar, syrup, salt and pepper as will give the sauce a sweet-sour taste. If the meat is to be stewed in this, add 2 ounces of currants, 4 bay leaves and a few ground cloves.

B. COLD SAUCES AND GRAVIES.

55. A La Diable Sauce. Served with all Kinds of Cold Meats. Grate the yolks of 4 hard boiled eggs, add 6 tablespoonfuls of claret, 4 spoonfuls of salad oil, 2 spoonfuls of mustard, juice of 2 juicy lemons, a little fine white pepper, salt, chopped eschalots, ¼ of a finely sliced apple, a little sugar and if the sauce is not sour enough a little wine vinegar. Rub the yolks of 2 hard boiled eggs with a little vinegar until smooth, add the oil, a little at a time, then the other ingredients and stir the sauce until the oil no longer appears.

56. Remoulade Sauce. 2 large grated onions, the finely grated yolks of 3 hard boiled eggs, 8 teaspoonfuls of mustard, 4 tablespoonfuls of salad oil, 1 tablespoonful of sugar, 1 cupful of wine vinegar, white pepper and salt, and if liked 3—4 finely chopped anchovies. This is all stirred together, but not boiled, then stir briskly through a sieve. Capers can also be added if wished.

This sauce is appropriate with all cold fish, roasts and pickled meats.

57. Mayonnaise with all Kinds of Cold Fish and Meat, and different Meat Salads. No. 1. Take the yolks of 3 hard boiled eggs and the yolk of 1 raw egg, rub smooth with 2 teaspoonfuls of mustard, 1—2 teaspoonfuls of sugar, 1 teaspoonful of grated eschalots, salt, a very little white pepper and the juice of a lemon or a little wine vinegar. Then add to it, constantly stirring, a very small cupful of salad oil, pouring in a very little at a time, and when this is all stirred together, gradually add ½ cupful of strong bouillon and as much vinegar as is deemed necessary. The sauce must be well bound and smooth. The flavor of the mayonnaise can be changed by adding some anchovy butter, capers, finely sliced vinegar pickles, tarragon or parsley.

Some people prefer the mayonnaise made of the yolks of raw eggs only. Take the yolks of 5 eggs, rub them until fine, add a little pepper, salt and mustard and stir with the yolks of the eggs. 1 small cupful of salad oil is added to this drop by drop, stirring constantly, finally adding a few drops of lemon juice. If the sauce is quite thick stir to it according to taste a little wine vinegar.

For lobster- or fish mayonnaise the eggs of the lobster are stirred with the mayonnaise, which gives it a deep red color.

For elaborate dinner parties the above mayonnaise is often served with caviar to cold fish in jelly. Put the caviar on a sieve, rinse in cold water until the roes are separated into single kernels and just before serving mix with the mayonnaise. For poultry or veal rolls in jelly, stir into the mayonnaise, according to the French style, about 3 spoonfuls of finely chopped boiled ham, first passing the ham through a sieve, then adding it to the mayonnaise.

58. Boiled Mayonnaise. No. 2. (Very nice and easily digestible.) Stir 4 raw eggs, 3 spoonfuls of salad oil, 1 spoonful of vinegar, salt, pepper and 3 spoonfuls of bouillon in a double kettle until thick, whip the sauce until it has cooled somewhat and stir through it 4 tablespoonfuls of thick sour cream. Another way is to take the yolks of 6 eggs, 2 spoonfuls of flour, 1 pint of sweet cream, 4 spoonfuls of oil, 4 spoonfuls of vinegar, salt and pepper, and stir until smooth, whip in a double kettle until thick and then pass through a sieve. Butter is often used instead of oil in this mayonnaise, but does not taste as well. Fine soup herbs, capers, cucumbers, etc., can also be used.

59. Sauce for Cold Grouse and Pork Rolls in Jelly. 2—3 tablespoonfuls of calves' foot jelly or gelatine, 3—4 tablespoonfuls of olive oil, 3 tablespoonfuls of tarragon vinegar or sharp wine vinegar and tarragon, peppermint and eschalots, all finely chopped, white pepper and salt. Stir this all together until it is a thick sauce and well bound.

60. Cumberland Sauce for Pig's Head, etc. Stir 1 teaspoonful of mustard with 1 tablespoonful of olive oil, add ½ bottle of Burgundy, 1 large cupful of thick brown sauce No. 2 or 3, and 6 ounces of currant jelly; whip the sauce until all the ingredients are well mixed. Then add salt, pepper and lemon juice and put the sauce into a cool place until wanted.

61. Prepared Mustard for various Kinds of Meats.
Slice 4 onions, 4 pieces of garlic, and 8 bay leaves very
fine and cook for 10 minutes in 1 quart of sharp wine
vinegar, add some sifted mustard meal and rub with a
wooden spoon until it is thick. Then add 6 ounces of
fine sugar, a few cloves, some cinnamon and put into a
covered glass.

62. Sour Mustard. Cook some vinegar with finely
cut onions, garlic, tarragon, bay leaves, dill, peppermint or wide leaved cresses, whole pepper, cloves and
salt, pass through a sieve, and after it is cold stir into
it some mustard meal.

Served with cold meats. Will keep for a long time
when bottled.

63. Herring Sauce. Freshen a herring in milk, bone
and then chop it together with 3 hard boiled eggs and
a few onions. Stir to a sauce with pepper, oil and
vinegar. Served with cold roasts.

64. Raw Horseradish Sauce. Stir ½ cupful of vinegar and 1 cupful of sweet cream or water with salt and
sugar, and mix with sufficient horseradish, which must
be grated just before wanted, to make a thick sauce.
Serve with melted butter with boiled fish, especially
carp.

65. Raw Radish Sauce. Wash and peel black radishes and grate them; mix with a little salt, vinegar
and oil, and serve with soup meat. A good sauce can
also be made by taking 4 spoonfuls of grated horseradish, 2 grated apples, omitting the oil and adding
a little sugar to the vinegar. Serve with bread and
butter.

66. Chives Sauce for cold or warm boiled Beef.
Take the yolks of a few hard boiled eggs, grate them,
mix with thick sour cream, add a little vinegar and a
few spoonfuls of oil, stirring constantly until well
bound; then add a little more vinegar, pepper and salt.
This sauce served with thinly sliced veal is a nice side
dish for salads or potatoes.

67. Sauce for Meat Jelly and Cold Meats. No. 1.
Take the grated yolks of a few hard boiled eggs, also

Fruit — Früchte.

1 Barberry—Berberitze; 2 Currant—Johannisbeere; 3 Grape—Weinbeere; 4 Hazelnut—Haselnusz; 5 Nectrine—Nectarine; 6 Mango-fruit—Mangofrucht; 7 Pistachio-nut—Pistazie; 8 Date—Dattel; 9 Plum—Pflaume; 10 Fig—Feige; 11 Blackberry—Brombeere; 12 Apricot—Aprikose; 13 Mulberry—Maulbeere; 14 Cherry —Kirsche; 15 Prune—Zwetsche; 16 Damask-plum—Damascenerpflaume; 17 Quince— Quitte; 18 Pineapple—Ananas; 19 Orange—Orange; 20 Raspberry—Himbeere; 21 Almond—Mandel; 22 Raisin—Rosine; 23 Walnut—Wallnusz; 24 Chestnut—Kastanie; 25 Pomegranate—Granatapfel; 26 Citron—Limone; 27 Lemon—Citrone; 28 Gooseberry—Stachelbeere; 29 Cranberry—Preisselbeere; 30 Strawberry—Erdbeere; 31 Pear—Birne; 32 Melon—Melone; 33 Peaches—Pfirsiche; 34 Medlar—Mispel; 35 Apple—Apfel.

some wine vinegar, oil, sugar, mustard, a little pepper and salt. Stir the yolks of the eggs with the vinegar and add the other ingredients, constantly stirring. The sauce must have a tart flavor, but not too sour, and it must not taste too strongly of mustard. If wished capers, finely chopped anchovies and eschalots can be mixed through the sauce.

68. Sauce for Meat Jelly. No. 2. Grated sour apples with mustard, oil, vinegar, sugar and a very little salt stirred together.

69. Vegetable Butter. Take 1 tablespoonful of finely chopped parsley, eschalots and chervil, mix with ¼ pound of clarified and creamed butter, add the juice of a lemon and a little salt, pepper and nutmeg. Especially for beef steaks.

70. A good Salad Sauce. 1—2 fresh hard boiled eggs, the fresh yolk of 1 raw egg, a little wine vinegar, 4 spoonfuls of salad oil, 1 spoonful of mustard, a little salt, a very little white pepper, 2 finely chopped eschalots, 1 tablespoonful of claret, 2 teaspoonfuls of finely chopped tarragon. Rub the yolks of the eggs with the vinegar, then, constantly stirring, add mustard, pepper, eschalots, tarragon, a little salt (and if needed a little sugar), and by degrees the oil and wine. At last stir in as much vinegar as will give the sauce the required acidity; too much vinegar will spoil the salad. The sauce must be well stirred so that the oil will not be noticeable. By adding a little anchovy butter, the sauce will be much improved.

2. Wine, Milk and Fruit Sauces.

71. White Wine Sauce. Stir 1 heaping teaspoonful of flour with the yolks of 4 eggs and 1 pint of white wine; take 3 tablespoonfuls of sugar, lemon peel and a little cinnamon, stir all together and let it come almost to a boil, stirring constantly, then pour into another vessel, stir so that it will not curdle and put into a sauce boat.

72. White Cream Sauce. Take 4 fresh whipped eggs, 1 large cupful of wine, 1 teaspoonful of flour, 2 heaping tablespoonfuls of sugar, a few slices of lemon and some whole cinnamon (vanilla is better). This is whipped with an egg beater on the stove until it nearly boils, then pour into another vessel and whip for another minute so that it will not curdle.

73. White Cream Sauce with Rum. Take 1 large cupful of wine, 1 teaspoonful of fine flour, 2 eggs, the juice of 1 lemon, the thin peel of half of the lemon and 3 tablespoonfuls of sugar; whip constantly until the cream is thick, then pour into another dish and whip a small glassful of rum through it.

74. Cold Punch Sauce is made the same as the preceding, taking instead of the whole eggs the yolks of 3 large or 4 small eggs, stir the sauce until it nearly boils, then take from the fire, let it cool, and add a glassful of arrac. This is a good sauce for cold puddings.

75. Parisian Sauce for warm Puddings. Whip 1 pint of sherry with 2½ heaping teaspoonfuls of sugar, the yolks of 6 eggs and 3 spoonfuls of apricot jelly until it nearly boils, then quickly stir into it 6 tablespoonfuls of thick sweet cream. Serve immediately.

76. English Sauce for Plum Pudding. Stir 10 tablespoonfuls of apple jelly with 5 spoonfuls of brandy until it becomes watery, then add 2 cupfuls of thick sweet cream, whip on the stove until boiling hot and serve immediately.

77. Claret Sauce. Take 1 pint of claret, ¼ pound of sugar, a few pieces of cinnamon, the thin rind of half of a lemon and 2 tablespoonfuls of raspberry- or currant jelly, cover the dish and put it on the stove until it is boiling hot, then smooth some cornstarch in cold water and add as much of it to the sauce as will give it the proper consistency. Serve in a sauce boat.

78. Claret Sauce with dried Currants. Take 1—2 ounces of dried currants, ½ of a lemon cut into thin slices (being careful to remove the seeds), and a few pieces of cinnamon. Put this into 1 large cupful of water, cover and cook slowly for about a quarter of an hour, or until the currants have become softened. Then add 1 large cupful of wine and sugar and when it is boiling hot, add a little cornstarch smoothed in water, to bind the sauce.

79. Cold Claret Sauce with Rum. This sauce is made the same as claret sauce, only adding more sugar. After taking it from the fire and it has cooled somewhat, stir through it 1 small cupful of rum.

80. Red Cream Sauce. Follow the directions given for white cream sauce, but use claret. Instead of taking lemon slices use fruit syrup or currant jelly if preferred.

81. Pure Sago Sauce. For 6 persons take about 2⅓ ounces of sago, wash and cook slowly with a little water, whole cinnamon and lemon peel, then add some sugar, the juice of a lemon and some wine; boil until the sauce is of the proper thickness, let it come to a boil again and then strain. Pure sago must cook for at least 2 hours. Pearl sago can also be used and requires only ½ hour cooking.

82. Chocolate Sauce. After dissolving 2½ ounces of chocolate (see under V, Nos. 4 and 5), add 1 large cupful of sweet cream, 1 large cupful of milk flavored with a little vanilla, add sugar and stir the sauce with the yolks of 2 eggs.

83. Almond Sauce. 1 ounce of pounded almonds (2 or 3 can be bitter), are cooked slowly with milk and a little vanilla for a quarter of an hour, strain, then add 1 pint of milk or cream, 2 teaspoonfuls of flour and sugar, cook again, then stir with the yolks of 2—3 eggs.

84. Cold Cream Sauce with Jelly or Claret. Appropriate with milk dishes of all kinds. Take 1 cupful of dissolved raspberry or currant jelly—or the juice—whip with 1 large cupful of sweet cream until it is creamy. Or else whip half claret and half thick cream with sugar and cinnamon until it creams, and then stir through it a few spoonfuls of arrac.

85. Sauce made of Fresh Currants. Served warm or cold. Take 1 pint of fresh currant juice, ½ pound of sugar and a little cinnamon. Put the juice of the currants on the stove with 1 large cupful of water together with sugar and cinnamon, remove any scum that may appear and thicken the sauce with a little cornstarch smoothed in water.

86. Currant Juice Sauce. After the juice has been pressed from the currants as in making jelly, put it into a dish and stir with powdered sugar for a quarter of an hour before serving. To a pint of juice take ½ pound of sugar. This sauce, which has a pretty color and is very refreshing and delicious, is unexcelled for blancmangers and cold rice dishes.

87. Raspberry Sauce. Cook raspberry sauce or jelly with water and white sour wine, cinnamon and sugar and thicken a little with cornstarch smoothed in water.

88. Strawberry Sauce. Take fresh picked strawberries (wild berries are the best), press them through a strainer, mix with ¼ pound of sugar, the juice of 1 lemon and about 1 pint of Madeira, whip the sauce on the stove until it boils. This sauce is served warm with puddings.

If you wish to serve this sauce cold, with cold puddings, do not boil it but stir with strawberry juice, sugar and vanilla and about 1 pint of thick sweet cream for about half an hour. Both kinds are very good sauces.

89. Cream Sauce from Raspberry or Currant Juice. Whip 4 fresh eggs, 1 teaspoonful of flour and 1 pint of fresh raspberries or currant juice on the stove, sweeten with sugar and whip with an egg beater, but do not boil. When taking the juice of preserved berries mix with one-third the quantity of wine or water.

90. Sauce made of Fresh or Dried Cherries. Take dried sour cherries with a few stones, pound them in a mortar with the addition of a few lemon slices, and then strain through a large sieve. Then cook the sauce again, add sugar, ground cinnamon and a few cloves, thicken the sauce with cornstarch smoothed in water until it is of the proper consistency. If liked, a little arrac can also be added.

91. Sauce for Farina Pudding. Cook 1 pint of white wine, 1 pint of water, the juice of a lemon and a little of the peel with ½ pound of sugar and 1 tablespoonful of cornstarch smoothed in a little water for a few minutes, then stir through it a cupful of preserved tutti-frutti, (see N, No. 36).

92.   Sauce for Nos. 140, 141, 142 and 143, Division S.
1 small cupful of milk and ¼ pound of sifted flour, the yolks of 4 eggs, a little salt, then the beaten whites of the eggs with a tablespoonful of rum mixed through the sauce. Dip the bread or roll into this and bake in butter or lard.

S.—Pastry, Cakes, etc.

I. CAKES.

1. General Directions. To be successful with cakes, pastry, etc., their ingredients should be put into a warm place for a few hours—in the Winter for a night—to get them to the proper temperature, and the stirring and working should also be done in a warm place where there is no draught. With pie crust and puff paste this is not necessary. When the whites of eggs are to be frothed, they should not be brought where it is warm before they are to be used. Directions for frosting see A, No. 2.

The flour and cornstarch used must always be of the best quality. As soon as warm both the flour and sugar should be sifted; for very fine cakes the addition of some rice flour is recommended. Flour and sugar are more or less moist and should then be sifted after warming and drying.

The butter used should be of the best and unsalted. Cream the butter, put it on boiling water or on top of the stove until soft, but it must not melt, then with a wooden ladle rub it to a cream.

The eggs must be perfectly fresh; a single slightly stale egg will be sufficient to spoil the cake, and for this reason eggs should be broken into a separate dish. The extract of lemon can often be substituted for lemon peel and juice. Lemon peel used in too large a quantity will impart an unpleasant taste to any dish, and the same is the case with cardamom seeds, which are not liked by everybody. Cakes in which yeast is used can be nicely flavored with rose water. Before the dough is put into the mould be sure that the latter has been properly prepared, nicely cleaned, rubbed with butter and dredged with rolled crackers or grated bread so that it will not be necessary to first get the mould ready while the dough is waiting for it. Many a cake is spoiled through this cause. Puff paste does not require a buttered mould.

Puff paste must never be kneaded, because this will make it heavy. To have it light and flakey put the butter into the middle of the flour, stir and work the dough with a knife at first, then with the ball of the hand, turning the dough frequently and folding it from the sides to the center, often dusting with flour and continue in this manner until flour and butter are thoroughly mixed; then set aside in a cool place for a few hours.

The addition of baking powder in biscuits, bread and almond cakes and the like will tend to make them lighter.

When using yeast be cautious to get it fresh and sweet. For baking with yeast the milk must be lukewarm and the flour, butter, sugar and the baking dish should also be slightly warm. When using baking powder all of the ingredients should be cold. After the dough has been well stirred, it will be greatly improved, smoother and finer if the mass is vigorously and uninterruptedly beaten for a while. To beat a soft dough use the flat side of a ladle. Firm doughs are beaten on the moulding board; fold the dough and continue the beating and folding as long as indicated in the several receipts. Afterwards set the dough in a warm place where there is no draught, cover with a clean cloth and let it raise for 1½—2 hours. Slow fermentation produces a mild dough, whereas if it raises too quickly the dough will be tough.

The degree of heat in the oven can be tested by means of a piece of paper. If the paper soon turns to a yellow (not black) color in the oven, this indicates the *first* degree of heat and is sufficient for puff paste and yeast doughs; if it turns yellow slowly it indicates the *second* degree of heat, fit for most kinds of baking; the *third* degree must be still lower for cakes, etc., that should dry more than bake.

In the receipts for the cakes, the time for baking is given as precisely as possible, but the length of time to finish the baking depends largely upon the heat of the oven; there are various tests for determining how near the cake is done, such as piercing it with a straw or something similar, which, if dry when drawn out, indicates that the cake is done. Leaving the cake in the oven unnecessarily long is very detrimental to it, particularly if it is a yeast cake.

After the cake has been taken out of the oven let it stand in the mould for about 10 minutes where there is no draught. Then take it out of the mould but do not bring it into a cold room at once. Cake moulds made so that the outer rim is removable are the best, because then the cake can be taken out without shaking, which causes spongy cakes to fall. All kinds of cakes should be turned out of the mould onto a wire cake cooler, which will allow them to cool more readily. The mould should be cleaned with soft paper or a cloth immediately after being used.

Cakes will keep best in a tightly covered porcelain or glass dish. Tin cake boxes are also very good, but must be cleaned from time to time with hot water and frequently aired. Yeast or fruit cakes are the best when fresh, although they are good after a few days when placed in the oven for a few moments before serving. If it should happen that a fruit cake is not baked until done at first, it will not lose in taste if it is finished the next day in a hot oven.

2. Puff Paste. 1 pound of dry flour, 1 pound of good butter, 1—1½ cupfuls of cold water, 1 small glassful of rum or arrac and 1 whole egg.

The evening before wanted, wash the butter so that it will become firm, spread on a plate to about the thickness of 1 inch and put into the cellar. The next day put the flour on the bread board, make a depression in the center of the flour, put in the egg, water and rum, stir with a knife and work the dough with the hands as you would bread. It must not be too stiff, neither must it stick to the hands. Then roll out about ½ inch thick, put the butter on this, fold the dough and set aside in a cool place for a while. Then roll again, using but very little flour for dusting. Brush off any flour that may be on the dough, fold again and set aside for a second time. Proceed in this manner until the dough has been set aside four times. Before rolling the dough for the fourth time, cut off a piece for the edge, roll the larger piece until quite thin, lay on this a plate of the desired size and cut the dough, dust a very little flour over this and fold it, because it can be handled better that way, and put it onto the plate, brush off any flour that may be on the dough, wet the edge all around with egg or a little water, lay an edge of the rolled dough on this and with a knife cut into the dough in various places so that it will not blister. Proceed in this manner until all the dough is used and bake immediately, otherwise the puff paste will not be good. Bake to a golden brown.

3. Saarbruck Puff Paste. ⅔ pound of butter prepared as directed under No. 2, ⅔ pound of flour, 2 tablespoonfuls of arrac and a large half cupful of cold water. Half of the flour is made into a dough with water and the arrac, then the butter and the remaining flour kneaded into the dough, each part rolled separately, then lay one on the other and roll out three times more.

4. Good Crust for Pies and Pastry. To 1 pound of flour take ¾ pound of good freshened butter, 1 whole and the yolk of 1 egg, and 2 tablespoonfuls of brandy or rum. The flour is put into a pan, the butter broken into small pieces and mixe through the flour. Make a depression in the center of the flour, beat the egg in ½ cupful of water, add to the flour with the brandy, stir to a dough with a knife rolling it four times like puff paste.

REMARK.—This dough is especially nice in the Summer, because in warm weather a puff paste is hard to make for those not accustomed to it.

5. English Crust for Tarts, Cookies, etc. 1 pound of flour, ¼ pound of sifted sugar, ¼ pound of pounded almonds, the yolk of 1 raw egg, the yolks of 9 hard boiled eggs chopped very fine, 10 ounces of freshened butter broken into small pieces and enough white wine to make an easily rolled dough.

6. Good Batter for large Cakes. To 1⅛ pounds of flour take 1 pound of freshened butter, 2 ounces of sugar and ½ wineglassful of cold water. This is all worked together, but not kneaded. Then set the dough aside in a cool place, roll and bake in a moderately hot oven.

7. Yeast Batter for German Fruit Cakes. 1 pound of warmed flour, ½ pound of freshened butter, 1 egg, the yolks of 2 eggs, 3 spoonfuls of sugar, 1 small cupful of lukewarm milk, 2 tablespoonfuls of dissolved yeast. Mix the yeast with a very little sugar and a teaspoonful of salt, stir one-half of the flour with milk and one-half of the yeast, then add the remaining flour, the softened butter, yeast and salt, stir the dough as given under No. 1, roll or press it with the hands and set aside to raise in a warm place.

8. A Cream for large fresh Prune Cake. 1 quart of thick sour cream, 2 tablespoonfuls of sugar, 1 teaspoonful of cinnamon, vanilla or a little grated lemon peel. Whip up the cream with the whole eggs, and when the cake is almost done put it over the cake a spoonful at a time. After the cake is baked, strew some sugar thickly over it.

9. Frosting for Tarts or small Cakes and for Decorating. ¼ pound of powdered sugar, the white of an egg beaten to a froth, the juice of a large lemon or 1 tablespoonful of rum or arrac.

Stir the sugar and lemon peel together, then add the beaten white of the egg, a spoonful at a time, stirring constantly until as white as snow. This icing is poured over the cake after it has cooled, drying it in the sun or in the oven. The cake can be decorated with powdered sugar, but this must be done before the icing has cooled.

10. To color Icing. A portion of the icing can be colored, leaving part of it white for decorating: Brown—by grating into it a little chocolate; red—by stirring into it a little currant- or raspberry juice; dark red—by adding a trifle of cochineal; (do not season the icing with lemon or it will have a yellowish red color; a little dissolved red gelatine can also be used); blue—with kermes and a little lemon juice; violet—with extract of violet; yellow—lemon rind grated on sugar or saffron, dropping a little brandy on it; green—with a little spinach juice.

11. Colored Sugar for Decorating. Put ¼ pound of poppy seed into a dish, boil ¼ pound of sugar dissolved in a little water, and after it has cooled somewhat put 1 spoonful over the poppy seed and stir with the flat hand until it commences to get cold. Repeat 8—10 times, when all of the sugar will be used.

The coloring is done in the following manner; Red—with a little cochineal; yellow—saffron (using but very little), letting it draw in a few drops of brandy; some of the sugar remains white. Many colors are adulterated and none other than the above mentioned should be used.

12. Lubec Marzapan. 1 pound of fresh, sweet almonds, 1 pound of powdered sugar, orangeflower water and some sugar for dusting.

Blanch the almonds and dry them in a cloth, grate and then put them into a stewpan on a slow fire with orangeflower water and stir until they no longer adhere to the hands, but they must not be any dryer. Then put on a bread board dusted with sugar, roll, dusting enough sugar underneath and over the almond paste to prevent sticking, form into cakes with a nice edge or stamp out small figures and bake in a slow oven, not allowing the marzapan to become hard, but keeping it white and soft.

13. Almond Marzapan. 1 pound of the best sweet and ½ ounce of bitter almonds, 1 pound of powdered sugar and rosewater.

The almonds are prepared as in the above receipt. Then grate as fine as flour, mix with the sugar and rosewater to a stiff dough, which must not be too soft when rolling it out. Dust the bread board with sugar, divide the dough into round pieces, roll out to about the thickness of a table knife and cut into small round cakes or any other desired shape. In making the edge, roll the dough quite long, cut into narrow strips and brush with rosewater, and indent the edge with the thumb or with a knife. At this stage heat the cover of a tart pan with glowing coals, put the cakes on some paper, place the hot cover over them and bake to a light yellow. Let them cool on the paper and lay on a flat dish. In the meantime stir 1 pound of powdered sugar with rosewater for ¾ hour, fill the marzapan to the edge with this and as soon as the sugar is hard lay over it some preserved fruits.

14. Marseilles Tarts. 1 pound of flour, 6 ounces of sugar, the yolks of 4 and 2 whole eggs and 2 table-spoonfuls of butter are made into a dough, roll quite thick, cut into small cubes and bake in freshened butter to a light yellow color   Then melt 1¾ pounds of sugar and a little rose or orangeflower water and after skimming the sugar add 3 ounces of finely sliced candied orange peel, the sliced peel of a fresh lemon, 2 ounces of sweet and 1 ounce of bitter almonds cut into pieces, ½ ounce of cinnamon, ¼ ounce of cloves, ⅛ ounce of cardamom seeds, all finely pounded and mixed with the dough. Then press the whole into a warm mould which has been brushed with wax, let it cool and turn onto a dish.

15. Bride's Cake. 1 pound of fresh butter, 1 pound of fresh grated almonds, 1 pound of powdered sugar, 1 pound of warmed flour, 12 eggs, the grated rind of a lemor and a teaspoonful of mace. For brushing the cakes use the yolks of 4 eggs, ¼ pound of powdered sugar, ¼ pound of freshened butter and the juice of 4 lemons, using the grated rind of one of them.

Cream the butter (see No. 1) add sugar, spices, the yolks of eggs and almonds under constant stirring, and stir for ½ hour as directed under No. 1. Then slowly add the flour, also the beaten whites of the eggs, and bake four cakes of equal size with a moderate fire to a dark yellow, not brown, color.

Cover the cakes with a lemon cream, letting the butter melt on a slow fire, stir sugar, lemon peel, yolks of eggs and lemon juice to the butter until it is thick, take from the fire, stir for a while longer, spread three cakes with this, pour over the top the frosting given under No. 9, and decorate the top. This cake is much nicer when it is a few days old, which is the case with all layer cakes. Being very rich this cake is cut into fine slices when sent to the table. Remnants of the cake can be kept for some time by taking care of them as directed under No. 1.

CAKES. 377

16. Vienna Cake. For the cake use ½ pound of freshened butter, ½ pound of powdered sugar, ½ pound of sifted flour, 2 ounces of finely pounded almonds, the grated rind of a lemon and 10 eggs. For a cream to cover the cake take nice apples, the juice of a lemon, 1 cupful of arrac, 2 heaping tablespoonfuls of sugar, a piece of butter the size of 2 walnuts and the yolks of 3 eggs.

Stir butter, sugar and lemon peel together, gradually add, constantly stirring, the yolks of the eggs and the almonds, and stir for ½ hour as given under No. 1. Then stir into it the flour and the beaten whites of the eggs; this will make 3—4 cakes. Grate some sour apples, take the juice and put it into an enameled kettle, add sugar and cook, stirring often, until it begins to thicken, add lemon juice, butter and the yolks of the eggs, take from the fire and mix through it the arrac. Spread this over the cake and proceed as given under No. 15. Instead of this cream different fruit jellies can be used.

17. Geneva Cake. 1 pound of sifted flour, 1 pound of melted butter, 1 pound of powdered sugar, ¼ pound of grated almonds, the grated peel of a lemon and 26 eggs.

12 of the eggs are boiled until hard, grate the yolks, and mix them with the almonds; after the butter becomes hard it is creamed and then gradually add 6 whole eggs, constantly stirring, also the yolks of 8 eggs, sugar, lemon peel, almonds and at last the flour. This dough will make 6 cakes; bake them to a dark yellow color, spread with jelly, marmalade or fruit or with lemon cream as given under No. 15, and lay one on the other. After trimming the edges pour a frosting over the top.

18. Punch Layer Cake. ¾ pound of butter, ¾ pound of sugar, ¾ pound of cornstarch, 9 eggs, 1 lemon, ½ cupful of arrac. The butter is freshened, creamed and stirred with the yolks of the eggs, sugar, lemon peel and lemon juice for ½ hour, as given under No. 1. Then add the starch, lighty stir through it the beaten whites of the eggs, and after the arrac is stirred through the cake it is baked the same as sand cakes.

Cover the cakes with punch frosting.

19. Almond Cake. No. 1. 1 pound of fresh sweet and ½ ounce of bitter almonds, ¾ pound of sifted sugar, 12—15 eggs, 1 lemon, a slip of mace, 2 heaping spoonfuls of finely grated and sifted potato flour, or better still rice flour.

The almonds are hulled, washed, dried and grated, the yolks of the eggs stirred with the sugar on which half of the lemon is grated, then add the juice, mace and the almonds, constantly stirring for ½ hour (see No. 1). Mix the whites of the eggs lightly through this, then the flour and baking powder, pour into a form, put into a moderately hot oven and bake for 1¼ hours. Do not jar the form; the heat must not be stronger from the bottom than from the top. To make this cake look prettier pour over it a frosting as given under No. 9, and dot this with preserved or candied fruit sliced as thin as paper.

20. Almond Cake with Wheat Bread. No. 2. Take 10 ounces of sifted sugar, 8 ounces of fresh sweet and 1 ounce of bitter almonds, grated, 12—14 eggs, 6 ounces of not too stale grated and sifted wheat bread, and 1 lemon.

Grate some of the lemon peel on the sugar, stir it with the juice and the yolks of the eggs for ¼ hour as directed under No. 1, add the almonds to this and stir for ¼ hour longer. When this is done mix the wheat bread quickly through the mass and lightly stir through it the beaten whites of the eggs. The cake is baked and frosted the same as the above cake. It can also be baked in layers and spread with jelly. A very pretty way is to color one part green, one part red and one part brown.

21. Orange Cake. Make an almond dough of 6 ounces of grated almonds, ½ pound of sifted sugar, 12 eggs (the whites beaten to a froth), a little more than 2 ounces of flour, 2 tablespoonfuls of arrac, or else half of the puff paste as given under No. 3, and out of this bake two layers. Then on the stove beat to a thick cream 2 whole and the yolks of 4 eggs, ½ pound of sifted sugar, the juice of 4 oranges, the juice of 2 lemons and the rind of an orange grated on some sugar, spread over one layer, put the other layer on this and frost the latter with the following: The juice of 1 orange is stirred with ¼ pound of sifted sugar and 1 tablespoonful of water; then follow the directions as given under No. 9. By taking 1—2 teaspoonfuls of raspberry juice the frosting will be of a pretty red color; when using this omit the water so that the frosting will not be too thin. Decorate the top layer with candied orange slices.

22. Chocolate Cake. Stir ½ pound of butter to a cream and add 6 ounces of sugar, the yolks of 8 eggs, 6 ounces of dissolved chocolate, 1 spoonful of vanilla, 1 spoonful of lemon sugar and ¼ pound of flour, constantly stirring, and beat the dough for ¼ hour. Then stir through it the beaten whites of 6 eggs, pour into a buttered mould and bake in a moderately hot oven for 1 hour. Spread with an icing made of 2 ounces of chocolate, 4 spoonfuls of water and 3 ounces of sugar, and before serving spread over all some whipped cream.

23. Potato Cake. 1¼ pounds of grated potatoes, 16 eggs, ¾ pound of sifted sugar, 5 ounces of sweet and 1 ounce of bitter almonds, 1 lemon, 2 heaping tablespoonfuls of sifted potato flour.

Boil the potatoes in their jackets the day before, but not too tender, peel when cold, grate and then weigh them. Of this take 1¼ pounds, spread on a flat dish and set aside until the next day. Then stir the yolks of the eggs, and the sugar with the lemon peel grated over it, with the juice and the almonds for half an hour, gradually add the potatoes and then lightly stir through the mass the beaten whites of the eggs and the potato flour. The cake is immediately filled into a buttered form, put into the oven and baked the same as almond cake. Very mealy potatoes are necessary.

24. Farina Cake. Farina biscuits are easy to make and are nice for the sick, but the finest farina is required. To ½ pound of farina take 8—10 eggs, ¾ pound of sugar, 1 lemon and almonds if liked. Stir the yolks of the eggs to a cream with the sifted sugar, beat the whites of the eggs to a stiff froth, stir into the farina a little at a time, then season with lemon peel grated on sugar and the juice of 1 lemon.

Bake the cake in a buttered mould dusted with grated wheat bread, for 1 hour in a moderately hot oven.

25. Carrot Cake. 10 ounces of carrots, 14 eggs, 11 ounces of sifted sugar, 10 ounces of sweet and 2 ounces of bitter, grated, almonds, 2 heaping tablespoonfuls of sifted potato flour or cornstarch. Wash the carrots, cook them in water until about half done and then grate them; the heart is not used. Then stir the yolks of eggs with the sugar, the juice of a lemon and part of the grated rind of a lemon and the almonds, add the carrots, stir for half an hour as directed under No. 1, mix the beaten whites of 9 eggs with the potato flour and bake like almond cake for 1½ hours.

26. Ulm Cake. Mix ½ pound of creamed butter, the yolks of 6 eggs, ½ pound of sugar, lemon peel, 6 ounces of cornmeal and the beaten whites of the eggs to a dough, divide into two parts and bake each part in a moderate oven. In the meantime stir 1 pint of sour cream, 6 eggs, 6 ounces of sugar, 3 ounces of grated almonds and a little vanilla on a slow fire to a thick cream, let it cool and spread one of the layers of the cake with this. Cover with the other layer, pour over the whole a lemon icing, and decorate with preserved fruits.

27. Bread Cake. 16 eggs, 1 pound of sifted sugar, 1 pound of fresh grated almonds, 2 ounces of grated and sifted chocolate, 2 ounces of finely cut candied citron, ⅛ ounce of cloves, ⅛ ounce of cardamom, ¼ ounce of cinnamon, the juice of a lemon, ½ pound of toasted, rolled and sifted brown bread and 1 cupful of arrac.

The yolks of the eggs and the sugar, almonds and spices are stirred for ½ hour, then stir through it the brown bread and the beaten whites of 12 eggs and at last the arrac. This is put into a well-buttered mould, sprinkled with wheat bread crumbs and baked for 1½ hours, the same as almond cake. Pour over it an icing seasoned with lemon juice or chocolate. The bread cake can also be made without an icing; in this case use a little more chocolate.

28. Filled Sand Cake. A puff paste made of ½ pound of flour, also 6 ounces of sugar, 6 ounces of butter, ¼ pound of powdered sugar, 12 eggs, and apricot marmalade for filling. Cream the butter and stir it for ¼ hour with the yolks of the eggs and sugar, then lightly mix through it the beaten whites of the eggs and the powdered sugar. This is made into a thin round cake, baked and spread with the marmalade. The puff paste is perforated so that it will not blister, lay it on the baked cake, spread with the beaten egg and bake. Puff paste must bake quickly.

29. Spice Cake. This is made and baked the same as sand cake (No. 58), but stir the following spices into the batter with the yolks of the eggs: ⅛ ounce of cinnamon, 1 teaspoonful of ground cloves, ½ teaspoonful of cardamom seeds, the grated peel of a lemon. If liked add ½ ounce of chopped citron and ½ ounce of candied orange peel. Mix 1 teaspoonful of baking powder with the whites of the eggs (see No. 1).

30. Swiss Cream Cake. For the dough take ¾ pound of flour, ½ pound of freshened butter, a little more than 2 ounces of sifted sugar, 1 egg, ½ wineglassful of brandy and half as much cold water. Cover the top with 1 heaping soupplateful of sour cherries, ½ pound of sugar, 1 pint of thick sweet cream and a little vanilla.

The butter is broken into pieces, mixed with the flour, make a depression in the center of the flour, put in the egg, sugar, brandy and water, and mix with a knife in a cool place to a dough which can be worked a little with the hands and then set aside for a short time. Then roll out three-fourths of the dough, cut a round cake of the size desired, spread the outer edge with egg, cut the remaining dough into strips, lay on the edge and bake about ¼ hour. In the meantime stone the cherries, sweeten, lay them on the cake without the juice and keep in the oven with 1 degree of heat, (see No. 1), until the cherries are tender. Then whip some cream as directed under N, No. 22, season with vanilla and spread over the cherries shortly before serving.

31. Cream Cake. No. 2. A cream or a good puff paste, fruit jelly, the whites of 5—6 eggs, ¼ pound of sifted sugar and a little vanilla.

The under crust is baked like Swiss cream cake, then cover with fruit, or a marmalade which can be made of fresh plums. Beat the eggs to a froth, add sugar and vanilla, constantly beating, spread the cake with this and set in the oven until the frosting is of a light brown color.

32. Macaroon Cream Cake. Bake a macaroon cake as directed under No. 72; marmalade, the whites of 6 eggs, ¼ pound of sifted sugar and a little vanilla.

After the cake has cooled it is spread with the preserves, the whites of eggs are beaten to a stiff froth, then mix them with the vanilla and spread over it the preserved fruit. Strew sugar over the frosting and set in the oven until dry.

33. Plain Cake with Fruit Jelly. Cream ½ pound of butter, ½ pound of sugar and stir into it the yolks of 6 eggs. Beat for ½ hour, then mix with the flour and the beaten whites of the eggs and bake to a light brown color. After it is cool pieces of jelly are laid over the cake.

34. Suabian Cake. For this cake take a puff paste, cream- or tart crust No. 6, a rather thick compot made of green gooseberries, ripe currants, cherries, apples, or plums, and for the icing 6 eggs, ¼ pound of finely pounded almonds, ¼ pound of sifted sugar and the grated peel of half of a lemon, or some nutmeg.

Make a puff paste crust with standing rim, strew over the bottom of the crust some finely rolled crackers, spread the compot over the crust and over this the following icing: Stir the yolks of the eggs with sugar, almonds and lemon peel for ¼ hour as directed under No. 1, and mix with it the beaten whites of the eggs. Bake in a moderate oven. When the icing has turned yellow, lay a paper over the cake so that the icing will not become to dark.

35. Wellington Cake. ½ pound of flour, ¼ pound of butter, ¼ pound of grated almonds, ¼ pound of sifted sugar, 2 eggs for the dough, also 6 ounces of sweet almonds and 6 bitter ones finely chopped, and the whites of 6 eggs.

The dough is either rolled or else put into a form and pressed out. Bake until done, beat the whites of the eggs to a stiff froth, mix with sugar and almonds, spread over the cake and set aside to dry.

36. Linzer Cake. ½ pound of grated almonds mixed with 1 ounce of bitter ones, ½ pound of flour, ½ pound of sugar, 6 ounces of butter, the yolks of 2 raw eggs and the finely grated yolks of 3 hard boiled eggs, the thin peel of 1 lemon, and 2 tablespoonfuls of arrac or rum, made into a dough and rolled out. Put a border of the crust around the edge and then bake. Spread with any kind of preserved fruit.

37. Strawberry Cake with Vanilla Cream. For this make a puff paste, take plenty of fresh, ripe, sweetened strawberries, 6 ounces of sugar, 8 eggs, a little vanilla, ½ teaspoonful of cornstarch and a trifle of gelatine for the cream.

Bake the puff paste; the cream is made as follows: Stir 1 cupful of the cream with the yolks of the eggs, add sugar and vanilla and whip on a medium fire until just before it boils. After taking it from the fire stir in the dissolved gelatine, (when using cornstarch it should be put into the cream before), and then stir the beaten whites of 6 eggs through the cream until it begins to cool, but not until it is firmly set. Wash the berries carefully and sprinkle plentifully with sugar. When the cake is to be served stir the berries through the cream and pour them over the cake.

38. Gooseberry Cake. Make either a puff- or a cream paste—the latter is preferable. 1½ pounds of cleaned and washed green gooseberies, or the same quantity of ripe gooseberries, for which less sugar is necessary, about 1 pound of sifted sugar and a little cinnamon.

Roll the dough evenly about ⅛ inch thick, spread to the thickness of about ½ inch with cooked gooseberry compot, putting strips of dough over the top, and bake for ¼—½ hour. After the dough is rolled lay a round cover over it and trim with a knife. Then lay it on the cake dish, around the top put an edge of the crust of the remaining dough cutting into small strips and twisting them. Roll out the remainder of the dough quite thin, cut into strips about ½ inch wide and lay them on the fruit.

39. Norway Gooseberry Pie. Bring 3 pounds of green gooseberries to a boil in water, drain and cook with 1¼ pounds of sugar, lemon peel and 1 cupful of wine until done, and lay them on a sieve. Cream ¼ pound of butter, add the yolks of 10 eggs, ¼ pound of sugar, 6 ounces of grated almonds and ¼ pound of grated bread and then lightly stir through it the gooseberries and the beaten whites of 6 eggs. Bake in a buttered mould in a moderate oven and pour over it the icing No. 9.

40. Grape Pie. Prepare the crust as directed under No. 6, and take grapes and sugar in equal quantities.

Make the pie with an upper and lower crust if wished, or with only an under crust, put into a form and proceed as given in the receipt for plum pie. Then strew grated wheat bread quite thickly over the cake, lay the grapes on this, sprinkle with plenty of sugar, cover with the other crust if wished and bake in a moderate oven for 1—1¼ hours to a dark yellow.

41. Currant Cake. A cream or puff paste, 1—½ pounds of currants, 1 pound of sifted sugar and a few tablespoonfuls of grated wheat bread. Roll out the dough, strew over it plenty of grated bread and on this lay the currants. In forming the edge and in baking proceed as directed for gooseberry cake.

42. Cherry Pie. Make a cream dough and take a soupplateful of stoned sour cherries, ½—¾ pound of sugar, cinnamon, a few spoonfuls of grated bread. After rolling half of the dough for the under crust, and sprinkling it with grated bread, put in the cherries without the juice, with sugar and cinnamon, and from the remaining dough cut strips, lay them on the pie in lattice form and bake the pie in a moderate oven.

Thicken the juice of the cherries and when the pie is served put a teaspoonful of the juice into each opening in the lattice. The lattice can be omitted, and then mix with the juice 4 eggs, 1 cupful of thick sour cream, 2 spoonfuls of cornstarch and 6 spoonfuls of sugar, also a little lemon peel and pour over the cake when it is nearly done, and then set in the oven until entirely done.

43. Love Cake. Take 1½ pounds of flour for a puff paste or cream paste, of this make 3 cakes, spread with butter, sugar, cinnamon and bake to a golden brown.

After they are cold spread over the first cake a thick wine cream, over the second a raspberry or currant jelly, and then put one on the other, and on the following day trim the outer edge smooth with a sharp knife, cover the cake with any icing desired, such as chocolate or sugar and lemon juice, and decorate with preserved fruits.

44. Lemon Cake with Icing. Make a puff paste, take a few fresh lemons, sugar, biscuit and for the icing 4 eggs, 1 pint of sweetened thick cream.

Bake a cake, sprinkle sugar over it, cover with lemon slices freed from peel and seeds, sweeten with plenty of sugar, lay biscuit slices over this and then pour over it the eggs, cream and sugar whipped with a beater, and set in the oven until the icing is thick.

45. Puff Paste Pie. Make a puff paste of ½ pound of flour; take 4 fresh juicy lemons, ½ pound of grated almonds, ½ pound of sugar and 4 eggs. Peel the lemons very thin, boil the peel in water until tender, cut into long pieces, cook 2 heaping tablespoonfuls of sugar with 1 tablespoonful of wine or the water in which the peel was boiled, and cook the lemon peel in this to a thick syrup and until the peel is sugared. Press the juice out of the lemons and stir with the almonds, sugar, candied peel and eggs. Spread over the dough and bake quickly.

46. Rice and Lemon Cake. For this take a puff paste as given under Nos. 4 or 6, ½ pound of best rice, ½ pound of sifted sugar and 4 fresh lemons. Wash and scald the rice the evening before and let it soak over night in plenty of water; the next day put it on the fire in the same water, boil until tender and then pour on a sieve to drain. Grate a lemon on the sugar, cut the rind thinly from 3 lemons, cook the rind in water until tender, cut into strips and candy them the same as in the preceding receipt. Stir the juice of 4 lemons with the sugar and mix through the rice with a salad fork. In the meantime roll out the under crust and make an edge the width of a finger, brushing first with a little water so that the edge will stick. After the cake is baked and is cool, put the rice over it, and over this the candied lemon peel. Instead of this preserved apricots can be used.

The above quantities are for a large cake. This cake is very refreshing, and nice when fresh fruits cannot be had.

47. Orange Cake. ½ pound of sugar, 6 ounces of grated almonds, 12 eggs, 2 ounces of flour and 2 table-spoonfuls of arrac. After stirring this together as directed in the receipt for almond cake, bake 2 cakes. Then take 2 whole and the yolks of 4 eggs, the juice of 4 oranges, the grated rind of an orange, the juice of 2 lemons and ¼ pound of sugar, put on the fire and whip with a beater until it is quite thick. This cream is spread on one of the cakes, put the other on this, and pour the following icing over the top: Mix the juice of 1 orange with ¼ pound of sifted sugar and 1 tablespoon-ful of water for ¼ hour and spread smoothly.

48. Apple Cake made of puff paste. Make a puff paste, take nice apples, 2 ounces of almonds neatly sliced, 1—2 lemons, sugar, cinnamon and a few spoon-fuls of grated bread.

Roll one-half of the dough for an under crust and strew over it some grated bread and then put on the sliced and cored apples with the almonds, lemon slices, cinnamon and the necessary sugar; over the top put a crust, or a lattice as given for gooseberry pie (No. 39). The cake is baked in a quick oven to a nice yellow color.

49. A nice Apple Cake. Make a crust as given under No. 6, take some nice cooking apples of uniform size, 1 cupful of white wine, 1 lemon, plenty of sugar and some pounded almonds.

Roll the dough or else put it into a round mould and press it as given under No. 52. In the meantime peel the apples, halve them, and on the round side hack them with a knife (but this must be done quickly so that they will not discolor), and dip them into a mixture made of the wine, grated lemon peel and their juice, almonds and sugar. Lay the cut side of the apple to the bottom of the cake and bake in a moderate oven for 1¼ hours. When wished the cake can be dotted with any kind of preserved fruits, and make an edge of sugared orange slices. It can also be served without any further additions.

50. Apple Cake. For the dough take ¾ pound of flour, ½ pound of freshened butter, 3 ounces of sifted sugar, 1 egg, 2 spoonfuls of water, 2 spoonfuls of rum, good apples, wine, sugar, lemon peel and whole cinnamon.

Stir the butter to a cream, then add sugar, egg, rum, water and flour, stir all for a short time, put into a cake pan, and with a flat wooden ladle press out the dough, having it a little thicker on the sides so as to form an edge; sprinkle some grated bread over the bottom. In the meantime cook thickly sliced apples in wine, sugar, lemon peel and whole cinnamon until half done, and after they are cold lay them neatly on the cake and bake to a golden—not brown—color. Boil down the juice until quite thick, and when the cake is served pour it over the apples.

51. Plain Apple Cake. Butter a pan, sprinkle over it some grated wheat bread and fill with alternate layers of grated roll (or brown bread) and apple slices. Over each layer put sugar, pieces of butter and a little fruit jelly. Then bake the cake, having grated bread for the top layer, for 1 hour. Half an hour before the cake is done make a cream for it, using 1 cupful of sour cream, the yolks of 4 eggs, 3 ounces of sugar and 1⅔ ounces of grated almonds, pour this over the cake and then bake until done.

52. Plum Cake. Make a dough as given under No. 6; take fresh plums, sifted sugar, cinnamon and grated bread.

Lay the plums on a sieve and then put them into boiling water until the skin can be easily taken off with a knife and after this is done, stone and lay them into a dish. Then make the dough, which can be moulded immediately without being first set aside. To do this put it into the mould in pieces and press it with the hands (which should be dusted with flour) uniformly all around, a little thicker at the sides, however, so as to make the edge about 1½ inches high; all thin spots should be covered with pieces of dough. The projecting edge should be scolloped with the fingers and then bent upwards, all scollops pointing in the same direction. Dust the dough plentifully with rolled crackers, turn each plum in powdered sugar and arrange them in circular form, beginning at the edge and working towards the center, putting them in closely together. Sprinkle with cinnamon and then bake the cake for 1¼ hours with 1 degree of heat (see No. 1). The juice of the plums is put on a soupplate with some sugar, set on the back part of the stove until thick and pour it over the cake when the latter is to be served.

The above given quantities are for a large cake. This is very nice when warm and also very good when a few days old, first putting it into a hot oven for ¼ hour. When plums cannot be obtained use prune sauce and then bake for ¼ hour.

53. Dried Prune Cake. Make a dough as directed under No. 6, cut some of the dough into long strips, lay them over the fruit, or make the cake as given in the above receipt; then take 1 pound of prunes, ½ bottle of white wine, 7 ounces of sugar, ¼ pound of currants, 1 lemon and grated bread. The prunes are scalded (as directed for compots) and slowly boiled in a little water until the stones will come out. They are then put into an earthenware dish with the broth, wine, sugar, juice and half of the peel of a lemon; cover the dish and boil slowly until tender. ¼ hour before tender put in the washed currants and let them boil until there is but little broth. After this is cold spread it over the dough and bake the cake for 1¼ hours with one degree of heat to a dark yellow color.

54. Date Cake. (Arabian Receipt.) 6 ounces of flour, 3 ounces of creamed butter, 3 ounces of sugar, the yolks of 3 eggs, the beaten whites of the eggs and finely cut lemon peel are made into a light dough which is put into a dish and baked until about half done. In the meantime stir the whites of 8 eggs to a froth, add 10 ounces of sugar, 10 ounces of grated almonds, 10 ounces of nicely sliced dates and 1 glassful of Madeira, pour this over the cake and bake until done. At last cover the cake with a three colored icing seasoned with plenty of lemon juice, so that it will have an acidulous taste, and lay over this dates and preserved fruits.

55. English Plum Cake. Melt 1 pound of nice butter, clarify and let it cool again, take 1 pound of sifted sugar, 1 pound of cornstarch, 1 pound of nicely washed and dried currants, 12 eggs, 2 ounces of finely cut citron, ¼ ounce of cinnamon, ⅛ ounce of cloves, both ground, and a wineglassful of Madeira or arrac.

Stir the butter to a cream, add, one by one, the yolks of the eggs, spices, sugar, currants and stir all for half an hour as directed under No. 1. Lightly stir through it the beaten whites of the eggs, then the starch and finally the Madeira, put the cake into a moderate oven and bake for 1¼ hours. If baking powder is added to the flour it will greatly improve the cake.

56. Layer Cake. A layer cake that will keep fresh for a long time is made of 8 eggs, the weight of the eggs in sugar, butter and flour.

The butter is melted, poured from the settlings and then allowed to cool again, add the sugar by degrees, and stir until all is melted. Then gradually put in the eggs, and stir the whole for ½ hour as given under No. 1, mix the flour through this, and then bake three cakes to a dark yellow color, spread two with jelly and lay the third on this. The next day cut the edge smoothly and dust sugar over the top. Lemon peel and lemon juice can also be added to this cake making one cake and spreading it with jelly and then with the beaten whites of 3 eggs, seasoning with a little vanilla, and set it in the oven a few moments to dry.

57. Ribbon Cake. 1 pound of freshened butter, 1 pound of sifted sugar, 1 pound of warmed flour, 16 eggs, 1 lemon, 1 teaspoonful of mace, 2 teaspoonfuls of cinnamon, 3 ounces of sweet and ½ ounce of bitter grated almonds.

The butter is slowly melted, poured from the settlings and stirred with sugar. Add the yolks of the eggs, juice and grated rind of the lemon, mace, cinnamon and almonds, and this is stirred for ½ hour as given under No. 1. Then stir the beaten whites of the eggs, a spoonful at a time, with the flour to the cake. Spread on the pan to the thickness of about ⅛ inch, and bake to a yellow color, spread dough over this and bake again, and so on until 5 layers are baked, which must be evenly divided. After the first layer is baked the heat should not be quite so strong from the bottom of the oven, baking the cake principally from the top, but keeping up 2 degrees of heat (see No. 1). This mass can also be baked in one cake and then serve fruit jelly with it.

58. Sand Cake. 1 pound of fresh butter, 1 pound of sifted sugar, ½ pound of fine flour, ½ pound of sifted cornstarch, 10—12 fresh eggs, the juice of a lemon and 2 tablespoonfuls of arrac. All of this, with the exception of the eggs, must be set in a warm place for a few hours.

The butter is melted and freed from settlings; after it is cold rub to a cream, adding the sugar by degrees with a little lemon peel, stirring constantly. Then stir in one by one the yolks of the eggs, the grated lemon peel and the flour. a spoonful at a time. After this has been stirred for ½ hour, stir through it the arrac and lemon juice and the beaten whites of the eggs, together with a teaspoonful of baking powder. Put this into a prepared form and then into the oven and bake with 2 degrees of heat for 1½ hours, and if the cake is very thick, for 2 hours. During this time the form should not be moved.

This cake can also be divided into three parts, one of which is colored with chocolate, the other with cochineal, leaving the last yellow, putting one layer on the other, covering the top with a three-colored frosting seasoned with Marascino.

59. Cardamom Biscuits. Stir the yolks of 16 eggs with 1 pound of sugar, the peel of ¼ and the juice of a whole lemon and ½ teaspoonful of fine cardamom seeds until thick and full of bubbles. Mix through it the beaten whites of 9 of the eggs, and at last stir in about 1½ pounds of cornstarch. The mould is buttered thickly, then sprinkle with grated rolls, pour in the cake and bake slowly for 1 hour in a moderately but uniformly hot oven.

60. Biscuits No. 2. ½ pound of pulverized and sifted starch, 1 pound of sugar, grate the rind of a lemon on the sugar which is pulverized and sifted after the yellow is taken off, the whites of 10 and the yolks of 20 fresh eggs, juice of a lemon, 1 teaspoonful of baking powder, but the latter is not absolutely necessary. Starch and sugar are put into a warm place to dry and warm for ½—1 hour. Whip the whites of the eggs to a froth stiff enough to cut, but it should not be whipped any longer than this or else it will become lumpy. Then whip the yolks of the eggs, juice and lemon sugar into the whites of the eggs and also by degrees the remaining sugar; whip briskly for about ¼ hour. Put the dish into hot water or on hot coals and whip until lukewarm, then put in the starch and baking powder which must be stirred in as quickly as possible. When this is done put the mass into a moderately hot oven in a prepared mould. Bake for about 1 hour. To prevent the biscuit from getting yellow too soon put over the top a buttered paper in such a manner that it will not prevent the biscuit from raising.

61. Hasty Biscuit. 15 fresh eggs, 1 lemon, ½ pound of sifted sugar, ½ pound of cornstarch.

Whip the whites of 13 eggs to a stiff froth, stir the yolks of 15 eggs with the grated peel and juice of a lemon and let this run slowly into the beaten whites, whipping constantly. Put in the sifted sugar, then the starch and whip until all is mixed, but not longer. Then follow directions as given above.

62. Bohemian Biscuits. For each egg, take ½ ounce of sugar and ½ ounce of grated stale bread without the crust. Whip the yolks of the eggs with sugar, cinnamon, the juice and half of the rind of a lemon, then put in the bread and stir the beaten whites of the eggs lightly through it. Bake in a buttered mould for 1 hour. If the bread is old take less. For 6 persons 8 eggs will be sufficient.

63. Chocolate Biscuits. The whites and the yolks of 12 eggs, ¾ pound of sifted sugar, 2 ounces of bitter grated and sifted chocolate, a teaspoonful of cinnamon, a little vanilla and 6 ounces of sifted cornstarch. Prepare as given in No. 61 and bake.

64. Biscuit Roll. ¼ pound of sugar, the yolks of 6 eggs, a little salt and lemon peel are stirred to a frothy mass, then lightly stir through it the beaten whites of the eggs together with 3 ounces of flour, and spread on the pan to the thickness of $1/32$ of an inch. Bake to a light yellow, take out of the pan, turn, and spread with any kind of fruit marmalade. Roll, put into the oven for a few minutes, pour over it a sugar icing and cover with preserved fruits. This can also be used as a pudding, serving it cut into slices and cover with a wine sauce.

65. Chocolate Cake. 14 eggs, ½ pound of sifted sugar, ½ pound of grated almonds, 6 ounces of finely grated and sifted sweet chocolate, ⅛ ounce of cinnamon and a teaspoonful of baking powder.

The yolks of 12 eggs and 2 whole eggs are whipped with sugar, almonds and chocolate for ¼ hour, or stirred for ½ hour, then lightly stir through it the beaten whites of the eggs, quickly stirring in the baking powder and bake the cakes for 1 hour as directed for almond cake.

66. Currant Cake. 1 pound of melted butter, poured from the settlings, 1 pound of cornstarch, ¾—1 pound of sifted sugar, ¼ pound of washed and dried currants, the grated peel of a lemon, 1 grated nutmeg or a teaspoonful of mace, 12 eggs, ½ glassful of arrac or rum.

Cream the butter and stir in the sugar and spices, yolks of eggs one by one; then stir briskly for ½ hour longer. Add the currants, after these the beaten whites of the eggs, then the cornstarch and at last the arrac.

67. Grape Cake. Take 1 pound of flour, ¾ pound of butter, 1 cupful of sugar, cinnamon, salt and the yolks of 5 eggs, and knead quickly.

Roll out the dough, lay it into a buttered pan and sprinkle over it finely pounded almonds; then beat the whites of 12 eggs, mix with 1½ pounds of pounded sugar and 3 pounds of white grapes, fill into the pan and bake. This will make 2 medium-sized cakes.

68. Cup Cake. 4 eggs, 1½ cupfuls of butter, 2 cupfuls of sifted sugar, 3 cupfuls of flour, 1 cupful of milk, 3 cupfuls of raisins, currants, cloves and the grated peel of a lemon.

Stir the butter to a cream, add spices and eggs, then milk and flour and at last raisins and currants.

To this cake take 1 teaspoonful of baking powder, mixing it with the flour.

Bake the cake for 2 hours in a moderately hot oven.

69. Rice Cake. ¾ pound of rice, milk for boiling the rice, 6 ounces of butter, the yolks of 12 eggs, the whites of 10 eggs, ¼ pound of sweet and a few bitter almonds, ⅛ ounce of cinnamon, ½ pound of sugared and the grated peel of a lemon or some candied orange peel (see Division A, No. 48.)

The rice is scalded in water and boiled slowly in milk until tender and thick; the kernels must remain whole. Then cream the butter and add, constantly stirring, the sugar, the yolks of the eggs, almonds and spices and at last the beaten whites of the eggs. The whole is put into a buttered mould which has first been sprinkled with grated bread and sugar, and then baked in a moderately hot oven for 1¼ hours.

If the rice when cooked should not be thick enough, stir through it some finely grated bread before putting in the whites of the eggs. Instead of the almonds ½ pound of stoned raisins can be cooked with the rice for ¼ hour.

70. Nice Rice Cake. Boil ¼ pound of rice in sweet cream with salt and 2 ounces of sugar, flavored with vanilla, until thick. By the addition of a variety of ingredients a number of different kinds of the rice cake can be prepared. After stirring through the rice the yolks of 6 eggs and 2 ounces of grated roll, stir in 2 ounces of sliced citron or 3 ounces of scalded raisins or 3 ounces of any kind of scalded candied fruit, also almonds, spices or grated nuts. In the meantime bake a puff paste No. 3, two crusts of the same size, spread first with fruit marmalade or a thick wine cream, then with the rice, put on the top crust and serve immediately.

71. Almond Cake. No. 1. ½ pound of flour, ¼ pound of butter, ¼ pound of sifted sugar, ¼ pound of sweet and 6 grated bitter almonds, and 2 fresh eggs.

Melt the butter, then add the eggs one by one, sugar, almonds, and stir for ¼ hour, stir through this the flour, put into the pan, press out quite thin and bake to a nice yellow color.

Spread the cake with jelly; if sugar is preferred cut the cake into pieces of the size required and sprinkle with sugar.

72. Almond Cake. No. 2. Puff paste as given in No. 6, ½ pound of sifted sugar, ½ pound of pounded almonds, a few lemons, the whites of 2 eggs, 2—2¼ ounces of crushed rock candy.

Put the sugar into water, let it dissolve, stir in the almonds and the finely cut peel of a lemon with its juice, and then set aside to cool.

Make a puff paste, divide it into 2 parts, rolling it into an upper and lower crust, making the lower 1 inch wider than the upper crust, spread on the lower crust the almond syrup, leaving about 1 inch for an edge, put the top on this and bake the cake not too slowly. As soon as taken from the oven, spread over it the beaten whites of the eggs, cut the lemon into small cubes, taking out the seeds, lay the cubes on the cake together with a few whole lemon slices, sprinkle over it the rock candy, set in the oven for a few moments to dry.

73. Portuguese Coffee Cake. Rub ½ pound of butter to a cream, add the yolks of 6 eggs, ½ pound of sugar, 1 glassful of Madeira, 1 spoonful of orangeflower water, a little salt, ¼ pound of cleaned raisins, 10 ounces of rice- or wheat flour, 1 teaspoonful of baking powder, stir through it the beaten whites of the eggs, put into a buttered mould and bake for 1½ hours. Spread over it any kind of an icing.

74. King's Cake. ¾ pound of butter stirred to a cream, gradually add the yolks of 10 eggs, ¾ pound of sugar, a little salt, lemon extract, 2 ounces of sweet and ⅓ ounce of bitter almonds, and 1 spoonful of French brandy, stirring well together. Then mix ¾ pound of flour, 3 ounces of currants, 3 ounces of chopped citron and 2 teaspoonfuls of baking powder, stir the whites of 8 eggs through the dough, put into a mould and bake slowly for 2 hours.

75. Sexton's Cake. 1 pound of freshened butter, 1 pound of flour, ¾ pound of sifted sugar, ½ pound of grated almonds, 9 eggs and jelly.

Cream the butter, add sugar, eggs and almonds, and stir for ½ hour. Then mix through this the flour and put into a pan, so that it will only be about ½ inch thick and bake to a light brown color. After the cake is cold dot with jelly and sprinkle sugar over it.

76. Carmelite Cake. 9 whole and the yolks of 2 eggs, ¾ pound of sifted sugar, ½ pound of almonds coarsely pounded with rosewater, 3 tablespoonfuls of cherry cordial, the grated rind of a lemon, a little cinnamon and 1 nutmeg.

The whole eggs and the egg yolks are whipped together, adding the other ingredients. Then stir all together for ½ hour, ½ pound of flour is added and the cake baked in a moderate oven.

77. Macaroon Cake. ¾ pound of sweet and a few bitter almonds are coarsely pounded with a little white of an egg, ½ pound of sifted sugar, (sugar and almonds both warmed), the whites of 5 eggs, juice and part of the lemon peel or some orange peel grated on sugar.

Mix the almonds with the sugar and the whites of the eggs, add the juice and peel of a lemon, spread this on the wafers laid together in the form of a cake. Bake the cake in a moderate oven and spread with jelly.

78. Puff Paste with Lemon Cream. Make a puff paste of ¾ pound of flour; for the cream take ½ pound of sifted sugar, 4 lemons, white wine or cider in proportion, the yolks of 20 fresh eggs, the whites of 5 eggs and ½ tablespoonful of cornstarch. Roll out the dough, put it into the pan, having the edge not too thin and bake quickly. Then make the following cream: The yolks of the eggs are put into a glass, add the juice of the lemons and enough white wine to equal the bulk of the yolks of eggs. Then mix with it the sugar, grated peel of 2 lemons, the whites of the eggs and the dissolved starch; gelatine can also be used instead of the cornstarch. Set on the stove and whip constantly; after it is thick take from the fire and whip until it is cool; when using gelatine be careful to pour the cream on the cake before it is cold. When the cake is to be brought to the table put the cream on the cake and ornament with small "kisses".

79. Apple Cake with Almond Icing. Take 18—20 nice cooking apples of medium size and for the filling nicely washed currants, sugar, cinnamon, citron and a little butter. For icing, 6 fresh eggs, ¼ pound of sugar, ¼ pound of grated almonds and ½ teaspoonful of mace.

Pare the apples, take out the core and leave the apples whole, put them into a pan side by side and fill with currants, sugar, cinnamon, citron and a small piece of butter. Then take the yolks of the eggs, sugar, almonds and mace, stir together for ¼ hour, mix with the beaten whites of the eggs, pour over the apples and bake for 1—1¼ hours.

Serve this if possible when warm; if made the day before set in the oven for ¼ hour before serving.

80. Mannheim Apple Cake. 3 ounces of creamed butter, 6 ounces of sugar, 5 whole eggs, the peel of ¼ of a lemon and ½ pound of flour are stirred to a light dough, which is put into a buttered pan, sprinkled with grated roll, covered thickly with apple slices. Pour over this an icing made of 1 cupful of sour cream, 3 eggs, sugar and vanilla. Bake in a moderate oven.

81. Milan Apple Cake. Bake a cake as given under No. 36. In the meantime stew some nice cooking apples in wine with sugar and lemon peel until tender, but they must not fall to pieces. Also scald 6 ounces of rice and boil with cream, sugar and vanilla until tender and thick and stir until cold. The apples must be cold before putting them on the cake, which must also be cold. Spread the cake with apricot marmalade, mix a glassful of Marascino through the rice and spread evenly on the cake, lay the apple slices on this, cover with thinned apple jelly and dot the cake with preserved cherries.

82. Westphalian Butter, Coffee or Sugar Cake. No. 1. 3 pounds of flour, yeast, 7 eggs, 1 lemon, 2 pounds of butter, 2 cupfuls of sifted sugar, 1 large cupful of milk, ½ pound of stoned raisins or currants.

Put the flour into a pan, make a depression in the center, put in the eggs, sugar, raisins, the grated peel of a lemon, milk, and the dissolved yeast; and then by degrees the butter, and thoroughly whip the dough, which has been mixed in a warmed pan. Then butter a large cake pan with unsalted butter, put the dough into this about ½ inch thick and let it raise in a warm place. When this is done, spread the cake with melted butter, strew thickly over it coarse or finely pounded sugar and bake quickly.

83. Westphalian Cake. No. 2. All of the following cakes must be pierced with a fork before putting them into the oven, so that they will not blister. For the dough: 2 pounds of flour warmed and sifted, ¾ pound of freshened butter, 2 ounces of yeast, 2½ ounces of finely sliced citron, 1 teaspoonful of salt, 2 eggs, 1 pint of warm milk. For on the cake: ⅔ pound of coarse sugar, ½ pound of butter, 2 ounces of finely pounded almonds, and for sprinkling the cake, ½ cupful of rosewater, or if this is not liked the same quantity of white wine or sugar water.

The flour is put into a warmed dish and mixed thoroughly with the pieces of butter; make a depression in the center of the flour, add the dissolved yeast, milk, 2 ounces of sugar, eggs and spices, and with a wide knife mix the flour and ingredients together quickly, avoiding working the dough too much; this is an essential point to be observed in making this cake. The dough thus made is put into a warmed pan and smoothed with the hand, which should be dusted with a little flour, until it is about ½ inch thick, put over it a warm cloth and set aside in a warm place 1—1½ hours to raise.

After the cake has raised pour over it a mixture of sugar, almonds, cinnamon, lay pieces of butter over this and bake the cake in a quick oven for 15—20 minutes. The cake must be of a dark color, but not brown, nor should it dry in the oven, because it must be soft inside. When taking out sprinkle the cake with rose water, wine or sugar water.

REMARK.—These cakes are best when fresh. They can, if a day or so old, be put into the oven for a few minutes. They are cut into pieces 1 inch wide and three times as long.

84. Westphalian Cake. No. 3. For the dough take 2 pounds of warmed flour, ½ pound of washed and stoned raisins, ¼ pound of butter and lard slowly melted together, fresh yeast, 1 pint of warm milk, and if you have it 2 tablespoonfuls of thick sour cream; for the top, ¼ pound of melted butter, ¼ pound of sugar and a little cinnamon,

The dough is stirred in a warm dish and then mixed on the bread board with the necessary flour; proceed as noted under No. 1 of this Division, then roll out the dough, put it into the cake pan, and after it has raised, spread with butter, sprinkle sugar over it, put into a hot oven and bake quickly.

85. Bremen Butter Cake. For the dough 3 pounds of sifted flour, 1 pound of washed and stoned raisins, ½ pound of sifted sugar, 1½ pints of milk, 3 ounces of yeast, 1 teaspoonful of salt, 1 pound of freshened butter and spices according to taste. For filling take ¾ pound of washed and warmed currants, ¼ pound of sugar, 2 ounces of cut almonds and 1 ounce of citron.

Make the dough, warming all ingredients as given in No. 91, let it raise slowly for about 1½ hours, roll into a long narrow strip about 1 inch thick, press with the rolling pin in the center of this so as to have the sides thicker, fill with currants, citron, almonds, then fold the two sides together so as to have the cake shaped like a half moon, put into the pan, make a few incisions into the cake, let it raise, spread with egg, and bake in a moderate oven for 1 hour.

86. Silesian Cheese Cake. A dough is made as given under No. 84. For the top take a soupplateful of curds stirred with fresh cream but not too thin, 1 cupful of melted butter, sugar, cinnamon to taste, 2 eggs, with ½ pound of currants stirred through it.

Roll the dough quite thin, put on the pan, let it raise, warming the cheese a little and spread it on the cake and bake quickly. According to the size of the cake, the evening before wanted take 3 quarts of thick milk with the cream, put it into a cheese cloth bag and the next morning use for the cake.

This cake is very nice and refreshing when not left in the oven too long so that it will become dry; it should be eaten when still quite fresh.

87. Fruit Cake. 1 quart of milk, 2 pounds of freshened butter, 1 pound of stoned raisins sprinkled with a little rum, 1 pound of cleaned currants, yeast, 3 ounces of sweet, and ½ ounce of bitter chopped almonds, 2 ounces of finely sliced citron, the grated peel of a lemon, a little mace, the yolks of 6 eggs, 1 teaspoonful of salt, and flour enough to make a thick dough. Take 1 large or 2 small forms, butter them and sprinkle with sweet almonds, put in the dough, and set aside in a warm place. When the dough is raised, put it into a medium hot oven, spread with butter, strew sugar and cinnamon over it and bake.

88. Parisian Cake. Dissolve some yeast in a cupful of milk. Then stir 1 pound of butter to a cream, add 3 whole eggs, the yolks of 3 eggs, 5 ounces of sugar, ¼ pound each of currants and raisins, ½ teaspoonful of salt, 2 ounces of citron, ½ ounce of grated bitter almonds, 1 spoonful of vanilla, grated lemon peel, mace, 3 spoonfuls of cognac, the dissolved yeast, and at last add 1¼ pounds of sifted flour. Whip the dough hard until light, put it into a large buttered pan, set aside to raise and then bake in a moderate oven to a light brown color. Turn the cake out of the pan, sift over it some powdered sugar and then hold a red-hot shovel over it to glaze it.

89. Elberfeld "Kringle." 2 pounds of flour, ¾ pound of butter, ½ pound of sugar, 5 eggs, ¼ pound of cinnamon (if cinnamon is not liked, vanilla or cardamom seeds can be used), 1 cupful of milk, ¾ pound of currants or 2 cupfuls of jelly and fresh yeast.

Stir ½ of the flour with the warm milk, eggs, and yeast, let it raise and then take ¼ pound of sugar and enough flour so that the dough can be kneaded. Work in the butter and the remaining flour. Then roll out the dough, not too thin, strew over it the remaining sugar, currants and cinnamon, or spread with jelly, roll and form in the shape of a wreath. Lay on a pan, and when raised spread with butter and bake for ¾ hour in a hot oven.

90. Sweet Cake ("Rodon Kuchen"). 1 pound of sifted flour, ¾ pound of freshened butter, ¼ pound of coarsely pounded almonds, ¼ pound of sugar, 9 fresh eggs, 1 cupful of fresh warm milk, grated peel of a lemon, ½ teaspoonful of salt and yeast. Stir the butter to a cream, gradually add the eggs, almonds, milk, spices, sugar and the dissolved yeast, constantly stirring, and at last stir in the flour a spoonful at a time, and put into a buttered pan sprinkled with grated roll and raise as given under No. 1, and bake.

REMARK.— Instead of taking yeast, baking powder can be used for all of these cakes.

91. Roll Cake. For the dough take 1¼ pounds of flour, ¾ pound of butter, according to taste 2—3 ounces of sugar, 3 eggs, yeast, 1 cupful of lukewarm milk, 1 teaspoonful of salt; for on the dough ½ pound of currants, ¼ pound of sugar, 1 ounce of finely sliced citron or some candied orange peel (A, No. 48), and ¼ ounce of cinnamon.

After all of the ingredients have been warmed and the yeast dissolved with some sugar and milk, put the melted butter into the center of the flour, stir sugar, eggs, yeast, salt and milk together, first with a knife and then with the hand, beat the dough and set aside to raise. Then roll to a long strip 6 inches wide, sprinkle with currants washed and dried and then warmed in the oven, sugar the finely sliced citron and cinnamon, roll it out and lay the end of the roll into the pan and then keep on rolling until the cake is formed, but it must lay so that it will have room to raise. Put into a warm place to raise and bake in a moderate oven for 1—1¼ hours.

92. Plain Potato Cake. 2 pounds of flour, ¼ pound of butter, ¼ pound of raisins or pears sliced finely, 1—2 eggs, about 1 pint of warm milk, yeast, 2—3 cold, partly boiled, grated potatoes, 1 teaspoonful of salt and, if liked, some mace.

Whip the eggs, add yeast, potatoes, salt and milk and mix through the remaining ingredients. Beat the dough and put it into a buttered mould, cover and set aside to raise. When it has raised for about 1½—2 hours, put it into the oven, cover and bake slowly.

II. TARTS, COOKIES, ETC.

NOTE.—To take cookies, etc., out of the pan without breaking them, dry the pan, warm it and then line it very slightly with white wax. After the cookies are baked, take them out while still hot with a long thin knife; if the cakes are cold before you have taken them out of the pan, warm the pan again.

93. Marshall Tarts. Puff paste, the whites of 2 eggs, ¼ pound of sugar and 3 ounces of grated almonds.

Roll the puff paste quite thin; stamp out the tarts with a wineglass and with a teaspoon spread on them the beaten white of an egg, with almonds and sugar. Bake in a moderate oven to a light yellow color, then spread with frosting and set in the oven to dry for a minute. They are eaten fresh.

94. Fruit Tarts. Puff paste, egg, sugar and cinnamon, fresh or preserved fruits as liked.

Roll the dough quite thin, line a tart mould, spread with egg and bake quickly. Then fill with fruit without the juice, or with fresh sweet cherries cooked until thick.

95. Swiss filled Cakes. ("Kropfli"). For the dough take ½ pound of flour, 6 ounces of butter, 2 ounces of sugar, 3 spoonfuls of French brandy, 1 tablespoonful of water; for the filling take fruit or jelly.

After rolling out the dough cut out disks with a large goblet, put some fruit on each disk, fold once, press the sides a little, spread with egg and bake quickly.

96. Apple Cake. Any preferred dough, apples, rum or arrac, preserved currants or currant jelly, a few macaroons or almonds, dried currants, sugar, cinnamon, lemon peel and eggs.

Pare and core the apples and a few hours before using pour over them the arrac and sprinkle with sugar and cinnamon. After the dough is rolled it is cut into square pieces; mix the apples with the preserves, to which a few pounded macaroons may be added. The apples can also be filled with finely cut almonds, sugar, currants and lemon peel. Put an apple on each square, fold the corners of the dough to the center, brush the top with beaten egg, turn in pounded almonds and sugar, and bake in a quick oven.

97. Yeast Cakes. ¼ pound of freshened butter, the yolks of 5 eggs, 1 ounce of sugar, lemon peel, 1 cupful of thick sour cream, yeast dissolved in milk and sugar, and ¾ pound of warmed flour.

Stir the butter to a cream, add the other ingredients, then make into balls the size of a walnut, put them on a buttered pan, let them raise, put on each cake a preserved cherry or a raisin. Spread them with the beaten white of the egg, sprinkle with sugar and bake in a quick oven for 10 minutes.

98. Milan Tarts. ½ pound of flour, ¼ pound of butter, 6 ounces of sugar, 2 tablespoonfuls of thick sour cream or brandy and 1 egg.

Make into a dough, roll, cut into square pieces, if liked brush with egg, bake quickly and after they are cold dot with jelly.

99. Swiss Chocolate Bread. Stir the whites of 3 eggs to a froth; 6 ounces of sugar, 2 ounces of pounded almonds, 2 ounces of grated chocolate. Then spread this on wafers, cut them into long narrow pieces and bake in a slow oven.

100. Speculaci or Tea Tarts for the Christmas Tree. 1 pound of sifted flour, 1 pound of sifted sugar, ½ pound of freshened butter, 3 eggs, 2 ounces of cinnamon, the grated rind of 1 lemon, and a teaspoonful of baking powder.

Break the butter into small pieces, mix with the flour and the other ingredients—excepting the baking powder—to a dough, which is then set aside for a few hours, or over night; it will not hurt the dough to keep it for a few days in a cool place. Then flatten out the dough, sprinkle the baking powder over it, knead it and then roll the dough to the thickness of $\frac{1}{32}$ of an inch. Cut out any shape or figure desired, put them on a buttered pan and bake in a moderate oven.

101. Nice Anise Cake. (For the Christmas tree.) ¾ pound of flour and cornstarch, half and half, ¾ pound of sugar, both sifted, 12 fresh eggs, 2 tablespoonfuls of anise seed.

Beat the whites of the eggs to a stiff froth, the yolks are stirred together and slowly added to the whites, beating uninterruptedly, then mix the anise seed with the sugar, and add to the eggs, a spoonful at a time, and then the flour. This mass is put into a waxed pan and baked in a moderate oven to a golden brown.

102. Sugar Drop Cakes. ½ pound of cornstarch, ½ pound of sifted sugar, 4 fresh eggs, the grated peel of a lemon.

The eggs are stirred with sugar and spices, and beaten for ¼ hour; add the beaten whites of the eggs, and the cornstarch is then quickly stirred through it. This is put into a waxed pan, a spoonful at a time, and baked in a moderate oven.

103. Almond Drop Cakes. ½ pound of sifted flour, ½ pound of sifted sugar, 2 ounces of butter, 2 ounces of grated almonds, 4 eggs, the grated peel of half a lemon.

Cream the butter, stir in the eggs, sugar, spices and almonds, and beat for ¼ hour, mix the flour into the mass and put into a buttered pan, a teaspoonful at a time, and bake in a moderate oven.

104. Spiced Drop Cakes. 2 pounds of flour, 2 pounds of sugar, 12 large or 14 small eggs, the peels of 2 lemons, 2 ounces of citron, a little ground cloves, cinnamon and pounded cardamom seeds.

Eggs, sugar and spices are stirred for half an hour, and then gradually add the flour. The pan is waxed, the batter dropped in with a teaspoon and baked to a golden brown.

105. Cinnamon Stars. 1 pound of sifted sugar, 1 pound of almonds, washed, dried and grated with the brown skin, the whites of 6 eggs, cinnamon and the finely cut peel of a lemon.

Stir sugar and lemon peel together, beat the whites of the eggs and add sugar, stir for ¼ hour, add cinnamon, set part of the mixture aside, roll out the dough and cut it into stars with a cutter of that design, brush with the white of the egg and sugar and bake slowly on a waxed pan. The cakes will keep for a long time.

106. Coffee Pretzels. Make a dough of ¾ pound of flour, 1 ounce of freshly roasted and finely ground coffee, 2 whole eggs, the yolks of 2 eggs, 5 ounces of sugar, 3 ounces of butter, vanilla, grated lemon peel, a pinch of salt and a teaspoonful of baking powder. Make into small pretzels and bake in a moderate oven to a light brown color.

107. Hohenzollern Cakes. 1 pound of flour, 1 pound of sweet coarsely pounded almonds, 13 ounces of light brown sugar, 4 eggs, some vanilla, 2 ounces each of grated chocolate and finely sliced citron, a little nutmeg, baking powder; make into a dough that can be moulded without breaking, and roll it into long rolls the thickness of a thumb, press the top a little, indent the rolls every 4 inches, and when baked and still hot, break them apart at the places where they were indented.

108. Almond Cakes. Freshened butter, sifted sugar, grated almonds and sifted flour of each ½ pound, 2 eggs, grated peel of ½ lemon. Cream the butter, add the other ingredients, leaving half of the almonds and sugar for the top. Then roll the dough ¼ inch thick, cut into long pieces, spread with beaten egg, almonds and sugar, and bake in a moderate oven to a light yellow color.

109. Shavings. 1 pound of sifted flour, 1 pound of sifted sugar, ¾ pound of melted butter, 6 eggs, the rind of a lemon.

After this has been well stirred together, spread as thinly as possible on a buttered mould and bake for 8—10 minutes to a light yellow color. While still hot cut the cake into strips 2 inches wide and quickly wind them over a round stick, so as to shape them like shavings.

110. Berlingoes. (Excellent with wine and for Christmas). 1½ pounds of flour, 1 pound of sugar, 9 ounces of fresh butter, 5 eggs, grated peel of a lemon.

Cream the butter, add the eggs one by one, sugar, and lemon peel, and at last the flour. Out of this dough form small wreaths which are put not too close together into a buttered pan, and dusted with a little flour. They must be baked to a light brown color.

They can also be spread with the white of an egg, coarsely pounded almonds, sugar and cinnamon, which makes them very nice.

111. Vienna Crusts. ½ pound of flour, ½ pound of sugar, 3 eggs, cinnamon, a trifle of cardamom seeds, cloves, grated peel of a lemon, 3 finely chopped preserved walnuts.

After the flour and sugar have been sifted, stir all the ingredients together excepting the flour, for $\frac{1}{4}$ hour; then add the flour, a spoonful at a time. Take a teaspoonful of the dough at a time, turn in sugar and form into long pieces, and bake on a waxed pan in a moderate oven to a light brown color.

112. Burnt Almonds. 1 pound of almonds rubbed in a cloth, (but not peeled), 1 pound of sugar, and if liked a little cinnamon.

The sugar is melted in a little water, and boiled in a copper stewpan until the sugar strings. Then add the almonds, which are stirred constantly until they are sugared. Then take the pan from the stove and stir until the almonds are dry; then put the pan on the stove again until they are glazed. Pour onto a flat dish and while still hot mix through them the cinnamon and then pick the almonds apart.

113. Muscadine Almonds. $\frac{3}{4}$ pound of almonds with the shells, $\frac{3}{4}$ pound of sifted sugar, the whites of 8 eggs, cinnamon, cloves, and lemon peel.

Clean the almonds in a cloth, grate and put them on the stove with the whites of the eggs, sugar and spices, and stir until they are no longer sticky when handled; then cool, form into small almonds and bake in a slow oven.

114. Kisses. For these cakes the finest powdered sugar only can be used. Take 1 pound of powdered sugar, a little vanilla, 4—6 fresh eggs (the whites only). Beat the whites to a froth stiff enough to cut, add sugar and vanilla, whipping constantly. Drop the batter onto a waxed pan with a teaspoon, bake in a slow oven. Some people prefer the kisses filled with whipped cream. Form the dough into balls the size of an egg, bake, hollow them, form the bottom and just before serving, fill them with cream.

115. Sweet Macaroons. $1\frac{1}{2}$ pounds of sifted sugar, 1 pound of grated almonds, the whites of 4 eggs, the grated rind of a lemon. Stir the almonds with sugar, lemon peel and the beaten whites of the eggs for a time, form into long or round balls with a spoon, put into a hot waxed pan and bake in a slow oven until light yellow. If the macaroons are wanted bitter, use three parts of sweet and one part of bitter almonds.

116. Spiced Macaroons. 1 pound of grated almonds, 1½ pounds of sifted sugar, the grated peel of a lemon, cinnamon, cloves, nutmeg or mace and the whites of a few eggs.

The ingredients are stirred with enough white of egg to bind the mass, beating the dough with a spoon, not stirring it. Bake as directed in the above receipt.

117. Almond Nuts. ½ pound of flour, ½ pound of sugar, ½ pound of pounded almonds, 2 ounces of butter, 4—6 eggs, lemon- or orange peel.

Cream the butter and stir with eggs, sugar, spices and almonds for ¼ hour, stir in the flour, make into little balls and bake slowly until a light yellow.

118. White Rifle Nuts (Pfeffernuesse). 1 pound of flour, 1 pound of sugar, both sifted, 4 large eggs, 3 ounces of citron, the peel of a lemon, 1 nutmeg, 1 tablespoonful of cinnamon, 1 teaspoonful of ground cloves, baking powder and white pepper.

Eggs, sugar and spices are stirred well together, mix the baking powder with the flour, mix all together, form into little balls and bake slowly.

119. Brunswick Rifle Nuts. 1 pound of flour, 1 pound of honey, baking powder, 1½ ounces of cinnamon, ½ ounce of ground cloves and the necessary flour.

Put the honey on the fire until it comes to a boil, stir into a deep dish, rinse the dish in which the honey was boiled with 1 cupful of water, add this to the dough and knead into the latter enough flour to make it very stiff. Cover the dough and set it aside for a few weeks or so in a cool place. When ready to bake put the dough on the board, add the spices and baking powder, knead the dough, roll it, fold it together again, roll again until soft and elastic. Then roll a small piece of the dough to the thickness of a finger, cut into pieces ½ inch thick, put these side by side into a buttered pan. After the little cakes are all made, take the rolling pin, lightly roll it over them to make them even and bake in a moderate oven until done, but not too dark nor too hard. After taking from the oven let the cakes remain in the pan so that they will harden like crackers, but they must not brown. The cakes are best when baked in this way, fcr if put into the oven to bake and dry at the same time they are apt to become too brown and are then bitter. To make them nicer sprinkle sliced almonds over the bottom of the pan before putting in the cakes. When put into a dry place they will keep for a long time.

120. Anise Cakes. 1 pound of flour, 1 pound of sugar, both sifted, 4 whole eggs, a piece of butter the size of a walnut, baking powder and anise seed.

Sugar, butter and eggs are stirred for ¼ hour and mixed to a dough with the flour and baking powder, setting aside a little of the flour. Put the dough on a board, knead, roll out to the thickness of half a finger, dust with a little flour and with a cutter stamp out the desired figures. After this is done lay them on a board sprinkled with anise, and leave them over night in a dry place. The next day wax a pan, put the cakes on it and bake in a moderate oven to a light yellow color.

121. Basil Honey Cakes ("Lebkuchen"). 1 pint of honey, which must be at least a year old, 2¾ pounds of flour, 1⅓ pounds of sugar, 7 ounces of almonds, the same quantity of orange peel and also citron, and the peel of 2 lemons all coarsely cut, furthermore about 2 ounces of cinnamon, ¼ ounce of cloves, 2 teaspoonfuls of mace, baking powder, 1 glassful of cherry cordial or arrac.

Honey and sugar are put on the stove; when the mass begins to raise put in the almonds and roast them for some time. Then take the pan from the fire, add the spices and when cool the cherry cordial and at last the flour and baking powder. As long as the dough is warm roll it to the thickness of ¼ of an inch, cut it into oblong pieces, lay close together on a pan dusted with flour and set aside over night. Then bake in a moderate oven; they are cut with a knife while still hot and when cold broken apart. For an icing boil sugar until it threads and then spread the cakes with it.

122. Basil Honey Jumbles ("Leckerli"). 1 pound of honey, 1 pound of sifted sugar, 1 pound of almonds, cut lengthwise, 1 pound of flour, 2 ounces of citron, the finely cut peel of a lemon, ½ of a nutmeg, cloves, and ½ wineglassful of rum or arrac.

Melt the honey on the stove, into this pour the sugar and almonds, stir together, add the other ingredients and knead to a dough which is set aside for a week. Then roll the dough about ½ inch thick, lay it on a waxed pan and bake in a hot oven. Cut the cake into pieces about 1 inch wide and 2 inches long.

123. Honey Cakes. 2 pounds of honey, 2 pounds of flour, ½ pound of butter, 6 ounces of almonds, the peel of a lemon, ⅛ ounce each of ground cloves and cardamom, and some baking powder.

Cook honey and butter together, take the dish from the fire, stir in the flour, spices and the coarsely pounded almonds, and when the dough has cooled mix the baking powder through it and set aside over night. Roll the dough to the thickness of about ½ inch and make into small square cakes, put an almond on each, also a piece of citron and bake to a nice yellow color.

124. Holland Pretzels. For the dough take ½ pound of flour, ½ pound of sugar, the yolks of 2 eggs, 1 tablespoonful of sour cream and 1 tablespoonful of coriander. Roll pieces of it with the hands into the shape of little pretzels or wreaths, and bake.

125. Holland Cakes. 1 pound of flour, 1 pound of sugar, 4 eggs, cloves and baking powder. Work the dough well, make into balls the size of a walnut, put an almond or a piece of orange peel on each and bake.

126. Small Cream Cakes. ½ pound of flour, 1 egg, 6 ounces of butter, 2 ounces of sifted sugar, 2 tablespoonfuls of thick sour cream.

Make into a dough, roll, cut with a wineglass or a round cutter, spread the cakes with lightly browned butter, sprinkle with sugar and cinnamon and bake to a light brown color.

127. Small Crackers ("Zwieback"). 2¾ pounds of flour, ½ pound of sifted sugar, 6 ounces of butter, or half lard and half butter, a little more than 1 pint of milk, 2 ounces of fresh yeast, 3 eggs, a little mace and cloves. Warm the flour, stir in the warmed milk with eggs, spices and the dissolved yeast, work to a soft dough, cover and let it raise for about 1 hour. Then add the sugar and butter, mix with the remaining flour and knead the dough as directed under No. 1.

Break small pieces from the dough, form round and smooth with the hands, put them on a buttered pan and let them raise again in a warm room. When this is done, bake them in a moderate oven for 10—15 minutes, and let them cool in the pan. Then cut them in two with a sharp knife—not pressing the crackers—and lay the cut side to the top and bake again in the oven to a nice yellow color.

To have the crackers crisp and fresh, after they are cut and baked warm them again in the oven.

128. Nice Almond Cakes. For the dough, 1¾ pounds of flour, 1 pound of freshened butter, 2 ounces of yeast, 1 cupful of warm milk and the yolks of 2 eggs; for on the cakes, 6 ounces of pounded almonds, the whites of 2 eggs; sugar and cinnamon. Cut the butter into small pieces, mix with the flour, stirring in the milk, sugar and dissolved yeast, and work to a soft dough, but it must not stick to the hands. Take small pieces of the dough, roll them out long and pinch the ends together, spread with beaten whites of eggs, dip into a mixture of sugar, almonds and cinnamon and lay them into a pan not too closely together. After they have raised bake in a moderate oven to a dark yellow color. The above quantity will make 60—70 cakes.

129. Cinnamon Rolls or Waffles. 1 pound of flour, 1 pound of sugar, both sifted, ½ pound of clarified butter, 7 eggs, cinnamon and grated lemon peel. When the butter is cold cream it, add the eggs and sugar, stir for a short time, mix with spices and flour. Then heat the waffle iron, put a spoonful of the batter into the iron, close it and bake first on one side and then on the other. The iron need not be buttered. These and the following cakes are nicer when the dough is prepared the day previous.

130. New Years' Cake. 1 pound of flour, ½ pound of pounded rock candy, 6 ounces of fresh butter, 1 egg, grated lemon peel, ground cinnamon, and if liked a tablespoonful of anise seed.

Dissolve the pounded sugar in a little more than 1 pint of boiling water, cool, add the melted butter, flour, spices, and egg, and stir for a while; it is best to bake it the following day. Put a tablespoonful into the iron (lined with butter) at a time, or enough to nicely cover the bottom, bake for 2—3 minutes on both sides and when done, quickly roll them around a smooth round piece of wood. For baking them have a slow wood fire, a charcoal fire is the best if it can be had. To keep these cakes, put them into a covered tin or basket and set into a warm place, because dampness will soften them.

131. German Waffles. ¾ pound of flour, ½ pound of fresh butter, 1 pint of lukewarm milk, 7 fresh eggs, fresh yeast dissolved in milk, 1 teaspoonful of arrac or rum, mace and lemon peel.

Cream the butter, add to it eggs, flour, milk, yeast and spices, beat the dough thoroughly, add the rum, cover, set aside 3—4 hours to raise. Then bake the cakes with a slow fire, and grease the iron with a piece of fresh pork fat. Then put a small spoonful of dough into the iron and bake both sides to a golden brown. Sprinkle sugar over the waffles.

III. CAKES BAKED IN BUTTER, LARD AND OIL.

132. Rules for Baking. Slow raising of the dough will greatly improve it and make it smoother. For doughnuts and the like, the dough should not be too soft, at the same time it must not be compact, and for this reason a few eggs should be added to prevent absorption of the fat; salt must not be forgotten. The moulding board must always be carefully dusted with flour so that the dough will not adhere to it, which would also cause the fat to penetrate.

Butter, of course, always makes the finest baking. The method of preparing it for the various receipts in this subdivision has been explained in Division A. No. 8. Good lard is also well adapted for the various kinds of baking in this subdivision.

A sufficient quantity of lard or butter should always be taken because when plenty of it is used the articles baked in it will not absorb so much and have a pleasanter flavor; a pound or two will generally be sufficient. After being used once it can be used again with the addition of some fresh butter or fat, and whatever is then left can be utilized in cooking. Take it from the fire as soon as the baking is done, pour it into a dish and when cold take off the settlings, melt the fat and set aside.

A medium fire is necessary for baking in fat. The kettle should be deep enough that boiling over need not be feared, and quite wide so that a quantity of the baking can be done at one and the same time. Before beginning to bake get the fat so hot that when a piece of the dough is dropped into it, it will at once rise to the top. The quicker the cakes brown in the fat, the less the latter can penetrate the dough and make it greasy. Should the fat become too hot, however, take the kettle from the fire a few minutes before commencing to bake; it is advisable to always reserve about one-fourth of the fat and to add a small quantity of it whenever the contents of the kettle become too hot.

When baking cakes in which yeast is used, for instance "Berlin pancakes", the upper side is put into the fat first. Shake the kettle occasionally and when brown from below turn the cakes with a fork, and when the top is brown also take them out, lay them on a piece of absorbent (blotting) paper for a while, turn in powdered sugar and dust some of this over the top.

133. Berlin Pancakes ("Berliner Pfannkuchen"). For the dough take 1 cupful of milk, ½ pound of clarified butter, 1 whole egg and the yolks of 5 eggs, scant 2 ounces of yeast, 2 ounces of sugar, a teaspoonful of salt and flour. For filling, currants, cherries, jelly or marmalade.

Flour and butter are warmed. Then whip the eggs, stir the lukewarm milk with the eggs, yeast, butter, sugar, salt and flour into a dough which is beaten until it bubbles, and no longer sticks to the spoon. Then set it aside to raise. When this is done roll it out to about the thickness of one-half inch and put a teaspoonful of the fruit jelly or marmalade 2 inches apart on half of the dough and lay the other half over this, and then with a glass cut so as to have the dots of jelly in the center of the cakes, and let them raise again. Then heat the fat, put the cakes in side by side with the tops to the bottom, putting in just enough cakes to cover the fat. They must be of a dark yellow color, and when done turn in powdered sugar or sprinkle with sugar and cinnamon; serve fresh. If wished they can also be frosted.

134. Doughnuts. 1 pint of water is boiled with 3 ounces of butter, then stir in 1 pound of flour and cook until it no longer adheres to the sides of the kettle. After it has cooled somewhat, beat in 10 eggs, make the dough into balls with a teaspoon, fry in fat and turn in sugar and cinnamon.

135. Brunswick Cakes ("Prillken"). 1½ pounds of warmed flour, ½ pound of melted butter, 3 ounces of sugar, 1 cupful of lukewarm milk, 2 eggs, yeast, the grated peel of a lemon and a little salt. Make into a dough and let it raise; when this is done, dip the hands in flour, form the dough into rings and put them on a bread board, let them raise; fry in fat to a light brown color and while hot, roll in sugar and cinnamon.

136. Snow Balls. ½ pound of flour, 2 ounces of butter, 1 cupful of water, 8—9 eggs, a little salt.
Water, butter and flour are stirred together as given in the above receipt; when cool stir in the eggs, and whip the dough until it is smooth. Make into balls and bake the same as given for "Berlin pancakes" to a yellow color. While still hot roll in sugar and cinnamon.

137. Butter Rings. 1 pound of warmed flour, 2 ounces of butter, the same quantity of pounded almonds mixed with a few bitter ones, 1 cupful of milk, 1 whole and the yolks of 4 eggs, 2 tablespoonfuls of rosewater, 1 tablespoonful of sugar, a little salt, yeast dissolved in a little milk.
Warm the milk and the butter, stir in eggs, rosewater, almonds, spices, yeast and flour, beat the dough and lay it on a moulding board dusted with flour. Then take small pieces of the dough, form them into little

rings and set aside to raise. Then bake in lard the same as "Berlin pancakes", beginning with those which were make first. They must be of a light yellow color. While hot roll in sugar and cinnamon.

138. Silesian Farina Cakes. 1 quart of milk, 2 cupfuls of farina, the yolks of 2 eggs, 1 tablespoonful of sugar, a trifle of grated lemon peel, cinnamon, mace and salt, also a few eggs, sifted sugar and rolled crackers.

Boil the milk, stirring in the farina, spices, sugar and salt. Then stir in the yolks of 2 eggs, put the dough, about 1 inch thick, into a dish dusted with flour, after it is cold cut into strips about 1½ inches wide and dust these with flour. Then beat a few eggs with sugar, turn the rolls in this, sprinkle with rolled crackers, and bake in lard to a dark brown color.

139. Swiss Rolls. Small rolls or milk breads are cut in two in the center, soaked in milk so that they are soft all through, and then put on a dish to drain. They are then fried in hot lard to a yellow brown color, sprinkled with sugar and cinnamon or powdered sugar, and brought to the table hot. They are nice with tea, also for dessert with whipped cream or a wine sauce.

140. Baked Wheat Loaf. 1 large fresh wheat loaf, 1 pint of milk, 4 eggs, 2 tablespoonfuls of sugar, cinnamon, mace and a cream sauce, seasoned with a little rum if desired. After cutting away the crust, let it soak in the above mixture, dip in the cream sauce, bake in butter as given under No. 132 to a yellowish brown color, and while hot sprinkle with sugar and cinnamon.

This is served as a dessert with a cream or fruit sauce. The bread can also be sprinkled with almonds and baked in a hot oven to a nice yellow color, basting often with butter.

141. Filled Bread. Cut the crust from a wheat loaf, then cut it in two and hollow each half a little.

Prepare a nice apple sauce with lemon, sugar and wine, stir into it the yolks of a few eggs, and a few bread crumbs, pour on a dish, stir in some chopped almonds or pounded macaroons and fill into the bread. Lay the pieces of bread together, spread the outside all round with egg, dip the bread into a sauce and bake in butter as in the above receipt.

142. Cherry Bread. 1 pound of stoned sour cherries, pound a few stones and cook the cherries with 1 cupful of Portwine and 6 ounces of sugar until thick, and rub them through a sieve. In the meantime soak small milk breads in milk, cutting off the crust, dip into a sauce and bake as given in No. 132. After the breads have dried set them side by side in the cherry sauce, sprinkled with sugar and if liked spread with whipped cream. Bake in a moderate oven for ¼ hour.

143. Apple Slices Baked in Butter or Lard. Peel large cooking apples and cut into slices ½ inch thick, take out the core. Soak in arrac and sugar for a short time, dip them into a sauce as given in R., No. 92, fry in butter and when done sprinkle with sugar seasoned with vanilla. Instead of apples, pears, peeled and sliced oranges, plums and apricots can be used.

In order that the apples may absorb but little fat, do not put more into the fat than will swim on the top.

144. English Pie Crust. 3 ounces of flour, 6 eggs, 1 pint of water and milk, (1 part water and 2 parts milk), 1 cupful of thick sour cream. mace and a little salt.

Flour, the yolks of the eggs, milk and spices are beaten together, mixed with the whipped whites of the eggs, and slightly baked in the oven with butter. Cut into oblong pieces about the size of a playing card, bake again in lard and butter half and half, sprinkle with sugar and vanilla. These cakes taste like waffles and are served with coffee or tea.

IV. BREAD.

145. Rolls or Milk Bread. To 1 quart of fresh milk take 4 pounds of flour, yeast and a little salt.

Set the flour in a warm place for a few hours, and have the milk lukewarm; add the dissolved yeast to the milk and stir enough flour to the milk to make a not too thin dough; then set aside. After this has raised, add the salt, and work in the remaining flour until the dough no longer sticks to the hands. The kneading must be done with the flat hand. Then beat the dough as given under No. 1, form into loaves which must be smooth on the top, let them raise again, cut into the dough, spread with beaten egg, put into a hot oven and bake until done.

Milk breads can be greatly improved by adding to the above 4 eggs and ¼ pound of butter.

146. Sour Rye Bread. To 1 quart of water add 5 pounds of rye flour and some sour dough (leavening) the size of an apple.

The evening before baking warm the water and mix the leavening with part of the flour into a thin dough, dust with flour and set aside to raise until the next morning. Then knead in the salt and the remaining flour, make into a long loaf, set to raise again and bake in a hot oven for 2 hours.

If the dough should not have raised enough, work in a little yeast when kneading; if buttermilk is used instead of water, the bread will be nicer; then use only half of the leavening.

147. Rice= and Wheat Bread. Boil 1 pound of rice in milk until tender and while warm mix with it 4 pounds of wheat flour, some dissolved yeast, 1 spoonful of salt and enough water to make a stiff dough, which is beaten, set aside to raise and then divided into 2 loaves. Spread with beaten egg and bake in a hot oven.

T.–Preserved and Dried Fruits and Vegetables.

1. Rules to be observed in Preserving Fruits. Particular care should be taken that all fruit which is to be preserved is well cleaned, and when possible always rub clean with a cloth.

The kettle in which the fruits are cooked must not have been used for preparing fatty food. A new double kettle filled with cold water, put on the fire and brought to a boil, or an enameled kettle is the best, Spoons and skimmers must not be greasy, and whenever possible the kitchen utensils used in making preserves should be devoted to this purpose only.

The vinegar should always be of the very best quality obtainable.

During the time the fruits are on the fire nothing else should be cooked that will emit a strong or pungent odor, such as cabbage or other vegetables, fat, etc., because this will act deleteriously on the fruit. The fire should be well attended to at the beginning, and if you have a coal fire it should not be disturbed, because the gas thereby liberated is also harmful to the fruit.

The fruit jars must be scrupulously clean and should be rinsed thoroughly a day or so before using, and dried in the sun or open air. When the jars are filled be careful to have the fruit covered with juice as much as possible; a teaspoonful of arrac or French brandy poured in at the top, or a circular piece of paper cut the size of the mouth of the jar, soaked in these liquors and placed on top of the fruit, will be found of great advantage.

Cloves are used in numerous varieties of preserves, but are apt to produce black spots on light colored vegetables or fruits, such as pumpkins, walnuts, etc.; to prevent this the heads of the cloves must be removed.

Fruits and vegetables such as pickles, prunes, cherries, etc., preserved in vinegar should be covered with an inverted saucer and weighted with a small stone, which must not be heavy enough to produce much pressure, but enough to keep the fruit or pickles under the juice or brine. A small muslin bag containing mustard seeds, the bag large enough to cover all of the pickles, is a good medium for preserving them.

Pickles and preserves should always be set aside in a cool, airy, dry place. The cellar is not usually well adapted for this purpose on account of dampness, especially in the Winter.

If a scum forms on the surface of the liquor containing the pickles, which is commonly caused through the inferior quality of the vinegar, wash the jar carefully and dry it, rinse the pickles in cold water, boil the vinegar and take off the scum, add some fresh vinegar, put part of the pickles into it for a few minutes, let them cool on a flat dish, then put them into the jar again and cover with the vinegar. Should the vinegar, however, have become flat without spoiling the pickles, it is of no further use and should be thrown away. Take fresh vinegar, put it on the fire with the rinsed pickles and the spices (which should be rinsed on a sieve) and as soon as the vinegar is hot take out the pickles, bring the vinegar to a boil, and as soon as it is cool pour it over the pickles.

Directions for keeping dill in good condition will be found under A. No. 41.

2. Clarifying Sugar for Preserves. The sugar should always be of good quality. It is clarified as follows: Put it on the fire in a very clean copper or enameled kettle in the proportion of 1 pound of sugar to ½ pint of water, and let it boil until clear, taking off any scum that may appear.

If the sugar is to boil until it beads, have a slow fire, but then do not use an enameled kettle, because the enamel will crack.

3. To Prevent Preserves from becoming candied.
Fruits candy because they were either too dry or because
the sugar was boiled down too much. The latter diffi-
culty can be obviated by exercising due caution; if it is
impossible to obtain any other than dry fruits that are
not juicy, add a trifle of citric acid diluted with a little
water to the fruit juice, after it is poured from the fruits
and brought to a boil.

I. FRUITS PRESERVED IN FRENCH BRANDY.

Remark.—It is important to use the best, genuine French Brandy; if adulterated or inferior qualities are taken, the preserves will spoil.

4. Mixed Fruits in Brandy. 1 cupful of pure brandy
and to every pound of fruit 1 pound of sugar. The fruit
must not be over-ripe and should be carefully wiped with
a cloth. Begin by putting in the strawberries first, then
the raspberries, currants, cherries with the stems half
cut away, apricots, peaches, pears, peeled and sliced
melon, grapes, and whatever other fruits are desired.
Pour the brandy into a clean dish which can be
tightly covered. Put in 1 pound of strawberries and at
the same time 1 pound of pulverized sugar; set the dish
aside in a very cool place. With every pound of the
succeeding fruits put in 1 pound of sugar, stirring very
carefully. If any considerable quantity of the fruit is to
follow it will be necessary to add another cupful of
brandy. After the last lot of fruit has been stirred
through, fill the preserves into jars and follow general
directions in No. 1 of this division.

5. Fruit in Brandy (French method). For 1 quart
of brandy, 1 pound of the best sugar.
The fruit, which ought not be too ripe, must be
wiped clean with a cloth and put into cans in layers
with the sugar, then pour in as much brandy as will
cover the fruit, cover the jar and proceed as given
under No. 1. Put into a boiler with cold water, between
straw, and put on the fire. Let the fruit cook for ¼
hour and then cool in the water.

6. Cherries in Brandy. 3 pounds of sweet cherries, 1½ pounds of sugar, 1 pint of brandy, cinnamon and cloves.

Put the fruit into cans after having been cleaned and half of the stems taken off. Then clarify the sugar as directed under No. 2, let it cool, stir the brandy through it, put a few pieces of cloves and cinnamon into the syrup, pour it over the cherries and cover the cans.

7. Quinces in Cognac. For each pound of quinces (weighed after cooking) take ¾ pound of sugar, cognac, lemon peel and cinnamon.

Peel the quinces, cut each one into eight parts, and after taking out the seeds put them into cold water. In the meantime bring some water to a boil and cook the quinces in this until they can easily be pierced with a fork, but they must not become soft.

Then take them out with a skimmer, lay them on a colander to drain, put a fine slice of lemon peel and cinnamon on each piece of citron. Then clarify the sugar as given under No. 2, cook for a while with the citron water, pour hot over the quinces and after 48 hours boil the juice. Then stir in as much cognac as wanted, and pour over the citron.

II. PRESERVED FRUITS.

8. Preserved Strawberries with Currant Juice. For 1 pound of strawberries take 1 pound of sugar, put one-half of the sugar over the berries and leave them over night. The next day cook the sweetened berries with currant- or apple juice, which has been boiled until thick, that is, not the berries but the juice is to be boiled; put the juice and berries on the fire together, and as soon as the berries are heated through take them out and cook the jelly for a few minutes longer. This is served with roasts, also with biscuits and sand cakes; served also alone with sweet cream.

9. Strawberries preserved in English Style. The fresh berries are put into glasses in layers with sugar (6 ounces of sugar with 1 pound of fruit), pour over the fruit some boiling hot Madeira or Malaga, and close the glasses tightly, wrap them in hay so that they will not touch one another, put them into a kettle, bring the water to a boil and cook the fruit until about one-fourth is boiled away; then take the kettle from the fire and leave the glasses in it until quite cool. Take them out and set aside in a cool place.

10. Strawberry Marmalade. 1 pound of strawberries, 1½ pounds of sugar; cook the strawberries in the clarified sugar under constant stirring until they become pulpy and the juice is thick. Can as directed under No. 1.

Or the heated berries may be passed through a sieve and stirred with sugar (to 1 pound of berries take 2 pounds of sugar), fill the marmalade into glasses, which must be covered immediately, cook in a double boiler for ¼ hour, leaving them in the boiler until cold.

11. Strawberry Juice for Invalids. 1 quart of fresh ripe strawberries, 1 pound of sugar. Cook the sugar to a syrup, lay in the fruit, stir carefully through the syrup with a silver spoon without breaking the berries, let them heat through but they must not boil. Then spread over a dish a thin muslin cloth, which must first be rinsed in fresh boiling water, and pour the fruit into the muslin so that the juice will drip through. The berries must not be pressed nor crushed. Pour the juice from the settlings into small bottles. 3 quarts of berries will give ¾ quart of juice, which is very nice for invalids. The berries will make a good compot. They can also be put into glasses until currants and raspberries are ripe, and then cooked to a marmalade with these fruits, taking for 3 pounds of fresh fruit 2 pounds of sugar.

12. Grape Juice. Mash white grapes, set aside for a few days and then press them. Boil the juice, taking ¾ pound of sugar for each 1 pound of juice, skim carefully, let it cool and pour through a muslin cloth. Put into bottles and cork tightly.

13. Gooseberry Marmalade. 1 pound of ripe gooseberries, ½ pound of sugar, lemon peel or cinnamon. Fully ripe gooseberries are weighed, washed, drained and then mashed with a silver spoon and pressed through a sieve. Then put them into the sugar and spices, which have been boiled to a syrup, stir constantly and cook to a thick marmalade. In case it should turn watery after about a week it must be boiled again.

14. Preserved Walnuts. 1 pound of walnuts, 1 pound of sugar, cinnamon and cloves. The nuts must be spotless and they should be freed from the inner skin. They are perforated in a few places with a sharp bodkin or larding needle, and left in cold water, which must be renewed three times daily for about a fortnight. Then change the water, boil the walnuts until tender, let them lay over night in cold water and the next morning put them on a sieve to drain. Instead of sticking cloves all over the walnuts, whereby they lose their nice appearance, cook the spices with sugar and the walnuts, which will give them a nice spicy flavor. Some people prefer them without spices. The juice of a lemon and citron peel for every pound of sugar will also give the walnuts a pleasant flavor. Clarify the sugar as given under No. 2, and let the walnuts boil for a few minutes. After 3—4 days cook the sugar syrup again, put the walnuts into a jar and pour the hot juice over them.

15. Raspberries are preserved the same as currants, but they must not be washed.

16. Raspberry Jelly. Prepare the same as currant jelly (No. 22), adding a little currant juice, because the jelly will become thicker. Berries for jellies should not be quite ripe.

17. Raspberry Marmalade is prepared the same as strawberry marmalade, No. 10.

18. Good Raspberry Vinegar. 2 quarts of raspberries, 1 quart of vinegar, for each quart of juice 1½ pounds of sugar.

Mash the berries a little, pour the vinegar over the berries, set aside for 24 hours and then press them. The next day pour the juice from the settlings, put on the fire with sugar, skim, set aside over night and then proceed as given under No. 1. All fruits must be kept in porcelain dishes.

19. Currant Jelly. For each pound of juice take 1 pound of sugar. Take the currants from the stems, mash them and then squeeze the juice through a cloth. After the juice is pressed out let it run through a conical bag, set it aside until the next day and pour from the settlings. Put the juice on a slow fire, gradually adding the sugar, stirring constantly. When the sugar has all been put into the juice it must be ready to boil, then take from the fire, set aside for ½ hour, take off the skin and fill into glasses, and after 48 hours put over the top a paper dipped in brandy or arrac, and tie carefully.

20. French Currant Jelly. ¾ pound of red and ¼ pound of white currant juice, and 1 pound of sugar. Put the currants on the fire until they are heated through, then pour on a new sieve, let the juice run through, pour it over the berries and let it run through the sieve again. Then boil sugar until it threads as given under No. 2, add the juice and skim carefully and cook for ¼ hour. Proceed as given under No. 1.

21. Black Currant Preserves. For every pound of fruit take ½ pound of sugar, clarify and boil the berries in this, stirring a few times. Pour into the glasses while still hot.

22. Black Currant Jelly. Prepare the same as for currant jelly, taking only half the quantity of sugar.

23. Preserved Cherries. 2 pounds of cherries freed from stems and stones, and 2 pounds of sugar.
Boil the sugar with 1 cupful of water until clear, stirring often, put the cherries into the syrup and set aside in a porcelain dish until the next day. Then pour into a colander, cook the juice again and pour it boiling hot over the cherries. The third day bring the juice to a boil until it becomes a thin syrup, stir the berries into this and fill into glasses while still hot.

24. Cherries for the Sick. 2 pounds of sour and 2 pounds of sweet cherries, 1 pound of sugar and a little cinnamon.
Dissolve the sugar in water, boil and skim; cook the sweet cherries with the cinnamon in this until about

half done, then put in the sour cherries and cook until tender, take out the juice, pour some of the juice into fruit jars, let the remaining juice boil for a while and pour over the cherries. To the cherry juice add for each half jar a piece of cinnamon and 2—3 cloves, and proceed as given under No. 1.

25. Cherry Juice. For each pound of juice take 6 ounces of sugar and 6 cherry pits.

Stone sour cherries and set them aside until the next day. Then press through a scalded cloth, weigh the juice, add the sugar, cook and skim for ¼ hour, fill into small dry bottles, cork tightly and set in a cool place.

26. Pineapple Peel Juice. Cut the peels of the pineapples into small pieces, weigh, and take three times as much sugar as you have fruit, boil and skim; cook the peel in this for 10 minutes. Set the juice aside until the next day, then pour it through the cloth and fill into bottles. After carefully corking the bottles steam them in a double boiler for 10—15 minutes. Another way is to take the peel, cut it up, sprinkle thickly with sugar and fill into glasses; cover tightly. The juice will keep for a long time.

27. Preserved Apricots. For each pound of stoned apricots take 1 pound of sugar. The apricots are washed, peeled, halved and the stones taken out. They can also be left whole. Put the apricots into an enameled dish, the round side to the bottom, and sprinkle sugar over them. The next day put them on a slow fire until hot, but they must not become soft, pour them on a colander to drain, then put a few of the stones into a can, cook the juice a little while longer, then pour over the fruit and fill into glasses. After about a week cook the juice again and then pour cold over the fruit.

28. Apricot and Peach Marmalade Marmalades should be cooked in very clean enameled kettles, stirring often, add the necessary sugar and as soon as done fill into fruit jars. The fruit, which must not be too ripe, is scalded so that the peel will easily come off. Halve and stone them, take as much sugar as fruit, put into an enameled kettle with the thinly peeled rind of a lemon and a few pieces of ginger; this will tend to keep the marmalade longer. Cook to a thick marmalade until tender, stirring constantly with a new wooden spoon, as it is apt to scorch. Should it became watery after about a week, it will have to be cooked again.

29. Cranberry Jelly. 1 pint of juice, 1 pound of sugar. Wash and clean the berries, put them into a moderately hot oven, stirring often until the juice is extracted. Squeeze through a muslin cloth, pour from the settlings, and for each pint of juice take 1 pound of sugar. Skim carefully and cook for about 15 minutes, take from the fire, and if any scum arises take it off. Fill the jelly into glasses. If cooked too long the jelly loses its nice red color; it must be thick enough to cut, as it is very nice for decorating. Try a little of the jelly after it has cooked to ascertain if it is thick enough.

30. Apple Marmalade. Pare and core the apples, and put them into a pan of fresh water acidulated with the juice of a lemon, so as to keep the fruit nice and white. For every pound of fruit take ½ pound of sugar, let it boil, skim carefully, add the thinly peeled rind of a lemon cut into small pieces, put in the apples, stirring constantly on a quick fire until thick. Take but little water, and the apples should be of a variety which will not become pulpy in cooking.

31. Preserved Blackberries. 3 pounds of ripe blackberries, 1 pound of sugar, cinnamon and a few cloves. Clarify the sugar, add the berries and spices and cook on a slow fire, stirring often, but carefully, so that the berries will remain whole. Then take them out, let the juice boil for a while longer, and pour over the berries. Fill into cans and cover tightly.

32. Prune Marmalade for Compots, also for spreading over or filling into Cakes and small Drop Cakes. 6 pounds of ripe prunes, stoned and skinned, 2 pounds of sugar, a few tablespoonfuls of vinegar, cinnamon, and cloves with the heads removed. Skin the prunes and stone them. Then boil sugar with the vinegar until clear, add the prunes, spices and cook, stirring often, because this compot is apt to scorch, for 2—2½ hours, or until the marmalade is thick.

33. Preserved Pears. For each pound of pears take 1 pound of sugar and a piece of ginger the length of a finger.

Take nice juicy pears, peel, core and wash them. In the meantime boil the sugar, put in the pears and ginger and cook until clear; they must not be too tender. Then lay them on a porcelain dish to cool, and let the juice boil, lay the fruit into the cans and pour over them the hot syrup. Cover tightly and set aside in a cool place.

They can also be preserved in cranberry juice, taking 1 quart of cranberry juice, 12 ounces of sugar and ¼ ounce of cinnamon for each 1½ pounds of fruit.

34. Preserved Pears, French Method. Peel the pears according to size, leave them whole or halve them, and as soon as peeled put them into water acidulated with lemon juice. Cook the pears in this water until they can easily be pierced with a fork, take them out with a skimmer, throw into cold water and let them drain. For every 2¼ pounds of pears take not quite 1½ pounds of sugar. Pour the clarified sugar over the pears and let them stand for 6—8 hours, pour off the juice, cook it until thick and then pour it over the pears again, after which set aside until the next day. Then pour off the juice once more, put a piece of lemon peel and a vanilla bean into a little bag and cook with the juice, put the pears into this and set on the stove for ¼ hour. Then put into cans and cover tightly. This is a very nice way of preserving pears; they have a brilliant white color and taste deliciously.

35. Apple Jelly. 3 pounds of juice, 3 pounds of sugar, ½ tumblerful of white wine and 1 lemon.

Take nice, juicy, not quite ripe apples, wipe them with a cloth, take out the stems, quarter without paring them, and cook in water until tender. Set the apples aside for 24 hours and then pour them into a jelly bag and let the juice drip into an enameled kettle. Boil the juice with sugar and after a while add wine and lemon juice and cook until the juice, when cold, is thick. Fill into small glasses and cover tightly as given under No. 1.

Instead of lemon peel, a vanilla bean tied in a little bag can be used; citron slices can also be taken so as to make the jelly thicken quicker, but when using this it will lose its clear color and taste stronger.

36. Apple Marmalade. 2 pounds of apples, 1 pound of sugar and 1 lemon.

Peel the apples, wash twice and weigh them. Then clarify the sugar, add the apples and the juice of a lemon with the peel, cook quickly in an enameled kettle until done. Then mash the apples and cook to a thick marmalade, stirring often from the bottom. If after a week the marmalade has become watery, boil again, skimming carefully.

37. Crab Apple Jelly. 1 pound of juice, ½ pound of sugar. Wash the apples, put them into a copper or an enameled kettle, cover with cold water, cook until tender and then press them through a sieve with the juice. The next day pour from the settlings, weigh, put on the fire with the sugar, skimming carefully, and cook for 1 hour, whereby this jelly obtains a nice red color. Fill into glasses and proceed as given for currant jelly. This jelly can be nicely moulded, and is well adapted for decorating, and can be cut into any desired ornament.

38. Preserved Citron. 1 pound of citron, ¾—1 pound of sugar, cinnamon and if liked a few pieces of preserved ginger.

Wipe the citron, peel, cut in two once and cook in water with the peel and core until nearly tender. The core will give the citron a nice yellowish-red color. Then let them drain, cooking the juice for an hour longer, strain, add sugar and skim. Let the citron cook in this until tender, lay into a glass with cinnamon and ginger, cook the juice until thick and pour over the citron while still hot. The juice must cover the fruit the same as with all preserves. If they are liked slightly sour, add to each pound of citron, while cooking, the juice of a lemon.

39. Quince Jelly. No. 1. 14 quinces and 2 pounds of sugar. The quinces are quartered, put into an enameled kettle, nearly covered with water and cooked until tender. Then pour the juice through a cloth; it will amount to about 1 quart. Clarify the sugar, pour the juice of the quinces from the settlings, add to the sugar and cook for about ¼ hour, skimming carefully. The juice will by that time have the required consistency.

40. Quince Jelly. No. 2. Clean 1 dozen quinces and grate them to the core with the peel, squeeze the juice through a cloth and set aside over night and pour from the settlings. For each pint of juice take 1 pound of sugar, clarify and boil it until it threads and then pour in the juice; put the seeds of the quinces into a little bag and boil with the juice. The seeds give the jelly a nice color. Skim carefully and let the juice boil for ½ hour. The fruit must not be too ripe, otherwise it will be difficult to have it jelly perfectly. This jelly is of a very pretty color and tastes nicely.

41. Quince Marmalade. 1 pound of quinces, ¾ pound of sugar and 1 lemon.

Cook the quinces in water until tender, peel and grate them, clarify the sugar, add the quinces, the finely cut peel of half a lemon and the juice of a whole lemon, and stir on a moderate fire until thick. If it should become watery after about a week, boil again.

III. FRUITS PRESERVED IN SUGAR AND VINEGAR.

42. Sweet Black Cherries in Vinegar and Sugar for Compot or Cherry Cake. 6 pounds of stoned cherries, 1 pound of sugar, ¼ ounce of stick cinnamon, ¼ ounce of cloves, 1 cupful of strong wine vinegar. Boil together, skimming carefully, until the cherries are tender. Put the cherries into a jar with a skimmer and cook the juice for a while longer. Then stir the juice through the cherries, cover the jar tightly and set aside in a cool place.

REMARK.—This compot is very nice in the Winter for cherry cake. When used for this purpose, let the juice, which will make a nice sauce for almond jelly, drip off the cherries and pour over the baked cream or puff paste.

43. Pickled Apricots. 4 pounds of ripe apricots, 1 cupful of wine vinegar, ⅛ ounce of cinnamon, some dried ginger, 2 pounds of sugar, cloves.

Boil and skim the vinegar and sugar, take from the fire, put the peeled and stoned apricots into this and heat them through. Let them drain, put them into a fruit jar with the apricot stones, cinnamon and cloves, the vinegar, sugar and ginger until thick, and pour hot over the apricots. After a few days the juice is cooked again, and this must be repeated a short time after. Cover the glasses tightly

44. Pickled Green Beans. 1 pound of small beans, ¾ pound of sugar, not quite 1 pint of vinegar and ⅛ ounce of cinnamon. String the beans and cook until about half done, and lay them on a cloth to drain. Then boil vinegar and sugar, skim, add cinnamon and the beans, cook for a while and fill into jars, boil the vinegar for a few moments, pour it hot over the beans and close the jars tightly.

45. Small Green Beans in Mustard. Small beans, good vinegar and to each quart of vinegar take ½ pound of sugar; mustard seeds, cinnamon, white pepper and horseradish according to taste.

String the beans, cook in salted water until nearly tender, and fill into jars in layers with mustard seeds, white pepper and sliced horseradish. In the meantime boil sugar and vinegar together and pour boiling hot over the beans. The beans must be covered with the liquid and then pressed down with a plate weighted with a stone. After a week boil the vinegar again and pour it over the beans, which must be repeated after another week. The third time let the vinegar boil for a while and pour over the beans so that they will be just covered.

46. Sweet Cucumbers. 3 pounds of cucumbers, 1 pound of sugar, 1 pint of water, ¼ ounce of stick cinnamon, a few pieces of ginger, ¼ ounce of cloves (taking off the heads). Take cucumbers which have become yellow, peel, quarter them and take out the seeds. Throw them into cold water so that they will remain white. Bring vinegar, sugar and spices to a boil and put in the cucumbers, which have lain in vinegar for a time, cook in this, but they must not be too tender. Then put into jars and cover.

47. Pickled Pears. 9 pounds of fruit, 3 pounds of sugar, 1¼ quarts of vinegar, ¼ ounce of cinnamon and the peel of 1 lemon.

Peel the pears, halve, take out the core, weigh, wash quickly in cold water so that they will keep their color. In the meantime boil sugar and vinegar, skim and put as many pears into this as can lay side by side, add the spices and cook on a quick fire until they can easily be pierced; if cooked too long they lose their nice color and will become dark brown. After they are cooked lay them into a glass, the round side to the top—do not pierce them with a fork—and pour the thick juice over them. Set them aside for a few days, boil down the juice again, pour hot over the pears and shake the glass once in a while so that they will settle. and cover tightly.

A number of the foregoing preserves can be served to invalids; Nos. 8, 9, 11, 16, 19, 21, 22, 23, 24, 27, 34, 35, 38, 39 and 40 are particularly nice.

IV. PICKLED VEGETABLES.

49. Pickled Red Cabbage. Take cabbages that are firm and have fine leaves; remove the loose and coarse outer leaves, then quarter the heads and put them into medium-sized stone jars in layers, sprinkling pepper-corns, cloves, bay leaves and dill between the layers, cover with a weak brine, placing a bag containing mus-tard seeds on top. Put a weight over all and cover the jar tightly.

When preparing for the table shred the cabbage very finely, pour over it a dressing made of olive oil, vinegar and pepper; if served with roasts omit the dressing.

Red cabbage can be finely shredded the same as white cabbage and then pressed into a stone jar with a little salt, covering with the above-named spices and some small pieces of ginger, or some sliced horseradish. Put a mustard seed bag on top and press down with a weight, after pouring a liquor of vinegar and water boiling hot over the whole. Cover tightly and set aside as directed above. When preparing for the table, take some of the cabbage, press it out and pour over it a dressing of salad oil and pepper.

50. Pickled Onions. Small onions, white pepper, horseradish and tarragon. Wash the onions, and to take off the skin easily lay them into lukewarm water and let them cool in this, then with a knife take off the skin. If possible, a silver knife should be used for this purpose, because the onions will receive dark spots if a common knife is taken. After they are rinsed, boil the onions for a few moments in vinegar with white pepper, take them out and fill in layers into cans, with tarragon and horseradish, pour in the cooled vinegar and cover tightly.

51. Pickled Eschalots and Onions. Select small onions. After they have been washed and peeled, strew salt over them, let them stand over night, the next day wash, heat the vinegar and put in the onions, stirring often; let them boil until tender. Then fill into a jar in layers with dill, tarragon, horseradish and peppercorns, and pour in the vinegar after it has cooled; press down with a plate and cover closely.

52. Pickled Beets. Use only the dark red beet. Cut off the tops, but none of the root, because the juice will then run out; wash the beets very clean, bake in the oven or else cook them in plenty of boiling water for 3—4 hours until they are tender. Do not pierce them with a fork and always add boiling water to replenish that which has boiled away. Then take off the skin, cut the beets into thin slices, lay them into a very clean jar with peppercorns, cloves, (see No. 1), horseradish, coriander or a few pieces of ginger, and a very little salt, and, if liked, a few bay leaves. Pour over them enough vinegar so that they will be covered, and close the jar tightly. Serve them with soup meats, roasts, potato- and endive salad, and also, chopped fine, in herring salad.

53. Preserved Mushrooms. Cut off the stems from small closed mushrooms, wash the latter in cold water and lay on a cloth to dry. Then heat plenty of clarified butter (see Division A, No. 8), lay the mushrooms with

white peppercorns into this and boil them, constantly
stirring. When they are hot enough so that the juice
will run out, take from the fire, put them into glasses
with the juice and cover them with melted butter about
½ inch thick. After the butter has cooled put a layer of
salt ½ inch thick over this, cover the glasses and set
aside in a cool, airy place.

54. Pickled Mushrooms. Take cloves, pepper, bay
leaves, tarragon, dried ginger and wine vinegar. Take
the heads off the cloves as directed under T, No. 1.

Large or small mushrooms can be used; clean and
then wash them quickly so that they will not absorb
too much water, and dry on a cloth. In the meantime
boil some vinegar with spices, let the mushrooms come
to a boil in this, lay them into glasses, boil the vinegar
for a while longer and pour over the mushrooms. After
a fortnight boil the vinegar again for a while and proceed as directed under No. 1.

55. Small Vinegar Pickles. For a 5-quart jar of
pickles take 6 ounces of salt, ¾ pound of small onions
(laying the onions in salt with the cucumbers), ¼ pound
of horseradish cut into smooth, uniform slices, 1 ounce
of dried ginger, ½ ounce of peppercorns—the white are
best—¼ ounce of cloves, 12 bay leaves, 2 handfuls of
dill and 1 handful of tarragon. A handful of peppergrass or cresses will improve the pickles; some unripe
grapes may also be added. In order that the dill may
be nice and fresh, observe the directions for keeping it
given in a preceding Division.

Select the pickles carefully, rejecting all that are
spotted or damaged, wash in fresh water with salt, and
set aside for 12 hours. Clean the onions in the same
manner as directed for pickling them. The heads of the
dill are either braided in three parts down as far as the
seed, or else cut off short and neatly arranged around
the edge of the dish when serving. Then lay the cucumbers on a cloth to dry and put them into jars in layers
with the spices. The jars, which must be new, should
be used only for pickles; they should be scalded before
using. Then pour over the pickles raw wine vinegar,
whereby they will retain their green color. After about
a fortnight pour off the vinegar, boil and skim it, pour

it over the pickles when cold and then press them down with a plate weighted with a stone, tie a cloth over them and set aside in a cool, airy place.

56. Cucumbers pickled in Vinegar and Water. For each 2 quarts of vinegar take 1 quart of fresh water, 1 cupful of salt and the spices as given in the above receipt.

Take nice, fresh cucumbers having small seeds, and leave them in fresh water for 12 hours. Then dry them in a cloth, put them into a stone jar with the spices, dissolve the salt in water, pour this, with the vinegar, over the pickles, which must be covered with plenty of the brine. put a mustard seed bag over them and cover as in the preceding receipt.

REMARK.—Cucumbers pickled in this way taste very nicely and keep for a long time. They are excellent for Cucumber Salad (Division Q).

57. Russian Cucumbers. 30 large cucumbers without seeds, 1 pound of eschalots, 2 ounces of mustard seeds, 1 ounce of garlic, 1 handful of fine sweet basil, dill and tarragon, 1 red pepper, fresh if possible, otherwise use a dried pod.

Wash the cucumbers, salt them thoroughly and let them stand for 48 hours. After they are washed and drained, dry and lay them side by side into a jar and cover with the above-named spices. Then boil as much vinegar as will cover the cucumbers and pour the boiling vinegar slowly over them. After about two weeks boil the vinegar and pour it cold over the pickles, which can be used after about six weeks.

58. Boiled Russian Pickles. For 2 quarts of wine vinegar take ½ ounce of pepper and ½ ounce of cloves; for between the pickles, ¾ pound of eschalots or small onions, ¼ pound of sliced horseradish, ¼ pound of mustard seeds, 1 ounce of garlic, ¼ ounce of bay leaves and a couple of handfuls of dill.

Take cucumbers of medium size, wash and then sprinkle plenty of salt over them and set aside for 24 hours. After this rinse off in the brine and wipe dry. In the meantime boil as much wine vinegar as will cover the pickles and add the cloves and pepper. When the vinegar boils, pour in part of the cucumbers, let them cook through, take out with a skimmer, throw in the others and put into the jar in layers with the spices and pour the hot vinegar over them. If after a few days they are not wholly covered with the vinegar add cold vinegar. The cucumbers can also be peeled and prepared in this way; both kinds will keep for a long time.

59. Mustard Pickles. For a 5-quart jar take ½ pound of salt, ½ pound of eschalots, ¼ pound of horse-radish, ¼ pound of mustard seeds, 1 ounce of ginger, ½ ounce of pepper, ¼ ounce of cloves (taking off the heads), bay leaves and two handfuls of dill.

Cucumbers which have turned yellow are the best, because they are not so apt to get soft. Peel, cut in two lengthwise, take out the seeds with a silver spoon, strew over them the salt and set aside over night. After they are drained, cut them into pieces two inches long and one inch wide, put into a jar and pour cold wine vinegar over them. After a week or a fortnight boil the vinegar and skim it, lay the cucumbers into the jar in layers with the spices and pour the cold vinegar over them (the vinegar must cover the pickles), lay a mustard bag over them, over this a plate weighted with a stone, and tie a cloth over the top.

60. Samba. Peel large cucumbers, finely slice them lengthwise (to the seeds), let them lay in salt for 3 hours, then put them into a scalded bag and hang up to drain. When they are dry put them into glasses in layers with mace, white peppercorns and some eschalots, and pour over them vinegar which was boiled and then cooled. A nice way to serve this is with small pickled onions, heaping them in the center of the dish and putting a wreath of the Samba around them.

Excellent with beef or mixed with herring salad.

61. Preserved Cucumber Salad. Half ripe peeled cucumbers are sliced as for salad, salted and then put on a sieve to drain, after which put them into a dish with wine vinegar to draw out the salt. Then lay a cloth into the sieve, pour the cucumbers into this, press out well, fill into a glass with onions and ground pepper, pour cold vinegar over them and at last add some salad oil.

U.—Dried and Pickled
Vegetables.

1. Pickling in Kegs and Stone Jars. The kegs should be carefully cleaned with a whisk broom and then filled with cold water, which must be renewed a few times during the week. Then scrub them thoroughly, scald with hot water, let them dry in the air and put them into the cellar, slightly raised from the floor. Before putting in the vegetables the kegs should be scalded again. Vegetables scalded before they are pickled should receive the scalding in a copper kettle, which will give them a nice green color, and this is not by any means deleterious, if the vegetables are not allowed to remain in the kettle after they are scalded, but are at once taken out and the water is changed. Should you, nevertheless, feel any hesitancy about using a copper kettle, take nickel or enameled ware, adding a little piece of alum to the water, which will also give the vegetables a fresh green color. After the vegetables are pickled, they should be covered with a linen cloth, putting some horseradish leaves or grape leaves on top of this; at last put in a plate large enough to cover the entire upper surface and weight it down sufficiently to bring the vegetables under the liquor, but not enough to press them. Clean the keg once a week, washing out the cloth every time. Be careful that there is always sufficient liquor to cover the vegetables, and if there should not be enough, pour in some (cooled) boiled water after each cleaning.

If the vegetables were allowed to stand dry, carefully remove all that may have spoiled before adding any water as above, running the fingers around the edges, taking up all that may have become soft. Wipe the interior of the keg with a clean cloth, rinse the cloth in fresh water and repeat this until the keg is entirely clean. Then pour the liquor into the center of the vegetables, rinse the top cloth and put it on again together with some fresh leaves, and weight it down with the clean plate and stone.

When taking out any of the vegetables, gather the cloth all around and lift it out carefully so that none of the scum which has gathered on it will drop into the keg. Press the vegetables, being cautious not to do this over the keg, rinse the top cloth, the plate and the stones, and put them back as before. In this manner the vegetables will remain sweet and wholesome.

2. Salted Green Peas. Fill 3 parts of green peas and 1 part of salt into a small, clean, scalded linen bag; dry the bag after it is scalded. Tie the bag securely, put it into a stone jar and weight it with a wine bottle filled with water.

To prepare the peas for the table take them out of the salt and cover with boiling water, which is poured off after the elapse of half an hour. Repeat this three times, then put the peas into boiling water with small carrots cut into cubes, and a piece of butter. Cook until tender, which will take about 1½ hours. When done, stir through it a finely rolled cracker, some sugar and finely chopped parsley. Send to the table at once, because the dish will lose its flavor if allowed to stand for any length of time.

3. Dried Green Peas. For this purpose take early marrow-fat peas, shell them and scald in boiling water for 5 minutes, after which spread them out on cloths to dry. Then put them on frames covered with clean white paper and dry them slowly in a slightly heated oven. Fill them into paper bags and hang in a dry, airy place. When preparing them for the table, let them stand over night, and parboil them the next day. Then put a piece of butter and a little sugar into water and bring it to a boil, cook the peas in this until tender and serve after adding the necessary salt, parsley, some sugar and another piece of butter rubbed in flour.

4. Salted Beans. Shell the beans and follow directions for salted peas. When preparing for the table it is best to first rinse the beans thoroughly in lukewarm water, then bring to a boil in hot water after which let them stand in hot water for a while longer. Boil in bouillon until tender and finish in the same manner as fresh vegetables.

5. String Beans Salted. For each 100 pounds of shredded beans take 7½ pounds of salt, which is partly sprinkled and stirred through the beans. Let the beans remain in the vessel over night and fill them into the keg without the liquor the next morning. Enough liquor will still appear to cover the tops of the beans. After three or four weeks take off the scum and, if necessary, pour in some boiled brine. Cover and weight the beans as directed in No. 1.

Remark.—The evening before the beans are to be cooked put them on the fire in cold water, cook for 1 hour and let them remain over night in fresh, cold water. The next morning rinse them carefully and put them on the fire in water with a piece of butter, to simmer. They will be done in an hour and taste very nicely.

6. String Beans salted after parboiling. Wash the beans, shred them, bring to a boil in a copper or nickel kettle, leaving them in the kettle for a few minutes only, even if they do not become entirely tender. Pour into a basket or colander and drench with plenty of cold water until cold. Put a thin layer of salt into the bottom of the keg and press every lot of parboiled beans into the keg, using fresh water for parboiling each succeeding layer. When all of the beans have been packed into the keg, sprinkle some salt over the top and cover with cold water; put a weight on them not any heavier than enough to hold them down. After a while a heavier weight may be used. After a fortnight pour off the liquor and replenish with cold water, repeating this from time to time, say about once in two weeks.

Beans salted as above directed will have a very nice color, need no further salting, will cook tender in a short time, have no unpleasant odor and in flavor are almost equal to beans brought in from the garden.

7. Salted Small Salad Beans. Take 3 pounds of salt for each 30 pounds of beans, string the beans, wash them, throw on a sieve, sprinkle the salt through them and let them stand in a clean keg over night. The next day mix them thoroughly, press tightly into the keg and cover as directed in the preceding receipts. Remove the scum with great care. If the beans should not be covered with liquor pour in some cold brine.

8. Salad Beans in Brine. Boil the beans, either whole or broken in two, until nearly tender, and when cold press them into a keg; prepare a brine strong enough to bear an egg, taking about 3 pounds of salt to 6 quarts of water, and when cold pour it over the beans. This quantity will be sufficient to cover about 17 quarts. Cover the keg as directed in No. 1.

9. Salad Beans in Vinegar. 2 quarts of wine vinegar, 1 quart of fresh water, a handful of salt, plenty of horseradish, or else some dry ginger, bay leaves, pepper, ground cloves.

The beans, which can be of any size desired, are carefully cleaned, string and throw part of them into a copper kettle containing boiling hot water; leave the beans in the water for ten minutes only, otherwise they will become soft and are apt to spoil. Spread them apart to dry, but this should not be done in the open air, otherwise they will lose their natural color. Press them in layers into a jar with the spices, dissolve the salt in water, and pour this over the beans with the vinegar. The beans should be fully covered, put on top a bag containing mustard seeds large enough to cover the entire surface of the beans, add the weight, close the jar tightly and set it aside in an airy cool place.

REMARK.—The beans are served as a salad with oil and vinegar, or after being parboiled, or as a vegetable with an egg sauce, after they have simmered sufficiently.

10. White Cabbage. For about 9 gallons, take about two dozen medium-sized firm heads; if the cabbage is to be shredded very finely 30—34 firm heads will be necessary. Winter cabbage should never be selected for pickling because it is tough and has a strong taste. The cabbage should be shredded as soon as possible after being cut from the stalk because it is then the juiciest; cover the bottom of the keg with some salt and put in the cabbage in thin layers without any salt, pressing it in quite compactly. Cleaning and covering the keg, etc., should be done as given in No. 1.

11. Salted Endives. For this purpose take only the smooth yellowed Summer endives. After removing the yellow leaves from the stalks, wash and then cut them into rather short lengths. Wash again and set aside to drain. After this put them into a clean keg or stone jar with plenty of salt, and cover with a rather heavy weight.

Remark.—For the table the endives are parboiled, drained, well pressed, then stewed with butter, salt, some rolled cracker and a little nutmeg; if desired, stir the yolk of an egg through it.

12. Dried Butter Beans. For this purpose take the large, so-called butter beans, fully grown and tender, cut them into pieces about 2 inches in length and parboil them for a few minutes, and slightly dry them in a moderately hot oven. They must retain a light green color and remain tough, consequently should not break.

13. Dried Salad Beans. Take small sized beans, not too early, at all events not before small beans have begun to form in the pods. Carefully string them, bring to a boil once and let them dry carefully, not too slowly, nor too quickly. The beans should be tough and not brittle. The stringing is most readily done after the beans are taken from the fire. To prepare them for the table, soak them over night in cold water and renew this the next morning. Put the beans on the fire in cold water and when tender, which will be after the elapse of 1—2 hours, they are finished in the same manner as fresh beans.

Vegetables permissible for invalids are noted in Division C.

V.—Beverages, Cordials, etc.

I. BEVERAGES.

1. The Various Kinds of Coffee, Directions for Roasting, etc. Coffee to be good should be roasted at home. It must be carefully browned, for when too brown, the coffee will be bitter, and if not roasted enough it will have an insipid taste. The cylinder in which the coffee is roasted should be only half filled, turn it slowly over a moderate fire until it emits a strong aroma. After this the turning should be done quicker, because the berries are then heated through and they will be browned too much if slowly finished. When the coffee has a uniform light brown color, which can be ascertained by opening the slide in the cylinder, spread it quickly on a flat dish and cover with a cloth. When cold, put the coffee into canisters or bottles and close tightly, so that it will not lose its aroma; for this reason it is best not to roast too large a quantity at a time.

2. To Prepare Coffee. For a strong cup of coffee, take about ½ ounce for each person. Put boiling water into the pot and set it on the top of the hot stove before putting in the coffee, which should not be ground too soon beforehand. Then pour in the necessary quantity of boiling water, take a few cupfuls out of the pot and immediately pour them back. Then put the pot on the top of the hot stove again until the coffee bubbles. After the coffee has settled it can be poured into another pot if desired. Coffee should never, under any circumstances, draw too long. The coffee can be improved if it is put into a perforated coffee funnel and then gradually pour boiling water over it.

It will be found advantageous to put a conical bag, so made that it will nicely fit on the inside of the funnel, to hold the coffee. It will strain better and clearer.

It is perhaps unnecessary to state that the milk served with the coffee should be of the very best. When cream can be obtained it is of course preferable to milk, and will make the coffee ever so much the better.

3. Tea. Formerly green and black teas mixed were much in vogue, but the black varieties are receiving greater favor at present, largely because the green teas are more injurious to health. Tea should always be kept in tightly closed canisters, and the latter will preserve the flavor of the tea ever so much better if they are first scalded with an infusion of tea, letting it cool in the canister.

The teapot should first be rinsed with boiling water, then put it on top of the hot stove, filled with boiling water. As soon as the pot is very hot, pour out the water and put in the tea—about 1 heaping teaspoonful for each person; for more people a proportionately less quantity can be taken. Add a small quantity of boiling water, let it draw for a while, fill the pot with boiling water, let it stand on the hot stove for a few minutes and then stir it with a teaspoon.

Tea prepared in the manner here described will contain considerable tannin and is neither well flavored nor pleasant to drink, but it is the usual method of preparing it and is therefore inserted in this place. The proper way to prepare tea is to let it draw in the boiling water for not longer than ½ minute. The resulting golden, transparent, aromatic beverage contains the principal constituent part of the tea—the theine—almost entirely in solution, and also the greater part of the ethereal oils, without the disagreeable tannic acid.

4. Chocolate with Milk. As there are so many different kinds of chocolate it will depend upon the quality how much to take. However, 2½ ounces of sweet chocolate to a quart, or ⅓ of an ounce to a cupful is the usual quantity. When using bitter chocolate take less. Put the chocolate on the fire, barely covered with water. After it is entirely dissolved, stir it until it is nicely smooth and then turn in the milk, which can be thinned, taking about ⅓ part water. The chocolate will be more agreeable in taste and easier to digest than when made with pure milk. Then add the necessary sugar and boil for about 10 minutes, stirring constantly.

5. Chocolate with Water. To 1 quart of water take ¼ pound of chocolate, or ½ ounce for each cupful of water. Prepare the same as chocolate with milk, but it must boil for 10 minutes on a good fire, stirring, or, better still, twirling it, which will cause it to bind.

6. Imperial Punch. 1 pineapple cut into very thin slices, 1 bottle of champagne, 1 bottle of Rhinewine, not quite 1 bottle of arrac, 1 quart of boiling water, about ½ pound of sugar with the peel of a lemon grated over it, if wished the fine peel of an orange, 4 oranges, the juice of 4 fresh lemons, a small teaspoonful of ground cinnamon and a little vanilla. Put the cinnamon into boiling water to draw, pour through a fine sieve into the punch bowl, add sugar, lemon juice, the oranges peeled and divided, and the pineapple. When cold, pour in the Rhinewine, arrac and champagne and a dash of vanilla.

7. Strawberry Punch. Mash 2 pounds of strawberries in a stoneware- or glass vessel which can be tightly covered, add 1 bottle of rum, and let the mixture stand 2—3 days, stirring it occasionally during this time. Then pour through a fine sieve into another vessel. The pulp of the strawberries is then also rubbed through the sieve. This strawberry rum should be bottled, covering the corks with sealing wax, when it will keep for a long time; the bottles must not stand, but lie on their sides. Should it jelly in the bottles, it can easily be shaken out and will readily dissolve when put into the boiling water.

When making the punch take the juice of two good lemons without the seeds, according to taste 1 to 1½ pounds of sugar, and nearly 3 quarts of water to a bottle of the strawberry rum. Put the sugar into the punch bowl, squeeze the lemon juice over it, pour in the rum, and finally the boiling water. When the punch is done, the bowl must be covered and set aside until cold; it will taste better if made in the morning and served in the evening than when it is served immediately after it is made. The punch can also be filled into bottles, let them lay on their sides for a few days and it will then be much better.

8. Holland Punch. 1 part of strained lemon juice, 2 parts of pulverized sugar, 4 parts of arrac, all measured in a glass. Put this mixture into a small vessel, let it dissolve on the fire and stir through it 8 parts of boiling water.

9. Wine Punch. No. I. 6 bottles of wine are mixed with sugar, taking 3 to 4 ounces to the bottle, heat until it nearly boils, then add ½ to ¾ bottle of arrac or better still Jamaica rum, leaving it on the stove for a short time, but it must not boil.

10. Wine Punch. No. 2. 1 bottle of Bordeaux, a little over 3 ounces of sugar, 2 bottles of water, ½ bottle of fine arrac and the juice of a lemon. Get the wine and sugar seething hot but do not let them boil. Add the boiling water and at last the arrac and the juice of a lemon.

11. Wine Punch. No. 3. Heat 3 bottles of Rhine-wine to the boiling point, then add 1 bottle of strong tea (using about ½ ounce of tea), also ⁴/₅ pound of sugar on which grate the peel of a lemon, using the juice in the punch. After this mixture has been poured into the bowl, add about ¼—½ quart of arrac, according to the strength desired.

12. Polish Royal Punch. Grate ½ of a lemon and ½ of an orange over a pound of sugar, cook this with ¾ quart of water to a thin syrup, then add the juice of 2 oranges and ½ of a lemon, 3 spoonfuls of pineapple syrup, ½ bottle of Chablis, the same quantity of Rhine-wine and Burgundy; let this all get very hot, but it must not boil. Then dip a piece of sugar into rum, lay it into a silver spoon, hold it over the punch and light it. As soon as the sugar burns, pour on more rum until ½ bottle has been poured into the punch in this way. Then pour in ½ bottle of champagne and serve the punch.

13. Mecklenburg Punch. For this punch take 1 bottle of good tea, 4 bottles of good claret, 1 bottle of

Portwine, 1 bottle of cognac, ½ bottle of Madeira and 2 pounds of sugar, grating the rind of 2 lemons on the sugar.

14. American Punch. Cream the yolks of 6 eggs with ½ pound of sugar, add nearly 1 pint of arrac and stir lightly through this the beaten whites of the eggs. When all is stirred together, mix through it 1½ quarts of whipped cream, and serve in punch glasses.

15. Jenny Lind Punch. Grate the rind of ½ of an orange on ½ pound of sugar, then press out the juice of 2 oranges and melt the sugar with the juice. Then pour onto this 2 bottles of Rhinewine and heat the punch until it is at the boiling point. Then let it cool, add a little vanilla, and at last ¼ bottle of Madeira; put the punch on ice until wanted to serve.

16. New Year's Eve ("Sylvester") Punch. This punch is to be prepared the last morning in the year, so that it can be served cold, which adds greatly to its taste. Scald ⅛ ounce of black tea for ½ minute in hot water, in a closely covered dish. Melt 1½ pounds of sugar in ¼ quart of water, add the peel of ½ of a lemon, some vanilla and ¼ ounce of dried orange blossoms, add to the sugar and set it on the back part of the stove. Then strain through a sieve and add to the tea, also pour in 1 bottle of Rhinewine, 1 bottle of Bordeaux, ½ bottle of Madeira, ¼ bottle of arrac, the juice of 2 oranges, 2 spoonfuls of raspberry juice, 1 spoonful of pineapple extract, all heated. As soon as the punch is good and cold add a glassful of Marascino.

17. Roman Punch. Grate the peel of ½ orange and ½ lemon on 1 pound of sugar. Melt the sugar with ¼ quart of water and the juice of 1 lemon and 2 oranges, pour in ½ bottle of Rhinewine, ½ cupful of arrac, ⅛ cupful of Marascino, and ⅛ bottle of champagne. Put this into a freezer and turn it constantly until it freezes. About ½ hour before serving, stir through it the beaten whites of 4 eggs, (⅕ pound of sugar seasoned with vanilla having first been stirred into the beaten whites of the eggs), let it freeze for ½ hour longer, and serve the punch, which must be as white and creamy as thick cream, in champagne glasses.

18. Egg Punch. 1½ bottles of good French wine, ½ quart of boiling water, ½ pound of sugar, grate the rind of 1 lemon on the sugar and use the juice of 2 lemons, some tea, nutmeg and a few cloves, 8 fresh eggs, and some arrac.

Let the spices draw in the boiling water, take them out, add the other ingredients and whip on the stove over a good fire until the cream rises, but it must not boil. Then take from the stove, whip for a while longer, and add a little arrac according to taste.

19. Ice Punch. Grate the rind of 1 lemon on 1 pound of sugar, put on the stove with a little water, to which add the juice of 2 lemons, and when it boils, skim. After it has cooled, add the juice of 6 oranges. Put into a freezer; after it is frozen quite thick add 1 bottle of champagne, 1 glassful of arrac and ½ glassful of Jamaica rum.

20. Mulled Wine. For 4 bottles of claret, take 1 pound of sugar, 1 ounce of cinnamon broken into pieces, also a few cloves; if after the wine is mulled it is not sweet enough, more sugar can be added. Put the mixture on the fire in a covered stone jar and pour it into a bowl while boiling hot.

21. Hot Egg Punch. To each pint of white wine take 1 fresh egg and 1⅔ ounces of sugar. Beat this on a quick fire until it is quite hot; it must not boil, otherwise it will curdle.

22. Cold Egg Punch. A refreshing beverage. For 1 pint of white wine or claret take the yolks of 2 very fresh eggs, beat with pulverized sugar and grated nutmeg and then gradually add the wine.

23. Bishop. For 1 bottle of claret take the thinly peeled rind of an orange and 3 ounces of sugar. The peel must be removed in about 10 minutes.

24. Punch Extract. 1½ pounds of sugar, the juice of four fresh lemons, 1 bottle of arrac. Boil the sugar in 1½ cupfuls of water, add the juice of the lemons, and after it has cooled, add the arrac. When using take 1 part of the extract to 2 parts of boiling water.

25. Parisian Cardinal Extract. ⅘ quart of arrac, the rind of 4 oranges, 2 ounces of cinnamon, and vanilla.

Break the cinnamon into small pieces, peel the oranges thinly, cut into small pieces, mix with the arrac, add vanilla, put into a covered vessel and shake often. Filter through blotting paper, and then bottle.

For every bottle of Rhinewine take about 2 table-spoonfuls of the extract, and sweeten with 3 to 4 ounces of sugar.

26. Bowl=Cups. For the preparation of all kinds of bowl-cups it is desirable to add a bottle of the heavier varieties of Rhinewine to the light Moselle or Rhine-wines used. The beverage will not thereby become too strong, but will gain very much in flavor. When using preserved fruits, only half of the quantity of sugar given in the various receipts should be used. The sugar easily dissolves in the water with which it is moistened before the addition of the wine, but a prepared sugar syrup is preferable. Sugar syrup can be prepared by bringing about 2¼ pounds of sugar to boil in 1 pint of water, let it boil for 5 minutes and strain through a scalded, rinsed and dried napkin into little bottles, where it will keep for a long time if well corked. When convenient, prepare the bowl several hours before it is sent to the table, cover tightly and set in a cold place, if possible on ice.

The use of claret does not improve the flavor of the beverage but will give it a pretty color. Appolinaris or selters water is also not to be recommended on account of the salts it contains in solution; if the beverage is not to be strong, use carbonated water to dilute it. Bowl-cups that are to be entirely agreeable should never contain any rum, arrac, cognac and the like. If champagne or sparkling Rhinewine is to be added, it should be poured into the bowl just before it is brought to the table.

27. Pineapple Cup. Thinly peel the pineapple and cut into fine slices, and according to the size of the fruit take 8—12 bottles of Rhine- or Moselle wine and 1 bottle of claret, and sweeten according to taste; for 1 bottle of wine take about 3—4 ounces of sugar.

Sprinkle the sugar over the pineapple in layers, pour over it a glassful of Madeira or water, and set aside for 24 hours. Then lay them into a bowl and add the wine and the remaining sugar. When using preserved pineapple, pour over it a bottle of wine 10—12 hours before serving.

28. Orange Cup. Take 1—2 oranges, 6 bottles of Rhine- or Moselle wine, 1 bottle of Burgundy or claret, according to taste ½ bottle of carbonated water, and 2 ounces or so of sugar to each bottleful of wine.

Thinly pare the oranges with a thin knife, put the peel into a wineglass which was half filled with water, cover with paper and set aside for a few moments to draw. The given quantity of sugar syrup is put into a bowl, add the wine and the extract of the orange peel according to taste; a bottle of Burgundy will improve the flavor of the bowl-cup.

29. Peach Bowl-Cup. After skinning the peaches, cut them into thin slices, sprinkle with sugar, and if possible set aside in a covered dish for a few hours or a day to draw, and then proceed as given for strawberry bowl-cup.

30. Strawberry Bowl-Cup. Take 1 heaping plateful of fresh strawberries—wild strawberries are preferable if they can be obtained—put them into a bowl, sprinkle ⅔ to 1 pound of sugar through them, add a trifle of water, and shake a little so that the sugar will mix through the berries. Set the bowl aside for 6 to 8 hours, cover tightly and then pour in 6 to 8 bottles of Moselle wine.

31. Champagne Bowl-Cup. Dissolve 1 pound of sugar in 2 bottles of Moselle wine, 1 bottle of Burgundy and 2 bottles of champagne or sparkling Rhinewine, and set the bowl aside on ice until wanted.

32. May Wine. Take fresh woodruf ("Waldmeister") before it blossoms (in April or May), pick it over carefully, remove the lower leaves and lower parts of the stalks. Just before using rinse it quickly in water, put it into a bowl containing sugar previously dissolved —about 2 to 3 ounces of sugar for each bottle of wine. Pour in as much Rhine- or Moselle wine as desired. The herbs must be taken out of the bowl after a few minutes, otherwise they will flavor the beverage too strongly. Sliced oranges with the seeds removed are a pleasing addition to May wine.

May wine when filled into bottles will keep for a few days, but great caution must be exercised, so that not the least bit of the herbs comes into the bottle.

Or the "Waldmeister" can be covered with a bottle of wine, letting it draw for 10 to 15 minutes. This extract can be filled into bottles and then is used in the above beverage according to taste.

In the months of July, August and September make a bowl-cup of mignonette-heads, taking about 15 heads for each bottle of wine with ¼ pound of sugar, letting the flowers draw in the wine somewhat longer than "Waldmeister."

REMARK.—The "Waldmeister" will gain in flavor very materially if it is not allowed to stand in water, but let it wilt in a cool place the day before using. The stalks of the herbs should not come into the wine; tie a bunch of the "Wald-meister" together wiih a cord and let only the heads of the bunch hang into the wine.

33. Apple Bowl=Cup. Select good dessert apples, pare, core and slice them. Pour 2 glassfuls of sugar syrup over the apple slices, cover and set aside for a day to draw. The next day add 2 bottles of Rhinewine, 1 glassful of Tokay and ¼ bottle of Burgundy. Strain after a few hours. Can be sent to the table with the further addition of ½ bottleful of champagne.

34. Whip. 2 bottles of white wine, about ½ pound of sugar with the peel of 1—2 lemons grated over it, a pinch of finely ground cinnamon, ½ dozen whipped fresh eggs. Beat briskly on a quick fire with an egg beater until it begins to boil. Pour into a warmed bowl, fill into glasses and serve while hot.

35. Grog. To each part of arrac or rum and sugar, add according to taste 3—4 parts of boiling water.

An excellent grog, which will also prove very palatable in cold weather to ladies, is made of genuine old Jamaica rum with plenty of sugar and boiling water, taking 4—5 times as much water as rum.

36. Warm Cream Bowl=Cup ("Hoppelpoppel.") Take 1 quart of sweet cream, the yolks of 4 eggs, ½ pint of arrac and sugar according to taste.

Bring the cream to a boil with the sugar, then take it from the fire, stir the yolks of the eggs with some milk, slowly add to the cream, constantly stirring, and then stir in the arrac.

37. Celestial Drink. (For hot Summer days.) Set 2 quarts of milk on ice, add a teaspoonful of vanilla, 4 small glassfuls of cherry juice, ½ plateful of mashed strawberries and ½ of a preserved pineapple cut into small pieces; add the necessary sugar, set aside for 3 hours to draw, pour through a sieve, put into champagne glasses, and into each glass put a piece of ice, a few preserved strawberries, pineapple pieces, and serve.

38. Cream Beer. For each person take 1 cupful of beer, 1 fresh egg, 1 ounce of sugar and, if liked, a little lemon peel or cinnamon.

The egg is beaten and put on the stove over a quick fire with beer and sugar, and whipped with a beater until it is at the boiling point, (it must not boil), take from the stove, whip for a while longer and serve.

39. Pineapple Sherbet. Take preserved pineapples, cut into very small pieces with a silver knife and lay them into a bowl with their juice, add 1 pint of water and the juice of 1—2 lemons, and cover tightly. A few hours before serving add 2 quarts of water, stir the juice and taste in order to ascertain whether sweet enough or if more lemon juice is to be added; pack in ice and serve in glasses with teaspoons, and with the fruits.

For 2—3 quarts of water take 1 pound of pineapple.

40. Peach or Apricot Sherbet. Peel 2 pounds of very ripe fruit, quarter, take out the stones, put the fruit into a dish, cover with ¼ pound of sugar, 1 pint of water, the juice of 1 to 2 lemons, and cover the dish. Then crush 1 pound of peaches with the stones and boil with 2 quarts of water for ½ hour, pour through a very fine sieve, and mix with the peaches. 2 hours before serving put the sherbet into a bowl and set it on ice, or else put small pieces of ice into the sherbet and serve as directed in the above receipt.

41. Nectar Sherbet with Champagne. Thinly pare 3 pounds of very nice apples, remove the stems and cut into very thin slices. Pour 2 quarts of water over the apple slices, add $2/5$ pound of sugar with the juice of a few lemons, with a little of the rind, and leave the apples in this for $\frac{1}{2}$ day, covered tightly. Then press the apples though a thin, very clean cloth, pour into a glass bowl, put on ice and shortly before serving add 1 bottle of champagne. Serve in glasses.

42. Orange Sherbet. Peel 1 dozen juicy oranges, cook the peel in plenty of water until tender, and drain. Then with a thin sharp knife remove the white inner skin from the outer peal and cut the latter into narrow strips or little squares. Dissolve about $6\frac{1}{2}$ ounces of sugar in a pint of water, put in the pieces or slices of orange peal, boil slowly for $\frac{1}{4}$ hour, then let it cool in the syrup. Cut 6 thin slices from the oranges, take out the seeds and lay the slices into a glass dish. Press the remaining oranges into a bowl through a fine sieve, add 2 quarts of water and 1 bottle of Mosellewine and at last enough of the peel of the oranges with the juice to give the sherbet the required flavor. Then set on ice, or else put small pieces of ice into the sherbet.

43. Cherry Sherbet. Stone 2 pounds of the finest cherries. Then dissolve 6 ounces of sugar in 1 quart of water, bring the cherries to a boil in this and let them simmer until tender. Mash 1 pound of cherries with the stones and boil with 2 quarts of water for 25 minutes, and then press through a very clean cloth. Let both cool, put the cherries into a bowl first, mix the cherry juice and 1 glassful of Marascino together and pour over the cherries, and then set the sherbet on ice.

This sherbet can also be made of strawberries, raspberries, figs and raisins, using different seasoning.

44. Lemonade for the Sick. (In cases of fever.) To 1 quart of boiling water add the juice of 1 lemon (not the peel), removing all the seeds. Put into bottles and when serving mix with a little sugar.

45. Almond Milk for the Sick. $\frac{1}{4}$ pound of peeled, washed, and pounded almonds are finely pounded in a mortar with a very little water, gradually add 1 quart of cold water, and then press through a very clean cloth which was first rinsed in boiling water; sweeten with sugar. Almond milk will keep for 3 days when put into a cool place. The almonds can also be mixed with 4 to 6 bitter ones.

46. Arrow Root Drink for the Sick. ⅔ quart of water is boiled with 2 ounces of sugar, a pinch of salt, and a little lemon peel, stir about 2 ounces of arrow root with ½ pint of cold water, boil until clear and then mix with fruit juice, claret or cognac. Can be served either warm or cold.

47. Oatmeal Gruel for the Sick. 1 ounce of oatmeal is stirred with a little water, and then boiled for about 20 minutes in 1 pint of boiling water, into which put a little ginger. This is passed through a sieve; take the yolks of 2 eggs and beat with 2 ounces of sugar and 1 pint of Porter until creamy and stir through the gruel.

48. Egg=Nogg for Invalids. The yolks of 4 eggs are whipped for ¼ hour with 2 ounces of sugar, then add 1 cupful of warm water and a large tablespoonful of lukewarm orange water. Mix thoroughly and serve lukewarm.

49. Barley Water for Invalids. Put pearl barley on the stove in boiling water with the juice of a lemon, which will give the barley a white color. After it has boiled for an hour it is poured (not pressed) through a sieve, and sweetened if liked.

50. An excellent Beverage in case of Bowel Com=plaint. ¼ pound of best rice is scalded and seasoned with ½ ounce of stick cinnamon, put into an earthenware dish with 2 quarts of boiling water, cooked until it is reduced to one quart, and poured through a sieve without stirring. Drink with or without sugar.

51. Barley Tea for Invalids. Put 1 tablespoonful of barley into a teapot filled with boiling water, and after it has cooled add a little raspberry juice.

52. Bread Water for Invalids. Cut the bread into slices, toast, pour cold water over it, add lemons lices without seeds—in case of fever only the juice—pour off the water and sweeten.

53. Apple Beverage. Take 8 washed apples divided into 4 parts with the peel, the yellow rind of ½ and the juice of a whole lemon, 1 piece of cinnamon and ½ cupful of washed raisins, and ½ cupful of currants.

This is boiled with 2 quarts of water until the apples are tender, then pour through a sieve, sweeten and serve cold.

With the spices left out, this is also a very nice drink for the sick. Instead of raisins and currants, a crust of brown bread can be cooked with the apples, omitting the lemon peel.

54. Violet Vinegar. A soothing drink for the sick, especially in cases of nervous disorders and headache. Take 2—3 handfuls of blue fragrant violets, remove the stems, put the flowers into a bottle, fill with wine vinegar and set aside in the sun, well corked, or near the stove, pour the vinegar through blotting paper and put into a corked bottle.

Take a teaspoonful in a small glassful of water and sweeten according to taste.

55. Beverage of Preserved Fruit Juice for Invalids. Raspberry-, currant- or cherry juice, particularly raspberry vinegar mixed with water, are very refreshing and beneficial in cases of fever, but the latter should not be given to those having lung troubles. Strawberry juice with selters (or appolinaris) water is particularly palatable and quite harmless.

56. Refreshing and beneficial Beverage of Coffee and Selters Water. Mix 1 cupful of good coffee with a small bottle of selters water, sweeten according to taste and drink cold.

Among these drinks, coffee, tea and chocolate can almost always be given to invalids, if the physician does not object. Nos. 18, 20, 21, 22, 29, 33, 34, 36, 37 and 39 may also be given to invalids, besides those beverages noted above as being adopted for the sickroom.

II. LIQUORS AND CORDIALS.

57. In General. Liquors and cordials of every description are readily obtainable from dealers in goods of that kind. It is possible, however, that some housekeepers may desire to be instructed how to prepare home made cordials.

The fruit, etc., should be filled into a large, wide-mouthed bottle or jar together with the brandy or other spirits selected. Cork the bottle carefully, let it stand in the sun or other warm place for 3—4 weeks, shaking often. Moisten some sugar, bring to a boil, skim, let it cool, stir the brandy to it and strain through blotting paper. · The cordial thus prepared is filled into clean, dry bottles and well corked. Add to each $\frac{4}{5}$ quart of French or cherry brandy, $\frac{1}{5}$ quart of boiled water and add this to the sugar. In the following receipts this proportion of brandy, water and sugar will be designated as 1 quart of brandy.

58. Clove Cordial. 1 quart of brandy, $3\frac{2}{3}$ ounces of sugar, $\frac{1}{4}$ ounce of cloves, $\frac{1}{2}$ ounce of coriander, both coarsely pounded, and 20 dried cherries.

59. Cinnamon Cordial. 1 quart of brandy, $3\frac{2}{3}$ ounces of sugar, $\frac{1}{4}$ ounce of best ground cinnamon.

60. Spiced Cordial. $1\frac{1}{2}$ quarts of brandy, 7 ounces of sugar, $\frac{1}{2}$ ounce of fennel, anise seed, elderberries or coriander, a little cinnamon, 6—7 cloves.

61. Walnut Cordial. 1 quart of brandy, 1 pound of sugar, 1 pound of fresh walnuts.

62. French Walnut Cordial. 30 walnuts, 30 cloves, a little cinnamon and a bottle of cognac. Set this in the sun for 7 weeks, shaking every day. Then filter through a woolen cloth, add a few pieces of rock candy, set aside for a few days and then fill into small bottles.

63. French Strawberry Cordial. Half fill a cordial bottle with small ripe strawberries and then fill with pounded rock candy; pour in arrac or brandy until the bottle is full to the cork, set daily in the sun and after a few months pour through a cloth and then the cordial can be used.

64. Curacao. 2 quarts of brandy, 3½ ounces of orange peel, 7 ounces of light brown rock candy. Put the peel into water so that the white part can easily be taken from the yellow rind, cut the peel into small pieces and put into jugs with the brandy. Cork tightly and set near a warm oven for 2 weeks, or in the cellar for 3 weeks, shaking daily. Then take out the peel, break the rock candy into small pieces, add to the liquor and .fill into bottles. Shake daily and when the sugar is dissolved filter the brandy through blotting paper.

65. Quince Cordial. 1 quart of quince juice, 10 ounces of white sugar, and as much brandy as you have juice and sugar, and for every quart of this liquor add ½ ounce of bitter almonds, and ⅔ ounce of coriander. Wipe the quinces with a cloth, grate and set in the cellar for 24 hours. Then press through a woolen cloth, boil the sugar until clear and then cook on a moderate fire with the juice of the quinces for ¼ hour, let it cool somewhat and pour in some brandy without any water. For each 1 quart of liquor add ½ ounce of bitter almonds, and ⅔ ounce of coriander, whole, pour into clean bottles or jugs, set in a warm place, turning frequently. Then filter through blotting paper, put into clean dry bottles and cork tightly.

66. Cherry Cordial. 1 quart of brandy, 11 ounces of sugar, 1 pound of sweet and 1 pound of black cherries pounded together, 1 cupful of black currants and a little cinnamon. Fill into bottles and set aside for 24 hours.

67. Raspberry Cordial. 1 quart of brandy, a little cinnamon, ½ pound of sugar, and 1 cupful of raspberries.

68. Black Currant Cordial. Is made the same as in the above receipt, taking 8 ounces of sugar.

69. Vanilla Cordial. Take a few vanilla beans and let them stand in a bottle of brandy for a fortnight, then add ½ pound of sugar and color the cordial with the juice of black cherries.

W.—Pressed and Smoked Meats, Meat Jellies, etc.

1. Headcheese. Take two parts of chopped sausage meat without fat, season with salt, pepper, ground cloves and cardamom, a little pepper and finely ground majoram; if liked, garlic may be used in this sausage. Add one part of rinds boiled until tender and chopped fine, 1 soup ladleful of blood, 2 pork tongues boiled until tender. This is all mixed together, and if necessary add a little more seasoning and then fill into a case. Let this boil slowly for 2 hours in slightly salted water or else boil in some broth, press over night and smoke for 2 to 3 weeks.

Can be served cold with bread and butter, also warmed with potato salad.

2. Bremen "Pinkel" Sausage. Mix with some finely chopped beef kidney suet the same quantity of oatmeal, add salt, pepper, cloves, ground cloves and plenty of finely chopped onions, fill into cases—leaving room for the oatmeal to swell—and then smoke. This sausage is cooked in brown cabbage, also in bean soup.

3. Panhas. The panhas is best when half beef and half rather fat pork is used; but it can be made just as well when either kind of meat is used alone. Boil the meat until tender, cut it into pieces and chop fine after taking out all the bones, and then bring it to a boil with the broth, which is passed through a sieve. Season with salt, pepper and cloves, and then add sufficient buckwheat flour (about 2 pounds for 2 pounds of meat) constantly stirring, so that after the panhas has cooked for ½ to ¾ hour it will be thick and not adhere to the sides of the kettle. Then put into clean and dried earthenware dishes and set aside in a cool and airy place. To fry the panhas proceed as given under Meats (Division D, No. 57).

4. Sour Beef Rolls. 10 pounds of beef, 4½ ounces of fine salt, ½ ounce of pepper and ½ ounce of cloves.

Cut lean and fat beef into long, thin slices, remove all the skin, mix and sprinkle the spices mentioned through the meat. Carefully clean and rinse a beef stomach, cut it into large, oblong pieces, put the meat on these and sew them closely, so that the strength of the meat and spices will not be lost, but they should not be filled too tightly, else they will burst. Then cover the rolls with plenty of water, add some salt, put on the fire, boil and skim for about 3—4 hours, or until the rolls can be easily pierced with a straw. Take the rolls out of the broth, mix some of the latter with sharp vinegar, and pour enough of this broth over the rolls after they are cold to cover them.

5. Pork Rolls in Jelly. The rind of the pork is loosened from the fat, leaving a little of the latter on the rind and then cut into pieces 2 inches wide and 6 inches long, also cut up some thin slices of lean pork of the same size. Lay the latter on the rinds, sprinkle with pepper and finely chopped lemon peel, roll them up tightly and tie with a thread. Put them into an enameled kettle with a few pigs' feet, knuckles and a small piece of beef, cover with vinegar and water half and half, add a few bay leaves, peppercorns, cloves and a piece of lemon peel, and cook until tender, skimming carefully. Then put the meat into a jar, pour the broth through a sieve into another vessel and after it has settled pour over the rolls. The latter are sent to the table sliced and dotted with meat jelly. Serve cold with bread and butter or salads. The jelly in which the rolls lay can also be utilized in a sauce for cold chicken or grouse.

6. Jellied Pork. No. 1. Put the nose, feet, ears and knuckle of a pig on the fire in an enameled kettle with 1½ pounds of lean beef, salt, 1 quart of wine vinegar

and enough water so that all of the scum can be taken
off; add a few bay leaves, plenty of peppercorns and
ground cloves, and cook until the meat is so tender that
it will drop from the bones.   Pour the broth through a
fine sieve and let it stand until the next day. Remove
the bones from the meat, and when the latter is quite
cold, cut it into narrow slices; do not take any of the
beef.   The next day remove the fat and settlings from
the jelly, put it on the fire with the sliced meat and a
sliced lemon without the seeds, let it cook for 15 minutes
and then fill into dishes or moulds that have first been
rinsed with cold water.   The jelly should be set aside,
uncovered, in an airy place. When preparing the jelly
for the table scrape off the fat with a knife and turn the
jelly on a dish, serving it with boiled potatoes, bread
and butter or salads. It will keep fresh for several weeks
and is a handsome, refreshing and palatable addition
to the table.

    7. Jellied Pork. No. 2. Take the ears and the
front feet and if wished part of the head, removing the
fat, clean all very carefully and put on the fire with
plenty of water and salt.   After skimming, add peppercorns, cloves, ground cloves and a few bay leaves, and
let the meat cook thoroughly until tender.   Then take
out the bones, cut the meat into long thin slices and
pour the broth through a sieve after it is cold, take off
the fat and put it on the fire with the meat, add a little
grated lemon peel and ground cloves, and boil. After it
has been boiled sufficiently pour into a dish or mould
to cool.

    8. Jellied Pork No. 3. To 2 pounds of pork from
the head add 3 cleaned calves' feet, and cook in salted
water until tender.   The broth must not be too thin
and is cooked with whole onions, cloves, pepper and
lemon peel, a few bay leaves and a cupful of sharp
vinegar for a while, and then poured through a sieve.
In the meantime cut the meat into cubes, add the broth
poured from the settlings, also the juice of a lemon, and
boil thoroughly.   Rinse a mould or deep dish with cold
water so that the jelly will come out easier, ornament
with lemon slices, carefully pour in the mass and proceed as directed in the above receipt.

9. Jellied Spare Ribs. Crack the ribs in two in the middle and then cut so that the ribs remain together two by two. They are cooked in water and vinegar half and half, with some pigs' feet, and skimmed. Then add lemon peel, plenty of whole pepper, 1—2 onions, salt, cloves, a few bay leaves and cook the meat until tender. Pour the broth through a sieve and after it has settled pour it over the meat into a porcelain dish. The ribs are served with some of the jelly in which they lie, with bread and butter, salad, and with potatoes. Decorate the dish with grated horseradish colored with beet juice, sprigs of parsley, putting some chopped hard boiled eggs in the center.

10. Headcheese in Jelly. No. 1. 2 pigs' noses, 3 ears and 4 feet, 2 calves' feet, $\frac{1}{4}$ of a beef jowl and the rinds of the pork are boiled in water and vinegar, half and half, and skimmed carefully; add 1 bottle of wine, 4 onions picked with cloves, peppercorns and a sliced lemon.

Cook until the meat is tender, take it from the bones and cut it into slices. After the rinds have become tender put them into a clean, wet cloth, cover the rinds with sliced beets and the meat alternately, then cover the top with another rind, tie the cloth tightly, press with a little slab and some weights and pour the broth through a fine sieve. The day following cut the headcheese into slices, put them into a dish, remove the fat and settlings from the jellied broth, then add the meat.

11. Headcheese. No. 2. Split the head of a young pig, clean carefully and boil until tender in water and vinegar, half and half, with the tongue and a few pigs' feet, salt, onions and spices. When tender put it on a slab, take the meat with the rind from the bones and lay the rind on a scalded but still wet napkin, keeping the rind whole. Take all sinews and gristle out of the meat and cut the latter into strips, also the tongue. Put the tongue and meat on the napkin in layers, sprinkle with pepper, a very little salt, thyme and cloves, fold the napkin closely around the meat, tie in a roll and cook this in the broth for $\frac{1}{2}$—1 hour. After taking the headcheese from the broth, let it cool, press between two slabs, and the following day take off the napkin. Serve in slices with jelly or Remoulade sauce.

The broth in which the headcheese was cooked is poured through a sieve, freed from settlings, adding a little salt if necessary, and then use as jelly.

12. Smoked Breast of Goose. When smoking goose breast use only the breasts of fat, large geese. After the breast is loosened from the breast bone cut off the legs at the first joint, salt the breast and legs, rub with a little saltpeter and after 3 days smoke them.

They must not smoke longer than a week, and during this time they should have more air than smoke.

They are cut into thin slices with their fat and served raw with bread and butter.

13. Smoked Geese in Pommeranian Style. Well fatted young geese are the best for this purpose. After they are thoroughly cleaned cut off the feet, neck and wings. Divide them in two lengthwise in the middle, rub with saltpeter and a little salt, pack them tightly into a small clean cask, and cover. Let them lay in this for not longer than 3 days. Then take them out and sprinkle thickly with wheatbran, being careful not to lose any of the moisture or the salt adhering to the meat; turn the meat in the bran so that all of it and the fat will be completely covered. Then smoke them, being careful that the pieces do not touch one another, neither must the heat from the fire affect them in any way. After the elapse of about a week take the meat out of the smoke, hang it in a cool place and after a short time wipe off all of the bran with a dry linen cloth.

Geese smoked in this way will have a very good color and keep for a long time.

Z.—Fruit Wine and Vinegar.

1. Apple Wine. (Cider). When preparing fruit wines, great care and cleanliness are necessary. All the utensils, such as tubs, casks, ladles, funnels, etc., should be of wood, stoneware or glass, because the acids corrode iron easily, and they should never be used for any other purpose.

The fruit used in making wine must be ripe, but perfectly sound, tart and of fine quality. Sweet apples are not good for wine. The apples can be of mixed varieties, and juicy pears may also be mixed with them. About 1½ cwt. of fruit will make in the neighborhood of 10 gallons of wine. After all of the vessels used for fermenting have been thoroughly cleaned, wash the fruit carefully and throw it into baskets to drain. Pick over the apples, rejecting any that are wormy or not perfectly sound. Mash the apples with a pounder in a tub or heavy wooden trough. Do not take too many apples in the trough at once, for then they will not mash easily. Then put the mashed apples into a vat, letting them stand until the next day, stirring occasionally so that the pulp will absorb some of the oxygen from the air. If there should only be fruit enough to make about 10 gallons, the juice can be pressed through a loose linen bag; for greater quantities a press will be found necessary.

Let the juice run into a keg which has first been rinsed with hot and then with cold water. The pressed pulp should be broken up, moistened with warm water and then pressed again the following day. Both lots of juice are mixed together, fill the keg and pour what is left of the juice into a keg. Put both keg and jug to ferment in a place having a temperature of about 25 to 30 degrees.

The opening of the keg and the mouth of the jug are lightly covered with a little piece of linen cloth, simply to keep out insects; the froth arising through fermentation must be carefully removed every day and the cloths cleaned or replaced by new ones. When the temperature is too low, a week may elapse before fermentation begins, usually, however, it will begin in 3—4 days. When the frothing stops, cover the opening in the cask with a small sandbag, which will be sufficiently tight, and then daily pour in some of the juice in the jug in order to keep the keg well filled. After fermentation is done close the cask tightly and replenish its contents every week with some of the juice contained in the jug, it being essential that the keg should be kept completely filled. In order that the juice in the jug may not spoil, it should be filled into bottles, which are kept well corked and the juice used to keep the keg filled.

After the elapse of about 8 to 10 weeks it will be advisable to change the cider into another keg. Filter the settlings or put them into bottles to clear. If there should not be enough juice to fill the keg, sweetened water must be added, but this ought not to occur because when pressing the first juice enough should be provided for replenishing purposes.

By Spring time the wine will be clear enough so that it can be filled into bottles, and is also fit for use, but if it can be kept until the Fall it will be much finer in appearance and flavor. In the early Summer it will prove to be a delicious, wholesome and refreshing drink. It is of great importance that no brandy nor spirits of any kind be added; plenty of fruit of good quality is the prime factor in making fruit wines.

2. Currant Wine. Currant-, gooseberry-, raspberry and huckleberry wines need plenty of sugar and the acidity of the currants must be reduced with water. Take the currants when ripe but not overripe, strip them from the stems and press out the juice, which is best done in a large bowl with a potato masher. For about 10 gallons take 30 to 40 pounds of berries; the quantity need not be exact because there must be enough juice for replenishing purposes. The pressed berries are set aside for 2 to 3 days in an open stoneware jar or wooden vessel, and then press out the juice with either a fruit press or with the hands through a coarse cloth bag. This juice may be thinned with water which has been on the currants over night and has run through the press clear.

To each quart of the juice first pressed, add 2 quarts of the second pressing and 2 pounds of sugar. When all is well mixed put the juice into a clean cask and fill the surplus into a jug or bottles for replenishing purposes. Then put the juice into the cellar to ferment and proceed in other respects as directed in the foregoing receipt.

A plentiful addition of sugar will make this a very fiery wine. Although fit for use after a twelve-month or so, this wine will be almost equal to Tokay if kept in the bin for 3 years, particularly so if white and black currants mixed were used in making it.

3. Gooseberry Wine. Is made of fully ripe berries; currants can also be mixed with them. Unripe berries may also be used, adding sugar and water as directed for currant wine.

The water can be hot when poured on the pressed gooseberries and then proceed as previously directed. Gooseberry wine will have a deliciously mild flavor if it is stored until the Fall before being bottled. Replenishing the contents of the keg with some of the surplus juice, tightly closing the cask after fermentation has ceased, and carefully corking the bottles are points which must be observed in order to be fully successful in making wine.

4. Huckleberry Wine. The preparation is the same as directed for currant and gooseberry wine, but less sugar is necessary. If the wine is not wanted very sweet, add either a little currant juice or tartaric acid.

5. Fruit Vinegar. The apples used to make the vinegar should be nicely washed, all unsound parts cut away, mash them thoroughly, and press until the pulp is quite dry. The apples need not be entirely ripe and pears may also be used; all blackened fruit should be rejected because it gives the vinegar a bitter taste. The fruit is put into open kegs for 8 to 10 days. All impurities will rise to the top during the process of fermentation and must be carefully removed. After this run the juice into casks, which should be half filled only in order that the air can act upon the juice, and then put the casks in a warm place. As soon as fermentation has entirely ceased, close the casks at the bung with a piece of linen of medium thickness and let them lay undisturbed until the Spring, when the vinegar can be drawn into bottles. There will always be a thick sediment at the bottom of the cask. It is a favorable indication when a thick tough skin (mother-of-vinegar) forms on the surface, and this should by no means be disturbed before bottling.

6. Sugar Vinegar. For 6 bottles or 5 quarts of water take 1½ pounds of sugar, boil for ½ hour, skimming carefully, and then pour it into an open keg. When cool throw in a slice of wheat-bread thickly spread with yeast. Let it ferment for 2 days and then add a piece of mother-of-vinegar if you have it.

Then pour the liquid into another keg, which should be put into a warm dry place. Close the bung with a piece of linen cloth, which should be perforated so that the air can easily enter the cask. If it is desired that the vinegar receive a nice Rhinewine color, add a quantity of primroses to the water and sugar at the beginning, and let them boil with the rest.

7. Currant Vinegar. Press the berries, let the juice stand until the next day and when clear fill into bottles, being careful to keep back all of the settlings; then let the bottles stand open in the sun or other warm place and do not cork them until fermentation has entirely ceased.

The American Kitchen.

In this division, receipts are given for various dishes prepared in styles peculiar to cooking as done in the United States.

SOUPS.

1. Oyster Soup. 1 quart of sweet milk and 1 quart of oysters. Bring the juice of the oysters and the milk to a boil; add a tablespoonful of butter, and salt and pepper to taste. Then add the oysters and bring to a boil again. Serve immediately. Too much boiling hardens the oysters.

2. Lobster Chowder. Mix with ¼ cup of butter 3 crackers which were rolled fine, and the green fat of the lobster. Then boil 1 quart of milk. Season with a scant teaspoonful of salt, some white pepper and a saltspoonful of cayenne pepper. Pour the boiling milk gradually over the lobster paste. Put it into a double boiler, add the lobster meat cut into dice, let it come to a boil and serve.

3. Clam Chowder. Boil 50 clams in their own juice for 3 minutes, strain and return the juice to the fire. Fry 1 onion in butter and cut a small piece of fat salt pork into dice and fry with the onion; add 2 tablespoonfuls of flour and stir well together. When well cooked add the clam juice, 1⅓ cupfuls of cream, a little ground mace, a little thyme, cayenne, 8 ounces of potatoes, and salt if necessary. When the potatoes are tender, add the clams, whole or cut into pieces, and 4 ounces of biscuits cut into pieces and soaked in milk. Boil until the clams are firm and serve in a deep dish or tureen.

4. Corn Chowder. Scrape from the cob 1 quart of raw sweet corn. Put the cobs in water enough to cover them, boil for 20 minutes and skim them. Take 1 pint of pared sliced potatoes, soak and scald them. Fry an onion in a small piece of pork fat and strain the fat into the kettle with the corn water. Add the potatoes, corn, 1 teaspoonful of salt, 1 saltspoonful of white pepper, 1 pint of sliced tomatoes. Simmer for 15 minutes, or until the corn and potatoes are tender, then add 1 large tablespoonful of butter and 1 pint of milk, and serve very hot with crisped crackers.

5. Mock=Turtle Soup. Take 1 calf's head and wash thoroughly; remove the brains and tongue, which keep for a separate dish. Put the head and 4 calf's feet into a soup kettle with cold water. Skim carefully, then add 2 carrots, a bunch of soup herbs, juice of a lemon, 4 onions, salt and 2 celery stalks. When boiled for about 3 hours or until the meat comes off the bones, take out the best parts and press. Take out all bones from the coarser meat and simmer for 3 hours; when cold, strain and skim thoroughly. The next day cut the pressed meat into cubes, to garnish the soup. Flavor the soup with sherry and plenty of pepper and lemon juice. Simmer with meat for half an hour and serve.

6. Fish Soup. Fry 4 sliced onions in salad oil for a few minutes or until they are light brown; then add 6 sliced tomatoes, 3 pints of water, parsley, thyme, 3 bay leaves and savory, all tied in a bunch, pepper and salt, blending the flour with a little water. Boil for ½ hour; then put in the slices of fish; as soon as they are firm remove the herbs and serve the soup with bits of bread. Curry powder may also be added if desired.

7. Chicken Soup. Cut a grown chicken as for frying; boil gently in 3 quarts of water and remove all scum carefully. To 2 quarts of soup use ½ pint of rice, a few sprigs of parsley, pepper and salt to taste. Boil until the chicken is tender. Then add ½ pint of sweet milk and 1 tablespoonful of arrow root stirred into a spoonful of butter. Old fowls when in good condition are best for soups.

8. Milk Soup. 1 quart of milk, the yolks of 4 eggs, salt and sugar to taste, and small pieces of bread.

Put the dried bread, cut into pieces, into the bottom of the tureen. Bring the milk to a boil, add sugar and salt. Rub the yolks of eggs with a very little milk or water. When the milk is boiling remove it from the fire and stir in the yolks of eggs. Put on the back part of the stove where it will not boil, and stir for a few minutes or until it thickens. Pour over the dried crusts and cover. Set aside for about 5 minutes and then serve. If the soup is boiled after the eggs are added, it will curdle.

9. Canned Tomato Soup. Stew 1 can of tomatoes until they are soft enough to strain, rub all but the seeds through a strainer, add 1 teaspoonful of sugar, 1 saltspoonful of pepper and 1 teaspoonful of salt, and add all to 1 quart of boiling stock. Serve with croutons.

10. Mixed Vegetable Soup. Take 1 cupful each of chopped celery, onions, carrots and strained tomatoes, ½ cupful each of chopped cabbage, turnips, parsnips and 1 tablespoonful of chopped parsley. If you have only a few of the vegetables, substitute macaroni, rice or pearl barley, using altogether about one-half the amount of vegetables that you have liquid. The vegetables should all be chopped very finely and cabbage, cauliflower, parsley, potatoes, parsnips or onions must be parboiled for 5 minutes and carefully drained. Fry onions and carrots, then put all with 1 quart of boiling water and 1 quart of stock and let it simmer until tender. For seasoning add 1 teaspoonful of sugar, 1 teaspoonful of salt, and 1 saltspoonful of pepper. Serve without straining.

VEGETABLES.

1. Potato Puffs. Put 2 cupfuls of cold mashed potatoes into the frying pan, adding the yolks of 2 eggs, 3 tablespoonfuls of cream and 1 tablespoonful of butter. Stir until well mixed and hot. Take from the fire and stir in carefully the beaten whites of the eggs. Heap on a well-greased tin or in gem pans, and bake with a quick fire until well done.

2. Potato Croquettes. Beat the yolks of 2 eggs to a cream and to this add 2 cupfuls of mashed potatoes, 1 teaspoonful of grated onion, 1 teaspoonful of powdered majoram, 1 tablespoonful of chopped parsley, cayenne, 1 teaspoonful of salt and 2 tablespoonfuls of cream. Put into a saucepan and stir until the mixture leaves the sides of the kettle. When cold form into balls or long croquettes. Dip first into egg and then into bread crumbs, making them very smooth and even. Set aside in a cool place for 1 hour, then fry to a golden brown. The lard should be deep enough to cover them. When fried to a golden brown, dry in the oven. Serve as a garnish to meat of any kind or as a vegettable.

3. Fried Potatoes. The potatoes must be raw, large, unblemished and of a good round shape. First take off a thin paring of the skin. Then pare the whole potato round and round, (not too thin), till you have gone through it all, and nothing is left unpared but a little lump in the centre. Then put these continuous rings of potatoes into a frying-pan, in which is boiling plenty of fresh butter, or butter and lard mixed. Fry them brown and tender, and arrange them handsomely in a dish for breakfast.

Another Way. Slice thin a sufficiency of fine raw potatoes and lay them into a pan of cold water to soak for an hour or more. Then pour off that water entirely and replace it with fresh. Let them remain in this for another hour, or till it is time to cook them. Put them into a frying pan that has in it plenty of fresh butter or lard, enough, while frying, to keep the potatoes near the surface. Fry them till perfectly well done and tender.

4. Cauliflower with White Sauce. Take off all outside leaves; wash thoroughly. Put in a bag and boil gently for half an hour in salted water. Pour over melted butter with a spoonful of cream, or make this white sauce: Cook together 1 ounce of flour and 2 ounces of butter, add 1 pint of sweet cream or milk, simmer for 5 minutes. Season to taste with salt and pepper.

5. Baked Beans. Anyone can have nice baked beans if he secures a bean pot and follows these directions: The large red kidney variety of beans is largely used, but the small white pea bean is more generally popular.

1 quart of beans is sufficient when cooked for two meals for an average family. They should be soaked in cold water for an hour or so. Then salt and pepper should be added, together with ½ teaspoonful of mustard and ½ teacupful of molasses. The molasses gives the beans a delicious flavor and at the same time it is not too pronounced, nor is it possible to detect the molasses. When the beans are in the pot, ½—¾ pound of salt pork well streaked with lean should be placed on top, and then enough warm water poured into the pot to just cover the beans.

Beans should be baked in an oven of even temperature for either a day or a night, or, in other words, about 12 hours. It is better to bake them in the daytime, for then they can receive more attention. As the water gradually evaporates more should be added from time to time, but care should be taken to keep the beans covered. This must be done until the beans are nearly ready to be taken out, when no more water should be added, so that they will not be so moist as to become mashed or broken.

The pot can remain in the oven, where it will simply keep hot, for an indefinite time without injury. Beans should be served in a covered dish. Beans that have been left over are delicious warmed up in a stewpan with a little water added, and many bean epicures think the more times beans are warmed over the better they are.

Good, old-fashioned brown bread is the proper accompaniment for baked beans, and it is as difficult to get the genuine article as it is to find good baked beans. Here is a famous recipe for Boston brown bread of the proper kind: 1 cupful of rye or graham flour, 1 cupful of white flour, 2 cupfuls of Indian meal, 1 cupful of molasses (scant), 2 teaspoonfuls of soda, ½ teaspoonful of salt, 1 cupful of sour milk and 1½—2½ cupfuls of water.

Steam for 3 hours and then dry in the oven for half an hour. The brown bread should be eaten warm and what is left over can be either steamed again or toasted.

6. Winter Succotash. Wash 3 cupfuls of dried corn and 2 cupfuls of lima beans; put the beans into a kettle and cover with cold water. Cover the corn with cold water and set on the back of the stove to heat and swell. Boil the beans for about 15 minutes, then drain off the water, pour boiling water on them and when tender add the corn, cooking both together for about 15 minutes. Just before serving add a little salt, pepper and butter and flour rubbed together, or ½ teacupful of cream or milk thickened with a little flour.

7. Summer Succotash. String ¼ peck of young green beans, and cut each bean into three pieces (not more), and do not split them. Throw the beans into a pan of cold water, as you cut them. Have ready over the fire a pot or sauce-pan of boiling water; put in the beans and boil them rapidly for nearly 20 minutes. Afterwards take them up and drain them well through a colander. Take ½ dozen ears of young but full-grown Indian corn, (or 8—9, if they are not all large) and cut the grains down from the cob. Mix together the corn and the beans, adding a very small teaspoonful of salt, and boil them about 20 minutes. Then take up the succotash, drain it well through a sieve, put it into a deep dish, and while hot mix in a large piece of butter (at least the size of an egg), add some pepper and send it to the table. It is generally eaten with salted or smoked meat.

Fresh Lima beans are excellent cooked in this manner with green corn. They must be boiled for half an hour or more before they are cooked with the corn.

Dried beans and dried corn can also be used for succotash, but they must be soaked all night before boiling. The water poured on them for soaking should be hot.

8. Stewed Tomatoes. To a dozen large tomatoes mince a good-sized onion (or less if preferred), and if the flavor of onion is not liked omit it altogether; a tablespoonful of good brown sugar, a teaspoonful of pepper, salt to taste, a teacupful of bread crumbs, a large heaped tablespoonful of good butter. Put into a covered stew-pan and cook for 1 hour; shake the pan well and frequently. Beat up the yolks of 2—3 eggs, and, just before serving, stir them rapidly to the tomatoes; let them remain a minute and serve in a small tureen or covered dish. This is a fine accompaniment to all kinds of baked or roast meats. Tomatoes are best when cooked for a long while.

9. Baked Tomatoes. Peel and mince enough to fill a quart dish; season them with sugar, mace, pepper, salt and a little minced onion. Put a layer of bread crumbs upon the bottom of the dish, then a layer of tomatoes, a little butter, another of bread crumbs, until the dish is full; bread crumbs must be strewn thickly over the top; lay over bits of butter. Bake in a moderate oven for 2 hours.

10. Parsnip Fritters. Boil enough parsnips to make 2 tumblerfuls when mashed and rubbed through the colander, season with salt and pepper, add 1 well-beaten egg and flour enough to hold it together (½ teacupful will be sufficient), fry in thick cakes. Serve as fast as they are fried.

11. Baked Egg=Plants. Prepare several fine, large, unblemished egg-plants by scooping out the inside or pulp with a spoon, leaving the rind standing. To do this you must cut off very nicely and evenly a round piece from the top, (afterwards to be tied on again). Make a sufficient quantity of forcemeat or stuffing of soaked bread pressed and dried slightly, fresh butter, minced sweet majoram leaves, a little pepper and salt, some powdered mace and the yellow rind of a lemon grated off very fine. Mix all these with the pulp or inside of the egg-plant. When thoroughly mixed stuff with it the rind or outside into a perfectly round shape, and with a thread tie on the top piece which was cut off. Put the egg-plants into a dish, the bottom covered with thin slices of cold ham. Bake them for an hour or more, and then send them to the table whole, with the slices of ham laid round on the dish. Remove the strings.

12. Old Fashioned Boiled Dinner. Take 4 pounds of corned beef and soak it in cold water, then put it on to boil in fresh cold water; skim carefully, then let it simmer until tender, but not until it falls to pieces.

Then let it cool in the liquor in which it is boiled. **Pour** it into a flat shallow dish and press with a slab. Take the fat from the liquor and save the latter, but do not let it stand in an iron kettle or tin pan. Boil 2 to 3 beets the day before and cover them with vinegar, the next day take a small cabbage, a couple of small carrots, a small white turnip, 6 to 8 potatoes and a small crooked-neck squash. Wash all of the vegetables, scrape the carrots and quarter the cabbage; the squash and turnips should be pared and then cut into slices three-quarters of an inch long; the potatoes should also be pared. About 2 hours before dinner time put the meat liquor on to boil; as soon as it boils throw in the carrots, then the cabbage and turnips and one-half hour before dinner add the squash and potatoes. When tender take the vegetables up carefully and drain the cabbage by pressing it in a colander. Slice the carrots. Put the cold meat into the center of a large dish and serve the carrots, potatoes, and turnips around the edge with the other vegetables in separate dishes. Or else put each vegetable into a separate dish by itself. If the meat is put on to boil quite early, and the fat taken off with the vegetables added to the boiling liquor, putting in those that take the longest time to cook, this may all be done the same day. The beets must always be boiled alone, take out the meat and fat before putting in the vegetables, sending each to the table as whole and daintily as possible.

MEATS.

1. Beef Roll. Remove the tough skin from 5 pounds of beef. Sprinkle ½ teaspoonful of pepper, a little ground cloves, salt to taste, 1 tablespoonful of sugar, 3 tablespoonfuls of vinegar and 1 teaspoonful of Summer savory over the meat and then roll up and tie with a narrow piece of muslin. Put into a stewpan, cover with cold water and stew for 3½ hours. Thicken the gravy and then cook for ½ hour longer. Cornstarch can be used instead of flour, adding it a few minutes before taking it from the fire. This is very good when cold.

2. Kidneys Stewed. Take 1 pair of perfectly fresh kidneys, split them, take out the white part and the sinews from the center. Put them into a kettle, cover with cold water and set on a moderate fire until the water nearly boils. Drain, cut into pieces, cover again with cold water and heat again. Bring to a boil with fresh water each time, being careful that the water does not boil or the kidneys will harden. In the meantime put one tablespoonful of butter and 1 tablespoonful of flour into a frying pan, and brown, then gradually stir in ½ pint of stock. Stir with a wooden spoon until it has boiled 3 minutes. Then add 1 tablespoonful of Worcestershire sauce, 1 tablespoonful of mushroom catsup, salt, pepper and the kidneys. Stir until the kidneys are heated through, take from the fire, stir in some sherry and serve with chopped parsley, sprinkled over the top. Kidneys must never boil, for like eggs, the more they boil the harder they become.

3. Scalloped Chicken. Put equal parts of cold chicken, boiled rice, macaroni and tomato sauce in layers into a shallow dish and cover them with buttered crumbs, and then bake until brown.

Cold roast turkey using stuffing and gravy may be prepered in the same manner.

4. Thanksgiving Chicken Pie. For the crust take 3 pints of cream, a heaping teaspoonful of salt and enough flour so that it will make a stiff enough dough to roll out easy. A deep earthen dish with flaring sides should first be lined with a thin layer of past, and the remainder of the latter rolled about ½ inch thick. ¾ of a pound of butter are cut into small pieces and put on the dough close together, a little flour is then sprinkled over the butter and the paste rolled over and over, after which it is rolled out again to the thickness of a finger and rolled up. Cut the ends from the roll, turn the pieces over and roll out to the thickness of a finger for rims. Use milk to moisten the paste lining in the dish and place the rims around the sides of the dish, put on 2 to 3 or 4 rims, one above the other having the inside rim the highest. Parboil 2 chickens and fill into the center of the dish after taking out some of the larger bones. Season the liquor with pepper and salt and pour it over the chicken, enough to nearly cover. Cut a quarter of a pound of butter into pieces the size of a chestnut putting them over the meat. Roll the remainder of the crust to fit the top, cutting a slit in it which should be turned back to let the steam escape. If you can bake this in a brick oven the time required will be about 3 hours; if baked in a stove it will take about 2 hours only and then use only 2 rims of crust.

5. To Boil Corned Beef. Soak the beef over night in plenty of water to cover it well. The following morning, wash the piece well, put it in the kettle and cover with cold water; boil slowly and skim frequently. If it is to be served cold, let it remain in the kettle until it becomes so.

To prepare it for luncheon or as a supper dish, remove all the bones when thoroughly done, pick the meat as for salad and pack in a deep dish, putting in alternately fat and lean. Skim the liquor, removing all fat; boil this broth until reduced one half; pour into the dish as much of it as may be needed to fill all the spaces left in packing the meat; lay over this a flat cover that will just fit it, and place a heavy weight upon this. It is best to prepare this dish in cold weather, or put upon ice the dish it was prepared in. Serve it upon a plate or round dish, and garnish with green sprigs of parsley, or celery; serve with it chow-chow, or any good pickle.

6. Beef Hash. Finely chop cold roast beef or cold steak, and about twice the quantity of potatoes. Put into a frying pan with a large piece of butter, pepper and salt; moisten with beef gravy or with hot water; cover and let it steam through thoroughly, stirring often. When done it should not be watery. Onion may also be added if liked. If onion is used, it should first be cooked a little in butter before it is added to the hash.

7. Veal Croquettes. Chop cold veal very fine, take a cupful of the meat, adding a little cold boiled chopped ham, two or three slices of onion, a pinch of mace, powdered parsley and a little pepper and some salt. Bring a pint of milk to the boiling point, then add a tablespoonful of cold butter and then the chopped meat. Beat up two eggs and stir in a teaspoonful of cornstarch or flour and add to the rest. Cook about 10 minutes, stirring often. Remove from the fire, spread it on a platter, roll into balls, flattening each when cool; dip them in bread crumbs, fry in a wire basket, dipped in lard.

8. Veal Pot Pie. Take a brisket piece of veal, about 5 pounds to 1 quart of water, and stew over a slow fire; just before it boils, skim it well and pour in a cupful of water, then turn over the meat so that all of the scum will rise to the surface. Season with pepper and salt to taste. Make a dough of raised yeast. Take 3 pints of flour, 2 ounces of butter and wet with milk sufficient to make a soft dough, knead it well and set aside to raise; when quite light mould and knead again; when it is light cut the dough in pieces of equal sizes (do not mould or roll it), lay them on top of the meat so as to cover it, and cook the whole slowly for one hour. Cover the kettle slowly and do not allow the meat to stop boiling.

9. Pot Roast. Take a piece of beef weighing about 5—6 pounds. Do not have it too fat. Put it into the kettle with barely sufficient water to cover it, and set over a slow fire; after it has stewed an hour add salt and some pepper. Then stew it slowly until tender, and add a little onion if liked. Do not add more water but let it nearly all boil away. When tender all through take the meat from the kettle and pour the gravy into a bowl. Put a large piece of butter into the kettle, take each piece of meat and dredge in flour, return to the kettle to brown, turning it often so that it will not burn. Skim off the fat from the gravy, pour this with the meat and stir in a large tablespoonful of flour, smoothed in water; let it boil for about 10 minutes and pour into the gravy dish.

10. Beefsteak Rolls. Make a dressing as for turkey; take a steak from the round and slightly pound it, spread the dressing on the steak, sprinkle with salt, pepper and a few bits of butter; lap over the ends, roll the steak up tightly and tie; spread butter over the rolls, then dip into well beaten egg, put into a sauce pan containing a little water, but the steaks must not lay in the water, and bake, basting often. A half hour in a well heated oven will suffice. Make a brown gravy and sent to the table hot.

11. Fried Beef Liver. Cut the slices rather thin and pour boiling water over them, which keeps the rich juices in the meat. Roll in flour or fine bread crumbs, seasoned with salt and pepper, dipped in egg and fried in hot fat and butter mixed.

12. Beef Croquettes. Chop cold roast or corned beef until very fine. Mix with the meat about twice the quantity of potatoes (hot), mashed and seasoned with butter and salt. Beat up an egg and stir well into the potato and meat, and make into balls, flattening them a little. Roll in egg and cracker crumbs, fry in butter and lard mixed, and brown on both sides. Serve very hot.

13. Roast Beef. When roasting beef, it is very essential that the oven is well heated when the meat is put in; this causes the pores to close up quickly and prevents the escape of the juices.

Take a rib roast weighing 6—8 pounds. Lay it in a dripping pan, and baste it well with butter. Set in the oven and baste it frequently with drippings. When partly done, season with salt and pepper, as meat will harden when salted when it is raw, and it also draws out the juices, then dredge with flour. Roast about two hours, leaving the inside a little rare. Take the meat out of the pan, skim off all the fat and set the meat where it will keep hot; smooth a tablespoonful of flour in a little water and add to the gravy, stir in a little pepper and a teacupful of boiling water. Boil up once and serve hot in a gravy boat.

14. Yorkshire Pudding. This is a very nice accompaniment to a roast of beef; take about 1 pint of milk, 4 eggs, beating the yolks separately, a little salt, and two tablespoonfuls of baking powder sifted with 2 cups of flour. Stir together until smooth. Have the roast about two-thirds done when the pudding is put into the oven. Take the roast from the oven and set where it will keep hot. Then take some of the gravy and put into two common sized tins, pour half the pudding into each, set into a hot oven and keep them until the dinner is ready to be dished up. Take the pudding out of the oven the last moment and send to the table hot.

15. Welsh Rare=Bit. Cut thin slices of bread, remove the crust and toast quickly; butter and cover with thin slices of rather new cheese, spread over this a little mustard and place on a tin in a hot oven until the cheese is melted, then cut into square pieces of any size, and serve at once on a hot dish, as it is spoiled if allowed to get cold. If mustard is not liked it may be omitted. Some think it more delicate if the toast is first dipped into a pan of boiling water; have some cheese melted in a cup and pour some over each slice. Have the plates hot and serve a slice to each person.

16. Veal Loaf No. 1. Take a cold fillet of veal, and (omitting the fat and skin) mince the meat as fine as possible. Mix with it a quarter of a pound of the fattest part of a cold ham, also chopped small. Add a tea-cupful of grated bread-crumbs, a grated nutmeg, half a dozen blades of mace, powdered, the grated yellow rind of a lemon, and two beaten eggs. Season with a salt-spoonful of salt, and half a salt-spoonful of cayenne. Mix the whole well together, and make it into the form of a loaf. Then glaze it over with beaten yolks of eggs, and strew the surface evenly, all over, with grated bread-crumbs or with pounded cracker. Set the dish into an oven, and bake it half an hour, or till hot all through. Have ready a gravy made of the trimmings of the veal, stewed in some of the gravy that was left when the fillet was roasted the day before. When sufficiently cooked, take out the meat, and thicken the gravy with beaten yolk of an egg, stirred in about three minutes before you take it from the fire.

Send the veal loaf to the table in a deep dish, with the gravy poured round it.

Chicken loaf, or turkey loaf, may be made in the same manner.

17. Veal Loaf No. 2. Chop 3 pounds of raw veal very fine, 3 eggs, 3 tablespoonfuls of milk or cream and butter the size of an egg; mix all together, roll 4 crackers until fine and mix with the meat. Season with salt and pepper and form into a loaf. Bake about 2½ hours. Baste with butter and water while baking. Serve cold, cut into thin slices.

18. Braised Veal. Take a piece of veal from the shoulder weighing about 5 pounds, take out the bones, and tie up the meat. Put a piece of butter into a kettle with a few slices of onion. Put the meat into this and let it get hot. Salt and pepper the meat, put on a medium fire, let it brown on one side, then turn and brown on the other side. Then put the kettle where it will simmer slowly, and if there is not juice enough for the gravy, add a few tablespoonfuls of water and a little more butter. This can be served either warm or cold.

19. Roast Spare Ribs. Crack the ribs through the middle and trim off all the ends, rub with salt and sprinkle with pepper, fold over, stuff with a dressing, sew up tightly, place in a dripping pan with a little water, and baste frequently. Brown on one side and then turn so that both sides will be equally brown.

20. Potted Ham. For 2 pounds of lean ham, take one of fat pork, mace, half of a nutmeg, grated, and a half teaspoonful of cayenne pepper. Mince the ham very fine, chopping fat and lean together, then pound in a mortar, adding the seasoning; put into a dish and bake for about ½ hour; then press it into a stone jar, fill up the jar with clarified lard, cover closely and paste over it a piece of thick paper. This will keep a long time in the Winter.

FISH.

1. Baked Pickerel. Wash and wipe the fish carefully, and lay into dripping pan with a very little water. Bake slowly, basting often with butter and water. Take a cupful of rich milk or sweet cream, add a few spoonfuls of hot water, stir in two large spoonfuls of butter and a little chopped parsley; heat by setting the dish into boiling water, stir in the gravy from the fish, and let it come to a boil. Place the fish into a hot dish and pour the sauce over it.

2. Baked White Fish. Clean the fish thoroughly, cut off the head, cut out the back-bone from the head to within a few inches from the tail, and stuff with the following dressing: Soak stale wheatbread in water and squeeze dry; finely chop an onion and fry in butter; then add the bread, about 2 ounces of butter, salt, pepper, and a little sage; heat thoroughly, then add the well beaten yolks of two eggs, stuff the fish, sew together. Cover the bottom of the pan with water and put a little butter over the top of the fish. Bake and when done serve with the following sauce: Smooth the yolks of 2 hard boiled eggs to a smooth paste with 2 tablespoonfuls of good salad oil, stir in a half teaspoonful of mustard and add pepper and salt to taste.

3. Baked Halibut. Lay the halibut into salted water for a few hours. Wipe it dry and cut the outer skin, then put it into a dripping pan, basting often with butter and water, and bake for an hour. It should have a nice brown color, and when it can be easily pierced with a fork it is done. Add a little water to the gravy in the dripping pan, stir in a tablespoonful of walnut catsup, a teaspoonful of Worcestershire sauce, the juice of a lemon, and thicken the sauce with browned flour, smoothing the flour with a little water. Bring to a boil and serve in a sauce boat.

4. Boiled Salt Mackerel. Wash the mackerel in clear water and put to soak in cold water over night, having the meat side down, and in the morning rinse again. Wrap each mackerel in a cloth and put into a kettle with considerable water, having the water cold, and cook about ½ hour. Carefully take it out of the cloth, take out the back bones and pour over it a little melted butter and cream, sprinkle lightly with pepper.

5. Baked Salt Mackerel. Soak the mackerel over night, put into a pan and pour on enough boiling water to cover. Let them stand a couple of minutes, drain off the water, and put them back into the pan, adding a few lumps of butter; pour on a cupful of sweet cream or rich milk, and a little pepper, set into the oven and bake until brown.

6. Fried Salt Mackerel. Wash and cleanse the mackerel well, and put them into cold water to soak, changing the water every two hours; then put them into fresh water. In the morning drain off the water, wipe them dry, roll in flour and fry in butter on a thick-bottomed frying pan. Serve with melted butter and garnish with parsley.

7. Potted Fish. Take out the backbone of the fish; for a fish weighing about 2 pounds take a tablespoonful of allspice and cloves mixed; put the spice into a little bag, put sufficient salt on the fish, then roll in a cloth, over which sprinkle a little cayenne pepper; put layers of fish, spice and sage in alternate layers into an earthen jar, cover with the best vinegar, close the jar closely with a plate, over this put a covering of dough about ½ inch thick. Have the edges of the crust adhere closely to the jar so as to make it air-tight. Put the jar into a pot of cold water and let it boil from 3—5 hours. Serve when cold.

8. Codfish Balls. Take a pint of codfish picked fine, two pints of whole raw peeled potatoes, sliced thickly; put them together in plenty of cold water and cook until the potatoes are thoroughly cooked; take from the fire and drain. Mash, add a piece of butter the size of an egg, and about 3 spoonfuls of rich milk. Make into little balls, put butter and lard half and half into a frying pan, and when hot put in the balls and fry to a nice brown.

9. Stewed Codfish. Take a piece of codfish and lay it into cold water for a few minutes. Pick it into small pieces, put it on the fire in a stewpan with cold water, let it come to a boil, drain off the water, and then add a pint of milk to the fish. Set it on the fire again, and let it boil slowly for a few minutes, then add a large piece of butter, a little pepper, and flour enough to thicken the milk to make a cream. Stew a few minutes longer, and just before serving stir in the well beaten yolks of two eggs.

10. Baked Codfish. Soak and pick the fish the same as for codfish balls. Take the same quantity of cold mashed potatoes as you have fish, a large piece of butter and milk to make it soft. Put into a buttered dish, put bits of butter over the top, and bake for about ½ hour.

11. Boiled Salmon. After carefully emptying the salmon, wash it very clean from the blood inside, and remove the scales. To preserve the fine color of the salmon, or to set the curd or creamy substance between the flakes, it should be put into boiling water, allowing to a gallon of water a handful of salt. After the water has been boiling a few minutes, and has been skimmed, put in the fish, (laying it on the drainer,) and let it boil moderately fast, skimming it well. It must be thoroughly boiled. Underdone fish of every kind is disgusting and unwholesome. Before it is taken from the fish kettle ascertain if it is sufficiently cooked, by trying if the back-bone easily loosens from the flesh. A quarter of an hour may be allowed for each pound, for a large thick salmon requires as much cooking as meat. When you take it up, drain it well, and serve it up immediately. Have ready some lobster sauce, or shrimp, if more convenient. To make it, mince the meat of a boiled lobster, mashing the coral with it, and mix it with melted or drawn butter, made very thick, and having but a very small portion of water. For shrimp sauce, boil the shrimps, take off their heads, and squeeze out their bodies from the shells. Thicken with them the drawn butter. Nothing should go with salmon that will interfere with the flavor of this fine fish, or give it any taste that will overpower or weaken its own.

12. Baked Fish. Make a stuffing by using the following receipt, and fill into the fish, which was first cleaned and wiped dry. After the fish is stuffed, sew it together with a needle and thread. Lay it on an earthen-ware dish or a platter on which it can be served, for it is difficult to remove the fish after it is baked. Sprinkle flour over the fish, and put a few slices of salt pork on top of the fish, and sprinkle salt over it. Baste it in the liquor in which it is baked. Add a little water, if there should not be enough. Bake in a moderate oven. When the fish can easily be pierced with a fork, take it from the oven, remove the pork and the thread and serve.

13. Stuffing for Baked Fish. Soak dry bread or crumbs in water. Press dry, and add the following ingredients: A piece of butter the size of an egg, 1½ tablespoonful of Summer savory, 1 tablespoonful of thyme, ¾ tablespoonful of majoram, salt to taste, and 1 teaspoonful of pepper. A beaten egg may also be added.

SHELL FISH.

1. Lobster Croquettes. Take remnants of lobster and pound until the dark and the light meat and coral are well mixed; add to the fish not quite as much bread crumbs as you have fish, season with salt and pepper; add some melted butter—about 2 tablespoonfuls—form into round balls, roll in egg, then in fine bread crumbs and fry in hot lard.

2. Deviled Crabs. Boil and mince ½ dozen fresh crabs, 2 ounces of butter, 1 teaspoonful of mustard, cayenne pepper and salt to taste. Put the meat into a bowl and carefully mix through it an equal quantity of fine bread crumbs. Cream the butter, mix the mustard well with it, then stir in carefully (a handful at a time) the mixed crabs, a teaspoonful of cream and the crumbs. Season with pepper and salt, fill the crab shells with the mixture, sprinkle bread crumbs over the tops, put small pieces of butter over the tops of each, and brown them quickly in a hot oven.

3. Crab Pie. Throw some live crabs into boiling salted water, boil for ¼ hour. When cold pick the meat from the claws and body. Chop together and mix with it bread crumbs, pepper, salt and a little butter. Put this into the shells and brown in the oven. A crab shell will hold the meat of two crabs.

4. Fried Oysters. Take large oysters and dry them in a napkin; then heat an ounce each of butter and lard in a thick frying pan. Season with pepper and salt, and then dip each one into egg and cracker crumbs. Place them into the hot grease and fry a delicate brown. Serve them crisp and hot.

5. Boston Fried Oysters. Turn the oysters in fine cracker meal and egg batter; fry for about 10 minutes over a slow fire in butter; cover the hollow of a hot platter with tomato sauce and place the oysters in it, but they must not be covered; garnish with chopped parsley.

6. Oyster Fritters. Select good-sized oysters, drain off the liquor, and to a cup of this juice add a cupful of milk, a little salt, four well-beaten eggs, and enough flour to make a batter. Surround the oysters in the batter, then fry in butter and lard, turning them so as to brown them on both sides. Serve very hot.

7. Scalloped Oysters. Roll crackers very fine so as to have about one pint of crumbs. Butter a deep earthen-ware dish, pour in a little of the oyster liquor, then put in a layer of oysters, sprinkle with salt and pepper, and lay small pieces of butter upon them, then another layer of cracker crumbs and oyster juice, then oysters, pepper, salt and butter, and so on until the dish is filled; the top layer to be of cracker crumbs. Beat an egg and add to it one cupful of milk, and turn this over the oysters. Cover the dish and bake for one-half hour. When baked through uncover the dish, and set on the top grate to brown.

8. Clam Fritters. Take 25 large sand clams from their shells; cut each in two, and lay them on a folded napkin. Put a pint of flour into a basin, add to it one-half pint of sweet milk, 3 well-beaten eggs, and nearly as much of their liquor as you have milk, beat the batter until smooth, then stir in the clams. Put plenty of lard into a pan, let it become boiling hot, and then put in the batter by the spoonful, fry to a delicate brown on one side and then turn on the other.

POULTRY.

1. Dressing or Stuffing for Fowls. Cut off the crust from stale slices of wheatbread, and pour warm water on the bread. Then press until dry, put into another dish, add pepper, salt, a teaspoonful of powdered savory, the same amount of sage and ½ cupful of melted butter, and a beaten egg. Work all together thoroughly and fill into the fowl.

2. Oyster Dressing. Use the same ingredients as given above, adding drained and chopped oysters. This stuffing is used in dressing turkey and chicken. Use the liquor and some of the oysters to make a sauce to pour over the turkey when served; or else it may be served separately in a sauce boat.

3. Turkey Scallop. Take a cold turkey, and pick out all of the bones and chop fine. Butter a dish, put in a layer of bread crumbs moistened with milk, then put in a layer of turkey with some filling, and put small pieces of butter over the top, sprinkle with pepper and salt; then another layer of bread crumbs, turkey and so on until the dish is filled; add a little hot water to the gravy, and pour this over the scallop. Then beat 2 eggs with 2 tablespoonfuls of milk, 1 tablespoonful of melted butter, a little salt, and cracker crumbs so that you can spread it over the scallop with a knife, dot with bits of butter and cover with a plate. Bake for an hour. A few moments before serving remove the plate and let the scallop brown on the top.

4. Boned Turkey. Carefully clean and wash the fowl. Take a sharp pointed knife, and beginning at the end of the wing, pass the knife down close to the bone, cutting all the meat from the bone, leaving the skin whole; run the knife down on each side of the breast bone, and up the legs close to the bone; fill the places where the bones were with a stuffing, keeping the fowl in its natural shape. Sew all the incisions made in the skin, then lard with rows of fat bacon, basting often with broth and a little butter. Carve across in slices, and serve with tomato sauce.

5. Fricassee of Chicken. Cut up two young chickens, and put them into a stew pan with just enough cold water to cover them. Bring them slowly to a boil, and then cook them for an hour or until they are tender. When they are tender, season them with salt, pepper, a piece of butter, and a little celery if liked. Smooth a little flour in water and add to the stew, also the well beaten yolks of two eggs; bring to a boil. Lay the chicken on a platter, and pour some gravy over it. Serve the remainder in a sauce boat. Stir a little of the hot gravy with the egg before adding it to the chicken.

6. Chicken Patties. Finely chop some cold chicken, season it with pepper and salt, some minced parsley and onion. Moisten this with chicken gravy, fill into scalloped shells that are lined with crust, and sprinkle with bread crumbs over the top. Dot with small pieces of butter and bake in a hot oven.

7. Chicken Croquettes. Chop cold roast chicken very finely, and add an equal amount of smoothly mashed potatoes, season with butter, salt, pepper and a little mustard. Make into cakes, dip into beaten egg and bread crumbs, and fry to a light brown.

8. Chicken Pot Pie. Cut up a large chicken, cover with cold water, and boil gently until tender. Season with salt and pepper, and thicken the gravy with 2 tablespoonfuls of flour, mixed smooth with a piece of butter the size of an egg. Roll out light bread-dough about an inch thick, and cut with the top of a small wine-glass; set them aside to raise for about ½ hour, then drop them into the boiling gravy. Put the cover on the pot, and cover very closely so as not to have the steam escape, and the water must not stop boiling. Boil for three-fourths of an hour.

BREAD, FRITTERS, CRULLERS, Etc.

1. Sponge for Winter Use. Peel and boil 4—5 medium-sized potatoes in 2 quarts of water; when done take out of the water, and press through a sieve or mash very fine in the dish in which the sponge is to be made, make a depression in the center into which put a cupful of flour, and pour over it the boiling water from the potatoes. Stir thoroughly, and when cool add a pint of warm water to make a thin batter, and a cupful of yeast. This sponge will make very moist bread.

2. Bread Raised Twice. Measure out 4 quarts of flour, take out about 1 cupful and put the remainder into a pan. Make a depression in the middle, into which put 1 tablespoonful of sugar, 1 tablespoonful of salt and 1 cupful of yeast; then mix in 1 pint of milk which was made lukewarm by adding 1 pint of warm water. Beat well with a strong spoon, and knead for 20—30 minutes; let it raise over night; in the morning knead again, mould into loaves, let them raise until about twice their size, and bake not quite 1 hour.

3. Salt=Raising Bread. Prepare the leaven in the following manner: Put 1 pint of lukewarm water into a bowl, and stir up a thick batter, adding only a teaspoonful of salt; beat the batter thoroughly, set in a pan of warm water and keep warm, and in 2—4 hours it will begin to raise. When it is nearly light enough, take 1 pint of milk and a pint of boiling water, mix the sponge in a bread pan, and when cooled about lukewarm stir in the leaven. The sponge will be light in about 2—4 hours if kept warm. The dough does not require as much kneading as yeast-raised dough. Bread made in this way should be made oftener, as it dries more quickly than bread made with potatoes. Some people object to it because of the odor in raising, which is the result of acetous fermentation, but the more of that the more sure you are of having sweet bread when raised.

4. Raw Potato Yeast. Peel 3 large potatoes and lay them into cold water. Then grate one potato in a large dish, pour over it at once one pint of boiling water to cook the potato. Grate the next potato, and pour on another pint of water, then grate the third, and over this also pour 1 pint of boiling water. Do not grate them all at once as the potato will turn dark. Stir quickly with a silver spoon, adding salt and about ½ cupful of sugar. When it is lukewarm stir in 1 cupful of yeast. When light it will be covered with a thick foam. This yeast makes delicious bread.

5. Brown Bread. 2½ cupfuls of sour milk, and ½ cupful of molasses; put into this 1 heaping teaspoonful of soda, 2 cupfuls of cornmeal, 1 cupful of graham flour, and 1 teaspoonful of salt. Steam 3 hours and afterwards brown in the oven.

6. Graham Bread. To a little more than 1 quart of warm water add ½ cupful of brown sugar or molasses, ¼ cupful of yeast and 1½ teaspoonfuls of salt, thicken the water with flour to a thin batter, then add yeast, salt and sugar, and stir in more flour until thick. In the morning add a small teaspoonful of soda and flour enough to make a stiff batter, pour it into pans and let it raise again, then bake in a moderate oven. Keep in a warm place while raising.

7. Soda Biscuits. Put 1 quart of flour into a sieve with 1 teaspoonful of soda and 2 teaspoonfuls of cream of tartar, and sift 1 teaspoonful of salt and 1 table-spoonful of white sugar, mix all well together, mix in 1 even tablespoonful of lard or butter, wet with ½ pint of sweet milk, put on the board and roll 1 inch thick, cut with a biscuit cutter and bake in a quick oven. Handle as little as possible and bake quickly.

8. Vienna Rolls. Stir a tablespoonful of butter in a bowl until soft. Then to 1 quart of unsifted flour add 2 heaping teaspoonfuls of baking powder, mix and sift, and then place in the bowl with the butter. Take enough milk to make a dough of usual stiffness, put into the milk a teaspoonful of salt, and stir it into the flour, turn on the board and knead until smooth. Roll about ½ inch thick, and cut with a cutter, fold each one over so as to form a half-moon, wetting them a little so as to make them stick; place them on buttered pans, brush the top with milk to give them a gloss, and bake immediately in a hot oven for about 20 minutes.

9. Buns. Break an egg into a cupful of sweet milk, mix with it 1 cupful of sugar, ½ cupful of butter, 1 cupful of yeast, and flour enough to make a soft dough; flavor with nutmeg. Let it raise until very light, then mould into biscuits. Let it raise again, bake, and when nearly done, glaze with a little molasses in milk.

10. Buttered Toast. Take bread which is not too fresh, slice thin and evenly; trim off the edges; warm each side of the bread, then present the first side to the fire and brown, then toast the other side, butter and serve immediately.

11. Apple Fritters No. 1. Sift 2 cups of flour with 1 teaspoonful of baking powder, then add ½ teaspoonful of salt. Beat the yolks of 2 eggs with 1 teaspoonful of sugar and 1 cupful of sweet milk. Stir this into the flour to make a smooth batter, then add the beaten whites of the eggs. Then stir in 3 chopped apples and fry in hot fat. Serve with maple syrup.

12. Apple Fritters No. 2. Make a batter in proportion of 1 cupful of sweet milk to 2 cups of flour, 1 heaping teaspoonful of baking powder, 2 eggs, 1 tablespoonful of sugar, and a little salt. Have the milk lukewarm, slowly add to the beaten yolks and sugar, then the flour and the whites of the eggs; stir all together, and throw in some slices of good sour apples, covering the apple slices well with the batter; drop into the hot lard with a spoon, and fry to a golden brown. Serve with Maple sugar or with syrup made of sugar.

13. French Pan=Cakes. Sift together ½ cupful of flour and 1 teaspoonful of baking powder and stir to a batter with 1 cupful of milk, 1 teaspoonful of sugar, 3 eggs, the whites beaten separately and added last, and 1 teaspoonful of melted butter. Put a piece of butter into a frying-pan, pour in enough of the batter to cover the surface. When brown on both sides spread with jelly, roll, and sift powdered sugar over the top.

14. Buckwheat Griddle Cakes. 2 cupfuls of buckwheat flour, ½ cupful of wheat flour, 2 teaspoonfuls of baking powder, 1 teaspoonful of salt, and make into a batter with 1 pint of sweet milk. Bake brown on both sides on a well greased griddle. Beat the batter well before baking.

15. Buckwheat Cakes. Sift together 1 quart of buckwheat flour and a teacupful of corn meal. In cool weather make up a moderately thin batter with lukewarm sweet milk; salt to taste. In warm weather it is best to use water as the milk would sour; add half a tumblerful of good yeast; make it up in a jar (covering closely), and let it raise over night. The next morning beat in three eggs; let it set 15 or 20 minutes; just before frying stir in a teaspoonful of soda, first sprinkling it over the batter. Dip out with a ladle, putting the same quantity in each cake but not enough to make them very large. Hot separate plates should be placed for serving them in, and nice syrup and drawn butter put upon the table, to be eaten with them (if liked); only one or two for each person should be sent in at once. And in taking them from the griddle, always put them upon a hot plate.

16. Strawberry Short=Cake. Sift together 1 quart of flour, 2 teaspoonfuls of baking powder, a little salt, and 1 tablespoonful of white sugar. Then mix in 3 tablespoonfuls of butter, beat 2 eggs into 1 cupful of milk, and mix all together as quickly as possible. Divide the dough into two parts, roll each part into a sheet about ½ of an inch thick, lay the sheets on a well greased pan, put the other sheet on this one, and bake in a hot oven. When they are done, separate them, put between the crusts a thick layer of strawberries, sprinkle with sugar. Any kind of berries may be used in this way.

17. Crullers. Take 2 cupfuls of sugar, 1 cupful of sweet milk, 3 eggs, 1 tablespoonful of butter, 3 teaspoonfuls of baking powder mixed with 6 cupfuls of flour, nutmeg and cinnamon. Beat the eggs, sugar and butter together, add milk, spices and flour; put some flour on the moulding board, turn the dough on this, and mix until stiff enough to roll out. Cut into squares, make 3—4 long incisions in each square, lift by taking alternate strips between the finger and thumb, drop into hot lard and bake quickly.

18. Cornmeal Puffs. Stir 8 tablespoonfuls of cornmeal into 1 quart of boiling milk, 4 tablespoonfuls of powdered sugar, and a little nutmeg. Let this boil for 5 minutes, stirring constantly; then take from the fire.

19. English Crumpets. 1 quart of warm milk, 1 teaspoonful of salt, ½ cupful of yeast, and flour enough for a not very stiff batter. When light add half a cupful of melted butter, let it stand about 20 minutes, and bake in muffin rings.

20. Corn Dodgers. To 1 quart of cornmeal add a little salt and a small tablespoonful of lard, scald with boiling water, and beat hard for a few minutes, and drop with a tablespoon into a well greased pan. The batter should be thick enough to flatten on the bottom, leaving then quite high in the middle.

21. Johnny Cake. 1 pint of butter-milk, 1 pint of cornmeal, 1 tablespoonful of melted butter, 3 eggs, 1 teaspoonful of soda, and 1 teaspoonful of salt. Beat the eggs and add to the butter-milk, then stir in the cornmeal, the melted butter and salt. Dissolve the soda in a little boiling water, and add to the batter, mix thoroughly and pour in a greased shallow pan. Bake in a moderately quick oven for ½ hour.

22. Graham Gems. Take 3 cupfuls of sour milk, 1 teaspoonful of soda, 1 teaspoonful of melted lard, and 1 beaten egg; add the milk to the egg, then the sugar and salt, and then the Graham flour, mixing the soda with the flour together with the lard; make a stiff batter so that it will drop from the spoon. Have the gem pans very hot, fill and bake for 15 minutes in a hot oven.

23. Graham Muffins. 2 cupfuls of sour milk, 2 tablespoonfuls of brown sugar, a little salt, 1 teaspoonful of soda, and enough Graham flour to make the batter moderately stiff.

24. White Hominy or Grits. Take 2 cupfuls of grits to 2 quarts of salted water, and soak over night, and boil for ¾ of an hour in a custard kettle; serve with milk and sugar, or when cold slice and fry.

25. Snow Flakes. One quart of sifted flour, one quart of sweet milk, salt to taste, six eggs beaten separately, one tablespoonful of melted lard. Just before baking, stir in one heaping dessertspoonful of baking powder. Bake in small patty-pans in a quick oven; grease the pans slightly. This is a delicate, and, when well made and baked, a beautiful dish.

26. Soda Biscuit. Put in the sifter one quart of flour and one even teaspoonful of soda, sift these together; rub into the flour thoroughly a piece of butter the size of a hen's egg; salt to taste; wet the flour with sour milk until a soft dough is formed; make it into thin biscuits, and bake in a quick oven. Work it very little.

Always reserve a little flour before putting in the soda to work into the dough, and flour the board.

27. Boston Brown Bread. Mix 1 cupful of cornmeal, 2 cupfuls of Graham flour, 1 teaspoonful of salt, 4 tablespoonfuls of molasses. 1 pint of milk, 1 teaspoonful of dissolved soda, and beat hard with a wooden spoon. Butter a large pudding mould or tin pail, put in the dough, filling about one-half full. Put on the cover and set the pail in boiling water. Be careful not to allow a drop of water to get inside of the pail. Boil for 3 hours. At the end of that time, set it in the oven to dry for one half hour.

CAKES, COOKIES, Etc.

1. Fruit Pound Cake. 1 pound of sugar, ¾ pound of butter, ½ cupful of water, 1 pound of raisins, ½ pound of currants, ½ pound of seedless raisins, ¼ pound of citron, 10 eggs, 1 pound of flour, and 1 teaspoonful of baking powder. Cream the butter and sugar, then add the yolks of eggs and a pinch of mace. Then add the flour and the beaten whites of the eggs. Then add the fruit, first sprinkling it with a little flour. Mix all together, and bake in two pans in a moderate oven.

2. Fruit Cake No. 1. 1 pound of butter, 1 pound of brown sugar, 12 eggs, ½ pound of figs, 1 whole orange chopped fine, 6 tablespoonfuls of molasses, 1 wine-glass of wine, ½ wine-glass of brandy, a little rose water, spice to suit the taste, 4 pounds of raisins, 3 pounds of currants. 1 pound of citron, 1 teaspoonful of soda, and flour enough to make a stiff dough. Beat butter, sugar and eggs together. Chop the orange fine and mix with it 1 tablespoonful of sugar. Stir in the orange with the raisins, currants, figs and citron. Then add the other ingredients, dissolve the soda with a little hot water, and stir in enough flour to make a very stiff dough.

3. Fruit Cake No. 2. ½ pound of butter, 1 pound of brown sugar, 3 eggs, 2 pounds of raisins, 2 nutmegs, 1 tablespoonful of allspice, 1 cupful of sour milk, 2 even spoonfuls of soda, and 2 pounds of flour. Beat sugar, butter and eggs together, then add the milk and the spices, the raisins and at last the soda dissolved in a little hot water, and then the flour.

4. Fruit Cake No. 3. 1 cupful of sugar, ½ cupful of butter, 3 eggs, 1 pound of raisins, 1 pound of currants, 2 ounces of citron, spices to suit the taste, 1 teaspoonful of ground coffee, 2 wine-glasses of wine, 1 lemon, 1 cupful of coffee, ½ pound of almonds, ½ cake of chocolate, 1 teaspoonful of vanilla, and 2 teaspoonfuls of soda. Flour enough to make a stiff dough. Beat sugar, butter and eggs together, add spices, coffee and wine, then the flour, the raisins, currants and citron, stir in the dough, add the other ingredients, dissolve the soda in a little hot water, and at last stir in enough flour to make a very stiff dough.

5. White Fruit Cake. The whites of 12 eggs beaten to a stiff froth, 2 cupfuls of sugar, 1 cupful of butter, stirred together, 1 cupful of sweet cream, 5 cupfuls of flour mixed with about 5 teaspoonfuls of baking powder, 1 pound of citron, 1 pound of almonds, all finely chopped, 1 pound of grated cocoanut, 2 tablespoonfuls of rose water, and 1 piece of candied orange peel, sliced. Bake carefully in a moderate oven until thoroughly done.

6. Whipped Cream Cake. 1 cupful of sugar, 2 eggs, 2 tablespoonfuls of softened butter and 4 tablespoonfuls of milk; beat well together; then stir in a cupful of flour, in which has been mixed a teaspoonful of baking powder. Bake in dripping pans. When the cake is cold have ready a pint of whipped cream, sweetened to taste, spread over the cake and serve while fresh.

7. Hickory=Nut Cake No. 1. 1 pound of sugar, ¾ pound of butter, 6 eggs, 1 nutmeg, 1 pound of raisins, ½ wine-glass of wine, 1 pound of hickory-nut meats, 1 pound of flour, and 1 teaspoonful of baking powder. Beat sugar, butter and yolks of eggs to a cream, then add nutmeg and wine, flour the raisins, stir them in and then add the flour mixed with the baking powder, and at last the beaten whites of the eggs. This makes 1 large cake.

8. Hickory-Nut Cake No. 2. 1 cupful of sugar, ½ cupful of butter, 2 eggs, ½ cupful of milk, 1 large cupful of raisins, 1 cupful of nut-meats, 2 cupfuls of flour, and 2 teaspoonfuls of baking powder. Beat sugar, butter and yolks of eggs to a cream, then add the milk, flour the raisins, stir in with the nuts, then add the flour and the baking powder.

9. Delicate Cake. 1 cupful of sugar, ½ cupful of butter, the whites of 4 eggs, 1 cupful of milk or water, ½ teaspoonful of rose and almond extract, 2½ cupfuls of flour, and 2 teaspoonfuls of baking powder. Cream the butter and sugar, add flavoring and milk, sift the flour and baking powder together and stir into the cake, and at last add the beaten whites of the eggs.

10. Silver Cake. The whites of 8 eggs, ¾ cupful of milk, ¾ cupful of butter, 1½ cupful of sugar, 1 teaspoonful of baking powder, and 3 cupfuls of flour. Cream the butter, beat in the sugar, then the milk; sift the flour and baking powder together 3 times, stir in the dough. and then carefully stir in the beaten whites of the eggs. Bake in a large loaf.

11. Gold Cake. The yolks of 8 eggs, 1 cupful of sugar, ½ cupful of milk, ¼ cupful of butter, 1 teaspoonful of lemon extract, 1½ cupfuls of flour and 2 teaspoonfuls of baking powder. Cream the butter, beat in the sugar and yolks of eggs; add the extract and beat the mixture; add the milk. Sift the flour and baking powder and stir into the dough. Bake in a tube-pan for about 40 minutes.

12. Fig Cake. The whites of 6 eggs, ¾ cupful of milk, 1½ cupfuls of sugar, ½ cupful of butter, 2 cupfuls of flour, and 1 teaspoonful of baking powder. Cream the butter and sugar, add milk, then sift the flour and baking powder, add to the dough, and at last add the whites of the eggs. Bake in layer tins.

13. Fig Filling. One-half pound of figs and one-half pound of raisins, chopped fine. Add enough boiling water to make a smooth paste. Spread evenly between the layers, and frost the top with white icing.

14. Angel Cake. Sift 1 cupful of flour and 1 teaspoonful of baking powder five times. Beat the whites of 11 eggs to a very stiff froth, and add a little salt to the beaten whites; then add sugar and flavoring and beat thoroughly. Stir the flour in carefully. Bake in an ungreased pan slowly for 40 minutes. Place on a cake cooler, so that the air will circulate underneath.

15. Chocolate Jelly Cake. 1 cupful of sugar, the white of 1 egg and the yolks of 2 eggs, 1 cupful of milk, 1 tablespoonful of butter, 1 teaspoonful of vanilla, 2 cupfuls of flour and 2 teaspoonfuls of baking powder. Thoroughly sift together the flour and the baking powder. Beat the sugar, yolks of eggs and butter; then add the milk, flavoring and flour. Beat together well, and lastly stir in the beaten white of an egg. Bake three layers and put together with a chocolate jelly.

16. Jelly for Filling. Shave 2 ounces of chocolate, and add to 1 cupful of boiling water 1 even tablespoonful of butter, and ¾ cupful of sugar. Let it come slowly to the boiling point, stirring until smooth, then add 1 heaping tablespoonful of cornstarch dissolved in water, and 1 teaspoonful of vanilla. When nearly cool spread between the layers and cover the top and sides.

17. Roll Jelly Cake. 1 cupful of sugar, 3 eggs, 1 tablespoonful of butter, 1 tablespoonful of warm water, a little salt, 1 cupful of flour, and 1 teaspoonful of baking powder. Sift flour and baking powder together, beat the yolks of the eggs, add the sugar and water and beat hard. Beat the whites of the eggs until very stiff, stir in the flour and then lightly stir in the beaten whites of the eggs. Spread very thin on a large shallow tin, and bake in a moderate oven. When done turn on the board, sprinkle with fine sugar, spread with jelly and roll.

18. Black Cake. 1 cupful of butter, 1 cupful of sugar, 1 cupful of molasses, 1 cupful of milk, 3 eggs, 1 cupful of raisins cut into halves, 1 teaspoonful of baking powder, ½ teaspoonful each of cloves and nutmeg, and 4 cupfuls of flour. Cream the butter and sugar, add the molasses, spices and the milk; then the eggs beaten lightly, and the raisins dredged in the flour. Mix all together and bake in one loaf.

19. Orange Cream Cake. 1 cupful of sugar, 2 eggs, ¼ cupful of butter, ⅔ cupful of sweet milk, 1½ cupfuls of flour, and 2 teaspoonfuls of baking powder. Cream the butter and the sugar, add eggs beaten light, then the milk and the flour sifted with the baking powder. Bake in three layers in a quick oven.

20. Cream for Filling. The grated rind and the juice of one orange. Then stir in as much powdered sugar as will give it the required consistency to spread. Stir until like cream.

21. Marble Cake. (WHITE PART.) 1 cupful of sugar, ½ cupful of milk, the whites of 4 eggs, ¼ teaspoonful of vanilla, ¼ cupful of butter, 1½ cupfuls of flour, and 1 teaspoonful of baking powder. Sift the flour and baking powder together, cream butter and sugar, add the milk and the vanilla, stir in the flour and lastly the whites of the eggs beaten to a stiff froth.

YELLOW PART. ¾ cupfuls of sugar, the yolks of 4 eggs, ¼ teaspoonful of vanilla, ¼ cupful of milk, 1 tablespoonful of butter, 1 cupful of flour, and 1 teaspoonful of baking powder. Cream butter, sugar and the yolks of the eggs, then add the milk, lastly the flour and vanilla, and beat well together.

DARK PART. Dissolve ¼ cake of sweet chocolate in a little hot milk, add 1 tablespoonful of sugar and 1 teaspoonful of vanilla. Stir this into a cupful of the batter, taking part of the light and part of the dark batter. Drop by tablespoonfuls into a well buttered pan, first one color and then another. This will make a large cake, and is very good.

22. Cocoanut Cake. 1 cupful of sugar, ½ cupful of butter, 2 eggs, ½ cupful of milk, ½ teaspoonful of vanilla, 2 scant cupfuls of flour, and 1 heaping teaspoonful of baking powder. Cream the butter and sugar, then add the yolks of the eggs, the flavoring, the sifted flour and at last the well beaten whites of the eggs. Bake in three layers in a quick oven.

23. Cocoanut Frosting. Boil 1 cupful of granulated sugar in a few tablespoonfuls of water until the syrup hairs, then pour the syrup into the beaten white of one egg. Beat constantly until it is nearly cool, then spread

494   THE AMERICAN KITCHEN.

over the cake; cover quickly with grated cocoanut. Pile the cakes together and cover the whole with grated cocoanut.

24. Chocolate Cake. 1¾ cupfuls of sugar, ½ cupful of butter, ½ cupful of milk, 3 eggs, 1 teaspoonful of vanilla, 3 squares of grated chocolate, 2 cupfuls of flour, and 1 heaping teaspoonful of baking powder. Cream the butter and the sugar, then stir in the milk, eggs, chocolate, and then the flour sifted with the baking powder. Pour into shallow pans, and bake about ½ hour. Pour a white icing over the top.

25. Soft Gingerbread. 1½ cupfuls of molasses, ½ cupful of sugar, 1 cupful of milk, 1 tablespoonful of ginger, ¼ cupful of butter, 2½ cupfuls of flour, and 2 teaspoonfuls of baking powder. Stir the sugar, butter and molasses together, then add the eggs and the milk. Sift the baking powder and the flour together, and mix with it the ginger and the cinnamon. Stir all well together and bake in a shallow pan.

26. Rich Cookies. 1 cupful of butter, 2 cupfuls of sugar, 4 eggs, 3 tablespoonfuls of water, 4 cupfuls of flour, 1 even teaspoonful of baking powder, and nutmeg. Sift the flour, baking powder and nutmeg together. Cream the butter and sugar, add yolks of eggs, beaten lightly, then the water and the well beaten whites of the eggs. Mix with the flour and roll out thin; cut into cakes of any shape desired, and bake quickly. These will keep fresh a long time.

27. Drop Cookies. ½ cupful of butter, 1½ cupfuls of sugar, 2 eggs, ½ cupful of milk, ¼ teaspoonful of cinnamon, 2½ cupfuls of flour, and 1 teaspoonful of baking powder. Sift flour, baking powder and cinnamon together. Cream the sugar and butter, add eggs and milk and mix with the flour to a soft dough that will drop from the spoon. Drop on buttered tins two inches apart. Sprinkle with powdered sugar and cinnamon before putting it into the oven.

28. Molasses Drop Cake. 1 cupful of sugar, 1 cupful of molasses, ¾ cupful of butter and lard, ¾ cupful of water, 2 eggs, 1 teaspoonful of ginger, cloves, cinnamon, and 1 teaspoonful of dissolved soda. Flour enough to drop.

29. Potato Cake. 2 cupfuls of powdered sugar, 1 cupful of butter, 4 eggs, ½ pound of sweet chopped almonds, 2 ounces of grated chocolate (sweet), 1 cupful of grated not freshly boiled potatoes, 1½ cupfuls of sweet milk, 1 grated lemon peel, ½ teaspoonful of cinnamon, cloves and allspice, 2½ cupfuls of flour, 2 teaspoonfuls of baking powder. Bake for two hours in a slow oven.

30. Coffee Cake. 1 cupful of brown sugar, 1 cupful of molasses, ½ cupful of butter, 1 cupful of strong coffee, 1 egg, 4 even cupfuls of flour, 1 heaping teaspoonful of soda sifted with the flour, cinnamon, cloves, 2 pounds of raisins, and ¼ pound of citron. Beat the butter, sugar and eggs together, add spices, molasses and coffee, then the flour and lastly the fruit. Bake for one hour in a moderate oven.

31. Drop Cakes. Beat the yolks of 4 eggs, 1 cupful of sugar, ½ cupful of butter, 1 cupful of cornstarch and 2 teaspoonfuls of baking powder together. Then lightly stir in the beaten whites of the eggs. Bake in small tins; a raisin or almond can be placed on the top of each cake after they are put into the tins.

32. Lady Fingers. Beat together 2 eggs, 1 cupful of sugar, ½ cupful of butter, then stir in 4 tablespoonfuls of sweet milk. Add enough flour to make a stiff dough, which can be stirred with a spoon, mixing with the flour 2 tablespoonfuls of baking powder. Flavor with vanilla. Flour the moulding board well, and with your hand take a piece of the dough and roll as large as your finger, cut off in 4-inch lengths, and put closely on buttered lady finger tins. Bake in a quick oven.

33. Jumbles No. 1. Stir ¾ cupfuls of butter, 1½ cupfuls of sugar, and 3 eggs together, then add 3 tablespoonfuls of milk, and 1 teaspoonful of baking powder. Roll, and sprinkle with granulated sugar, which should be gently rolled in. Cut with a jumble cutter and bake quickly.

34. Jumbles No. 2. 2 cupfuls of sugar, 1 scant tablespoonful of melted butter, 1 cupful of milk, 2 teaspoonfuls of vanilla, 4 eggs, 1 saltspoonful of salt, 1 quart of flour, and 1 teaspoonful of baking powder. Beat the eggs very light with the sugar, then add butter, milk, and vanilla, lastly the flour sifted with the baking powder, making a very stiff dough. Drop little portions of it into a greased pan with plenty of space between them. Bake quickly. If the heat is right, and the batter stiff enough, they will raise in the middle, giving them a very pretty shape.

35. Wafers. ¼ pound of butter, ½ pound of pulverized sugar, and 3 even tablespoonfuls of flour. Flavor with rosewater, and spread in thin cakes in a dripping pan. Bake, and while still hot roll them and powder with sugar. They must be rolled at once as they bake quickly.

36. Vanilla Snaps. 1½ cupfuls of sugar, 2 large teaspoonfuls of milk, 2 eggs, 3 teaspoonfuls of vanilla, 1 cupful of butter, 1 teaspoonful of baking powder, and 3 cupfuls of flour. Cream butter and sugar, add milk, eggs beaten lightly, and vanilla. Sift together the flour and the baking powder. Mix with the flour to a soft dough, and roll thin. Sprinkle with pulverized sugar before baking.

37. Spice Ginger Cake. 5 eggs, 2 cupfuls of butter, 4 cupfuls of flour, 2 cupfuls of sugar, 1 cup not quite full of molasses, with a teaspoonful of soda stirred into it until it foams from the bottom; a wine-glass of brandy, 1 tablespoonful of ginger, 1 tablespoonful of cinnamon, and 1 tablespoonful of allspice and cloves mixed. Add the beaten whites of the eggs last, then the molasses. Fruit may be added.

38. Fruit Ginger Cake. 1 pound of flour, 1 cupful of sugar, 2 cupfuls of molasses, ½ pound of butter, 6 eggs, 1 pound of currants, the same of raisins, ½ pound of citron, 1 tablespoonful of ginger. 1 teaspoonful of cinnamon and allspice, 1 teaspoonful of soda, and 2 teaspoonfuls of cream of tartar.

39. Ginger Nuts. 3½ pounds of flour, 1 pound of butter, ½ pound of sugar, 1 quart of molasses, 5 even tablespoonfuls of ginger, 3 teaspoonfuls of allspice, 1 teaspoonful of cloves, and 2 teaspoonfuls of cinnamon.

Make a smooth dough, roll out, and cut about the size of a cent piece; wash over with molasses and water and bake in a moderate oven.

40. Ginger Snaps. 1 egg, 1 cupful of molasses, 1 cupful of sugar, 1 cupful of butter and lard mixed, ½ cupful of boiling water, 1 even tablespoonful of soda dissolved in the water, and 1 tablespoonful of ginger. Flour to mould out soft. Roll out thin, and bake in a quick oven.

41. Cinnamon Drop Cakes. Take 1 egg, 1 cupful of sugar, 1 cupful of molasses, ½ cupful of butter, 1 cupful of water, 2 teaspoonfuls of cinnamon. 1 heaping teaspoonful of soda, and 3 cupfuls of flour. Bake in small cups half full.

42. Sugar Cookies. 1 cupful of sugar, 1 cupful of butter, 1 cupful of water, 1 teaspoonful of soda, 1 teaspoonful of cream of tartar or 1 tablespoonful of baking powder. Flour enough to make a stiff dough. Roll out and cut into any desired shape, and bake in a quick oven.

43. Eggless Cookies. 1 cupful of sugar, ½ cupful of butter, 1 cupful of water, 1 tablespoonful of baking powder, and flour enough to roll out. Cut into any desired shape, and bake in a quick oven.

44. Boiled Frosting No. 1. 1 cupful of granulated sugar, and 5 tablespoonfuls of water boiled over a hot fire until it threads. Beat the white of 1 egg until very stiff; turn the boiling sugar into it, and stir rapidly for a few minutes. Then put in the beater and beat until light and creamy. When cooled put on the cake.

45. Boiled Frosting No. 2. Put 1 cupful of sugar and ¼ cupful of milk over the fire until it boils. Boil for five minutes without stirring, then place into a pan of cold water, and whip until white and light; add flavoring to taste, as it stiffens, but before it is quite cold, spread on the cake, and smooth with a knife.

46. Sauce for Pudding. Beat 1 large tablespoonful of butter, 1 cupful of pulverized sugar, and 1 teaspoonful of vanilla until light and creamy. Put 1 large cupful of water into a sauce pan, and add the flour mixed with a little cold water. Cook this until like thin starch, then take up the butter and sugar mixture, and while you are beating it briskly, have some one pour into it gradually the hot flour sauce. If the beating is not stopped for a moment the whole sauce will rise and be foamy.

47. Cream Sauce. Put 1 pint of milk into a double boiler, and let it just come to the boiling point, then stir in 1 heaping teaspoonful of cornstarch dissolved in a little cold milk, and add 1 tablespoonful of sugar. Cook for a few minutes, and then let it get cold, then add 2 tablespoonfuls of sherry or 1 teaspoonful of vanilla, and just before serving stir in the beaten whites of 2 eggs. This is to be served cold.

48. Strawberry Sauce. Beat ½ cupful of butter with 1 cupful of sugar, then add the white of 1 egg beaten stiff. Mash the strawberries, and beat all well together.

49. Wine Sauce. 1 cupful of sugar, and ½ cupful of butter are beaten to a cream, add 1 well beaten egg, then stir in ¾ cupful of sour wine, a little nutmeg, and ½ teaspoonful of lemon extract. When ready to serve set in a dish of hot water, but do not boil; let it get quite hot.

50. Apple and Lemon Filling. The juice and grated rind of 1 lemon, 1 large sour apple grated, and 1 cupful of sugar boiled together for five minutes. Let it cool, and it is ready for use.

51. Walnut Filling. Boil ½ cupful of milk and 2 cupfuls of sugar steadily for five minutes. Take from the fire and add 1 pound of walnuts chopped fine, and beat until it will spread nicely.

52. Cooked Orange Filling. Strain the juice of 1 lemon and 2 oranges, and put them on to boil. When boiling add 1 tablespoonful of cornstarch moistened with a little water; let it cook for 10 minutes. Then add ½ cupful of sugar and the yolk of 1 egg beaten together, and a little grated orange rind. Take from the fire, and stir in 1 teaspoonful of butter, and let it cool. Put between the cakes and dust sugar over the top layer.

PIES AND PUDDINGS.

1. Squash Pie No. 1. 1 pint of cooked squash, ½ cupful of sugar, 1 cupful of milk, 1 egg, ½ teaspoonful of salt, and ½ teaspoonful of mace. Press the squash through a sieve, add sugar, salt, mace, the well-beaten egg, and the milk. Beat all together, and fill into a pie plate lined with a good crust.

2. Squash Pie No. 2. Cook the squash and press through a sieve. Take 1 pint of this squash, add 1 cupful of milk, 1 egg, ½ cupful of sugar, ½ teaspoonful of salt, and ½ teaspoonful of mace. Beat all together, and fill into a deep plate, lined with a good crust. Bake with one crust.

3. Mince=Meat Pies. To prepare the meat: Chop fine 2 pounds of lean, tender beef, cold, boiled, or baked; remove all skin and gristle. (The tongue and heart of a very young beef, boiled tender, makes the best mince-meat.) Mince fine ½ pound of suet, 1 pound of raisins, seeded; 1 pound of dried currants, washed and picked; ½ pound of citron, sliced thin; the same of candied orange or lemon peel; 1 pound of clean, moist brown sugar; the juice of 6 lemons, the rinds grated (throw away the pulp); 2 nutmegs grated, 1 ounce of salt, 1 ounce of ground ginger, the same of coriander seed, pounded and sifted; ½ ounce of allspice and cloves each; Mix the meat, fruits, and spices well. Pour upon the sugar a pint of wine and ½ pint of brandy; add the fruits to the meat; pour over the wine and brandy. When it is well mixed, pack it in small jars, and pour over the top of the meat the best syrup an inch thick; cover closely, and keep the jars in a cool place. When ready to make the pies, line the pie-plates with a good crust; add to a pint of the mixture a pint of tart apples chopped, and a wine-glass of rose-water. Fill the crust half full; lay over bits of butter; put in more meat to nearly fill the plate; cover with puff paste; cut a slit in the middle, and bake. They keep well. Warm them before serving. Cold fowls are sometimes used to make pies for immediate use. An excellent way to keep the meat a few weeks is to spice the meat, pack it away, covering closely with syrup, and add the fruits, wine, and brandy when the pies are made.

4. Lemon Pie. 1 cupful of sugar, 1 cupful of thick sweet cream, 4 eggs and 2 lemons. Grate the rind of the lemons, squeeze out the juice, add the sugar and the yolks of the eggs, and beat to a cream; add the cream, and bake in a rich undercrust. Beat the whites of the eggs to a stiff froth, beat in a few tablespoonfuls of powdered sugar, spread on the top of the pie when the pie is baked, then set it in the oven to set the meringue.

5. Cocoanut Pie. 1 cupful of sugar, 1 cupful of sweet milk, the grated rind of a lemon, 4 eggs, 1 tablespoonful of butter, 1 grated cocoanut. Stir the sugar with the butter, and add the yolks of the eggs, then stir in the cocoanut, the milk and the grated rind of a lemon, and lastly the whites of the eggs beaten to a stiff froth. Bake in a deep dish lined with paste.

6. Boiled Apple Dumplings. ½ pint of cold milk or water, 2 quarts of finely chopped apples, 1 tablespoonful of butter, 1 teaspoonful of salt, 1 quart of flour, and 2 teaspoonfuls of baking powder. Stir together flour, baking powder and salt. Rub together the butter and the flour, then stir in the apples, and make into a loaf with the milk or water. Any kind of fruit may be used instead of the apples. Serve with a brandy or a lemon sauce. The water must be boiling when the pudding is put in to boil, and must not stop boiling until the pudding is done.

7. Steamed Suet Pudding. 1 cupful of molasses, 1 cupful of water or milk, 1 cupful of chopped raisins or currants, ⅔ cupful of butter, 1 cupful of chopped suet, ½ teaspoonful of nutmeg, ½ teaspoonful of cinnamon, ½ teaspoonful of salt, 1 teaspoonful of soda, and 2½ cupfuls of flour. Sift the soda, the salt and the spices into the flour, rub the butter in the flour and then add the raisins. Mix the milk with the molasses, and stir into the flour. Steam in a buttered pudding mould for two hours. Serve with a brandy sauce.

8. Boiled Corn=Meal Pudding. Warm a pint of milk and a pint of molasses, and stir well together. Then beat together 4 eggs, and stir these with 1 cupful of chopped beef suet and corn-meal enough to make a stiff batter. Stir in a teaspoonful of soda dissolved in a little water, a little cinnamon and nutmeg. Then dip a cloth into boiling water, wring out, sprinkle a little flour over it, and put in the pudding and tie, leaving room for the pudding to swell. Cook for about three hours.

9. Apple Dumplings. Remove the peel and core from some good cooking apples. Make a rich biscuit dough of baking powder; roll the dough about ½ inch thick, and enclose an apple in each, filling the core of the apple with a little sugar, cinnamon and a small piece of butter. Butter a dripping pan, and set the dumplings into it side by side. Then put in a cupful of hot water, put a piece of butter over each dumpling, and sprinkle over them a handful of sugar. Baste the dumplings once while baking with the liquor, and serve with cream and sugar.

10. Baked Apple Pudding. The yolks of 4 eggs, 6 large grated apples, 3 tablespoonfuls of butter, ½ cupful of sugar, the juice and half of the peel of a lemon. Beat the sugar and butter to a cream, stir in the yolks and lemon with the grated apples. Pour in a deep pudding dish and bake. Whip the whites and pour over the pudding. Grate a little nutmeg over the top. Set in the oven for a moment. Serve with cream. Eat cold.

11. Apples Baked Whole. Never bake apples without paring and coring. They will be found nearly all skin and core, and are troublesome and inconvenient to eat. Have fine large apples, take off a thin paring and extract the core with a tin corer. Fill up the holes with brown sugar. Place the apples side by side in a square tin pan, set them in on oven and bake until, when tried with a fork, you find them soft all through. Send them to table warm, but not hot, and serve with sweet cream.

12. Fruit Dumplings. 1 pint of flour sifted, and 1 heaping teaspoonful of baking powder. Rub the butter with the flour and then mix with enough milk until quite soft. Spread this on the bottom of a round tin baking dish, and cover with sliced apples or peaches. Steam for ½ hour and serve with sugar and cream.

13. Lemon Pie. Grate off the rinds of 2 lemons, squeeze out the juice, add 1 cupful of sugar and the yolks of 4 eggs and beat to a cream. Then add 1 cupful

of cream and bake in a rich undercrust. Beat the whites
of the eggs to a stiff froth, beat in a few tablespoonfuls
of powdered sugar spread on the top of the pie and set
the pie into the oven for a few seconds to brown.

14. A Brown Betty. Pare, core and slice thin some
fine juicy apples. Cover the bottom of a large deep
dish with the apples. Sweeten them well with plenty
of brown sugar, adding grated lemon or orange peel.
Strew over them a thick layer of bread crumbs and add
to the crumbs a very few bits of fresh butter. Then put
in another layer of cut apples and sugar, followed by a
second layer of bread crumbs and butter. Next more
apples and sugar, then more bread crumbs and butter;
repeat this until the dish is full, finishing with bread
crumbs. Bake until the apples are entirely done and
quite soft. Send to table hot. It will be improved by
adding to each layer of apples a very little sweet unfer-
mented cider, fresh from the press.

15. Cranberry Puffs. 2 cupfuls of flour, 2 teaspoonfuls of baking powder, 2 tablespoonfuls of butter, ½ teaspoonful of salt, 2 eggs, 1 pint of cranberries and 1 cupful of milk.
Sift flour and baking powder together, rub the butter into the flour, add the salt to the eggs and beat to
a thick cream. Add the cranberries to the flour, then
the eggs and milk. Fill buttered cups about half full
of the mixture, set in a steamer closely covered and
steam for 1 hour. They should come out perfect puff
balls. They are spongy and absorb a great deal of
sauce. Serve with plain pudding sauce.

16. Peach Cobbler. ¾ cupful of milk, 1 egg, 2 tablespoonfuls of butter, ½ teaspoonful of salt, 2 cupfuls
of flour and 2 teaspoonfuls of baking powder, also
1 quart of peeled peaches. Sift together the flour, salt
and the baking powder, rub in the butter, then beat
the egg and milk together and stir into the flour to
make a nice batter. Turn on a well-floured board and
roll to the thickness of about an inch. Line an earthenware dish with the paste, invert a cup in the center of
the dish and fill the peaches around it. Sprinkle with
sugar and put on a top crust. Bake ½ hour in a hot

oven. When the pudding is cut the cup will be found to contain a very rich juice, which is used as a sauce for the pudding.

17. Fig Pudding. Mince very fine ½ pound of suet and the same quantity of figs; then mix with them ½ pound of finely grated bread crumbs, with a little sugar and enough golden syrup to make a nice paste. Butter a mould, fill it with the mixture and boil or steam it for 1½ hours. Turn it out and serve either plain or with whipped cream or syrup sauce. The latter is made by flavoring a little white sauce with some lemon rind and a spoonful of golden syrup.

18. Tapioca Pudding, No. 1. Pour a quart of milk over a cupful of tapioca. The milk should be boiling hot and sweetened to taste. Beat 6 eggs well and when the milk is nearly cold pour it slowly upon the eggs, stirring rapidly; season with nutmeg and cinnamon. Bake for ¼ hour and serve with rich sauce.

19. Tapioca Pudding, No. 2. Soak a cupful of tapioca for 1 hour in 2 cupfuls of milk. Put in a stew-pan half a dozen medium-sized tart apples, peeled and cored; the cavities filled with sugar and a little powdered cinnamon. Pour to them a cupful of water; cover the stew-pan and stew until the apples are tender. Take them up, put them into an enameled dish, pour over them any syrup that may remain in the stew-pan, add to the tapioca another cupful of rich, sweet milk; pour over the apples and bake. Eat with rich, solid butter sauce.

20. Floating Island. For one common-sized floating island have a round thick jelly cake, lady cake or almond sponge cake, that will weigh 1½—2 pounds. Slice it downwards, almost to the bottom, but do not take the slices apart. Stand up the cake in the center of a glass bowl or a deep dish. Have ready 1½ pints of rich cream, make it very sweet with sugar and color it a fine green with a teacupful of the juice of pounded spinach, boiled 5 minutes by itself; strained and made very sweet. Or for coloring pink you may use currant jelly, or the juice of preserved strawberries. Whip to a stiff froth 1½ pints more of sweetened cream, and flavor it with a large glass of mixed wine and brandy. Pour round the cake as it stands in the dish or bowl, the colored, unfrothed cream, and pile the whipped white cream all over the cake, highest on the top.

PRESERVES, JELLIES AND PICKLES.

1. Currant Jelly. Currants should not be over ripe, neither should they be gathered after a rain, as they are then apt to be watery. Remove all the leaves and the poor fruit, and if gritty wash and drain, but do not stem them. Put them into a porcelain kettle, mash them with a wooden spoon but do not heat the fruit, as this will darken the jelly. Then put the fruit into a flannel bag and drain over night. Do not squeeze them, or the jelly will be cloudy. The next morning take a bowl of sugar for each bowl of juice. Heat in an earthenware dish in the oven, stirring often to prevent burning. Boil the juice for about 20 minutes, skimming thoroughly. Then add the hot sugar and boil for 5 minutes, or until it will thicken in a spoon when exposed to the air. Pour into glasses and set aside for 24 hours, then dip a paper in brandy and tie it over the top.

2. Quince Jelly. Remove all dark spots, take off the stem and wipe the fruit carefully. The best part of the fruit is used for canning, the core, peel and other parts not used for canning are used for making jelly. The seed contains a large part of gelatinous substance and also gives the jelly a nice color. Boil in enough water to cover until soft, then mash and drain. Then take as much sugar as fruit juice when it is boiling, and boil until it jellies.

3. Tomato Catsup. Boil 1 bushel of ripe tomatoes until soft, strain through a colander. Then stir in 1 cupful of salt, 2 pounds of brown sugar, about ½ ounce of cayenne pepper, 3 ounces each of ground allspice, mace and celery seed, and 2 ounces of ground cinnamon. Then add 2 quarts of the best vinegar, stir all well together, and strain through a sieve. Boil slowly until reduced about one-half. Put into bottles, seal, and keep in a dark, cool place.

4. Watermelon Preserves. Select a melon with a thick rind; cut in any desired shape and lay the pieces into strong salt water for 24 hours, then soak in clear water for 24 hours, changing the water often. Then put them into alum water for an hour to harden them. Then to every pound of fruit take 1 pound of sugar. Make a syrup of the sugar, a few small pieces of white ginger root and 1 lemon, sliced. After the syrup has boiled take out the ginger root and the lemon, and put in the watermelon. Let it boil until transparent, then carefully take out the melon, put it into jars and pour the syrup over it.

5. Quince and Citron Preserves. Pare and cut the citron into small pieces; boil hard in medium-strong alum water for about ½ hour; drain and boil in fresh water until the color is changed and they are tender. Carefully wash the quinces and pare, quarter, core and halve them, boil the core and parings in water enough to cover them, for 1½ hours; remove and add the quinces to the liquid; boil, and when they begin to be tender add the citron and ¾ pound of white sugar to every pound of the fruit.

6. Canned Pumpkins. Peel the pumpkins or squash, cut into small pieces and stew until tender. Do not add any seasoning. Then mash them very fine. Have the cans hot, fill them with the hot pumpkins or squash, seal them tight and put in a dark, cool place.

7. Peach Jelly. Pare and slice the peaches, taking out the stones. Put the peach slices into a kettle with water enough to cover them, adding about one-fourth of the kernels. Stir often and when the fruit is well cooked strain it and to every pint of peaches add the juice of 1 lemon; then measure again and for each pint of peach juice add 1 pound of sugar. Heat the sugar and add the juice after it has boiled about 20 minutes. Then let it come to a boil and take it immediately from the fire. Fill into glasses and keep in a dark, cool place.

8. Pie=Plant Butter. For each pound of peeled and cut up pie-plant allow 1 pound of sugar. Let this sugar and pie-plant cook for an hour, then put into cans and seal.

9. Apple Jelly. Use apples that are pleasantly acid. Peel and core, and, as you cut them, throw the pieces immediately into cold water to prevent their being discolored by the action of the air. When you have prepared as many as you wish to use, put them into the preserving-kettle, and pour over them just enough water to cover them. Cover closely and let them boil without interruption until the apples are soft; then strain through a thin linen bag into some vessel that can be kept covered. The proportion for making the jelly is to 2 tumblers of the juice use 1½ tumblers of sugar. Measure the juice and the sugar in this proportion and put into the kettle. Let this syrup boil for a few minutes; then strain through a jelly bag. Return to the kettle 2 tumblerfuls of the syrup; this, boiled to the proper consistency, will form 1 tumblerful of jelly. After preparing the juice and measuring the proportions, it is safe to make the jelly thus in small quantities.

Quince jelly is made in the same manner. Strawberries, blackberries, raspberries and grapes all make very pleasant jellies. After washing the fruit, put it on to boil without any water, and when the juice is all extracted strain and proceed as in apple jelly.

10. Preserved Crabapples. Take the finest Siberian crabapples, which, being always red and pleasantly acid, are the only sort now used for preserving. Rub each crabapple with a dry, clean flannel and then prick every one in several places with a large needle to prevent their bursting. To every pound of fruit allow 1½ pounds of double-refined loaf sugar, and a pint of water. First make a syrup of the sugar and water, boiling it in a porcelain kettle, and skimming it until perfectly clear. Put in the crabapples, adding for each pound the juice and grated yellow rind of a large lemon. The lemon is indispensable to this sweetmeat. Simmer them slowly in the syrup until tender all through, so that they can be pierced with a twig of broom-corn, but do not allow them to break. When done put them up warm in glass jars more than half full, and the syrup over them.

11. Candied Orange and Lemon Peel. Remove the pulp and inside skin, cut the peel in strips lengthwise, boil in clear water until tender. Make a syrup in the proportion of ½ pound of sugar to 1 pound of the peel, adding to the sugar as much water as will melt it. Put in the peel and boil over a slow fire until the syrup candies, then take them out, strew powdered sugar over them and set in the sun to dry, or, if the weather will not admit of this, dry them in a warm oven. These will be found very useful in making fruit cakes or puddings.

12. Orange Syrup. Use sweet, thin-skinned oranges, squeeze the juice, add sugar enough to make a thick syrup. Boil and skim until clear. Pour off when clear and bottle when cool. A tablespoonful in a glass of water is delicious. Flavor with a little of the grated rind put in before boiling; a little in pudding sauce is good. Lemons may be prepared in the same way. Flavor the sugar by rubbing lumps upon the outside of the fruit and then add it to the juice; this is better than adding the peel.

13. Pineapples Preserved. Take 6 fine large pineapples, as ripe as you can get them. Clean them very nicely, but do not, at first, pare off the rind or cut off the leaves. The rind and leaves being left on while boiling will keep in the flavor of the fruit. Put the pineapples whole into a very large and very clean iron pot. Fill it up with cold water and boil the pineapples until they are so tender that you can pierce them through the rind to the core, with a splinter skewer or a twig from a broom. Then take them out of the pot and drain them. When they are so cool as to be handled without inconvenience, remove the leaves and pare off the rind. Cut them into round slices about ½ inch thick, extracting the cores from the center so as to leave a small round hole in every slice. Weigh them and to each pound of fruit allow a pound of sugar. Cover the bottom of a large dish or dishes with a thick layer of the sugar. On this place a layer of pineapple slices, then a layer of sugar, then a layer of fruit, and so on until the slices are all thickly covered, finishing with a layer of sugar at the top. Let them stand 24 hours. Then drain the slices from the syrup and lay them in wide jars. Put all the syrup into a clear porcelain kettle, and boil and skim it until the scum ceases to rise. Then pour it hot upon the pineapple. While warm, cover the jars closely with white paper cut to fit, and dipped in brandy, and cover tightly. There is no better way of preserving pineapples, or that retains the flavor so well.

Quinces may be preserved in the same manner.

14. Preserved Tomatoes. This is an excellent and popular sweetmeat, when flavored well with lemon, which is indispensable to making it palatable. Also, it should be well penetrated with sugar, therefore it is best not to attempt preserving tomatoes whole. The most convenient for preserving are those with smooth, even surfaces. If fluted or cleft they are difficult to peel when scalded, as the skins do not strip off so easily. Having weighed the tomatoes (which must be full-grown and quite ripe) allow to every 2 pounds, 2 pounds of the best brown sugar, a large spoonful of ground ginger and the juice and grated rind of 1 large ripe lemon, rolled awhile under your hand. Having scalded and peeled all the tomatoes, and mixed with the sugar a little beaten white of egg, put them into a porcelain-lined preserving kettle (uncovered), and add, gradually, the sugar. Boil the tomatoes and sugar slowly together until the scum ceases to appear. Then add, gradually, the lemons (peel and juice) and boil slowly for an hour or more. The tomatoes must all have bursted, otherwise they will not keep, from the sugar not getting sufficiently into them. When done, take them off the fire, put the tomatoes with their syrup into glass jars and seal.

15. Canned Pears. To every 3 pounds of fruit allow 1½ pounds of sugar and ½ pint of water. Peel the pears and lay them in cold water to keep them from turning dark before they are wanted. When the syrup is boiling, put the pears in and cook until they look clear or a fork can be stuck into them easily. Have the jars standing in a pan of hot water, and carefully fill them with the fruit. Pour the hot syrup over them, filling the jars to the top. Cover and seal.

16. Brandied Pears. In making brandied pears, Bartletts are the only variety that will give entire satisfaction when brandied, as they have a more decided flavor than any other. Select firm, but ripe pears, peel, and boil in a weak syrup until they can be pierced with a straw. Take the fruit out, drain and put into jars. Have ready a rich, hot syrup, made with 3 pounds of sugar and ½ pint of water and fill the jars containing the fruit with equal parts of the syrup and white brandy. Cover immediately.

17. Ginger Pears are a delicious sweetmeat. Use a hard pear, peel, core and cut the fruit into very thin slices. For 8 pounds of fruit after it has been sliced use the same quantity of sugar, the juice of 4 lemons, 1 pint of water and ½ pound of ginger root, sliced thin. Cut the lemon rinds into as long and thin strips as possible. Place all together in a preserving kettle and boil slowly for an hour.

18. Spiced Pears are an excellent relish. To make them, place in a porcelain kettle 4 pounds of sugar, 1 quart of vinegar, 1 ounce of stick cinnamon and ½ ounce of cloves. When this comes to a boil add to it 8 pounds of pears that have been peeled and cook until tender. Skim out the fruit and put in glass jars. Boil the syrup until thick and pour it over them. Apples may be used in the same manner.

19. Pickled Pears. Boil together 3 pounds of sugar, 3 pints of vinegar and 1 ounce of stick cinnamon. Use 7 pounds of sound pears, wash, and stick 3—4 cloves in each pear, put them into the hot syrup, cook slowly 25 minutes, turn them into a stone jar with the syrup and cover. The following day pour off the liquid and heat and turn over the fruit again. It may require heating the second time.

20. Grape Preserves. To make grape preserves press the pulp from the fruit with the fingers and put it over the fire to boil. When boiling rub it through a sieve to remove the seeds. Put the juice, pulp and skins into a preserving kettle, and to every pint add 1 pound of granulated sugar and boil until as thick as required.

21. Grape Jelly. Grapes are one of the best fruits we have for jellies. Wild grapes are considered by many as even better than the cultivated fruit. To make jelly stem the grapes carefully and wash well. Put them into a preserving kettle, cover and heat slowly. Stir frequently and cook until the fruit is well broken and has boiled. Take from the fire and squeeze through a jelly bag. Measure the juice into a porcelain kettle and set upon the stove to boil. For each pint of juice allow 1 pound of granulated sugar, and while the juice is boil ing place the sugar on tin pans and put it in the oven, stirring often. When the juice has boiled steadily 20 minutes add the hot sugar and stir rapidly until it dissolves. It will make a hissing sound as it falls in, and melt quickly. Let the jelly boil up once and take from the stove. Have the glasses heated by standing them in hot water and pour the liquid jelly into them. When it is perfectly cold cover the glasses. Jelly of two colors and different flavors may be made with the same grapes by separating the pulp and skins from the grapes and cooking each one by itself. One will be purple and the other amber.

22. Spiced Grapes. Grapes make an excellent spiced fruit. To prepare them, pick from the stems 7 pounds of ripe grapes and separate the pulp from the skin. Put the skins into a preserving kettle over the fire with enough water to prevent them from burning. In another kettle place the pulp and cook until it will press easily through a sieve to remove the seeds. Add the strained pulp to the skins with ½ pint of sharp vinegar and 1 ounce each of white cloves, allspice and cinnamon. Boil together until it is thick and put into jelly glasses.

23. Grape Sherbet. Grape juice makes a fine sherbet. Put into a saucepan ½ pound of granulated sugar and 1 quart of water. Let it boil a few moments. Take from the fire and add the juice of 1 lemon and a tablespoonful of gelatine that has been dissolved in a gill of water. When cool add ½ pint of juice from any dark, rich grape, and turn into a freezer and freeze. When frozen, and before you remove the beater add the white of an egg beaten to a froth with 1 tablespoonful of powdered sugar. Stir thoroughly into the sherbet. Cover and repack. Stand in a cool place for 2 hours.

24. Canned Green Gages. For canning green gages or blue plums prick the fruit with a fork to prevent bursting. Prepare a syrup, allowing 2 pounds of granulated sugar and ½ pint of water to every 3 pounds of fruit. When the sugar is dissolved put in the fruit and heat slowly to boiling point. Let it cook 10 minutes. Skim out the fruit and place in jars. Let the syrup boil another 10 minutes, then pour over the fruit and cover at once.

25. Canned Blue Plums make delicious pies for Winter use. Spiced plums are fine with meats. The damson plums have the best flavor. To 7 pounds of fruit add 3½ pounds of brown sugar, 1 pint of sharp vinegar and 1 ounce each of cinnamon, cloves and allspice. Scald them three times and put into jars.

26. Grape Jelly. Take the grapes from the stems and rub through a sieve, stir well together and boil slowly for 20 minutes, then add 1 pound of sugar to 1 pound of juice after it has boiled for a while. Then boil for 15 minutes. Put into glasses, seal, and set aside in a cool place.

27. Walnuts or Butternuts Pickled. Gather them in early summer when they are full-grown, but so tender that a large needle will easily pierce them all through. Rub off the outer skin with a coarse cloth, and then lay them in salt and water for a week, changing the brine every other day. Allow for this brine a small ¼ pound of salt to a large quart of water. Make enough to cover all the nuts well. Place a large lid over the pan, and keep them closely from the air. The last day take them out of the brine, drain them and prick every one quite through in several places with a large needle. Drain them again, spread them out on large flat dishes, and set them to blacken for two days in the hot sun. For 100 nuts allow 1 gallon of excellent cider vinegar, ½ ounce of black peppercorns, ½ ounce of cloves, ½ ounce of allspice, 1 ounce of root ginger, and 1 ounce of mace. Boil the spice in the vinegar for 10 minutes, tied up in eight small muslin bags. Then take them out, and having divided the nuts in four stone jars, distribute among them, equally, the bags of spice, and pour on the vinegar hot, an equal portion in each jar. While warm, secure them with flat corks and tie leather over them. Done this way you may begin to use them in a

week.   If you have not enough of vinegar to fill the jars
up to the top, add some cold, and strew among the
nuts some blades of mace.   Finish with a large spoonful of salad oil at the top of each jar.

28. Pickled Cauliflowers.   Take large, ripe, full-
blown cauliflowers.   Remove the leaves and stalk, and
divide the blossoms into pieces or clusters of equal size
Throw them into a porcelain kettle of boiling water,
(adding a little salt) let them simmer and skim then
well.   When they come to a boil, take them up with a
perforated skimmer, and lay them on a sieve to drain
Put them into stone jars, (three parts full).   Season
with mace and nutmeg infused in sufficient of the best
cider vinegar, and simmer it for ¼ hour.   When it comes
to a boil take it off the fire and pour it hot over the
cauliflower in the jar, filling quite up to the top and
adding sweet oil at the last.   Cover tightly.

29. Mixed Pickles.   2 quarts of cauliflower slips
2 quarts of onions, English celery, carrots sliced, 300
small pickles, 4 ounces of radish seed, 4 ounces of nas
turtium seeds, brine strong enough to carry an egg and
poured over each article separately, boiling hot, and
leave in the brine for 48 hours.   Then drain and fill into
jars or glasses.   8 quarts of vinegar, scalded, 1 quart o
vinegar to dissolve 3 cupfuls of flour, 3 cupfuls of sugar
¼ cupful of mustard powder, 2 ounces of curry powder
and stir this into the boiling vinegar and pour over th
pickles.

30. Chow-Chow.   ¼ peck of small string beans
¼ peck of tomatoes, 3 dozen ears of corn, 2 dozen very
small cucumbers, 1 quart of small onions, 1 dozen green
peppers, 1 head of cauliflower, ¼ pound of white must
ard seed, ¼ pound of black mustard seed, 1 tablespoon
ful of celery seed, ½ pound of ground mustard, 2 tea
spoonfuls of tumeric powder, 2 tablespoonfuls of salad
oil.

Salt the beans, tomatoes, peppers and onions, and
set aside for 12 hours.   Make a brine for the cucumber
and cauliflowers, pour it over them and set aside fo
the same length of time.   When all is ready to mix, cu
the corn from the cob, mix all together in a kettle

whole with strong cider vinegar and boil 1 hour. As soon as done, take from the stove, add the tumeric powder, mixing thoroughly; add the oil at the last, mixing it well with the other ingredients. This is best made during the first part of October.

BEVERAGES, CANDIES, Etc.

1. **Grape Wine.** The grapes should be gathered on a dry, clear day, after the morning dew has disappeared. Pick them carefully from the stems, selecting only ripe and perfect fruit. Mash them thoroughly, taking care not to bruise the seeds, as that would impart a bitter taste. After bruising, let the mass remain for 24 hours. Strain through a colander or sieve, taking care that there is no grease about it. Sweeten the juice (for this the crushed sugar is best) until it will float an egg so as to show about the size of a twenty-five cent piece. Put into jugs, filling them and leaving the mouths unstopped, reserving a bottle of the juice to replace that which escapes from the jugs by fermentation. When fermentation ceases, pour the wine off into a large bowl and clarify in the following manner: Wash sand (½ pint will be sufficient for 5 gallons of wine) until the water will run clear from it. Beat to this the whites of 4 eggs, and stir into the wine. When it has settled and the wine looks perfectly clear, pour off carefully into clean jugs, putting a piece of muslin inside of the funnel. Cork the jugs tightly and set in a cool place where they will not be disturbed until the last of October or first of November.

A few days before bottling, have the bottles that you wish to use well washed, dried and sunned. Provide new corks. Have everything in readiness before the bottling begins, including cement for sealing. Strain the wine again into large pitchers, taking particular care not to turn the jug back after beginning to pour from it, as it stirs up the sediment which is at the bottom of the jug. Cover inside of the funnel with a piece of muslin before placing it in the mouth of the bottle; fill the bottle and cork immediately, driving in the cork with a wooden mallet or light hammer. Never use old corks. Cover the neck of the bottle with cement. Keep in a cool, dry place.

2. Blackberry Cordial. Put very ripe berries in a jar; cover them with good peach brandy. Cover well with oil-cloth; let it stand a week. Strain the brandy from the fruit. Put in a kettle a pound of crushed sugar for every quart. Add spices—1 teaspoonful of allspice, 1 of cinnamon and the same of cloves; do not beat the spices. Pour on the sugar as much of the liquor as will dissolve it; as soon as it boils up pour to the rest of the liquor; mix well and bottle.

Peach cordial is good in the same way, only cut up the peaches and scald them when the sugar and spices are scalded. Any cordial may be made in this way.

3. Ginger Beer (Superior). To 6 quarts of water add 1 ounce of cream of tartar and 2 ounces of white Jamaica ginger; boil it 10 minutes. Strain it and add to the liquor a pound of loaf sugar. Put it on the fire; let it simmer until the sugar is dissolved. Pour into an earthenware vessel, into which has been put 2 ounces of tartaric acid and the rind of 1 lemon. When lukewarm add ½ tumblerful of strong hop yeast. Stir all well together and bottle, tie down the corks tightly. Use in a few days.

4. Molasses Candy, No. 1. 1 quart of molasses, ½ cupful of vinegar, 1 cupful of granulated sugar, butter the size of an egg, 1 teaspoonful of soda. Dissolve the sugar in the vinegar, put in with the molasses and butter, and boil, stirring often. As soon as it hardens when dropped in water it is done. Then stir the soda in quickly and pour in buttered pans to cool. Pull until white.

5. Molasses Candy, No. 2. 1 quart of best New Orleans molasses, 1 cupful of granulated sugar. Boil 15 minutes, then add butter the size of an egg. Stir to keep from burning. Drop a little in cold water and if it hardens it is done. Before taking from the fire add 1 teaspoonful of soda made very fine. Stir quickly, take from the fire and pour into buttered tins to cool. As soon as you can handle it pull white.

6. Lemon Taffy, No. 1. 3 pounds of best brown sugar, ¼ pound of butter and 1 pint of vinegar. Boil all together until it hardens in water. Add 1 teaspoonful of lemon extract. Pour on buttered tins to cool.

7. Lemon Taffy, No. 2. Put into a porcelain-lined preserving kettle 3 pounds of the best loaf sugar, and pour on it 1½ pints of very clear water. When it has entirely dissolved, set it over the fire and add a tablespoonful of fine cider vinegar to assist in clearing it as it boils. Boil and skim it well, and when no more scum rises add the juice of 4 large lemons or oranges. Let it boil until it will boil no longer, stirring it well. When done, transfer it to square tin pans, that have been made very clean and bright, and that are slightly greased with sweet oil. Set the taffy away to cool, first marking it with a knife while soft. Mark it in straight lines the broad or crossway of the pans. If marked lengthways the pieces will be too long. When the taffy is cold cut it according to the lines in regular slips, like cocoanut candy. Serve it up in glass dishes.

Orange taffy is made in the same manner. These candies should be kept in tin boxes.

Cocoanut candy is made in the manner of taffy, using finely grated cocoanut instead of lemon or orange.

8. Maple Cream. 3 cupfuls of grated maple sugar, 1 cupful of thick sweet cream. Boil until it hardens when dropped into cold water. Remove from the fire and beat with a silver fork until it is of the consistency of very thick cream. Pour in buttered tins and when cool cut in squares.

9. Chocolate Creams. 1 pound of confectioner's sugar, the white of 1 egg, 2 tablespoonfuls of water, 1 teaspoonful of vanilla; mix well and make into balls. Melt ½ cake of baker's chocolate, dip the balls into this and lay on buttered paper to harden.

10. Chocolate Caramel. Take ½ pint of rich milk and put it to boil in a porcelain kettle; scrape down 1½ squares of chocolate, put it into a very clean tin cup and set on the top of a stove until it becomes soft. Let the milk boil up twice. Then add, gradually, the chocolate, and stir both over the fire until thoroughly mixed and free from lumps. Stir in ½ pint of the best powdered sugar, and 4 large tablespoonfuls of molasses. Let the whole boil fast and constantly (so as to bubble) for at least 1 hour or more, till it is nearly as stiff as good mush. When all is done add a small teaspoonful of essence of vanilla, and transfer the mixture to shallow tin pans, slightly greased with very nice sweet oil. Set it on ice or in a very cool place, and while yet soft mark it deeply in squares with a very sharp knife. When quite hard cut the squares apart. If it does not harden well it has not been boiled long enough or fast enough.

TABLE OF MEASURES.

2 saltspoonfuls	make	1 coffeespoonful.
2 coffeespoonfuls	"	1 teaspoonful.
4 teaspoonfuls (liquid)	"	1 tablespoonful.
3 teaspoonfuls (dry)	"	1 tablespoonful.
4 tablespoonfuls (liquid)	"	1 wineglassful.
2 tablespoonfuls (liquid)	"	1 ounce.
2 wineglassfuls	"	1 gill.
2 gills (or ½ pint)	"	1 cupful.
2 cupfuls	"	1 pint.
4 cupfuls	"	1 quart.
1 cupful butter (solid)	makes	½ pound.
1 cupful granulated sugar	"	½ pound.
1 round tablespoonful butter	"	1 ounce.
1 heaping teaspoonful sugar	"	1 ounce.
1 ounce salt	"	1 teaspoonful.
1 quart sifted flour	"	1 pound.

A dash of pepper is ¼ saltspoonful.

TIME TABLE FOR COOKING.

Loaf Bread, - - -	40—60 minutes.
Rolls and Biscuits, - -	10—20 "
Grahams, - - -	30 "
Gingerbread, - -	20—30 "
Sponge Cake, - - -	45—60 "
Plain Cake, - - -	30—40 "
Fruit Cake, - - -	2—3 hours.
Cookies, - - -	5—10 minutes.
Bread Pudding, - - -	1 hour.
Rice and Tapioca, - -	1 "
Indian Pudding, - -	2—3 hours.
Steamed Pudding, - -	2—3 "
Steamed Brown Bread, - -	3 "
Custards, - - -	15—10 minutes.
Pie Crust, - -	about 30 "
Plum Pudding, - - .	2—3 hours.

CHARACTERISTIC GERMAN DISHES IN GERMAN, WITH ENGLISH TRANSLATION.

(Stating Number of Recipes and Page Where They Can Be Found.)

B. SOUPS—SUPPEN.

D. MEATS—FLEISCH.

Beef, Veal, Mutton, Hares, Game—Rind- und Kalbfleisch, Hammelfleisch, Kaninchen und Wildbret.

E. MEAT AND GAME PIES—FLEISCH- UND ANDERE PAS-TETEN.

F. FRESH AND SALT WATER FISH—FLUSS- UND SEE-FISCHE

G. RARE DISHES OF VARIOUS KINDS—SELTEN VORKOMMENDE SPEISEN.

H. HOT PUDDINGS—WARME PUDDINGE.

English-German Vocabulary

Comprising the

Most important technical terms and expressions of the Culinary Art, Foods, Beverages, etc., as applied in Kitchen, Household and at the Table. With translations in both languages.

Compiled by C. N. Caspar.

a la carte (Fr.)—chosing bill of fare—Wahl nach dem Speisezettel

a la jardiniere (Fr.)—with vegetables—mit Gemüse

a la mode (Fr.)—.braized—geschmort

absinthe (Fr.)—Absynth, Wermutbranntwein

absorbent paper—Fliesspapier

acorn coffee—Eichel-Kaffee

adam's apple—Paradiesapfel, Pompelmus

aitchbone—edgebone—Knochenstück aus dem Schwanzstück

ale—starkes Bier

aleberry—Warmbier

almonds—Mandeln

almond buns—Mandel-Brezeln

almond cake—Mandel-Kuchen

almond cookies—kleine Mandelkuchen

almond knobs—Mandel-Kolatschen

almonds, sweet—süsse Mandeln

alose (fish)—Alse, Maifisch

anchovy—Anchovies

anise (Indian)—Sternanis

anise cake—Aniskuchen

anise rusks—Anisbrod

appetizers—hors d'oeuvres (Fr.)—Appetitanreizer

apple—Apfel

apple fritters—Apfelstrudel, Apfelkrapfen

apricot—Aprikose

Armenian cherry—Amorrellen, Kirschen

arrac (liquor)—Arrak

artichoke, green—grüne Artischocke

artichoke, Jerusalem—Erdartischoke, Artischoke

asparagus—Spargel, Schnittspargel

aspic jelly—Fleisch- oder Fischsulz

au four (Fr.)—bake in oven—im Ofen überbacken

au gratin (Fr.)—browned—mit Kruste und Käse überbacken

au nature (Fr.) plain, simple—ohne Zutat

bacon—Speck, geräuchertes Bauchstück vom Schwein

bacon grieves—Grammeln. Speckgriefen

baiser (Fr.)—buns—Schaumgebäck. Krapfen

baked—gebacken

baked chicken—Huhnpastete

baked chowder—Gericht aus gebackenen frischen Fischen, Schweinefleisch, Schiffszwieback, etc.

baked faggots—crepinettés—Netzwürstchen

baked fillets of flounder (fish)—Flunderbraten

baked hominy—gebackener Maisbrei

baked salmontrout, with cream gravy—gebratene Lachs-Forellen mit Rahmsose

baked veal resembling veal cutlets—Wiener Schnitzel

baked venison—gebratenes Hirschfleisch

bakery—Bäckerei

ball—Knödel. Klösse. Spatzen, Knöpfle Knöpflein

balm—Melisse

bananas—Paradiesfeigen, Bananen

bannocks, Scotch oatmeal cakes—Bannocks, Schottischer Hafermehl-Kuchen

banquet (Fr.)—Festessen

barbel (fish)—Barbe

barberries—Berberitzen, Sauerdorn

baron of beef—zwei ungeteilte Lendenstücke

baron of hare—Hinterviertel und die Lenden vom Hasen

basil, sweet—Basilikum, Basilienkraut

bass (fish)—Flussbarsch

basting—begiessen

batter—geschlagener dünner Teig (Mehl, Eier, u. s. w.)

Béchamelsauce, cream sauce—Rahmtunke

butter puffs—Pfitzauf, Eierkuchen

bay leaves—Lorbeerblätter

beans—Bohnen

beans, French—Türkische oder Wälsche Bohnen, Schnittbohnen.

beans, green—grüne Bohnen

beans, haricot—Stangenbohnen

beans, Lima—grosse weisse Bohnen

beans, scarlet—scharlachfarbige Bohnen

beans, string—Wälsche Bohnen; Schneidebohnen; Brechbohnen

beans sautés (Fr.)—in Butter aufgeschwitzte Bohnen

beantressel, savory— Bohnenkraut Saturei, Bohnenkölle, Wurst- oder Pfefferkraut

beef, braized—boeuf a la mode (Fr.)—gedämpfter Rostbraten

)eef, collared—gerolltes und zusammengebundenes Fleisch

beef collops—gedünstete Fleischstücke, Klops von Rindfleisch

beef extract—Fleischextrakt

beef marrow—Rindermark

beef pot roast—Rinderschmorbraten

beef, pressed—gepresstes Fleisch, stark gewürzt und 12 Tage abgelegen

beef, rolled—Roulade von Ochsenfleisch

beef (rolled) with farces, meat birds— Fleischvögel

)eef, sour—Sauerbraten

beefsteak—Rindstück, Lendenbraten

beefsteak a la Tartare (Fr.)—scraped beef with onions, etc., eaten raw—feingeschabtes Ochsenfleisch mit Zwiebeln, u. s. w., wird roh gegessen

)eefsteak, braized— Schmorbraten

beef, stewed, boeuf a la mode (Fr.)— gedämpftes Rindfleisch

beefsteak, broiled—am offnen Feuer gebratnes Lendenstück

beefsteak, chateaubriand—Doppelrindslendenstück mit Muscheln

beefsteak, double tenderloin—Doppelrindslendenstück

beefsteak, Hamburg— gehacktes Rindfleisch

beefsteak, not too much done—nicht durchgebratenes Rinds-Lendenstück

beefsteak, porterhouse or rumpsteak—bestes Beefsteak, zarter Lendenbraten, Rumpfstück

beefsteak, rare—nicht durchgebratenes, blutendes Rindsstück

beefsteak, rump (porterhouse)—Fleisch vom Schenkel, nächst dem Rumpf

beefsteak, scraped, raw —geschabtes rohes Rindfleisch

beefsteak, underdone— nicht durchgebratenes Rindsstück

beefsteak, well done— gut durchgebratenes Rindsstück

beef tallow—Rindsnierentalg

beef-tea—Rindfleisch-Tee, klare Rindfleisch-Brühe

beer—Bier

beer vinegar—Bier-Essig

beet rave—rote Rübe

beet root—rote Rübe

beignets (Fr.)—mit Schmalz gebackene Fritten

beignets, potato—in Schmalz gebackene Kartoffelklösschen

Belgian hare—belgischer Hase

berian (Fr.) teacakes— Berian (Fr.) Teebackwerk

best cuts of Mutton:— loin, saddle and leg —bestes Hammelfleisch, Rückenstück

beverage—Getränk

bilberries— Heidelbeeren .

bill of fare—menu (Fr.)—Tafel-Speisekarte, Speisezettel

bischoff, beverage of bitter oranges, wine. sugar. etc.—Getränk aus bitteren Pomeranzen, Wein, Zucker u. s. w.

biscuit—Zuckerbrot·

biscuit, caraway— Kümmel-Zuckerbrot

bisque (Fr.)—beliebtes Mus von Krebsen, Reis, Gemüse, Fischen, Geflügel; gewöhnlich Krebs- oder Muscheltiersuppe

berlingos, small teacakes—kleine Teekuchen

black bass (fish)— Flussbarsch

blackberry. brambleberry—Brombeere

black currant jelly— schwarzer Johannisbeeren-Gelee

black sausage—Blut-Wurst

blacktail (fish)—Kaulbarsch

blade-bone—Schulterblatt

blanc (Fr.)—white— weiss

blanc (Fr.)—clear soup —helle Fleischbrühe

blanchir (Fr.)—scald —abbrühen

blanquette (Fr.): white meat warmed and thickened with eggs —Ragout von Kalbfleisch mit weisser Sose

bleak fish, play—Blei, Blicke. Plötze.

blini, Russian pancake —russischer Pfannkuchen

bloater (fish)— geräucherter Hering, Bücking, Böckling, Bückling, Bittling

block sugar—Stück-Zucker, Granitzucker

blueberries—Heidelbeeren

blue fish—Goldmakrele, Rossmakrele

boar—männliches Wildschwein

board—Kost

board and lodging— Kost und Logis

boarding house—Kosthaus

bodschwene, a polish soup, containing beets, beef, onions— Bodschwene, polnische Suppe, rote Rüben, Rindfleisch, Zwiebel enthaltend

boeuf a la mode (Fr.) —gedämpftes Rindfleisch

boeuf piquant (Fr.)— gebeiztes Ochsenfleisch, Milchsauerbraten

boil—kochen

boiled—in siedendem Wasser gekocht

boiled salad dressing— zubereitete gewürzte Salatsose

bologna: large sausage made of veal, pork, bacon, etc., chopped fine and enclosed in a skin— Bolognawurst, Mettwurst

bon bons, candies—
Bon Bons, Zuckerwerk
borage—Borretsch
borecole, kale—Grünoder Winterkohl
boronia, a Spanish dish
of tomatoes, pumpkins, etc., diced—
spanisches Gericht
aus Tomaten, Kürbis, u. s. w. in Würfel geschnitten
bottle—Flasche
bouillon (Fr.)—
Fleischbrühe, Kraftsuppe
bouillon, chicken—
Huhnkraftsuppe
boulette (Fr.)—ball—
Bällchen, Klösschen,
Knöpfle.
bouquet (Fr.)—sprig of
herbs—ein Sträusschen von Küchenkräutern
bourbon—amerikanischer Maisbranntwein
bowl—Bowle, ein terrinenartiges Gefäss
für Punsch
braiser, braising pan—
Schmorpfanne,
Schmortopf
braized—geschmort,
geröstet, braisirt
braized beef—boeuf a
la mode (Fr.)—gedämpfter Rostbraten
braized beefsteak—
Schmorbraten
braized calf's liver—geschmorte Kalbsleber
braized carbonade of
mutton—gedämpfte
Hammelkarbonade
braized neck of veal—
geschmorter Kalbsbraten vom Hals
bramble-berry—Brombeere
brandy—Branntwein,
Cognac, Kognak
brasse (fish)—Zander
brawn—Presswürste
brayed, grated—
gerieben
bread—Brot;
new bread—frisches
Brot; stale bread—
altbackenes Brot
bread and butter—
Butterbrot
bread, rye—Schwarzbrot, Roggenbrot
bread, thin pieces of—
Brotschnitte
bread, white—Weissbrot
breakfast—Frühstück

breakfast rolls—Frühstücksbrötchen,
Semmeln
bream (fish)—Brasse,
Fogas, Fogasch, Fogosch
breast of veal—Kalbsbrust
brill (fish)—Steinbutte
brisket—Bruststück
brisolettes—veal—
Kalbsbrisoletter
broach—Spiess
broccolli (It.)—Winterblumenkohl,
Broccoli
brochet (fish)—Hecht
broiled—auf offenem
Feuer gebraten
broiled woodcock—gebratene Waldschnepfe
broiler—Brat-Rost
brook or garden cresses—Brunnen-oder
Garten-Kresse
brook trout—
Bachforelle
broth—Brühe, Gemüsebrei, steife Suppe,
Fleischbrühe
brown bread—Schwarzbrot, Roggenbrot
brown George, brown
Tommy—Kommissbrot
browned—au gratin
(Fr.)—mit Kruste
gebacken
Brunswick sausage—
Braunschweiger
Leberwurst
Brussels sprouts—
Rosenkohl, Kohlsprossen, Brüssler
Kohl
bubble and squeak—geschmortes Rindfleisch und Kohl
buckwheat—
Buchweizen
bull—Stier
buns—Brezeln, Milchbrötchen, Moppen,
Krapfen
butcher—Fleischer,
Metzger
butler—Kellermeister
in vornehmen
Häusern
butter—Butter
buttermilk—Buttermilch
butter and flour thickening—roux (Fr.)—
Einbrenne, Mehlschwitze, braune
Butter
buttered toast—mit
Butter bestrichene,
geröstete Brotscheiben

butternut pickles—eingelegte Butternüsse
butterpaste—Butterteig
buttock—Hinterbacke
buttock of a fowl, etc.
—Sterz, Steiss
button-mushrooms—
Edelpilze, Tafelpilze,
Champignons
cabbage—Welschkohl,
Wirsingkohl, Kraut
cabbage, curled—Wildkohl
cabbage, red—Rotkraut
Blaukraut
cabbage, savoy—Wirsing, Savoyerkohl,
Sommerkohl
cabbage, sour pickled—
Sauerkraut
cabbage sprouts—
Schnittkohl
cabbage, summer—
Schnittkohl
cabbage, turnip—Kohlrabi, Kohlrübe,
Wruke
cabbage, white—Weisskraut, Kabis, Kappis, Kapus, Kopfkohl
café (Fr.)—coffee house
—Kaffeehaus
cake—Kuchen
cake, almond—Mandelkuchen
cake, anise—Aniskuchen
cake, buckwheat—
Buchweizenkuchen
cake, caramel—Art Gebäck mit gebranntem Zucker übergossen
cake, citron layer—
Zitronenkuchen
cake, cocoanut—Kokosnusskuchen
cake, Madeira—Sandtorte
cake mould—Kuchenform
cake, small drop—
Maken
cake, sponge—Schaumtorte
cake, strewed—
Streuselkuchen
caldo, Spanish soup—
Caldo, spanische
Suppe
calf—Kalb, Kalbfleisch
calf's brain—Kalbsbregen, Kalbshirn
calf's liver—Kalbsleber
calf's liver a la jardiniere (Fr.)—Kalbsleber mit Gemüse
calf's tripe—Kalbsgekröse
can—Kanne, verlötete
Büchse

candied fruit—Confitui-
ren

candied lemon—citron-
nat (Fr.)—einge-
machte Zitronen-
schale

candies—Zuckerwerk,
Naschwerk, Süssig-
keiten, Leckerei

canella—weisser Zimmt

canned fruits—in verlö-
teten Büchsen einge-
machte Früchte

canned meat—Büchsen-
fleisch

canned string beans—
Welsche Bohnen in
Büchsen

canned truffles—Büch-
sentrüffeln

canned vegetables—
Büchsengemüse, ein-
gemachte Gemüse

cannelon (Fr.)—stuffed
meat rolled up and
roasted—gefülltes
Fleisch, gerollt und
gebraten

capers—Kapernsträuch-
er, beim Einmachen
benutzt

capon—Kapaun,
kastrirter Haus-
hahn, Kapphahn

capsicum—Paprika,
spanischer Pfeffer

caramel (Fr.)—
gebrannter Zucker,
Karamelle

caramel cake—
Karamellenkuchen

caraway—Kümmel

caraway biscuits—
Kümmel-Zuckerwerk

carbonade (Fr.)—
Karbonade

carbonade of mutton—
Hammelkarbonade

cardamom (spice)—
Kardamom

cardinal, a beverage of
whitewine and bit-
ter oranges—Kardi-
nal, ein Getränk aus
Weisswein, mit bit-
teren Pomeranzen

carnival fritters—
Faschings-Krapfen

carp—Karpfen

carrots—gelbe Rüben,
Möhren, Carotten

carrot sauté (Fr.)—ge-
schmorte Rüben

casserole (Fr.)—
Kasserolle, Schmor-
pfanne, Schmortopf

catawba—
amerikanische rote
Weintraube

catsup—eine Würze aus
Tomaten, Morcheln
etc.

catsup, mushroom—
Würzsose aus
Pilzen

caudle—Warmbier,
mischen

caudle, English oat-
meal soup for inva-
lids—englische Ha-
ferschleimsuppe für
Kranke

cauliflower—Blumen-
kohl

cauliflower—au gratin
(Fr.)—mit Kruste
gebackener Blumen-
kohl

caviar—Kaviar

Cayenne pepper—
Cayennepfeffer,
roter Pfeffer,
spanischer Pfeffer

celery—Sellerie

celery, knob—Knollen-
sellerie

celery salad—Sellerie-
salat

celery, turnip—Wurzel-
sellerie

cervelat—Cervelat-
wurst, Schlackwurst

champagne (Fr.)—
Schaumwein, Sekt

champignon (Fr.)—
button-mushroom
Edelpilze

chanfania, Spanish dish
of pig's or lamb's-
liver—spanisches
Gericht von
Schweins- oder
Hammelsleber

chantilly soup, green
pea soup—Chantilly
Suppe, grüne Erb-
sen-Suppe

charlotte russe (Fr.)—
geschlagener Rahm
mit Biscuit

charlottes (Fr.)—made
of fruit, butter,
sugar, eggs, etc.—
Charlotten

chartreuse (Fr.)—of
vegetables—arran-
girte Gemüse

chateaubriand (Fr.)—
Doppelrindslenden-
stück

cheek (pertaining to
meat)—Backe

cheese—Käse

cheese bisques—Käse-
mus

cheese curds—Quark

cheese, Roquefort (Fr.)
—fester, weisser,
grün marmorierter
Käse

cheese sandwich—
Käse-Brötchen

cheese, Swiss—
Schweizerkäse

chef (Fr.)—head cook—
Küchenmeister

cherries—Kirschen

chestnuts,—marrons
(Fr.)—essbare Kas-
tanien

chestnut bread—
Kastanien-Brot

chestnuts, roasted—ge-
röstete Kastanien,
Maronen

chevin (fish)—Aland,
Altfisch

chicken—Huhn, Hühn-
chen

chicken, baked—Huhn-
pastete

chicken bouillon—
Huhnsuppe

chicken, fried—
gebratenes Huhn

chicken omelet—
Hühnerfleisch-Ome-
lette

chicken pie—Hühner-
pastete

chicken, pilau of—
Huhn mit Reis
gekocht

chicken pot pie—Huhn-
fleischpastete

chicory, endives—Endi-
vien, Cichorie

chiffonade, green pea
soup—grüne Erbsen-
suppe

chilli—Schote des spa-
nischen Pfeffers

chine—Kreuz, Rücken-
stück

chips—Späne

chives—Schnittlauch,
kleine Zwiebel

chlodnik, Polish cold
soup—polnische
Kaltschale

chocolate—Chocolade

chocolate pudding—
schwarzer Pudding

chop—zerhauen, zer-
hacken

chop, shoulder—rundes
Rippenstück

chopped, minced—
gehackt

chopped beefsteak—
gehacktes rohes
Rindfleisch

chopped meat—gehack-
tes Fleisch

chops, cutlets—côtelette
(Fr.)—Kotelette,
Lendenrippchen,
Hals

chops, mutton or cut-
lets—Hammelkote-
letten

chops, pork—Stück
vom Nierenende der
Lende mit etwas
Niere daran

chou (Fr.)—cabbage—
Kohl
chow-chow (Chin.)—
Tomaten, Sellerie,
Zwiebel, kleinge-
hackt, in Zucker
und Essig einge-
macht
chowder—ragoutarti-
ges Gericht aus
Fischen, Schweine-
fleisch, Muscheln,
Schiffszwieback, etc.
chowder, baked—
Gericht aus geback-
enen frischen
Fischen, Schweine-
fleisch, Schiffszwie-
back, etc.
chowder, scalloped—
ragoutartiges Aus-
terngericht
Christmas loaf—Striez
chuck roast—Mittel-
rippe
chuck-steak—Schulter-
stück vom Rind
chutney—scharfe
ostindische Würze
cicely, sweet—
spanischer Kerbel,
cider—Apfelwein
cinnamon—Zimt
cinnamon bark—
Kaneel, Zimmtrinde
cinnamon buns—Milch-
brötchen mit Zimt
cinnamon flowers—
Zimmetblüten
citron—Limone, Zitrone
citron layer cake—
Zitronenkuchen
clabber, sour milk—
sauere Milch
clam—amerikanische
Venusmuschel,
Jakobsmuschel
clam bisque—Muschel-
mus
clam chowder—ragout-
artiges Gericht aus
Muscheln
clams, creamed—ra-
goutartiges Gericht
aus Muscheln mit
Rahm
claret, Bordeaux wine,
light red wine—
Bordeaux Weine,
blass-rote Weine
clarified—geläutert, ab-
geklärt
clarify—abklären
clear soup—Kraftbrühe
clotted—geronnen
clotted milk—
geronnene Milch
clove—Gewürz-Nelke
clovebark—Nelken-
pfeffer, Neugewürz,
Piment
coal fish—Weissling

cobbler—
amerikanisches ge-
mischtes Getränk
cochineal (a red dye)
—Kochinelle
cock—Hahn
cock-a-leekie
englische Hühner-
suppe
cockles—Muscheln
cocktail—amerikani-
sches gemischtes
Getränk
cocoa—Kakao
cocoanut—Kokosnuss
cod, cured—Stockfisch
cod, dried—Stockfisch
cod, fresh—Lengfisch
cod, salted Aberdeen
fish—Kabeljau
Laberdan
codfish—Dorsch,
Kabeljau
coffee—Kaffee; black
coffee—schwarzer
Kaffee; coffee with
milk—Milchkaffee
coffee, acorn—Eichel-
kaffee
coffee house—Kaffee-
haus; café (Fr.)
cognac—französicher
Branntwein
colander—Seiher, Sieb
cold beef—kaltes Rind-
fleisch
cold entrees—kalte
Speisen
cold soup—Kaltschale
collared—gerollt
cold meats mixed—
kalter Aufschnitt
collared beef—gerolltes
und dann zuzam-
mengebundenes
Fleisch
collared head—Schwar-
tenmagen, gefüllter
Schweinsmagen
collops—Fleischschnitte
collops, beef—gedün-
stete Fleischstücke,
Klops von Rind-
fleisch
collops, minced—
Klops: Klösschen
oder kleine Kotelet-
ten von gehacktem
Rindfleisch, etc.
comfit—Konfekt,
Zuckerwerk
comfitures, preserves—
Dauerspeisen, Dau-
erfrüchte, Büchsen-
gemüse
compote—Kompott,
Eingemachtes
cones (ice cream,
whipped cream)—
kleine Düten aus
Oblatenteig mit

gefrorenem Rahm-
schaum gefüllt
confectioner—Konditor,
Zuckerbäcker
confitieres, marmelade
of preserved fruits,
candied fruits—Con-
fitieren, Marmelade
von Früchten in
Zucker eingekocht,
ganz gelassene
Früchte
conger (fish)—Meeraal
consommé (Fr.)—
gravy-soup—Kraft-
brühe
contents of soups—Ein-
lagen für Suppen
cony, rabbit—Stallhase,
Kaninchen
cook—kochen, Koch
cookies—kleine Tee-
kuchen, Gebäck,
Backwerk
cooking pot—Kochtopf
cooking stove, range—
Kochofen, Herd
cooking utensils—
Kochgeschirr
coquilles, dishes of cur-
ried meats, served
on shells—Coquillen,
Muschelschalen in
welchen Ragouts
servirt werden
coriander (spice)—
Koriander
corn—Korn, Mais
corn flour—Maismehl
corn meal—Maismehl
corn meal cake—Mais-
kuchen
corn salad—Rapünz-
chen, Mausohrsalat
corn starch—Korn-
stärke
corn (unground) soup
—Graupensuppe
corned—mit gekörntem
Salz zubereitet
corned meat—einge-
salzenes Rindfleisch
cornelian cherry—Kor-
nelkirsche
cornet, paper bag—
Düte, Tüte
cornet wafers—Hohl-
hippchen
couvert (Fr.)—cover—
Tischzeug; Gedeck
crab and tomato salad
—Krebssalat mit
Tomaten
crab bisque—Krebs-
mus, Krebssuppe
crab butter—Krebs-
butter
crabs, shrimp—Krebse,
Taschenkrebse
crabs and champignons
—Krebse und Pilze

crackers—Schiffszwie-
back, dünner trock-
ener Zwieback
cracklings—Fettwürfel
cracknels—Brezel
Pretzel, Kringel
cracknels, egg—Eier-
kringel
cranberry—Krons-
beere, Moosbeere
crawfish, crabs—Fluss-
krebs
cream—Sahne, Rahm
cream bun, meringue—
baiser—Schaum-
gebäck
cream cake—Rahmtorte
cream gravy—Rahm-
sose
cream puff, cream bun,
meringue—Baiser,
Schaumgebäck,
Windbeutel
cream tart—Rahmtorte
creamed clams—zube-
reitete Muscheln mit
Rahm
crecy soup, vegetable
soup—Crecy-Suppe,
Gemüsesuppe
crepinettes (Fr.)—flat
sausage—Netz-
würstchen
cress—Kresse
crevettes, brown or
shrimp soup—
Crevettes, Garnelen-
Suppe
crop—Kropf
croquants, crisp baked
cakes—Croquants,
spröde gebackenes
Zuckerbackwerk
croquette (Fr.)—Krus-
teln; aus den Spei-
sen Figuren herstel-
len; Schnittchen,
Frikandellen
croustades (Fr.)—
dough filled with
various dishes—
Krustaden
crouton (Fr.)—kleine
Stücke Weissbrot-
Krummen geröstet
crucian (fish)—
Karausche (Fisch)
crumpets—weiche
Kuchen
crushed—gestossen
crust—Kruste
crust, flaky—Blätter-
teig
crust, short—mürber
Teig
crustacea—Weichtiere:
Krebse, Muscheln,
Austern
cucumber—Gurke,
Kukummer
cucumber salad—Gur-
kensalat

cucumbers, stewed—ge-
schmorte Gurken
cuisine (Fr.)—kitchen—
Küche
culinary—kulinarisch
cup—Tasse, Becher
curaçao (Liquor)—
Curaçao
curdled milk—
geronnene Milch
curds—Molken
cured—eingepökelt,
eingelegt, zubereitet
curled cabbage—Wild-
kohl
currants—Johannis-
beeren, Korinthen
currant-black jelly—
schwarzer Gelee von
Johannisbeeren
curried—mit sehr
scharfen Gewürzen
zubereitet
curried fowl—gedünste-
tes und stark ge-
pfeffertes Huhn
curries: stews of meat
or fish—Ragout von
Fleisch oder Fischen
mit Würzpulver ge-
würzt
cutlet—Kotelett, Kote-
lette,—Cotelettes
(Fr.)—Rippchen
cutlets, mutton or
chops—gebratene
Hammelkoteletten
cutlets, pork—
Schweinskoteletten
cuts—Schnitte
damask plum—
Damascenenpflaume
dandelion—Löwen-
zahn, Butterblume
date—Dattel
deer—Hirsch, Rehwild
dé'jeuner—breakfast
—Frühstück
dé'jeuner a la four-
chette—luncheon—
Gabelfrühstück
demitasse (Fr.)—small
cup—kleine Tasse
dessert—Dessert, Nach-
tisch
deviled—sehr stark ge-
pfeffert und mit
Senf, etc., geröstet
diced—in Würfeln
dill—Dill
dinner—diner (Fr.)—
Mittagessen, Haupt-
mahlzeit, Mahl
dinner—a part—Einzel-
Mahlzeit
dinner mat—Tellerun-
terlage
dinner party—Tischge-
sellschaft
dinner service—Tafel-
geschirr

dinner time—Mittag-
essenszeit
dish—Teller, Platte,
Gericht
dishes for invalids—
Tafel für Kranke
dissolve—auflösen
dolpettes—baked meat
dumplings—geback-
ene Fleischklösschen
dorse (fish)—Dorsch
double refined sugar—
feinster raffinierter
Zucker
double tenderloin—
Doppelrindslenden-
stück
dough—Teig
doughnuts—Kringel,
Berliner Pfann-
kuchen
dredge, strew—
bestreuen
dress (prepare for a
roast, etc.)—dressi-
ren, zubereiten, an-
richten
dresser—table d'hôte
(Fr.)—gemeinschaft-
liche Wirtstafel
dressing—Zubereiten
von Speisen
dressing of poultry,
meats, etc., with
twine to keep them
in shape while
roasting—bridieren
oder dressieren, zu-
sammenbinden des
Geflügels, Fleisches,
u. s. w. beim Braten
dreux a la (Fr.)—
larding of meat
with bacon, tongue,
mushrooms—das
Spicken eines
Fleischstückes mit
Speck, Zungen,
Trüffeln
drippings—herab-
tropfendes Braten-
fett
drop cakes (small)—
Maken
dry—trocken, herb
duck—Ente
duck, wild—Wildente
duckling—junge Ente
dumpling—Kloss
dumplings, ham—
Schinkenknödel
dumplings, little—
Nocken, Nockerln
Dutch buns—holländi-
sche Moppen
Dutch cheese—hollän-
discher Käse
echandés (Fr.)—a kind
of steamed cake—
eine Art gedünsteter
Kuchen

edgebone—aitchbone—
Knochenstück aus
dem Schwanzstück
eel, collared—gerollter
Aal
eel pouts—Aalraupen
eel, river—Flussaal
egg cracknels—Eier-
Kringel
egg, white of—Eiweiss;
yolk of—Eigelb, Ei-
dotter
eggs, boiled—gesottene
Eier
eggnogg—Eiertrank
eggplant—Eierpflanze
eggs, fried—Spiegel-
eier, Eier in Butter
gebraten
eggs, poached—ohne
Schale, halbweich
gesottene Eier,
verlorne Eier
eggs, scrambled—
Rührei
eggs, turned over—ge-
stürzte Eier
elder vinegar—
Holunderbeeren-
essig
Endives, chicory—
Endivien, Cichorie
endive salad—Endivien-
Salat
entrées (Fr.)—dishes
served between
courses—
Zwischengericht
epanada, Spanish pas-
try—Epanada,
spanische Pastete
escallops—Eskolop
eschalots—Schalotten,
oder Schalottenzwie-
bel, Eschlauch
essence—Essenz,
Extrakt
faggots, baked—crepi-
nettes (Fr.)—Netz-
würstchen
flat sausage—Netz-
würstchen
farce, forcemeat—
Füllsel, Fülle, ge-
füllte Fleisch-
schnitte
farferl paste—Farferl-
teig
farin sugar, casson-
ade, sugar used in
the manufacture of
liquor, compots, etc.
—Farin-Zucker,
Cassonade, Zucker
welcher zu Likör-
fabrikation, Com-
pots, etc. verwandt
wird
farina—Gries
fattened chicken—Mast-
hühnchen
feet—Füsse

fennel—Fenchel
fennelflower seed—
schwarzer Kümmel,
Mutterkümmel
field fares—Kramets-
vögel
fig—Feige
fig and bread pudding
—Feigen- und Brot-
klösse
filet beef—
Lendenbraten
filet steak—aus Len-
denbraten zuberei-
tetes Steak; Rinds-
stück von der Lende
filled breast of veal—
gefüllte Kalbsbrust
fillings and frostings—
Füllungen und Gla-
sur
fillet—filet (Fr.)—
Rindsbraten
fine, first class table—
table recherches
(Fr.)—gewählter
feiner Tisch
fish bisque—Fischmus
fish chowder—ragout-
artiges Gericht aus
Fischen
flaky—blätterig
flaky crust, puff paste
—Blätterteig
flamery, flumery, sweet
dishes of cornstarch,
semolina, etc.—süsse
Speisen aus Stärke-
mehl Gries, u. s. w.
flank (meat)—untere
Flanke
flat baked ryebread—
Flammplatz
flavored—schmackhaft
zubereitet, gewürzt
flawns—Plätzchen
flip—warmes Mischge-
tränk; Eierbier
flounder (fish)—
Flunder
flour—Mehl
fondant (Fr.)—sugar
boiled and beaten to
a creamy paste—
im Munde zerlau-
fend, saftreich,
saftig
foot—Fuss
forcemeat, farce—Füll-
sel, Fülle, Farce
forcemeat of fish—
Farce von Fisch
Frankfurters—Frank-
furter Würstchen
French barley—Perl-
graupen
French beans—
türkische oder wäl-
sche Bohnen,
Schnittbohnen,Veits-
bohnen

French dressing: sim-
ple salad dressing
of oil, vinegar, salt,
etc.—einfache Salat-
zubereitung mit Oel,
Essig, Salz, etc.
French roll—Kipfel
French salad—franzö-
sischer Salat
fricandellas (Fr.)—
Frikandellen,
Fleischschnitte
fricassée (Fr.)—
Frikassee
fricassée (Fr.), of veal
—Kalbsfricasse
fried—in einer Pfanne
gebraten
fried chicken—gebrate-
nes Huhn
fried potatoes—Brat-
kartoffeln
fried sausage—Brat-
wurst
fritter—Krapfen, Krus-
teln
fritters a la créme
(Fr.)—Krapfen mit
Rahm
fritters, apple—Apfel-
strudel
fritters, carnival—
Faschingskrapfen
fritters, rice—
Reisstrudel
Frittura (Italian hotch
potch)—italieni-
sches Fleischragout
mit Gemüse
frogshanks—Frosch-
schenkel
front shank—vorderes
Knochenstück
fruit—Frucht, Obst
fruit cake, a cake made
of raisins, currants,
almonds, citron;
cake made of yeast
dough with layer of
fruit, apple, etc.—
Kuchen mit Rosi-
nen, Korinthen,
Mandeln, Zitronat,
u. s. w. gebacken;
Frucht- oder Obst-
kuchen
fruit, canned—Conser-
ven in verlöteten
Büchsen, eingemach-
te Früchte
fruit sirup—Fruchtsaft
fruits de la saison
(Fr.)—frisches Obst
wie es die Jahres-
zeit bietet
fruits, stewed—Compot
frumenty—Weizenbrei
fry—in Butter auf-
schwitzen,
umschwenken
frying pan—Bratpfanne
game—Wild

garden cress—Garten-
kresse
garden rue—Weinraute
garlic—Knoblauch
gastronomer—Speise-
kundiger, Liebhaber
von Leckerbissen,
Feinschmecker
gauffres (Fr.)—weiche
Kuchen
gazpacho, a Spanish
cold soup—
Gazpacho,
spanische Kaltschale
gelatine—Gelatin, sehr
reiner Knochenleim;
Gallert
gelée (Fr.)—jelly—
Sulze, Gallert
German fried potatoes
—Bratkartoffeln
German pot roast—
Pfannkuchen mit
gebratenem Rind-
fleisch, gedämpftes
Rindfleisch
German wax beans—
deutsche Wachs-
bohnen
gherkins—Pfeffer-
gurken
giant perch (fish)—
Schill, Zander, gros-
ser Barsch
giblet soup—Suppe aus
Gänseklein
gin—Genever, Wach-
holderbranntwein
ginger—Ingwer
ginger bread—
Lebkuchen
glacé (Fr.)—ice—Eis,
gefrorene Speisen,
Gefrorenes
glazed—glasirt
goby (fish)—Meer-
grundel
godiveau (Fr.)—meat
farce—Fleischfarce
gold fish—Goldfisch
gold plover—Gold-
brachvogel
goose—Gans
gooseberries—Stachel-
beeren
goose breast—
Gänsebrust
goose giblets—Gänse-
klein
goose grease—Gänse-
fett, Gänseschmalz
goose liver—Gänseleber
goose liver pie—Gänse-
leberpastete
goose, stuffed—gefüllte
Gans
goulasch—Gollasch,
Gulasch
Graham bread—
Weizenschrotbrot
Graham and cornmeal
griddle cakes—aus

Weizenschrot und
Maismehl geback-
ener Pfannkuchen
granite sugar—Stück-
Zucker
granulated sugar—
körniger Streuzu-
cker
grapes—Weintrauben
grapefruit—Abart von
Traubenpomeranze
grape vinegar—Trau-
benessig, Weinessig
grated—gerieben
gratin (Fr.)—left-
overs—Ueberbleib-
sel, verbrannte
gravy, broth—sauce
(Fr.)—Brühe, Jüs.
Sose, Tunke, Sauce
gravy, cream—Rahm-
sose
gravy soup—Kraft-
brühe
gravy, white cream,
made of chicken—
supréme (Fr.)—Ge-
richt aus den fein-
sten Stücken eines
Huhnes
grayling (fish)—
Aesche
greaves—Grieben
green artichoke—grü-
ne Artischoke
green beans—grüne
Bohnen
greengages—Reine
Clauden, Ringlots,
Weinpflaumen
green goose—junge
Gans
green lettuce—grüner
Salat
green peas—grüne
Erbsen
green pea pancakes—
Pfannkuchen aus
grünen Erbsen
green plover—grüner
Brachvogel
green string beans—
Schneide- oder
Brech-Bohnen
green turtle—Schild-
kröte
gribolettes (Fr.)—
larded cuts of
roasted meat—ge-
spickte Fleisch-
schnitte auf dem
Rost gebraten
griddle—Brat-Rost,
auch Kuchenpfanne
grilled—auf einem
Rost gebraten
grilled on the spit—
braten am Spiess,
grillieren
grit, semolina—Gries

groats—Weizen-
grütze; Hafergrütze
grog—Getränk aus
Rum, Zucker und
Wasser
groundling (fish)—
Gründling
grouse—Waldhuhn,
Birkhuhn
grouse, mountain—
Auerhahn
grouse, white—Schnee-
huhn
grunter (fish)—Knurr-
fisch, Alse
gruyère—Swiss
cheese—Schweizer-
käse
guinea fowl—Perlhuhn
haberdine (fish)—
Klippfisch
haddock—Schellfisch
haggis (Scotch)—pud-
ding made of the
pluck of lamb or
calf—ein Pudding
aus Kalbs- oder
Lammsgeschling
halibut (fish)—Helli-
butte, Heilbutt
ham—Schinken
ham and eggs—gebra-
tener Schinken mit
Spiegeleier
ham sandwich—Schin-
ken-Brötchen
Hamburg steak—ge-
hacktes Rindfleisch
gebraten
hard sausage (Italian)
—Salami
hare—Hase
hare jelly—Hasensülze
hare ragout—schwar-
zer Hase; Hasen-
k'ein
haricot—dish of mut-
ton and beans—ein
Gericht aus Ham-
melfleisch und Boh-
nen
haricot beans—Stan-
genbohnen
hash—hachis—Ha-
sche, Gehäck, ha-
cken
hashed—kleingehackt,
nachdem es gekocht
wurde
hashed meat—gekoch-
tes Fleisch, gehackt
head cabbage—Kohl-
kopf
head cheese—collared
head—gefüllter
Schweinsmagen
head lettuce—Kopf-
Salat
head waiter—Ober-
kellner

heathcock—heathgame—heathpout—Birkhahn

heath hen—Birkhuhn

heel—Rinde am Käse

herbs—Kräuter

herbs for soup—Suppenkräuter

herring—Hering, Häring

herring, collared—Rollmops, Rollhering

herring, marinated—marinierter Hering

herring, pickled—marinierter Hering

herring, roe—Rogenhering. Milchhering

herring salad—Herings-Salat

hickory nut—weisse amerikanische Walnuss

hind loin—hintere Lende

hind quarter—Schenkel

hind shank—hinteres Knochenstück, Keule

hip—Hagebutte

hip sauce—Hagebuttensose

hochepot (Fr.)—dish of mutton or oxtail with vegetables—ein Gericht aus Hammelfleisch oder Ochsenschwanz mit Gemüsen

hodge, podge, hotchpotch—Fleischragout mit verschiedenen Gemüsen

hogsbean—Puffbohne, Saubohne

hogshead, split in the middle—Presskopf

homely supper—einfache Abendmahlzeit

hominy—grob gemahlener Mais; Maisbrei

honey—Honig

hops—Hopfen

hors d'oeuvres (Fr.)—relishes—Vorgericht, Beigericht, Imbiss

horseradish—Meerrettig oder Märrettig

hot pot—beverage of ale, whitewine, sugar, etc.—Getränke aus Ale, Weisswein, Zucker u. s. w.

hot punch—heisser Punch

hot wine—Glühwein

huse—sturgeon—Hausen

icebox—Eisschrank

ice cream—Eis, Gefrorenes—glacé (Fr.)

ice lemonade—gefrorene Limonade, Gramolata

icing for pastry—Backwerk-Glasur

Indian corn—Mais, Welschkorn

Indian cress—Kapuzinerkresse

ingredients—Zubehör

Irish stew—Ragout von Hammelfleisch, Zwiebeln und Kartoffeln u. s. w.

isinglass—Hausenblase

jack snipe—Becassine

jam—Frucht-Marmelade, Jam

Jamaica pepper: pimento—Beissbeere, Nelkenpfeffer

jardiniere (Fr.)—Fleischsuppe mit Gartengemüse

jelly—Sulze, Gelee

Jerusalem artichoke—Erdartischoke

jug—dämpfen, im Wasserbad schmoren

jugged hare—Zubereitung des Hasen in Stücke mit Zuthat von Wein

julep—amerikanisches gemischtes Getränk

julienne (Fr.)—Sommersuppe: eine dünne Fleischsuppe

junket—Milchspeise

jus, meatjuice—Jus, Fleischsaft

Kail—Kale—Scotch green soup—schottische Grünkohl-Suppe

Kale—borecole (Fr.)—Winterkohl, Grünkohl

kassolettes—cupshaped pastry of rice, etc.—Kassolettes, becherförmige Pastetchen aus Reis u. s. w.

kebob—East Indian dish of mutton or fowl—ostindisches Gericht aus Hammelfleisch oder Geflügeln

kernels—seeds—Kerne

kidneys—Nieren

kidney suet—Talg, Nierenfett

kingfish—Weissbarsch

kitchen—Küche

knobs (cakes)—Kolatschen

krambambuli—beverage of arrac, etc. Getränk von Arrak u. s. w.

kohlrabi—Kohlrabe, Kohlrabi

koumiss (Russ.)—Kefir, Kumys—durch Hefe gegorene Stutenmilch

lace paper—Spitzenpapier

lake trout—Seeforelle

lamb—Lamm

lamb's fry—Lamm-Bouillon

lamb's pluck—Lammsgeschlinge und Kopf

lamb roast—Lammbraten

lamprey—Lambrete, Meerneunauge

land rail (poultry)—Wachtelkönig

lard—Schmalz

lard, to lard—spicken, bardieren. mit Speckscheiben belegen

larded—gespickt

larded braised calf's liver—gespickte, geschmorte Kalbsleber

larded leg of mutton—gespickter Hammelschlegel

larding of fowl—Barden, dünne Speckschnitten, mit denen man Geflügel beim Braten umbindet

larks—Lerchen

laver—Meerlattich

leaven—Sauerteig

leaves—Blätter

leek (with small onions)—Perlzwiebel. Pr auch

leeks—porret (vegetable)—Porre, Stangenlauch, Lauch, spanischer Lauch

left overs—Uebriggebliebenes

leg—Keule, Schlegel, Bein

leg of mutton—Hammelschlegel

leg of veal—Kalbs-
keule
legumes—Hülsen-
früchte
lemon—Citrone, Li-
mone
lemon pie—Citronen-
pastete
lemonade—Limonade
lentils—Linsen
lettuce—grüner Salat,
römischer Salat,
Lattich
lightly fry—sauté (Fr.)
—in Butter auf-
schwitzen
Lima beans—grosse
weisse Bohnen
Limburger cheese—
Limburger Käse
limeflower tea—Lin-
denblütentee
liqueur (Fr.)—liquor—
Likör
liver—Leber
liver, calf's—Kalbs-
leber
liver sausage—Leber-
wurst
loaf sugar—Hutzucker
lobster—Hummer,
See-Krebs
lobster a la Newburg
—Hummergericht
lobster salad—Hum-
mersalat
lodging—Logis, Woh-
nung
loin—Nierenbraten,
Lendenstück
loin, hind—hintere
Lende
loin, lower—bestes
Lendenstück
loin, upper—geringe-
res Lendenstück
long nose skate (fish)
—Glattroche
long roll—Stolle oder
Striezel
lukewarm—lauwarm
lunch—luncheon—Im-
biss: zwischen
Frühstück und Mit-
tagessen
macaroons—Macaro-
nen
macaroons, almond—
Mandelmacaronen
maccaroni (It.)—Hohl-
nudeln, Röhrnudeln
mace—Muskatblüte
macedoene (Fr.)—
mixed dish of veg-
etables and fruit—
ein Mischgericht
aus Gemüsen und
Früchten
mackerel (fish)—
Makrele

Madeira cake—Sand-
torte
maize—Welschkorn,
Mais
malakoff—sausage or
rolled meat—Wurst-
oder Fleischroulade
Malta sugar—Melis-
Zucker
mango fruit—Mango-
Frucht
mangold—Dickwurz
marbled—durchwach-
sen (vom Fleisch)
mangold stalks—Man-
gold-Stiele
maple sugar—Ahorn-
Zucker
marchpane—Marzipan
margarin, oleomar-
garine, artificial
butter—Margarin,
Oleomargarin,
Kunstbutter
marinade (Fr.)—Salz-
lake, eingepökeltes
Nahrungsmittel
marinade—marinate—
mariniren
marinated herring—
marinierter Hering
marjoram—Meiran,
Marjoram, Dost
marmade (Fr.)—Likör
von Gewürzen, Es-
sig u. s .w., in wel-
chem Fleisch einge-
taucht, ehe es ge-
kocht wird
marmelade (Fr.)—
Obstmus
marmelade of plums—
Powidel, Pflaumen-
mus
marrons—chestnuts—
essbare Kastanien
marrow—Mark
marrow, beef—Rinder-
mark
marrow peas—Mark-
erbsen
mash—Puree: Brei von
durchgeschlagenen
Hülsenfrüchten,
Kartoffeln, Fleisch
u. s. w.
mashed—pounded—
gestampft.
mashed apples—Apfel-
brei
mashed meat—Fleisch-
puree
mashed potatoes—Kar-
toffelbrei, Stampf-
kartoffel
mashed vegetables—
Gemüsebrei
maskinonge, muskel-
lunge (fish)—ame-
rikanische, unge-

wöhnlich grosse
Hechtart
master cook—Küchen-
meister
matie—Jungfern-
hering, Matjes-
hering
matze—matzes—
crackers of the Is-
raelites—ungesäuer-
ter Osterkuchen der
Israeliten
maycup—Maibowle,
Maitrank, Maiwein
mayonnaise (Fr.)—rich
salad dressing—
kalte Sose von Ei-
gelb, Salz, Senf, Oel,
u. s. w.
meat—Fleisch
meat birds—Fleisch-
Vögel, gerollte
Rindfleischstücke
mit Füllsel
meat, canned—Büch-
senfleisch
meat, chopped—ge-
hacktes Fleisch
meat, corned—einge-
salzenes Fleisch,
Pökelfleisch
meat extract—Fleisch-
extrakt
meat, hashed—gehack-
tes gekochtes Fleisch
meat jelly—aspic—
Fleischsulze
meat, mixed—ge-
mischter Aufschnitt
meat, mixed, cold—kal-
ter Aufschnitt
meat of the neck—
Kammfleisch
meat pie—Fleisch-
pastete
meat roasted in gravy
—Saftbraten
meat, rolled, Roulade
(Fr.)—Fleischrollen
meat salted—Pökel-
fleisch
meat, smoked—Rauch-
fleisch
meat soup with veg-
etables—jardiniere
(Fr.)—Fleischsuppe
mit Gartengemüse
melon—Melone
menu (Fr.)—bill of
fare—Tafel- Spei-
sekarte, Tafelfolge
meringues (Fr.)—egg-
kisses—Eierschaum-
Nacken, Krapfen,
Baisers
merluche (Fr.)—hake,
merluce (fish)—
kleiner Stockfisch,
Meerhecht, Hecht-
dorsch

merveilles (Fr.)—sugar cookies—Zucker-backwerk

met—mead—beverage of ancient Germans consisting of fermented honey—Met, ein Getränk der alten Deutschen aus gegorenem Honig

milk roll—Kipfel, Milchbrötchen

milk, sour—clabber—sauere Milch

millet—pannicle—Hirse

millet (fish)—Seebarbe

milter (fish)—Milcher, Milchner, männlicher Fisch

mince—blätterig geschnittenes Würzfleisch

mince, baked—gehackter Braten

mince pie—Pastetchen aus Fleisch, Obst und Branntwein

minced—kleingehackt, geschabt

minced beef, pork—Hackebraten, Fleischfarce aus Rindfleisch oder Schweinefleisch

minnow (fish)—Elritze, Pfrille, Bitterfisch

mint (fish)—Minze

mirabeau a la (Fr.)—dishes made of sardels and butter—mit Sardellen und Butter zubereitete Gerichte

mirabelle plum—Mirabelle, kleine gelbliche Pflaume

mixed cold meats—gemischter kalter Aufschnitt

mixed drinks—gemischte Getränke, besonders die sogenannten amerikanischen, wie Cobbler, Cocktail, Cup, Flip, Julep, Sour, Tom and Jerry, u. s. w.

mixed pickles—sauer eingemachte Gurken, Wurzelwerk

mocha—Mokka-Kaffee

mocha cake—Kaffeekuchen

mock—nachgemacht, unecht

mock turtle soup—nachgemachte Schildkrötensuppe aus Kalbsfüssen

molasses—Zucker-sirup, ungereinigter

molasses candy—Melasses-Kandis; Zuckersirupleckereien

morel—Morille, essbarer Pilz

mortar—Mörser

mother's doughnuts—Fettkringel, Berliner Pfannkuchen

mould—Form

mountain grouse—Auerhahn

mousebuttock—Maus, unteres stück vom Schenkel

mugget—Gekröse von Kalb oder Schwein

mugwort—Beifuss, Estragon

mulberry—Maulbeere

mulled ale—Warmbier

mullet (fish)—Meerbarbe, Meeräsche

mushrooms—Tafelpilze, Champignons, Trüffel, Edelpilze, Morcheln, Steinpilze

mushroom catsup—Würzsose aus Pilzen zubereitet

must—Most: Saft der Trauben vor der Gährung

mustard—Senf

mustard pickles—Senfgurken

mutton, best cuts: loin, saddle and leg—bestes Hammelfleisch von Lende, Rücken und Schenkel

mutton, braized carbonade—gedämpfte Hammelkarbonade

mutton cutlets or chops—gebratene Hammelkoteletts

mutton, larded leg of—gespickter Hammelschlegel

mutton roast—Hammelbraten

napfkuchen—a German cake baked in a bowl having a cylinder in the center—Napfkuchen, Aschkuchen, Topfkuchen, Babe, Rodonkuchen

napkin—Mundtuch, Serviette

nasturtium seeds—Nasturz, Brunnenkresse

navel piece—dünne Flanke

navy beans—getrocknete weisse Bohnen

neat's foot—Rindsfuss

neck—Hals

neck of veal—Kalbsbraten vom Hals

neck piece—Halsstück: dünnes Stück am Ende des Halses; oberer Kamm

nectar (beverage)—Nektar (Getränk)

nectarine (fruit)—Nectarine (pfirsichartige Frucht)

noodles—macaroni (It.)—Nudeln, Hohlnudeln

nougat—Mandel- und Zuckerteig

nut—Nuss

nut jelly—Nuss-Sulze

nutmeg—Muskatnuss

nutmeg melons—Muskatnussmelone

oats—Hafer

oatmeal—Hafergrütze, Hafermehl

olive—Olive

olive oil—Olivenöl

omelet—Eierkuchen, Omelette

omelette soufflé (Fr.)—Eierauflauf, geschlagene Omelette

onion—Zwiebel

onion custard—Eierrahm mit Zwiebeln

onions, Spanish—spanische Zwiebeln

orange—Apfelsine, Pomeranze, Orange

orange blossom—Orangenblüte

orange sauce for wild ducks—Pomeranzen-Sauce für wilde Enten

ordinary kitchen—Garküche

oval wood dish cookery—Kochen auf Hölzteller

ox tongue—Ochsenzunge

oysters—Austern

oyster bisque—Austermus

oyster plant—Schwarzwurzel

panada—Brotbrösel

panade—a dough made of grated rolls—Panade, Semmelteig

pancake strudels—Flädchen-Strudel

pancakes—Pfannkuchen, Plinzen

pancakes, green pea—
Pfannkuchen aus
grünen Erbsen
pancakes, thin—Plin-
zen mit Obst
pantry—Speisekammer
pap—Kinderbrei
paper bag—Düte,
Tüte
paperbag cooking—
Kochen in Papier-
beuteln
parmesan (Italian
cheese)—Parmesan-
Käse, ein italieni-
scher Käse
parsley—Petersilie
parsnip—Pastinake
partridge—Rebhuhn
passed—durchgeseiht,
durchgetrieben,
durch ein Sieb
getrieben
paste—Teig
pastilla—a Russian
dried fruit mar-
melade—russische
getrocknete Obst-
marmelade
pastille—sugar wafers
—Zuckerplätzchen
pastry cook—Pasteten-
bäcker
pastry—light puff,
baked in a mold and
filled with chicken,
sweet breads, etc.—
vol-au-vent (Fr.)—
Blätterteigpastete
von Wild u. s. w.
pastry—pie—Pastete
patties—Pastetchen
patty paste—Pasteten-
Teig
peach trifle—Pfirsich-
Auflauf
peeled barley—Grau-
pen
pearl (fish)—Brill,
Glatt-Butte
pears—Birnen
peas—Erbsen
pease-meal—Erbs-
mehl, Erbsbrei,
Erbsengericht
pea soup—pease soup
—Erbs-Suppe
pepper gherkins—
Pfeffer-Gurken
pepper grass—Pfeffer-
kraut
peppermint—Pfeffer-
minze
perch, bass—Fluss-
barsch, Barse
perch, fried (fish)—ge-
bratener Barsch
perch, pike (fish)—
Zander, Schill,
Barsch

petersfish (fish)—
Goldfisch, Peters-
fisch
petito fours (Fr.)—
small cookies—klei-
nes Backwerk
pheasant—Fasan
piccalilli (It.)—nach
Art von Pickles ein-
gelegtes Gemüse
pickerel (fish)—Grass-
hecht, amerikani-
sche Art Hecht
pickle (to pickle)—
marinieren, einma-
chen
pickled fruits—sauer
eingelegtes Obst
pickled meat—Pökel-
fleisch
pickled pork—ge-
pökeltes Schweine-
fleisch
pickled sour cabbage—
Sauerkraut
pickles—Essigfrüchte
und Essiggemüse
pickles, butternut—
eingelegte Butter-
nüsse
pickles, mustard—
Senfgurken
pickles, small—kleine
eingemachte Gurken
pickles, sweet sour—
Gurken, süss-sauer
eingemacht
pie—Pastete
pie (small)—baked in
a mold and turned
out while hot: tim-
bale—becherför-
mige Pastete
piece—Stück
pièce de resistance
(Fr.): principal
dish at a meal—die
Platte, welche der
Suppe folgt
pig—Schwein
pig, sucking—Span-
ferkel
pig's fry—gebratene
Leber, Herz, Milz
u. s. w.
pig's trotters—
Schweinsfüsse
pigeon—Taube
pigeon sauté (Fr.)—
geschwungene Tau-
be
pike (fish)—Schill,
Zander, Hecht
pilau: East Indian or
Turkish dish of
meat and rice—
Reisspeise mit
Fleisch, ein Haupt-
gericht in der Tür-
kei und Ostindien

pilau of chicken—
Huhn mit Reis ge-
kocht
pimente: Jamaica pep-
per—Weissbeere,
Nelken-Pfeffer
pimolas: small olives
stuffed with sweet
red pepper—kleine
Oliven gefüllt mit
süssem rotem Pfef-
fer
pimpernell—Pimper-
nell, Bibernellkraut
pineapple—Ananas
piquante (Fr.)—sharp-
ly flavored—scharf
gewürzt
piquant beef—Milch-
Sauerbraten
piquant roast beef—
gebeiztes Ochsen-
fleisch
pirog, pie of fish, eggs,
sour cabbage, mush-
rooms, etc.—Pastet-
chen von Fisch,
Eiern, Sauerkraut,
Pilzen u. s. w.
plain boiled—blau ge-
sotten (beim Fisch)
plain table—table fru-
gale (Fr.)—ein-
facher Tisch
plover—Brachvogel
pluck of lamb—
Lammsgeschlinge
plum—Pflaume
plum tart—Pflaumen-
kuchen
plums, marmelade of—
Powidel, Pflaumen-
mus
poached eggs—verlo-
rene Eier
podware—Hülsen-
früchte
pop—Sodawasser: ein
leicht gärendes Fla-
schengetränk, des-
sen Kork beim Her-
ausziehen einen
Knall gibt
poppy—Mohn
pork—Schweinefleisch
pork and beans—Speck
und Bohnen
pork chops—Schweins-
rippchen
pork cutlets—Schweins-
coteletten
pork, fresh—ungesal-
zenes Schweine-
fleisch
pork knuckles—
Schweinsknochen
pork, pickled—gepö-
keltes Schweine-
fleisch

pork roast—Schweins-
braten
pork roast, braised—
geschmorter
Schweinsbraten
pork, roasted—gebra-
tenes Schweine-
fleisch
pork, salted, pickled
pork—gepökeltes
Schweinefleisch
pork sausage—Brat-
wurst
pork skin—Speck-
schwarte
pork, smoked, after-
wards cooked—
Selchfleisch
porterhouse—Speise-
haus, Restaurant
porterhouse beefsteak,
rumpsteak—Len-
denbraten
pot—Topf
pot au feu (Fr.)—na-
tional soup—fran-
zösische National-
Suppe, Fleischbrühe
mit Fleisch und Ge-
müse
pot-hellion—amerika-
nische Fleisch-
pastete
pot herbs—Suppen-
kräuter
pot house—Bierhaus,
Kneipe
pot pie—Fleischpastete
pot pie, chicken—
Hühnerfleisch-
pastete
pot roast—Schmorbra-
ten
pot roast beef—Rin-
derbraten, der in
einem Topf zuge-
richtet wird
potage: a family soup
—Familiensuppe
potatoes—Kartoffeln
potatoes—a la
duchesse (Fr.)—
Kartoffelgericht
potato balls (dump-
lings)—Kartoffel-
klösse
potato chips—Kartof-
fel-Spähne
potato flour—Kartof-
felmehl
potatoes, German
fried—Bratkartof-
feln
potatoes, mashed—
Kartoffel zu Brei
zerrieben. Kartof-
felbrei, Stampfkar-
toffel
potatoes, sweet—Süss-
kartoffeln

potatoes with parsley
—Petersilien-Kar-
toffeln
potpourri (It.)—Misch-
masch, Allerlei
potted—in Töpfen ein-
gelegt
poularde—Masthuhn
poultry—Geflügel
poultry bisque—Geflü-
gelmus
poultry stew—blan-
quette (Fr.)—Ra-
gout von Geflügel
mit weisser Sose
pounded—gestampft
pounder—Schlegel,
Keule
powdered sugar—
Staubzucker, Streu-
zucker
prairie chicken—Prai-
riehuhn, Feldhuhn
prawn, small shrimp—
Garneele
preparation—Zube-
reitung
prepare—anrichten
preserved fruit—einge-
machtes, eingeleg-
tes, conservirtes
Obst
preserves—Dauer-
speisen, Dauer-
früchte, Büchsenge-
müse
pressed beef—gepress-
tes Fleisch stark
gewürzt
pretzels—cracknels—
Brezel, Pretzel,
Kracklinge
provisions—Nah-
rungsmittel
prune, dried plum—
Pflaume, Zwetschge,
gedörrt
prunellas—prunel-
los—Prünellen
prunes and nut jelly—
Pflaumen- und
Nuss-Sulze
public dinner—Zweck-
essen
pudding—Pudding,
Hüllkloss
puff paste—Blätter-
teig, Butterteig
puff paste cane—Blät-
terteigröhrchen mit
Schlagsahne oder
mit Fleischfarce ge-
füllt
puffs, batter—Pfitzauf,
Eierkuchen
pulverized—pulverisirt
pumpernickel—un-
salted bread made
of shredded rye—
schwarzes, ungesal-

zenes Roggenbrod
aus Ganzmehl
pumpkin—Kürbis
punch—Punsch
purée (Fr.)—puree—
Gemüsebrei, dicke
Suppe
puree soups—durch-
getriebene Suppen
purslane—Portulac
pute—Truthenne
puter—Truthahn, Pu-
ter
pyramidal cake—
Baumkuchen
quails—Wachteln
quarter—Viertel
quarter of mutton—
Hammelviertel
quinces—Quitten
rabbit—hare—Kanin-
chen, Hase
radish—Rettich, Ret-
tig
radish, little red—Ra-
dieschen
radish, Spanish
—schwarzer Rettich
radish—turnip—Rü-
benrettig, Rettig
ragout (Fr.)—stewed
meat in rich gravy
—gaumenreizendes
Fleisch-Gericht mit
reicher Sose
ragout, hare—schwar-
zer Hase, Hasen-
klein, Hasenpfeffer
rarebit—mit im Bier
aufgeweichtem Kä-
se übergossene
heisse Brotschnitte
raspberries—Himbee-
ren
ratavia—fruit liquor—
Fruchtlikör
rechauffé (Fr.)—any-
thing warmed over
—wieder aufge-
wärmt
red beet—rote Rübe
red cabbage—Rotkraut
red pepper—Spanish
pepper—Paprika,
roter Pfeffer
red wine vinegar—
Rotweinessig
relishes—hors
d'oeuvres (Fr.)—
Vorgericht, Beige-
richt, Imbiss
rémoulade sauce (Fr.)
—a piquant meat-
gravy—pikante
Fleischsose
remove—relevé (Fr.)—
Platte, welche bei
einer geordneten
Tafel der Suppe
folgt

restaurant—Restauration, Speisehaus
rhubarb—Rabarber
rib roast—Vorderrippe
rice—Reis
rice flour—Reismehl
rice fritters—Reispfannkuchen
rich salad dressing—mayonnaise (Fr.)—kalte Sose von Eigelbem, Salz, Senf, mit Oel verrührt
rissoles (Fr.)—Maultaschen, Blätterteig-Halbmonde. Rissolen, Krapfen
rissotto—rice and cheese cooked together (Italian dish)—Reis in Fleischbrühe und Butter gebrüht mit Käse
river fish—Flussfisch
river lamprey (fish)—Bricke oder Neunaugen
roach (fish)—Rotauge
roast—braten, rösten
roast beef—Rostbraten
roast beef piquant—gebeiztes Ochsenfleisch
roast fillet of beef—Lendenbraten
roast lamb—Lammbraten
roast loin of veal—Nierenbraten vom Kalb
roast mutton—Hammelbraten
roast spareribs—Rippenbraten
roast stuffings—Bratenfüllungen
roast turkey—gebratener Truthahn
roast veal—Kalbsbraten
roast veal filled—gefüllter Kalbsbraten
roast venison—Hirschbraten
roasted—in einem Ofen gebraten
roasted chestnuts—Kastanien, Maronen, geröstet
roasted meat in gravy—Saftbraten
roasted sugar—caramel (Fr.)—gebrannter Zucker
rocambole—Graslauch, Rocambole, Sandlauch, Perlzwiebel

roe—spawn—Rogen
rolled beef—Roulade von Ochsenfleisch
rolled beef with farces—meat birds—Fleischvögel
rolled meat—roulade (Fr.)—Fleischrollen, Roulade
rolls—rundes Brötchen. Weck, Semmel
rolls, French—Kipfel
rolls, long—Stollen, Striezel
rolls, milk—Kipfel, Milchbrötchen
rolls, white round—Kipfel
Roman lettuce—Bindsalat, römischer Salat, Spargelsalat
roots—carrots, turnips, etc.—Wurzelwerk
Roquefort—brand of fancy cheese—fester, weisser, grün marmorirter Käse
rosemary—Rosmarin
roulade (Fr.)—gefüllte Fleischröllchen
round—Schwanzstück, Rundstück
round roll, white—Kipfel
roux (Fr.)—butter and flour thickening—Einbrenne, Mehlschwitze, braune Butter
rum—Zuckerrohrbranntwein
rump—Rumpf, Hinterteil, Kreuz, Schwanzstück
rump steak—porterhouse steak—zartestes Ochsenfleisch vom Hinterviertel
rusk—Zwieback
rye bread—Schwarzbrot, Roggenbrot
saddle—Rückenstück
saddle of veal—Kalbsrücken
saffron—Saffran
sage—Salbei
salad—Salat
salad, apple—Apfelsalat
salad, celery—Selleriesalat
salad dressing, boiled—zubereitete Salat-Gewürzsose
salad, endive—Endiviensalat
salad, French—französischer Salat

salad, herring—Heringsalat
salad, lobster—Hummernsalat
salmi (Fr.)—warmed over dish of game, well seasoned—braunes Ragout von gebratenem wilden Geflügel
salmon—Lachs, Salm
salmon-trout—Lachs-Forelle
saloop—arrowroot—Salep, Pfeilwurzel
salt—einsalzen, Salz
salt meat—Pökelfleisch, Salzfleisch
salted and boiled pig's trotters—Schweinsfüsse
salted cod—Bakeljau, Stockfish
sandat—sandre (Fr.)—zander, perch pike, giant perch—Zander, Sander
sandwich—belegtes Brötchen, Butterbrot. Butterstulle
sandwich, cheese—Käsebrötchen
sandwich, ham—Schinkenbrötchen
sardelles (Fr.)—anchovy—Sardellen
sardine (fish)—Sardine, Pilchard
sauce (Fr.)—Sose. Brühe, Tunke, Salse, Guss, Beiguss
sausage—Wurst, Knackwurst, Bratwurst
sausage, black—Blutwurst
sausage, Bologna—Mettwurst, Bologna
sausage, Brunswick—Braunschweiger Leberwurst
sausage, fried—Bratwurst
sausage, German—Mettwurst, Bologna
sausage, Italian, hard—Salami
sausage, liver—Leberwurst, Weisswurst
sausage, pork—Bratwurst
sausage, white—Leberwurst, Weisswurst
sausage (Wiener)—Wiener Würstchen
sausages, skins for—Därme für Würste

sauté (Fr.)—to mix by shaking, to lightly fry, to stew—in Butter aufschwitzen, umschwenken, schmoren, gesotten

sauté, carrot—geschmorte Rüben

sauté, pigeon—geschwungene Taube

sauté, turnip—leichtgebratene Rüben

saveloy—Cervelatwurst

savory—Bohnenkraut

savoy cabbage—Welschkohl, Savoyer Kohl, Wirsing-Kohl

scalded—abgebrüht

scallop—Speisen, welche einen zick-zackartigen Rand haben

scallop chowder—ragoutartiges Austerngericht

scarlet beans—scharlachfarbige Bohnen

schalet or scholet—a jewish dish—isrealitisches Gericht

schmarn—fruit pancake—Schmarrn

scorpion grass—cornsalad—Ackersalat, Rapünzchen, Mausohr

scorsonera—Schwarzwurzeln

scraped—minced—shredded—geschabt

sea bass (fish)—Seebarsch

sea cabbage—Meerkohl

sea mullet (fish)—Meeräsche, Meerbarbe

seasoned—dem Geschmacke entsprechend gewürzt

seeds—kernels—Kerne

seed cake—Mohnkuchen, Kümmelkuchen, Streuselkuchen

selterswater—Selterwasser

servants' table—table du commun (Fr.)—Gesindetisch

shad (fish)—Alse

shaddock—Citrone, Pampelmuscitrone

shank—Schenkel

shank, front—vorderes Knochenstück

shank, hind—hinteres Knochenstück

sharply flavored—piquante (Fr.)—scharf gewürzt

shavings—Späne

sheat (fish)—Waller, Wels

shelled almonds—Krach- oder Knackmandeln

shellfish, shells—Weichtiere: Krebse, Muscheln, Austern

sherry—Xereswein

shiners—whitelings (fish)—Weisslinge

shirred eggs—Setzeier, Spiegeleier in Sahne

short-cake—Erdbeerkuchen

short crust—mürber Teig

shoulder (pertaining to meat)—Blatt, Schulter, Kamm

shoulder and bladebone—Schulterstück beim Schlachtvieh

shoulder butt—Rippenstück

shoulder chop—rundes Rippenstück

shoulder of veal, larded—gespickte Kalbsschulter

shred—klein schneiden, in Streifen schneiden

shredded, minced—geschabt

shredded wheat—geschrotener Weizen

shrimp—Taschenkrebs

shrimp, white (fish)—Seeheuschrecke

side board—Büffet, Silber- und Gläserschrank

side dishes—éntrées (Fr.)—Zuspeise, Beigericht

sieve—Sieb

sifted sugar—Puder- oder Staubzucker

silurus—sheat (fish) Waller, Wels

simmer—gelinde kochen

sirloins—Lendenstücke

sirlóin steak—Fleisch vom Schenkel, nächst dem Rumpf

skate—Flachfisch

skim—abschäumen

skimmer—Schaumlöffel, Rahmkelle

skins for sausages—Därme für Würste

skippered salmon—Räucherlachs

sloe—Schlehe

small cakes—Confekt, Zuckerbackwerk

small dishes served between courses—entrées (Fr.)—Zwischengericht

small drop cakes—Maken

small dumplings—Nocken

small pickles—kleine eingemachte Gurken

smelt (fish)—Stintfisch

smoke—rauchen, räuchern

smoked—geräuchert

smoked eel—Spickaal

smoked fish—geräucherter Fisch

smoked goose—Spickgans

smoked meat—Rauchfleisch

smoked sausage—Knackwurst, geräucherte Wurst

snail—Schnecke

snipe—Landschnepfe —becassine (Fr.)

soda and brandy—Sodawasser und Cognac

soda-lemonade—Brauselimonade

soda water—Sodawasser, Syphon

sole (fish)—Seezunge

sorrel—Sauerampfer

soufflé (Fr.)—Auflauf, Omelette

soup—Suppe

soup, giblet—Suppe aus Gänseklein

soup, meat—julienne (Fr.)—dünne Fleischsuppe mit vielerlei Gemüsen

soup, puree—durchgetriebene Suppe

soup, thick—dicke Suppe

soup, unground corn—Graupensuppe

soup with vegetables—Suppe mit Gartengemüsen

sour—amerikanisches gemischtes Getränk

sour beef—Sauerbraten

sour cabbage, pickled—Sauerkraut

sour milk—clabber—sauere Milch, dicke Milch

southern wood—Citronenkraut, Stabwurz, Eberraute

spareribs, roasted—Rippenbraten

spelt—Spelz, Dinkel
spice—Gewürz
spice nuts—Pfeffer-Nüsse
spiced—gewürzt
spinach—Spinat
spiny lobster—spring lobster—Languste
spit—Spiess
spit pin—Spicknadel
spitch cockerel—gebratener Aal
sponge cake—Schaumtorte
spoon—Löffel
spouted cake—fritter—Spritzkuchen
spring chicken—junges Huhn
sprout—Spross, Sprössling
squash—Melonenkürbis
squirrel—Eichhorn
stalks—Stiele
stall-fed hen—Masthühnchen
steak—see beefsteak
steak, stewed—gedünstetes Rindfleisch
steam—Dampf, Dampf erzeugen
steam table—Behälter zum Warmhalten der Speisen
steamed—gedämpft
stew—Frikassee, weiss Eingemachtes, in Butter aufschwitzen, umschwenken, schmoren
stew, poultry—blanquette (Fr.)—Ragout von Geflügel mit weisser Sose
stewed beef—beef a la mode (Fr.)—gedämpftes Rindfleisch
stewed—braized—geschmort
stewed cucumbers—geschmorte Gurken
stewed fruits—Compot, Mus, Dunstobst
stewed meat in rich gravy—ragout (Fr.)—gaumenreizendes Gericht aus Fleisch
stewed steak—gedünstetes Rindfleisch
stewing pan—Schmorpfanne, Schmortopf
strawberries—Erdbeeren
strewed—bestreut
strewed cake—Streusel-Kuchen

string beans—welsche Bohnen, Schneidebohnen, Brechbohnen
stuffed—gefüllt
stuffings for roasts—Bratenfüllsel
sturgeon—Stör
Suabian biscuits—Schwabenbrot
succotash beans—Gericht aus jungem Mais mit Bohnen
sugar—Zucker
sugar, block—Granitzucker
sugar boiled and beaten to a creamy paste—fondant (Fr.)—im Munde zerschmelzend, saftig
sugar loaf—Zuckerhut
sugar peas—Zuckerschoten
sugar, roasted—caramel (Fr.)—gebrannter Zucker
sugar, sifted—Staubzucker, Puderzucker
summer cabbage—Schnittkohl
Sundae (Am.)—Fruchteis; gefrorener Rahm mit Fruchtmus
supper—Abendessen, Abendbrot, Nachtmahlzeit
supreme: white cream gravy made of chicken—Gericht aus den feinsten und ausgesuchtesten Stücken
sweet—süss
sweet basil—Basilikum, Basilienkraut
sweet bread—Kalbsbrüse, Kalbsmidder, Kalbsmilch, Saum
sweet cicely—spanischer Kerbel
sweet marjoram—Meiran
sweet fruit sauce—süsses Fruchtmus
supper time—Abendbrotzeit
sweet pickled gherkins—süss eingemachte Gurken
sweet toast—Zwieback
Swiss cheese—schweizer Käse
Swiss turnovers—schweizer Kröpfli
table—Tisch, Tafel
table d'hôte (Fr.)—regular table board—gemeinschaftliche Wirtstafel

table du commun (Fr.)—servant's table—Gesinde-Tisch
table frugale (Fr.)—plain table—einfacher Tisch
table napkin—Mundtuch, Serviette
table recherché (Fr.)—fine, first class table—gewählter, feiner Tisch
tapioca—Tapioka
tarragon—Dragun, Dragon, Estragon, Kaisersalat
tarragon vinegar—Dragun-Essig
tart—Torte
tartare (Fr.)—tartaric—roh, tartarisch (vom Rindsstück
tea, green tea, black tea—Tee, grüner Tee, schwarzer Tee
tea, limeflower—Lindenblütentee
tea, peppermint—Pfefferminztee
Teltow turnips—Teltower Rüben
tench (fish)—Schleie
tenderloin—Lendenstück; Filet (Fr.)—Möhrbraten, Mürbebraten
tepid—lau
terreen—Terrine, Napf
terrine (Fr.)—tureen—tiefe Schüssel
thyme—Timian
timbale (Fr.)—small pie baked in a mold—becherförmige Pastete
toast—Weissbrotscheiben, am Feuer geröstet
toast (to)—rösten
toast rack—silbernes Gerät mit rostartigen Querstäben
toast, sweet—Zwieback
toasted anchovy crackers—gerösteter Zwieback mit Sardellenteig überstrichen
tomato—Tomate, Liebesapfel
tongue—Zunge
torsk (fish)—Dorsch
tourté (Fr.)—tart—Torte
trevet—Dreifuss
trifle—Art Auflauf, Weihnachtsleckerei
tripe—Kuttelflecke, Gekröse
trout (fish)—Forelle, Bach-Forelle

trout, baked—gebratene Forelle
true marjoram—Meiran
truffle, mushrooms—Trüffel, Pilze, Morcheln
turbot, grilled (fish)—gebratene Steinbutte
tureen—Terrine, tiefe Schüssel, Napf
turkey—Truthahn, welscher Hahn, Puter
turkey roast—gebratener Truthahn
turmeric—Gelbwurzel, Curcuma, ostindisches Gewürz
turnip—Kohlrübe, Kohlrebe, weisse Rübe, Mairübe, Steckrübe
turnip cabbage—Kohlrabi, Kohlrübe
turnip celery—Wurzelsellerie
turnip radish—Rübenrettig
turnip sauté (Fr.)—geschmorte Rüben
turnover—halbrundes Apfeltörtchen
turtle—Schildkröte
tusk (fish)—Dorsch
tutti frutti (It.)—Fruchteis, allerlei Früchte, Fruchtallerlei
twirl—quirlen
umber (fish)—Aesche
underdone—halb durchgebraten
unground corn soup—Graupen-Suppe
uniformly—gleichmässig
upper loin—geringeres Lendenstück
vanilla—Vanille, tropische Frucht
vanilla—blanc manger—Milchsulze mit Vanilla
vanilla—blanc mange
vanilla sugar—Vanille-Zucker
veal—Kalbfleisch
veal breast—Kalbsbrust

veal brisolettes (Fr.)—Kalbs-Brisoletten
veal cutlets, baked—Wiener Schnitzel
veal, filled—gefüllter Kalbsbraten
veal pot pie—Napfpastete von Kalbfleisch
veal kidneys—Kalbsnieren
veal, leg of—Kalbsschlegel
veal or calf's tripe—Kalbsgekröse
veal saddle—Kalbsrücken
veal, shoulder of—Kalbsschulterstück
vegarade, bitter orange—bittere Pomeranze
vegetables—Gemüse
vegetables, canned—Büchsengemüse, eingemachtes Gemüse
vegetable marrow—Kürbisfrucht
venison—Hirschbraten
vermicelli (It.)—Fadennudeln
Vienna rolls—Wienerbrötchen
vinegar—Essig
vol-au-vent (Fr.)—puff paste patty—Blätterteigpastete aus feinem Ragout von Wild, Geflügel, etc.
wafer—Waffel, Hohlhippchen, Plinsen
waffle, wafer—Waffeln
warmed up—rechauffé (Fr.)—aufgewärmt
Water—Wasser
watermelon—Wassermelone, Arbuse
wax beans—Wachsbohnen
well done—gut durchgebraten
well done beefsteak—gut durchgebratenes Rindsstück
Welsh rarebit—mit im Bier aufgeweichten Käse; übergossene heisse Brotschnitte
wheat—Weizen

wheat bird—Weizenvogel
whip, beverage of whitewine, sugar, eggs—Getränk aus Weisswein, Zucker, Eier
whipped cream—Schlagobers, Rahmschnee, Rahmschaum, geschlagene Sahne, Schlagsahne
whiskey—Getreide-Branntwein
white bait (fish)—Breitling
white braise—helle Schmorbrühe
white bread—Weissbrot
white cabbage—Weisskraut
white grouse—Schneehuhn
white round roll—Kipfel
white sausage, liver sausage—Leberwurst
white shrimp (fish)—Seeheuschrecke
white wine vinegar—Weinessig
whitings (fish)—Weisslinge
widgeon (game)—Pfeifente
wild boar—Wildschwein
wild duck—Wildente
wild pigeon—wilde Taube
wine, hot—Glühwein
with vegetables—a la jardiniere (Fr.)—mit Gemüse
woodcock—Waldschnepfe, auch Auerhahn
woodcock, broiled—gebratene Wildschnepfe
yeast—Hefe
yeast dough—Hefenteig
yeast dumplings—Hefenklösse, Hefenknödel
zander (fish)—Schill, Zander

Deutsch - Englisches Wörterverzeichnis

umfassend die

wichtigsten Fachausdrücke über Speisen und Getränke,
etc., wie dieselben in der Küche, der Tafel, sowie
im Wirtschaftsbetrieb angewandt werden.
Mit Uebersetzung in beiden Sprachen.

Zusammengestellt von C. N. Caspar.

Aal—eel
Aal, gebratener—
 spitchcock
Aal, gerollter—collared
 eel
Aalraupen—eel pouts
Abendbrot—supper
Abendbrotzeit—supper
 time
Abendessen—supper
abgebrüht—scalded
Abklären—to clarify
Absinth—Wermut-
 branntwein—
 absinthe
Abschäumen—skim
Aesche (Fisch)—gray-
 ling, umber
Ahornzucker—maple
 sugar
Allerlei Mischmasch—
 potpourri
Alse (Fisch)—shad,
 grunter
Alse, gebratene—baked
 shad
am Rost gebraten—
 grilled
am Spiess gebraten—
 roasted on the spit
Amarellen-Kirsche—
 Armenian cherry
amerikanische ge-
 mischte Getränke—
 mixed drinks
amerikanische rote
 Weintraube—
 Catawba
amerikanische Venus-
 muschel—clam
amerikanischer Mais-
 branntwein—
 bourbon
Ananas—pineapple
Ananas-Bowle—pine-
 apple punch
Anis—anise
Anisbrod—anise rusk
Aniskuchen—anise cake
anrichten, zubereiten—
 to dress, prepare
Apfel—apple

Apfelmus—mashed
 apples
Apfelsalat—apple salad
Apfelsine—orange
Apfelstrudel—apple
 fritters
Apfelsulze—apple jelly
Apfelwein—cider
Appetitanreizer—appe-
 tizer
Aprikose—apricot
Arbuse—watermelon
Arrak (Likör)—arrack
arrangierte Gemüse—
 chartreuse of vege-
 tables
Artischocke—artichoke
au naturel (Fr.)—ohne
 Zutat—plain, simple
Auerhahn—mountain
 grouse, woodcock
auf einem Rost gebra-
 ten—grilled, broiled
aufgelöst—dissolved
aufgewärmt—réchauffé
 (Fr.)—warmed over
Auflauf—soufflé (Fr.)
 —puff, light pud-
 ding, trifle
Auflauf, Pfirsich—
 peach trifle
au four (Fr.)—im Ofen
 überbacken—baked
 im oven
Aufschnitt, gemischter
 —various kinds of
 cold meats mixed
Aufschnitt, kalter—
 mixed meats
au gratin (Fr.)—ge-
 backene Gerichte
 mit einer bräun-
 lichen Kruste—
 baked dishes with a
 brown crust
aus Schmalz gebacke-
 ne Speisen—beig-
 nets (Fr.)—fruit
 fritters
aus Weizenschrot und
 Maismehl geback-
 ene Kuchen—Gra-

ham and cornmeal
 griddle cakes
Austern—oysters,
 shells, crustacea
Austerngericht, ragout-
 artiges—scallop
 chowder
Austernmus—oyster
 bisque
Bachforelle—brook
 trout
Backe (vom Fleisch)—
 cheek
backen—to bake
Bäckerei—bakery
Backwerk-Glasur—
 icing for pastry
Baiser, Schaumgebäck
 —meringue (Fr.)—
 cream puff, cream
 bun
Bakeljau—salted cod
Bällchen—ball, boulette
Banane—Banana
Bannocks, schottischer
 Hafermehlkuchen—
 Scotch oatmeal
 cakes
Barbe (Fisch)—barbel
Barberize (Beere)—
 barberry
Barden, dünne Speck-
 schnitten mit denen
 man Geflügel beim
 Braten umbindet—
 larding of fowls
bardieren, belegen mit
 Speckscheiben—to
 lard
Barse oder Barsch
 (Fisch)—perch
Basilikum, Basilien-
 kraut—sweet basil
Batate—Carolina pota-
 to; sweet potato
Baumkuchen—pyrami-
 dal cake
Bauern-Krapfen—ex-
 cellent buns
Becassine—jack snipe
Béchamelsauce, Rahm-
 tunke—cream sauce

beefsteak a la Tartare (Fr.)—fein geschabtes Ochsenfleisch mit Zwiebeln, u.s.w., wird roh gegessen—scraped beef with onions, etc., eaten raw

begiessen—basting

Beifuss—mugwort

Beigerichte, Nebengerichte— hors d'oeuvre (Fr.) sidedishes

Beignets . von Kartoffeln—potato beignets

Beiguss—sauce, gravy

Beissbeere, Nelkenpfeffer—pimento— Jamaica pepper

belegte Brötchen— sandwiches

Berberitzen, Sauerdorn —barberries

Berian (Fr.)—Teebackwerk—teacakes

Berliner Pfannkuchen —doughnuts

Berlingos, kleine Teekuchen—berlingos, small teacakes

bestes Lendenstück— lower loin

bestreut—strewed, dredged

Bier—beer

Bierhaus—saloon, pothouse

Bindsalat, römischer Salat, Spargelsalat —Roman lettuce

Birkhahn—heathgame, heathpout, heathcock, grouse

Birkhuhn—heath hen

Birnen—pears

Bischoff, Getränk aus bitteren Pomeranzen, Wein, Zucker, u. s. w.—bischoff, beverage of bitter oranges, wine, sugar, etc.

Bittling, geräucherter Hering—bloater

blanc, helle Fleischbrühe—clear soup

blanchieren, abbrühen —scald

Blatt—(pertaining to meat), shoulder

Blätter-Ragout: blätterig geschnittenes Würzfleisch—mincemeat

Blätter-Teig—flaky crust, puff paste

Blätterteig-Halbmonde, Farce oder fein gehacktes Fleisch, in einer dünnen Teig-

hülle, paniert und gebacken—Rissoles (Fr.)—mince-meat fritters

Blätterteig-Hohlröhrchen das mit Schlagsahne einer Creme oder mit Fleischfarce gefüllt ist—cannelon

Blätterteig-Pastete mit Deckel, feinem Ragout oder Frikassee von Wild-Geflügel, etc.—vol-au-vent (Fr.)—puff paste patty

Blättertorte mit Créme —puff-paste tart with cream

blau gesotten (beim Fisch)—plain boiled

Blaubeeren, Heidelbeeren—blueberries

Blei, Blicke, Plötze— bleakfish, play

Blini, russischer Pfannkuchen—blini Russian pancake

Blumenkohl—cauliflower

Blumenkohl, mit Kruste gebackener—au gratin (Fr.)—cauliflower baked with crust

Blut-Wurst—black sausage

Bodschwene, polnische Suppe—bodschwene, a Polish soup, containing beets, beef, onions

Boeuf a la Mode (Fr.) —braized beef

Bohnen—beans

Bohnen, geschwungene —stewed beans

Bohnen, getrocknete weisse—navy beans

Bohnen, grüne—green beans

Bohnen, scharlachfarbige—scarlet beans

Bohnen, türkische— French beans

Bohnen, weisse—haricot beans

Bohnen, welsche— string beans, French beans

Bohnenkraut—savory

Bohnenkraut, Saturei, Bohnenkölle, Wurst oder Pfefferkraut— beautressel, savory

Bökling, Böcklhering, geräucherter Hering —bloater

Bon Bons, Zuckerwerk bon bons, candies

Boronia, spanisches Gericht aus Tomaten, Kürbis, u. s. w. in Würfel geschnitten—boronia, a Spanish dish of tomatoes, pumpkins, etc., diced

Borretsch—Gurkenkraut—borage

Boulette (Fr.)— Fleischschnitte von gekochtem oder gebratenem und rohem Fleisch gemischt—boulettes (Fr.)—Fricandells made of cooked or roasted or raw meat and rolls

Bowle; ein terrinenartiges Gefäss für Punch—bowl cup.

Brachvogel—plover

braisirt, geschmort— braized

Branntwein—brandy, cognac

Branntwein, französischer—cognac

Brasse (Fisch), Bresse oder Brackse— bream

braten—to roast

braten am Spiess— grilled on the spit

Braten auf dem Rost —grilled on the roast

Bratenfett—drippings

Bratenfüllsel—stuffings for roasts

Braten, gehackter— baked mince meat

Bratkartoffeln—German fried potatoes

Brat-Rost—grill, griddle, gridiron, broiler

Bratwurst—pork sausage, fried sausage

Braunschweiger Wurst, Cervelatwurst— Brunswick sausage

Brauselimonade—soda lemonade

Breitling (Fisch)—. white bait

Brezel, Kracklinge, Milchbrötchen— pretzels, buns, cracknels

Bricke, Neunaugen— river lamprey

bridieren oder dressieren, zusammen binden des Geflügels beim Braten—dressing of poultry with twine while roasting

Brill (Fisch)—pearl
Broccoli, Winterblu-
menkohl—broccoli
(It.)—Italian cauli-
flower
Brombeere—bramble-
berry, blackberry
Brot—bread; Weiss-
brot—white bread;
Schwarzbrot—rye
bread; frisches Brot
—new bread; alt-
backenes Brot—
stale bread
Brot und Feigenklösse
—fig and bread
dumplings
Brotbrösel—panada
Brötchen, belegte—
sandwiches
Brotschnitte—thin
pieces of bread
Brühe—broth, sauce,
gravy
Brunnen oder Garten-
Kresse—brook or
garden cress
Brüssler Kohl—
Brussels sprouts
Bruststück—brisket
Büchsen, verlötete
Kannen—preserving
cans
Büchsenfleisch—canned
meat
Büchsengemüse—
canned vegetables,
preserves, comfit-
ures
Büchsen-Trüffeln—
canned truffles
Buchweizen—
buckwheat
Buchweizenkuchen—
buckwheat cake
Bückling; geräucherter
Hering—bloater
Büffet, Silber- und Glä-
serschrank—
sideboard
Butterbrot—bread and
butter
Buttermilch—butter-
milk
Butternüsse—butter-
nuts
Butterstulle, belegtes
Brötchen—sandwich
Butterteig—puff paste
Caldo, spanische Suppe
caldo, Spanish soup
Cardinal-Essenz—
cardinal essence
Carotten, gelbe Rüben
—carrots
Caudle, englische Ha-
ferschleimsuppe für
Kranke—caudle,
English oatmeal
soup for invalids

Cayennepfeffer; roter
Pfeffer—Cayenne
pepper
Cervelatwurst, Braun-
schweiger Wurst—
cervelat, saveloy,
Brunswick sausage
Chanfania, spanisches
Gericht von
Schweins- oder
Hammelsleber—
Spanish dish of pigs
or lambsliver
Champignons, Mor-
cheln—mushrooms
Chantilly Suppe, grüne
Erbsensuppe—chan-
tilly soup, green
pea soup
Charlotten—charlottes,
made of fruit, but-
ter, eggs, sugar, etc.
Chiffonade (Fr.)—
grüne Erbsensuppe
—green pea soup
Chlodnik, polnische
Kaltschale—chlod-
nik, Polish cold
soup
Cichorie, Endivie—
chicory, endives
Citrone—lemon
Citronenkraut, auch
Stabwurz oder
Eberraute—
southernwood
Citronnat—candied
citron (Am.),
candied lemon
Claret, Bordeaux
Weine, blassrote
Weine—Bordeaux
wine, light red wine
Cock-a-Leekie, engli-
sche Hühnersuppe—
Cock-a-Leekie, Eng-
lish chicken soup
Cognac, Kognak—
brandy
Compot—stewed fruits
Confekt, Zuckerback-
werk—small cakes,
cookies, sweets,
sweetmeats
Confitieren, ganz gelas-
sene Früchte in
Zucker eingekocht
—candied fruits
Conserven—preserved
fruit
Coquillen, Muschel-
schalen in welchen
Ragouts serviert
werden—coquilles,
dishes of curried
meats served on
shells
Coriander—Coriander
Corinthen—currants
Cornets, kleine Düten
aus Oblatenteig mit

Gefrorenem gefüllt,
ice cream cones
Cotelettes—cutlets
Crecy-Suppe, Gemüse-
suppe—crecy soup,
vegetable soup
créme crue (Fr.)—rohe
Sahne
crepinettes (Fr.)—
baked faggots
Crevettes, Garnelen-
suppe—crevettes,
brawn, shrimp
Croquants, spröde ge-
backenes Zucker-
backwerk—crisp
baked cakes
Curaçao—curacao
Curcuma, ostindisches
Gewürz—turmeric
Damascenenpflaume—
damask plum
Dampf, Dampf erzeu-
gen—steam
dämpfen, im Wasser-
bad schmoren—to
stew, jug
Därme für Würste—
skins for sausages
Dattel—date
Dauerspeise, Dauer-
früchte, Büchsenge-
müse—preserves,
comfitures
Dessert, Nachtisch—
dessert
déjeuner la four-
chette—Gabelfrüh-
stück—luncheon
deutsche Art des Beef-
steaks—filet steak
deutsche kleine Man-
delkuchen—German
almond cookies
deutsche Wachsbohnen
—German wax
beans
Dickbein—shank
dicke Milch—sour milk
Dill—dill
Dolpettes, gebackene
Fleischklösschen—
baked meat dump-
lings
Doppelrindslenden-
stück—chateau-
briand; double ten-
derloin
Doppelstulle, belegtes—
sandwich
Dorsch (Fisch)—dorse,
torsk, tusk, codfish
Dost, Meiran, Marjo-
ram—majoram
Dragun-Essig—tarra-
gon vinegar
Dreifuss—trevet
Dressieren (zum Braten
u. s. w. vorrichten,
fertigmachen)—to
dress

Dreux a la (Fr.)—das Spicken eines Fleischstückes mit Speck, Zunge und Trüffeln—larding of meat with bacon, tongue, mushrooms

dünne Flanke (Fleisch) —navel piece

dünne Fleischsuppe mit vielerlei Gemüsen—julienne (Fr.) —meat soup

dünne Speckschnitte— bacon

dünner trockener Zwieback—crackers

durchgebraten—well roasted

durchgebratenes Rindsstück—beefsteak well done

durchgeseiht—strained

durchgetriebene Suppen—puree soups

durchwachsen (vom Fleisch)—marbled

Dunstobst—stewed fruit

Düte, Tüte—paper bag, cornet

Echaudes (Fr.)—eine Art gebrühter Kuchen—a kind of steamed cake

echte Sardine—pilchard

Edelpilze—mushrooms, champignons

Eier—eggs

Eier, gesottene oder gekocht—boiled eggs

Eier, gestürzt—turned over eggs

Eier in Butter gebraten —fried eggs

Eier, ohne Schale in Wasser halb-weich gekocht, verlorene Eier—poached eggs

Eierauflauf—omelette, souffle

Eierbier—flip

Eierkuchen—omelet

Eierrahm mit Zwiebeln —onion custard

Eiertrank—eggnog

Eigelb, Eidotter—yolk of egg; Eiweiss— white of egg

Einbrenne, Mehlschwitze, braune Butter— roux (Fr.)—butter and flour thickening

einfacher Tisch—table frugale (Fr.)—plain table

eingekochte Suppe— Purée (Fr.)—mash

eingelegt—cured

eingelegte Butternüsse —pickled butternuts

eingelegtes Obst: Conserven—preserved fruit

eingemachte Früchte— canned fruits

eingemachte Gurken— gherkins, sweet pickled pickles

eingemachtes Kompott —compote

Eingemachtes, sauer— mixed pickles

eingemachtes Obst: Conserven— preserved fruit

eingepökelt—corned, cured

eingepökelte Nahrungsmittel— salted foods

einkochen—to stew

Einlagen—contents of soup

Einzel-Mahlzeit—dinner for one

Eis, Gefrorenes—glacé (Fr.)—ice, ice cream

Eisschrank—icebox

Elritze (Fisch)— minnow

Ende des Halses, das dünne Stück—neck piece

Endivien, Cichorie— endives, chicory

Ente—duck

Eichel-Kaffee—acorn coffee

Ente, junge—duckling

Ente, wilde—wild duck

Entrées (Fr.)—side dishes

Epanada, spanische Pastete—Spanish pastry

Erbsen—peas

Erbs-Suppe—pea-soup, pease-soup

Erdartischoke—Jerusalem artichoke

Erdbeersaftsauce— strawberry sauce

Escalope (Fr.)—small pieces of meat, collops

essbare Pilze—mushrooms, eatable

Essenszeit—dinner time

Essenz, Extrakt— essence

Essig—vinegar

Essigfrüchte, Essiggemüse—pickles

Estragon, Dragon, Dragun, Beifuss (Pflanze)—dragon, tarragon

Fadennudeln—vermicelli

Familiensuppe—potage

Farce, Fasch, Füllsel— forcemeats, filling

Farce von Fisch—forcemeat of fish

Farin-Zucker oder Cassonade, Zucker welcher zu Likörfabrikation und Compots verwandt wird, etc.—sugar used in the manufacture of liquor, compots, etc.

Fasan—pheasant

Faschings—Krapfen— carnival fritters

Feige—fig

feiner, gewählter Tisch —table recherchés (Fr.)—fine first class table

Feinschmecker—gastronomer

feinster Raffinade-Zucker—double refined sugar

Feldhuhn, Prairiehuhn prairie chicken

Fenchel—fennel

fertigmachen, zubereiten, anrichten, vorrichten—to dress

Festessen—banquet

Festmahl, Schmaus— dinner

Fettwürfel—cracklings

Filet (Fr.)—Braten— fillet, leg of veal (and other meat)

Fisch—fish

Fisch-Farce—forcemeat of fish

Fische, ragoutartiges Gericht aus—fish chowder

Fischmus—fish bisque

Flachfisch—skate

Flamery, süsse Speisen aus Stärkemehl, u. s. w.—flamery, sweet dishes of cornmeal

Flammplatz—flat baked rye-bread

Flädchen, Fladen, Strudel—a farinaceous food of thin wound paste with a stuffing of sliced apples, raisins, etc.; pancake strudels

Flanke, dünne (Fleisch)—navel piece

Flanke, untere Flasche—bottle (Fleisch)—flank

Fleisch, eingesalzenes, Pökelfleisch— corned meat

Fleisch, gehacktes— chopped meat

Fleisch (gehacktes) gebraten oder gedünstet—minced collop
Fleischbrühe—bouillon, broth—consommé (Fr.)
Fleischer—butcher
Fleischextrakt—beef extract, meat extract
Fleischpastete—meat pie, pot pie
Fleischpastete, amerikanische—pothellion
Fleischpuree—mashed meat
Fleischragout, italienisches—Frittura (It.)—Italian hotch potch
Fleischragout mit verschiedenen Gemüsen—hotch potch
Fleischröllchen, gefüllte—Roulade (Fr.)—rolled or collared meat
Fleischrollen—Roulade (Fr.)—meat, rolled
Fleischschnitte—chops, cutlets
Fleischstücke, gedünstete, ähnlich wie das ungarische Gulyasch—beef collops
Fleischsulz—aspic jelly
Fleischsuppe mit Gartengemüse—jardiniere (Fr.)—meat soup with vegetables
Fleisch-Vögel—rolled beef with farce
Fliesspapier—absorbent paper, blotting paper
Flunder (Fisch)—flounder
Flunderbraten—baked fillets of flounder
Flussaal—river eel
Flussbarsch—bass, perch
Flussfisch—river fish
Flusskrebs—crawfish
Fogas, Fogasch, Fogosch (Fisch)—kind of brasse
Forelle—trout, brook trout
Frankfurter Würstel—Frankfurters, two long and thin sausages bound together
französischer Branntwein—cognac
Frikandellen—croquettes
Frikassee—fricassee, stew

Frisolen, grüne Bohnen—green beans
Frittura (italienisches Fleischragout)—Italian hotch potch
Froschschenkel—frog shanks
fromage a la créme (Fr.)—Sahnenkäse
Frucht, Obst—fruit
Fruchteis—Sundae icecream
Frucht-Essig—fruit vinegar
Frucht-Marmelade—jam, marmalade
Fruchtsaft—fruit sirup
Früchte, eingemachte—canned fruits
Frühstück—breakfast
Frühstück, zweites—luncheon
Fülle, Füllsel—farce, forcemeat
Füllung und Glasur—filling and frosting
Füsse—feet
Gabelfrühstück—lunch
Gallerte, Sulze—Gelée (Fr.)—jelly, gelatine
Gans, gefüllte—stuffed goose
Gänsebrust—goose breast
Gänsefett, Gänseschmalz—goosegrease
Gänseklein—goose giblets
Gänseleber—goose liver
Gänseleberpastete—goose liver pastry
Garküche—ordinary kitchen
Gartenkresse—garden cress
Garneele—prawn, small shrimp
Gazpacho, spanische Kaltschale—a Spanish cold soup
Gebäck—cookies
gebacken—baked
gebeiztes Ochsenfleisch—roast beef piquant
gebrannter Zucker—caramel (Fr.)—browned sugar
gebraten—broiled, grilled
gebratene Hammelkoteletts—mutton cutlets or chops
gebratene Leber, Herz, Milz, etc.—pig's fry
gebratene Makrelen (Fisch)—fried mackerel
gebratene Steinbutte (Fisch)—grilled turbot

gebratener Aal—spitchcock
gebratener Schinken mit Spiegeleiern—ham and eggs
gebratener Truthahn—roast turkey
gebratenes Schweinefleisch—roast pork
gedämpft—steamed
gedämpfte Hammelcarbonade—braized carbonade of mutton
gedämpfter Rostbraten—braized beef
gedämpftes Rindfleisch—beef á la mode (Fr.)—stewed beef
gedörrter Fisch—dried fish
gedünstetes Rindfleisch—stewed beef
gedünstetes und stark gepfeffertes Huhn—curried fowl
Geflügel—poultry
Geflügelmus—poultry bisque
Geflügel (Ragout von) mit weisser Sose—blanquette (Fr.)—poultry stew
Gefrorenes, Eis—glacé (Fr.)—ice, ice cream
gefüllt—stuffed
gefüllte Fleischschnitte—farces
gefüllte Gans—stuffed goose
gefüllter Kalbsbraten—roast veal, filled
gedünstete Fleischstücke—beef collops
gefüllte Kalbsbrust—filled breast of veal
gefüllter Schweinsmagen; Schwartenmagen—pudding of swarts
Gehäck—hash
gehackt—minced, chopped
gehackter Braten—baked mince
gehacktes Fleisch—chopped meat, hashed meat
gekocht und gedünstet—jugged, cooked and steamed
gekochte Eier—boiled eggs
Gekröse von Kalb oder Schwein—mugget
Gelatine; sehr reiner Knochenleim—gelatine
geläutert—clarified
gelbe Rübe; Möhre, Mohrrübe—carrot

gelbliche Pflaume:
Mirabelle—
mirabelle plum
Gelbwurzel: ostindi-
sches Gewürz—
turmeric
gelinde kochen—
simmer
gemischte Getränke,
besonders die ameri-
kanischen—mixed
drinks
gemischter Aufschnitt
—various kinds of
cold meats mixed
Gemüse—vegetables
Gemüse, sauer einge-
machte—mixed
pickles
Gemüsebrei—purée
(Fr.)—broth
Gemüsemus—vegetable
bisque
Gemüsesuppe mit But-
ter und Rahm—Ger-
man soup
Genever—gin
gepökeltes Schweine-
fleisch—pickled
pork, salted pork
geräuchert—smoked
Gericht—dish
Gericht aus jungem
Mais mit Bohnen—
succotash
Gericht (ragoutartiges)
aus Fischen, Schwei-
nefleisch, Muscheln,
Schiffszwieback, etc.
—chowder
gerieben—grated,
brayed
geringeres Lendenstück
—upper loin
gerollt—collared
geronnen—clotted
geronnene Milch—
cheese curds, clotted
milk, curdled milk
geröstet—braized,
toasted
Gerste—barley
geschabt—minced,
shredded, scraped
geschabtes rohes Rind-
fleisch—scraped raw
beefsteak
geschlagene Sahne,
Schlagsahne—
whipped cream
geschlagener Rahm mit
Biscuit—charlotte
russé (Fr.)—whipped
cream with lady fin-
gers
geschmort, braisirt—à
la mode (Fr.)—
braized, stewed
geschmorte gespickte
Kalbsleber—larded
braized calf's liver

geschmorte Gurken—
stewed cucumbers
geschmorter Kalbsbra-
ten vom Hals—
braized neck of veal
geschmorter Schweine-
braten—braized
pork roast
geschmortes Rind-
fleisch und Kohl—
bubble and squeak
geschrotener Weizen—
shredded wheat
Gesindetisch—table du
commun (Fr.)—ser-
vants' table
gesotten—sautée (Fr.)
—boiled
gesottene Eier—boiled
eggs
gespickt—larded
gespickte geschmorte
Kalbsleber—larded
braized calf's liver
gespickte Kalbsschale—
shoulder of veal,
larded
gespickter Hammels-
schlegel—larded leg
of mutton
gestampft—mashed,
pounded
gestossen—crushed,
pounded, brayed
gestürzte Eier—turned
over eggs
Getränk—drink, bever-
age
Getränke, gemischte,
besonders die ameri-
kanischen—mixed
drinks
getrocknete Pflaumen—
prunes
getrocknete weisse
Bohnen—navy beans
gewählter, feiner Tisch
—table recherches
(Fr.)—fine first
class table
Gewürz—spice
Gewürz-Nelke—clove
Gewürz, ostindisches—
—turmeric
gewürzt—spiced
glasirt—glazed
Glasur und Füllungen
—frostings and fill-
ings
Glatt-Butte (Fisch)—
pearl (fish)
Glattroche (Fisch)—
long nose skate
Glühwein—hot wine
Goldbrachvogel—gold
plover
Goldfisch—gold fish
Goldmakrele—blue fish
Grammeln, Speckgrie-
fen—bacon greaves

Gramolata, gefrorene
Limonade—ice
lemonade
Granit-Zucker—granite
sugar, block sugar
Grashecht—pickerel
Graslauch—locambole
Graupen, Gerstel,
Gräupchen—peeled
grain or barley
Gribolettes (Fr.)—ge-
spickte Fleisch-
schnitten auf dem
Rost gebraten—
larded cuts of
roasted meat
Grieben, Griffen—
greaves, scraps
Gries—grit, semolina,
farina, groats
Grillade, geröstete
Fleischschnitte—
cuts of meat roasted
grillieren, braten von
Fleisch an dem
Spiess—roasting of
meat on the spit
grobe Cervelatwurst:
Schlackwurst—
cervelat, saveloy
Gründling, Grundel,
Kresse, Kressling,
(Fisch)—ground-
ling, gudgeon
grüne Bohnen—green
beans
grüner Brachvogel—
green plover
grüner Salat—lettuce
Grütz-Würste—barley
sausages
Gulasch (stark gewürz-
tes Ragout, ungar-
isches Nationalge-
richt—goulasch
Gurken, eingemachte—
gherkins, sweet
pickles
Gurken, geschmorte—
stewed cucumbers
Gurkensalat—cucumber
salad
Gurken, süss-saure—
sweet pickles, gher-
kins
Guss—sauce, gravy,
frosting
Guss-Torte—a fruit
cake
gut durchgebraten—
well done
gut durchgebratenes
Rindsstück—beef-
steak well done
Hackebraten oder
Fleischfarce, fein ge-
hacktes, rohes Rind-
fleisch, Schweine-
fleisch mit Semmeln,
u. s. w.—minced
beef, pork with rolls

Hafer—oats
Hafergrütze—groats, oatmeal, gruel
Hagebutte (Fisch)—hip
Haggis, schottisch, ein Pudding bereitet aus Kalbs- oder Lamms- geschling—a pudding made of the pluck of calf or lamb
Hahn—cock, rooster
halb durchgebraten— underdone
Hals—neck
Halsstück—neck piece
Hammel-Braten—roast mutton
Hammelcarbonade, gedämpft—braized carbonade of mutton
Hammelfleisch, bestes: Lenden, Rücken und Beine—best cuts of mutton
Hammel-Koteletten— mutton chops; mutton cutlets
Hammelsschlegel, ge- spickter—larded leg of mutton
Hammelviertel—quar- ter of mutton
Hasche, Hachis—hash, hachis
Haricot (Fr.)—Gericht von Hammelfleisch und Bohnen—dish of mutton and beans
Häring-Salat—herring salad
Hase—hare
Hase, belgischer—Bel- gian hare
Hase, Hinterviertel und Lenden—baron of hare
Hase, schwarzer—hare ragout
Hasenklein—hare ragout
Hasenpfeffer—ragout of hare
Hauptmahlzeit—dinner
Hausen (Fisch)—huse, sturgeon
Hausenblase—isinglass
Hausmannskost— daily fare
Hecht, amerikanischer —pickerel
Hecht, gebratener— baked pickerel
Hechtdorsch (Fisch)— hake, merluce
Hederich—dandelion
Hefenknödel—yeast dumplings
Hefen-Kolatschen— little buns

Hefen-Seelen—tea rolls
Hefen-Teig—yeast dough
Heidelbeeren, Blau- beeren, Besinge, Bickbeere, Schwarz- beere, Waldbeere— blueberries, bilber- ries
Heilbutte (Fisch)— halibut
heisser Punsch—hot punch
herb, trocken—tart, dry
Hering, Häring— herring
Hering, geräucherter Bückling—bloater
Hering, marinierter— marinated herring, pickled herring
Herz, Leber, etc., ge- bratene (vom Schwein)—pig's fry
Himbeere—raspberry
Himbeersaftsauce— raspberry sauce
Hinterbacke—buttock
hintere Lende—hind loin
hinteres Knochenstück —hind shank
Hinterteil—rump
Hinterviertel und die Lenden vom Hasen —baron of hare
Hirsch—stag, hart, deer
Hirsch-Braten— venison
Hirse—millet, pannicle
Hochepot (Fr.)—Ge- richt aus Hammel- fleisch oder Ochsen- schwanz mit Gemü- sen—dish of mut- ton or oxtail with vegetables
Hochwild—venison
Hohlhippchen—wafers
Hohlnudeln— maccaroni, noodles
holländische Moppen— Dutch buns
holländischer Käse— Dutch cheese
Holunderbeeressig— elder-vinegar
Holzdecke, kleine— dinner mat
Honig—honey
Hopfen—hops
hors d'oeuvres (Fr.)— appetizers
Hot Pot, Getränk aus Ale, Weisswein, Zucker, u. s. w.— beverage of ale, whitewine, sugar, etc.

Hotsch Potsch: Fleischragout mit verschiedenen Ge- müsen—hodge podge
Huhn—hen, fowl, chicken
Huhn, gebratenes— fried chicken
Huhn, gedünstetes und stark gepfeffer- tes—curried fowl
Huhn mit Reis ge- kocht—pilau of chicken
Huhneierkuchen— chicken omelet
Huhnfleischpastete— chicken pot pie
Huhnpastete—baked chicken; chicken pie
Huhnsuppe—chicken bouillon
Hüllkloss—pudding
Hülsenfrüchte— legumes, podware, cereals
Hummer, Seekrebs— lobster
Hummernsalat— lobster salad
Hutzucker—loaf sugar
im Wasserbad schmoren—to jug
Imbiss (zwischen Frühstück und Mit- tagessen)—lunch
in Butter aufschwitzen —sauté (Fr.)—to stew
in einem Ofen ge- braten—roasted
in einer Pfanne ge- braten—fried
in Essig legen—to marinate, to pickle
in siedendem Wasser gekocht—boiled
in Streifen schneiden— shred, mince
in Töpfen eingelegt— potted
in verlöteten Büchsen eingemachte Früch- te—canned fruits
in Würfel—diced
Ingwer—ginger
Jam, Fruchtmarmelade —jam, fruit marma- lade
Johannisbeeren—cur- rants
junge Ente—duckling
Jungfernhering, Matjeshering— matie
Jus (Fr.)—Fleisch- brühe—meatjuice

Kabeljau, Kableiau: wenn gedörrt Stock-fisch, erst gesalzen und dann getrock-net, Klippfisch, La-berdan am Fangort gesalzen—codfish
Kaffee—coffee; schwarzer Kaffee—black coffee; Milch-kaffee—coffee with milk
Kaffeehaus—café (Fr.) coffee house
Kaffeekuchen—coffee cake, mocha cake
Kail, Kalebroth, schottische Grün-kohlsuppe—kale, Scotch green soup
Kaisersalat, Dragun, Dragon, Estragon—tarragon
Kakao—cocoa
Kalb—calf
Kalbfleisch—veal
Kalbfleisch (Ragout von) mit weisser Sose—blanquette (Fr.)—veal stew with white gravy
Kalbfleisch von der Keule—veal of the leg
Kalbsbraten—roast veal
Kalbsbraten, gefüllter —filled roast veal
Kalbsbraten vom Hals —neck of veal
Kalbsbregen, Kalbs-hirn—calf's brain
Kalbsbrüse—sweet bread
Kalbsbrust—breast of veal
Kalbsbrust, gefüllte—filled breast of veal
Kalbsfricassee—fricassee of veal
Kalbsgekröse—veal or calf's tripe
Kalbsleber—calf's liver
Kalbsleber, gespickte, geschmorte—larded braized calf's liver
Kalbsmidder, Kalbs-milch, Bröschen, Milchling, Milcher, Briesle, Schweser—sweet bread
Kalbsniere—veal kid-neys
Kalbsrücken—saddle of veal
Kalbsschale, gespickte —larded shoulder of veal
Kaldaunen oder Kuttelflecke—tripe
kalte Mahlzeiten—cold entrees

kalter Aufschnitt—cold mixed meat
kaltes Rindfleisch—cold beef
Kaltschale—cold soup
Kamm (meat)—shoulder
Kamm, oberer—neck piece
Kammfleisch—meat of the neck
Kanel, Zimmetrinde—cinnamon bark
Kaninchen, Stallhase—rabbit, cony
Kanne—can
Kapaun, Kapauner (kastrirter Haus-hahn)—capon
Kapern—capers
Kapernsträuche—capers
Kapuzinerkresse—Indian cress
Karamelle, gebrannter Zucker—caramel (Fr.)—browned sugar
Karausche (Fisch)—crucian
Karbonade (beim Hammel oder Schwein das zwischen Rippen-stück und der Keule befindliche Stück)—carbonade, cutlets
Kardamom (Gewürz)—cardamom
Kardinal, ein Getränk aus Weisswein mit bitteren Pomeran-zen—a beverage of whitewine, with bitter oranges
Karneolkirsche, Tier-lein, Dürrhitze, Her-litze—cornelian cherry
Karotten, gelbe Rüben —carrots
Karpfen—carp
Kartoffel, Erdäpfel—potatoes
Kartoffel zu Brei ge-stampft—mashed potatoes
Kartoffelklösse—potato dumplings
Kartoffelmehl—potato flour
Kartoffel-Späne—potato chips
Käse—cheese
Käsebrötchen—cheese sandwich
Käse, holländischer—Dutch cheese
Käse, Limburger—Limburger cheese

Käsemus—cheese bisque
Käse, Parmesan, italienischer Käse —Italian cheese
Kasserolle—stewpan
Kassolettes, becherför-mige Pastetchen aus Reis—cup shaped pastry of rice
Kastanien, essbare; marrons (Fr.)—chestnuts
Kastanien-Brod—chestnut bread
Kaulbarsch (Fisch)—black-tail ruff, pollard
Kaviar—caviar
Kebob, ostindisches Gericht aus Ham-melfleisch, Geflügel —East India dish of mutton or fowl
Kefir, Kumys—koumiss: fermented milk from mares
Kellermeister in vor-nehmen Häusern—butler
Kerbel, spanischer—sweet cicely, chervel
Kerne—kernels, seeds
Keule, Schlegel—pounder, hind shank, leg
Kinderbrei—pap
Kipfel—milk roll,
Kirschen—cherries white round roll, French roll
klein schneiden—shred, mince
kleine Holzdecke—din-ner mat
kleine Rosinen—cur-rants, small seed-less raisins
kleine Tasse—demitasse (Fr.)—small cup
kleine Teekuchen—cookies
kleine Zwiebel—chives
kleingehackt—minced
kleingehackt nachdem es gekocht wurde—hashed
Klops, von dem Aus-druck Escalloupes entstanden—minced collops
Klops von Rindfleisch —beef collops
Kloss—dumpling
Klösschen—small dumpling, boulette
Klösschen oder kleine Koteletten von ge-hacktem Rindfleisch, etc.—minced collops

Knackwurst—smoked sausage

Knoblauch—garlic

Knochen—bones

Knochenstück aus dem Schwanzstück— edgebone, aitchbone

Knochenstück, hinteres —hind shank

Knochenstück, vorderes—front shank

Knödel—balls, boulettes, dumplings

Knollensellerie—knob celery

Knöpfle, Knöpflein, Knödel—balls, boulettes

Knurrhase (Fisch)— grunter

kochen, gelinde— simmer

kochen, in Holztellern —oval wood dish cookery

kochen, in Papier- beuteln—paperbag cooking

kochen, langsam—stew

Kochgeschirr—cooking utensils

Kochinelle (Färbe- mittel)—cochineal

Kochofen, Herd— cooking stove, range

Kochtopf—cooking pot

Kognac, Cognac— brandy

Kohl—cabbage

Kohl, brüssler— Brussels sprouts

Kohl, römischer— Roman cabbage

Kohlkeimchen— sprouts

Kohlkopf—cabbage head

Kohlrabi, Kohlrabe— kohlrabi, cabbage turnip

Kohlrübe, Kohlrebe, Wruke—turnip, cabbage turnip

Kohlsprossen— Brussels sprouts

Kokosnuss—cocoanut

Kolatschen—a Bohemi- an pastry

Kommissbrot—brown George; brown Tommy

Kompott—compote

Konditor (Zucker- bäcker)— confectioner; pastry cook

Konfekt—comfit sweets, sweetmeats

Konserven—canned food or fruits

Kopf-Salat—head let- tuce

Koriander (Gewürz)— coriander

Korinthen—currants

Kork—cork

Korkzieher—corkscrew

Kornbranntwein— corn brandy, whiskey

körniger Streuzucker— granulated sugar

Kornstärke—corn starch

Kost—board

Kost und Logis— board and lodging

Kosthaus—boarding house

Kotelett, Kotelette— cutlet, chop

Koteletten (kleine) von gehacktem Rind- fleisch, auch von an- derem Fleisch ge- braten oder gedüns- tet—minced collops

Krabben, Taschen- krebse—crabs, shrimps

Krach- oder Knack- mandeln—shelled almonds

Kracklinge, Brezel— pretzels, cracknels

Kraftbrühe—clear soup, gravy soup— consommé (Fr.)

Krambambuli, geistiges Getränk, Arak, u. s. w.— beverage of arac, etc.—

Krametsvögel, Drossel —field fares

Krapfen—meringues, rissoles, kind of a bun made of flour and eggs

Krapfen mit Rahm— fritters a la créme (Fr.)—fritters with cream

Krapfen (schmalz- gebackene)—fritters

Kraut, weisses oder rotes, Weisskohl, Rotkraut, Blau- kraut, Kabis, Kappis—white or red cabbage

Kräuter—herbs; Sup- penkräuter—herbs for soup

Krebse—shells, crusta- cea, crabs, crawfish

Krebse und Cham- pignons—crabs and champignons

Krebsbutter—crab butter

Krebsmus, Krebssuppe —bisque

Krebssalat—crab salad

Kresse—cress

Kreuz—chine, rump

Kropf—crop

Krustaden— crustades: dough filled with various dishes

Kruste von geschabtem Brot—gratin (Fr.)— browned crust

Krusteln—fritters, croquette

Küche—kitchen— cuisine (Fr.)

Kuchen—cake

Kuchen, weiche— gauffres (Fr.)— crumpets

Kuchenblech—griddle cake tin

Küchenkräuter— kitchen herbs

Küchenmeister—mas- ter cook—chef (Fr.)

Kuchenpfanne— griddle

Kukummer—cucumber

kulinarisch, auf die Küche bezüglich, zur Kochkunst ge- hörig—culinary

Kümmel—caraway

Kumys, Kefir— koumiss: fermented milk from mares

Kürbis—pumpkin

Kürbisfrucht—vege- table marrow

Kuttelflecke—tripe

Kwas—kvass

Laberdan—salted cod- fish, Aberdeen fish

Lachs, Salm—salmon

Lachs-Forelle— salmon-trout

Lachs, gepflückter— picked salmon

Lammbraten—roast lamb

Lammfleisch (Ragout von) mit weisser Sose—blanquette (Fr.)—stew with white gravy

Lammgeschlinge und Kopf—lamb's pluck and head

Landschnepfe—snipe

langsam kochen—stew, simmer

Languste—spiny lobster, spring lobster

Lattich-Gemüse— lettuce

Lattichsalat—lettuce salad

lau—tepid

Lauch, Stangenlauch oder Porree—spanischer Lauch—leek, porree
lauwarm—lukewarm
Lebensmittel—provisions
Leber—liver
Leberwurst—liver sausage; white sausage
Lebkuchen, Honigkuchen—ginger bread
Lebkuchen, Basler—Basle gingerbread
Leckerei, Naschwerk, Zuckerwerk, Süssigkeiten—candies, sweets
Lende—loin
Lende, hintere—hind loin
Lende, Rindsstück von der—fillet steak, rump steak
Lenden und Hinterviertel vom Hasen—baron of hare
Lendenbraten—fillet beef, roast fillet of beef
Lendenrippchen—chops
Lendenstück—sirloins, tenderloins, loins
Lendenstück, bestes—lower loin, rump steak
Lendenstück, geringeres—upper loin
Lengfisch—fresh cod
Lerchen—larks
Liebesäpfel—tomatoes
Liebhaber vom Leckerbissen, Feinschmecker—gastronomer
Likör—liquéur (Fr.)—liquor
Lima Bohnen—Lima beans
Limburger Käse—Limburger cheese
Limonade—lemonade
Limone—citron, lemon
Lindenblütentee—limeflower tea
Linsen—lentils
Linsenklösse—lentil dumplings
Löffel—spoon
Lorbeeren—bay leaves
Löwenzahn—dandelion
Lunch, Imbiss—lunch
Lungenmus—hash made of calf's lungs
Macédoine (Fr.)—ein Mischgericht von Gemüsen u. Früchten—mixed dish of vegetables and fruit

Macronen—macaroons
Mahl—dinner, breakfast or supper
Mairübe—turnip
Mais, Welschkorn—Indian corn, maize
Mais, grob gemahlener—hominy
Maisbranntwein, amerikanischer—bourbon
Maisbrei, gebackener—hominy
Maiskuchen—corn meal cake
Maismehl—corn flour, corn meal
Maitrank; Maibowle, Maiwein—maycup
Makaroni, Hohlnudeln, Röhrnudeln—macaroni
Maken—small drop cakes
Makrelen—mackerel
Malakoff, Wurst oder Fleischroulade—sausage or rolled meat
Malakoff-Suppe, bereitet aus Kartoffeln, Gelbrüben, Schinken, u. s. w.—malakoff soup, made of potatoes, carrots, ham, etc.
Mandeln—almonds
Mandeln, süsse—sweet almonds
Mandel-Kolatschen—almond knobs
Mandelkuchen—almond cake
Mandelmilch—almond milk
Mandel- und Zuckerteig—nougat
Mango-Frucht—mango fruit
Mangold, Dickwurz—mangold
Mangold-Stiele—mangold stalks
männlicher Fisch: Milcher, Milchner—milter
Margarin, Oleomargarin, Kunstbutter—margarine, oleomargarine, artificial butter
Marinade (Fr.)—Sose, Brühe oder Beize, um Fleisch mürber zu machen—a juice to make meat tender
mariniren—to marinade, to marinate, to pickle
marinirter Hering—marinated herring, pickled herring

Marjoram, Meiran, Dost, Wurstkraut—marjoram
Mark—marrow
Markerbsen—marrow peas
Mark-Klösse—marrow dumplings
Marmade (Fr.)—liquor made of vinegar, spices, etc. in which fish are dipped before cooking
Marzipan—marchpane
Masthähnchen—fattened chicken; stallfed hen
Masthuhn—poularde
Matjeshering, Maatjeshering—herring which have not spawned, matie
Matze, Matzes, ungesäuerter Osterkuchen der Israeliten—crackers of the Israelites
Maulbeere—mulberry
Maultaschen—rissoles; little mouthfuls
Maus: unteres Stück vom Schenkel—mouse, buttock
Mayonnaisensauce—mayonnaise dressing
Meeraal—conger
Meeräsche (Fisch)—sea mullet
Meerbarbe (Fisch)—mullet
Meerfische—seafish
Meergrundel—goby, rockfish
Meerhecht—hake, merluce
Meerkohl—sea cabbage
Meerlattich—laver
Meerrettig oder Märrettig—horseradish
Mehl—flour
Mehrbraten, Möhrbraten, Mürbebraten—tenderloinroast
Meiran, Dost, Marjoran—marjoram
Melasse, Zuckersirup—molasses
Melis-Zucker—Malta sugar
Melisse—balm
Melone—melon
Melonenkürbis—squash
menu (Fr.)—Speisekarte, Tafelfolge, —bill of fare

meringue (Fr.)—
Meringeln, Konfekt
aus versüsstem Ei-
weissschnee—sweets,
made of whipped
cream
merveilleo (Fr.)—
Zuckerbackwerk—
sugar cookies
Met, oder Meth, das
Getränk der alten
Deutschen, beste-
hend aus gegohre-
nem Honig, u. s. w.
mead, a beverage of
the ancient Germans
consisting of fer-
mented honey etc.
Mettwurst—German
sausage
Metzger, Fleischer—
butcher
Milch, geronnene—
clotted milk, cheese
curds, curdled milk
Milch, sauere—sour
milk, clabber
Milchbrötchen—bun
Milchbrötchen mit
Zimmt—cinnamon
buns
Milcher, Milchner:
männlicher Fisch—
soft roed fish,
milter
Milchhering—herring
with a soft roe
Milch-Sauerbraten—
piquant beef
Milchsuppe—milk soup
Milchspeise—junket
Minze—mint
Mirabeau, a la (Fr.)—
mit Sardellen und
Butter zubereitete
Gerichte—dishes
made of sardels
and butter
Mirabelle: gelbliche
Pflaume—mirabelle
plum
Mirliton (Fr.)—Tört-
chen von Butterteig
—pastry of butter-
dough
Mischgetränk, warmes
—flip
Mischmasch, allerlei—
potpourri
mit Butter bestrichene
und geröstete Brot-
scheibe—buttered
toast
mit Gemüse—a la
jardiniere (Fr.)—
with vegetables
mit gekörntem Salz
zubereitet—corned
mit Kruste gebacken—
au gratin (Fr.)—
browned

mit sehr scharfen Ge-
würzen zubereitet—
curried
Mittagessen, Mittags-
tisch—dinner—
diner (Fr.)—
Mittagessenszeit—
dinner time
Mittagstisch oder ge-
meinschaftliche
Wirtstafel—table
d'hôte (Fr.)—to eat
at the ordinary
table
Mittelrippe—chuckroast
Mohn—poppy
Möhren, Gelbrüben,
Mohrrüben—carrots
Mokka-Kaffee—Mocha
Molken—curds
Mörbraten, Lenden-
braten—grandfilét
(Fr.)—roastloin
Morcheln, Cham-
pignons—mush-
rooms
Morille: essbarer Pilz
—morel
Mörser—mortar
Most: der Saft der
Trauben vor der
Gärung—must
Mundtuch, Serviette
—table-napkin
Mürbebraten: Lenden-
braten—roast fillet
of beef
mürber Teig—short
crust
Mus—pinée (Fr.)—
mash
Mus von Krebsen,
Reis, Gemüse,
Fischen, Geflügel—
bisque
Muschelmus—clam
bisque
Muscheln—shells, crus-
tacea, cockles
Muscheln mit Rahm—
creamed clams
Muscheln, ragoutar-
tiges Gericht aus—
clam chowder
Muskatblüte—mace
Muskatnuss—nutmeg
nachgemacht, unecht—
mock
Nachtmahlzeit, Abend-
essen, Abendbrot—
supper
Napf—terreen, tureen
Napfkuchen, Asch-
kuchen, Topf-
kuchen, Babe,
Rodonkuchen—a
German cake baked
in a bowlshaped
form having a
cylinder in the
center

Napfpastete von Kalb-
fleisch—veal hotpie
Naschwerk, Zucker-
werk, Süssigkeiten,
Leckerei—candies,
sweets
Nastürz—nasturtium
seeds
Nektarin (süsses Ge-
tränk)—nectarine
Nelkenpfeffer, Neuge-
würz, Piment—
clove bark
nicht durchgebratenes,
noch blutendes,
englisches Rinds-
stück—beefsteak
underdone, beef-
steak rare, beef-
steak not overdone
Nieren—kidneys
Nierenbraten—loin,
sirloin roast
Nierenbraten vom
Kalb—roast loin of
veal
Nierenfett, Talg—
kidney suet
Nocken, Nockerln—
little dumplings
Nougat—Mandelkonfekt
almond cookie
Nudeln—macaroni,
noodles, vermicelli
Nuss—nut
Nuss-Sulze—nut jelly
oberer Kamm—neck
piece
Oberkellner—head
waiter
Oblatengebäck, tüten-
förmiges dünnes—
wafers
Obst, conservirtes—
preserved fruit
Obst, eingelegtes—pre-
served fruit, pickled
fruit
Obst, eingemachtes—
preserved fruit
Obstkuchen, Kuchen
aus Rosinen, Korin-
then, Mandeln, u. s.
w.—fruitcake, a
cake made of yeast
dough with layer of
fruit, a cake made
of raisins, currants,
almonds, etc.
Obstmus—marmalade
Obstschaum für Mehl-
speisen—sweet or
fruit sauces
Ochsenfleisch, gebeiz-
tes—roast beef
piquant
Ochsengaumen—ox
palates
Ochsenschweif—ox tail
Ochsenzunge—ox
tongue

Offleten—wafers
ohne Zutat—au naturel
(Fr.)—prepared
plain
Oliven—olives
Oliven (kleine) gefüllt
mit Nelkenpfeffer—
pimolas
Olivenöl—olive oil
Omeletten—omelets—
soufflé (Fr.)
Orangenblüte—
orangeflower
Pampelmuscitrone—
shaddock
Panade, Semmelteig—a
dough made of
grated rolls
Paprika, Pfeffer—red
pepper, capsicum
Paradiesfeige—
banana
Pastetchen—pastries
Pastete—pie, pastry,
pasty (meat)
Pastete, becherförmige,
—timbale (Fr.)—
small pie baked in
a mold
Pastetenteig—dressing
paste
Pastilla, russische, ge-
trocknete Obstmar-
melade—a Russian
dried fruit marma-
lade
Pastille, Zuckerplätz-
chen—sugarwafer
Pastinake—parsnip
Perlgraupen—French
barley
Perlhuhn—guinea fowl
Perlzwiebel, Perllauch
—leek with small
onions
Petersilie, Peterling,
Peterlein—parsley
Petersilien-Kartoffel—
potatoes with pars-
ley
petits fours (Fr.)—
kleines Backwerk—
small cookies
Pfannkuchen—pancakes
Pfannkuchen, Berliner
—ball doughnuts
with fruit filling
Pfeffer—pepper
Pfeffer, roter—Cayenne
Pfeffergurken—
gherkins
Pfefferkraut—pepper
grass
Pfefferkuchen—
gingerbread
Pfefferminze—pepper-
mint
Pfefferminztee—
peppermint tea
Pfeffer-Nüsse—spice
nuts

Pfeifente—widgeon
(game)
Pfirsich—peach
Pfitzauf—batter puffs
Pflaumen—plums
Pflaumen, getrocknete
—prunes
Pflaumenkuchen—
plum tart
Pflaumen- und Nuss-
Sulze—prunes and
nut jelly
Pfrille (Fisch)—
minnow
pikant—piquant (Fr.)
—sharply flavored
Pilaw (Pilau): Reis-
Speise mit Fleisch—
pilau, stewed meat
with rice
Pilchard: echte Sardine
—pilchard
Pilze, essbare—mush-
rooms, edible
Pimpernell, Bibernell-
kraut—pimpernell
Pirog, Pasteten von
Fisch, Eiern, Sauer-
kraut, Pilzen, u. s.
w.—pie of fish,
eggs, sour cabbage,
mushrooms, etc.
Plätzchen—flawns
Plinsen—wafers
Plinzen mit Obst—thin
pancakes
Pökelfleisch—salt
meat, pickled meat,
corned meat
Pökellachs—salted
salmon
Pomeranzen-Sauce—
orange sauce
Pompelmuse, Paradies-
äpfel—Adam's apple
Porrei oder porrée
(Fr.)—(Gemüse)—
—leeks
Portulac—purslane
pot au feu (Fr.)—
Nationalsuppe—
French national
soup
poularde (Fr.)—junges
verschnittenes und
dann gemästetes
Huhn—young, cas-
trated, wellfed hen
Prairiehuhn—prairie
chicken
Preiselbeer-Gelee—
cranberry jelly
Presskopf, der Länge
nach gespaltener
Schweinskopf—
hog's head split in
the middle
Presswürste—brawn
Prise Muskatnus—a
pinch of nutmeg

Prünellen—prunellas,
prunellos
Pudding, Hüllkloss—
pudding
Puffbohne, Ackerbohne,
Dickbohne, Sau-
bohne—broadbean
or hogsbean
pulverisirt—pulverized
Pumpernickel, schwar-
zes, ungesalzenes
Roggenbrod aus
Ganzmehl—un-
salted bread made
of shredded rye
Puree—mash, broth
Quargel, Quärgel—
finger-shaped cheese
Quark—cheese-curds
quirlen—twirl
Quitten—quinces
Rabarber—rhubarb
Radieschen—little red
radish
Ragout (Fr.)—stewed
meat in rich gravy
Ragout (braunes) von
gebratenem, wildem
Geflügel—salmi
(Fr.)—warmed over
dish of game, well
seasoned
Ragout von Fleisch
oder Fischen mit
Würzpulver gewürzt
—curries
Ragout von Hammel-
fleisch, Zwiebeln
und Kartoffeln—
Irish stew
Ragoutartiges Gericht
aus Fischen,
Schweinefleisch,
Muscheln, Schiffs-
zwieback, etc.—
chowder
Rahm—cream
Rahmkelle—skimmer
Rahmschaum—whipped
cream
Rahmschnee—whipped
cream
Rahmsose—cream
gravy
Rahmtorte—cream
cake
Rapünzchen—corn
salad
Ratavia, Fruchtlikör
—fruit liquor
rauchen, räuchern—
smoke
Räucherlachs—
smoked salmon
Rauchfleisch—smoked
meat
Rebhuhn, Feldhuhn—
partridge
Rehwild—venison, deer
Reis—rice
Reismehl—rice flour

Reismus—rice bisque
Reisstrudel—rice fritters
Rémouladen-Sauce, pikante Fleischsauce—a piquant meat gravy
Rettig, Rettich—radish
Rettich, schwarzer—Spanish radish
Rheinlachs—Rhine salmon
Rind, Schulterstück vom—chuck-steak
Rinderbraten (in einem Topf zugerichtet)—pot roast beef
Rindermark—beef marrow
Rinderschmorbraten—beef potroast
Rindfleisch, gedämpftes—beef a la mode (Fr.)—stewed beef
Rindfleisch, gedünstetes—stewed steak
Rindfleisch (gehacktes) gebraten oder gedünstet—minced collop
Rindfleisch, gerolltes—collared beef
Rindfleisch, geschabtes, rohes—scraped raw beefsteak
Rindfleisch, geschmortes, und Kohl—bubble and squeak
Rindfleisch, kaltes—cold beef
Rindfleisch-Tee—beef tea
Rinds-Fuss—cow heel, or neat's foot
Rindsnierentalg—beef-tallow
Rindsstück, Lendenstück—beefsteak
Rindsstück, englisches, nicht durchgebratenes noch blutendes—beefsteak not overdone
Rindsstück, geschabtes—scraped raw beefsteak
Rindsstück, gut durchgebratenes—beefsteak well done
Rindsstück vom zarteren Hinterviertel—rump-steak, porter house steak
Rindsstück von der Lende—fillet steak
Ringlots: Weinpflaumen—green gages
Rippchen—cutlets
Rippen—ribs

Rippenstück—shoulder butt
Rippenstück, rundes—shoulder chop
Rippenstückchen—pork chops
Rissolen—fine chopped mincemeat, rissoles
Rocambole, Sandlauch, Perlzwiebel—rocambole,
Rogen—roe, spawn
Rogenhering—roe herring
Roggenbrod mit Sauerteig—rye bread with leaven
rohe Sahne—créme crue (Fr.)—crude cream
rohes, gehacktes Rindfleisch—chopped beefsteak
Röhrnudeln—macaroni noodles
Rollhering, Rollmops: zum Knäuel geballter halbirter Hering—collared herring
Rollmops, Heringsroulade—herring roulade
römischer Salat, Lattich—lettuce
Rosenkohl—Brussels sprouts
Rosinen, kleine—small seedless raisins
Rosmarin—rosemary
Rossmakrele, Goldmakrele—blue fish
Rostbeef—roast beef
Rostbraten, gedämpfter—braized beef
rösten—to toast
Rotauge (Fisch)—roach
rote Rübe—red beet, beet rave, beet root
roter Pfeffer: spanischer Pfeffer—Spanish pepper, Cayenne
Rotkraut, Rotkohl—red cabbage
Rotwein-Essig—red wine vinegar
Roulade von Ochsenfleisch—rolled beef
Rüben, gelbe—carrots
Rübe, rote—beet rave, red beet, beet root
Rübe, weisse—turnip
Rübenrettig—turnip radish
Rückenstück—chine, chine of pork, saddle
Rührei—scrambled or buttered eggs
Rum—rum

Rumpf—rump
rundes Rippenstück—shoulder chop
Rundstück—round
Saffran—saffron
Saftbraten—roasted meat in gravy
saftig, saftreich, im Munde zerlaufend—fondant (Fr.)—mellow, juicy
Sago—sago
Sahne—cream
Sahne, geschlagene—whipped cream
Sahnenkäse—fromage a la créme (Fr.)—cream cheese
Salami—Italian hard sausage
Salep—saloop, arrowroot
Salat—salad
Salat, grüner—lettuce
Salatsose, gewürzte—boiled salad dressing
Salatzubereitung von Essig, Salz, Pfeffer, etc.—French dressing
Salbei—sage
Salbei-Sauce—sage sauce
Salm, Lachs—salmon
Salmis, Wildgeflügelragout—ragout of wild fowl
Salse—sauce
Salzlake—marinade (Fr.)—salt lick
sandieren, schnelles Garmachen dünner Schnitte von Fleisch, Fisch, u. s. w.—quick cooking of meat, fish, etc.
Sandtorte—Madeira cake
Sardellen—anchovy, sardels
Sardine—sardine, pilchard
sauer—sour
sauer eingelegtes Gemüse—mixed pickles
Sauerampfer—sorrel
Sauerbraten—sour roast beef
Sauerdorn—barberries
sauere Milch—sour milk, clabber
Sauerkraut—pickled sour cabbage
Sauerteig—leaven
Saum (Fleisch)—sweetbreads
Savoyer Kohl—savoy cabbage

Schalet oder Scholet, israelitisches Gericht—a Jewish dish
Schalotten oder Schalottenzwiebel, Eschlauch—eschalots
Schaltiere—shells, crustacea
scharfe Würze—chutney
scharlachfarbige Bohnen—scarlet beans
Schaumgebäck, Baiser —meringue, cream puff, cream bun
Schaumkuchen—sponge cake
Schaumlöffel—skimmer
Schaumwein—champagne
Schellfisch—haddock
Schenkel—hind quarter
Schiffszwieback—crackers
Schildkröte—turtle, green turtle
Schildkrötensuppe (nachgemachte) aus Kalbsfüssen—mock turtle soup
Schill, Zander—zander, perch, pike, giant perch, brasse
Schinken—ham
Schinken, gebratener, mit Spiegeleiern—ham and eggs
Schinken-Brötchen—ham sandwich
Schinkenknödel—ham dumplings
Schlackwurst: grobe Cervelatwurst—cervelat, saveloy
Schlagobers—whipped cream
Schlagsahne—whipped cream
Schlagteig—batter
Schlegel, Keule—pounder
Schlehe—sloe
Schleie (Fisch)—tench
schmackhaft zubereitet —flavored
Schmalz—lard
Schmarn—schmarn, fruit pancake
Schmaus, Festmahl—dinner
Schmorbrühe, helle—white braise soup
schmoren, im Wasserbad—jug
Schmorfleisch—stewed meat
Schmorpfanne, Schmortopf-casserole, frying, stewing or braising pan; braiser

Schnecke—snail, also a sort of bun
Schneehuhn—white grouse
Schneide- oder Brechbohnen—green beans
Schnittbohnen—French beans
Schnittchen: belegte Brötchen—little slices of bread—Croquettes (Fr.)
Schnitte—cuts
Schnittkohl—cabbage sprout, summer cabbage
Schnittlauch—chives, leek
Schnittspargel—asparagus
Schnitzel (kleine)—escalope (Fr.)—collops
Schnitzel, Wiener—baked veal resembling veal cutlets
Schokolade—chocolate
Scholle, Steinbutte (Fisch)—turbot, flounder
Schöps, Hammel—mutton
Schulter, Schulterstück—shoulder
Schulterblatt—bladebone
Schulterstück vom Rind—chuck-steak
Schüssel, tiefe—terrine, tureen
Schüsselunterlage—dinner mat
Schwaben-Brod—Suabian biscuit
Schwamm, essbarer: Pilze—mushrooms
Schwanzstück—round, rump
Schwartenmagen: gefüllter Schweinsmagen—collared head, pudding of swarts—head cheese
Schwarzbrot—rye bread
schwarzer Gelee—black currant jelly
schwarzer Hase—hare ragout
schwarzer Pudding—chocolate pudding
Schwarzkümmel, Mutterkümmel—fennel flower seed
Schwarzwurzel—oyster plant
Schweinefleisch, gebratenes—roast pork or roast pig

Schweinefleisch, gepökeltes—salted pork, corned pork
Schweinefleisch, ungesalzenes—fresh pork
Schweinsbraten—roast pork
Schweinsbraten, geschmorter—braized pork roast
Schweinsfüsse—pig's trotters, salted or boiled pig's feet
Schweinskoteletten—pork cutlets
Schweizerkäse—Swiss cheese, gruyére
Schweizer Kröpfli—Swiss turnovers
Scorzoneren—oysterplant
Seebarbe (Fisch)—millet
Seebarsch—seabass, bass, perch
Seeheuschrecke (Fisch) —white shrimp
Seezunge (Fisch)—sole
Seiher—colander
Selchfleisch—smoked pork, afterwards cooked
Sellerie—celery
Selterswasser—seltzerwater
Semmel, Milchbrötchen —rolls
Senf, Mostrich—mustard
Senf und Kresse—mustard and cress
Senfgurken—mustard pickles
Sieb—sieve or colander
Sodawasser—soda water
Sommerkohl—savoy cabbage
Sommersuppe: eine leichte Fleischsuppe —julienne (Fr.)—clear bouillon
Sooleier—salt brine eggs
Sose—sauce, gravy
Sose (kalte) von Eigelbem, Salz, Senf, mit Oel verrührt und mit Dragunessig abgeschmeckt —mayonnaise (Fr.) —rich salad dressing
Spanferkel—sucking pig
spanische Zwiebel—Spanish onions or Bermuda onions

spanischer Kerbel—
sweet cicely
spanischer Pfeffer:
Paprika—red pepper
Cayenne pepper
spanischer Pfeffer, die
Schote davon—chilli
Spargel—asparagus
Spargelkohl—broccoli
(It.)—Italian cauli-
flower
Spatzen—dumplings,
boulette
Speck—bacon
Speck und Bohnen—
pork and beans
Speckschwarte—pork
skin
Speisehaus—restaurant
Speisekammer—pantry
Speisekarte—bill of
fare, menu
Speisekundiger—
gastronomer
Spelz, Dinkel—spelt
Spickaal—smoked eel
spicken—to lard
Spickgans—smoked
larded goose
Spicknadel—spit pin
Spiegel-Eier—shirred
eggs
Spiess—spit, broach
Spinat—spinage
Spitzen-Papier—lace
paper
Springerle oder Tirgeli
—anise-seed biscuits
Spritzkuchen—spouted
cake, fritters
Stachelbeeren—goose-
berries
Stangenbohnen—hari-
cot beans
stark gepfefferter Käse
mit Zwieback—
devilled cheese and
crackers
Stärkemehl—
cornstarch
Staubzucker—
powdered sugar,
sifted sugar
Steckrübe—turnip
steife Suppe—broth
Steinbutte (Fisch)—
brill, turbot
Steinpilze, oder Cham-
pignons—mush-
rooms
Steiss, Sterz—buttock
of a fowl
Sternanis—badiane,
Indian anise
Stier—bull
Stintfisch—smelt
Stockfisch—dried cod,
cured cod
Stockfisch, kleiner—
hake, merluce

Stollen—loaf-shaped
cake
Stör—sturgeon
Streifen schneiden—
shred, mince
Streusel-Kaffeekuchen
—seed cake, strewed
cake
Streuzucker—
granulated sugar,
strew sugar
Striez—Christmas loaf
Striezel—a long roll
Strudelflädchen—
pancake strudels
Stück—piece
Stück-Zucker—block
sugar
Sulze—jelly
Sumpfschnepfe—snipe
bécassine (Fr.)
Suppe—soup, broth
Suppe aus Gänseklein
—giblet soup
Suppe, dicke: Purée—
thick soup, broth
Suppe, durchge-
triebene—puree
soup
Suppe, gebundene,
Purée—mash
Suppenkräuter—pot
herbs
süss—sweet
süsse Kartoffel, Batata
—sweet potatoes
süsse Limone—limette
süsse Mandeln—sweet
almonds
süsser Blätterteig—
sweet puff paste
süss-saure Gurken—
gherkins, sweet
pickles
Süssigkeiten, Nasch-
werk, Zuckerwerk,
Leckerei—sweets,
candies
Syphon—soda water
Tafel—table
Tafel für Kranke—
dishes for invalids
Tafelgeschirr—dinner
service
Tafelkarte—menu, bill
of fare
Tafelpilze—mushrooms,
champignons
Tapioca—tapioca
tartarisch, roh—a la
tartare (Fr.)—
tartaric
Taschenkrebs—shrimp
Tasse—cup
Taube—pigeon
Taube, geschwungene
—pigeon sauté
Tee, grüner Tee,
schwarzer Tee—
tea, green tea, black
tea

Teekuchen, kleiner—
cookie
Tellerunterlage—
dinner mat
Teltower Rüben—Tel-
tow turnips
tiefe Schüssel—terrine,
tureen
Timian—thyme
Tisch—table
Tischgesellschaft—
dinner party
Tischzeug—cover,
couvert
Tomaten, Liebesäpfel
—tomatoes
Torte—tart
tranchiren, zerlegen—
carving
Trauben-Essig—grape
vinegar
trocken, herb -dry
trockene Brotscheibe—
dry slice of bread
trockener, dünner
Zwieback—crackers
Trüffeln—truffles,
mushrooms
Truthahn, Puter—
turkey-cock
Truthahn, gebratener
—roast turkey
Tunke—sauce, gravy
türkische oder welsche
Bohnen: Schnitt-
bohnen—French
beans
Tüte—paper bag
Uebriggebliebenes—
left overs
umschwenken—sauté
(Fr.)—to fry
unecht, nachgemacht—
mock
Unschlitt, Talg—tallow
untere Flanke
(Fleisch)—flank
unteres Stück vom
Schenkel—mouse-
buttock
Vanille: tropische
Frucht—vanilla
Vanille-Zucker—vanilla
sugar
Vegarade, bittere
Pomeranze—
vegarade, bitter
orange
Veitsbohne, türkische
Bohne, welsche
Bohne, Schnitt-
bohne—French
beans
Venusmuschel, ameri-
kanische—clam
verlötete Büchsen—
preserving cans
vorderes Knochenstück
—front shank
Vorderrippe—rib roast

Vorgericht, Beigericht, Imbiss: hors d'oeuvres (Fr.)—relishes
vorrichten, fertigmachen, anrichten, zubereiten—to dress
Vorspeisen—entrées (Fr.)—side dishes
Wachholderbeeren—juniper berries
Wachtelkönig (Geflügel)—land rail
Wachteln—quails
Waffel—wafer, waffle
Waldhuhn—grouse
Waldschnepfe—woodcock
Waller, Wels—sheat fish, silurus
Walnuss—walnut
weisse amerikanische Walnuss—hickory nut
Warmbier—mulled ale, aleberry
Wasser—water
Wassermelone—watermelon
Weck, Semmel, rundes Brötchen—rolls
weiche Kuchen—gauffres, crumpets
Weichtiere, Schaltiere—shells, crustacea
Weinpflaumen—green gages
Weinraute—garden rue
Weintrauben—grapes
Weintrauben, rote amerikanische—Catawba
Weissbarsch—kingfish
Weissbrot—white bread
weisse Bohnen—haricot beans
weisse Bohnen, getrocknete—navy beans
weisse Rübe—turnip
weisser Zimmt—canella
Weisskraut—white cabbage
Weisslinge—whitings, shiners, coal fish
Weisswein-Essig—white wine vinegar
Weizen—wheat
Weizenbrei—frumenty
Weizengrütze—groats
Weizenschrotbrot—Graham bread
Weizenvogel—wheat bird
Wels, Waller—sheat fish, silurus

Welschkohl: Wirsingkohl—cabbage, savoy
Welschkorn: Mais—maize, Indian corn
Wermutbranntwein—absinthe
Wiener Brötchen—Vienna rolls
Wiener Schnitzel—baked veal, resembling veal cutlets
Wild, Wildbret—game, venison
Wildente—wild duck
Wildkohl—curled cabbage
Wildschwein—wild boar
wilde Taube—wild pigeon
Windbeutel—cream puff
Winterblumenkohl—broccoli
Wirsingkohl, Welschkohl—cabbage, savoy
Wirtstafel, gemeinschaftliche—table d'hôte (Fr.)—regular table
Wruke, Kohlrübe—cabbage turnip
Wurst—sausage
Wurst, Braunschweiger—Brunswick sausage, cervelat
Würstel, Frankfurter—Frankfurters
Würze aus Tomaten, Morcheln, etc.—catsup
Würze, scharfe—chutney
Würzfleisch, blätterig geschnittenes—mince
Würzpulver aus Pfeffer, Piment, Kurkuma, Gewürznelken und Muskat—curry
Würzsose aus Pilze zubereitet—mushroom catsup
Würzsose (aus Tomaten, etc.)—catsup, catchup
Wurzelsellerie—turnip, celery
Wurzelwerk—turnip, carrots, parsley, celery roots
Zander, Sander—sandre, sandat,

perch pike, giant perch, brasse
zerriebene Kartoffel—mashed potatoes
Ziege—goat
Ziegenmilch—goatmilk
Zimmt—cinnamon
Zimmetblüte—cinnamon flowers
Zitrone, Limone—lemon, citron
Zitronenkuchen—citron layer cake
Zitronenpastete—lemon pie
Zubehör—ingredients
zubereiten, anrichten—to dress
Zucker—sugar
Zucker, gebrannter: Karamelle—caramel (Fr.)—browned sugar
Zuckerbäcker (Konditor)—confectioner, pastry cook
Zuckerbranntwein—rum
Zuckerbrot—biscuit, caraway biscuits
Zuckergebäck—caramel cake
Zuckerhut—sugar loaf
Zuckerschoten—sugar peas
Zuckersirup, Melasse—molasses
Zuckerwerk, Naschwerk, Süssigkeiten, Leckerei—candies
Zunge—tongue
Zweckessen—public dinner
zwei ungeteilte Lendenstücke—baron of beef
zweites Frühstück—lunch
Zwetschge, Pflaume—prune, plum
Zwieback—rusk, sweet toast, crackers
Zwieback (gerösteter) mit Sardellenteig überstrichener—toasted anchovy crackers
Zwiebel—onion
Zwiebel, kleine—chives
Zwiebel, spanische—Spanish onions
Zwischengericht, entrée (Fr.)—dishes served between courses